What's New in the Second Edition

The second edition of this book is almost all new. Although I treat many of the same topics that I did in the first edition, I've tried to compress the more basic material from nine days to seven. This leaves room for work on table creation, more trigger information, and lots of new features in SQL Server versions 7.0 and 2000.

I've changed some of the examples and exercises to address the Northwind database instead of pubs. Northwind has a better variety of data and datatypes, some larger tables, and Unicode strings.

I've tried to go a little deeper on each topic, and get a little closer to real life with each problem. Even in the earlier days, I'm trying to give you, the reader, a better chance to succeed with SQL Server.

Here are some new topics in this edition:

- New SQL Server datatypes
- Designing and using computed columns
- Indexing with computed columns
- Indexing views
- Working with table variables
- Using table hints to control locking
- Using the stored procedure debugger
- Triggers on views
- User-defined functions

Lowell Mauer
with David Solomon
and Bennett Wm. McEwan

SAMS
Teach Yourself

Transact-SQL in 21 Days

SECOND EDITION

SAMS
201 West 103rd St., Indianapolis, Indiana, 46290 USA

Sams Teach Yourself Transact-SQL in 21 Days, Second Edition

Copyright © 2001 by Sams Publishing

International Standard Book Number: 0-672-31967-5

Library of Congress Catalog Card Number: 00-102594

Printed in the United States of America

First Printing: March 2001

04 03 02 01 4 3 2 1

Trademarks

All terms mentioned in this book that are known to be trademarks or service marks have been appropriately capitalized. Sams Publishing cannot attest to the accuracy of this information. Use of a term in this book should not be regarded as affecting the validity of any trademark or service mark.

Warning and Disclaimer

Every effort has been made to make this book as complete and as accurate as possible, but no warranty or fitness is implied. The information provided is on an "as is" basis. The author and the publisher shall have neither liability nor responsibility to any person or entity with respect to any loss or damages arising from the information contained in this book.

Executive Editor
Rosemarie Graham

Acquisitions Editor
Sharon Cox

Development Editor
Robyn Thomas

Managing Editor
Charlotte Clapp

Project Editor
Dawn Pearson

Copy Editor
Michael Henry

Indexer
Erika Millen

Proofreader
Daniel Ponder

Technical Editor
Tim Whalen

Team Coordinator
Pamalee Nelson

Media Developer
JG Moore

Interior Designer
Gary Adair

Cover Designer
Aren Howell

Page Layout
Darin Crone
Steve Geiselman

Contents at a Glance

Contents

About the Authors

Lead Author

Lowell Mauer has been in data processing for more than 20 years as a programmer, instructor, and consultant. He has taught programming at Montclair State College in New Jersey and has developed and marketed several Visual Basic applications, including a SQL Server–based reservation system for a private golf course. As a manager of technical support, he has attended seminars and training sessions in several countries and is an expert in more than six computer languages. He currently is the Manager of Consulting for Cognos Corporation in New York.

Contributing Authors

David Solomon, President of Metis Technologies, LLC: I've been working in, on, and around SQL Server (in its incarnations from Sybase and Microsoft) since 1990, and I can't believe that I can still make a living in this technology. I consult and teach courses on SQL Server, and write books like this one from time to time.

When I'm not wasting my time working, I coach youth soccer enthusiastically. If you come to Troy, you'll probably find me on a soccer field, shouting and chasing kids and pretending I'm one of them.

I save the best of my time for my kids, Adam and Luke, my wife Carola, and my three cats, Lucifer, Sam, and Daisy. Right now, Lucifer is sitting in my desk chair, which leaves me standing.

Bennett McEwan is president of Geist, LLC, a company in scenic upstate New York, specializing in explaining SQL Server. The work Ben enjoys most is mentoring, where he helps programmers or database administrators through the tough spots in mission-critical applications.

Ben also teaches SQL Server training classes, writes, and designs Visual Basic client/server applications, and consults on difficult SQL Server performance issues. You can catch him on `comp.databases.ms-sqlserver` and in the pages of *Microsoft SQL Server* Professional (Pinnacle Publishing).

Dedication

Of all the books I have worked on in the past few years, this is my first non-Visual Basic–related book. So, I would like to dedicate this book to my wife Patti, who allowed me the time to research the material and work on the book. To my parents Aileen and Donald, who always knew I could do it before I did. And to Divott, my Scottish Terrier who kept me company while I worked.

-Lowell Mauer

Tell Us What You Think!

As the reader of this book, *you* are our most important critic and commentator. We value your opinion and want to know what we're doing right, what we could do better, what areas you'd like to see us publish in, and any other words of wisdom you're willing to pass our way.

As an Executive Editor for Sams, I welcome your comments. You can fax, email, or write me directly to let me know what you did or didn't like about this book—as well as what we can do to make our books stronger.

Please note that I cannot help you with technical problems related to the topic of this book, and that due to the high volume of mail I receive, I might not be able to reply to every message.

When you write, please be sure to include this book's title and author as well as your name and phone or fax number. I will carefully review your comments and share them with the author and editors who worked on the book.

Fax: 317-581-4770

Email: `feedback@samspublishing.com`

Mail: Rosemarie Graham
Executive Editor
Sams Publishing
201 West 103rd Street
Indianapolis, IN 46290 USA

Introduction

This book is designed to help you teach yourself how to access data in a SQL Server database by using Transact-SQL. In just 21 days, you will learn about such fundamentals as retrieving, modifying, and updating data in the database. Lessons provide sample listings—complete with sample output to illustrate the topics of the day. Syntax examples are clearly marked for handy reference.

To help you become more proficient, each lesson ends with a set of common questions and answers, a quiz, and exercises. You can check your progress by examining the quiz and exercise answers provided in Appendix A, "Answers to Quizzes and Exercises."

Who Should Read This Book

You do not need any previous experience in programming to learn how to program in Transact-SQL.

Conventions

These boxes highlight information that can make your SQL programming more efficient and effective.

These focus your attention on problems or side effects that can occur in specific situations.

NEW TERM These boxes provide clear definitions of essential terms.

Do	Don't
DO use the "Do/Don't" boxes to find a quick summary of a fundamental principle in a lesson.	**DON'T** overlook the useful information offered in these boxes.

This book uses various typefaces to help you distinguish SQL code from regular English. Actual SQL code is typeset in a special `monospace` font. Placeholders—words or characters temporarily used to represent the real words or characters you would type in code—are typeset in *`italic monospace`*. New or important terms are typeset in *italic*.

In the listings in this book, each real code line is numbered. If you see an unnumbered line in a listing, you'll know that the unnumbered line is really a continuation of the preceding numbered code line (some code lines are too long for the width of the book). You will also see a line continuation character like this ➥. In this case, you should type the two lines as one; do not divide them.

The listings are also included on the CD-ROM with file names that begin with lst, followed by the two-digit chapter number, a dash, and then the two-digit listing number within that chapter. For example, the first example in day one is `Listing01-01.sql`.

What's New in SQL Server 2000

As with every new release of a software product, things change; some features are added, others are removed, and still others are enhanced. SQL Server 2000 is no different in this respect. SQL Server 2000 has extended its performance, reliability, quality, and ease-of-use over SQL Server version 7. This new release includes several new features that now make it a great choice for large-scale online transactional processing, data warehousing, and e-commerce applications.

Language Features

The language of SQL Server 2000 is Transact-SQL, which provides several new and enhanced statements, stored procedures, functions, data types, DBCC statements, and other information about the database you would use. This provides you with the ability to enhance the way your application uses and works with the data stored in the database. Many of these enhancements are in the system maintenance command areas, including new stored procedures and console commands. In addition, many new informational log tables have been added to SQL Server 2000. Two of the more interesting additions are User Defined Functions (covered in Day 20, "User-Defined Functions in SQL") and computed columns (covered in Day 8, "Defining Data"). Many other features have been added to allow your Transact-SQL programs to be more efficient.

Server Features

Microsoft SQL Server 2000 has introduced several server improvements and features that bring SQL Server into alignment with the World Wide Web, the Internet, and the new technologies that this requires, such as XML support. To move SQL Server 2000 toward an enterprise-wide corporate solution, there have been many enhancements including the enhancement that enables you to partition tables across multiple servers.

For performance, you can control the actions that SQL Server 2000 takes when you try to update or delete a key that is used in other tables. In addition, you can now create indexes on computed columns or specify whether indexes are built in ascending or descending order.

There are, of course, many more enhancements than I can list here. For more information on the changes to SQL Server, check the "What's New" section in the SQL Server Online Books that are installed with SQL Server 2000.

WEEK 1

Working with Rows and Columns

Learning SQL to extract data from SQL Server is as simple as using the `Select` statement. On Day 1, "Introduction to SQL and the Query Analyzer," I will start by explaining what SQL really is and how it relates to databases. In addition, you will install the Query Analyzer and see how to use it to access data in SQL Server by using SQL.

On Day 2, "Filtering and Sorting Data," you will learn how to retrieve specific data and how to sort the data by using `SELECT`, `WHERE`, and `ORDER BY`.

Day 3, "Working with Columns," will discuss how to manipulate the data columns and what different types of data are available, such as integers and dates.

Day 4, "Working with Row Aggregates and Grouping," will show you how to get aggregate data from the database, such as an average value in a column. In addition, you'll learn how to use the `GROUP BY` and `HAVING` clauses of SQL.

On Day 5, "Joining Tables," you will see how to specify relationships between tables. Then on Day 6, "Using Subqueries," you will discover how subqueries are used to create a nested SQL statement.

Finally on Day 7, "Adding, Changing, and Deleting Rows," you will learn how to add new data, update existing data, or delete data from the database.

Does this all sound confusing? Don't worry; it will all make sense. Don't forget to try the exercises at the end of each day to reinforce what you have read. Well, good luck and see you at the end of the week.

WEEK 1

DAY 1

Introduction to SQL and the Query Analyzer

Congratulations, you have decided to learn one of the most widely used computer languages in use around the world today. Because there are many books for you to choose from, I am glad that you chose this one. *Sams Teach Yourself Transact-SQL in 21 Days, Second Edition* will assist in getting you started on your road to database programming. You will start with the basics and progress to some of the more advanced topics in Transact-SQL or, as most database programmers call it, T-SQL. At the end of the three weeks, you will have everything that you need to access information that is stored in a SQL Server database like a seasoned professional.

This book is going to teach you the basics of the SQL language using many examples, workshops, and screenshots to show you exactly what you should see when doing this on your own computer. In the process, you will also learn a few things about the new SQL Server 2000 and one of its many included tools. The first week covers how to access data on the server by using queries. The second week is about SQL programming concepts and techniques to manipulate data and transaction control. The third and final week covers stored procedures, triggers, and the newer features of user-defined functions and working with BLOBs (Binary Large Objects).

This book will teach you SQL by using examples, both going through them and by showing you the syntax of a statement. Although I must show you the syntax, I will also describe the problem, how to use the statement or statements to solve that problem, and give you the actual example and its explanations.

Today, you will learn the following:

- A brief history of SQL Server
- How SQL is used in real applications
- Getting connected using the New Query Analyzer
- How to write and execute your first SQL query

SQL and SQL Server

If you have read the Introduction and the weekly description, you have seen the terms *SQL* and *SQL Server* many times. Well, here is where we define them. SQL stands for Structured Query Language. This language was created back in the mid-1970s by IBM and was originally called SEQUEL. SEQUEL was an acronym of the initials that stood for Structured English QUEry Language. The SQL used today is often pronounced "SEQUEL" as well; it is the accepted name for this method of accessing data from a database. SQL provides you with a standard method for accessing data contained within a relational database. No matter what type of database you use, SQL is the standard language to access that data within it.

The American National Standards Institute (ANSI) developed and published the standard for SQL languages back in 1989, and updated this standard in 1992 and in 1999. Having standards enables you to learn a single language and apply it to many different databases including Oracle, Access, Sybase, Visual Foxpro and SQL Server. In this book, you will be using Transact-SQL, the SQL variation associated with SQL Server, to do all the examples and workshops.

The SQL language is used to execute commands on the database server. In the case of this book, the database server that you will be working with is Microsoft SQL Server. The server is one-half of a client/server or Web-based system. The client can be either an application running on a desktop or laptop computer, or any user accessing the application across the World Wide Web. The server is responsible for physical storage of the data and the enforcement of any business rules while ensuring data integrity.

The client application is responsible for getting data from the server, formatting it, and displaying it to the user for analysis or manipulation. As an example, during a national election, you might have an application that retrieves data from a SQL Server. This server would store a table full of state voting information, and the client workstation would request that data and then build a graphical chart to display it. This division of responsibility is good because it lets each computer be specific to the task needed: You don't really need a 21-inch monitor on a SQL Server and your desktop doesn't really need 50–100GB of disk space.

What Is T-SQL?

Transact-SQL is one of the dialects of SQL. As you go through this book and learn how to use T-SQL, I will mention where the SQL standard is being followed and where the topics you are learning are in addition to the standard. Some of the most ordinary items are actually additions to the ANSI standard SQL, such as indexes and any program flow-of-control statements that you learn about later.

The SQL-99 standard does not mention indexes at all. This is because the standard SQL language is not focused on performance issues on specific databases. The standard is written generically to ensure that you can manipulate and access the data contained on any relational database. The result is that every different database platform has developed its own version of SQL that is slightly different from the others. This was done so that items such as indexes—which the overall standard does not account for—can be added as functionality for your database. Another example of an individual database "tweaking" the SQL standard for its own use is Oracle's PL/SQL.

Retrieving Data with Query Analyzer

The SQL Server Query Analyzer is your primary interface for executing T-SQL queries and stored procedures. You will be using this utility throughout the rest of your 21 days, and it's a good idea to get comfortable with several of the available options in this tool. For those of you who might have used previous versions of Microsoft SQL Server, it should be noted that for historical reasons, the Query Analyzer is named `ISQLW.exe`. This was the program name of the older version of the interactive SQL processor (see Figure 1.1). Although this older version was useful, the changes that have been made to the new Query Analyzer in SQL Server 2000 make it a much easier tool to use.

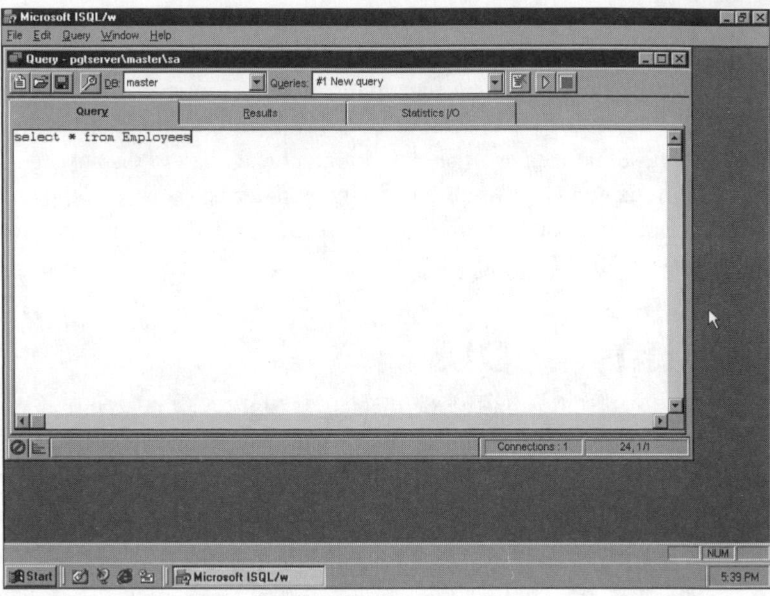

FIGURE 1.1
The old ISQL SQL processor.

You can run SQL Query Analyzer either from inside the SQL Server Enterprise Manager or directly from the Start menu. You can also run SQL Query Analyzer from the command prompt by executing `isqlw.exe` itself. Some of the functions and features of Query Analyzer are

- Create and execute queries and other SQL scripts
- Quickly create commonly used database objects
- Copy existing database objects
- Execute stored procedures without knowing the parameters
- Debug stored procedures
- Debug query performance problems
- Locate objects within databases or view and work with objects
- Insert, update, or delete rows in a table
- Create keyboard shortcuts for frequently used queries
- Add frequently used commands to the Tools menu

Installing the Query Analyzer

Installing the Query Analyzer is actually done automatically during the full installation of the SQL Server product. However, if you want to use the Query Analyzer on a computer other than the one where SQL Server was installed, you need to run the SQL Server installation and select the Client Tools Only option (see Figure 1.2).

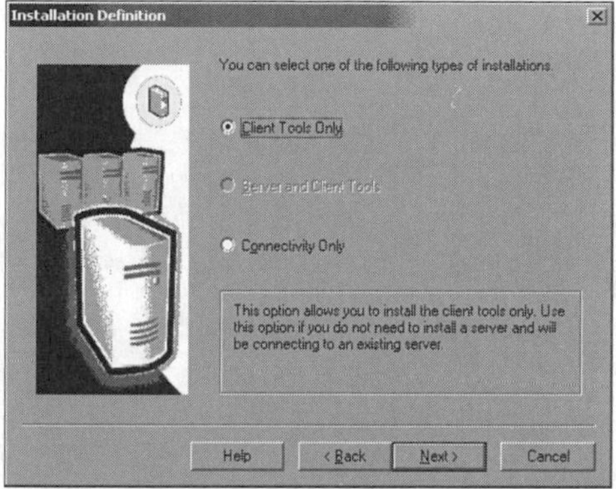

FIGURE 1.2

Installing the Query Analyzer on a client PC.

After you select the installation option, click Next to select the components you want to install on your computer (see Figure 1.3).

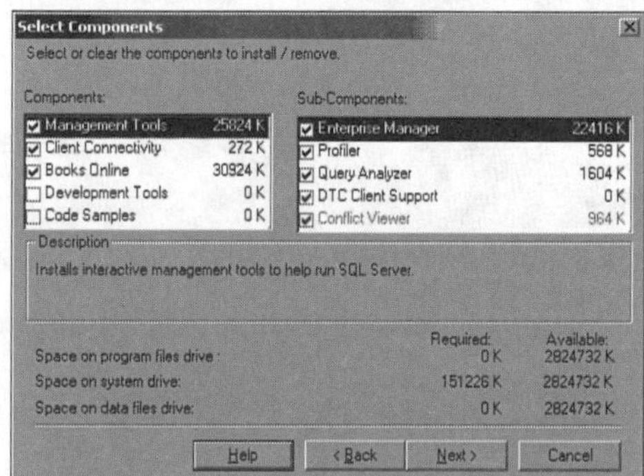

FIGURE 1.3

Selecting the components of SQL Server 2000 for installation.

Of the components available, the ones you want to select are the Enterprise Manager, Profiler, and the Query Analyzer. After you have made your selections, click Next to start copying the files (see Figure 1.4).

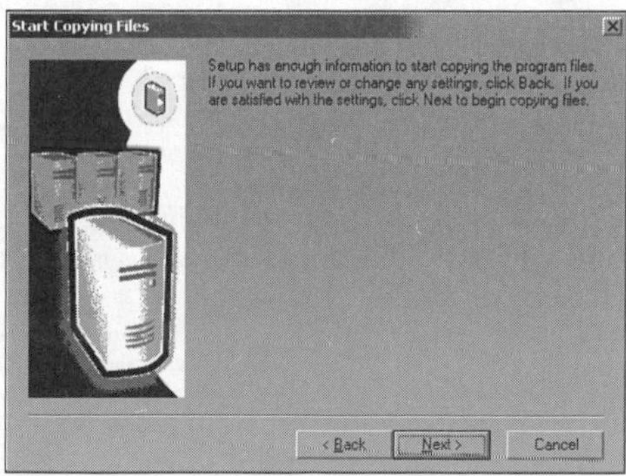

FIGURE 1.4

The SQL Server 2000 installation in progress.

After the installation is complete, you will find the Query Analyzer on the SQL Server menu list, as shown in Figure 1.5.

FIGURE 1.5

Finding the Query Analyzer start icon in the SQL Server menu list.

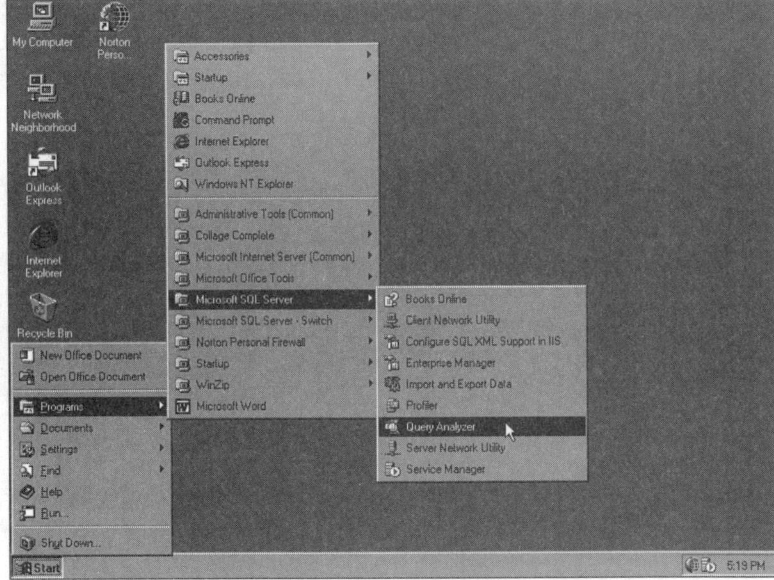

When the install is complete, you are ready to start using the Query Analyzer.

Logging In to and Changing the Database

Now that you have the Query Analyzer ready to go, let's start the program by selecting it from the SQL Server menu list. After you click OK, you are logged in to the appropriate instance of SQL Server (this is assuming that you entered in a correct login ID and password). You will then see the main work area of the Query Analyzer, as shown in Figure 1.6.

Login IDs are created and maintained by the SQL Server 2000 administrator. If you are using SQL Server 2000 at work, you should contact this administrator for a login account.

If you want to learn more about the management of SQL Server 2000, which includes the administration of user ID's and passwords, refer to *Sams Teach Yourself SQL Server 2000 in 21 Days*.

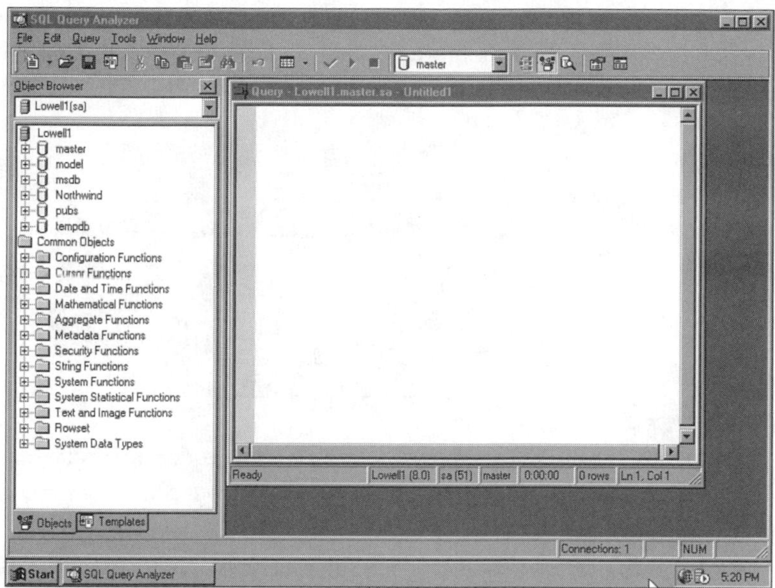

FIGURE 1.6

The SQL Server Query Analyzer main work area.

If there is a problem with your login, you might see a dialog similar to Figure 1.7. Usually you will see this if you've mistyped your password. Simply try again. You should also verify that you have entered your login ID correctly. If you've changed the password, be sure to type in the newest one.

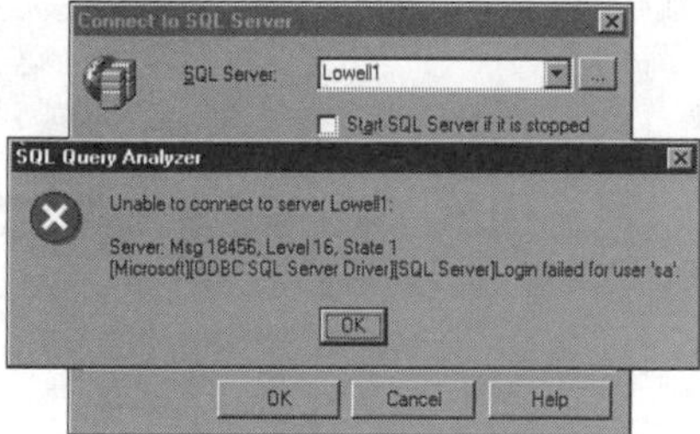

FIGURE 1.7

SQL Server notifying you of a login failure.

Figure 1.8 shows another error that you might see. If you do get this error, there are several things to look for to correct it. First, verify that the SQL Server service is running on the computer to which you are trying to log in. If it is, the problem might be with your client setup. Otherwise, make sure that you type in the server name correctly. To see a list of servers on the network, rather than type one in, click the three dots next to the SQL Server name box to display the list of active SQL Servers that are on your network.

Don't be alarmed if your server doesn't show up; you can still connect to it by typing in its computer name. In this case, I tried to connect to a server named Oracle, which doesn't exist on my network.

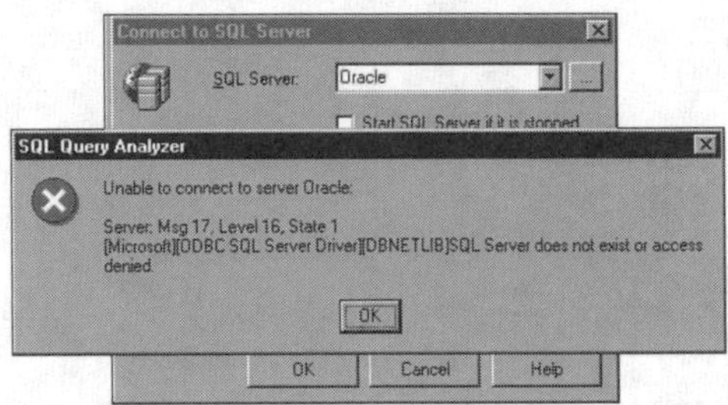

FIGURE 1.8
Network connectivity error message.

Figure 1.9 shows the empty Query Analyzer workspace. You should be able to see that there are really two connections open. Each connection that you open has a title bar that displays the following:

- Which computer you are logged in to
- What database you are currently using
- Your login
- The title of any query you have opened
- Which window number is displayed

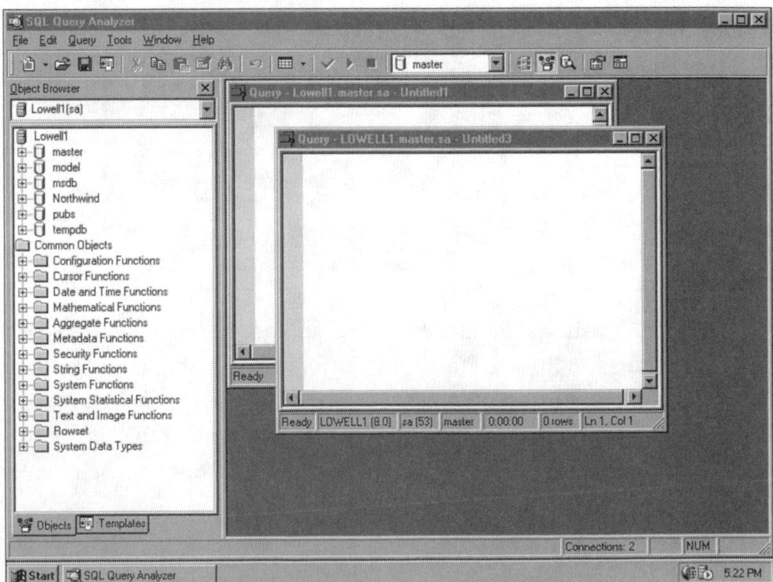

FIGURE 1.9
Seeing multiple connections in a single instance of the Query Analyzer.

1

As you might have guessed by now, having this information in the title bar when you have many open connections can be extremely handy. So, back in Figure 1.9, you see both connections are open using the Login ID 'SA', which is the default login for SQL Server.

Caution

> If you are using SQL Server 2000 at work, this login might not work because the administrator probably changed the password. Check with the administrator for the login to use.

Both are connected to my computer, LOWELL1, in the master database, and each one is connected to the same instance. There's no reason they couldn't be connected to different database instances.

The Query Toolbar

You can start running T-SQL queries by selecting the New Query button (leftmost button on the toolbar in Figure 1.10). Each new query window that you open is a separate connection to SQL Server; if you open too many, you might be wasting resources on your SQL Server.

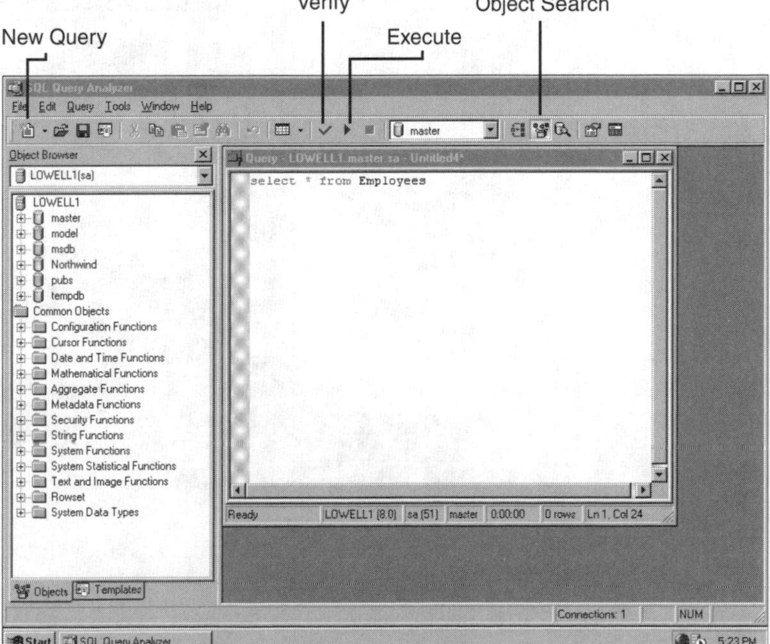

FIGURE 1.10

The Query Analyzer toolbar.

If you select the second button (which looks like a standard Windows File Open button), it will open a standard dialog box to find saved SQL scripts (which, by default, have a `.SQL` extension). The next button, the Save Query/Result button, will either save the text in your query window or, if you have run a query and clicked in the Results window, save the results of a query you have run. The next button loads a "template" SQL query so that you can quickly develop variations of work you've done before. The next several buttons have the standard Windows functionality.

The Execute Mode button is next, and it's pretty powerful. When you click this button, you are presented with a drop-down list of options that determine how and where your results will appear when you run a query. The default option, Results in Grid, is easier to read because many names in SQL Server 2000 can be 128 characters long. The default display option will usually pad the text to the complete 128 characters with spaces if the names aren't fully used. The Results in Grid option typically leaves enough space only for the widest data column to be displayed. You can also switch to Results in Text, which can be nice when you want to look at all that long text. You can even automatically have the results of your queries routed directly to a file. These options are shown in Figure 1.11.

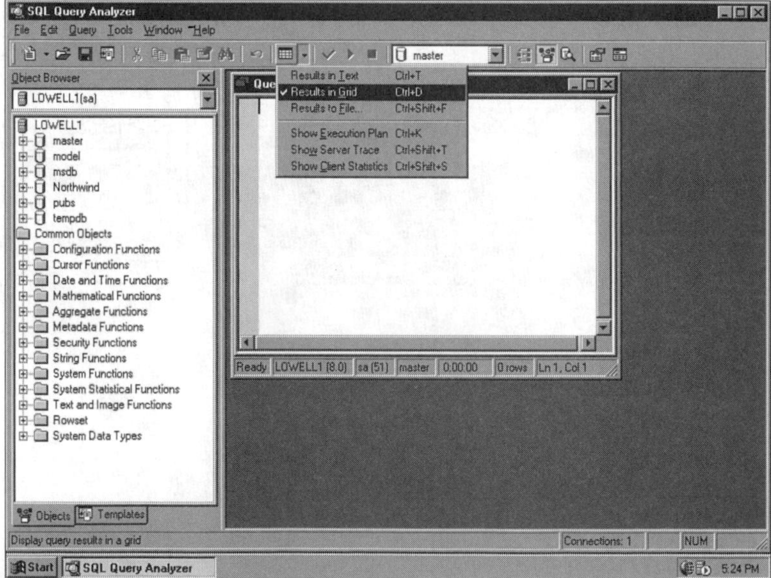

FIGURE 1.11

The Query mode selection drop-down list.

The next option on the menu shown in Figure 1.11 is Show Execution Plan. This option shows you the methods and indexes SQL Server will use to find the data you requested in your query. After you have logged in to the server, you then need to select the database with which to work. A drop-down box provides a list of the installed databases on the server to which you are connected. If you change the value here, the SQL script you run will use this database unless you specify a different database in the SQL script itself with the `USE` command. When you do specify a different database in your SQL, the changed database will be reflected in this list box.

Executing Your First Query

The easiest way to see how this all works is by using the Query Analyzer. Click the New Query button to open a new query window. Now type the following statement into the window as shown in Figure 1.12:

```
Use Northwind
Select * From Employees
```

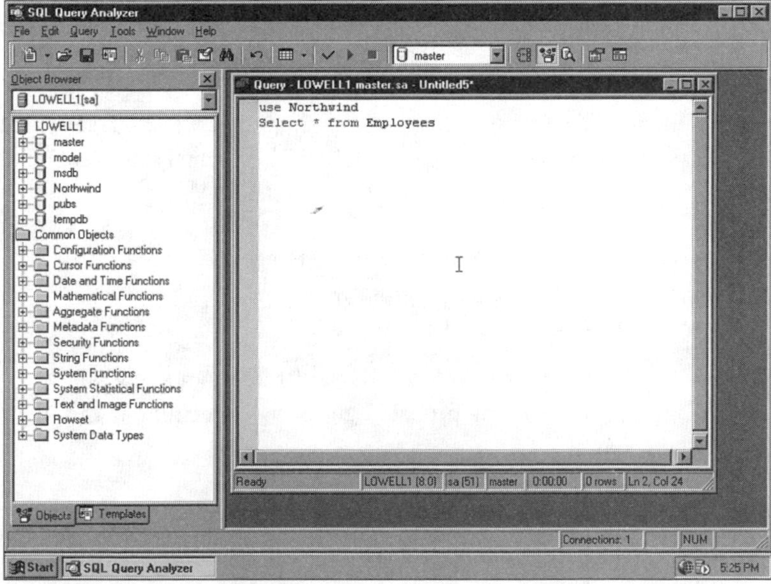

FIGURE 1.12

Entering a SQL statement into the query window.

This query is pretty easy after you understand what the commands mean. The first statement, `USE Northwind`, tells the server to switch to the Northwind database, which is a sample database that is installed along with SQL Server 2000. The second statement, `Select * From Employees`, requests that SQL Server return all the rows and columns of data from the table or view named Employees (and because you explicitly switched to the Northwind database, you know this table is in Northwind). So, to translate these statements into English, the following is what these statements mean:

```
Switch to the Northwind database
Return all the data about the employees
```

After you type the two preceding commands, you can verify that they've been entered correctly. Notice that several other buttons on the toolbar are now available. Click the blue check mark on the toolbar to verify that everything is typed in correctly. This will check that the SQL you entered is syntactically correct. If everything is okay, you will see the following:

```
The command(s) completed successfully.
```

Understanding `SELECT` and `FROM`

The keywords `SELECT` and `FROM` are used in SQL programming more than any other words. They aren't as interesting as `CREATE` or as ruthless as `DROP`, but they are the backbone for any conversation you hope to have with the computer when asking for data from the database. Of course, data retrieval is the reason that you have stored data in the database in the first place. What follows is a brief discussion of the `SELECT` keyword. Almost every SQL statement you will code will start with `SELECT` as shown:

```
Select <column name(s)>
```

The basic `SELECT` statement is very simple. However, `SELECT` doesn't work alone, as you saw earlier when entering your first SQL statement. If you typed in this SQL statement

```
Select EmployeeID
```

you would get the following error message:

```
Server: Msg 207, Level 16, State 3, Line 1
Invalid column name 'EmployeeID'.
```

This message tells you that SQL Server does not know where to find the column name EmployeeID. You can probably guess that something is missing. That something is the `FROM` clause:

```
From <table>
```

Together, the `SELECT` and `FROM` clauses begin to unlock the power that is contained in your database.

I have used a couple of terms that you are probably wondering about. SQL has three main elements: keywords, clauses, and statements. SQL *keywords* refer to individual SQL elements, such as `SELECT` and `FROM`. A *clause* is a part of a SQL statement; for instance, `SELECT` *`column1, column3`* is a clause. SQL clauses combine to form a complete SQL *statement*. For example, your first SQL statement was the combination of the `SELECT` and `FROM` clauses, which are themselves a combination of keywords.

Finally, the asterisk (*) that you used in your first SQL statement tells the database to return all the columns associated with the table that you listed in the `FROM` clause.

Using the Query Analyzer Editor

Another thing you might have noticed (see Figure 1.12) as you entered the earlier SQL statement is that some of the words you typed in have changed color. The Query Analyzer editor changes the color of the code entered based on the category the code word is found in. Table 1.1 lists the different colors that are used.

TABLE 1.1 Color Coding in SQL Query Analyzer

Color	*Category*
Red	Character string
Dark Red	Stored procedure
Green	System table
Dark Green	Comment
Magenta	System function
Blue	Keyword
Gray	Operator

You can change these defaults by selecting the Fonts tab on the Query Analyzer Options dialog box.

Now, to actually run the query, click the Execute Query button. You can also select Query, Execute from the menu, press F5 on your keyboard, or press Alt+E. After you run the query, the results pane appears with all the information about the employees in the Northwind database, as shown in Figure 1.13.

Notice that while your query was executing, the red Stop button became available. You can cancel a query while it's still running by clicking on the Stop button. However, your queries should run so fast that you will never get a chance to cancel them—at least until you work with a larger production database that contains many entries.

Now, let's go back to the text and grid options that we discussed in the previous section. Click the current mode button on the toolbar and switch to the Results in Text option. You can also press Ctrl+T to set this option. Now, rerun the query and examine your results pane. Notice that all the same tabs are listed, but your query results are formatted a bit differently.

FIGURE 1.13
Displaying your query results.

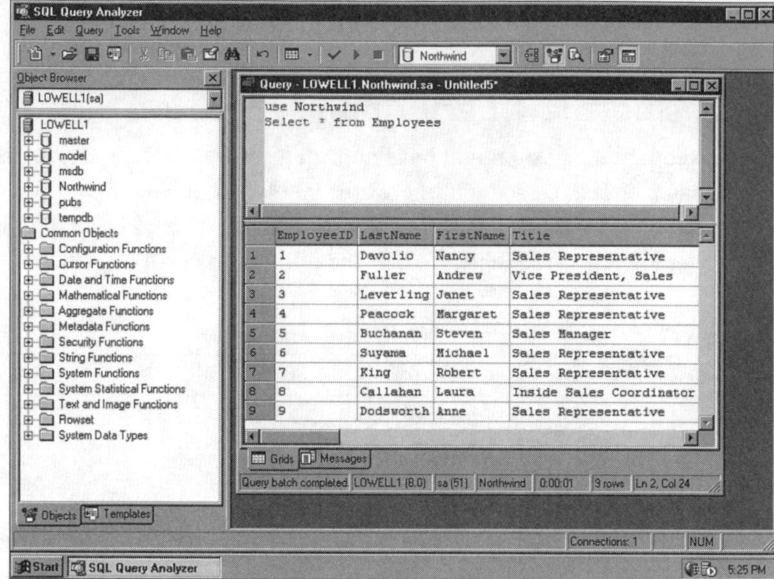

Using Query Analyzer to Learn About Tables

Besides using Query Analyzer to run queries, you can also use it to view information about the tables in the database, such as the columns in the table or indexes that are defined. The Object Browser, when turned on, enables you to easily browse all database objects for each connection that you have open. It's much more powerful than it first appears. You can drag and drop any object into your query window. That's pretty useful, but try clicking on the object and dragging it into your query window as shown in Figure 1.14. In addition, right-clicking on an object enables you to choose from different SQL statement options, such as writing a create table script or a select query script.

Another useful option is the object search. Click it to bring up the screen that is shown in Figure 1.15. If you can't remember where the table is that you had the salary column in, just use this feature and the Query Analyzer will search for it and the highlight it if found. This can be very useful when working on a large or complex system, or just a system you haven't seen in a while.

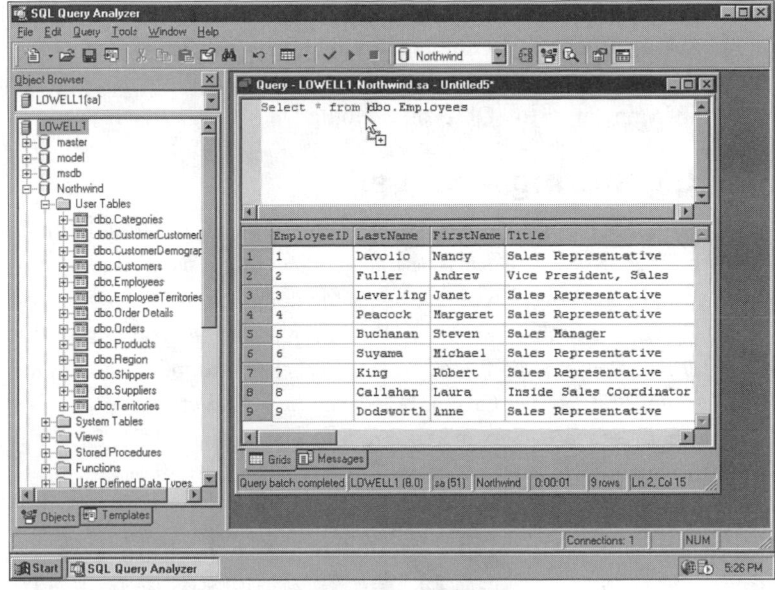

FIGURE 1.14

Dragging and dropping objects from the Object Browser.

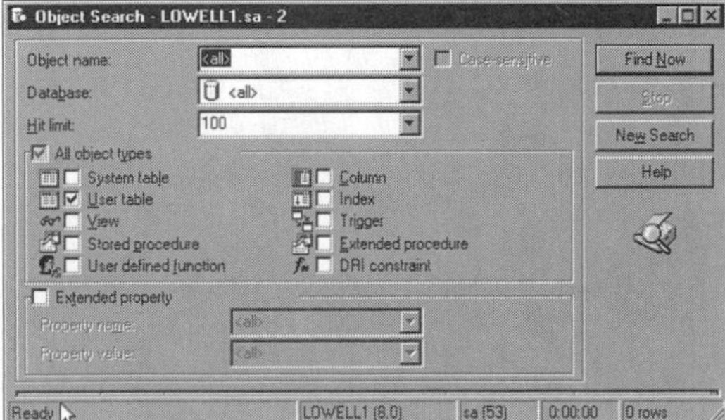

FIGURE 1.15

Using the Object Search dialog.

Well, you've gotten a good look at the Query Analyzer that you will be using for the remainder of this book. You will quickly see how important a tool the Query Analyzer really is.

Introducing SQL Server 2000 Enterprise Manager

As you have just seen, the Query Analyzer is a very powerful tool. It has been greatly enhanced in SQL Server 2000 to be a SQL programmer's best friend. However, you still have the SQL Server Enterprise Manager, which is meant to be the primary graphical interface. There's very little that the Enterprise Manager can do that you can't accomplish from a T-SQL command in the Query Analyzer. However, using the Enterprise Manager is sometimes more convenient, especially when you are new to the SQL Server environment or to SQL programming.

Registering a Server

If you are using SQL Server on your computer, and it is the first time you have started the SQL Server Enterprise Manager, you might need to register the server with which you are working. If you are using the computer where SQL Server is installed, your local SQL Server computer name will be registered for you during the setup process. To register a server, expand the Microsoft SQL Servers option, and you should see the default group, SQL Server Group. Select the SQL Server Group and then from the Action menu, select New SQL Server Registration. The Register SQL Server Wizard appears as shown in Figure 1.16.

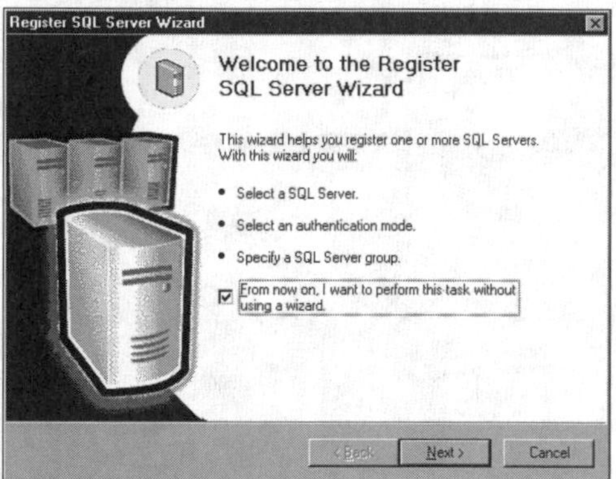

FIGURE 1.16
Registering a SQL Server by using the SQL Server Wizard.

I suggest that you choose not to use the wizard in the future because registering a SQL Server is one of the easiest tasks you can perform. Click Next to be presented with the default dialog box to register a SQL Server (see Figure 1.17).

Enter your computer name in the Server box (as shown in Figure 1.17), and then select the security mode you want to use. Select the SQL Server login option, and complete your SQL Server login credentials if you select to use SQL Server authentication. Now, click the OK button to configure your first registration for Enterprise Manager.

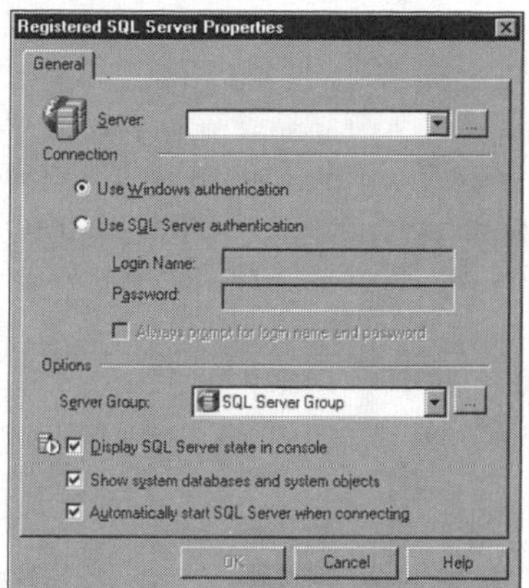

FIGURE 1.17

The Registered SQL Server Properties dialog box.

Seeing How Enterprise Manager Works

Close the Registered SQL Server Properties dialog by clicking the Cancel button, and you will see that your servers are already registered in the left pane of Enterprise Manager when you expand the SQL Server Group. Then expand each server (see Figure 1.18). You can tell when you are connected by the presence of the green circle with the white arrow in it. So, in Figure 1.18, you can see that I am connected to my default instance (Lowell1) and not connected to the Oracle instance. Recall that we generated an error message earlier today by asking for the Oracle server, but because it is not registered, we were unable to see it.

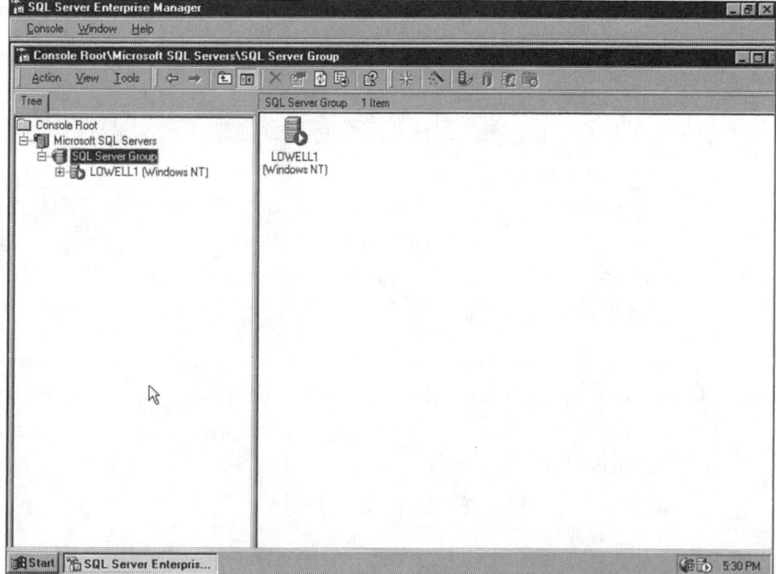

FIGURE 1.18

Enterprise Manager with your registered servers.

Within each server, the Databases folder lists the databases installed on your server. The Data Transformation Services folder shows any DTS packages that you have set up, as well as Meta Data Services packages. The Management folder shows the administrative management features of SQL Server. The Replication folder shows the replication configuration changes that you've made to your server. The Security folder enables you to configure security in SQL Server. The Support Services folder enables you to control other SQL Server–related services on your computer, such as the Distributed Transaction Coordinator and full-text search. Figure 1.19 shows an expanded view of each folder. Notice that when I highlight my server, information about that server is displayed as an HTML page on the right side of the screen.

FIGURE 1.19

The console display of the Enterprise Manager.

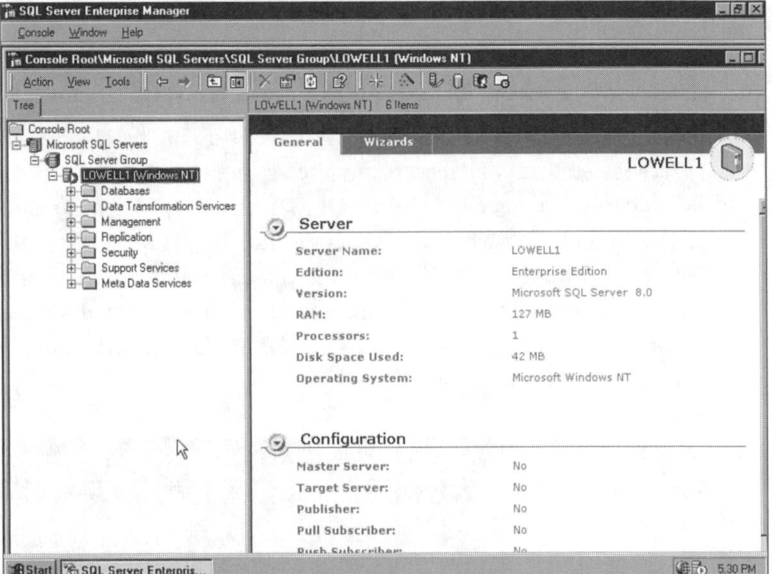

Now expand the Databases folder, and then highlight the Northwind database in the left pane. Notice how a new page then displays in the right pane, as shown in Figure 1.20. This is how Enterprise Manager works: Container objects are typically shown on the left and the contents of the container objects, or other information, are displayed on the right.

Some dialog boxes also open separate windows or dialog boxes for you to work with. For example, right-click the Northwind database folder on the left and select Properties from the pop-up menu. Notice that you are presented with a new dialog on top of Enterprise Manager (see Figure 1.21). *Property sheets* (dialogs with the descriptions of properties of an object) often appear as separate dialogs.

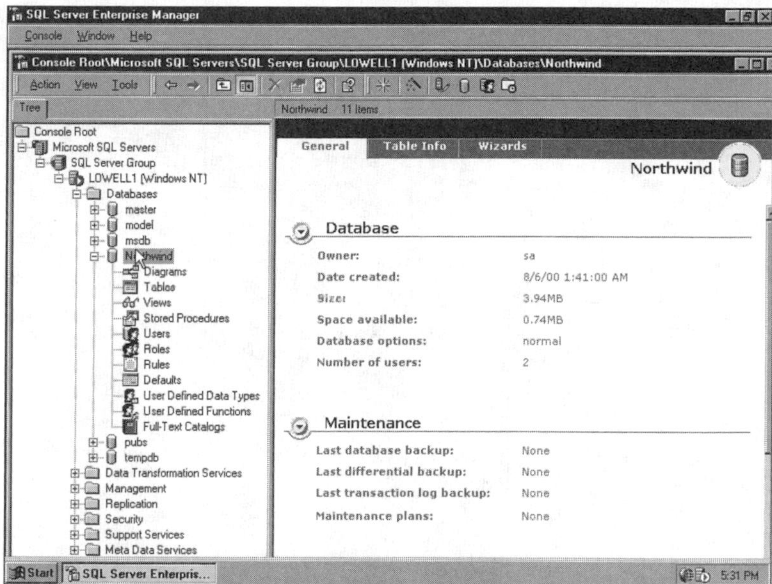

FIGURE 1.20

The Northwind database and its objects.

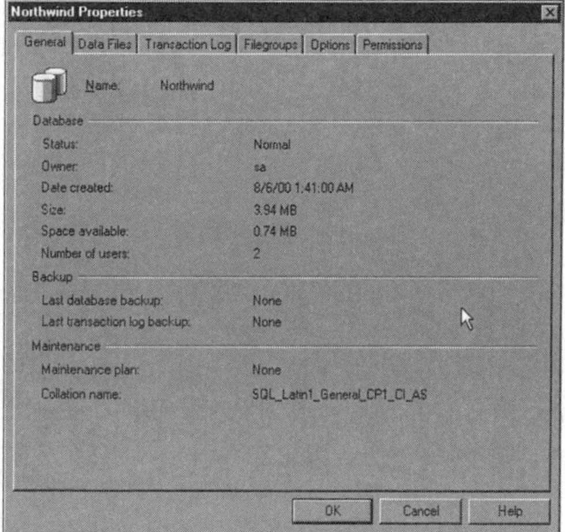

FIGURE 1.21

The properties of the Northwind database.

Click Cancel to dismiss the Northwind database's property sheet without making any changes. Another feature that's worth examining is the menu options. The options available will change depending on what you've highlighted. For example, you will see Figure 1.22 if you click the Tools menu with the Northwind database highlighted. Don't worry about these options; as a SQL programmer, you will not need to work with them. The database system administrator is the person who maintains these options.

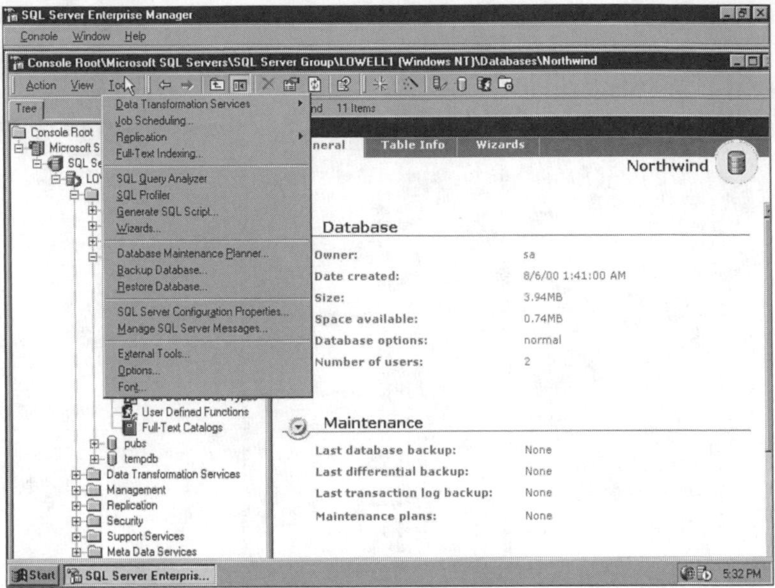

FIGURE 1.22
Menu options in SQL Server Enterprise Manager.

To fully understand the Enterprise Manager would take at least another 30 to 40 pages. However, because you will mostly be using the Query Analyzer in this book, you can read up on the Enterprise Manager in *Sams Teach Yourself SQL Server 2000 in 21 Days* at a later date.

Summary

In today's lesson, you learned what SQL is and how it relates to the SQL Server database that you will be using. In addition, you wrote your first SQL query using the new SQL Server tool, Query Analyzer. The Query Analyzer is used to enter, execute, and modify SQL code. Finally, you took a brief look at the new Enterprise Manager that comes with Microsoft SQL Server. You saw how to use these tools to view table information and the columns that they contain. In tomorrow's lesson, you will learn how to modify the `SELECT` statement you used today in order to filter and sort the data that you are requesting from the database.

Q&A

Q I don't have a Microsoft SQL Server available to me, what can I use instead?

A You could use a personal database such as Microsoft Access, but this book is about T-SQL, and although some of the examples in this book will work in Access or some other database, many will not.

Q I'm new to programming, but I need to learn SQL. Is this book for me?

A Absolutely. I've included notes and sidebars for people who have never programmed before. If you have programmed before, just skip over these as you see fit.

Q Why is SQL pronounced "sequel?"

A SQL is a descendant of IBM's SEQUEL language. The pronunciation has stuck from this earlier name.

Workshop

The Workshop provides quiz questions to help you solidify your understanding of the material covered and exercises to provide you with experience in using what you've learned. Try to answer the quiz and exercise questions before checking the answers in Appendix A, "Answers to Quizzes and Exercises," and make sure you understand the answers before continuing to the next lesson.

Quiz

1. How can I tell whether the words I type into the Query Analyzer editor are keywords?
2. Identify the column and table names in the following `SELECT` statement:

```
select OrderID,
        CustomerID,
        OrderDate,
        ShipName,
        ShippedDate
From Orders
```

3. The following query does not work. Why?

```
Select * Employees
```

Exercise

1. Using the `Employees` table from earlier today, write a query to return just the `EmployeeID` and title for each employee.

WEEK 1

DAY 2

Filtering and Sorting Data

In yesterday's lesson, you learned a little about what SQL is and how it relates to the SQL Server database. In addition, you were introduced to the Query Analyzer and some of its features. Using the Query Analyzer, you executed your first SQL query, returning all the data in the `Employees` table of the Northwind database.

Today, you will learn how to limit the number of rows you get back, and to sort those rows in a particular order, based on one or more columns returned in the query. These actions are the backbone of almost every SQL query that you will run. In fact, you can see an example of this at home in your bank statement. Each month you get a report (statement) that shows only the last month's data (filtering) and it is listed in date order (sorting).

Today, you will learn how the `WHERE` and `ORDER BY` clauses that can be used in the `SELECT` statement. You will cover the following topics along the way:

- How and when to use the equality and inequality conditions in the `WHERE` clause
- Using Boolean logic in the `WHERE` clause

- Comparing a list of values with `IN` and `NOT IN`
- Searching a range with `BETWEEN` and `NOT BETWEEN`
- How to compare dates in SQL
- What Null values are and how to use them
- How to order or sort the data when it is returned

Filtering Data with WHERE Clauses

The first half of today's lesson will show you how to use a `WHERE` clause to restrict the rows returned from a table. Learning to limit rows with `WHERE` will improve system performance by reducing the amount of data returned to (and processed by) your application programs.

Queries that don't include a `WHERE` clause operate on all rows in a table. Later, when you learn to `UPDATE` and `DELETE` data, you will use `WHERE` clauses to determine what data in your tables is deleted and/or updated. If you don't include a `WHERE` clause in a `DELETE` statement, you will delete every row in the table, which is not a good idea. An example of an update that affects all the rows in a table is

```
Update Orders Set OrderDate = '1/1/2000'
```

This will modify every `OrderDate` in the table, regardless of what you really might have wanted to do.

`WHERE` clauses provide a test for each row to determine whether some condition is true or false for that row. The true or false answer is generated from criteria you initially set up in the test, which determines whether a row is returned. If a row meets the requirements you set for return, that row will be displayed. Subsequently, if a row does not meet the criteria, it will not be returned. Setting up the test and criteria generally follows this format:

```
<expression> <comparison-operator> <expression>
```

The *`expression`* can be any combination of columns, constants, variables (more on variables in the second week), functions, and operators. `The WHERE` clause must follow the table list (the `FROM` clause) in the `SELECT` statement, as shown in the following example:

```
use northwind
select EmployeeID, FirstName, LastName, city
From Employees
Where city = 'London'
```

Results:

```
EmployeeID  FirstName  LastName             city
----------- ---------- -------------------- ---------------
5           Steven     Buchanan             London
6           Michael    Suyama               London
7           Robert     King                 London
9           Anne       Dodsworth            London

(4 row(s) affected)
```


The *comparison-operator* defines the type of comparison that will occur between any given row and the criteria set forth for return. Here are the comparisons we'll learn about today:

- Equality (=) and inequality (<>, !=)
- Range search (>, >=, <, <=, BETWEEN, NOT BETWEEN)
- List membership (IN, NOT IN)
- Pattern match (LIKE, NOT LIKE)

Matching Column Data with Equality Statements

We'll work with the Products table, from the Northwind database, today for our exercises. Imagine that you would like a complete price list for all the items listed in the table. You could write this query inside your query analyzer:

```
select ProductName, UnitPrice
from Products
```

This query returns 77 rows, but I am interested in only the price of tofu today. To request a price for a particular product, you would include a WHERE clause that restricts the output to only rows having a value of 'Tofu' in the ProductName field. The following code example shows the WHERE clause in action:

```
select ProductName, UnitPrice
from Products
where ProductName = 'Tofu'
```

Results:

```
ProductName                              UnitPrice
---------------------------------------- ---------------------
Tofu                                                   23.2500

(1 row(s) affected)
```

The output includes a single row, with the price of tofu. When you execute a query with a WHERE clause, the server searches the table for rows matching your conditions. Only rows matching the search conditions are then returned in the result set (see Figure 2.1).

What if you use double quotes to define a string? Here's the same query, but I've identified the string with double quotes instead of single quotes to set off the string data:

```
select ProductName, UnitPrice
from Products
where ProductName = "Tofu"
```

Sometimes, double quotes work fine and the results are exactly the same as with single quotes, but in other cases, you might get a message like this:

```
Server: Msg 207, Level 16, State 3, Line 1
Invalid column name 'Tofu'.
```

The server did not recognize that `"Tofu"` was a string value. The string value passed in double quotes has been interpreted as a (nonexistent) column name.

The server behaves differently with double quotes depending on your current version of the server (prior to version 7, SQL Server did not differentiate between single and double quotes). Server behavior also changes based on settings that you choose or your administrator chooses for you.

The short explanation is that the ANSI SQL standard (we discussed this standard yesterday) requires that identifiers (table names, database names, column names, and so forth) be optionally identified with double quotes. That's useful when a table name includes a space or other special character, as in this query:

```
select OrderID, ProductID
from "Order Details"
where OrderID = 12345
```

Without the quote marks, the server wouldn't know where the table name ended and the next word in the query began. This behavior can be changed with the set option, `set quoted_identifier <on|off>`. (You can also use brackets, as in `[Order Details]`, to set off identifiers whenever you need to.)

When `quoted_identifier` is on (which is true by default), double quotes identify column names and table names, but not character strings. When it's off, double quotes identify character strings but not columns and tables.

Here's the bottom line. Use brackets to identify table and column names if necessary (as in `[Order Details]`). Use single quotes to identify strings (as in `'Tofu'`). Never use double quotes. Ever. To help you out, SQL Query Analyzer turns single-quoted strings (but not double-quoted strings) red in the text window.

FIGURE 2.1

The condition described in the `WHERE` *clause limits the result set to the rows in the table that match the condition.*

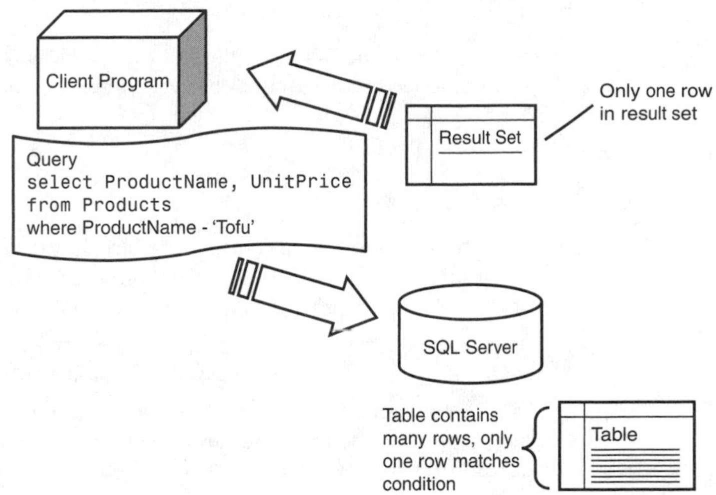

2

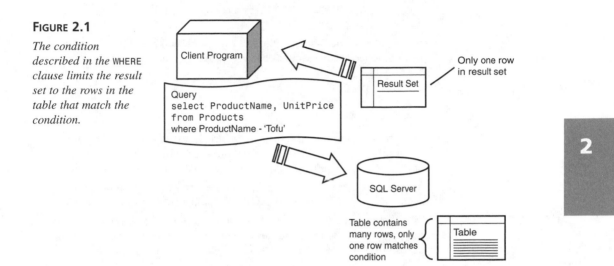

Uppercase and Lowercase Strings

Case sensitivity is a function of the server and database configuration. By default, SQL Server is not case sensitive. That means in most instances the server does not distinguish between uppercase and lowercase character strings.

What that means in a `WHERE` clause is that uppercase and lowercase won't matter there either. For example, in the query we tried earlier, it doesn't matter how the search string is capitalized. If we pass the string as `'tofu'` (lowercase `'t'`), the query will still work:

```
select ProductName, UnitPrice
from Products
where ProductName = 'tofu'
```

Results:

```
ProductName                              UnitPrice
---------------------------------------- ---------------------
Tofu                                                   23.2500

(1 row(s) affected)
```

This is important to remember. If you received different results from this query than those shown here, the SQL Server you are connected to is running in case-sensitive (binary sorted) mode. This will make your queries case sensitive. This will also affect table and column naming and sort orders. You should ask the database administrator to find out for sure.

However, before you panic, try the following test. Run this query that checks whether the server distinguishes between uppercase and lowercase 'A':

```
if 'A' = 'a'
    print 'Dictionary'
else
    print 'Binary'
```

If the return message is 'Dictionary', you're using dictionary sorting and case sensitivity is not an issue. If you did not specify this setting when you installed SQL Server 2000, the default is used, which is dictionary sorting.

If the message is 'Binary', your results might differ from those shown in a number of places throughout the book. You will want to keep that in mind.

Changing this setting is not hard, but it does require the SQL Server administrator to perform the task. You can find out how to do this in Books Online by going to the following topic: "How to rebuild the master database."

Matching Rows Using Not Equals (!= or <>)

Matching rows when they do *not* equal a value is very similar to the test for equality. SQL Server accepts two different symbols for not equals: <> (which is familiar to BASIC programmers) and != (which is more familiar to C programmers). The two operators behave identically in your query, so use whichever one is more comfortable for you.

The following code is an example of using a not equals operator with a numeric value to find some needed data. Imagine that you are looking for all discontinued products. To find this information, you will need to query the Discontinued column in the Products table. The Discontinued column is considered a bit column, and can accept a value of only 0 or 1. The typical convention is to use 0 for false and 1 for true. In this case, a value of 0 in the Discontinued column means the product was not discontinued and a value of 1 means that it was; note that in the WHERE clause that follows.

```
select ProductName, UnitPrice
from products
where discontinued = 1
```

Results:

```
ProductName                              UnitPrice
---------------------------------------- ---------------------
Chef Anton's Gumbo Mix                                  21.3500
Mishi Kobe Niku                                         97.0000
Alice Mutton                                            39.0000
Guaraná Fantástica                                       4.5000
Rössle Sauerkraut                                       45.6000
Thüringer Rostbratwurst                                123.7900
```

```
Singaporean Hokkien Fried Mee                               14.0000
Perth Pasties                                               32.8000
```

By using a WHERE clause that checks whether the Discontinued column contains a 1 (meaning the product was discontinued), I can list only those products that match that condition. Notice that I didn't include the Discontinued column in the result set. It's quite common to exclude criteria columns in a final result presented to a user.

Not equals is slower than most other conditions in almost all situations. The server usually cannot find a way to "optimize" (that is, run efficiently) queries based solely on not equals conditions. If you can find a way to restate a condition without a not equals clause, it will probably be faster.

For example, because you know that Discontinued is limited to 0 and 1, change the WHERE clause from

```
where discontinued <> 0
```

to

```
where discontinued = 1
```

or

```
where discontinued >= 1
```

In general, use what you know about the data to simplify the server's work.

Searching for Numeric Values

In the previous query, we looked for rows by matching the product name to a string constant. (You will learn how to match strings using wildcards later today.) In addition to searching for string values, you can also search for numeric values. To find books with a price of $23.25, use the WHERE clause with a numeric comparison, as shown in the following example:

```
Select ProductName, UnitPrice
from Products
where UnitPrice = 23.25
```

Results:

```
ProductName                              UnitPrice
---------------------------------------- --------------------
Tofu                                                  23.2500

(1 row(s) affected)
```

Notice that the numeric value is passed without quotes. What if you use quotes here?

```
select ProductName, UnitPrice
from Products
where UnitPrice = '23.25'
```

Results:

```
Server: Msg 260, Level 16, State 1, Line 1
Disallowed implicit conversion from data type varchar to
data type money, table 'Northwind.dbo.Products', column
'UnitPrice'. Use the CONVERT function to run this query.
```

The query failed because the server tried to compare a number (the UnitPrice column) to the character string, `'23.25'`. By using the quotes, you changed 23.25 from a number value to a string value, and the comparison caused an error because the server cannot perform implicit (that is, automatic) conversions between these data types. So, to properly query for numbers, you will be best served by not putting the numbers in quotes. Tomorrow, we'll learn how to convert these data types by using the `cast()` and `convert()` functions.

Returning Multiple Rows

All the queries have so far returned only one row. What if the condition applies to multiple rows? All rows matching the conditions are returned in the result set. Here's an example of a query that returns multiple rows:

```
select ProductName, UnitPrice
from Products
where UnitPrice = 12.5
```

Results:

```
ProductName                              UnitPrice
---------------------------------------- ---------------------
Gorgonzola Telino                                      12.5000
Scottish Longbreads                                    12.5000

(2 row(s) affected)
```

Although the preceding query looks the about the same as the others we have seen so far, the difference is in the actual data. Because there is more than one row where the unit price matches 12.50, they are all returned by the `SELECT` statement. Also, as you can see, you can use columns in the `WHERE` clause that are not requested in the `SELECT` columns list.

2

> **Note**
>
> This is the last time that I will include the message
>
> ```
> (2 row(s) affected)
> ```
>
> in sample output unless it is important to see the server response. By now, you have probably realized that these messages come back every time, and that they provide an accurate count of the number of rows returned by the query.
>
> If you want to suppress the rowcount report at the end of every query, you have two methods available.
>
> One method is to execute this statement in the SQL Query Analyzer window:
>
> ```
> set nocount on
> ```
>
> That will suppress the count messages for that window, but it won't affect any other window you might open. You will also need to remember to run it every time you start the SQL Query Analyzer.
>
> You can also use the Connections tab in the Options dialog box of the SQL Query Analyzer (Tools, Options, Connections). Click Set Nocount to suppress the count display for all new connections. This option is retained after you exit and return to the SQL Query Analyzer.
>
> There are times when you will find the rowcount display useful. To switch it back on, use
>
> ```
> set nocount off
> ```

Numeric Data and Display Formats in the `WHERE` Clause

Each of the products in the previous result set has a price of $12.50. It's important to notice that the formats of the price in input and output are different. The server interprets numbers by converting the value into an internal arithmetic format. It doesn't matter if we enter **`$12.50`**, **`12.50`**, or **`12.5`**. If the number (which is converted internally by the server to an internal numeric value) matches the value in the column, the condition is true.

On the other hand, output format depends entirely on the software that you are using to display the data. UnitPrice is defined as `money`, which allows four decimal positions (and permits numeric values up to about 900 trillion). The SQL Query Analyzer displays all four digits of `money` type data.

The `UnitsInStock` column is defined as a small integer (`smallint`, permitting no decimal positions and values ranging up to about `32000`). Because a `smallint` value never includes decimal data, the default display for these values in SQL Query Analyzer only shows the integer part of the number. This example shows how the SQL Query Analyzer displays `UnitsInStock` values for the rows we just looked at a moment ago:

```
select ProductName, UnitsInStock
from Products
where UnitPrice = 12.5
```

Results:

```
ProductName                              UnitsInStock
---------------------------------------- ------------
Gorgonzola Telino                                   0
Scottish Longbreads                                 6
```

In your own applications, you can modify how the any of the data returned is displayed. Most report builders and application development environments are able to determine whether to display the data in a result set. As the developer, you are free to override the way data is displayed so that it makes the most sense for your users. This is usually done within the software you are using to display the data.

Retrieving Empty Result Sets

Sometimes you will present a condition that matches no rows. For example, a query asking for products with a negative price will never return any rows:

```
select ProductName, UnitPrice
from products
where UnitPrice = -10
```

Results:

```
ProductName                              UnitPrice
---------------------------------------- ---------------------

(0 row(s) affected)
```

In spite of the fact that no rows were found, a result set will still be returned. The result set just won't have rows of data in it.

Combining Conditions with `OR` and `AND`

You will often need to combine conditions in the `WHERE` clause to find rows that meet multiple criteria. For example, you might want to see the price of several products, as in this query:

```
select ProductName, UnitPrice
  from Products
 where ProductName = 'Konbu'
    or ProductName = 'Cream Cheese'
```

```
    or ProductName = 'Tofu'
    or ProductName = 'Pavlova'
```

Results:

```
ProductName                              UnitPrice
---------------------------------------- --------------------
Konbu                                                  6.0000
Pavlova                                               17.4500
Tofu                                                  23.2500
```


The four comparisons in the query are joined with the keyword OR. As in all programming environments, when you use OR, the condition is true when any of the joined conditions is true. For each row, the server tests each of the conditions. As long as the row matches any one condition, it will be included in a result set. (Notice that no row came back for 'Cream Cheese'. This company doesn't sell cream cheese.)

You can also combine conditions affecting different columns. Here is a query combining a price condition and a product name condition:

```
select ProductName, UnitPrice
  from Products
 where ProductName = 'Konbu'
    or UnitPrice = 10.00
```

Results:

```
ProductName                              UnitPrice
---------------------------------------- --------------------
Aniseed Syrup                                         10.0000
Konbu                                                  6.0000
Sir Rodney's Scones                                   10.0000
Longlife Tofu                                         10.0000
```

This query returns four rows from either the ProductName column or UnitPrice column, or both. There is one row matching the 'Konbu' condition, but the other three match only the price condition. If a row matches both conditions, it still appears in the result set only one time.

The AND Condition

Like the OR condition, AND works as it works in all programming environments. When conditions are connected with the AND keyword, all the conditions must be met for the row to appear in the result set. Each row will be compared to all the conditions in turn; only when all conditions are true will the SQL Server include the row.

In the previous query, we connected the conditions with OR. Rebuilding the same query with AND, we find that there are no rows whose ProductName is 'Konbu' and whose UnitPrice is 10.00:

```
select ProductName, UnitPrice
  from Products
 where ProductName = 'Konbu'
   and UnitPrice = 10.00
```

Results:

```
ProductName                              UnitPrice
---------------------------------------- --------------------
```

The query returns an empty result set.

The next example combines the `CategoryID` and `SupplierID` to provide a narrow list. There are 12 products where the `CategoryID` is `2` and three products whose `SupplierID` is `1`. When the conditions are combined, we find the only row where both conditions are true:

```
select ProductName, CategoryID, SupplierID
  from products
 where CategoryID = 2
   and SupplierID = 1
```

Results:

```
ProductName                              CategoryID  SupplierID
---------------------------------------- ----------- -----------
Aniseed Syrup                                      2           1
```

Combining AND and OR

What happens when the `AND` and `OR` conditions appear in the same query? For example, what if you wanted to see everything with a `CategoryID` of `2` from suppliers with an ID of `1` and `3`. Here's how you might write it:

```
select ProductName, CategoryID, SupplierID
  from products
 where CategoryID = 2
   and SupplierID = 1
    or SupplierID = 3
```

Results:

```
ProductName                              CategoryID  SupplierID
---------------------------------------- ----------- -----------
Aniseed Syrup                                      2           1
Grandma's Boysenberry Spread                       2           3
Uncle Bob's Organic Dried Pears                    7           3
Northwoods Cranberry Sauce                         2           3
```

The third row in the results is in the wrong category. I wanted rows in category 2, but somehow something from category 7 appeared in the list.

The problem occurs because of *operator precedence* or, in English, because AND conditions are evaluated before OR conditions. In this case, the server first evaluated each row for the combination of category 2 and supplier 1 (using AND), and then used OR to include any rows from supplier 3 (regardless of category).

To override the default precedence, use parentheses to group together conditions you want evaluated first. In this example, wrap parentheses around the two SupplierID conditions, forcing them to be evaluated before the CategoryID condition, like this:

```
select ProductName, CategoryID, SupplierID
  from products
 where CategoryID = 2
   and (SupplierID = 1
    or SupplierID = 3)
```

Results:

```
ProductName                              CategoryID  SupplierID
---------------------------------------- ----------- -----------
Aniseed Syrup                                      2           1
Grandma's Boysenberry Spread                       2           3
Northwoods Cranberry Sauce                         2           3
```

The parentheses allow the server to correctly remove the incorrect row. Sometimes it's difficult to remember the rules for precedence. In general, when combining OR and AND conditions, use parentheses to clarify what you want. Your code will work more often on the first try, and the logic will be easier for others to understand and modify later.

Searching for Ranges of Values with Inequalities (>, <, BETWEEN)

SQL Server enables you to search for a range of values with greater than and less than operators, and with the BETWEEN keyword. These comparison operators work just like the equals and not equals comparison methods, so I'll just show you a couple of examples. After that, we'll look at a couple of specific issues with range searching.

SQL Server supports the four basic inequality operators: > (greater than), < (less than), >= (greater than or equals), and <= (less than or equals). All these operators work with a variety of data types (numeric, string, date, and binary). Let's start by looking at numeric comparisons.

This first query looks for products whose price is less than $7:

```
select ProductName, UnitPrice
  from Products
 where UnitPrice < 7
```

Results:

```
ProductName                              UnitPrice
---------------------------------------- --------------------
Konbu                                                  6.0000
Guaraná Fantástica                                     4.5000
Geitost                                                2.5000
```

Notice that any products costing exactly $7 are omitted from this result set because of the open comparison (less than). Here's the same query, allowing items costing exactly $7 because of the closed comparison (less than *or equals*):

```
select ProductName, UnitPrice
from Products
where UnitPrice <= 7
```

Results:

```
ProductName                              UnitPrice
---------------------------------------- --------------------
Konbu                                                  6.0000
Guaraná Fantástica                                     4.5000
Geitost                                                2.5000
Filo Mix                                               7.0000
```

`Filo Mix` appears in the second result set but not in the first.

Combining Inequality Conditions

You can combine equalities and inequalities, as in this query:

```
select ProductName, UnitPrice, CategoryID
  from Products
 where CategoryID = 3
   and UnitPrice < 10
```

Results:

```
ProductName                    UnitPrice            CategoryID
------------------------------ -------------------- -----------
Teatime Chocolate Biscuits                   9.2000           3
Zaanse koeken                                9.5000           3
```

You can combine two inequalities on the same column to get a list of values in a specific range. The next query lists products whose unit price is more than $12 but less than $13.

```
select ProductName, UnitPrice
  from Products
 where UnitPrice > 12
   and UnitPrice < 13
```

Results:

```
ProductName                              UnitPrice
---------------------------------------- --------------------
Gorgonzola Telino                                     12.5000
Chocolade                                             12.7500
Scottish Longbreads                                   12.5000
```


Searching for Ranges of Values with BETWEEN

The previous query provided a list of rows where the UnitPrice was in a range that excluded the endpoints. In other words, rows having values of 12 and 13 were left out of the result set.

That query could be rewritten to *include* the endpoints by using less than or equals (<=) and greater than or equals (>=) conditions.

```
select ProductName, UnitPrice
  from Products
 where UnitPrice >= 12
   and UnitPrice <= 13
```

Results:

```
ProductName                              UnitPrice
---------------------------------------- --------------------
Gorgonzola Telino                                     12.5000
Spegesild                                             12.0000
Chocolade                                             12.7500
Scottish Longbreads                                   12.5000
Original Frankfurter grüne Soße                       13.0000
```

Notice that rows with prices of $12 and $13 appeared in this result set after we included the endpoints; this is referred to as a closed-ended range. SQL provides a keyword, BETWEEN, that enables us to define closed-ended range searches in a single condition. Here is the same query with the UnitPrice inequality conditions restated as a single condition using BETWEEN:

```
select ProductName, UnitPrice
  from Products
 where UnitPrice between 12 and 13
```

If you take the time to try this out, you will find that the results are identical to the prior query.

A technical note here: Not only are the results identical, but query performance is also identical. It simply does not matter whether you use BETWEEN or connect two closed inequalities with AND. From the perspective of the server, they are the same query.

This is an important point. As you work with Transact-SQL, you will find a variety of methods to achieve the same purpose. Even though all the avenues reach the same correct result, often one of the choices provides better performance. I'll point these out to you as we come across them.

Transact-SQL also supports `NOT BETWEEN`, which is the opposite of the `BETWEEN` comparison operator. The `WHERE` clause

```
where UnitPrice not between 12 and 13
```

returns all rows with unit price less than `12` and all rows with unit price greater than `13`. The endpoint values (`12` and `13`) are excluded. The `NOT BETWEEN` query is the same as using `OR` with less than and greater than:

```
 where UnitPrice < 12
    or UnitPrice > 13
```

Using Inequalities with Strings

So far, all our comparisons have been based on numeric data. As I said earlier, inequalities work with all types of data, but we'll have to look closely to understand the implementation.

What do we mean when we ask for all products whose name is greater than `'T'`? Here's the query and result set:

```
select ProductName
  from Products
 where ProductName > 'T'
```

Results:

```
ProductName
----------------------------------------
Tarte au sucre
Teatime Chocolate Biscuits
Thüringer Rostbratwurst
Tofu
Tourtière
Tunnbröd
Uncle Bob's Organic Dried Pears
Valkoinen suklaa
```

```
Vegie-spread
Wimmers gute Semmelknödel
Zaanse koeken
```

All these values appear later than the letter T in a sorted list, so they are all greater than `'T'`.

Here's the rule: *A string is greater than another string if it appears after it in an alphabetical listing.*

Things become complicated when you start looking for ranges of values with strings. When you want a list of products that start with Q or R, you might consider using this query:

```
select ProductName
  from Products
 where ProductName between 'Q' and 'R'
```

Results:

```
ProductName
----------------------------------------
Queso Cabrales
Queso Manchego La Pastora
```

I can see the products starting with Q, but nothing with R. Remember that the `BETWEEN` query is the same as two inequalities joined with `AND`, as in this query:

```
select ProductName
  from Products
 where ProductName >= 'Q'
   and ProductName <= 'R'
```

Any product name starting in R would appear after the letter R itself in a sorted list. Therefore, product names starting with R are not between Q and R.

To get products starting with Q and R, you need to use the letter S as your second endpoint, as in this query:

```
select ProductName
  from Products
 where ProductName >= 'Q'
   and ProductName < 'S'
```

Results:

```
ProductName
----------------------------------------
Queso Cabrales
Queso Manchego La Pastora
Raclette Courdavault
Ravioli Angelo
Rhönbräu Klosterbier
Röd Kaviar
Rogede sild
Rössle Sauerkraut
```

Don't use `BETWEEN` here. `BETWEEN` conditions include both endpoints, so a product named S would be included in your result set.

One more note about `BETWEEN`. The low and high ends of the range must be stated in that order. If the low value is greater than the high value, the condition is always false. For example, this condition will never return any rows:

```
where ProductName between 'D' and 'A'
```

Getting Correct Results from Date Comparisons

The discussion about string inequalities got us started in understanding date comparisons. In fact, I avoided addressing dates at all until you understood inequalities. That's because almost all date processing on SQL Server is done with inequalities, not equalities.

SQL Server doesn't really store dates. It stores `datetime` data, which is a composite data type made up of date information and time information. There are two data types for storing dates: `datetime` and `smalldatetime`. Both types consist of a date component and a time component.

In Transact-SQL, all dates are quoted strings formatted as dates and/or times. (We'll look at some date functions tomorrow in the section "Using Functions.") The output of dates includes both a date and time component, as in this query from the `Employees` table:

```
select LastName, HireDate
from Employees
```

Results:

```
LastName             HireDate
-------------------- ---------------------------
Davolio              1992-05-01 00:00:00.000
Fuller               1992-08-14 00:00:00.000
Leverling            1992-04-01 00:00:00.000
Peacock              1993-05-03 00:00:00.000
Buchanan             1993-10-17 00:00:00.000
Suyama               1993-10-17 00:00:00.000
King                 1994-01-02 00:00:00.000
Callahan             1994-03-05 00:00:00.000
Dodsworth            1994-11-15 00:00:00.000
```

As you can see, the hire dates are all entered as dates with a zero time (00:00:00.000), which is midnight. In all these cases, we can use an equality to find employees by hire date. Here's an example:

```
select LastName, HireDate
  from Employees
 where HireDate = 'Jan 2, 1994'
```

Results:

```
LastName             HireDate
-------------------- ---------------------------
King                 1994-01-02 00:00:00.000
```

You probably noticed the date format: `'Jan 2, 1994'`. You can also use almost any date format. Here are some of the valid ways to present the same date, all to be enclosed in single quotes in the `WHERE` clause:

- `1/2/94`
- `01/02/1994`
- `1-2-94`
- `1994-01-02`
- `19940102`
- `January 2 1994`
- `1.2.94`

Dates in Other Languages and Formats

What about month names in other languages, or day-month-year ordering preferences? These are essentially localization issues that can be resolved by installing and selecting a different national language for your server or user profile.

A dateformat option in T-SQL changes the interpretation of date strings for your current session. To allow the database server to accept dates in day-month-year format, use this query:

```
set dateformat dmy
```

Every time you log in, you will need to set this setting. It's easier to set a national language for your login and use that to define your default dateformat.

The date *output* format reflects the choice of the developer of the SQL Query Analyzer tool itself. When you write your own applications, you will use your software development tools and report writers to improve the appearance of date information. T-SQL provides several functions that you can use with dates to change how dates are displayed as shown in the following example:

```
Select     Convert(varchar,OrderDate,107)
From Orders
```

This SQL statement would format the date as shown:

```
Jul 04, 1996
```

You will be learning how to use these later in this book.

Experimenting with datetime Values

The Employees table doesn't have any nonzero times, so we need to fabricate a more lifelike situation. Let's create a temporary table and add some dates with nonzero times. This will enable us to experiment with real-life examples of datetime data to understand better how it works.

Note

You're about to do a little extra work to get a table with more realistic datetime values, so I ought to explain why you're going to all this trouble. The Northwind database contains several date fields, but all the dates in every table have a zero time component. That's probably because this database is provided as a sample database for all of Microsoft's database application environments, not just SQL Server.

The reality is that all your dates (except birth dates and hire dates) will have time components. Most systems populate a column such as OrderDate by using the getdate() system function, which returns the date and time from the server system clock (down to the millisecond). Audit trails use full date and time values, as do trading systems, banking systems, and so forth.

Unfortunately, new T-SQL programmers constantly make mistakes with dates, often because their learning and test environment does not include dates with time components. So, take the time now to learn this well and you can avoid a major headache later.

Listing 2.1 provides the script to create and populate a temporary table with some date values. (It's also on the CD-ROM if you don't want to type this much stuff.)

LISTING 2.1 CHAP02_1—Create and Populate a Temporary Table to Test `datetime` Behavior

```
create table #TempDate
(
    OrderNum int not null primary key,
    OrderDate smalldatetime not null
)
go
set nocount on
insert #TempDate (OrderNum, OrderDate)
values (1, '7/12/2000')
insert #TempDate (OrderNum, OrderDate)
values (2, '7/12/2000 5:00pm')
insert #TempDate (OrderNum, OrderDate)
values (3, '7/12/2000 5:15pm')
insert #TempDate (OrderNum, OrderDate)
values (4, '7/12/2000 11:59pm')
insert #TempDate (OrderNum, OrderDate)
values (5, '7/13/2000')
insert #TempDate (OrderNum, OrderDate)
values (6, '7/13/2000 7:15pm')
insert #TempDate (OrderNum, OrderDate)
values (7, getdate())
set nocount off
go
select OrderNum, OrderDate
  from #TempDate
go
```

You haven't formally learned how to create a temporary table or to insert data, but this code listing shows you how it's done. A temporary table is just what its name implies: a place to store data temporarily. The table is private to your session (so, if you open another SQL Query Analyzer window, you won't be able to see #TempDate there). The `INSERT` statement adds rows to the table. We'll learn more about `INSERT` on Day 7, "Adding, Changing, and Deleting Rows."

For now, just run the code listing as it's written and you should get this output:

```
OrderNum    OrderDate
----------- ---------------------------
          1 2000-07-12 00:00:00
          2 2000-07-12 17:00:00
          3 2000-07-12 17:15:00
```

```
          4 2000-07-12 23:59:00
          5 2000-07-13 00:00:00
          6 2000-07-13 19:15:00
          7 2000-06-07 18:16:00
```

The last row of data that was inserted in this table used the system function `GetDate()`. This means that the last row will always display the current date and time when the query was executed.

Generally, when you use date criteria, you are interested in retrieving data for a given time period: an hour, a day, a week, perhaps a year. The key in constructing all these queries is to learn to write date conditions that properly reflect the time period in which you are interested.

We want to see a list of orders in the `#TempDate` table from July 12, 2000. First, we'll try this query:

```
select OrderNum, OrderDate
  from #TempDate
 where OrderDate = '7/12/2000'
```

Results:

```
OrderNum    OrderDate
----------- --------------------------
          1 2000-07-12 00:00:00
```

Even though there are four rows whose date value falls on the 12th of July, this query returns only one row. The other three rows are left behind. When you don't pass a time component in your `datetime` expression, the server assumes that you mean midnight, time zero. Only one order was entered on the stroke of midnight; the rest were entered at various other times during the day.

You saw the correct solution to this problem in your work with string inequalities. You might be tempted to use this query with `BETWEEN`:

```
/* Incorrect date searching method */
select OrderNum, OrderDate
  from #TempDate
 where OrderDate between '7/12/2000' and '7/13/2000'
```

Results:

```
OrderNum    OrderDate
----------- --------------------------
          1 2000-07-12 00:00:00
          2 2000-07-12 17:00:00
          3 2000-07-12 17:15:00
          4 2000-07-12 23:59:00
          5 2000-07-13 00:00:00
```

The results of this query are incorrect. The last row in the set is from July 13, not July 12. The problem with using `BETWEEN` is seen in the closed-end comparison at the high end of the range.

> **Note**
>
> I can just hear you saying to yourself, "Sure, but how much data really gets entered right at the stroke of midnight? Nobody's even at work."
>
> Remember, any date value that is not assigned a time automatically is assigned the zero time: midnight. You could have your entire table all piled up on that little instant.

The correct way to retrieve date range information is to use two inequalities joined with `AND`. Notice how, in this example, the second inequality leaves the high end of the range open (less than but not equal):

```
/* Preferred date searching method */
select OrderNum, OrderDate
  from #TempDate
 where OrderDate >= '7/12/2000'
   and OrderDate < '7/13/2000'
```

Results:

```
OrderNum    OrderDate
----------- ---------------------------
          1 2000-07-12 00:00:00
          2 2000-07-12 17:00:00
          3 2000-07-12 17:15:00
          4 2000-07-12 23:59:00
```

Searching for a Time

How do you search for a time? For example, I want a list of orders taken between 5 and 6 p.m. on any day. Will this query work?

```
/* Incorrect method of searching for a time */
select OrderNum, OrderDate
  from #TempDate
 where OrderDate >= '5:00pm'
   and OrderDate < '6:00pm'
```

Why didn't this query return any rows? Try inserting one more row into the `#TempDate` table, and then retrieve the new row:

```
insert #TempDate (OrderNum, OrderDate)
values (8, '4:00pm')
select OrderNum, OrderDate
from #TempDate
where OrderNum = 8
```

Results:

```
OrderNum    OrderDate
----------- ---------------------------
          8 1900-01-01 16:00:00
```

When you pass a time without a date, the server applies the *system zero date*, January 1, 1900, to the time. In the prior query, when we were looking for data between 5 p.m. and 6 p.m., the server was trying to find rows between 5 p.m. and 6 p.m. on January 1, 1900.

The only way to search a `datetime` column for a time value independent of the date is to use the `datepart()` function, which extracts a part of a `datetime` value. To find all orders between 5:00 p.m. and 6:00 p.m., you would use this query:

```
select OrderNum, OrderDate
  from #TempDate
 where datepart(hh, OrderDate) = 17
```

Results:

```
OrderNum    OrderDate
----------- ---------------------------
          2 2000-07-12 17:00:00
          3 2000-07-12 17:15:00
```

Although searching for dates is pretty straightforward, it's complicated to look for times. A new feature introduced in SQL Server 2000—computed fields—can make it easier. We'll learn more about `datepart()` and other date functions in the function discussion tomorrow.

It's considered good behavior to drop temporary tables when you are finished working with them. If you don't need to continue working with the `#TempDate` table, drop it by executing this statement:

```
drop table #TempDate.
```

Looking for Values in a List: The `IN` Operator

Earlier, when you were looking at multiple comparisons with `AND` and `OR`, you ran a query to find products whose product names matched one of several values. This is the query:

```
select ProductName, UnitPrice
  from Products
 where ProductName = 'Konbu'
    or ProductName = 'Cream Cheese'
    or ProductName = 'Tofu'
    or ProductName = 'Pavlova'
```

The IN operator allows you to compress the four conditions into a single condition like this:

```
select ProductName, UnitPrice
  from Products
 where ProductName in
            ('Konbu', 'Cream Cheese', 'Tofu', 'Pavlova')
```

Both forms of the query return the same results, and they are identically processed by the server. The second form with IN is more compact and easier to read.

In combination with other conditions connected by AND, you are less likely to make grouping mistakes that will throw off the logic of your queries. Do you remember the problems that occurred in the query you wrote earlier combining conditions on both CategoryID and SupplierID? The original query required parentheses to group the SupplierID conditions in order to avoid mistakes in the result set membership:

```
select ProductName, CategoryID, SupplierID
  from products
 where CategoryID = 2
   and (SupplierID = 1
    or SupplierID = 3)
```

Rewritten, the query requires no extra parentheses:

```
select ProductName, CategoryID, SupplierID
  from products
 where CategoryID = 2
   and SupplierID in (1,3)
```

The set of rows emerging from the SupplierID test is automatically resolved before the CategoryID condition is applied.

Using the NOT IN Operator

You can use NOT IN to ask for rows *not matching* any element in a list. This query asks for all products whose category doesn't match a long list of possible categories:

```
select ProductName, CategoryID
  from Products
 where CategoryID not in
    (1, 3, 5, 6, 7, 8)
```

Results:

```
ProductName                              CategoryID
---------------------------------------- ----------
Aniseed Syrup                                     2
Chef Anton's Cajun Seasoning                      2
Chef Anton's Gumbo Mix                            2
```

```
Grandma's Boysenberry Spread                    2
Northwoods Cranberry Sauce                      2
Genen Shouyu                                    2
Gula Malacca                                    2
Sirop d'érable                                  2
Vegie-spread                                    2
Louisiana Fiery Hot Pepper Sauce                2
Louisiana Hot Spiced Okra                       2
Original Frankfurter grüne Soße                 2
Queso Cabrales                                  4
Queso Manchego La Pastora                       4
Gorgonzola Telino                               4
Mascarpone Fabioli                              4
Geitost                                         4
Raclette Courdavault                            4
Camembert Pierrot                               4
Gudbrandsdalsost                                4
Flotemysost                                     4
Mozzarella di Giovanni                          4
```

The result set consists entirely of products in categories 2 and 4. If you know the range of possible values, it usually makes sense to present a `NOT IN` query as the opposite `IN` query:

```
select ProductName, CategoryID
  from Products
 where CategoryID in
    (2, 4)
```

Not only is the query more readable, but it will probably run faster.

A `NOT IN` condition is the same as a set of inequality conditions connected with `AND`. The last example could be rewritten in this way to derive the same results:

```
select ProductName, CategoryID
  from Products
 where CategoryID <> 1
   and CategoryID <> 3
   and CategoryID <> 5
   and CategoryID <> 6
   and CategoryID <> 7
   and CategoryID <> 8
```

Using `IN` and `NOT IN` improves the readability of your code. On Day 6, when we look at subqueries, you will see another application of `IN` that does a lot more than that. Subqueries will allow you to check for the existence of a value in another table.

I can't tell you how many bitter debates I've seen among new users of SQL over the usage of the NOT IN condition. Many people want to argue that it's actually a series of inequalities connected with OR, not AND. If you're feeling that way, take the time to prove it to yourself. Understand why you need to connect the conditions with AND. Try a number of combinations on small tables so that you can predict the result sets. After a few trials, you will start to see it.

Wildcard Searches with LIKE

So far, you have been able to do simple string comparisons. But when working with strings, you will often need to search patterns within strings. To do that, you will need wildcard characters.

SQL supports two basic wildcard characters:

- The percent sign (%) stands for any number of characters (or no characters).
- The underscore (_) stands for any single character.

Let's see a few examples.

In an earlier query, we searched for the value 'Tofu' with an equality condition. Let's repeat that query, but change the condition to look for anything starting with 'T'. I'll use the % wildcard and the LIKE keyword:

```
select ProductName, UnitPrice
  from Products
 where ProductName like 'T%'
```

Results:

```
ProductName                              UnitPrice
---------------------------------------- --------------------
Tarte au sucre                                        49.3000
Teatime Chocolate Biscuits                             9.2000
Thüringer Rostbratwurst                              123.7900
Tofu                                                  23.2500
Tourtière                                              7.4500
Tunnbröd                                               9.0000
```

I can also search for anything with the word 'tofu' in the product name by using two wildcards, at the beginning and end of the word:

```
select ProductName, UnitPrice
  from Products
 where ProductName like '%tofu%'
```

Results:

```
ProductName                              UnitPrice
---------------------------------------- --------------------
Tofu                                                   23.2500
Longlife Tofu                                          10.0000
```

As long as the word `'tofu'` appears anywhere in the string, the row is included in the result set.

There are a couple of key points to keep in mind with the wildcard operators:

- First, the wildcards are active only in a comparison using the `LIKE` comparison operator. With other comparisons, the wildcard characters are simply characters. In this condition, the server will look for a product name that is the literal string `'%Tofu%'`.

  ```
  where ProductName = '%Tofu%'
  ```

- Wildcard comparisons work only with strings. If you try to use a wildcard on a number (`where price like %.95 ???`), you will get a nasty error message from SQL Server.
- For the best performance with wildcard comparisons, use simple comparisons in which you search for a constant expression with the percent sign wildcard at the end, as in this form:

  ```
  where ProductName like 'Tofu%'
  ```

The single character wildcard (_) can be used to check formatting in input masks. For example, if you want to check telephone numbers to see whether they match the U.S. telephone pattern, you might try this query:

```
select Phone
  from Suppliers
 where Phone like
    '(___) ___-____'
```

Results:

```
Phone
------------------------
(171) 555-2222
(100) 555-4822
(313) 555-5735
(161) 555-4448
(503) 555-9931
(617) 555-3267
(514) 555-9022
(514) 555-2955
```

The parentheses, space, and hyphen are fixed in their positions. The underscores each stand for a single position that can be occupied by any character (number, letter, punctuation mark, or symbol).

The pattern in the last query could also match this value, which is clearly not a telephone number:

```
(RX#) N*Y-P{+M
```

2

SQL Server provides a more selective single-character wildcard by using brackets ([]) to provide a list or range of characters for each position. Here is the telephone number query with the bracket notation limiting each character position to a numeric digit:

```
select Phone
  from Suppliers
 where Phone like
    '([0-9][0-9][0-9]) [0-9][0-9][0-9]-[0-9][0-9][0-9][0-9]'
```

Each instance of `[0-9]` stands for a single position in the string.

Use the carat (^) character within the brackets to exclude a character or range of characters from appearing in a position. To see all postal codes *not* starting with a digit, but including a digit in the second position, use this query:

```
select PostalCode, Country
  from Suppliers
 where PostalCode like
    '[^0-9][0-9]%'
```

Results:

```
PostalCode Country
---------- ---------------
M14 GSD    UK
H1J 1C3    Canada
J2S 7S8    Canada
```

The `NOT LIKE` Operator

SQL Server supports the `NOT LIKE` operator. You can use `NOT LIKE` to see all non-US phone numbers in this example:

```
select Phone
  from Suppliers
 where Phone not like
    '(___) ___-____'
```

Results:

```
Phone
------------------------
(03) 3555-5011
(98) 598 76 54
(06) 431-7877
(03) 444-2343
031-987 65 43
(11) 555 4640
(010) 9984510
(069) 992755
(04721) 8713
(0544) 60323
(0)2-953010
08-123 45 67
(1) 03.83.00.68
555-8787
43844108
(12345) 1212
(953) 10956
(02) 555-5914
(089) 6547665
85.57.00.07
38.76.98.06
```

The returned data set contains only phone numbers that do not match the pattern.

Searching for Wildcard Characters

Sometimes you need to search for a wildcard (percent sign, underscore, bracket) as a character in its own right. You can declare an escape character in a `LIKE` condition (you will see how later in this section), and then use the escape character to allow the wildcard to behave like any normal character.

An *escape character* is used to prevent a special character from exercising any special behavior.

An example will help make this clear. How can you use a wildcard to search for the phrase `'50%'` in the following strings?

```
Take 50% off today and tomorrow!

Ice cream sandwiches only 50 cents!

500 marchers converge on courthouse steps
```

To search for the phrase `'50%'` anywhere in a string, you might try this condition:

```
where thestring like '%50%%'
```

Unfortunately, the server takes the `%` after `50` to be a wildcard for any number of characters (just as with the other two wildcards in the expression), so the search condition is true for all three strings. We need to tell the server to treat the second percent sign as a literal character. To do that, define an escape character in the search clause. Then insert the escape character in the string before the wildcard you want to treat as a literal. Here's the corrected search condition:

```
where thestring like '%50\%%' escape '\'
```

You can see in the preceding code that you define the new escape character after you use it in the statement. You won't use an escape character often, but it's useful when you need it.

2

Summary of Search Conditions

Before we start sorting data, let's review what you've learned so far about search conditions:

- To improve overall system performance, do all your data filtering on the server. That will reduce network traffic (from transferring unnecessary rows) and simplify application programming.
- Search conditions appear in a `WHERE` clause. The `WHERE` clause must follow the table list. If no `WHERE` condition is specified, your query operates on the entire table.
- You can use equality, inequality, and range comparisons to test values of any data type. Range searches with `datetime` values should avoid using `BETWEEN`.
- You will need to combine search conditions with `OR` and `AND`. When you combine more than two conditions, especially when `OR` is present, use parentheses to clarify the logical grouping of your conditions.
- Use `IN` and `NOT IN` to test for membership in a list of values.
- Use `LIKE` to check for pattern matches. Remember that the wildcards only work with `LIKE` (not with equality or `IN` comparisons). Wildcards can be used only with strings.

Take a quick break. You've worked through the majority of this today's lesson. Compared to searching for data, the next two sections will be a snap.

Sorting Data (ORDER BY)

The `order by` keywords enable you to define the sort order for a result set. Notice that `ORDER BY` affects the result set, *not the original table*. This is crucial. To affect the sorting of a table, you need to modify its indexes (see Day 9, "Indexes and Performance,"), but you can change the order of the data you are reviewing.

It's important to do as much of the sorting as possible in SQL Server instead of sorting data locally in a client application. The server has resources to improve sort performance and to handle very large sorts. Take advantage of these resources and your overall performance will improve.

Sorting by One Column

To sort data, add an `ORDER BY` clause to your `SELECT` statement after the `WHERE` clause, as in this example:

```
select CompanyName, Region
  from Suppliers
 where Country = 'USA'
 order by Region
```

Results:

```
CompanyName                              Region
---------------------------------------- ---------------
New Orleans Cajun Delights               LA
New England Seafood Cannery              MA
Grandma Kelly's Homestead                MI
Bigfoot Breweries                        OR
```

The suppliers are listed in order by the `Region` column (state).

You can sort on any data type. In this example, employees are sorted by `HireDate`:

```
select LastName, HireDate
  from Employees
 where HireDate >= '1/1/94'
 order by HireDate
```

Results:

```
LastName             HireDate
-------------------- ---------------------------
King                 1994-01-02 00:00:00.000
Callahan             1994-03-05 00:00:00.000
Dodsworth            1994-11-15 00:00:00.000
```

Sorts can be ascending (lowest to highest) or descending (highest to lowest). The default order is ascending, so you will seldom see the ASC keyword used. The DESC keyword reverses the order of the sort:

```
select LastName, HireDate
  from Employees
 where HireDate >= '1/1/94'
 order by HireDate desc
```

Results:

```
LastName             HireDate
-------------------- --------------------------
Dodsworth            1994-11-15 00:00:00.000
Callahan             1994-03-05 00:00:00.000
King                 1994-01-02 00:00:00.000
```


Now the data is sorted with the most recent hire at the top of the list.

Sorting by Multiple Columns

You can perform multilevel sorts by providing a list of columns in the ORDER BY clause. The order the columns are listed in the ORDER BY clause is the order in which they will be sorted. In this example, data is sorted first by supplier, and then by product ID:

```
select ProductName, SupplierID, ProductID
  from Products
 where CategoryID = 3
 order by SupplierID, ProductID
```

Results:

```
ProductName                              SupplierID  ProductID
---------------------------------------- ----------- -----------
Pavlova                                            7          16
Teatime Chocolate Biscuits                         8          19
Sir Rodney's Marmalade                             8          20
Sir Rodney's Scones                                8          21
Scottish Longbreads                                8          68
NuNuCa Nuß-Nougat-Creme                           11          25
Gumbär Gummibärchen                               11          26
Schoggi Schokolade                                11          27
Zaanse koeken                                     22          47
Chocolade                                         22          48
Maxilaku                                          23          49
Valkoinen suklaa                                  23          50
Tarte au sucre                                    29          62
```

Within each supplier set, the products are sorted by product ID.

In a multilevel sort, the ASC and DESC keywords apply only to the column or expression they follow. In the following example, suppliers are sorted in ascending order, but within each supplier list, the products are listed in descending order by price (highest-priced item first):

```
select ProductName, SupplierID, UnitPrice
  from Products
 where CategoryID = 3
 order by SupplierID, UnitPrice desc
```

Results:

```
ProductName                 SupplierID  UnitPrice
--------------------------- ----------- ---------------------
Pavlova                               7               17.4500
Sir Rodney's Marmalade                8               81.0000
Scottish Longbreads                   8               12.5000
Sir Rodney's Scones                   8               10.0000
Teatime Chocolate Biscuits            8                9.2000
Schoggi Schokolade                   11               43.9000
Gumbär Gummibärchen                  11               31.2300
NuNuCa Nuß-Nougat-Creme              11               14.0000
Chocolade                            22               12.7500
Zaanse koeken                        22                9.5000
Maxilaku                             23               20.0000
Valkoinen suklaa                     23               16.2500
Tarte au sucre                       29               49.3000
```

Notice that, within the set of four rows from Supplier 8, the first item listed is Sir Rodney's Marmalade, which costs $81 (eighty-one dollars? for marmalade?). The DESC keyword affected only the sorting of the prices, not the supplier IDs.

You don't have to sort by a column or columns in the SELECT list. You could sort a list of products by price, but not display the price, as in this example:

```
select ProductName, SupplierID
  from Products
 where CategoryID = 3
   and SupplierID in (11, 8)
 order by UnitPrice desc
```

Results:

```
ProductName                              SupplierID
---------------------------------------- -----------
Sir Rodney's Marmalade                             8
Schoggi Schokolade                                11
Gumbär Gummibärchen                               11
NuNuCa Nuß-Nougat-Creme                           11
Scottish Longbreads                                8
Sir Rodney's Scones                                8
Teatime Chocolate Biscuits                         8
```

I don't recommend sorting on invisible fields often. Most people are troubled by lists that are unsorted, as this one appears to be.

Sorting by Column Number

You can also designate a sort column by its position in the select list. Here's the multi-level sort that we were looking at earlier:

```
select ProductName, SupplierID, UnitPrice
  from Products
 where CategoryID = 3
 order by SupplierID, UnitPrice desc
```

SQL Server would return the same results if you changed the `ORDER BY` clause to designate the sort columns by position, like this:

```
select ProductName, SupplierID, UnitPrice
  from Products
 where CategoryID = 3
 order by 2, 3 desc
```

This query format belongs in a category I call "breakable SQL." *Breakable SQL* is code that would be easy to ruin by making a simple and predictable change. What if I inserted ProductID at the front of the select list, like this:

```
select ProductID, ProductName, SupplierID, UnitPrice
  from Products
 where CategoryID = 3
 order by 2, 3 desc
```

Now products are sorted by name, and then by supplier ID (in descending order).

Unfortunately, SQL Server tempts you with a number of shorthand techniques like this one. Avoid using shorthand when it can lead to difficult maintenance and reliability problems later.

Retrieving Unique Rows

The last element we'll learn about today is the `DISTINCT` keyword. `DISTINCT` asks SQL Server to remove all duplicate rows from your result set.

Most of the time, you won't need to use `DISTINCT`. Sometimes, when you think you need `DISTINCT` you really have a problem somewhere else in your code. But there are legitimate situations where duplicate rows can emerge from a table. In the next pages, we'll learn how to use `DISTINCT` and how to avoid it.

Using `DISTINCT` to Find Unique Rows

The keyword `DISTINCT` is placed optionally between `SELECT` and the select list. When you include `DISTINCT`, the server removes duplicate rows from your results.

What if you wanted a list of countries where you have suppliers? Consider this query:

```
select Country
from Suppliers
```

Results:

```
Country
---------------
UK
USA
USA
Japan
...
France
France
Canada
```

(I removed some of the rows from the output. There were 29 in my original result set.) The output lists the country value for each supplier; however, you are really interested only in a list of countries. To remove the duplicates and see only unique rows, add `DISTINCT`:

```
select distinct Country
from Suppliers
```

Results:

```
Country
---------------
Australia
Brazil
Canada
Denmark
Finland
France
Germany
Italy
Japan
Netherlands
Norway
Singapore
Spain
Sweden
UK
USA
```

The new result set includes only the 16 unique values for the `Country` column instead of all 29 values that contains duplicates.

Here is a similar example based on the `Country` and `City` columns in `Suppliers`. Again, we want to find unique values, but in this case, we are interested in *unique combinations* of the two columns. (Athens, USA (Georgia) is different from Athens, Greece.)

```
select distinct Country, City
from Suppliers
where Country in ('Italy', 'UK', 'Spain', 'France')
```

Results:

```
Country         City
--------------- --------------
France          Annecy
France          Montceau
France          Paris
Italy           Ravenna
Italy           Salerno
Spain           Oviedo
UK              London
UK              Manchester
```

The list includes multiple rows for France, Italy, and the UK. The keyword `DISTINCT` removes duplicate rows, so if there were multiple suppliers in any of these city/countries, only one row would appear for each city/country combination.

Avoiding DISTINCT

Some point-and-click code generators (as in older versions of Access) always add `DISTINCT` to every SQL query. Is there anything wrong with adding `DISTINCT` to every `SELECT` statement? Actually, there could be a substantial performance penalty to pay. To find unique rows, the server needs to sort the data. Adding an extra sort step when it's not necessary can be expensive.

How can you tell that `DISTINCT` is unnecessary? In one-table queries where an ID column or other unique identifier (Company Name might be unique, for example) is in the `SELECT` list, `DISTINCT` is unnecessary. Remember, `DISTINCT` is looking for *duplicate rows,* not duplicate columns. So, any unique column or combination of columns in the `select` list makes the `DISTINCT` operation unnecessary.

Summary

Today you learned how to filter and sort rows from a table in SQL Server. You used the `WHERE` clause to define search conditions for result sets, and then used the `ORDER BY` clause to sort those result sets. Finally, you used the `DISTINCT` keyword to remove unwanted duplicate rows from the results.

Here's the syntax for the `SELECT` statement so far:

```
select [distinct] <ColumnName> [, <ColumnName> ...]
from <TableName>
[where <expression> <comparison-operator> <expression>
[and|or <expression> <comparison-operator> <expression> ...]  ]
[order by <ColumnName> [, <ColumnName> ...]  ]
```

In conclusion, I leave you with the following list of items:

Do	Don't
DO define search criteria in your `SELECT` statement.	DON'T use `DISTINCT` when it's unnecessary.
DO use parentheses to group comparisons.	
DO use range criteria to retrieve information by date.	
DO use wildcards with `LIKE`.	
DO sort data on the server.	

Q&A

Q You keep talking about some methods being fast and others being slow. What's that all about?

A When a database administrator implements a database, query performance is usually the primary concern. How fast can users get their results from typical queries? How many users can input data at once?

To improve query speed, the administrator creates indexes that are available for use by any query. The server compares the query and the indexes and, through a process called *optimization,* finds the fastest way to resolve it.

Your job as a Transact-SQL programmer is to (1) make your queries easy for the server to understand so that it can optimize them efficiently, and (2) avoid SQL techniques that can't be optimized. On Day 9, we'll talk in detail about indexing methods and SQL Server optimization.

Q Sometimes it seems as though my data has already been sorted the way I need it, without using the `ORDER BY` clause. When can I leave out `ORDER BY`?

A One of the basic precepts of the relational database model is that data in tables is not predictably sorted. In the real world, the data is almost always sorted in some way, but the result set sort is based on the index the server uses to retrieve the data. The problem is, you can't always predict the order of data when you execute a query unless you specify the sort order in the `ORDER BY` clause.

Q Does the order of the clauses in the `SELECT` statement matter? Can I put the `WHERE` clause after ORDER BY clause?

A The order does matter. You need to present the various clauses in the correct order or the statement will fail.

Q I need to do pattern matching with numeric data. For instance, we store Social Security numbers (SSNs) as data, but I need to check the last four digits for security purposes. How can I do that?

A You will need to convert the SSN to a character string before you can do the pattern match. The `convert()` and `cast()` functions both change data from one data type to another. Here's a `WHERE` clause to see whether the last four digits of the SSN are `'1234'`:

```
where cast(SSN as nchar(9)) like '%1234'
```

Workshop

The Workshop provides quiz questions to help you solidify your understanding of the material covered and exercises to provide you with experience in using what you've learned. Try to answer the quiz and exercise questions before checking the answers in Appendix A, "Answers to Quizzes and Exercises," and make sure you understand the answers before continuing to the next lesson.

Quiz

1. Can you use wildcards with `IN`, as in this example?

```
select ProductName, UnitPrice
from Products
where ProductName in ('%tofu%', '%cereal%', '%grain%')
```

2. When do you need to group conditions using parentheses?
3. In this query, is the sort order on the `EmployeeID` ascending or descending?

```
select EmployeeID, OrderDate, OrderID
from Orders
order by EmployeeID, OrderDate desc
```

4. In this query and result set featuring `DISTINCT`, why are there multiple rows with the value `'Sales Representative'` in the title column? Isn't `DISTINCT` supposed to eliminate those duplicates?

```
select distinct title, lastname
from employees

title                          lastname
------------------------------ --------------------
Inside Sales Coordinator       Callahan
Sales Manager                  Buchanan
Sales Representative           Davolio
Sales Representative           Dodsworth
Sales Representative           King
Sales Representative           Leverling
Sales Representative           Peacock
Sales Representative           Suyama
Vice President, Sales          Fuller
```

Exercises

In all these exercises, I'll ask you to find some fact or set of facts. I'll pose a problem, and then I'll provide you with the answer. If your results match mine, you probably found a correct method of resolving the query. In the answers, you'll see my SQL solution.

1. List all customers in Mexico. How many are there?
2. Find Andrew Fuller's home phone number.
3. What product costs the same as Chang?
4. Produce a list of different countries shipped to in May 1998.
5. Find the youngest employee. When was he or she born?

Week 1

Day 3

Working with Columns

Yesterday, you took your first step in understanding the unique language of database access. Learning how to filter and sort the data returned by a SELECT statement provides you with the skills to get data from your database. Of course, this has only scratched the surface of what you can do with a SELECT statement.

In today's lesson, you will extend your knowledge of the SELECT statement by working with the columns in the database tables. We will cover a lot of information today, so prepare yourself. As you read this, you might ask yourself, "What will this do for me?" The answer to that question might not become clear until later in this book. Much of this lesson will help you throughout your career as a SQL programmer. The topics that will be discussed today are

- Data types
- Column manipulation
- The CONVERT and CAST functions
- Arithmetic and string operators
- String functions
- Date functions

- Numeric functions
- System functions
- The CASE statement

Column Characteristics

When a column is added to a database table, you set several parameters that define the characteristics of that column. These include the name of the column, its data type, its length, and a default value. In this section, you will learn all about data types, what they are and how you should use them. In addition, you will see how empty or null columns are treated by the SQL processor.

Data Types

In a database, every column, variable, expression, and parameter has a related data type associated with it. A *data type* is an attribute that specifies the type of data (integer, string, date, and so on) that object can contain. All the data that a specific column holds must be of the same data type. A data type also determines how the data for a particular column is accessed, indexed, and physically stored on the server.

Tables 3.1 and 3.2 describe each of the available data types in Microsoft SQL Server 2000 and provide an example of what each might be used for. If the data you are working with is of different lengths, such as names, addresses, and other text, you should use variable-length data types. Fixed-length data types are best used for data, such as phone numbers, Social Security numbers, and ZIP Codes.

TABLE 3.1 Data Types in SQL Server 2000

Long Name	*Syntax*	*Example*	*Description*
Variable character	`varchar(6)`	`"John"`	Variable-length character fields are best for most strings.
Character	`char(6)`	`"John"`	Fixed-length character fields are best for most strings.
National variable characters	`nvarchar(6)`	`"John"`	Variable-length Unicode data with a maximum length of 4,000 characters.
Datetime	`datetime`	`Jan 1, 2000 12:15:00.000 pm`	`Datetime` fields are used for precise storage of dates and times. `Datetimes` can range from Jan 1, 1753 to Dec 31, 9999. Values outside this range must be stored as character.

TABLE 3.1 continued

Long Name	*Syntax*	*Example*	*Description*
Small datetime	`smalldatetime`	`Jan 2, 2000 12:15pm`	Small datetimes are half the size of datetimes. They use increments of one minute and represent dates from Jan 1, 1900 to Jun 6, 2079.
Precise decimal	`decimal(4,2)` or `numeric (4,2)`	`13.22`	Decimal/numeric data types store fractional numerics precisely. The first parameter specifies how many digits are allowed in the field. The second parameter specifies how many digits may come after the decimal. In this example, I could represent numbers from –99.99 to 99.99.
Big floating point	`float(15)`	`64023.0134`	Floating-point numbers are not guaranteed to be stored precisely. SQL Server rounds up numbers that binary math can't handle. Floats take a parameter specifying the total number of digits.
Little float	`real(7)`	`16.3452`	Half the size of a float; the same rules apply.
Integer	`int`	`683423`	Integers are four bytes wide and store numbers between plus or minus two billion.
Small integer	`smallint`	`12331`	Small integers are half the size of integers, ranging from –32,768 through 32,767.
Tiny integer	`tinyint`	`5`	Tiny integers are half again the size of small integers, a single byte, and may not be negative. Values run from 0 to 255. Perfect for an age column.
Bit	`bit`	`1`	Bits are the smallest data type available today. They are one bit in size, one-eighth of a byte. Bits may not be null and can have a value of 0 or 1. This is the actual language of all computers.
Binary	`binary`	`0x00223FE2…`	Fixed-length binary data with a maximum length of 8,000 bytes.
Money	`money`	`$753.1132`	Money types range from +/- 922 trillion. Money types store four digits to the right of the decimal and are stored as fixed-point integers.

3

TABLE 3.1 continued

Long Name	*Syntax*	*Example*	*Description*
Small money	`smallmoney`	`$32.50`	Small money can handle about +/ $214,000, with four digits to the right of the decimal. Half the size of Money.
Text	`text`	`"We the people…"`	Text fields can be up to 2GB in size. Text fields are treated at Binary Large Objects (BLOBs) and are subject to a great many limitations They cannot be used in an `ORDER BY`, indexed, or grouped, and handling the inside an application program takes some extra work. (BLOBs will be discussed on Day 21, "Handling BLOBs in T-SQL.")
Image	`image`	`0x00223FE2…`	Image data can be used to store any type of binary data, including images (gif, jpg, and so on), executables, or anything else you can store on your disk drive. Images are also BLOBs, subject to the same limitations.

TABLE 3.2 New Data Types in SQL Server 2000

Long Name	*Use*	*Example*	*Description*
Big integer	`bigint`	`983422348`	A large integer that can hold a number +/- 2 raised to the 63rd power. Twice as large as an integer.
Sql_variant	`sql_variant`		A data type that stores values of other supported data types, except `text`, `ntext`, and `sql_variant`. You can use this to hold data from any other data type without having to know the data type in advance.
Table	`table`		This is a special data type that can be used to store a result set for later processing. It is primarily used for temporary storage of a set of rows.

Data Type Precedence

When two expressions of different data types are combined using one or more operators or functions, the data type precedence rules specify which data type is converted to the other. The data type with the lower precedence is converted to the data type with the higher precedence. If the conversion is not a supported implicit conversion, an error is returned. If both expressions have the same data type, the resulting object has the same data type. The order of precedence for the data types are shown in Table 3.3.

TABLE 3.3 Data Type Order of Precedence

Precedence Number	*Data Type*
1	sql_variant
2	datetime
3	smalldatetime
4	float
5	real
6	decimal
7	money
8	smallmoney
9	bigint
10	int
11	smallint
12	tinyint
13	bit
14	ntext
15	image
16	timestamp
17	uniqueidentifier
18	nvarchar
19	nchar
20	varchar
21	char
22	varbinary
23	binary

An example of the precedence can be seen when you add two unlike numbers together as shown here:

```
Select quantity * price as Sale_Total from "Order Details"
```

The quantity column is an integer data type, whereas the price column is a money data type. When this calculation is performed, the result would be a money data type.

Don't worry about how to use the multiplication operator, or what the as Sale_Total means. We will cover these issues later in this lesson.

Using Null Data

When a column is empty, it is treated differently than when a column is blank or zero. These might sound the same to you, but to the computer, they are very different. A blank is an actual character that takes a position in the column. Of course, zero is its own explanation. A null means that the column actually contains nothing. To see how a null is displayed, try executing the following SQL statement in the Query Analyzer:

```
use pubs
select title_id, advance
from titles
order by title_id
```

Results:

```
title_id advance
-------- ---------------------
BU1032   5000.0000
BU1111   5000.0000
BU2075   10125.0000
BU7832   5000.0000
MC2222   .0000
MC3021   15000.0000
MC3026   NULL
PC1035   7000.0000
PC8888   8000.0000
PC9999   NULL
...
TC4203   4000.0000
TC7777   8000.0000

(18 row(s) affected)
```

You should see that null values are displayed using the string NULL. However, most standard comparisons will not recognize the null value. The next example shows you what happens when I add a where clause to the SELECT statement. I am looking for all title IDs where the advance amount is less than $5,000. You might think that 'null' or 'empty' are identical, but they're not. Although you will be covering functions later in this lesson, I want to cover one in this section.

The `isnull()` function permits a way to include null values in aggregate calculations. The function requires two arguments and its syntax is shown here:

```
Isnull(<expression>, <value>)
```

The first argument is the expression on which the calculation will be performed; usually this is a column from the database. The second argument is the value that will replace the null value for display or calculation purposes. If the expression contains a null, the second parameter is returned by this function. If the expression is not null, the value in the expression is returned.

The following SQL query shows the effect of the `isnull()` function on the titles table in the `pubs` database.

```
use pubs
select title_id, price, isnull(price, $45)
from titles
order by price
```

The output of this query shows which prices were null:

```
title_id price
-------- -------------------- --------------------
MC3026   NULL                 45.0000
PC9999   NULL                 45.0000
MC3021   2.9900               2.9900
BU2075   2.9900               2.9900
PS2106   7.0000               7.0000
...
PS3333   19.9900              19.9900
PC8888   20.0000              20.0000
TC3218   20.9500              20.9500
PS1372   21.5900              21.5900
PC1035   22.9500              22.9500

(18 row(s) affected)
```

As you can see in the output, there are two titles in the table that have null in their `price` column. When the `isnull()` function evaluates those columns, it returns `$45` for the third column in the result set. For the other columns, it simply returns the value of the column.

You can use the `isnull()` function inside an aggregate function. If you want to know the average price of a book, you would ask for the `avg(price)` on the `titles` table. However, the two books that have null for a price would be excluded from the calculation. Suppose that you know that those books will be priced at $29 each. You could use the `isnull()` function to include those books in the calculation. The example shows you the query without the `isnull()` function and then with the `isnull()` function.

```
select avg(price)
from titles
```

Results:

```
--------------------
14.7662

(1 row(s) affected)

Warning: Null value is eliminated by an aggregate or other SET operation.
```

As you can see, the server displays a warning message informing you that there were null values found and they were not used.

```
select avg(isnull(price, $29))
from titles
```

Results:

```
--------------------
16.3477

(1 row(s) affected)
```

In the second version of the query, you can see that the average returned is different because the two books with nulls were included in the calculation. The `isnull()` function doesn't change the value of the row in the table; it only assumes a value for the purposes of a single query.

Changing Result Sets

So far, every column you have requested has been retrieved and displayed as the data was stored. However, there will be many times when you will need to change the way the data is displayed. This next section will discuss the different ways that you can change the labels of the displayed columns or modify the data in the columns by using operators and functions.

Using Column Aliases

You will find that the names of the columns as defined in the database are not exactly easy to read as shown in the following example:

```
use pubs
select emp_id, job_id, job_lvl, pub_id
from employee
```

Results:

```
emp_id    job_id job_lvl pub_id
--------- ------ ------- ------
PMA42628M 13     35      0877
PSA89086M 14     89      1389
VPA30890F 6      140     0877
H-B39728F 12     35      0877
L-B31947F 7      120     0877
F-C16315M 4      227     9952
```

As you can see, the column names are not very descriptive. SQL provides you with the ability to change the names of the columns in the SELECT statement to make it easier for you to understand the output. To change a column name, you would use the following syntax:


```
SELECT <column name> as <new name> FROM <table>
```

Using the previous SQL example, I could change it to make the output more readable as shown in the next example.

```
use pubs
select emp_id as 'Employee Number',
       job_id as 'Job Number',
       job_lvl as 'Job Pay Level',
       pub_id as 'Publisher ID'
from employee
```

Results:

```
Employee Number Job Number Job Pay Level Publisher ID
--------------- ---------- ------------- ------------
PMA42628M       13         35            0877
PSA89086M       14         89            1389
VPA30890F       6          140           0877
H-B39728F       12         35            0877
```

You can also see that I used single quotes to define the new column names that include blanks in the SQL statement.

Using column aliases is one of the best ways of creating easy to understand T-SQL scripts, especially long, complex scripts.

Using String Constants

Now that you have seen how to change the names of the columns that you select, you will see how to add new columns of text to your output that are not included in the database. String constants enable you to add labels and comments to your output easily. You can use a string constant in your SQL statement in the same way you would reference a column. The following example shows how to add a constant to your SQL query:

```
use northwind
select 'Hi! My Name is: ', FirstName
from employees
```

Results:

```
                  FirstName
---------------- ----------
Hi! My Name is:  Nancy
Hi! My Name is:  Andrew
Hi! My Name is:  Janet
Hi! My Name is:  Margaret
Hi! My Name is:  Steven
Hi! My Name is:  Michael
Hi! My Name is:  Robert
Hi! My Name is:  Laura
Hi! My Name is:  Anne

(9 row(s) affected)
```

You can see from the output that there are two columns being displayed. The first column has the words, `Hi! My name is:` for every row in the `Employees` table. The second column contains the first name of each employee. Adding these strings to your SQL enables you to produce more readable output. In fact, you will see in the next section how you can manipulate strings even further using operators and functions.

Using Operators

All programming languages, including T-SQL, contain a set of operators that enable you to specify an action to be performed on one or more expressions. These operators fall into several different categories, which are listed in Table 3.4.

TABLE 3.4 Available Operators in T-SQL

Category	*Operator*	*Description*
Arithmetic	+ (Add)	Addition.
	- (Subtract)	Subtraction.
	* (Multiply)	Multiplication.
	/ (Divide)	Division.
	% (Modulo)	Returns the integer remainder of a division.

TABLE 3.4 continued

<table>
<tr><th>Category</th><th>Operator</th><th>Description</th></tr>
<tr><td>Bitwise</td><td>&</td><td>Bitwise AND.</td></tr>
<tr><td></td><td>|</td><td>Bitwise OR.</td></tr>
<tr><td></td><td>^</td><td>Bitwise exclusive OR.</td></tr>
<tr><td>Comparison</td><td>=</td><td>Equal to.</td></tr>
<tr><td></td><td>></td><td>Greater than.</td></tr>
<tr><td></td><td><</td><td>Less than.</td></tr>
<tr><td></td><td>>+</td><td>Greater than or equal to.</td></tr>
<tr><td></td><td><=</td><td>Less than or equal to.</td></tr>
<tr><td></td><td><></td><td>Not equal to.</td></tr>
<tr><td>Logical</td><td></td><td>Tests for the truth of some specified condition. All the logical operators return a Boolean data type with a value of <code>TRUE</code> or <code>FALSE</code>. These operators are <code>ALL</code>, <code>AND</code>, <code>ANY</code>, <code>BETWEEN</code>, <code>EXISTS</code>, <code>IN</code>, <code>LIKE</code>, <code>NOT</code>, <code>OR</code>, and <code>SOME</code>.</td></tr>
<tr><td>Unary</td><td>+ (Positive)</td><td>Positive number.</td></tr>
<tr><td></td><td>- (Negative)</td><td>Negative number.</td></tr>
<tr><td></td><td>~ (Bitwise NOT)</td><td>Returns the ones complement of the number.</td></tr>
<tr><td>Assignment</td><td>= (Equal sign)</td><td>Used to assign a value to a variable.</td></tr>
<tr><td>String Concatenation</td><td>+ (Concatenation)</td><td>Appends two strings together to form one string.</td></tr>
</table>

In the next section, you will see how to manipulate the columns you request in a SQL statement.

Using the Addition Operator

If we want to add two or more numbers together, we can use the addition sign. This will add the numbers together and display the single result as shown in the following example:

```
use northwind
select UnitPrice, Discount,
       UnitPrice + Discount as Total
from "order details"
```

Results:

```
UnitPrice            Discount                 Total
-------------------- ------------------------ --------
14.0000              0.0                      14.0
9.8000               0.0                      9.8000002
```

```
34.8000              0.0                  34.799999
42.4000              0.15000001           42.550003
16.8000              0.15000001           16.949999
16.8000              0.0                  16.799999
```

You can see how using an alias here helps to make the output more readable.

You can use any of the arithmetic operators in this fashion.

What about string values? If you want to add two or more strings together, you can use the addition operator for this as well. When used between two strings, the addition operator enables you to concatenate the strings (that is, to add the second string on to the end of the first). This functionality gives you the ability to create new strings using the data in multiple columns.

This next example requires both the string and the first name from the database table to appear as the column called `Introduction`. To make the output pretty, you have to add an extra space in the constant string. Otherwise, the first names of all the employees will be pushed up against the word `is`.

```
use northwind
select 'Hello, my name is ' + firstname as Introduction
from employees
```

Results:

```
Introduction
----------------------------
Hello, my name is Nancy
Hello, my name is Andrew
Hello, my name is Janet
Hello, my name is Margaret
Hello, my name is Steven
Hello, my name is Michael
Hello, my name is Robert
Hello, my name is Laura
Hello, my name is Anne

(9 row(s) affected)
```

Although this looks a lot like the example using string constants earlier in this section, in this query we retrieved the static string plus the data in a single column instead of two columns. Then we used the + sign to concatenate the strings.

Manipulating Multiple Columns and Using Constants

Besides adding a constant to one column value, you can use constants to manipulate multiple columns to display information in standard format styles. A common example of this is when you need to print usernames. In the `Employees` table, the first name is stored in the `FirstName` column and the last name in `LastName`. Suppose that you wanted a list of employee names, listed with last name first, first name last, and separated by a comma. You also want to call this column `Employee Names`. The following example shows how to perform this request:

```
use northwind
select lastname + ', ' + firstname as 'Employee Names'
from employees
Order by "employee names"
```

Results:

```
Employee Names
--------------------------------
Buchanan, Steven
Callahan, Laura
Davolio, Nancy
Dodsworth, Anne
Fuller, Andrew
King, Robert
Leverling, Janet
Peacock, Margaret
Suyama, Michael

(9 row(s) affected)
```

Using the + operator with strings enables you to put multiple columns and constants together in a single column of the result set. I used an alias to name the column, and then I used the alias in the `ORDER BY` clause.

Tip

I could have sorted this last example by using the original column names as shown:

```
use northwind
select lastname + ', ' + firstname as 'Employee Names'
from employees
Order by lastname, firstname
```

When you ask for an ordering to occur on a calculated result, such as the concatenated string, the server first builds the result set and then sorts it.

Using Functions

You have briefly used a couple of functions in yesterday's lesson on filtering dates. In this next section, you will learn about the different types of functions available to you in SQL Server 2000. There are four types of built-in functions that you can use in T-SQL. The types of functions are

- Mathematical
- String
- System
- Niladic

I will provide an example of each of these functions in the next section. *Niladic* functions work exclusively with the `INSERT` statement, which will be covered on Day 7, "Adding, Changing, and Deleting Rows." They include functions such as `CURRENT_TIMESTAMP()` to insert the current date and time automatically.

Whenever a function is performed on a column, the server cannot use an index to resolve a query based on that column. To answer your query in the least amount of time, the server must act based on information available to it before the query runs. Because a function will take some action on a column, the server can't know what the data will be until after the query runs. Using functions in the `SELECT` list is okay, but using them in the `WHERE` clause can cause performance problems.

The purpose of this section is to provide you with a list of examples in order to understand how each set of functions are used in real-world situations. In each of the following groups, you will see how to use several of the more useful functions available. Remember that there are more functions than what I will cover in this section.

As you work with these functions, remember that you can use them with columns you are retrieving, or you can use them in the `WHERE` clause to modify the data you are comparing.

Using String Functions

String functions enable you to manipulate character data from the database. These functions perform an operation on a string value and then return either a string or numeric value, depending on the type of function being used.

UPPER() and LOWER()

These two functions are the direct opposites of each other. The UPPER() function will return a character expression with any lowercase characters converted to uppercase. The LOWER() function will return a character expression with any uppercase characters converted to lowercase. The following example shows how to use the UPPER() function. Remember that the syntax for the LOWER() function is exactly the same.

```
use northwind
select firstname,
       upper(firstname) as "All Caps"
from employees
where lastname = 'Fuller'
```

Results:

```
firstname  All Caps
---------- ----------
Andrew     ANDREW

(1 row(s) affected)
```


SUBSTRING() and RIGHT()

The SUBSTRING() function enables you to extract a string from anywhere in a larger string, whereas the RIGHT() function returns a string from the end of another string. There is no LEFT() function. Both functions are useful for manipulating strings in columns where several fields have been concatenated into a single column. Although this is a bad database design practice, this type of data often occurs in the real world.

Suppose that you have a table of product information where a column contains a combination of two unique values, as we can see in the title_id column in the titles table of the pubs database. The first two positions in the column represent the book type and the rest of the column represents the unique book number. You might need to separate these values out in order to work with them independently. To do this, you could use the SUBSTRING() or RIGHT() function as shown in the following example:

```
use pubs
select title_id,
       type,
       substring(title_id,1,2) as Book_Type_Code
from titles
```

Results:

```
title_id type         Book_Type_Code
-------- ------------ --------------
BU1032   business     BU
BU1111   business     BU
```

```
BU2075   business     BU
BU7832   business     BU
MC2222   mod_cook     MC
MC3021   mod_cook     MC
MC3026   UNDECIDED    MC
PC1035   popular_comp PC
PC8888   popular_comp PC
PC9999   popular_comp PC
PS1372   psychology   PS
PS2091   psychology   PS
PS2106   psychology   PS
PS3333   psychology   PS
PS7777   psychology   PS
TC3218   trad_cook    TC
TC4203   trad_cook    TC
TC7777   trad_cook    TC

(18 row(s) affected)
```

`SUBSTRING()` takes three arguments: the source string, where to start (1 is the first character), and how many characters to take. The `RIGHT()` function takes two arguments: the source string and how many characters to take. The syntax for each follows:

```
SUBSTRING(source, start, length)
```

```
RIGHT(source, start)
```

RTRIM and LTRIM

These two functions trim any extra blanks off the beginning of a string (`LTRIM`) or the end of a string (`RTRIM`). There is no function that performs both at the same time. However, you can nest functions, so that if I were inserting some data into a table, and that data included blanks at both the beginning and end, I could trim off the extra blanks.

This example doesn't insert anything into the database table (that is covered in Day 7). Instead, this is how you might trim the blanks off the front and back of a column at the same time:

```
Select ltrim(rtrim(title))
From Titles
```

Both of these functions accept a single parameter, which is the string to be trimmed.

STR

The `STR()` function will convert numeric data into string data. There is no `VAL()` function to convert strings to numbers as you might have seen in Visual Basic, but the generic `CONVERT()` function will accomplish both goals. The `STR()` function accepts three parameters: source number, length of the new string to be created, and number of digits to the right of the decimal. The following example shows how to use this function:

```
use pubs
select 'The price is ' + str(price, 6,3)
from titles
```

Results:

```
------------------
The price is 19.990
The price is 11.950
The price is  2.990
...
The price is  7.990
The price is 20.950
The price is 11.950
The price is 14.990

(18 row(s) affected)
```

Caution

If you try to execute the preceding SQL query without using the `STR` function, you will receive the following error from the server:

```
Server: Msg 260, Level 16, State 1, Line 2
Disallowed implicit conversion from data type
varchar to data type money, table 'pubs.dbo.titles', column
'price'.
Use the CONVERT function to run this query.
```

As you can see from the message, the server is telling you to use the `CONVERT()` function instead of the `STR()` function. The `CONVERT()` function will convert numeric data to a string, but it won't add insignificant zeroes or line up all the decimal points.

The syntax for the `STR()` function is

```
STR(<source number>, [length of output], [scale])
```

The `STR()` function is useful for converting numeric data in a way that looks good when displayed.

ASCII() and CHAR()

These functions convert a single character into its ASCII code or an ASCII code into its character. If you pass more than one character to the ASCII function, it will return the code for only the first letter. The following example shows both the `ASCII()` and `CHAR()` functions in one query:

```
select ascii('B'), char(66)

----------- ----
66          B

(1 row(s) affected)
```

The `CHAR()` function can be useful for inserting keycodes that cannot be easily typed in, such as the Tab and CR/LF codes.

PATINDEX() and CHARINDEX()

`PATINDEX()` returns the first occurrence of a string inside a larger string. You can use this function to search a `BLOB` text field. Wildcards are available for use in the pattern field. `CHARINDEX()` works the same way, but wildcard characters are not permitted, and it cannot be used to search text types.

The `titles` table contains the text field `notes`. The query that follows will search for books that have a note containing the word `Computer` in it, and return the character position where that word appears.

```
select title_id,
       patindex('%Computer%', notes) as 'Starts at'
from titles
where patindex('%Computer%', notes) <> 0
```

Results:

```
title_id Starts at
-------- -----------
BU7832   28
PC8888   45
PC9999   17
PS1372   94
PS7777   97

(5 row(s) affected)
```

As you can see, the `PATINDEX()` function was used in two places in the query. The use in the `WHERE` clause searches through all the text data looking for the word `Computer`. If a match is found, the title ID is returned along with the starting position of the word. The syntax for both of these functions is the same:

```
PATINDEX(<pattern>, <source string>)

CHARINDEX(<pattern>, <source string>)
```

The CAST and CONVERT Functions

To combine columns and constants, they must be of the same underlying data type. The server will convert varchar and char columns without your help. However, if you tried a query where you wanted a numeric and character type in the same column, you would have a problem, as shown in the following example:

```
use pubs
select title_id + ' is priced at $' + price
from titles
```

Results:

```
Server: Msg 260, Level 16, State 1, Line 2
Disallowed implicit conversion from data type
varchar to data type money, table 'pubs.dbo.titles',
column 'price'.
Use the CONVERT function to run this query.
```


To overcome this, as the error message suggests, you must use the CONVERT function. There are actually two functions that you could use: the CONVERT() and CAST() functions. These functions provide similar functionality in T-SQL.

The CAST() function will change the data type of the expression being passed to it. It will not allow you to specify the style or length of the new expression. The syntax for the CAST() function is

```
CAST (expression AS data_type)
```

The CONVERT() function, besides allowing you to specify the new data type as the CAST() function does, also enables you to specify the length and style of the new expression.

Both functions are useful for many more applications than the example. You can also convert character data to numeric data for use in mathematical calculations. To perform the concatenation in the current example, you must convert the price column (datatype money) into a variable character format:

```
use pubs
select title_id +
       ' is priced at $' +
       convert(varchar(10), price)
from titles
```

Results:

```
-------------------------------
BU1032 is priced at $19.99
BU1111 is priced at $11.95
BU2075 is priced at $2.99
...
```

```
TC3218 is priced at $20.95
TC4203 is priced at $11.95
TC7777 is priced at $14.99

(18 row(s) affected)
```

In this example, I converted the `price` column, containing small money data, into a variable character. When a data type is converted to a variable character, the length of the resulting string is only as long as it needs to be, up to the maximum specified in the function call. In this case, I asked for a `varchar(10)`. So, if the price were 132.55, the converted `varchar` string would be exactly six characters long.

However, if I had converted the price to a fixed-length character string (a `char(10)`), the total string length would have been the maximum size of 10 characters no matter how many characters were needed. The data is left justified, and spaces are added on the end to round out the remainder of the field.

In either case, if the price data were too large to fit in the maximum length, the server would place an asterisk in the character field to indicate that it didn't have enough room to convert the data. If you convert a long string to a shorter string, the data is truncated, meaning that only as much of the string as fits in the new length will be converted; the rest is thrown away.

If you do not specify a length for data types, such as `char` and `varchar` fields, the server will default to the data type specific value. In the case of `char` and `varchar` types, this default is 30 characters.

In addition to converting data types, the `CONVERT()` function also helps you format date fields in several different ways. By default, when you select a `datetime` value, the output would be displayed as

```
Oct  6 2000  3:00PM
```

As you know, `datetime` values are stored out to the millisecond. This presents you with some pretty ugly output. The `CONVERT()` function can be used to request some alternative date formats. When using the `CONVERT()` to format the `datetime` values, you should always convert the data to a `char` or `varchar` data type. Table 3.5 summarizes the different date formats that are usable with the `CONVERT()` function.

TABLE 3.5 Date Formats Available with CONVERT()

Code	*Description*
0	(default style) mon dd yyyy hh:mmAM
1	mm/dd/yy
2	yy.mm.dd
3	dd/mm/yy
4	dd.mm.yy
5	dd-mm-yy
6	dd mon yy
7	mon dd, yy
8	hh:mm:ss
9	mon dd yyyy hh:mm:ss:mmmAM
10	mm-dd-yy
11	yy/mm/dd
12	yymmdd
13	dd mon yyyy hh:mm:ss:mmmm (military time)
14	hh:mm:ss:mmm (military time)

These codes display the year without a century prefix. To get a century prefix, add 100 to the code. Note that styles 9 and 13 always provide a four-digit year.

Other String Functions

Other string functions are available for you to use in T-SQL; I have listed them in Table 3.6 as a reference.

TABLE 3.6 Other Available String Functions

Function	*Description*
SPACE(<*int*>)	Returns a string of *n* spaces.
REVERSE(<*source string*>)	Reverses the source string (that is, "Ben" becomes "neB"). Not sure what you would use this for.
REPLICATE(<*pattern*>,<*int*>)	Returns a string with the pattern repeated *n* times.

TABLE 3.6 continued

Function	*Description*
SOUNDEX(<*source string*>)	Returns a four-digit soundex code to represent the phonemes in the source string. This function would probably be used when searching for a string that sounds like…, as in a case when you are looking for a phone number. If you wanted to find the number for someone named Smith, the soundex code would match for the following names: Smythe, Smyth, Sumith, and Smith. The function knocks out any vowels in the string and uses the first letter to form its code.
DIFFERENCE(<*char1*>,<*char2*>)	Evaluates the soundex difference between *char1* and *char2* on a scale of 0 to 4, where 4 is an exact match and 0 is a complete mismatch.

Using Arithmetic Functions

Most math functions are used in very specific applications having something to do with engineering. However, there are times when you might need to use one in some more standard application areas. What follows is an accounting example. The function being used is

SIGN(numeric)	Returns 1 if the number is positive, 0 if 0, and -1 if the number is negative.

In this example, you have a table with two columns in it: CustID and InvAmt. The InvAmt column contains negative values for the amounts that you owe (credits) and positive values for amounts that are owed to you (debits). This query will display a report with four columns, labeled CustID, Debit, Credit, and Invoice Amount.

```
select CustID,
       InvAmt * ($0.5 *(sign(InvAmt) + 1)) as 'Debit',
       InvAmt * ($0.5 *(sign(InvAmt) - 1)) as 'Credit',
       InvAmt
from invoice
```

Note

This example uses a table that I have in my personal database; it will not work on a standard installation of SQL Server 2000.

Results:

```
CustID Debit            Credit           InvAmt
------ ---------------- ---------------- --------
1      0.00             500.00           -500.00
1      0.00             250.00           -250.00
2      75.00            0.00             75.00
3      35.00            35.00            35.00
```

This query uses some math functions to arrive at a clever answer to the problem of identifying which values are debits and which are credits.

Let's start from the inside out. First, get the sign of the data. For the `Debit` column, I want data that is positive. So, take the sign and add 1 to it. Positive values go to 2, negative values to 0, and zeroes to 1.

Now, multiply the result by .5. By using .5, the server thinks I want a float result, but if I multiply by 50 cents, the data type remains a `smallmoney`. Positive numbers go back to 1 (2*.5=1). Negative numbers go to zero because zero times anything is zero and zeroes go to zero (1 * .5 = 0). Now, multiply this product by the data. Only positive numbers retain a non-zero value.

3

In the `Credit` column, we start off the same way. This time, we are subtracting 1 from the sign. If you follow the logic through, this means only negative numbers retain a non-zero value.

Using Date Functions

Only nine date functions are available in T-SQL. Table 3.7 lists each of them along with a description.

TABLE 3.7 Date Functions

Function	*Description*
`DateAdd`	Adds a specified number of dateparts to the date
`DateDiff`	Calculates the difference between two dates
`DatePart`	Extracts the specified datepart from the date
`DateName`	Returns a part of the date as a string
`Day`	Returns the day number of the date
`GetDate`	Returns the current date and time of the computer
`Month`	Returns the month number of the date
`Year`	Returns the year of the date
`GetUTCDate`	Returns the current UTC (universal time, GMT) date and time

The first four date functions in Table 3.7 take an argument (the first argument) to tell it on what part of the date to operate. Table 3.8 shows the different date parts available for use in the date functions.

TABLE 3.8 Datepart Codes Used in Date Functions

Name	*Usage*	*Sample Values*
Year	yy	1999
Quarter	qq	1, 2, 3, 4
Month	mm	1–12
Day of year	dy	1–365 (366 in leap years)
Day	dd	1–31
Week	wk	1–53
Weekday	dw	1–7, where Sunday is 1
Hour	hh	0–23, midnight is 0
Minute	mi	0–59
Second	ss	0–59
Millisecond	ms	0–999

Refer to this table if you have any questions about these codes while you are working with the examples in this section. When providing arguments to these functions, do not use quotation marks around the datepart codes, but if you are specifying a constant date, use quotation marks around the codes.

GETDATE()

This is one function that you will find yourself using quite often, in many different applications. The `GETDATE()` function returns the current date and time as a `datetime` value. The following example shows only one of the many uses of this function:

```
Select GETDATE()
```

Results:

```
------------------------
2000-10-06 20:48:10.500
```

This function is most often used in stored procedures and triggers to test the validity of an operation. For example, an inserted row might be checked to see whether a due date is five days from now or if it has passed.

DATEADD()

To get the date that is 30 days from today, you would first need to use the `GETDATE()` function to get today's date. You would then use `DATEADD()` to add the 30 days. The function would then return the date that is 30 days later. The syntax of the functions is

```
DATEADD(<datepart>, <increment>, <source>)
```

The example shown adds 30 days to today.

```
Select Dateadd(dd,30,getdate())
```

Note

> You should note the use of the `dd` as the datepart to request that the addition be done in days. If you used `mm` accidentally, you would have added 30 months to today instead.

Results:

```
-----------------------
2000-11-05 20:53:44.670

(1 row(s) affected)
```

> The `DATEADD()` function takes into account the different days in a month and even a leap year when doing its calculations.

DATEDIFF()

This function calculates the difference between `date1` and `date2`, based on the datepart specified. The syntax of this function is

```
DATEDIFF(<datepart>, <date1>, <date2>)
```

The following example shows the difference between today and New Year's Eve:

```
Select getdate(), datediff(dd, getdate(), '12/31/2000')
```

Results:

```
--------------------------- --
2000-10-06 20:58:03.483    86

(1 row(s) affected)
```

If the second date is earlier than the first date, you will receive a negative number as the result.

DATEPART()

The DATEPART() function returns an integer that represents a specified datepart of the source date. The following query sums the total number of books sold in June, regardless of the year:

```
use pubs
select sum(qty) as 'June Sales'
from sales
where datepart(mm,ord_date) = 6
```

Results:

```
June Sales
-----------
80

(1 row(s) affected)
```

DATENAME()

This function works the same way as the DATEPART() function, except that it returns a string instead of an integer. It is most useful when you need to get the days of the week or months of the year. The following example shows how to get the day of the week from today's date:

```
Select 'Today is ' + datename(dw, getdate()) + '.'
```

Results:

```
----------------
Today is Friday.
```

GETUTCDATE()

The GETUTCDATE() function returns the datetime value representing the current UTC time (Universal Time Coordinate or Greenwich mean time). The current UTC time is derived from the current local time and the time zone setting in the operating system of the computer on which SQL Server is running. The example shows the current time and the corresponding UTC time.

```
Select getdate() as 'Today', getutcdate() as 'UTC'
```

Results:

```
Today                       UTC
--------------------------- -----------------------
2000-10-06 21:10:51.067     2000-10-07 01:10:51.067
```

DAY(), MONTH(), YEAR()

These three functions return an integer that represents the day, month, or year part of a specified date. The following example shows all three functions at once:

```
SELECT DAY(getdate()) as 'day',
       MONTH(getdate()) as 'month',
       YEAR(getdate()) as 'year'
```

Results:

```
day         month       year
----------- ----------- -----------
6           10          2000

(1 row(s) affected)
```


Using the CASE Statement

The last topic we will discuss today is the CASE statement. The CASE expression provides great performance and allows me to design very fast SQL code. The CASE expression compares a specified column in the SELECT statement against a list of possibilities and returns different results depending on which WHEN expression in the CASE statement is matched.

There are two ways that you can use the CASE keyword. The first way is the simplest; it enables you to take different actions against the same expression. The second method, which is called a searched CASE expression, enables you to specify a Boolean expression and to take actions on that expression depending on whether it is true or false.

The syntax for the CASE statement is as follows:

```
CASE input_expression
  WHEN when_expression THEN result_expression
    [...n]
  [
    ELSE else_result_expression
  ]
END
```

Using a Simple CASE Statement

A simple CASE statement uses a single column in the CASE and returns an expression based on the contents in the column. The following example uses the CASE function to alter the display of book categories to make them more understandable:

```
use pubs
SELECT   Category =
      CASE type
         WHEN 'popular_comp' THEN 'Popular Computing'
```

```
        WHEN 'mod_cook' THEN 'Modern Cooking'
        WHEN 'business' THEN 'Business'
        WHEN 'psychology' THEN 'Psychology'
        WHEN 'trad_cook' THEN 'Traditional Cooking'
        ELSE 'Not yet categorized'
     END,
   CAST(title AS varchar(25)) AS 'Shortened Title',
   price AS Price
FROM titles
WHERE price IS NOT NULL
ORDER BY type, price
```

Results:

```
Category            Shortened Title           Price
------------------- ------------------------- --------------------
Business            You Can Combat Computer S 2.9900
Business            Cooking with Computers: S 11.9500
Business            The Busy Executive's Data 19.9900
Business            Straight Talk About Compu 19.9900
Modern Cooking      The Gourmet Microwave     2.9900
...
Psychology          Computer Phobic AND Non-P 21.5900
Traditional Cooking Fifty Years in Buckingham 11.9500
Traditional Cooking Sushi, Anyone?            14.9900
Traditional Cooking Onions, Leeks, and Garlic 20.9500

(16 row(s) affected)
```

The CASE expression takes the place of a single column in an otherwise quite ordinary query. For each row in the titles table, the CASE expression is evaluated. The order of the WHEN expressions is significant: If a row satisfies the Boolean WHEN expression, the code following the WHEN's THEN clause is performed, and the next row is evaluated. If the row matches none of the WHEN clauses, the ELSE is evaluated.

The CASE expression has five keywords associated with it: The CASE keyword starts the statement; WHEN presents the Boolean expression to test; THEN precedes the expression return value that the CASE expression represents for a particular row; ELSE gives an expression that is returned when none of the WHEN conditions is true; the END keyword marks the end of the CASE statement. After a CASE statement satisfies an expression, the remaining CASE statements in the grouping are skipped.

Using a Searched CASE Statement

This type of CASE statement is basically the same as the simple CASE, except that the WHEN expression contains a complete Boolean expression as shown in the following example:

```
use pubs
select lname, job_lvl,
      case
   when job_lvl<100 then 'Dear Fellow Worker'
   when job_lvl<200 then 'Dear Honored Guest'
   else 'Dear Executive'
      end as 'Greeting'
from employee
order by Greeting, lname
```

As you can see, the WHEN keyword is followed by a Boolean expression which includes a column name, operator, and value to be tested.

Summary

Well, you made it through the day. Today, you learned how to manipulate data using operators, functions, constants, and the CASE statement. In addition, you learned how to create aliases for columns in the SELECT statement. These techniques will serve you well throughout the rest of this book and throughout your career in T-SQL programming.

You also learned how to manipulate and search date values. You explored how to use the CONVERT and CAST functions to change the data type of a value from one type to another, and to format dates differently.

Finally, you discovered how to use the CASE expression to evaluate the values in selected columns and return a different value based on those contents. If you find yourself asking, "How do I do that in SQL?", remember the CASE expression.

Q&A

Q If the server won't convert my data type to hold fractions, what happens when I get the sum of something too big to be held?

A The server is smart enough to promote the data type to the next larger data type to hold the result of an aggregate or calculation.

Q Functions look really interesting, but it seems like a lot of work to type in all that stuff just for a simple result set.

A Functions are frequently used in the production of stored procedures and triggers. They enable you to provide consistent code for particular actions that will be used in many places in an application.

Workshop

The Workshop provides quiz questions to help you solidify your understanding of the material covered and exercises to provide you with experience in using what you've learned. Try to answer the quiz and exercise questions before checking the answers in Appendix A, "Answers to Quizzes and Exercises," and make sure you understand the answers before continuing to the next lesson.

Quiz

1. What function enables you to provide a value for nulls?
2. What is the result of this query?

```
Use Pubs
Select 'My name is ' + au_fname
From authors
Where au_id = '172-32-1176'
```

3. What column name is displayed by this query?

```
Use Pubs
Select au_fname as 'First Name'
From authors
```

4. What would be the result of the following query?

```
Use Pubs
Select 'My price is ' + price
From titles
Where title like '%Computer%'
```

Exercises

1. When was the first employee hired by Northwind?
2. What is today's date and what day of the week is it?
3. How many hours until New Year's Day?

WEEK 1

DAY 4

Working with Row Aggregates and Grouping

Now that you have learned to combine and manipulate columns to change data, you are ready for the next major step in the data retrieval process. Today you will learn how to use the aggregate functions to display a set of information that describes a group of rows. The topics we will discuss are

- Using the aggregate functions: `SUM()`, `AVG()`, `MIN()`, `MAX()`, `COUNT()`, and `COUNT_BIG`
- Understanding how nulls affect aggregate functions
- Finding subtotals (and subaverages and so forth) with `GROUP BY`
- Using `HAVING` to select from aggregate result sets
- Displaying summary values with `ROLLUP` and `CUBE`
- Using `CASE` to build a pivot table

Working with Aggregate Functions

All the functions you learned about yesterday are row-based: The function acts only on columns in the current row. *Aggregate functions* act on a set of rows. What are aggregate functions? You probably know them better as the summary, average, minimum, maximum, and count functions. "To aggregate" means to collect or to bring together. So, aggregate functions gather together data from many rows and report it in a single row (see Figure 4.1).

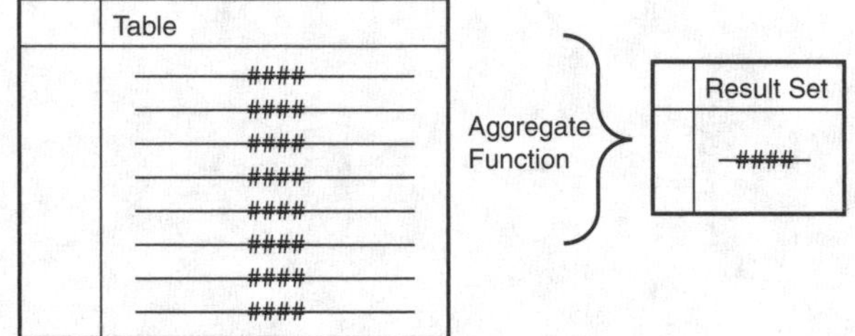

FIGURE 4.1
Aggregate functions gather values from many rows in a table into a single row in the result set.

SQL Server supports six aggregate functions:

- `SUM()`—Total of all values; works with numeric data types
- `AVG()`—Average of all values; works with numeric data types
- `MIN()`—Minimum value; works with all data types
- `MAX()`—Maximum value; works with all data types
- `COUNT()`—Number of values; works with all data types
- `COUNT_BIG()`—Number of values; works with all data types; returns a value of type `bigint`

In addition, SQL Server supports four additional numeric functions for statistical aggregation:

- `STDEV()`—Standard deviation for the matching rows
- `STDEVP()`—Standard deviation for the entire population
- `VAR()`—Variance for the matching rows
- `VARP()`—Variance for the entire population

Note

The statistical functions are used the same way you would use any aggregate functions.

We'll go through a number of examples, and then we'll look at how aggregates interact with `DISTINCT`, null values, and a variety of data types.

Using `SUM()` and `AVG()`

The `SUM()` and `AVG()` functions work with numeric expressions. As a quick review, here is the list of rows in the `Order Details` table for the product tofu (`ProductID 14`).

```
OrderID     ProductID   UnitPrice             Quantity Discount
----------- ----------- --------------------- -------- ------------------------
10249       14          18.6000               9        0.0
10325       14          18.6000               9        0.0
10333       14          18.6000               10       0.0
10375       14          18.6000               15       0.0
10393       14          18.6000               42       0.25
10409       14          18.6000               12       0.0
10412       14          18.6000               20       0.1
.
.
.
10794       14          23.2500               15       0.2
11076       14          23.2500               20       0.25
11077       14          23.2500               1        2.9999999E-2

(22 row(s) affected)
```


As you can see, there are many orders for tofu. Now, here's the total quantity of tofu (`ProductID 14`) sales in the `Order Details` table:

```
select sum(Quantity)
  from [Order Details]
 where ProductID = 14
```

Results:

```
-----------
        404
```

For each row found that matches the criteria (`ProductID = 14`), SQL Server evaluates the expression within the `SUM()` function (`Quantity`) and adds that result to the running total. When all the rows have been evaluated, the server reports the value in the running total. In this case, SQL Server totaled 404 tofu sales.

You can have multiple aggregate requests in a single query. Each aggregate operates over the same set of rows. I've also added a column alias for each function:

```
select sum(Quantity) as 'Qty Sold',
       avg(Quantity) as 'Avg Qty'
  from [Order Details]
 where ProductID = 14
```

Results:

```
Qty Sold    Avg Qty
----------- -----------
        404          18
```

SQL Server returns an integer result for both the sum and average because the original `Quantity` column is stored as a small integer. You won't lose accuracy with a sum, but if you need the average of an integer data type to provide greater accuracy, you should change the expression to a floating point or numeric data type by using the `cast` or `convert` function. (See the section "Using Functions on Column Data" in Day 3, "Working with Columns.") You can also multiply the `Quantity` column by `1.0`, as in this example:

```
select sum(Quantity) as 'Qty Sold',
       avg(Quantity * 1.0) as 'Avg Qty'
  from [Order Details]
 where ProductID = 14
```

Results:

```
Qty Sold    Avg Qty
----------- ----------------------------------------
        404                                18.363636
```

If no rows are found in the result set, aggregates return null. This query looks for sales of product 1400, which doesn't exist:

```
select sum(Quantity) as 'Qty Sold',
       avg(Quantity) as 'Avg Qty'
  from [Order Details]
 where ProductID = 1400
```

Results:

```
Qty Sold    Avg Qty
----------- -----------
NULL        NULL
```

Using Aggregates with Expressions

You can also use complex expressions as arguments in an aggregate. In the next set of examples, we'll compute an extended price for a detail line in `Order Details`, and then sum those extended prices. To determine the total extended price, you need to multiply the `UnitPrice` by the `Quantity` sold, and then apply the discount. This detailed result set shows how `ExtendedPrice` is derived for each row in the `Order Details` table (please note that to save space on the page, I removed a number of rows from the result set):

```
select Quantity,
       UnitPrice,
       Discount,
       Quantity * UnitPrice * (1.0 - Discount)
                as 'ExtendedPrice'
  from [Order Details]
 where ProductID = 14
```

Results:

```
Quantity UnitPrice      Discount        ExtendedPrice
-------- ------------- ------------- -------------
       9       18.6000           0.0     167.39999
       9       18.6000           0.0     167.39999
      10       18.6000           0.0         186.0
      15       18.6000           0.0         279.0
      42       18.6000          0.25     585.90002
…
      20       23.2500          0.25        348.75
       1       23.2500  2.9999999E-2       22.5525
```

> **Tip**
>
> This result set is a critical step in developing complex queries with aggregates in Transact-SQL. The preceding result set shows the way a computation works. It details all the components of the computation and enables me to examine individual rows. That gives me a chance to make sure that the results are correct. After the data is rolled into an aggregate value, it's much harder to tell whether your results make sense.
>
> Take the time to write queries from the bottom up. Work with small sets of output. Examine a few rows. Ask yourself, "Does this result make sense?" Then you can go ahead and apply aggregates.

4

In the first several rows, the unit price is $18.60; in the last two, the unit price is $23.25. Discounts vary from no discount to 30% off (the last value). The extended price expression seems to work correctly.

To find out the total dollar value of the sales of this product, I need to sum the `ExtendedPrice` expression:

```
select sum(Quantity * UnitPrice * (1.0 - Discount))
                as 'Total Dollar Sales'
  from [Order Details]
 where ProductID = 14
```

Results:

```
Total Dollar Sales
-----------------------------------
                 7991.4900035858154
```

For each row matching the criteria, the server found the quantity and unit price, multiplied them together, applied the discount, and then added that result to the running total for `Total Dollar Sales`. After all the rows were processed, SQL Server reported the running total.

Why is the `Total Dollars Sales` column displayed so strangely? When SQL Server performs a mathematical calculation involving different data types, it follows specific rules on the target data type for the result. `Quantity` is a `smallint` data type, `UnitPrice` is `money` (four decimal places, range up to 900 trillion), and `Discount` is a `float` column (15 significant digits, range up to 10^308 power).

When you multiply an `integer` value and a `money` value, you get a `money` result. When you multiply anything by a `float`, you get a `float`. The rules seek to avoid arithmetic overflow (exceeding the maximum size of the value allowed in a data type) by always using the largest type of those involved.

Using Aggregates in Complex Expressions

You can use aggregate functions in expressions after they have been calculated, but those expressions should contain other aggregates and constants only. To determine the average unit price for all sales of product `14`, divide the `Total Dollar Sales` (the aggregate we created in the preceding example) by the `Qty Sold`:

```
select sum(Quantity) as 'Qty Sold',
       sum(Quantity * UnitPrice * (1.0 - Discount))
                    as 'Total Dollar Sales',
       sum(Quantity * UnitPrice * (1.0 - Discount)) /
                sum(Quantity) as 'Average Unit Price'
  from [Order Details]
 where ProductID = 14
```

Results:

```
Qty Sold    Total Dollar Sales       Average Unit Price
----------- ------------------------ ------------------------
        404       7991.4900035858154        19.780915850459941
```

First, the server determines the value for `Total Dollar Sales` and `Qty Sold`. As a last step before reporting the results, SQL Server performs the division to derive the `Average Unit Price`.

Using MIN() and MAX()

The functions `MIN()` and `MAX()` look for the lowest and highest values for a column or expression. Let's get the lowest and highest sale price for a product:

```
select min(UnitPrice) as 'Min Price',
       max(UnitPrice) as 'Max Price'
  from [Order Details]
 where ProductID = 14
```

Results:

```
Min Price             Max Price
--------------------- ---------------------
             18.6000               23.2500
```

Unlike `SUM()` and `AVG()`, `MIN()`, and `MAX()` work with any data type. This query reports the earliest recorded order date:

```
select min(OrderDate) as 'Earliest Order'
  from Orders
```

Results:

```
Earliest Order
---------------------------
1996-07-04 00:00:00.000
```

To find the earliest order date in February 1997, use this:

```
select min(OrderDate) as 'Earliest Order'
  from Orders
 where OrderDate >= '2/1/97'
   and OrderDate < '3/1/97'
```

Results:

```
Earliest Order
---------------------------
1997-02-03 00:00:00.000
```

`MIN()` and `MAX()` also work with binary data and with strings. This final example of `MIN()` and `MAX()` finds the last product name in the price list:

```
select max(ProductName)
from Products
```

Results:

```
----------------------------------------
Zaanse koeken
```

Using Aggregates in a `WHERE` Clause

You have just used an aggregate function to find the earliest order date, but after you find that date, you probably want to know more details about what happened on the date. It's tempting to insert the aggregate function into a `WHERE` clause like this:

```
/* WARNING BAD EXAMPLE DOESN'T WORK */
/* DANGER DANGER DANGER */
select OrderID, CustomerID, EmployeeID
from Orders
where OrderDate = min(OrderDate)
```

Go ahead and try it. Doing so will give you the chance to provoke another stern error message from the server:

```
Server: Msg 147, Level 15, State 1, Line 5
An aggregate may not appear in the WHERE clause unless
it is in a subquery contained in a HAVING clause or a
select list, and the column being aggregated is an
outer reference.
```

You probably have no idea what the error message is trying to tell you. So, let's simplify the message:

An aggregate may not appear in the WHERE clause unless it is in a subquery.

> What's a subquery? It's a query used within another query. Normally the server will get the value of the subquery first, and then use that value in the outer query. Day 6, "Using Subqueries," will go into detail on subqueries. For now, you need to learn just one way to use a subquery.

If you want to use the result of an aggregate function in the WHERE clause, you need to tell the server to retrieve the value of the aggregate first, and then use that value in the search condition in the main query. The subquery is enclosed in parentheses, as shown here:

```
/* This example works just fine */
select OrderID, CustomerID, EmployeeID
from Orders
where OrderDate =
      (
      select min(OrderDate)
        from Orders
      )
```

Results:

```
OrderID     CustomerID EmployeeID
----------- ---------- -----------
      10248 VINET                5
```

Armed with the earliest date, the server was able to find an order from that date. Notice that the minimum Order Date was never returned as part of the result set. The server uses results from subqueries internally; they are not displayed to the user. If you want to see the data being used, you need to add the `Order` date to the main `SELECT` statement as shown:

```
/* This example works just fine */
select OrderID, OrderDate, CustomerID, EmployeeID
from Orders
where OrderDate =
      (
      select min(OrderDate)
        from Orders
      )
```

Results:

```
OrderID     OrderDate   CustomerID EmployeeID
----------- ----------- ---------- ----------
10248     1996-07-04 00:00:00.000   VINET      5
```

I can also add the February 1997 condition to the subquery statement to find out information about the earliest order in that month.

```
/* This example works just fine */
select OrderID, CustomerID, EmployeeID
from Orders
where OrderDate =
      (
      select min(OrderDate)
        from Orders
       where OrderDate >= '2/1/97'
         and OrderDate <  '3/1/97'
      )
```

Results:

```
OrderID     CustomerID EmployeeID
----------- ---------- ----------
      10433 PRINI               3
      10434 FOLKO               3
```

The result set includes two rows, not one. Even though the aggregate function returned only a single value for the minimum date in February, there were two rows that matched the condition in the main query. After the subquery has derived the earliest date (February 3, 1997), that value is substituted for the entire subquery and this outer query runs:

```
select OrderID, CustomerID, EmployeeID
from Orders
where OrderDate = '1997-02-03 00:00:00.000'
```

Using COUNT()

The COUNT() function enables you to find the number of values or rows that match the search conditions. How many products are on the price list? How many employees are there? How many times was tofu purchased in February 1997? When you are interested in how many times a value appears in a list, you should use the COUNT() aggregate.

How many orders in February 1997?

```
select count(OrderID) as 'Num of Orders'
  from Orders
 where OrderDate >= '2/1/97'
   and OrderDate < '3/1/97'
```

Results:

```
Num of Orders
-------------
           29
```

How many employees?

```
select count(EmployeeID)
from Employees
```

Results:

```
-----------
          9
```

Using COUNT(*)

You might be wondering how to choose the column for the COUNT() function. The real question you asked in the previous queries was "How many rows are there?" The COUNT() aggregate enables you to use the asterisk as an argument to ask for a count of rows:

```
select count(*)
from Employees
```

Results:

```
-----------
          9
```

COUNT(*) is faster than COUNT(EmployeeID). SQL Server doesn't need to open up the row, and then find and parse the EmployeeID. It simply checks whether the row matches the search conditions, and then increments its internal counter.

When should you use COUNT() with a column name? When the column might contain nulls. In that case, you can count how many rows contain non-null values for that column. This query determines how many customers have a non-null value in the Region column:

```
select count(Region) "Customers with Region"
  from Customers
```

Results:

```
Customers with Region
---------------------
                   31

(1 row(s) affected)

Warning: Null value eliminated by aggregate or other set
operation.
```

The server warned me that the aggregate does not include some rows because the COUNT(Region) function skipped them.

Using COUNT_BIG()

The COUNT_BIG() aggregate function was introduced as part of the SQL Server 2000 release. It is intended to help in applications where row counts exceed the 2.1 billion limit imposed by the integer (int) data type.

The only difference between the COUNT_BIG() and COUNT() functions is their return type. The COUNT() function returns an int, so it can go as high as 2.1 billion (2^31). COUNT_BIG() returns a bigint, so it can count up to 9,223,372,036,854,775,808 (2^63 or *9 quintillion!*) rows.

4

Implementing Error Handling for Aggregates

The most common error with aggregates is arithmetic overflow during a sum or count operation. Arithmetic overflow occurs when the number assigned to a variable or column is out of the range of possible values for that data type. For example, a smallint data type is limited to +/- 32,677. Inserting a value of 40,000 into a smallint column will cause the insert statement to fail and report an arithmetic overflow.

SQL Server tries to avoid overflows by automatically changing numeric data types to the highest related data type. For example, if you are summing smallint values, the server automatically returns an integer (int). The greater range of the integer data type will usually prevent an overflow.

Numeric data types allow you to define both a precision (the number of digits in the number) and a scale (the number of decimal positions). When you sum numeric data types, the server automatically returns a sum with the highest number of digits that the data type can hold (38).

You will learn all about data types on Day 8, "Defining Data," when you learn how to define tables and columns.

Understanding Aggregates and Null

Aggregates act as if nulls don't exist. Nulls are not counted as zeros for sums or averages. They are ignored for mins and maxes. And they will be ignored for `COUNT()`.

To clarify this point, let's use a very simple temporary table called `#Samples`. Listing 4.1 provides the script to create and populate this table.

LISTING 4.1 Script to Create and Populate a `#Samples` Temporary Table

```
set nocount on
go
create table #Samples
(
    id int primary key,
    value int null
)
go
insert #Samples (id, value) values (1, 10)
insert #Samples (id, value) values (2, 15)
insert #Samples (id, value) values (3, 20)
insert #Samples (id, value) values (4, null)
go
set nocount off
go
select * from #Samples
```

Here's the result returned by the last SELECT statement:

```
     id          value
----------- -----------
          1          10
          2          15
          3          20
          4 NULL
```

Now we can work with the `#Samples` table to experiment with aggregates and null. Run the query in Listing 4.2 to see how aggregates treat the null in the `value` column:

LISTING 4.2 How Aggregates Treat Null Values

```
select
        sum(value) as 'Sum',
        avg(value) as 'Avg',
```

LISTING 4.2 continued

```
      min(value) as 'Min',
      max(value) as 'Max',
      count(value) as 'Count',
      count(*) as 'Count(*)'
from #Samples
```

Results:

```
Sum      Avg      Min      Max      Count    Count(*)
-------- -------- -------- -------- -------- ---------
      45       15       10       20        3         4

(1 row(s) affected)

Warning: Null value eliminated by aggregate or other set
operation.
```

The null value in the fourth row is not included in the aggregate results. Sum is `45` because the null in row 4 is ignored. Notice that null is neither the max value nor the min (null is not an implied zero). `COUNT()` returns `3` because only three rows have non-null values in them. Notice that the average is computed by deriving `SUM(value)` and `COUNT(value)`, and then finding the quotient (`SUM/COUNT`).

Why does `COUNT(*)` return `4` when one of the rows is null? `count(*)`counts only rows, not columns or other expressions.

Don't forget to drop the temporary table when you are finished using it.

```
drop table #Samples
```

Computing Aggregates with DISTINCT

You can use `DISTINCT` to compute aggregates of unique values for a column. `DISTINCT` appears most commonly with `COUNT()`, although it works the same way with the other aggregate functions.

The expression `COUNT(DISTINCT UnitPrice)` asks SQL Server to determine the number of unique values that are in a set of rows for the `UnitPrice` column. Use `COUNT(DISTINCT <column name>)` to answer questions such as "How many customers ordered in November 1997? How many dates are there in 1998 when we had sales? How many users visited our Web site?" Use `DISTINCT` when you are looking for the number of unique instances in a place where duplicates are permitted.

How many customers ordered in November 1997?

```
select count(distinct CustomerID) 'Customers'
  from Orders
 where OrderDate >= '11/1/1997'
   and OrderDate < '12/1/1997'
```

Results:

```
Customers
-----------
         27
```

How many dates are there in 1998 when we had sales?

```
select count(distinct OrderDate) as 'Number of Dates in 1998'
  from Orders
 where OrderDate >= '1/1/1998'
   and OrderDate < '1/1/1999'
```

Results:

```
Number of Dates in 1998
-----------------------
                     90
```

Remember that the sample data in the Northwind database is not representative of real life. The dates have no time component, which probably won't be true for all the dates in the databases you will build and support.

To find out the number of unique dates in a table where the dates include a non-zero time component, you need to change the argument for the COUNT() function to strip off the time component. Here's the query in real life:

```
select count(distinct convert(varchar(12), OrderDate, 101))
as 'Number of Dates in 1998'
  from Orders
 where OrderDate >= '1/1/1998'
   and OrderDate < '1/1/1999'
```

The convert function uses format 101 to return the date as a string in the form MM/DD/YYYY. If there were a time component, this conversion process would strip off the time, leaving only the date.

As it turns out, the formatted strings are never converted back to a date data type, but that doesn't matter. The query is interested only in how many different values appear in the table, not in the content of the data.

Avoid using `DISTINCT` with `MIN()` and `MAX()`. There is a performance penalty for using `DISTINCT`. The server must perform a sorting and elimination step before it can do the aggregate processing. That extra step is expensive, and `MIN()` and `MAX()` always return the same result with or without `DISTINCT`.

Reviewing Aggregates

In the next section, you will learn to generate subtotals and other sub-values by using aggregates while grouping the data. As you continue to work with these functions, remember these key points about aggregate functions:

- Aggregate functions return one value representing one or many rows.
- Aggregates never include nulls.
- Aggregates are not permitted in the `WHERE` clause.

Grouping Data

So far, you've learned how to use aggregates to get overall totals (and averages, and so on) for a set of rows. If you wanted to know the total dollar sales for product `14`, you could execute the query we wrote earlier:

```
select sum(Quantity * UnitPrice * (1.0 - Discount))
                    as 'Total Dollar Sales'
  from [Order Details]
 where ProductID = 14
```

What if you were also interested in products `11`, `12`, and `13`? You could reexecute the query several times, each time with a different product ID.

It would be better to write a single query and get a result set that looked like this:

```
ProductID   Total Dollar Sales
----------- ----------------------------------------
         11                       12901.770042419434
         12                       12257.660041809082
         13                       4960.4400224685669
         14                       7991.4900035858154
```

In the rest of today's session, you will learn how to use `GROUP BY` clauses to define groupings of aggregates for subtotalling.

`GROUP BY` Clauses

If you look closely at the last result set, you will notice that it combines both aggregate and nonaggregate data. The first column, `ProductID`, is a simple column value. The second column, `Total Dollar Sales`, is the result of a `SUM()` function.

If you execute the following query in which you combine aggregate and nonaggregate columns in the select list, you get the following error:

```
select ProductID,
       sum(Quantity * UnitPrice * (1.0 - Discount))
                    as 'Total Dollar Sales'
  from [Order Details]
 where ProductID between 11 and 14
```

Results:

```
Server: Msg 8118, Level 16, State 1, Line 1
Column 'Order Details.ProductID' is invalid in the select
list because it is not contained in an aggregate function
and there is no GROUP BY clause.
```

You need to instruct the server to group (*aggregate*) the data by the product ID:

```
select ProductID,
       sum(Quantity * UnitPrice * (1.0 - Discount))
                    as 'Total Dollar Sales'
  from [Order Details]
 where ProductID between 11 and 14
 group by ProductID
```

The `GROUP BY` clause instructs the server to build a worktable whose key is `ProductID`. The other column in the worktable is the aggregate. Each time SQL Server retrieves a row, it looks up the `ProductID` in the worktable. If the value for `ProductID` already exists, the server adds the `Quantity * UnitPrice` product to the running total. If the `ProductID` is not found in the worktable, the server adds a row with the new value, setting the running total equal to the `Dollar Sales` for the current row.

When SQL Server exhausts the rows in the source table, it presents the contents of the worktable to the user as the result set.

Grouping works with all the aggregate functions. Here is an example where we find the most recent order date for each customer:

```
select CustomerID, max(OrderDate)
from Orders
group by CustomerID
```

Results:

```
CustomerID
---------- ---------------------------
TOMSP      1998-03-23 00:00:00.000
LILAS      1998-05-05 00:00:00.000
GREAL      1998-04-30 00:00:00.000
HUNGO      1998-04-30 00:00:00.000
```

```
...
COMMI      1998-04-22 00:00:00.000
BONAP      1998-05-06 00:00:00.000
```

Each customer is listed along with the latest order date for that customer. Notice that the `CustomerID` values are not sorted.

One significant change to SQL Server 2000 occurred with the introduction of new methods of grouping data. In previous versions, grouped output would be sorted by the grouping column. SQL Server 2000 does not guarantee any specific order in grouped data.

Users should include an `ORDER BY` clause in every `GROUP BY` query in which the order of the result set matters. Existing systems that rely on the automatic sorting of grouped output must be fixed as part of the upgrade to SQL Server 2000 so that they do not rely on that sorting:

```
select CustomerID, max(OrderDate)
from Orders
group by CustomerID
order by CustomerID
```

4

Grouping with all

Transact-SQL allows the keyword `all` to force the result set to report rows for all possible grouping values. It makes sense to use `all` when the query includes a `WHERE` clause.

This query reports the number of employees hired since 1994. The report is organized by title.

```
select Title, count(*) 'Count'
  from Employees
 where HireDate >= '1/1/1994'
 group by Title
```

Results:

```
Title                          Count
------------------------------ -----------
Inside Sales Coordinator                 1
Sales Representative                     2
```

The report includes a row for a title only where an employee matches the search criterion. To get a complete report that includes a row for every job title, add the `all` keyword to the `GROUP BY` expression:

```
select Title, count(*) 'Count'
  from Employees
```

```
 where HireDate >= '1/1/1994'
 group by all Title
```

Results:

```
Title                          Count
------------------------------ -----------
Inside Sales Coordinator                 1
Sales Manager                            0
Sales Representative                     2
Vice President, Sales                    0
```

This is a complete list of job titles. Two rows show that no employees having those titles matched the search condition.

Using Multi-Level Grouping

You can group on multiple columns or expressions as well. In this example, we see the number of products for each supplier and category:

```
select SupplierID,
       CategoryID,
       count(*) as 'Num of Products'
  from Products
 where SupplierID in (1, 2, 4)
 group by
       SupplierID,
       CategoryID
```

Results:

```
SupplierID  CategoryID  Num of Products
----------- ----------- ---------------
          1           1               2
          1           2               1
          2           2               4
          4           6               1
          4           7               1
          4           8               1
```

With two levels of grouping, the server reports a count for every unique combination of supplier and category.

Grouping by Complex Expressions

So far, all the examples have used `GROUP BY` with a single column. You can also use a calculation or function for grouping. This query uses the `DATEPART()` function to extract the year from the date, and then reports the number of orders for each year:

```
select
      datepart(yy, OrderDate) as 'Year',
      count(*) as 'Orders'
  from orders
 group by
      datepart(yy, OrderDate)
 order by
      datepart(yy, OrderDate)
```

Results:

```
Year        Orders
----------- -----------
       1996         152
       1997         408
       1998         270
```

The key point in this example is that the expressions in the grouping clause and in the select list match exactly. If there were a mismatch between these expressions, the results would be skewed and difficult to understand.

Let's extend the year-by-year order breakdown we just worked on. In addition to grouping on the year, let's add the month. To do this, we'll use two levels of grouping: We'll group first on year, and then on month.

It's a simple extension of what we've done so far, add another expression for month to the select list along with the same expression in the `GROUP BY` clause. (Use the `DATENAME()` function with the month so that you can get the name of the date instead of its ordinal number.) Sort the data by year, and then by month, as shown in Listing 4.3.

LISTING 4.3 A Select Statement with Multi-Level Grouping

```
select
      datepart(yy, OrderDate) as 'Year',
      datename(mm, OrderDate) as 'Month',
      count(*) as 'Orders'
  from orders
 group by
      datepart(yy, OrderDate),
      datename(mm, OrderDate)
 order by
      datepart(yy, OrderDate),
      datename(mm, OrderDate)
```

When you run the query, you should get this result set:

```
Year        Month                          Orders
----------- ------------------------------ -----------
       1996 August                                  25
       1996 December                                31
```

LISTING 4.3 continued

```
1996 July                          22
1996 November                      25
1996 October                       26
1996 September                     23
1997 April                         31
1997 August                        33
1997 December                      48
1997 February                      29
1997 January                       33
1997 July                          33
1997 June                          30
1997 March                         30
1997 May                           32
1997 November                      34
1997 October                       38
1997 September                     37
1998 April                         74
1998 February                      54
1998 January                       55
1998 March                         73
1998 May                           14
```

You can see that the results are broken out by year, and then by month. However, there is a problem: The months aren't sorted chronologically, they are sorted alphabetically by name.

Why didn't SQL Server sort the months properly? From the server's standpoint, the month names are just strings that must be put in order. You sort strings by using an alphabet, not a calendar.

To correct this output, you must display the name of the month, but sort by the number of the month. Listing 4.4 shows the corrected query.

LISTING 4.4 This Query Attempts to Sort on the Month Number but Displays the Month Name

```
select
       datepart(yy, OrderDate) as 'Year',
       datename(mm, OrderDate) as 'Month',
       count(*) as 'Orders'
  from Orders
 where OrderDate < '1/1/2000'
 group by
       datepart(yy, OrderDate),
       datename(mm, OrderDate)
```

LISTING 4.4 continued

```
order by
        datepart(yy, OrderDate),
        datepart(mm, OrderDate)
```

The query fails with this error message:

```
Server: Msg 8127, Level 16, State 1, Line 2
Column name 'Orders.OrderDate' is invalid in the ORDER BY
clause because it is not contained in either an aggregate
function or the GROUP BY clause.
```

The message warns that the `OrderDate` column is referenced in the `ORDER BY` clause but has not been properly referenced in the `GROUP BY` clause. Of course, the `OrderDate` column is actually listed twice in the `GROUP BY` clause: once for the year and once for the date. But the new sorting expression based on the ordinal date number, `DATEPART(mm, OrderDate)`, contains a reference to `OrderDate`. `OrderDate` is not grouped.

Why must the server group by a value in order to sort on it? The server performs grouping activities first, and then sorts the grouped output. If `DATEPART(mm, OrderDate)` is not included in the temporary grouped output, SQL Server cannot sort on it.

Finally, to make this work, we must force the month `DATEPART()` expression into the grouped output. We can do that without displaying it in the ultimate result set, as shown in Listing 4.5.

LISTING 4.5 This Query Sorts on the Month Number but Displays the Month Name

```
select
        datepart(yy, OrderDate) as 'Year',
        datename(mm, OrderDate) as 'Month',
        count(*) as 'Orders'
  from Orders
 where OrderDate < '1/1/2000'
 group by
        datepart(yy, OrderDate),
        datename(mm, OrderDate),
        datepart(mm, OrderDate)
 order by
        datepart(yy, OrderDate),
        datepart(mm, OrderDate)
```

Here is the final output:

```
Year        Month                          Orders
----------- ------------------------------ -----------
       1996 July                                    22
       1996 August                                  25
```

LISTING 4.5 continued

```
        1996 September                              23
...
        1998 February                               54
        1998 March                                  73
        1998 April                                  74
        1998 May                                    14
```

By adding line 10 to the GROUP BY clause, the query worked. The data is sorted properly by year, and then sorted chronologically by month. The results are properly grouped. A little later today, you will learn how to turn this into a pivot table with months on the left and years along the top.

On Day 2, "Filtering and Sorting Data," we looked at the possibility of sorting on a column that is not included in the results. This is one time when it's appropriate not to display the ordering column (the month number). The name of the month enables a user to understand the sorting of the data without displaying the month number.

Using HAVING to Remove Grouped Rows

In the first half of this lesson, you have seen how a WHERE clause removes rows from a result set, but you could not use aggregates in WHERE clauses. A HAVING clause enables you to filter out rows after grouping has occurred, and you can refer to the results of aggregates in a HAVING clause.

Let's enhance what we did in Listing 4.4 by finding only months where there were 70 orders or more. To do that, add a HAVING clause that includes the condition

```
having count(*) >= 70
```

Notice that the HAVING clause appears between the GROUP BY and the ORDER BY clauses. To see this, check out line 11 in Listing 4.6.

LISTING 4.6 The HAVING Clause Removes Months with Fewer than 70 Orders

```
 1: select
 2:       datepart(yy, OrderDate) as 'Year',
 3:       datename(mm, OrderDate) as 'Month',
 4:       count(*) as 'Orders'
 5:   from Orders
 6:  where OrderDate < '1/1/2000'
 7:  group by
 8:       datepart(yy, OrderDate),
 9:       datename(mm, OrderDate),
10:       datepart(mm, OrderDate)
```

LISTING 4.6 continued

```
having count(*) >= 70
 order by
       datepart(yy, OrderDate),
       datepart(mm, OrderDate)
```

The results include only two months.

```
Year        Month                          Orders
----------- ------------------------------ -----------
       1998 March                                   73
       1998 April                                   74
```

Combining Subtotals and Totals with ROLLUP and CUBE

You often need to display both subtotals and totals in the same result set. Transact-SQL provides the ROLLUP and CUBE operators to provide this extension to the grouping options. Let's examine a result set to understand the effect of these operators.

Grouping with ROLLUP

Here's a result set from an earlier example. It includes an additional row now whose ProductID is null. That row contains the sum of all the TotalDollarSales for all ProductIDs.

```
ProductID   Total Dollar Sales
----------- -----------------------------------------
         11                         12901.770042419434
         12                         12257.660041809082
         13                         4960.4400224685669
         14                         7991.4900035858154
NULL                                38111.360110282898
```

To get that additional row, add the ROLLUP operator to the GROUP BY clause:

```
select ProductID,
       sum(Quantity * UnitPrice) as 'Total Dollar Sales'
  from [Order Details]
 where ProductID between 11 and 14
 group by ProductID with rollup
```

Here is another example that uses the MAX() function. The last entry with a null customer ID reports the latest date reported for a customer.

```
select CustomerID, max(OrderDate)
from Orders
group by CustomerID with rollup
```

Results:

```
CustomerID
---------- ---------------------------
ALFKI      1998-04-09 00:00:00.000
ANATR      1998-03-04 00:00:00.000
ANTON      1998-01-28 00:00:00.000
AROUT      1998-04-10 00:00:00.000
BERGS      1998-03-04 00:00:00.000
…
WOLZA      1998-04-23 00:00:00.000
NULL       1998-05-06 00:00:00.000
```

Notice that the data is sorted by `CustomerID` even though we did not include an `ORDER BY` expression. When you use `ROLLUP`, it's important not to include ordering. Otherwise, the `ROLLUP` lines will be sorted to the top of the list.

So far, we've limited the results to queries with a single grouping expression. When there are multiple grouping expressions, the `ROLLUP` operator provides subtotals at each grouping level and an overall total at the highest level.

```
select SupplierID,
       CategoryID,
       count(*) as 'Num of Products'
  from Products
 where SupplierID in (1, 2, 4)
 group by
       SupplierID,
       CategoryID with rollup
```

Results:

```
SupplierID  CategoryID  Num of Products
----------- ----------- --------------
          1           1              2
          1           2              1
          1 NULL                     3
          2           2              4
          2 NULL                     4
          4           6              1
          4           7              1
          4           8              1
          4 NULL                     3
NULL        NULL                    10
```

The `ROLLUP` operator has added a number of rows to this result set. The third row (`SupplierID 1` and `CategoryID null`) provides an overall count of products for supplier 1 (all categories). There are similar rows for suppliers 2 and 4. The last row is an overall total for all suppliers and all categories.

Grouping with CUBE

Whereas the ROLLUP operator provides subtotals and totals that follow the hierarchy of your grouping expressions, the CUBE operator provides subtotals and totals for all possible combinations of your grouping expressions.

With a single grouping expression, CUBE and ROLLUP provide identical results. Here is the first ROLLUP example, presented this time with CUBE:

```
select ProductID,
       sum(Quantity * UnitPrice * (1 - Discount))
               as 'Total Dollar Sales'
  from [Order Details]
 where ProductID between 11 and 14
 group by ProductID with cube
```

Results:

```
ProductID   Total Dollar Sales
----------- --------------------------------------
         11                     12901.770042419434
         12                     12257.660041809082
         13                     4960.4400224685669
         14                     7991.4900035858154
NULL                            38111.360110282898
```

The CUBE result set differs from ROLLUP when there are multiple grouping expressions. Here is the multi-level ROLLUP we looked at a moment ago, now implemented with CUBE:

```
select SupplierID,
       CategoryID,
       count(*) as 'Num of Products'
  from Products
 where SupplierID in (1, 2, 4)
 group by
       SupplierID,
       CategoryID with cube
```

Results:

```
SupplierID  CategoryID  Num of Products
----------- ----------- ---------------
          1           1               2
          1           2               1
          1 NULL                      3
          2           2               4
          2 NULL                      4
          4           6               1
          4           7               1
          4           8               1
          4 NULL                      3
```

4

```
NULL        NULL                10
NULL                  1          2
NULL                  2          5
NULL                  6          1
NULL                  7          1
NULL                  8          1
```

The first 10 rows of results match exactly the results from the ROLLUP query. They include the summaries for suppliers 1, 2, and 4, as well as an overall summary for all suppliers and categories. The last five rows provide category summaries across all suppliers. Grouped output includes all possible combinations of supplier and category, as well as totals across each supplier and each category.

Identifying ROLLUP and CUBE Rows with grouping

There might be instances when you need to know whether a row was created as part of a ROLLUP or CUBE operation. Use the grouping function to display a 1 or 0 in the result set.

```
select SupplierID,
       CategoryID,
       count(*) as 'NumProducts',
       grouping(CategoryID) 'CategoryGrp',
       grouping(SupplierID) 'SupplierGrp'
  from Products
 where SupplierID in (1, 2, 4)
 group by
       SupplierID,
       CategoryID with cube
```

Results:

```
SupplierID  CategoryID  NumProducts CategoryGrp SupplierGrp
----------- ----------- ----------- ----------- -----------
          1           1           2           0           0
          1           2           1           0           0
          1 NULL                  3           1           0
          2           2           4           0           0
          2 NULL                  4           1           0
          4           6           1           0           0
          4           7           1           0           0
          4           8           1           0           0
          4 NULL                  3           1           0
NULL        NULL                 10           1           1
NULL                  1           2           0           1
NULL                  2           5           0           1
NULL                  6           1           0           1
NULL                  7           1           0           1
NULL                  8           1           0           1
```

Each row is tagged to indicate whether there was a rollup on that row for the category or supplier column. If an actual null SupplierID or CategoryID were included in the result set, this would be the only way to distinguish between CUBE or ROLLUP rows and actual data. This enables you to identify the column on which the data is actually being aggregated.

Applying ROLLUP

Adding the ROLLUP operator to the year and month orders report will expose some real-life application issues. Listing 4.7 lists the new query, now including ROLLUP.

LISTING 4.7 Breakdowns by Year and Month with ROLLUP (First Try)

```
 1: select
 2:        datepart(yy, OrderDate) as 'Year',
 3:        datename(mm, OrderDate) as 'Month',
 4:        count(*) as 'Orders'
 5:   from Orders
 6:  where OrderDate < '1/1/2000'
 7:  group by
 8:        datepart(yy, OrderDate),
 9:        datepart(mm, OrderDate),
10:        datename(mm, OrderDate) with rollup
```


Notice that the ORDER BY clause has been removed from the query now that we've added ROLLUP in line 10. ROLLUP does its own sorting. The grouping order matters now, so make sure that the grouping is first by year, and then by numeric month (datepart), and last by alphabetic month (datename). Otherwise, ROLLUP will sort the data incorrectly.

Here are the results. ROLLUP added summary rows for each year as well as a grand total at the end. Unfortunately, it also appears to have added a duplicate row for each month with a month name of NULL.

```
Year        Month                          Orders
----------- ------------------------------ -----------
       1996 July                                    22
       1996 NULL                                    22
       1996 August                                  25
       1996 NULL                                    25
…
       1996 December                                31
       1996 NULL                                    31
       1996 NULL                                   152
       1997 January                                 33
       1997 NULL                                    33
…
       1998 May                                     14
       1998 NULL                                    14
       1998 NULL                                   270
NULL        NULL                                   830
```

We need to find a way to remove those extra rows. Let's display the DATEPART expression that finds the numeric month in the result set. Listing 4.8 provides the revised query with the additional expression included in the select list.

LISTING 4.8 Breakdowns by Year and Month with ROLLUP (Second Try). Displays the Value of the Month datepart Expression

```
select
       datepart(yy, OrderDate) as 'Year',
       datename(mm, OrderDate) as 'Month',
       datepart(mm, OrderDate) as 'Month Number',
       count(*) as 'Orders'
  from Orders
 where OrderDate < '1/1/2000'
group by
       datepart(yy, OrderDate),
       datepart(mm, OrderDate),
       datename(mm, OrderDate) with rollup
```

Results:

```
Year        Month          Month Number Orders
----------- -------------- ------------ -----------
       1996 July                      7          22
       1996 NULL                      7          22
       1996 August                    8          25
       1996 NULL                      8          25
…
       1996 December                 12          31
       1996 NULL                     12          31
       1996 NULL           NULL                 152
       1997 January                   1          33
       1997 NULL                      1          33
…
       1998 May                       5          14
       1998 NULL                      5          14
       1998 NULL           NULL                 270
NULL        NULL           NULL                 830
```

The query provides three levels of grouping, so ROLLUP provides three levels of output. The second and third levels of grouping (month name and month number) represent the same data. We need to suppress the extra grouped rows in the output.

To filter grouped data, we'll add a HAVING clause. (Rows created by ROLLUP aren't available at the time the WHERE clause is evaluated.) The extra rows have a non-null value for the month number and a null value for the month name. Listing 4.9 includes the HAVING clause to suppress the extra rows.

LISTING 4.9 Breakdowns by Year and Month with ROLLUP (Final). The HAVING Clause Suppresses Unnecessary ROLLUP Data Generated by the Extra Grouping Expression

```
select
       datepart(yy, OrderDate) as 'Year',
       datename(mm, OrderDate) as 'Month',
       count(*) as 'Orders'
  from Orders
 where OrderDate < '1/1/2000'
group by
       datepart(yy, OrderDate),
       datepart(mm, OrderDate),
       datename(mm, OrderDate) with rollup
having
       datepart(mm, OrderDate) is null
    or datename(mm, OrderDate) is not null
```

The HAVING clause eliminates rows where the numeric datepart is not null and the alphabetic datename is null. Those are the rows to be eliminated. The result set is now correct and complete:

```
Year        Month                          Orders
----------- ------------------------------ -----------
       1996 July                                    22
       1996 August                                  25
…
       1996 December                                31
       1996 NULL                                   152
       1997 January                                 33
…
       1998 May                                     14
       1998 NULL                                   270
NULL        NULL                                   830
```


Creating Pivot Tables

The last thing we'll do today is look at a method for generating a pivot table using aggregates and grouping. *Pivot tables*, also called *cross-tabs*, are different from regular result sets because the column headings are drawn from the data itself. One column in the data is selected to become the headings for the cross-tab report. To understand this better, you need to see the result set for a pivot table. Then we will step through the process of building it. The result set we will produce analyzes current (1998) and prior (1997) year orders for the first five months of the year:

```
Month     Orders 1998 Orders 1997 Percent Change
--------- ----------- ----------- ------------------------
January            55          33                66.666666
February           54          29                86.206896
```

```
March              73           30                143.333333
April              74           31                138.709677
May                14           32                -56.250000
NULL              270          155                 74.193548
```

The months (extracted from the export date) are displayed on the left. The years (also extracted from the export date) are displayed at the top. Each cell (intersection of a month and year) contains the result of an aggregate based on that month and year. At the right is the percent change from the prior year to the current year for each month. At the bottom is a year-to-date total.

Everything we have learned so far will end up in this query. Make sure that you feel pretty good about the material. You might even want to work on some of the exercises at the end before you go on.

We will take this example slowly, as we did the rest. Work through each stage of the code. Test it, change it, break it: It's the only way to learn.

The key to this query is the `CASE` operator. You learned about this yesterday, and now it's time to put it to good use.

We'll use `CASE` to examine the year of each order and decide whether the order belongs in a count of orders for 1998 or 1997. This query looks at 10 individual rows, performing that analysis:

```
set rowcount 10
select OrderDate,
       datepart(yy, OrderDate) as 'Year',
       case datepart(yy, OrderDate)
              when 1998 then 1
              else 0
       end as 'is1998'
from Orders
where OrderDate >= '12/30/97'
set rowcount 0
```

Results:

```
OrderDate                   Year        1998
--------------------------- ----------- -----------
1997-12-30 00:00:00.000            1997           0
1997-12-30 00:00:00.000            1997           0
1997-12-30 00:00:00.000            1997           0
1997-12-31 00:00:00.000            1997           0
1997-12-31 00:00:00.000            1997           0
1998-01-01 00:00:00.000            1998           1
```

```
1998-01-01 00:00:00.000          1998          1
1998-01-01 00:00:00.000          1998          1
1998-01-02 00:00:00.000          1998          1
1998-01-02 00:00:00.000          1998          1
```

The first and last lines set a limit on the number of rows returned by a query. I wanted to limit the output to just 10 rows.

The `WHERE` condition was specifically chosen to find rows that select rows in 1997 and 1998. This enables you to see that the `CASE` expression returns `0` for rows that do not fall in 1998 and `1` for rows that do fall in 1998.

The expression to find rows in 1997 uses the same logic. Here is a query that lists the orders and includes a column for each year. The left column displays the month of the order.

```
set rowcount 10
select datename(mm, OrderDate) as 'Month',
       case datepart(yy, OrderDate)
              when 1998 then 1
              else 0
       end as 'is1998',
       case datepart(yy, OrderDate)
              when 1997 then 1
              else 0
       end as 'is1997'
from Orders
where OrderDate >= '12/30/97'
set rowcount 0
```

Results:

```
Month                          is1998      is1997
------------------------------ ----------- -----------
December                                 0           1
December                                 0           1
December                                 0           1
December                                 0           1
December                                 0           1
January                                  1           0
January                                  1           0
January                                  1           0
January                                  1           0
January                                  1           0
```

Notice that there is still no grouping clause, so each row in the result reflects a single row in the `Orders` table.

4

If we had a table with the columns `Month`, `is1998`, and `is1997`, it would be a simple matter to produce the grouped result. We would add up all the ones and zeros in each column to come up with a total number of rows. Here's the query we would write:

```
/* query we would write if we could */
select
    Month,
    sum(is1998) as 'Orders 1998',
    sum(is1997) as 'Orders 1997'
  from
      Orders
 where
      OrderDate >= '1/1/97' and
      OrderDate <  '1/1/99'
 group by
      MonthNumber, Month with rollup
having
      MonthNumber is null or
      MonthName is not null
```

You should add the date condition to avoid working with rows that are outside the range of either year column. That will save processing time.

To get the overall totals, I've added the `ROLLUP` operator. Make certain to group first by the month number rather than the month name so that the data is sorted chronologically, not alphabetically. (You learned about that problem earlier today.) I've added the `HAVING` clause to suppress rows created by the extra grouping level.

Unfortunately, we don't have those columns in our table, but we already have expressions for them. Just write the same query, but substitute the expressions from the preceding code. Listing 4.10 has the integrated code.

LISTING 4.10 Summing the `CASE` Expressions Provides a Count of Rows Matching the Criteria

```
select
        datename(mm, OrderDate) as 'Month',
        sum(case datepart(yy, OrderDate)
               when 1998 then 1
               else 0
        end) as 'Orders 1998',
        sum(case datepart(yy, OrderDate)
               when 1997 then 1
               else 0
        end) as 'Orders 1997'
  from
        Orders
 where
```

LISTING 4.10 continued

```
            OrderDate >= '1/1/97' and
            OrderDate <  '1/1/99'
      group by
            datepart(mm, OrderDate),
            datename(mm, OrderDate) with rollup
     having
            datepart(mm, OrderDate) is null or
            datename(mm, OrderDate) is not null
```

The result set displays the month with the orders for each of the years:

```
Month                          Orders 1998 Orders 1997
------------------------------ ----------- -----------
January                                 55          33
February                                54          29
March                                   73          30
April                                   74          31
May                                     14          32
June                                     0          30
July                                     0          33
August                                   0          33
September                                0          37
October                                  0          38
November                                 0          34
December                                 0          48
NULL                                   270         408
```


Now we need to perform the year-to-year comparison. We'll limit the query to the first five months of the year (there's no data after May for 1998). To do that, use a `WHERE` clause.

We can calculate the percent change with this expression:

```
100 * Orders 1998 / Orders 1997 - 100 as 'Percent Change'
```

Again, it's just a matter of substituting the expressions we already have for `Orders 1998` and `Orders 1998` into this formula and adding it to the select list as shown in Listing 4.11.

LISTING 4.11 Final Query Displaying Percent Change from Prior to Current Year

```
select
        DateName(mm, OrderDate) as 'Month',
        sum(case DatePart(yy, OrderDate)
               when 1998 then 1
               else 0 end)      as 'Orders 1998',
```

LISTING 4.11 continued

```
        sum(case DatePart(yy, OrderDate)
              when 1997 then 1
              else 0 end)      as 'Orders 1997',
        (100. *
        sum(case DatePart(yy, OrderDate)
              when 1998 then 1.
              else 0. end)
        /
        sum(case DatePart(yy, OrderDate)
              when 1997 then 1.
              else 0. end)) - 100. as 'Percent Change'
   from Orders
  where OrderDate >= '1/1/1997'
    and OrderDate < '1/1/1999'
    and datepart(mm, OrderDate) <= 5
  group by
        DatePart(mm, OrderDate),
        DateName(mm, OrderDate) with rollup
 having
        datepart(mm, OrderDate) is null
     or datename(mm, OrderDate) is not null
```

In this code, it's worth noting that all the numbers in the percentage calculation have been converted to the `float` data type by adding a decimal point (`1.`, `0.`, `100.`). Otherwise, the percentage would be calculated by using integer arithmetic and would be incredibly inaccurate.

We will come back to this code again later in the book. This query and queries like it are very common requirements of SQL programmers. Tomorrow, after you have learned to join tables, you will be asked to produce a similar analysis of the total dollar activity for the company.

Later in the book, you will learn to use a number of methods that will simplify queries like this one. User-defined functions and computed columns will enable users to invoke the detailed `CASE` logic more simply. Views will enable you to predefine whole queries to access similar data more easily. Stored procedures will enable you to execute a query like this one by name.

Summary

Today you learned to use aggregate functions to get information about a set of rows in a single row or a grouped result. Aggregates are among the most powerful and frequently used tools in Transact-SQL.

You've seen the power and flexibility of the SELECT statement extended significantly in this lesson. With grouping, ROLLUP, and CUBE, you can get grouped and totaled data. In combination with the CASE operator, you've learned to build pivot tables to deliver data in a useful format.

What all these techniques share is the capability to condense vast amounts of data into a compact result. Whenever possible, use SQL Server aggregates to reduce the size of result sets. This will improve network efficiency, reduce the work required by client applications, and improve overall system performance.

Tomorrow you will learn how to join tables together to get result sets that include data from many tables.

Here is the syntax of the SELECT statement so far:

```
select [distinct] <select-list>
  from <table-name>
 where <condition-expression>
 [ and | or <condition-expression> … ]
 group by <group-expression>
 [ , <group-expression> … ]
     [ with rollup | cube ]
having <condition-expression>
 [ and | or <condition-expression> … ]
 order by <sort-expression> [asc | desc]
 [ , <sort-expression> [asc | desc] … ]
```


Q&A

Q Why does SQL Server tell me that only one row is affected when it returns an aggregate result? For instance, in this query where 31 non-null customer regions were found, the server only reported `(1 row(s) affected)`.

```
select count(Region) "Customers with Region"
  from Customers

Customers with Region
---------------------
                   31

(1 row(s) affected)
```

A The number of rows in the rowcount report is only the size of the ultimate result set. Regardless of how many rows are touched by an aggregate function, the final result is just the single reported value.

Q Can I use `ROLLUP` and `CUBE` in the same statement?

A No. You can only use one or the other.

Q How many columns can I include in my `GROUP BY` clause?

A There is no stated limit to the number of grouping columns you can use. The total length of a grouping key is limited to about 8KB. Depending on the length of the grouping expressions, the server will allow dozens of grouping keys in a single query. In real life, I've seldom seen a query need more than 16 grouping expressions.

You are limited to 10 columns in a **`GROUP BY`** query that uses `ROLLUP` or `CUBE`.

Workshop

The Workshop provides quiz questions to help you solidify your understanding of the material covered and exercises to provide you with experience in using what you've learned. Try to answer the quiz and exercise questions before checking the answers in Appendix A, "Answers to Quizzes and Exercises," and make sure that you understand the answers before continuing to the next lesson.

Quiz

1. Put the following keywords in order to make a `SELECT` statement work properly:
   - `GROUP BY`
   - `HAVING`
   - `SELECT`
   - `DISTINCT`
   - `WHERE`
   - `FROM`
   - `ORDER BY`
   - `ROLLUP`
2. What is the difference between `COUNT(*)` and `COUNT(`*`expression`*`)`?
3. Is the following query permitted? If not, how would you correct it?

```
select ProductID, ProductName
  from Products
 where UnitPrice > avg(UnitPrice)
```

4. Is the following query permitted? If not, how would you correct it?

```
select Country, Region, Count(*) as 'Customers'
  from Customers
 group by Country
```

5. What is the difference between HAVING and WHERE?
6. What is the difference between ROLLUP and CUBE?

Exercises

1. Who is the oldest employee, and when was he or she born?
2. How many customers are located outside the United States?
3. Prepare a report showing a breakdown of suppliers by country. Include a grand total in the report.

```
Country         Suppliers
--------------- ----------
Australia                2
Brazil                   1
Canada                   2
Denmark                  1
Finland                  1
France                   3
Germany                  3
Italy                    2
Japan                    2
Netherlands              1
Norway                   1
Singapore                1
Spain                    1
Sweden                   2
UK                       2
USA                      4
NULL                    29
```

4. Which countries have more than one supplier? Sort the countries by greatest to least occurrence.

```
Country         Suppliers
--------------- ----------
USA                      4
France                   3
Germany                  3
Australia                2
Canada                   2
Italy                    2
Japan                    2
Sweden                   2
UK                       2
```

5. How many different categories of product are there?
6. Display the top selling product ID (by dollars sold, including discounts) and the total dollar sales.

```
ProductID   Dollar Sales
----------- ------------------------------
         38               41396.73522949219
```

WEEK 1

DAY 5

Joining Tables

In the past several lessons, you might have noticed that the data you have been accessing has been from only one table at a time. You have been looking at order information, but the order is missing things such as the customer name and product number. The strength of a relational database is to be able to access more than one table at a time. Relational database systems get their name from the relationships that are defined between tables. Because most real data is spread out across several tables, you will see how to *join* tables together.

Table joins are the topic of the day. Understanding joins is central to your understanding of T-SQL, so today's lesson is as important a topic as you can find in this book. The discussions include

- Understanding Joins
- T-SQL syntax for Joins
- Primary and foreign keys
- Understanding cross joins
- Joining multiple tables
- Displaying data from multiple tables

A query that includes data from multiple tables requires you to join those tables together. You specify the names of the tables in the SELECT statement and the method of relating them. The server then performs the join by comparing the join data from each table and returns the final result set back to you.

Understanding Joins

I'm going to teach you a way to think about joins. This method of understanding joins will help you visualize what happens when you write multitable queries. This will make it easier to learn how to write joins and will help you through the more complex cases that you will confront in real life.

Although the method I will teach you will help you understand how queries with joins could be resolved, the server uses a number of efficient techniques to speed up joins. To be honest, the server cheats in any way it can. So, what you are about to learn might help you a lot, but don't expect the server to use this method.

To get a better handle on joins, let's improve one of the queries from yesterday's lesson. We were writing aggregate queries to report from the `Order Details` table. For example, this query, which doesn't include a join, will report the five best-selling products (by quantity) in the database:

```
select
    top 5 ProductID,
    sum(Quantity) 'Total Qty'
from
    [Order Details]
group by
    ProductID
order by
    'Total Qty' desc
```

Results:

```
ProductID   Total Qty
----------- -----------
         60        1577
         59        1496
         31        1397
         56        1263
         16        1158
```

Because we're going to rely on this query closely in the next part of today's lesson, let's take a moment here to talk about some of the more complex elements.

In line 2, `top 5` tells the server to report only the first five rows reported after the sort is performed. The data is sorted in descending order by the sum of quantity for each product. The report lists values for only the five rows with the highest quantity sales.

In line 3, we define a column alias for the sum expression in the second column. The alias, `'Total Qty'`, is used in the `ORDER BY` clause in place of the expression `sum(Quantity)`.

> **Note**
>
> You can reference column aliases in the `ORDER BY` clause, but they won't work elsewhere in the query. The `WHERE`, `GROUP BY`, and `HAVING` clauses require you to provide them with a complete expression rather than an alias.

This report really isn't very useful. A list of productIDs doesn't tell us much. To improve the report's readability, we should replace the `ProductID` column with the `ProductName`, but the product name is stored in the `Products` table. To include the product name in a report along with order quantity information from the `Order Details` table, we will need to join the `Order Details` and `Products` tables.

Up to this point, all your `SELECT` statements have been based on a single table. Far more often, the questions posed to you will not point to a specific table. Consider this question: *Have beverage sales in the Midwest been seasonal over the last several years?* First, you would determine which products are beverages. Next, you would need to define sales (What are the quantity sold and gross sales? What about the net sales after costs? What defines a season? How many years? How do I determine which sales were in the Midwest?).

5

Next, you would need to find the data elements that correspond to the report. Product categories are described in the `Categories` table. Regions are stored in the `Regions` table, and referenced in the `Territories` table. You will need to refer to the `Orders` table for dates, the `Order Details` table for sales information, and the `Products` table to get product category.

It's all very confusing, but there are tools to simplify your work. The most important reference tool for a T-SQL programmer is a good *entity relationship diagram*, or *ERD*.

Creating and Using Entity Relationship Diagrams (ERDs)

An *entity relationship diagram* is a drawing that shows a set of tables in a database, along with every column in each table. The ERD also shows how the tables relate to each other. Figure 5.1 shows a simple, two-table entity relationship diagram relating the `Products` and `Order Details` tables.

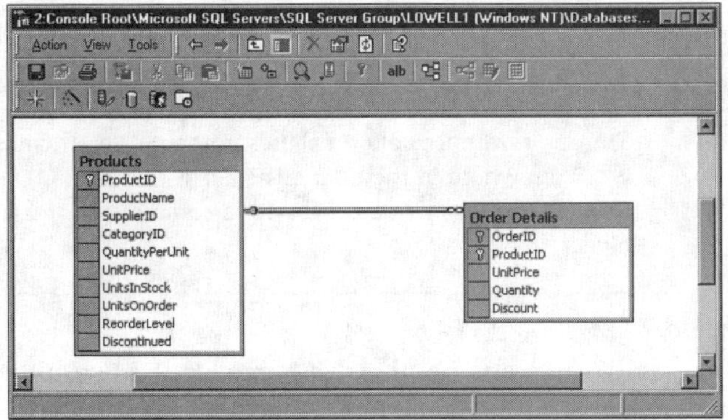

FIGURE 5.1
An entity relationship diagram showing the relationship between the `Order Details` *and* `Products` *tables.*

Note

The term *entity relationship diagram* comes from the field of data analysis. When data analysts work with their customers to understand the information that people use, the analysts' first job is to identify the "stuff" that makes up the business. These are "entities." Entities in a construction business are *projects, locations, deadlines, workers,* and *equipment*. In an ice-cream shop, the entities might include *products, flavors, menu items, purchases,* and *workers*.

The analysts' next job is to figure out how the entities relate to each other. Does a project have one deadline or many? Does a worker always go with a piece of equipment? Does each purchase have one or more flavors?

After that, the analysts draw up an entity relationship diagram to summarize the work they have done. Normally, there are a number of steps between the completion of the analysis and the definition of a database. There are usually changes to the database design, mostly focused on making the database fast and simple. When the database is ready to run, analysts draw a revised ERD as a reference for programmers and users.

I usually prefer to work with a single ERD that contains all the tables and columns in the system. When you're dealing with databases containing literally hundreds of tables, that's not feasible. In those cases, a complete ERD covers an entire wall of a conference room.

When you work in those environments, you use an ERD that shows just the group of tables you are working with. You can use the SQL Server Enterprise Manager (SQL-EM) to design and maintain your own ERDs. We'll take a moment now to produce an ERD that shows all the tables in the `Northwind` database.

On Day 1, "Introduction to SQL and the Query Analyzer," you learned how to log on to a server using Enterprise Manager. Your server should be listed in the tree under a SQL Server Group. Open the `Northwind` database so that the elements are displayed. You should see an element labeled `Diagrams` in the tree (see Figure 5.2).

FIGURE 5.2

The Enterprise Manager enables you to create and manage database diagrams (ERDs) based on your current database.

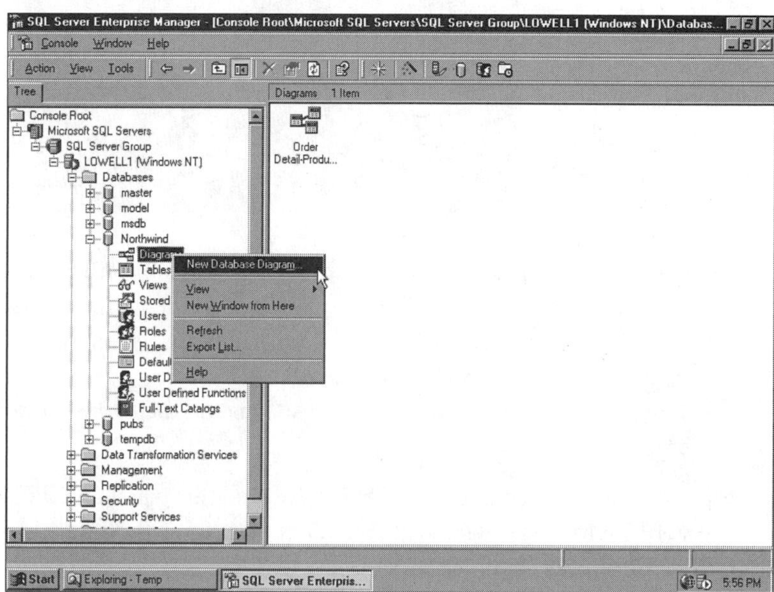

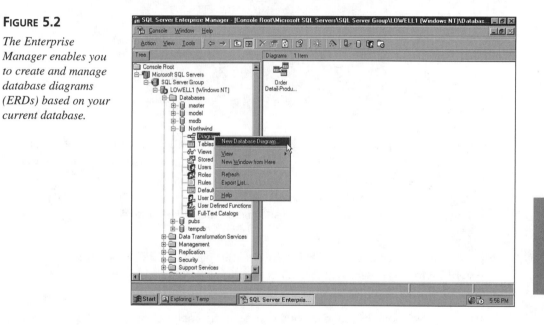

Right-click on the `Diagrams` item and choose `New Database Diagram`. That should start up the Create New Database Diagram wizard. Read the first panel, and then proceed. Figure 5.3 shows you the second panel in the wizard where you will choose the tables to include in the diagram.

Tip

> In most database environments, all the tables are related to each other, however distantly. Without getting all the tables, you might want to produce an ERD that includes a specific set of tables and all of their directly related tables.

5

The check box on this wizard enables you to add related tables automatically, and you can use the spin control to decide how many levels of related tables to bring along. You can include first-level relations, but not second, or second-level but not third. That way you get the information you need without drawing the diagram on the wall of a building or using 2.5-point type.

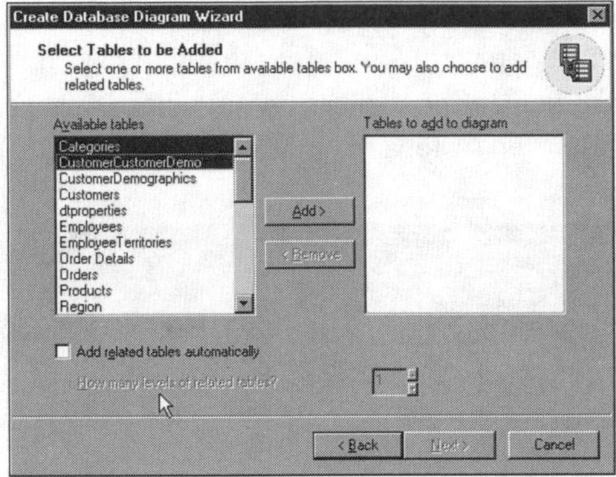

FIGURE 5.3

The second panel of the Create New Database Diagram wizard enables you to choose the tables in the ERD.

To choose several tables, you can hold down the Control key and select the tables, or click on a table, hold down the Shift key, and select another table and all tables between those two will be selected. Don't include any of the system tables (names starting with `sys`) or the `dtproperties` table. On my list, `Territories` was all the way at the bottom below the list of system tables. Click Add and all the tables are moved to the list box on the right side.

That's really all there is to it. Choose Next on this panel and Finish on the next, and Enterprise Manager will create an initial diagram with these tables. Figure 5.4 shows how mine looked.

If you right-click in the diagram window, one of the popup menu options is View Page Breaks. You'll see that the default diagram will print out on two pages. If you use this layout, you will need to get scissors and some tape to make your final ERD.

Instead, take the time now to rearrange the tables so that they are all visible in the display window without scrolling or zooming and none of the relationship lines cross. Try to make the entire ERD print out on one sheet of paper. Print out the diagram and tape it to your desk or pin it to the wall of your cubicle.

Figure 5.5 shows you my final drawing, zoomed to 50%. You can't read the table names at this zoom setting, but you can see how the tables are arranged. The output fits on a single sheet, so I don't need to start messing around with scissors and rubber cement.

FIGURE 5.4

The initial diagram includes all the tables I selected.

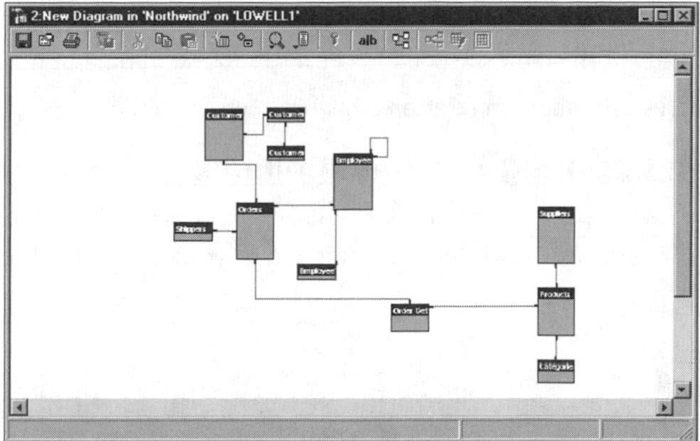

FIGURE 5.5

You can change the arrangement of the tables, and then save the diagram.

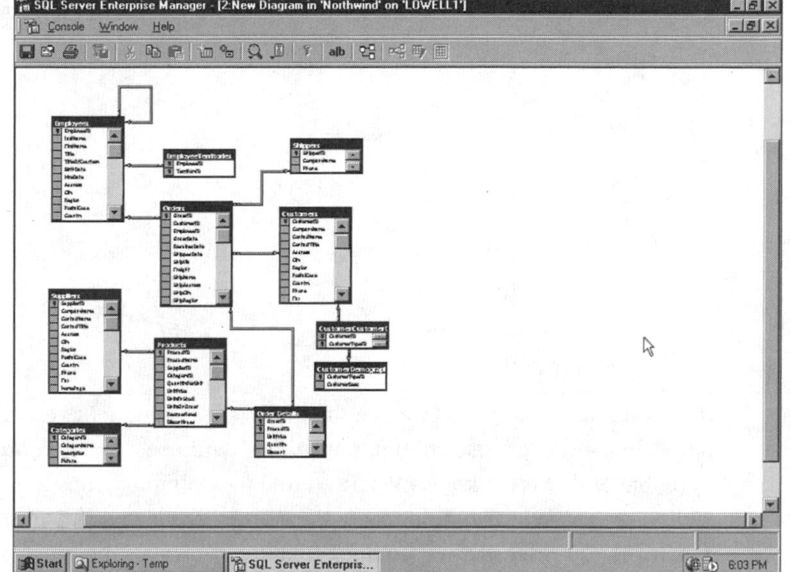

Writing Your First Join Using an Inner Join

Now that we have a good map (the ERD), we are ready to start joining data. First, we'll produce that report with the product names and total sales.

There's not much magic to joining tables. In fact, there's a simple three-step recipe that will help you write every join. First, I'll list the steps, and then we can work through each step in turn.

Step 1: Choose the columns to display in the select list or refer to in a `where` clause.

Step 2: List all the tables needed to retrieve those columns in the `from` clause.

Step 3: Describe the join relationships between the tables.

Step 1: Choosing Required Columns

The key to choosing the columns you need is to start with a good idea of how the final report or query result will look. In Figure 5.6, you see the final report we want to create.

FIGURE 5.6

Always start writing a query by having a good sense of the finished product.

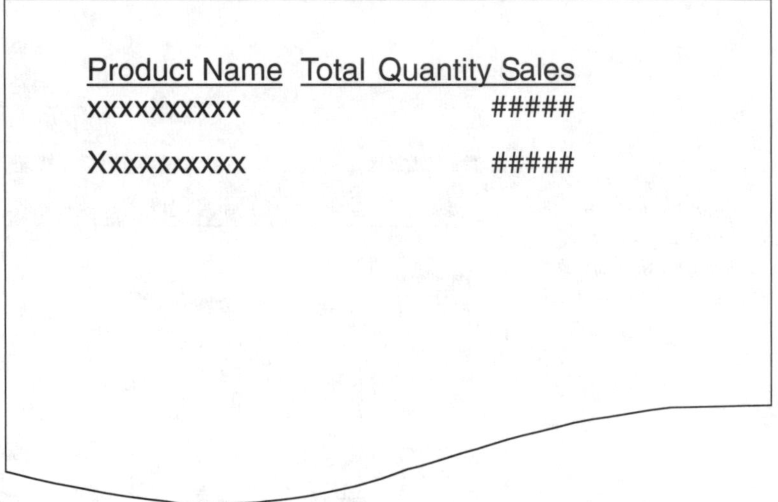

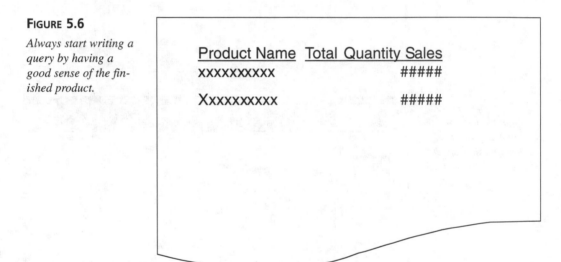

The columns we need to produce the query are `Product Name` and `Quantity`. In the select list, include those column names. You will need to *fully qualify* the names to make sure that SQL Server knows where to find the columns. You fully qualify names by providing the name of the table where the column is located as part of the column name wherever you refer to the column. I'll talk more about qualification in a little while.

The following lines display the select list for the query:

```
select
      Products.ProductName,
      sum([Order Details].Quantity) 'Total Quantity'
...
```

This code fragment includes references to column names from two different tables. The name of each column is preceded by the name of the table where it can be found. This is called *qualifying* a column name. (For more information on qualifiers, see the section "Understanding Qualifiers" later in this lesson.) Notice that the `Order Details` table name is enclosed in brackets because it contains a restricted character, the space.

You will notice that, aside from the table references, the select list is no different than any other. The columns are separated by commas, the `SUM()` function applies to the fully named column, and the column alias is the same as before.

Step 2: Listing Required Tables

The next step is to list the tables that are required to satisfy the report. In this report, we need only the `Order Details` and `Products` tables because the `ProductName` and `Quantity` columns are found in those two tables. Other reports might require several tables.

It's important to realize that the list of tables is not strictly limited by the columns named in the select list. Any column that is referenced during any part of the query must belong to a table in the list of referenced tables. For example, here is a `WHERE` clause to test for orders in August, 1998:

```
…
where Orders.OrderDate >= '8/1/98'
  and Orders.OrderDate < '9/1/98'
…
```

Even if you choose not to include the order date in the output, you would need to include the `Orders` table in the list of affected tables.

The tables for this query are `Order Details` and `Products`. Here is the first draft of a `FROM` clause for this query:

```
…
  from
      [Order Details]
        inner join
      Products
…
```


The order of the table list is irrelevant unless many tables are involved in a query (like 10 or 15—more on that when we discuss indexes on Day 9, "Indexes and Performance"). Notice that the keywords, `INNER JOIN`, connect the table names and that there are no commas.

Step 3: Describing the Join Relationships

The final step in building this query is to describe how the join is formed. This query includes two tables and one join relationship. Most of the time, a query will include one fewer join relationship than the number of tables. Sometimes there will be more.

Most join relationships are called *equijoins* or *equality joins*. These are relationships based on rows where select columns in each table match. For example, the order rows that correspond to a certain product include that product's ID value. You join order details and products on `ProductID`.

Let's look at some other tables and see how they are related. The `Shippers` and `Orders` tables share a `ShipperID` field. `Suppliers` and `Products` join on `SupplierID`; `Order Details` and `Orders` join on `OrderID`. These common keys provide a method for connecting the tables and getting more interesting and sophisticated results.

> How do I know, just from the names, that two columns are common keys? That's a good question. I don't. The fact is that any database administrator is free to name columns however he pleases. He could identify the two `ProductID` columns in `Order Details` and `Products` with completely different names.
>
> The fact is that most databases do adhere to naming conventions where common keys share a name. Where those conventions are missing or routinely ignored, chaos rules. However, just because a column in both tables has the same name doesn't automatically mean it is a key. An example of this is the `city` column. There is usually no reason to join two tables using a city name column. Remember that there are many cities with the same name (for example, Paris, NY and Paris, France).

The join condition, which compares the content of a column or group of columns, will determine membership in the final result set. Here is the join condition for the `Order Details` and `Products` tables:

```
...
    on [Order Details].ProductID = Products.ProductID
...
```

Notice that there are two columns named `ProductID` in the condition. To clear up uncertainty about which column is which, we are required to identify the table name for each column. The order of the columns in the join condition does not matter.

Understanding Qualifiers

Qualifiers enable you to fully identify a column or object name either to clear up uncertainty about the source of a column (because more than one column in a database has the same name) or to point to another location to find the table and column.

A fully qualified column name includes the name of the database, owner, table, and column, in this format:

```
<database-name>.<table-owner>.<table-name>.<column-name>
```

The fully qualified name of the `ProductName` column is

`Northwind.dbo.Products.ProductName`

In the example, the database name is `Northwind`. The owner of the table is the `dbo` (the database owner, who created the table in the first place). The name of the table is `Products` and the column name is `ProductName`.

We have managed so far to write queries without fully qualifying the names. That's because there are rules determining the default location of columns. Here is a summary of those rules:

- If a column name in a query is unqualified, SQL Server will find a column with that name in one of the tables in the query. If more than one table includes that column, the query fails and the server reports an `Ambiguous column name`.
- If the owner of a table is not specified, the server first tries to find a table with that name owned by the user executing the query. If a table is not found for that user, the server tries to find a table owned by the `dbo`. If no table is found using either method, the server reports an `Invalid object name`.
- If the database is not specified, the server looks in the current database. With temporary tables, the server looks only in the `tempdb` database.

Although the rules make it possible to avoid qualifying columns and table names, SQL Server is faster when you fully qualify everything. That makes sense, if you think about it. The server doesn't have to try searching for each column and table in the entire set of possible columns and tables.

Full qualification is also good programming practice. If you refer to a column without a table name, the query might work fine until someone adds a column with the same name to another table in your query. To make certain that your code works through every reasonable database modification, always qualify everything. Later on today, you will see how to simplify the qualification process by using table aliases.

Completing the Query

All we need to do now is put together the pieces of the puzzle. Here is the completed query. I've added the `GROUP BY` clause to make the aggregating and subtotaling work properly.

```
select top 5
      Products.ProductName,
      sum([Order Details].Quantity) 'Total Quantity'
  from
      [Order Details]
        inner join
```

```
        Products
          on [Order Details].ProductID = Products.ProductID
  group by
        Products.ProductName
  order by
      'Total Quantity' desc
```

Results:

```
ProductName                              Total Quantity
---------------------------------------- --------------
Camembert Pierrot                                  1577
Raclette Courdavault                               1496
Gorgonzola Telino                                  1397
Gnocchi di nonna Alice                             1263
Pavlova                                            1158
```

Well, that's it. You have written your first query that joins two tables. Notice how the columns that make up the join relationship (`ProductID`) are not included in the result, even though they are crucial to the query.

Understanding More About Joins

Now that you have written a join, let's take a moment to understand how joins work.

Listing 5.1 shows the code to create and populate two small tables in an automobile database. The first table is a list of car `Makes`; that is, manufacturers of automobiles. The second table is a list of `Models`. Each model corresponds to an entry in the `Makes` table.

LISTING 5.1 Create and Populate Small `Makes` and `Models` Tables to Practice Joining Tables

```
create table Makes (
      MakeID int identity primary key,
      MakeDescription nvarchar(10) not null
)
go
create table Models (
      ModelID int identity (101,1) primary key,
      MakeID int not null references Makes (MakeID),
      ModelName nvarchar(20) not null
)
go
insert Makes (MakeDescription) values ('Ford')
insert Makes (MakeDescription) values ('Chevrolet')
insert Makes (MakeDescription) values ('Chrysler')
insert Makes (MakeDescription) values ('Honda')
go
insert Models (MakeID, ModelName) values (1, 'Pinto')
```

LISTING 5.1 continued

```
insert Models (MakeID, ModelName) values (1, 'Thunderbird')
insert Models (MakeID, ModelName) values (1, 'Mustang')
insert Models (MakeID, ModelName) values (2, 'Caprice')
insert Models (MakeID, ModelName) values (2, 'Nova')
insert Models (MakeID, ModelName) values (3, 'Town and Country')
insert Models (MakeID, ModelName) values (3, 'Sebring')
go
```

Here's the content of the two tables, printed out with simple `SELECT *` statements:

```
select * from Makes
select * from Models
```

Results:

```
MakeID      MakeDescription
----------- --------------
1           Ford
2           Chevrolet
3           Chrysler
4           Honda

ModelID     MakeID      ModelName
----------- ----------- -------------------
101         1           Pinto
102         1           Thunderbird
103         1           Mustang
104         2           Caprice
105         2           Nova
106         3           Town and Country
107         3           Sebring
```


As you can see, both tables contain a `MakeID` column. This is the column that will define the join between the two tables. Each row in the `Models` table contains a value of `MakeID` that exists in the `Makes` table. For instance, the row for the Pinto model includes `MakeID` `1`, which references the row for Ford in the `Makes` table.

When you write a join between the tables, you need to tell the server how the tables connect. If you leave out the join condition, as in this failed query, the server gives you an error message:

```
/* error: inner join requires join condition */
select *
from
      Makes
        inner join
      Models

Server: Msg 170, Level 15, State 1, Line 5
Line 6: Incorrect syntax near 'Models'.
```

The incorrect syntax in this query is the lack of a condition, starting with the keyword, on. Let's write the query correctly:

```
select *
from
      Makes
        inner join
      Models
        on
      Makes.MakeID = Models.MakeID
```

Results:

```
MakeID  MakeDescription ModelID     MakeID  ModelName
------- --------------- ----------- ------- ----------------
1       Ford            101         1       Pinto
1       Ford            102         1       Thunderbird
1       Ford            103         1       Mustang
2       Chevrolet       104         2       Caprice
2       Chevrolet       105         2       Nova
3       Chrysler        106         3       Town and Country
3       Chrysler        107         3       Sebring
```

In this result, there are seven rows, one for each row in the `Models` table. The result includes two columns labeled `MakeID`. The first is the value in the `Makes` table; the second is from the `Models` table. It is no coincidence that the two `MakeID` values always have the same value; after all, the condition of the join was that the two `MakeID` values be equal.

Notice that there are no rows in the result set for Honda. Even though Honda exists in the `Makes` table, there are no `Models` in our list that refer to `MakeID` 4.

How does the server handle `SELECT *` in a join? The asterisk means "all columns," so `SELECT *` means display all columns from all tables in the query. Note that a table is limited to 1,024 columns and a select statement can return only 4,096 columns. If you use `SELECT *` with several wide tables (tables with lots of columns), you could run into that limitation.

If you want to access all the columns in a single table, you can qualify the asterisk with a table name, as in this query:

```
select Models.*
from
      Makes
        inner join
      Models
        on
      Makes.MakeID = Models.MakeID
```

The query will return only columns from the Models table.

Introducing Cross Joins

If you want to really understand joins, you have to break them. We'll break this join by using a cross join.

NEW TERM A *cross join* is a join of multiple tables where there is no logical column or key with which to join the tables together. The server provides all possible combinations of rows between the tables. Usually, a cross join gives you a lot of extra, incorrect information.

Here's the code for the cross join. When you use `CROSS JOIN`, the query doesn't allow a join condition.

```
select *
from
      Makes
        cross join
      Models
```

Results:

```
MakeID  MakeDescription ModelID     MakeID  ModelName
------- --------------- ----------- ------- --------------------
1       Ford            101         1       Pinto
1       Ford            102         1       Thunderbird
1       Ford            103         1       Mustang
1       Ford            104         2       Caprice
1       Ford            105         2       Nova
1       Ford            106         3       Town and Country
1       Ford            107         3       Sebring
2       Chevrolet       101         1       Pinto
2       Chevrolet       102         1       Thunderbird
2       Chevrolet       103         1       Mustang
2       Chevrolet       104         2       Caprice
...
4       Honda           106         3       Town and Country
4       Honda           107         3       Sebring

(28 row(s) affected)
```

In the result set, the server provides you with a complete set of all possible combinations of makes and models from the table. The value of the `MakeID` in the two tables is not considered. For instance, the fourth line in the results displays the Ford Caprice. (Ford has made a lot of strange cars, but they never made a Caprice.)

The `MakeID` of the Caprice is either `1` or `2`, depending on which `MakeID` column you look at. How is that possible? It happened because this join does not define any relationship between the rows in the two tables. It only asks for every possible combination.

Finally, notice that Honda shows up in this list. Even though there are no models that refer to `MakeID 4`, there is an entry in the result set for Honda in combination with each model.

How many rows are returned when you perform a cross join? In this case, we got 28 rows. There are four rows in the `Makes` table, and seven rows in the `Models` table. 4 times 7 is 28. To get the number of rows in a cross join result, multiply the number of rows in the joined tables.

Another name for a cross join is *Cartesian product*. These products are named after René Descartes, the famous French philosopher and mathematician, and a key player in the development of modern algebra.

Why would anyone be interested in a cross join? There are some specialized applications for cross joins. For instance, if I wanted to build a table of all possible months in all historical years, I could create a table of months (numbers or names) and a table of years, and then use their cross join to build a container table.

More often than not, cross joins or Cartesian products arise from a programmer's error than from an intentional act. When you make these mistakes, a few obvious things happen. First, the number of rows returned suddenly goes sky high (from 7 to 28 in this case, or from 10 thousand to 200 million in others). Second, performance suddenly slows. After all, the server might be working through a huge volume of data.

Sometimes, the mistakes can be subtle and difficult to find. What if we used a cross join rather than an inner join in the first join query we wrote previously in this lesson? Here's the revised code. I've replaced the inner join with a cross join, and left out the join condition.

```
select top 5
      Products.ProductName,
      sum([Order Details].Quantity) 'Total Quantity'
  from
      [Order Details]
        cross join
      Products
 group by
      Products.ProductName
 order by
     'Total Quantity' desc
```

Results:

```
ProductName                            Total Quantity
-------------------------------------- --------------
Chai                                            51330
Carnarvon Tigers                                51330
Camembert Pierrot                               51330
Boston Crab Meat                                51330
Aniseed Syrup                                   51330
```

In this result, even though we got the right number of rows in the result set, every value in the `Total Quantity` column is the same. If we removed the `top 5` condition and allowed rows for every product, you would see that every product had the same sales. This is an amazing coincidence that should make you suspicious of your query. (Other amazing coincidences: Sales are always the same, year after year. Every employee is making the same salary. All products are the same price. You get the idea.)

Why are all the `Total Quantity` values the same? The server calculates the total quantity *of all orders* for every product, regardless of which product was actually sold in the order.

Understanding More About Joins

I can just hear you saying to yourself, "Only an idiot would write `CROSS JOIN` when he meant `INNER JOIN`." In fact, if I hadn't told you about the cross join, you might never have discovered it or tried it. Still, this discussion has not been a waste of time. Here's why.

The ANSI SQL-94 standard provided us with the join syntax you have learned so far. The words `INNER JOIN`, `CROSS JOIN`, and the designation of a join condition with `on` are all part of that revision of the standard. Before that, joins were defined by using table lists, and join conditions were included in the `WHERE` clause. In fact, this syntax is still so widely used that you need to learn it now.

5

Here is the `Makes` and `Models` join, written using the original join syntax:

```
select *
from
      Makes,
      Models
where
      Makes.MakeID = Models.MakeID
```

There are some big differences in the format of the original join syntax. First, the tables are presented as a list in the `FROM` clause, with nothing describing their relationship. Second, the relationship between the tables is included as part of the `WHERE` clause.

In most circumstances, there is no difference in the result or the performance of the query, regardless of the query format. You can feel free to use this format in place of the SQL-94 format most of the time.

Problems arise with the older format when you fail to provide the join condition in the WHERE clause:

```
/* Bad news: join without join condition
         produces cross join result set */
select *
from
     Makes,
     Models
```

The good news is that this query works. It returns 28 rows, exactly the same result we got from the cross join.

The bad news is that it is a cross join. When the programmer omits a join condition, 99% of the time it's a mistake, but the server does not trap it as an error. That's a good reason to stick with the SQL-94 syntax. If you leave out the join condition, the server will trap a query without join conditions and display a programming error instead of displaying useless and incorrect data without any error message.

Using Table Aliases

Now that you have seen how to join tables, let's see how to reduce the amount of typing you used to do when qualifying a column name. You do this by using table aliases to improve the readability of queries. Table aliases work the same as column aliases, but for table names, and can only be used within the current query. These aliases are usually shorter than the original table names.

Here is the query we've worked on throughout today's lesson, modified to use table aliases:

```
select top 5
      p.ProductName,
      sum(od.Quantity) 'Total Quantity'
  from
      [Order Details] od
        inner join
      Products p
        on od.ProductID = p.ProductID
 group by
      p.ProductName
 order by
     'Total Quantity' desc
```

Here are the changes I've made. First, in the `FROM` clause, I've defined an alias for each of the two tables. The alias is a string that follows the table name. The alias for `Order Details` is `od`; the alias for `Products` is `p`. You can use the optional keyword, `AS`, for increased readability and to identify the alias if you like. Here is the `FROM` clause with `AS`:

```
from
    [Order Details] as od
      inner join
    Products as p
      on od.ProductID = p.ProductID
```

Second, everywhere that I refer to a column in the query, I preface it not with the table name but with the alias for that table. *After you define an alias for a table name, you cannot use the table name within the query.* Thus, the column expression `p.ProductName` says, "get the content of the `ProductName` column in the table whose alias is `p`" (that is, `Products`).

The query returns the same result as before. Table aliases do not have a performance impact, but they will save you some time typing. Later today, you will learn to use table aliases to write self-joins. A self-join is the only time a table alias is required.

Working with Multi-Table Joins

A multi-table join is nothing more than a join that includes three or more tables. There is no significant difference between multi-table joins and two-table joins. As long as you are using the SQL-94 syntax, writing the query will lead you through the definition of the necessary join conditions and will help you avoid confusion.

Multi-table joins can be chained or star-shaped. Chained joins are where each table connects only to the next table. Figure 5.7, a screenshot of a diagram drawn in the Enterprise Manager, shows you the chained relationships in the query.

A star-shaped query starts with a single, central table, and then gets information from several related tables. The `Orders` table in the `Northwind` database connects to four other tables: `Shippers`, `Employees`, `Customers`, and `Order Details`. A join of those five tables would focus on the relationship between the `Orders` table and each of the others. Figure 5.8 shows the relationship among the five tables in a star configuration.

Star-shaped joins are common in databases with a number of lookup tables, or code tables. The central table will include coded values in several columns, and then the lookup tables will provide the decoded values.

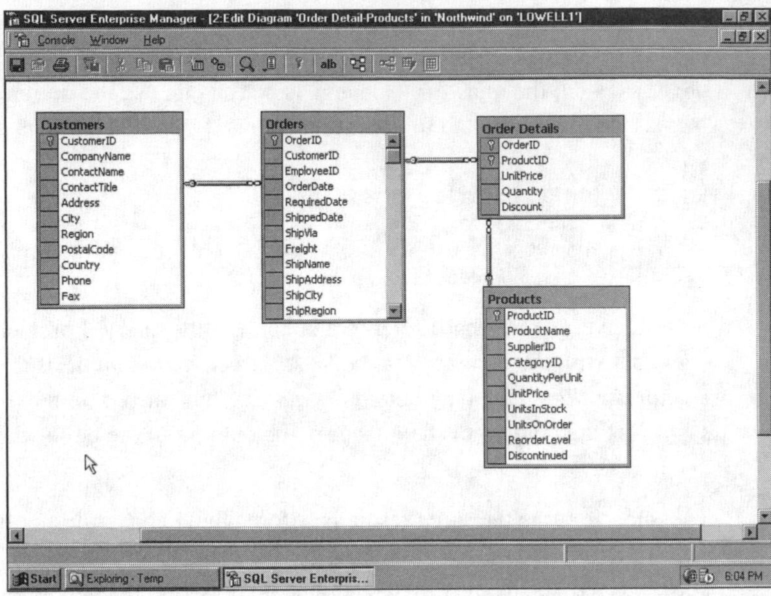

FIGURE 5.7

In a chained join, each table in the query joins only to the next table.

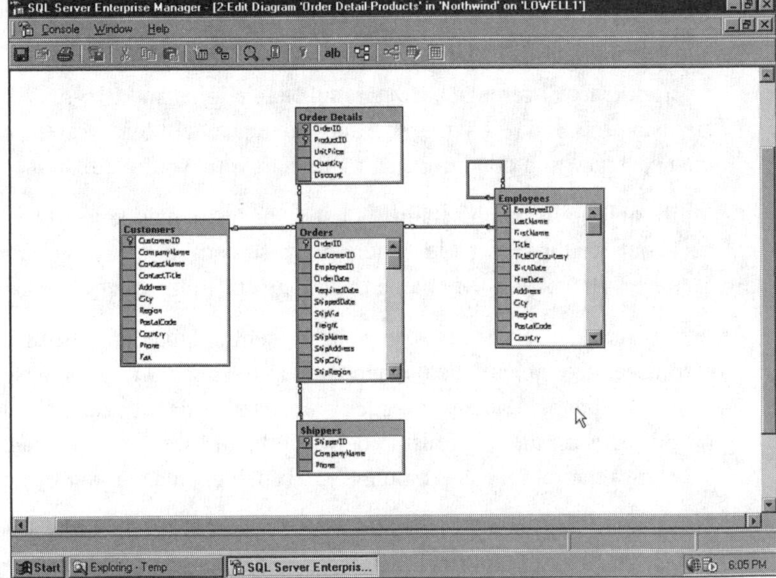

FIGURE 5.8

In a star-shaped join, a central table connects to several related tables.

Listing 5.2 provides an example of a query from the `Orders` table, with references to each of the related tables.

LISTING 5.2 A Star-Shaped Multi-Table Join with `Orders` as the Common Table

```
select top 5
        e.LastName as 'Employee',
        c.CompanyName as 'Customer',
        s.CompanyName as 'Shipper',
        sum(od.Quantity*od.UnitPrice*(1.-od.Discount))
                      as 'Total Dollars'
   from
        Orders as o
    inner join
        Customers as c
            on o.CustomerID = c.CustomerID
    inner join
        Shippers as s
            on o.ShipVia = s.ShipperID
    inner join
        Employees as e
            on o.EmployeeID = e.EmployeeID
    inner join
        [Order Details] as od
            on od.OrderID = od.OrderID
group by
        e.LastName ,
        c.CompanyName ,
        s.CompanyName
order by
    'Total Dollars' desc
```


Let's take a moment to look closely at this query. First, the order in which you present the tables in the query matters. You cannot refer to a table alias in the `FROM` clause before you define the alias. This clause would fail:

```
   from
        Shippers as s
    inner join
        Customers as c
            on o.CustomerID = c.CustomerID
    inner join
        Orders as o
            on o.ShipVia = s.ShipperID
```

The join condition in line 5 refers to the table alias `o`, but the alias is not defined until line 7. The server reports this error:

```
Server: Msg 107, Level 16, State 2, Line 2
The column prefix 'o' does not match with a table name
or alias name used in the query.
```

When it comes to table order, don't worry about performance. The server's own internal join order—the order in which it will actually process the tables—is determined separately from the query syntax.

It's worth noticing that the contents of the `Orders` table itself are not used in the query. No order data is included in the select list. No search conditions refer to those columns, either. Nevertheless, the `Orders` table is absolutely essential to the query. It contains the glue that enables you to relate the other tables in the query.

Joining Tables with Multi-Part Keys

Most of the tables in the `Northwind` database share a common characteristic: They have single-part keys. That means that a single column identifies a row in each table. The only tables that have multi-part keys are `Order Details` and `CustomerCustomerDemo`. To identify a row in the `Order Details` table, you need to provide both an Order ID and a Product ID. To identify a row in `CustomerCustomerDemo`, you need to provide both `CustomerID` and `CustomerTypeID`.

The Northwind design is a fairly common approach. Single-part keys greatly simplify joins and avoid common programming errors. Nevertheless, chances are that you'll come across systems that include many more tables with multi-part keys.

In order to look at multi-part keys, I'll change and extend the make and model database we were looking at earlier. Instead of numeric keys, I'll use the actual character strings as unique keys. The make of a car will become part of the key of a model. For example, the make `"Ford"` plus the model `"Mustang"` will define a model. Listing 5.3 provides the code to re-create the `Makes` and `Models` tables and add a new table, `Vehicles`.

Note

> Before you start sending me angry emails about model years of cars, I need to confess that I don't know a thing about them. In 1965, my mother was driving a cherry-red convertible Mustang. When she sold it in 1971 to buy a boxy little Fiat, my interest in cars died a quiet death.

Listing 5.3 Code to Create `Makes`, `Models`, and `Vehicles` Tables to Demonstrate Multi-Part Keys

```
if exists(select * from sysobjects where name='Vehicles')
      drop table Vehicles
go
if exists (select * from sysobjects where name = 'Models')
      drop table Models
go
if exists (select * from sysobjects where name = 'Makes')
      drop table Makes
go
create table Makes (
      Make nvarchar(10) not null primary key
)
go
create table Models (
      Model nvarchar(20) not null,
      Make nvarchar(10) not null references Makes (Make),
      YearIntroduced smallint null,
      constraint c_Models_PK primary key (Model, Make)
)
go
create table Vehicles (
      VIN nvarchar(10) not null primary key,
      Model nvarchar(20) not null,
      Make nvarchar(10) not null references Makes (Make),
      Year smallint not null,
      constraint c_Vehicles_Models_FK
         foreign key (Model, Make)
         references Models (Model, Make)
)
go
insert Makes (Make) values ('Ford')
insert Makes (Make) values ('Chevrolet')
insert Makes (Make) values ('Chrysler')
insert Makes (Make) values ('Honda')
go
insert Models (Make, Model, YearIntroduced) values
       ('Ford', 'Pinto', 1970)
insert Models (Make, Model, YearIntroduced) values
       ('Ford', 'Thunderbird', 1950)
insert Models (Make, Model, YearIntroduced) values
       ('Ford', 'Mustang', 1964)
insert Models (Make, Model, YearIntroduced) values
       ('Chevrolet', 'Caprice', 1970)
insert Models (Make, Model, YearIntroduced) values
       ('Chevrolet', 'Nova', 1970)
insert Models (Make, Model, YearIntroduced) values
       ('Chrysler', 'Town and Country', 1995)
```

LISTING 5.3 continued

```
48: insert Models (Make, Model, YearIntroduced) values
49:         ('Chrysler', 'Sebring', 1996)
50: go
51: insert Vehicles (VIN, Make, Model, Year) values
52:         ('F1234', 'Ford', 'Mustang', 1965)
53: insert Vehicles (VIN, Make, Model, Year) values
54:         ('F1235', 'Ford', 'Mustang', 1986)
55: insert Vehicles (VIN, Make, Model, Year) values
56:         ('F1227', 'Ford', 'Mustang', 1978)
57: insert Vehicles (VIN, Make, Model, Year) values
58:         ('F1267', 'Ford', 'Thunderbird', 1994)
59: insert Vehicles (VIN, Make, Model, Year) values
60:         ('F2540', 'Ford', 'Pinto', 1972)
61: insert Vehicles (VIN, Make, Model, Year) values
62:         ('CV435', 'Chevrolet', 'Nova', 1975)
63: insert Vehicles (VIN, Make, Model, Year) values
64:         ('CV436', 'Chevrolet', 'Nova', 1976)
65: insert Vehicles (VIN, Make, Model, Year) values
66:         ('CV938', 'Chevrolet', 'Caprice', 1993)
67: insert Vehicles (VIN, Make, Model, Year) values
68:         ('CH985', 'Chrysler', 'Sebring', 1999)
69: insert Vehicles (VIN, Make, Model, Year) values
70:         ('CH995', 'Chrysler', 'Sebring', 2000)
71: go
```

First, a quick description of the listing. The first few lines check for each table in the set and drops it if it already exists. (This technique makes a script "re-runnable," which is important if you want to make useful database maintenance scripts. Every time it is run, the script clears the way for another successful execution.)

Lines 10 to 30 define the three tables. The unique identifier or primary key in the `Makes` table is the `Make`, and the unique identifier of a model is the `Make` and `Model` combination, with the column `Make` in the `Models` tables acting as the foreign key (which is related to the primary key in the `Makes` table). Vehicles are uniquely identified by the vehicle identification number, or VIN. (I have dramatically shortened these. If you want to see a real one, check your dashboard.) To point to a model, the vehicle record also includes both the make and model.

Note

> All the table definitions include definitions of primary and foreign keys. These are the keys that define uniqueness within the table and the relationships among the tables. Line 11 requires that the `Make` column be unique within the `Makes` table. Line 16 requires that each value for `Make` in `Models` references an actual value in `Makes`.

Line 18 requires every combination of `Make` and `Model` to be unique. (That would allow both Ford and Chrysler to release a "Mustang" model.) Lines 24 through 26 require that every combination of `Make` and `Model` in a row in `Vehicles` correspond to an actual combination of `Make` and `Model` in the `Models` table.

This relationship among the tables is called *referential integrity,* or *RI*. In this case, I've implemented RI through constraints, although I could also have used a number of other methods. This method of using constraints to manage RI is called *declarative referential integrity,* or *DRI.* We'll learn how to use DRI to manage data as part of the data definition language (DDL) in Day 8, "Defining Data."

After you execute the script without getting any error messages, you can write queries that join the tables. If you want to list actual model years of vehicles with the year that a particular model was introduced, you will need to join `Models` and `Vehicles`. Here's the query written correctly:

```
select
        v.VIN,
        v.Make,
        v.Model,
        v.Year,
        mo.YearIntroduced
from
        Vehicles as v
    inner join
        Models as mo
            on mo.Make = v.Make and
               mo.Model = v.Model
where
        v.Make = 'Chrysler'
```

Results:

```
VIN        Make       Model      Year   YearIntroduced
---------- ---------- ---------- ------ --------------
CH985      Chrysler   Sebring      1999           1996
CH995      Chrysler   Sebring      2000           1996
```

The key point in this query is that the join requires two conditions, one for each key. Because the relationship key consists of two parts, the two conditions are considered to be a single join condition. Therefore, the relationship between two tables still requires only one join condition.

5

What if you leave out part of the key? Here is the same query, without the necessary join condition on the `Model` column:

```
/* incorrect query - part of the join key not specified */
select
        v.VIN,
        v.Make,
        v.Model,
        v.Year,
        mo.YearIntroduced
from
        Vehicles as v
    inner join
        Models as mo
            on mo.Make = v.Make
where
        v.Make = 'Chrysler'
```

Results:

```
VIN        Make       Model            Year  YearIntroduced
---------- ---------- ---------------- ----- --------------
CH985      Chrysler   Sebring          1999            1996
CH985      Chrysler   Sebring          1999            1995
CH995      Chrysler   Sebring          2000            1996
CH995      Chrysler   Sebring          2000            1995
```

There are only two Chrysler vehicles in the `Vehicles` table, but we have somehow gotten information about four vehicles. Notice that there are two rows for each VIN. The failure to include the second part of the join key creates another partial Cartesian product. In this case, extra rows in the `Models` table join to each vehicle.

It's important to check queries carefully when you are working with multi-part keys. These partial Cartesian products are hard to detect when the queries are more complicated and the result sets are larger.

Writing Outer Joins

So far, you've learned about inner joins and cross joins. Cross joins include all the combinations of rows in the tables. Inner joins include only rows where tables include common values. Outer joins include rows where the tables don't include common values.

Why do you need to find rows where tables fail to intersect? Here's a common problem: Find the worst performing customers to target them for a sales campaign.

The example that we will create will start by first developing the example using inner joins, and then modifying the example to use an outer join to see how they differ.

We're interested in customer information, so we'll display the names and total sales for each customer. I'll limit the output to the first five rows.

```
select top 5
        CompanyName
from
        Customers
```

Results:

```
CompanyName
----------------------------------------
Alfreds Futterkiste
Ana Trujillo Emparedados y helados
Antonio Moreno Taquerià
Around the Horn
Berglunds snabbköp
```

The next step is to integrate the `Orders` table into the query. Performance will be based on dollars in the `Order Details` table, but the `Customers` table doesn't connect directly to `Order Details`, so we need to join to `Orders` first. For the time being, just to include some data, we'll include the `OrderID` in the output:

```
select top 5
        c.CompanyName,
        o.OrderID
from
        Customers as c
    inner join
        Orders as o
            on o.CustomerID = c.CustomerID
```

Results:

```
CompanyName                              OrderID
---------------------------------------- -----------
Alfreds Futterkiste                            10643
Alfreds Futterkiste                            10692
Alfreds Futterkiste                            10702
Alfreds Futterkiste                            10835
Alfreds Futterkiste                            10952
```

All the rows apply to `Alfreds Futterkiste`. That's because there are multiple orders for that customer.

Now we can connect to the `Order Details` table. We'll display the dollar amount for each item in the order. That will demonstrate that we have the right join conditions and prepare us for the next step.

```
select top 5
        c.CompanyName,
        o.OrderID,
        od.ProductID,
        od.UnitPrice * od.Quantity *
                (1.0 - od.Discount)
                as 'Total Dollars'
from
        Customers as c
    inner join
        Orders as o
            on o.CustomerID = c.CustomerID
    inner join
        [Order Details] as od
            on od.OrderID = o.OrderID
```

Results:

```
CompanyName        OrderID     ProductID   Total Dollars
------------------ ----------- ----------- --------------
Alfreds Futterkis        10643          28          513.0
Alfreds Futterkis        10643          39          283.5
Alfreds Futterkis        10643          46           18.0
Alfreds Futterkis        10692          63          878.0
Alfreds Futterkis        10702           3           60.0
```

Notice that there are now multiple rows for the first order, number 10643. Each product included in the order requires a separate order detail row.

All that's required now is to total the dollars for each customer. The query will omit the `OrderID` and `ProductID` because I'm particularly interested in the total dollars for each customer, so I will group only on `CompanyName`. The last step is to order the customers based on the total dollars of business. Listing 5.4 shows the complete code for selecting customers by total sales.

LISTING 5.4 Customers by Total Dollar Sales

```
select top 5
        c.CompanyName,
        sum(od.UnitPrice * od.Quantity *
                (1.0 - od.Discount))
                as 'Total Dollars'
from
        Customers as c
    inner join
        Orders as o
            on o.CustomerID = c.CustomerID
    inner join
        [Order Details] as od
```

LISTING 5.4 continued

```
13:             on od.OrderID = o.OrderID
14: group by
15:         c.CompanyName
16: order by
17:         'Total Dollars'
```

Results:

```
CompanyName                              Total Dollars
---------------------------------------- -----------------
Centro comercial Moctezuma               100.79999923706055
Lazy K Kountry Store                                  357.0
Laughing Bacchus Wine Cellars                         522.5
North/South                                           649.0
Galerià del gastrònomo                   836.69999694824219
…
Rattlesnake Canyon Grocery               51097.800333023071
Save-a-lot Markets                        104361.9499206543
Ernst Handel                             104874.97871398926
QUICK-Stop                               110418.65497779846
```

This query displays customers in order by total dollars sold, as we wanted. The query returns only 89 rows, but a quick check of the `Customers` table shows that there are 91 total rows (use `SELECT COUNT(*)`). What happened to the other two rows?

The extra two rows have no sales at all. If we decide to focus on customers with low sales, the two customers with *no sales* might be the best place to start. We need a way to force the customers with no sales into the list.

That's where the outer join comes in. To get a complete list of customers, regardless of whether there are associated orders, you need to write an outer join.

Outer joins relate to the order of tables in your join clause. There are three types of outer joins: `LEFT OUTER JOIN`, `RIGHT OUTER JOIN`, and `FULL OUTER JOIN`. A `LEFT OUTER JOIN` asks that all data on the left of the join clause be included. A `RIGHT OUTER JOIN` asks that all data on the right of the join clause be included. A `FULL OUTER JOIN` asks that all data on both sides of the join clause be included. Figure 5.9 depicts which customers from the `Customers` table are included in an inner join and which are included in an outer join.

We'll change both inner joins in the original query to left outer joins (See lines 8 and 11) to force all rows from the `Customers` table into the final result set. Listing 5.5 shows how the left outer join replaces the inner join.

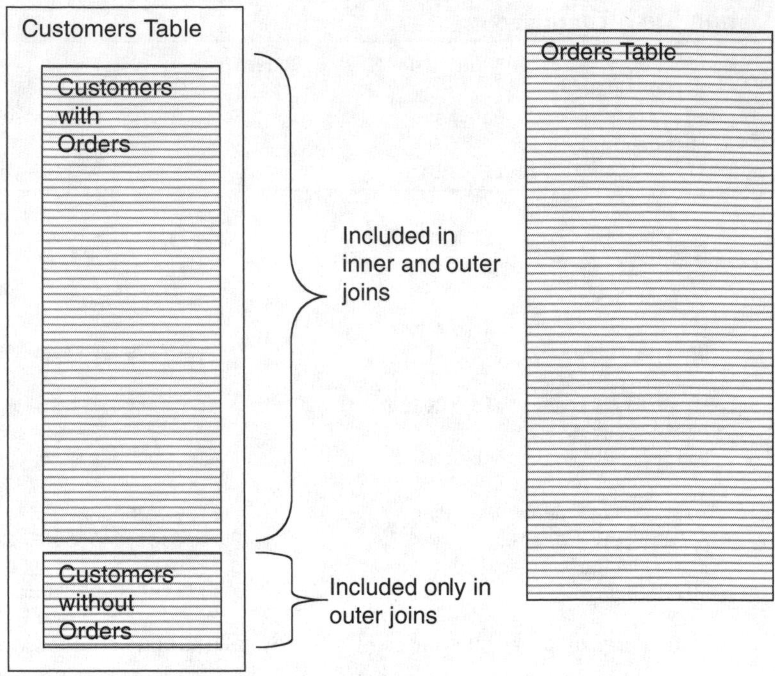

FIGURE 5.9
An outer join includes rows that have no match in the joined table.

LISTING 5.5 Customers by Total Dollar Sales, Includes All Customers

```
select top 5
        c.CompanyName,
        sum(od.UnitPrice * od.Quantity *
                (1.0 - od.Discount))
                as 'Total Dollars'
from
        Customers as c
    left outer join
        Orders as o
            on o.CustomerID = c.CustomerID
    left outer join
        [Order Details] as od
            on od.OrderID = o.OrderID
group by
        c.CompanyName
order by
        'Total Dollars'
```

Results:

```
CompanyName                              Total Dollars
---------------------------------------- ------------------
FISSA Fabrica Inter. Salchichas S.A.     NULL
Paris spécialités                        NULL
Centro comercial Moctezuma               100.79999923706055
Lazy K Kountry Store                                  357.0
Laughing Bacchus Wine Cellars                         522.5
```

This time, the query includes two rows with `NULL` values for `Total Dollars`. These are the customers we need to focus on, before customers with small but real sales.

How did I know to use a left outer join instead of a right outer join in the query? Because the `Customers` table was listed first, it was considered to be on the left side of the query. If I had written the query as a right outer join, the server would have reported `Order Details` where there was no corresponding order, and `Orders` where there was no corresponding customer. These situations both violate basic referential integrity, so they should not occur.

Joining a Table to Itself

Certain real-life phenomena require a database to store information about relationships within a single table. There are several examples of these types of tables. Manufacturers and parts distributors work with parts, but the parts can be gathered into kits, and the kits can often become assemblies. All those entities (parts, kits, and assemblies) are usually stored in a single table, which might be called `Products`. Table 5.1 lists a two-level parts and kits example.

5

TABLE 5.1 Table Containing Data in a Two-Level Structure

ItemNo	Description	PartOf
1	blue shirt	10
2	blue pants	10
3	red cape	10
4	yellow belt	10
5	red boots	10
10	Superman Suit	null

The key to the table is the `PartOf` column, which contains the self-referencing key. `PartOf` is not a unique key, but it does uniquely point to another row within the same table.

Using Parent-Child Relationships

A table of family members would display similar hierarchical relationships. Child rows would contain a pointer to their parents, but the parents would also be children to their own parents. If we tried to avoid the self-referencing, we would need a separate table for each generation.

The parent-child example (see Figure 5.10) is useful to keep in mind. We usually speak about *self-joins* in terms of parents and children. The parent record is a row that other rows point to. The child is the row that points to another row. It's very important to recognize that a single row can act as both a child and a parent with respect to different rows.

FIGURE 5.10

This sample `Products` *table contains parts and kits, and parts can belong to kits.*

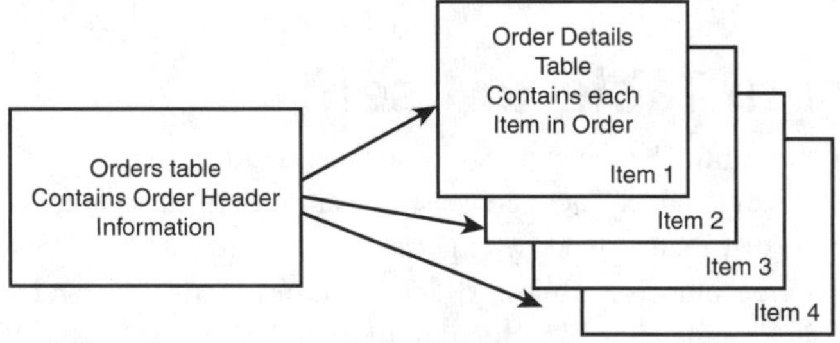

NEW TERM A *self-join* is a join that relates a table to itself. A self-join can use predefined parent and child keys.

If you look back at the completed diagram for the `Northwind` database in Figure 5.5, you will notice that the `Employees` table in the upper-left corner of the diagram has an arrow that points back to itself. `Employees` includes a parent-child relationship to handle management reporting. An employee reports to a manager, who is himself an employee reporting to another manager. The key columns in the relationship are `EmployeeID`, which uniquely identifies an employee, and `ReportsTo`, which uniquely identifies another employee.

We'll write a query to display the `EmployeeID` and name of each employee, along with the manager ID and manager name for that employee. When you are writing self-joins, it's often useful to act as if there were two different versions of the table. Sometimes even printing out the contents of "each" table will help you avoid confusion.

Let's start out simply. We'll list all the employees and their manager's ID number:

```
select
        EmployeeID,
        LastName,
        FirstName,
        ReportsTo
from
        Employees
```

Results:

```
EmployeeID  LastName             FirstName  ReportsTo
----------  -------------------- ---------  ----------
         1  Davolio              Nancy               2
         2  Fuller               Andrew     NULL
         3  Leverling            Janet               2
         4  Peacock              Margaret            2
         5  Buchanan             Steven              2
         6  Suyama               Michael             5
         7  King                 Robert              5
         8  Callahan             Laura               2
         9  Dodsworth            Anne                5
```

Based on the results, you can see that Nancy Davolio (along with others) reports to Andrew Fuller (ID 2) and Michael Suyama (and others) reports to Steven Buchanan (ID 5). Buchanan also reports to Fuller (ID 2).

The next step is to display the name of the person whose ID is listed in the `ReportsTo` column on each row. Before we can do that, I need to talk a little bit about aliases in self-joins.

5

Naming Standards in Self-Joins

The best way to help yourself when writing self-joins is to adhere to constructive naming standards. Use useful column and table aliases and everything will be clear. Use confusing or meaningless names and you will never know whether you got the right answer.

We already have a good list of employees. Now we need to add their managers' names to the list. To do that, first we'll add an inner join to the `FROM` clause. Self-joins are the only instance where table aliases are required, but I'll choose useful aliases to simplify the query.

```
…
from
        Employees emp
   inner join
        Employees mgr
            on emp.ReportsTo = mgr.EmployeeID
```

I've chosen to use the table aliases `emp` and `mgr`. The version of the `Employees` table that holds an employee is `emp`. The version that holds a manager is `mgr`. The join clause says, "the manager is the person whose employee ID is this `ReportsTo` value."

Notice how much more confusing the query is when the aliases are not constructive. In the following example, the aliases `e1` and `e2` are used to identify the two versions of `Employees`:

```
…
from
        Employees e1
   inner join
        Employees e2
            on e1.ReportsTo = e2.EmployeeID
```

When you use this aliasing method, it is almost impossible to decide which version of each column to reference elsewhere in the query.

After you have chosen useful aliases, the rest of the query is fairly easy to write. You will also want to choose useful column aliases for columns to avoid confusion. Listing 5.6 shows you a completed self-join.

LISTING 5.6 Using Constructive Table and Column Aliases to Make It Easier to Write Self-Joins

```
select
        emp.EmployeeID as 'EmpID',
        emp.LastName,
        emp.FirstName,
        emp.ReportsTo as 'MgrID',
        mgr.LastName as 'ManagerLast',
        mgr.FirstName as 'MgrFirst'
from
        Employees emp
   inner join
        Employees mgr
            on emp.ReportsTo = mgr.EmployeeID
```

Results:

```
EmpID  LastName      FirstName  MgrID  ManagerLast  MgrFirst
------ ------------- ---------- ------ ------------ --------
     1 Davolio       Nancy           2 Fuller       Andrew
     3 Leverling     Janet           2 Fuller       Andrew
     4 Peacock       Margaret        2 Fuller       Andrew
     5 Buchanan      Steven          2 Fuller       Andrew
     6 Suyama        Michael         5 Buchanan     Steven
     7 King          Robert          5 Buchanan     Steven
     8 Callahan      Laura           2 Fuller       Andrew
     9 Dodsworth     Anne            5 Buchanan     Steven
```

The completed self-join displays the name of each employee, along with the name of his or her manager. Notice that the column names of the columns that refer to data from the `mgr` version of the `Employees` table have all been aliased to avoid confusion (see lines 5, 6, and 7).

We have one more problem to solve. The employee list is incomplete. Andrew Fuller, the president of the company, is missing. In the `Employees` table, the row for Fuller has a `NULL` value for `ReportsTo`, so the row fails to appear as part of an inner join. We'll replace the inner join at line 10 with an outer join to force the last employee into the table. We will force the additional row on the employee side (we are looking for employees without managers, not managers without employees). Listing 5.7 displays the query with the outer join and the ensuing result set.

LISTING 5.7 The Outer Join Forces All Employees to Be Included, Even Those Without a Manager

```
 1 select
 2         emp.EmployeeID,
 3         emp.LastName,
 4         emp.FirstName,
 5         emp.ReportsTo as 'ManagerID',
 6         mgr.LastName as 'ManagerLast',
 7         mgr.FirstName as 'ManagerFirst'
 8 from
 9         Employees emp
10    left outer join
11         Employees mgr
12             on emp.ReportsTo = mgr.EmployeeID
```

Results:

```
EmployeeID  LastName      FirstName  ManagerID   ManagerLast    ManagerFirst
----------- ------------- ---------- ----------- -------------- ------------
          1 Davolio       Nancy                2 Fuller         Andrew
          2 Fuller        Andrew     NULL        NULL           NULL
          3 Leverling     Janet                2 Fuller         Andrew
          4 Peacock       Margaret             2 Fuller         Andrew
          5 Buchanan      Steven               2 Fuller         Andrew
          6 Suyama        Michael              5 Buchanan       Steven
          7 King          Robert               5 Buchanan       Steven
          8 Callahan      Laura                2 Fuller         Andrew
          9 Dodsworth     Anne                 5 Buchanan       Steven
```

This last result set includes all the employees, even Andrew Fuller, who has no manager. Notice the `NULL` values in the manager information columns. When no corresponding row is found, columns based on the inner table get no value.

Using Union to Merge Result Sets

When you join tables, you get a result set where each row can contain values from several tables. In this last section, you will learn to merge two or more result sets into a single result set by using the `UNION` keyword.

Consider the problem of developing a mailing list of suppliers and customers. You would want to produce a list of names and addresses for each table. You don't need to join the tables; after all, there are no corresponding columns to join the tables. Figure 5.11 shows how rows from two separate queries are merged into a single result set.

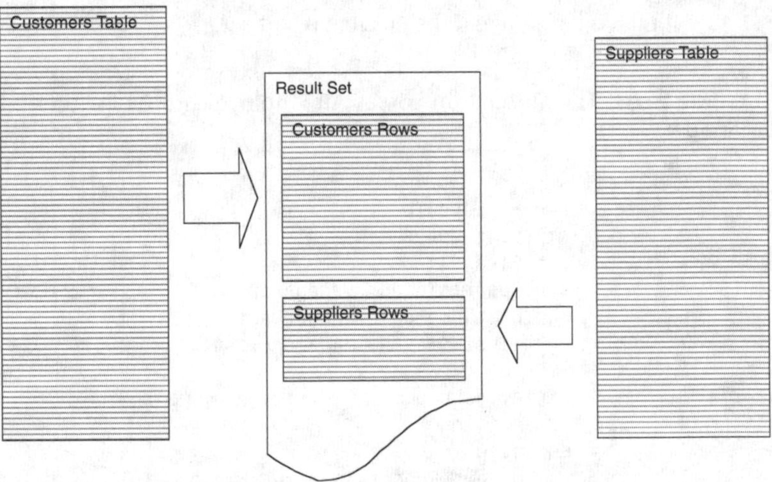

FIGURE 5.11
`UNION` *merges two result sets into a single result.*

Here is the `Customers` and `Suppliers` mailing list query. Notice how the `UNION` statement connects two complete, self-sufficient select statements. (I've limited it to `Customers` and `Suppliers` in the United States to shorten the output, and I've truncated every column to make the data fit on the printed page.)

```
select
        left(CompanyName, 20) CompanyName,
        left(Address, 20) Address,
        City,
        Region as St,
        PostalCode as Zip
from
        Customers
where
         Country = 'USA'
union
select
```

```
        left(CompanyName, 20) ,
        left(Address, 20) ,
        City,
        Region,
        PostalCode
from
        Suppliers
where
        Country = 'USA'
```

Results:

```
CompanyName          Address              City      St Zip
-------------------- -------------------- --------- -- -----
Bigfoot Breweries    3400 - 8th Avenue Su Bend      OR 97101
Grandma Kelly's Home 707 Oxford Rd.       Ann Arbor MI 48104
Great Lakes Food Mar 2732 Baker Blvd.     Eugene    OR 97403
Hungry Coyote Import City Center Plaza 51 Elgin     OR 97827
Lazy K Kountry Store 12 Orchestra Terrace Walla Wal WA 99362
Let's Stop N Shop    87 Polk St. Suite 5  San Franc CA 94117
Lonesome Pine Restau 89 Chiaroscuro Rd.   Portland  OR 97219
New England Seafood  Order Processing Dep Boston    MA 02134
New Orleans Cajun De P.O. Box 78934       New Orlea LA 70117
Old World Delicatess 2743 Bering St.      Anchorage AK 99508
Rattlesnake Canyon G 2817 Milton Dr.      Albuquerq NM 87110
Save-a-lot Markets   187 Suffolk Ln.      Boise     ID 83720
Split Rail Beer & Al P.O. Box 555         Lander    WY 82520
The Big Cheese       89 Jefferson Way Sui Portland  OR 97201
The Cracker Box      55 Grizzly Peak Rd.  Butte     MT 59801
Trail's Head Gourmet 722 DaVinci Blvd.    Kirkland  WA 98034
White Clover Markets 305 - 14th Ave. S. S Seattle   WA 98128
```


You can't tell from the final result whether any specific row started out as a customer or supplier.

Tip

If you needed to, you could include a column to indicate the source table. In each select list, add a column with a constant string, like this:

```
select
left(CompanyName, 20) CompanyName,
'Customer' as Type,
left(Address, 20) Address,
 …
union
select
left(CompanyName, 20) ,
'Supplier' as Type,
left(Address, 20) ,
…
```

> Now, each row will include a value for type. If the row emerges from the `Customers` query, the value for type will be `'Customer'`; otherwise, it will be `'Supplier'`.

The first query sets the stage for the number of columns, their data types (including length, precision, and scale), and column aliases. Each subsequent select statement must have the same number of columns as the first. When SQL Server matches up each successive query in a `UNION`, each column in a query must be a compatible data type to the corresponding column in the first query. Column names and column aliases in subsequent queries are ignored.

You have a lot of leeway when you use `UNION`. If you want to add the `Employees` table to the mailing list, you need to deal with the lack of a company name in that table. Also, in both `Customers` and `Suppliers`, the `ContactName` column is not separated into `FirstName` and `LastName`. You will need to address both of these issues. Listing 5.8 is the revised query with three result sets.

Listing 5.8 A Three-Query Union

```
select
        left(CompanyName, 20) CompanyName,
        left(ContactName, 20) ContactName,
        left(Address, 20) Address,
        City,
        Region 'St',
        PostalCode 'Zip'
from
        Customers
where
        Country = 'USA'
union
select
        CompanyName,
        ContactName,
        Address,
        City,
        Region,
        PostalCode
from
        Suppliers
where
        Country = 'USA'
union
select
```

LISTING 5.8 continued

```
26:         'Our Company Name',
27:         FirstName + ' ' + LastName,
28:         Address,
29:         City,
30:         Region 'St',
31:         PostalCode 'Zip'
32:from
33:         Employees
34:where
35:         Country = 'USA'
```

In Listing 5.8, you can see that the second `Select` statement on line 13 that retrieves data from the `Employees` table does not contain a company name. However, the `UNION` syntax requires that the position for company name contain data. To allow this to work, we have added a static string, `'Our Company Name'`, in that position.

SQL Keywords and `UNION`

To understand `UNION` clearly, you need to understand how it interacts with various keywords. I'll provide you with some guidance here, but you can work with these on your own.

UNION ALL

You should notice that the previous result set is sorted alphabetically by the first column, `CompanyName`. The server sorts the data to remove any duplicate values. None of the data here is duplicated, and in most cases, the results of `UNION` queries won't be.

You can suppress the sort step and the related search for duplicates by adding the keyword `ALL` after `UNION`. That will improve query performance with no loss of data integrity.

`WHERE, GROUP BY`, and `HAVING`

These three keywords are associated only with the local query prior to the `UNION` operation. `WHERE` clauses provide the conditions governing the current select statement. Grouping is performed within the individual query, and `HAVING` clauses are evaluated within the query as well.

`ORDER BY`

You can specify the order of a `UNION` query only after the final `SELECT` statement. That ordering will govern the entire result set.

Summary

In today's lesson, you learned how to join one or more tables together to produce useful collections of data for use by your application programs. You saw how to use the different types of joins depending on your needs. Inner joins can be used to gather information from multiple tables or from one table by restricting the number of rows that appear in a result set using the information contained in another table.

Understanding these different types of joins helps you to understand the concepts of T-SQL. You will need this understanding before going on to tomorrow's lesson on subqueries. Finally, I want to leave you with a few do's and don'ts pertaining to using joins:

Do	Don't
Be careful when using multipart keys	Include tables in a join if you don't need them
Use meaningful table aliases	Use `SELECT *` in a query
Qualify all columns in your queries	
Use constructive table aliases and column names in self-joins	

Q&A

Q What is normalization? Should my database be normalized?

A Normalization refers to the design of a database. Roughly speaking, a database is considered to be normalized when every table contains information specific to only that table. Well-normalized databases have less data duplication and are usually faster and easier to maintain.

Most real-life databases make some compromises about normalization. When you "denormalize," you store duplicate data so that it can be read more quickly. The choice to denormalize depends on the use of your system.

I'll discuss database design briefly in Day 8.

Q Should I qualify all my table names with database and owner?

A I tend to avoid full table qualification unless a table I am referring to is outside of the current database. It's not unusual to have several versions of the active database running on a single server in various stages of development and testing. If you hard-code database names in your applications, you won't be able to work in this kind of environment.

I'll discuss user names in more detail in Day 8. A simple summary of that discussion is this: All objects should be owned by the database owner, dbo. It simplifies database management, programming, and security administration. More on this later.

Q What does this table reference mean?

```
master..sysdatabases
```

A This notation refers to the `sysdatabases` table in the master database. There are two dots because the name of the owner of the table is omitted. When no owner is specified, the server searches first for a table owned by the current user. Next, it searches for a table owned by the database owner.

Q Why doesn't the server just know how to perform a join from the database design? Or join on commonly named columns?

A There are a couple of answers to this question. The academic answer is that the relational model calls for the tables in a relational database system to have only a logical relationship to each other. When you refer to the tables in a query, you need to spell out their relationship; the server will not do it for you.

The realistic answer is that there are circumstances where you don't want the server to perform the obvious join. It would be a nuisance at best if you had to constantly fight off the server's attempts to default a relationship among tables.

Q How do I indicate an outer join using the older join notation?

A Outer joins are indicated with an asterisk next to the equals sign in the join condition. The position of the asterisk denotes the outer table; that is, the table where all rows are to be returned, even those with no matches in the inner table. Here is an outer join in the older notation:

```
select
        c.CompanyName,
        max(OrderDate) 'Last Order'
from
        Customers c,
        Orders o
where
        c.CustomerID *= o.CustomerID and
        c.Country = 'USA'
group by
        c.CompanyName
```

Q Does SQL Server actually create a second copy of a table when it performs a self-join?

A No. It's useful to imagine a second table, but there is only one table involved in the query.

Q Can I join tables across databases?

A Yes, selecting across databases is common and does not typically affect performance. (Running data modification queries such as `INSERT`, `UPDATE`, and `DELETE` across databases might affect performance.)

Q Can I join tables across servers?

A Yes, but you can't use the approaches we have been looking at today. You will use table variables and stored procedures to do that work.

Workshop

The Workshop provides quiz questions to help you solidify your understanding of the material covered and exercises to provide you with experience in using what you've learned. Try to answer the quiz and exercise questions before checking the answers in Appendix A, "Answers to Quizzes and Exercises," and make sure that you understand the answers before continuing to the next lesson.

Quiz

1. For each of the following items, identify the database name, owner, table name, and column name (if available). Where the value will default, indicate that.
   a. `CompanyName`
   b. `Customers.CompanyName`
   c. `Northwind.dbo.Products.QuantityPerUnit`
   d. `Northwind..Products.UnitPrice`
   e. `dbo.Suppliers.City`
   f. `Mary.Suppliers.City`
   g. `Suppliers`
   h. `dbo.Suppliers`
2. How many join conditions are required to perform a three-table join?
3. What is a cross join?
4. How do you decide whether an outer join should be a right or left outer join?
5. How many `ORDER BY` clauses can appear in a query containing the `UNION` keyword?

Exercises

1. Display the names and hire dates of five sales representatives.

```
LastName             FirstName  HireDate
-------------------- ---------- ---------------------------
Davolio              Nancy      1992-05-01 00:00:00.000
Leverling            Janet      1992-04-01 00:00:00.000
Peacock              Margaret   1993-05-03 00:00:00.000
Suyama               Michael    1993-10-17 00:00:00.000
King                 Robert     1994-01-02 00:00:00.000
```

2. Modify the query in Exercise 1 to include a list of order numbers for each employee. Display the first five rows.

```
LastName             FirstName  HireDate   OrderID
-------------------- ---------- ---------- -----------
Davolio              Nancy      1992-05-01       10258
Davolio              Nancy      1992-05-01       10270
Davolio              Nancy      1992-05-01       10275
Davolio              Nancy      1992-05-01       10285
Davolio              Nancy      1992-05-01       10292
```

3. Modify the last query to include the product IDs and the total dollar value of each sale item. Display five total rows.

```
LastName    FirstName  HireDate   OrderID ProductID Dollars
----------- ---------- ---------- ------- --------- -------
Davolio     Nancy      1992-05-01  10258          2   608.0
Davolio     Nancy      1992-05-01  10258          5   884.0
Davolio     Nancy      1992-05-01  10258         32  122.88
Davolio     Nancy      1992-05-01  10270         36   456.0
Davolio     Nancy      1992-05-01  10270         43   920.0
```

4. Group the last result by employee and show the five employees with the worst sales overall.

```
LastName             FirstName  HireDate   Dollars
-------------------- ---------- ---------- ---------------
Suyama               Michael    1993-10-17        73913.12
Dodsworth            Anne       1994-11-15        77308.06
King                 Robert     1994-01-02       124568.23
Davolio              Nancy      1992-05-01       192107.60
Leverling            Janet      1992-04-01       202812.84
```

5. Challenge: Modify the previous query to display five employees with the worst average yearly performance. Hint: Use the employee hire date to determine the number of years the employee has worked for the firm.

5

```
LastName     FirstName  HireDate   Years Average Sales
------------ ---------- ---------- ----- ---------------
Suyama       Michael    1993-10-17     7        10559.01
Dodsworth    Anne       1994-11-15     6        12884.67
King         Robert     1994-01-02     6        20761.37
Davolio      Nancy      1992-05-01     8        24013.45
Leverling    Janet      1992-04-01     8        25351.60
```

WEEK 1

DAY 6

Using Subqueries

One of the capabilities of SQL is to nest one SQL query within another. If you want to select data from one table based on a list of values, you could enter the `WHERE` condition values manually using an `IN` clause, or you could use a second SQL `SELECT` statement to get the values. When you use the result set from one query to supply another query's conditions, you are using a *subquery*. Subqueries enable you to perform in one step what otherwise would require multiple steps. In today's lesson, you will learn

- How to write subqueries
- Why to use subqueries: what they do and why they're useful
- Subqueries returning a single value
- Subqueries returning multiply values
- Using the `IN` clause with a subquery
- Correlated subqueries
- Using `WHERE EXISTS` with a subquery

Understanding Subqueries

The first thing that we want to do is explain what a subquery really is. A subquery is a `SELECT` query that returns a single value and is nested inside a `SELECT`, `INSERT`, `UPDATE`, or `DELETE` statement or inside another subquery. A subquery can be used anywhere an expression is allowed.

The `INSERT`, `UPDATE`, and `DELETE` statements will be covered in tomorrow's lesson.

A *subquery* is a normal T-SQL query that is nested inside another query, using parentheses.

You may have a subquery nesting up to 32 levels deep. Thirty-two levels are more than enough for most queries that you will ever work with.

In prior versions of Microsoft SQL Server, you could have a maximum of 16 tables in a `SELECT` statement. This limit included the tables used in any subqueries. In SQL Server 2000, that limit has been raised to 256 tables, which is probably more than anyone would ever use in a single `SELECT` statement.

A Basic Subquery

In Day 4, "Working with Row Aggregates and Grouping," I gave an example that really required two steps to complete. The problem that the query needed to solve was to find the earliest order in the table. Here is the solution in two steps:

```
select min(OrderDate)
from Orders
```

Results:

```
-----------------------
1996-07-04 00:00:00.000
```

```
select OrderID, CustomerID, EmployeeID
from Orders
where OrderDate = '1996-07-04 00:00:00.000'
```

Results:

```
OrderID     CustomerID EmployeeID
----------- ---------- ----------
10248       VINET      5
```

To solve this in a single step, you can use a subquery (I actually showed you how to do this on Day 4):

```
select OrderID, CustomerID, EmployeeID
from Orders
where OrderDate = (
    select min(orderdate)
    from orders)
```

When you use subqueries, they are placed in parentheses. The entire query is resolved by evaluating the innermost query first and then working outward. In this case, the `SELECT MIN()` query is executed first, returning a single result (the earliest date in the table). This date is then used to search for the order that was the earliest entered. Although the outer query returns only a single row, it is okay for the outer query to return multiple rows because this is what you will receive as your final result set.

I used an equality operator in this example to compare the `orderdate` with the return value. You may use any operator, such as a >= operator, to match a subquery that returns a single row.

If the subquery being used in the SQL statement doesn't return any rows, you will not receive an error message. The end result of this would be an empty result set from the main or outer query.

Benefits of Using Subqueries

Subqueries enable you to resolve, in a single SQL statement, a problem that would usually require multiple statements. By combining everything in a single statement, you reduce the network traffic and avoid cutting and pasting results from one query's result set to another query's text.

The Rules of Using Subqueries

When using subqueries in your SQL statement, you need to be aware of a number of restrictions. Those restrictions are the following:

- The select list of a subquery introduced with a comparison operator can include only one expression or column name (except when used with an `EXISTS` or `IN` keywords which can operate on `SELECT *` or a list, respectively).
- If the `WHERE` clause of an outer query includes a column name, it must be the same data type as the column in the subquery select list.

- The `ntext`, `text`, and `image` data types are not allowed in the select list of subqueries.
- Because they must return a single value, subqueries introduced by an unmodified comparison operator (one not followed by the keyword `ANY` or `ALL`) cannot include `GROUP BY` and `HAVING` clauses.
- The `DISTINCT` keyword cannot be used with subqueries that include `GROUP BY`.
- The `COMPUTE` and `INTO` clauses cannot be specified.
- `ORDER BY` can be specified only if `TOP` is also specified.
- A view created with a subquery cannot be updated. Views are covered on Day 10, "Views and Temporary Tables."
- The select list of a subquery introduced with `EXISTS` by convention consists of an asterisk (`*`) instead of a single column name. The rules for a subquery introduced with `EXISTS` are identical to those for a standard select list because a subquery introduced with `EXISTS` constitutes an existence test and returns `TRUE` or `FALSE`, rather than data.

Matching a Value with Subqueries

Subqueries can be used in the `WHERE` clause as the left side of an expression following one of the comparison operators shown in Table 6.1. A subquery that is used with a comparison operator must return a single value rather than a list of values. If such a subquery returns more than one value, the server will display an error message.

TABLE 6.1 Comparison Operators Used with Subqueries

Operator	*Description*
=	Equality
<>	Not equal
>	Greater than
>=	Greater than or equal
<	Less than
!>	Not greater than
!<	Not less than
<=	Less than or equal

You would use a subquery with a comparison operator to select a value from either another table or the same table. You will realize rather quickly that subqueries will make your programming life much easier.

Creating Subqueries with Comparison Operators

To use a subquery with a comparison operator, you must know your data and understand the nature of the request you are making to know that the subquery will return exactly one value. Here's an example of this type of subquery: If you assume that each publisher is located in only one city, and you need to find the names of all the authors who live in the city in which `'Algodata Infosystems'` is located, you can create a `SELECT` statement with a subquery using the = comparison operator:

```
use pubs
select au_fname, au_lname
from authors
where city =
    (select city
     from publishers
     where pub_name = 'Algodata Infosystems')
```

Results:

```
au_fname             au_lname
-------------------- -----------
Cheryl               Carson
Abraham              Bennet

(2 row(s) affected)
```

If, however, `'Algodata Infosystems'` is located in multiple cities, an error message would have been displayed. Instead of the = comparison operator, you could use the `IN` clause (which is discussed later today) or you could use the `= ANY` variation of a comparison operator (which is discussed next).

Most subqueries that return a single value include an aggregate function. The reason for this is that an aggregate function returns only one value itself.

6

Using ALL and ANY

Any comparison operators that are introduced in a subquery can be modified by the keywords `ALL` and `ANY`. This is called a subquery with a modified comparison operator. These subqueries return a list of zero or more values and can include a `GROUP BY` or `HAVING` clause. After you understand how these modify a comparison operator, you will see that there are other ways to obtain the same results.

In the following example, you want to get a list of all authors who live in a city where there is a publisher. You might try the following SQL statement, but you will get a nasty error message from SQL Server:

```
use pubs
select au_fname, au_lname
from authors
where city =
    (select city
     from publishers)
```

Results:

```
Server: Msg 512, Level 16, State 1, Line 2
Subquery returned more than 1 value. This is not
permitted when the subquery follows =, !=, <, <= , >, >=
or when the subquery is used as an expression.
```

By modifying the comparison operator with the `ANY` keyword, you are asking the outer query to return any rows that match any of the values returned in the subquery (for example, `= Any (1, 2, 3)` any rows that contain a 1,2, or 3 in the comparison column). The following code shows the results of this SQL statement:

```
use pubs
select au_fname, au_lname
from authors
where city = any
    (select city
     from publishers)
```

Results:

```
au_fname             au_lname
-------------------- ---------------
Cheryl               Carson
Abraham              Bennet

(2 row(s) affected)
```

You will see in the next section how to obtain the same results by using the `IN` clause of the `SELECT` statement instead of a comparison operator.

The other modifier for comparison operators is the `ALL` keyword. This uses a subquery that returns a result set of one column but many rows. The data type of the returned column must be the same as the data type of the expression being compared.

To explain this, let's use the > comparison operator as an example. `>ALL` means greater than every value—in other words, greater than the maximum value (for example, `>ALL (1, 2, 3)` means greater than 3). The following is an example of how to use the `ALL` operator:

```
USE pubs
SELECT title
FROM titles
WHERE advance > ALL
   (
    SELECT MAX(advance)
    FROM publishers INNER JOIN titles ON
      titles.pub_id = publishers.pub_id
    WHERE pub_name = 'Algodata Infosystems'
   )
```

This SQL statement returns all titles where the value in the `advance` column is greater than the value returned in the subquery. In this case, the subquery returns the max value for the `advance` column in the `titles` table, which is joined to the `publishers` table, and where the publisher's name is `'Algodata Infosystems'`.

Checking for Membership

"Checking for membership" actually means that you want to return a set of data that matches another set of values that are specified in the `WHERE` clause. To work with a subquery that returns more than one value, you can modify the comparison operator as discussed in the previous section, or you can use the `IN` or the `EXISTS` clause of the `SELECT` statement.

So far, all the subqueries that you have seen have been written for you. In this section, you will write a subquery from scratch. Along the way, I will give you a couple of tips to help make the process easier.

> The result of a subquery that is used with an `IN` clause is a list of zero or more values. After the subquery returns the resulting information, the outer query will use them as if you typed them in yourself.

Writing Your First Subquery with IN

To see how to use the `IN` clause, let's suppose you need to find all the products that are supplied by companies in a selected country. You want to create the final query in steps. This will enable you to test each piece of the query to ensure that it works as desired. The first step is to create the inner query. Remember that the inner query will not return an error message if it fails. This is the reason for testing it before including it as a subquery. This query would return all the supplier ID codes based on the supplied country name (in this case, 'Germany') in the WHERE condition as shown:

```
Use Northwind
select supplierid
from suppliers
where country = 'Germany'
```

Before continuing, you should execute this query to see whether there are any suppliers in Germany. For the Northwind database, you should get the following results:

```
supplierid
-----------
11
12
13

(3 row(s) affected)
```

You can see that there are three unique suppliers in Germany. The next step is to create the outer or main query. This would be a SELECT statement that specifies the columns you want to return from the products table as shown:

```
select productid, productname
from products
```

You might want to execute this query to test it, but if your database is very large, this could return thousands or millions of rows from the products table.

The final step is to combine these two SQL statements together by using the IN condition with the WHERE clause. The following code is the final result of this combination:

```
select productid, productname
from products
where supplierid in
      (select supplierid
       from suppliers
       where country = 'Germany')
```

With the final result:

```
productid   productname
----------- ----------------------------------------
25          NuNuCa Nuß-Nougat-Creme
26          Gumbär Gummibärchen
27          Schoggi Schokolade
28          Rössle Sauerkraut
```

```
29          Thüringer Rostbratwurst
30          Nord-Ost Matjeshering
64          Wimmers gute Semmelknödel
75          Rhönbräu Klosterbier
77          Original Frankfurter grüne Soße

(9 row(s) affected)
```

To review, the inner query is evaluated first, producing the ID numbers of the three suppliers who meet the subqueries' `WHERE` condition. The outer query is then evaluated using these values in the `IN` clause. If I knew the ID numbers of the suppliers in Germany, I could have written the query as follows:

```
select productid, productname
from products
where supplierid in (11,12,13)
```

Using the `NOT IN` Condition

There is one variation of the `IN` condition in which you would return rows in the outer query where the comparison column does not match any of the values returned from the subquery. When using `NOT IN`, the subquery still returns a list of zero or more values. However, the final result will be the opposite of what you would expect. Using the previous example, the `NOT IN` would return all the products that are not supplied from Germany.

Creating Correlated Subqueries

Most queries are evaluated by executing the subquery once and then substituting the resulting value or values into the `WHERE` clause of the outer query. In queries that include a *correlated subquery* or repeating subquery, the subquery depends on the outer query for its values. This means that the subquery is executed repeatedly, once for each row that might be selected by the outer query. The following example finds the names of all the authors in the `PUBS` database who earn 100% of the shared royalty on a book:

```
USE pubs
SELECT au_lname, au_fname
FROM authors
WHERE 100 IN
   (SELECT royaltyper
   FROM titleauthor
   WHERE titleauthor.au_ID = authors.au_id)
```

The results of this query are

```
au_lname                                 au_fname
---------------------------------------- --------------------
White                                    Johnson
Green                                    Marjorie
```

6

```
Carson                                   Cheryl
Straight                                 Dean
Locksley                                 Charlene
Blotchet-Halls                           Reginald
del Castillo                             Innes
Panteley                                 Sylvia
Ringer                                   Albert

(9 row(s) affected)
```

Unlike most of the subqueries shown earlier today, the subquery in this example cannot be resolved independently of the outer query. It requires a value for `authors.au_id`, but this value is a variable. It changes as each row of the `authors` table is examined.

That is exactly how this query is evaluated: SQL Server considers each row of the `authors` table for inclusion in the results by substituting the value in each row into the subquery's `WHERE` condition. Then, if the value in the `royaltyper` column matches `100`, it is returned in the final result set. This evaluation occurs for each row in the `authors` table.

Things to Remember When Using `IN`

Using the `IN` condition allows you to search the data in the table for more than one value. However, when you are using the `IN` condition, there are a few things to watch out for. These are discussed in the following sections.

Removing Duplicate Values from the `IN` List

Do you really want duplicate values in the `IN` list? The answer depends on the size of the tables being accessed in the outer query and subqueries. There is one good reason for not wanting duplicates in the list. Suppose that the outer query is going against a very large table and the subquery is working on a small table, you should use the `DISTINCT` keyword to remove any duplicates in the subquery result set. This helps the server improve response time because each row in the outer query must be tested against the values in the subquery list. If you have fewer values returned, the server has fewer items in the list to compare against.

However, for every other instance, there is no real need to remove duplicates from the list. In fact, using the `DISTINCT` keyword when you don't really need it will slow down the response from the server. To summarize: There are only a few situations in which using `DISTINCT` in the subquery is warranted, but in general, it doesn't pay to use it.

Matching Data Types

You want to make sure that the data type of the list items being returned matches the data type of the column that they are being compared with. If you don't, the server must perform a conversion on the entire list of items for every row in the tables referenced in the outer query. In addition, if the data types are incompatible (for example, money and character), you will receive an error message from the server.

Returning an Empty Result Set

When you use a subquery that returns no rows, you will not receive an error message. In the case of an IN list, you are comparing values to an empty list, and no rows in the outer query will be in that list.

Writing Subqueries with EXIST

I want to discuss one other type of subquery today. The WHERE EXISTS test enables you to verify the existence of a row in a table and to take action only if a matching row exists. The EXISTS condition is really a type of correlated subquery. Suppose that you want to know which business titles have sold any books. To verify this, you need to look in the titles table for all titles that have a type of 'Business'. Then, you look in the sales table to find the rows for the titles that you previously found. You don't really want to select anything from the sales table; you just want to find those books that have at least one row in the sales table. The following example shows how to use the EXISTS condition to perform this task:

```
USE pubs
Select title_id
from titles
where exists (
      select *
      from sales
      where sales.title_id = titles.title_id)
```

The subquery in an EXISTS test works the same way as the correlated subquery: by referencing a table in the outer query. For every row in titles that matches the WHERE clause, the subquery is evaluated. If the subquery is true, the row is included in the result set.

Comparing Joins and Subqueries

6

Up to this point in this lesson, you have learned how to select information from one or more related tables by making use of subqueries. You can also use a subquery to resolve problems when information from another table is needed to complete a SELECT statement's WHERE condition. However, you must use a join to display information from more than one table.

Many T-SQL statements that include subqueries can be alternatively created using joins, with the reverse being true as well. Other questions can be posed only with subqueries.

In T-SQL, there is usually no performance difference between a statement that uses subqueries and a statement that uses joins instead. However, in some cases where existence must be checked, a join yields better performance. The following two code examples return the same result set, but you can see that one uses joins whereas the other uses a subquery. This first example uses the `INNER JOIN` syntax:

```
USE pubs
Select pub_name
from publishers as p inner join
     titles as t
     on t.pub_id = p.pub_id
where t.type = 'business'
```

This next example retrieves the same data by using a subquery:

```
Select pub_name
from publishers as p
Where p.pub_id in (
      select t.pub_id
      from titles as t
      where t.type = 'business')
```

When you execute these two SQL statements, you will see a different number of rows returned. This will probably confuse you just a little, until you take a closer look. You will see that the subquery version returns only unique values. To reproduce this exactly in the join version, you would need to include the `DISTINCT` keyword.

> **Note** Going back to the topic of performance, both SQL statements using joins and those using subqueries can return the same data, but when you need to use the `DISTINCT` keyword to eliminate duplicates, you are actually slowing down the processing. So, if you don't really care about duplicates, the join SQL statements are faster.

Summary

Congratulations, you have made it to the end of the day. If your head hurts, don't worry, it's temporary. Today, you learned everything you ever wanted to know about subqueries, but didn't know to ask. You saw how to use subqueries that return single results, as well as subqueries that return lists, and subqueries that do the work of inner joins. In addition, you saw how to use subqueries to return aggregate information, which you would then use in a normal query (one that doesn't use a `GROUP BY` clause).

You also learned how to use both the `IN` and `EXISTS` conditions in the `WHERE` clause to select data when using subqueries. In tomorrow's lesson, you will learn how to manipulate the data that is in the database by using the `INSERT`, `UPDATE`, and `DELETE` SQL statements.

Q&A

Q Can I use more than one subquery in a single statement?

A Yes. In fact, you can use as many subqueries as you like, just as long as you do not exceed the nesting level limit of 32.

Q Can I mix subqueries and joins in the same query?

A Why not? Some programmers find that doing this helps them understand how the server is actually creating their result set.

Q What happens if the subquery I am using returns a null, or if it returns no rows at all?

A If a subquery returns a NULL, the outer query will simply compare the specified column to a NULL value. This won't cause an error, but it might not be what you wanted. If the subquery returns no rows (empty set), again, there would be no error, but you would not get any rows back from the outer query either.

Workshop

The Workshop provides quiz questions to help you solidify your understanding of the material covered and exercises to provide you with experience in using what you've learned. Try to answer the quiz and exercise questions before checking the answers in Appendix A, "Answers to Quizzes and Exercises," and make sure you understand the answers before continuing to the next lesson.

Quiz

1. How many tables can appear in a single query?

Exercises

These exercises use the `Pubs` database.

1. List the authors who have at least one book priced above the average price.
2. Using a subquery, list the sales information for all books with the word `Computer` in the title.

WEEK 1

DAY 7

Adding, Changing, and Deleting Rows

In the past six days, you have seen how to retrieve data from the database by using the SELECT statement along with a variety of optional parameters. After this data is retrieved, you can use it in your application program or edit it. So far, the focus has been on retrieving the data. However, you might have wondered how to enter data into the database in the first place.

Today, you will learn several ways of manipulating the data within the database. These topics include

- Creating tables
- Inserting rows
- Updating rows
- Deleting rows

Creating Tables

Although you will completely cover how to create a table in tomorrow's lesson, you need to know a bit about it in order to work with the remaining topics in today's lesson. When creating a table, you must define several attributes for each column in the table. The first thing you need to decide and define is the data type for the column. The `title` table has a `title` column that is defined as `varchar` and a `price` column that is defined as `money`. If you execute an `sp_help` on the table, you will see the data types for each column.

The next attribute would be the length for the data types that require it. Data types such as `datetime`, `integer`, `smallinteger`, and `money` have fixed lengths, so you do not need to set a length. Character fields and variable length fields require you to set a maximum length.

The final attribute you need to specify is whether you want the column to be able to accept NULLs. If you want to allow a row of data to be inserted without specifying values for some of the columns, NULLs can be allowed in these nonessential columns.

The `customer_demo` table in the following example is a made-up table and is not part of the Northwind database. However, it will be used for the remainder of today's lesson.

The following is the code we will use to create the `customer_demo` table:

```
Use northwind
create table customer_demo(
    cust_id int not null,
    fname varchar(30) not null,
    lname varchar(30) not null,
    addr1 varchar(40) null,
    addr2 varchar(40) null,
    city varchar(40) null,
    zip char(9) null,
    )
```

As you can see in the preceding code, seven columns are being defined in the new `customer_demo` table. After the table is created, we can add new rows to the table by providing the `cust_id`, `fname`, and `lname`. The other columns are defined as NULL, so we do not have to specify them if we don't have that information. I will not go into any more detail today; you will cover the `CREATE TABLE` statement on Day 8, "Defining Data."

Deleting Tables

Now that you have seen how to add a table, you need to be able to remove or delete the table at the end of the lesson. To remove any object from the database, such as a table, you use the `DROP` operation. If you need to re-create a table or just remove it, you use the `DROP TABLE` statement as shown.

```
Drop table customer_demo
```

> After you drop a table, it is gone forever. If you had a million rows in the table, they're gone. The server will let you drop a table even if it has rows in it. Unless you have a backup of the data, you have lost it completely.
>
> Drop objects only when you are really sure that you don't need them.

Inserting Rows

To add data to a table in the database, you would generally use the `INSERT` statement. The `INSERT` statement appends one or more rows of data to a table. The syntax for the `INSERT` statement follows, with Table 7.1 describing the main arguments of the statement.

```
INSERT [ INTO]
    { table_name WITH ( < table_hint_limited > [ ...n ] )
        | view_name
        | rowset_function_limited
    }
    {     [ ( column_list ) ]
        { VALUES
            ( { DEFAULT | NULL | expression } [ ,...n] )
            | derived_table
            | execute_statement
        }
    }
    | DEFAULT VALUES
    }
```

TABLE 7.1 Insert Statement Arguments

Argument	*Description*
`[INTO]`	Optional keyword used to specify the table to be used when inserting data.
`table_name`	Name of the table where the data is being inserted.

TABLE 7.1 continued

Argument	*Description*
WITH (<table_hint_limited> [...*n*])	Specifies one or more table hints that are allowed for a target table.
view_name	Name of an optional view that can be used to insert data.
rowset_function_limited	Is either the OPENQUERY or OPENROWSET function. This argument is used to access data from a remote server. For most uses of the INSERT statement this argument is omitted.
(column_list)	A list of one or more columns in which to insert data. This list must be enclosed in parentheses and delimited by commas.
VALUES	Specifies the list of data values to be inserted in the order of the columns listed.
DEFAULT	Forces SQL Server to load the default value defined for a column.
expression	This provides a constant, a variable, or an expression to be used to as the source of the data to be inserted. The expression cannot contain a SELECT or EXECUTE statement.
derived_table	This is any valid SELECT statement that returns rows of data to be loaded into the table.
execute_statement	Any valid EXECUTE statement that returns data with SELECT or READTEXT statements.
DEFAULT VALUES	Forces the new row to contain the default values defined for each column.

The values that are specified in the INSERT can either be actual values or data retrieved using a SELECT statement.

Inserting Rows with INSERT...VALUES

The first method we will look at for inserting data into a table is the INSERT statement using the column list and VALUES clause to specify the data to be inserted. Using the customer_demo table that we created in the previous section, let's add some data to the table and then display it by selecting it. Listing 7.1 contains the code to

- Create the customer_demo table
- Insert data into the table
- Select the data
- Drop the table when finished

LISTING 7.1 Creating a Table and Inserting Rows

```
Use northwind
create table customer_demo(
  cust_id int not null,
  fname varchar(30) not null,
  lname varchar(30) not null,
  addr1 varchar(40) null,
  addr2 varchar(40) null,
  city varchar(40) null,
  zip char(9) null,
   )
 insert customer_demo
      (cust_id, fname, lname)
      VALUES(1,'John','Davolio')
 insert customer_demo
      (cust_id, fname, lname)
      VALUES(2,'Anne','Callahan')
 insert customer_demo
      (cust_id, fname, lname)
      VALUES(3,'Steven','Suyama')
 insert customer_demo
      (cust_id, fname, lname)
      VALUES(4,'Robert','Buchanan')
 insert customer_demo
      (cust_id, fname, lname)
      VALUES(5,'Janet','Peacock')
 insert customer_demo
      (cust_id, fname, lname)
      VALUES(6,'Andrew','Leverling')
 select * from customer_demo
 drop table customer_demo
```

Results:

```
(1 row(s) affected)

(1 row(s) affected)

(1 row(s) affected)

(1 row(s) affected)

(1 row(s) affected)

(1 row(s) affected)

cust_id    fname       lname        addr1  addr2  city   zip
---------- ----------- ------------ ------ ------ ------ ------
1          John        Davolio      NULL   NULL   NULL   NULL
1          Anne        Callahan     NULL   NULL   NULL   NULL
```

LISTING 7.1 continued

```
1           Steven      Suyama      NULL   NULL   NULL   NULL
1           Robert      Buchanan    NULL   NULL   NULL   NULL
1           Janet       Peacock     NULL   NULL   NULL   NULL
1           Andrew      Leverling   NULL   NULL   NULL   NULL

(6 row(s) affected)
```

You can see that there were six individual messages from the server, one for each of the `INSERT` statements that were executed. In addition, because we did not specify any address information, these fields display `NULL` to signify that these columns are empty.

If you don't want the row count displays in the output, you can turn them off by using the `NOCOUNT` option as the first statement at the beginning of a procedure:

```
SET NOCOUNT ON
```

The data that you have inserted is returned to you in the order in which you inserted it. Because you did not specify an `ORDER BY` clause in the `SELECT` and there are no indexes on your table, the data is kept in the table, and returned to you, in the order in which it was inserted.

To insert rows, you specify the columns you want to insert within parentheses following the table name. You then follow that list with the keyword `VALUES` and specify the values for the row in the parentheses. If you do not specify a column list, the values you specify must be in the order in which they appeared in the original `CREATE TABLE` statement.

If you are using the `INSERT` statement in an application program, you should always provide a column list. This will prevent any problems if the table is dropped and re-created with the columns in a different order.

When specifying data to be inserted into a table, you must specify it based on the data type of each column. In the previous example, you could see that the first and last name values are specified using quotes. Table 7.2 lists the different data types and how to specify the data, including what to watch for.

TABLE 7.2 How to Insert Different Data Types into a Table

Data Type	*Example*	*Quotes*	*Comments*
`Varbinary`	`values(0XA02D21A5)`	No	Binary values accept hexadecimal notation.
`Binary`	`values(0x1a)`	No	Binary values accept hexadecimal notation.
`Varchar`	`values('Jerry')`	Yes	Character values are specified in quotes.
`Char`	`values('Bill's Car')`	Yes	Character values are specified in quotes.
`Smalldatetime`	`values('12:39')`	Yes	
`Datetime`	`values('01/01/00 12:32 AM')`	Yes	Specifying a date without a time will default the time to midnight (0:00). Specifying a time without a date will default the date to January 1, 1900.
`Smallmoney`			
`Money`	`values($473000,16)`	No	Do not use quotes for `money` values. In addition, do not use commas to specify thousands.
`Bit`	`values(0)`	No	The possible values for a bit field are `0` and `1`.
`Bigint`	`values (9223372036854775807)`	No	
`Int`	`values(34038)`	No	
`Smallint`	`values(-318)`	No	
`Tinyint`	`values(24)`	No	
`Numeric`	`values(-23.075)`	No	
`Decimal`	`values(165.2)`	No	
`Float`	`values(165.2)`	No	
`Real`	`values(1125.31)`	No	

Inserting Rows with `INSERT...SELECT`

In this method of inserting data, we will use the `SELECT` subquery instead of specifying the columns and respective values. The `SELECT` subquery in the `INSERT` statement can be used to add values into a table from one or more other tables or views. Using a `SELECT` subquery also enables you to insert more than one row at a time. The example in Listing 7.2 shows how to create the `customer_demo` table using the data from the `employees` table as the input.

LISTING 7.2 Inserting Data Using a Subquery

```
Use northwind
set nocount on
create table customer_demo(
    cust_id int not null,
    fname varchar(30) not null,
    lname varchar(30) not null,
    addr1 varchar(40) null,
    addr2 varchar(40) null,
    city varchar(40) null,
    zip char(9) null,
    )
insert into customer_demo
       (cust_id, fname, lname)
       select employeeid,
              firstname,
              lastname
       from employees
select * from customer_demo
drop table customer_demo
```

The select list of the subquery must match the column list of the `INSERT` statement. If no column list is specified, the select list of the subquery must match the columns in the table or view being inserted into.

The resulting output of the statement in Listing 7.2 would be exactly the same as Listing 7.1, in which you specified the values to input. If you chose, you could have specified the address information from the `employees` table to insert into the `customer_demo` table.

Inserting Rows with `SELECT INTO`

There is one other method for inserting rows that you can use. The `SELECT INTO` statement provides a mixture of functionality. First, it creates a new table based on the structure of the existing table being specified in the statement. The following example provides the same functionality as the previous `INSERT INTO` statement. However, it does not need to define the columns in the new table, nor does it need to create the new table itself.

```
select employeeid,
       firstname,
       lastname,
       Address,
       city,
       PostalCode
Into customer_Demo
from employees
```

All the employees in the `employees` table were copied to a new table, `customer_demo`.

You may select specific columns by using the `SELECT INTO` statement to create a table with fewer fields than the original table (as shown earlier), or you could create a complete copy of the original table as shown here:

```
select *
Into customer_Demo
from employees
```

The `SELECT INTO` statement requires that the special option `'SELECT INTO.BULKCOPY'` be turned on in the database properties. This option is set by the SQL Server administrator to provide the ability to load an entire table from another table.

Choosing which of these different methods to insert data with is entirely up to you and your particular need in a given application.

If you need to create large amounts of test data for an application, you can do so very quickly by using the `INSERT...SELECT` version of the `INSERT` statement. Using the following example, you could copy the data in a table back to itself, thus duplicating the information:

```
Insert customer_demo
Select * from customer_demo
```

Updating Rows

Updating information in a database row is done in much the same way that you would retrieve data using the `SELECT` statement. The `UPDATE` statement is used to actually modify data in a table. The syntax of the `update` statement is

```
UPDATE <tablename> | <viewname> | <alias>
SET    <column> = <New value>[,
```

```
        <column> = <New value>…]
[FROM <table list>]
[WHERE <Boolean constraint>]
```

There are three basic sections to the UPDATE statement:

1. The table that the UPDATE is modifying.
2. The list of columns that will be updated and their respective new values.
3. Optionally, you can specify multiple tables if joining tables together to limit the number of rows being updated.

The following example searches the entire customer_demo table looking for a row that has a customer ID of 2. When it finds a row that matches, it updates the city column to the new value. Before performing the update, we display the row of data; after completing the update, we display the data again.

```
Use northwind
set nocount on
SELECT cust_id, city
FROM customer_demo
WHERE cust_id = 2
UPDATE customer_demo
SET city = 'Buffalo'
WHERE cust_id = 2
SELECT cust_id, city
FROM customer_demo
WHERE cust_id = 2
```

Results:

```
cust_id     city
----------- ----------------------------------------
2           NULL

cust_id     city
----------- ----------------------------------------
2           Buffalo
```

Caution

If you issue an UPDATE statement with no WHERE clause, the UPDATE updates the data in the entire table.

Tip

If you want to be sure that you are affecting the correct rows in the table, you should execute a SELECT * using the WHERE clause from your UPDATE statement before executing the UPDATE statement. I did this in the UPDATE example.

Updating Data Using Data in Other Tables

You have the ability to modify data in a table by using the information contained in other tables in the database. You can use data from one other table or, by using joins, you can use data from multiple tables.

This example (using the pubs database) will increase the prices of all titles by Stearns MacFeather by five dollars:

```
Use Pubs
update t
set t.price = t.price + $5
FROM authors as a inner join titleauthor as ta
     on a.au_id = ta.au_id
     inner join titles as t
     on ta.title_id = t.title_id
where a.au_lname = 'MacFeather'
```

In previous releases of Microsoft SQL Server, joins were defined in the WHERE clause, you would not have been able to write the update statement using the new INNER JOIN syntax.

This author has written two books. I used the last name of the author to identify him in the authors table. To complete this UPDATE request, the server finds the rows in the titles table that join to 'MacFeather'. It then reads the price column for those rows, adds five to it, and then writes the new value back to the table.

Note

You might be asking what the titleauthor table is doing in this example. Well, the titles table does not have any columns in it that relate directly to the authors table. The titleauthor table is where this relationship is stored. The titles table joins to the titleauthor table, and then the titleauthor table joins to the authors table.

Caution

After you update a column, the change is permanent. There is no "UNDO" feature.

What? Well, that is not entirely correct. On Day 13, "Programming with Transactions," you will see how to use the transaction processing capability of the server to "UNDO" an update.

Reviewing the Limits on the UPDATE Statement

You may update only one table at a time. If you are joining tables in your update, you must be sure to update columns from only a single table. In addition, if you are updating a view, and that view references multiple tables, you must perform the update in as many steps as there are tables in the view.

If you are working with large tables, try to perform as many column changes as you can in a single UPDATE statement. If you change two columns in one update, the row must be read into memory and written back to the table only once. If you change one column in two separate UPDATE statements, each row must be read and written twice.

Deleting Rows

The last of the action statements that we will cover today is the DELETE statement. You have already seen how to add and insert data into a table in the database. You also learned how to modify and update that data. Now, you will see how to remove or delete rows from a table. The syntax of the DELETE statement is

```
DELETE <table_name | view_name>
[WHERE <condition>]
```

The first thing that you will probably realize is that the DELETE command does not have a prompt. Users (yourself included) are accustomed to being prompted before doing something that can destroy data or files. The "Are you sure?" message box is a common sight before performing a delete operation.

The following example deletes a row from the customer_demo table:

```
Delete customer_demo
Where cust_id = 3
```

Just as with the UPDATE statement, be very careful about how you specify which rows you want to delete by using the WHERE clause.

A DELETE without a WHERE clause will delete all the rows in a table.

Ensuring a Successful Deletion

You should not turn on the NOCOUNT option when using the DELETE statement. Watch the row counts when you execute a DELETE command. Sometimes, you might delete no rows at all. If I tried to delete from the customer_demo table, and the cust_id that I specified in the WHERE clause didn't exist, I would see the following message from the server:

```
delete customer_demo
where cust_id = 8

(0 row(s) affected)
```

Issuing a DELETE that affects no rows does not cause an error. This is important to remember because in your application programs, you must be able to determine whether a delete operation completed successfully. If you intend to delete a row, issue a DELETE, and find that you haven't deleted anything, there is likely a problem in your logic or database.

Reviewing the Limits on the DELETE Statement

The same rules that apply to table joins and updates also apply to table joins and deletes. You may delete from only one table at a time, but you may join to other tables for information about which rows to delete.

In addition, you may not delete rows from any view that references more than one table.

Truncating Tables

If you plan to delete all the rows in a table, an unqualified DELETE will do the job. However, a faster way to do this is to use the TRUNCATE TABLE command as shown here:

```
Truncate Table customer_demo
```

TRUNCATE TABLE will remove all the rows in a table, but will leave the structure of the table intact. This means that you do not have to re-create the table when you use the TRUNCATE statement. The DROP statement would delete the table structure as well as the data.

Understanding Identity Columns and the TRUNCATE Statement

If there are identity columns in the table, a DELETE will remove any rows specified, but the next row that you add will continue where the identity value left off. Deleting rows from a table with identity columns means that those identity values will never be used again. The TRUNCATE statement actually resets the identity value back to its original starting value. Table 7.3 shows the differences between the DELETE, TRUNCATE, and DROP commands.

TABLE 7.3 Differences Between DELETE, TRUNCATE, and DROP

Operation	*Table Still Exists*	*Identity Reset*
TRUNCATE TABLE	Yes	Yes
DELETE w/o WHERE	Yes	No
DROP TABLE	No	N/A

Summary

In today's lesson, you took a quick look at creating and dropping tables. You saw that when creating a table, each column requires a name, a data type, a length (where needed), and an indication of whether it can be NULL.

After you had a table, you saw how to insert data into the table by using different versions of the INSERT statement. Data can be added to a table by specifying the input values directly, or by selecting information from other tables in the database. After adding information to a table, you saw how to use the UPDATE statement to modify that information.

Later, you took a brief look at how to delete one or more rows from a table. Finally, you learned how to use the TRUNCATE TABLE statement to remove all rows from a table and reset the identity column value at the same time.

Next week, you will learn how to create tables using the DDL (Data Definition Language). In addition, you will see how to enhance the performance of your database and how to prevent multiple users from accessing the same information at the same time.

Q&A

Q Can I copy data from a table into itself using the INSERT command? In addition, I want to change the value of one column.

A By using the INSERT statement with a SELECT statement, you can copy all the rows from the table into itself. However, you must modify the column in question as a separate step. You cannot update columns while performing this type of INSERT. The following code shows how to perform these tasks:

```
Insert customer_demo
Select * from customer_demo
Update customer_demo
Set Addr2 = 'unavailable'
```

Q You said that caution should be taken when using the INSERT, UPDATE, DELETE statements, but there seem to be some simple fixes to correct whatever I did wrong. Is this correct?

A Yes. For example, a simple way to fix a misspelled name is to do an update on that row to fix the name. Or you could delete the row and redo the insert with the corrected spelling of the name.

However, what if you inserted a thousand rows and didn't notice that you misspelled something until a couple of weeks later? You would not want to simply delete the rows, which probably include many new rows or multiple updates from your users. In most cases, you would probably not even know what rows to fix.

To fix something this drastic, I would print all of the rows that have the misspelled name in it using a WHERE clause. Then, I would slowly make the changes one row at a time.

Q What is the difference between the DROP TABLE and the TRUNCATE TABLE statements?

A The `DROP TABLE` statement will completely remove a table and its definition from the database, whereas the `TRUNCATE TABLE` statement will only remove the data in the table (much like a `DELETE` statement), resetting the identity column.

Workshop

The Workshop provides quiz questions to help you solidify your understanding of the material covered and exercises to provide you with experience in using what you've learned. Try to answer the quiz and exercise questions before checking the answers in Appendix A, "Answers to Quizzes and Exercises," and make sure you understand the answers before continuing to the next lesson.

Quiz

1. What is wrong with the following statement?

```
DELETE * FROM customer_demo
```

2. What is wrong with the following statement?

```
UPDATE customer_demo (
    'John', 'smith', 34)
```

3. What would happen if you executed the following statement?

```
DELETE * from customer_demo
```

4. Will the following SQL statement work?

```
INSERT INTO customer_demo
SET VALUES = 758
WHERE ITEM = 'CAR'
```

Exercises

1. Create a table called `customers_demo` with the following: an identity column called `cust_id`; fname and lname as required fields; `email`, which is an optional email address; and `cust_new` to specify whether the customer is new. The `cust_new` column should default to `'Y'` to specify that the customer is new to the company.
2. Insert the following data into your table.

First Name	*Last Name*	*Email*	*New Customer?*
John	Smith	Jsmith@aol.com	Y
Julie	Pinter		N
Bill	Buckley	BillyB@wb.com	Y
Seven	Nine	Sevenof9@st.com	N

3. Try inserting values with the incorrect data types into the table. Note the errors and then insert values with correct data types into the table.

WEEK 1

In Review

You've reached the end of the first week. To review what you have learned, let's quickly recap each day. If you see something you don't remember, go back to the day in question and review the topic.

Day 1, "Introduction to SQL and the Query Analyzer": This first day was really a startup day. It discussed what SQL is and how it relates to a database. However, you did learn several very important things in Day 1. You learned what the Query Analyzer is and how to use it with the Enterprise Manager. In addition, you wrote your very first SQL query and saw how the `SELECT` statement works.

Day 2, "Filtering and Sorting Data": You learned that the `WHERE` clause restricts the rows returned by your query. Each row that might pass the `WHERE` test is compared against the expression. The `WHERE` expression will return a Boolean result, either true or false, meaning that the row will either be kept in the result set, or it will be thrown away. While learning the `WHERE` clause, you saw how to use the `IN` and `BETWEEN` clauses. In addition, you learned how to sort the data being returned by using the `ORDER BY` clause to specify how you wanted the data sorted.

Day 3, "Working with Columns": In Day 3, you learned how to work with columns. Columns can contain any type of data. Microsoft SQL Server has many data types available, which were briefly discussed. You saw how to change the name of the column using an alias. This enables you to provide different names for the columns in the result set. Finally, you also saw how to change the data being returned by using operators and functions in conjunction with the data in the columns.

Day 4, "Working with Row Aggregates and Grouping": There are six unique SQL aggregates in T-SQL: `sum`, `avg`, `min`, `max`, `count`, and `count big`. These are called aggregates because they return only a single value that is calculated based on many rows. You saw that aggregates couldn't be used in a `SELECT` list along with non-aggregated columns, unless the data is grouped by the column you want to aggregate on. This showed you how to make use of the `GROUP BY` clause of the `SELECT` statement. In addition to the `GROUP BY` clause, you also saw how to provide different ways to display subtotals and totals in your output by using the `CUBE` and `ROLLUP` clauses in the `SELECT` statement. Finally, you learned how to use the `HAVING` clause with aggregates instead of the `WHERE` clause.

Day 5, "Joining Tables": Day 5 was probably one of the most important lessons that you learned for working with SQL and relational databases. Table joins enable you to pull together related data based on information in the tables that are used as keys. A *key* is a piece of data that exists in two tables and allows those tables to have a meaningful relationship. Most of the time keys are ID numbers, such as product IDs, which could join an order detail table together with a product table.

Day 6, "Using Subqueries": In Day 6, you learned how to nest one or more queries within others. Subqueries enable you to calculate aggregates and compare those results to an outer query, test the outer query against a list of values retrieved by the inner query, and join tables.

Day 7, "Adding, Changing, and Deleting Rows": The last day of the week covered how to insert, update, and delete information from the tables with which you are working. The `SELECT` statement that you learned at the beginning of the week allowed you to retrieve data, and Day 7 showed you how to manipulate the data directly.

WEEK 2

Programming with T-SQL

Congratulations on finishing your first week! You now have a pretty good working knowledge of SQL to get by in most common situations. The first week taught you quite a bit about the `SELECT` statement. In the second week, you will start learning some of the more advanced SQL topics.

On Day 8, "Defining Data," you will learn how to create databases, tables, and columns using DDL or Data Definition Language. This enables you to manipulate the database without having to use one of the Windows-based tools such as Enterprise Manager.

On Day 9, "Indexes and Performance," we will take a look at how adding indexes to your tables will affect the performance of your SQL queries. In addition, you will learn how to use a couple of the performance tools that come with Microsoft SQL Server 2000.

Day 10, "Views and Temporary Tables," is about temporary tables. Temporary tables are almost the same as permanent tables, but they exist for only a short period of time and are then dropped when you are finished with them. They are useful for holding temporary results, among other things. Finally, I will take a look at views, what they are, and how you can use them to look at existing data in the database.

On Day 11, "T-SQL Programming Fundamentals," I will present you with the fundamentals of SQL programming. You will learn what variables are, how to use them, and the concepts of conditional coding. I will also show you how errors occur and then how to deal with them.

Day 12, "Understanding Database Locking," covers the important topic of row and table locking. Locking is the server's way of ensuring that data isn't written while its being read, and vice versa. Locking can be a little confusing, but it is a necessary evil on any multi-user application system.

Day 13, "Programming with Transactions," covers transactions. A transaction enables you to group SQL statements so that they either succeed or fail as a group. Writing transactions is a critical skill in a SQL-based computer application. All serious application systems use transactions in some way to ensure the integrity of the data.

Finally on Day 14, "Using Cursors," we will discuss cursors. Cursors enable you to treat a result set on a row-by-row basis, instead of looking at it as a single chunk of data. However, cursors require a great deal of programming effort on your part and large amounts of CPU or processing time.

WEEK 2

DAY 8

Defining Data

In the previous week, you have seen how to use Transact-SQL to manipulate the data contained within columns. The columns were organized in tables and one or more of these tables are contained in a database. SQL can be divided into two types of SQL: DML (Data Manipulation Language) and DDL (Data Definition Language). All the SQL you have used so far is DML SQL. Today, you will see how to create and set up the databases and tables for your data by using DDL SQL statements. This enables you to automate the installation of your application by having the program itself create the required database on the user's computer and the needed tables and columns. In addition, you can have maintenance functions in the application modify some of the properties in the database by using the DDL statements you will learn today. The topics we will cover are

- Creating and altering databases
- Creating and altering tables
- Choosing column properties
- Defining constraints
- Discussing primary keys and foreign keys
- Defining table relationships

What Is Data Definition Language (DDL)?

Data Definition Language (DDL) comprises the SQL statements that are used to create, modify, and delete SQL-based databases and other SQL objects. DDL is used to define the properties of these objects at creation time, or to change the properties of any of these objects after they have been created. The database itself is considered just another object, and there can be many objects under or contained within the database. Some of these objects include

- Tables
- Views
- Stored procedures
- Triggers
- Users

Creating a New Database

When you installed SQL Server, several databases were created automatically. One of these is the master database. The *master database* holds information about each database that is added to SQL Server. This information is stored in the sysdatabases table. Another database that is added at install time is the model database. The model database is used as the template whenever you add a new database to SQL Server. A copy of the model database is used and renamed to the new database you have just added. The current settings of the model database are used to initialize the new database. You then change these settings as needed.

The master database stores information about each database as well as the SQL Server environment itself. By making a backup of the master database before altering it, you can recover from any damage accidentally made to the master. Damage to the master database can affect other databases as well as keep the SQL Server from initializing. If this happens without a backup of the master database, you would have to reinstall SQL Server and then restore your database, if you even have a backup.

When you create a new database, you need the following information before starting:

- Database name
- Filename for the database and log file
- Starting size of the database and log file

- Maximum size of the database
- Filegrowth for the database

The syntax of the `CREATE DATABASE` statement is as follows:

```
CREATE DATABASE database_name
[ On [PRIMARY]
[ <filespec> [,...n] ]
[, <filegroup> [,...n] ]
]
[ LOG ON [ <filespec> ] ]
[ FOR LOAD | FOR ATTACH ]

<filespec> ::=

( [ NAME = 'logical_file_name', ]
  FILENAME = 'os_file_name'
  [, SIZE = size]
  [, MAXSIZE = { max_size | UNLIMITED } ]
  [, FILEGROWTH = growth_increment] ) [,...n]

<filegroup> ::=

FILEGROUP filegroup_name <filespec> [,...n]
```

The arguments of the preceding syntax are described in Table 8.1.

TABLE 8.1 Definition of the `CREATE DATABASE` Arguments

Argument	*Explanation*
`database_name`	The friendly name for the new database as it will appear in SQL Server.
`logical_file_name`	The logical or physical name used for the database file. It must be a unique name in the database.
`os_file_name`	Actual location where the database will be stored on the computer and accessible by SQL Server.
`Size`	The size of the database file to be created. KB or MB can be used to specify the size. MB is the default increment. Only whole numbers are allowed and the minimum value is 512KB. The default size is 1MB.
`max size`	The maximum size to which the defined file can grow. This is also specified in either KB or MB. If the `max_size` is not specified or if it is set to `UNLIMITED`, the defined file will grow until there is no more free space available on the hard drive.

TABLE 8.1 continued

Argument	*Explanation*
`growth_increment`	The amount of space added to the file each time it needs to be expanded.
`FOR LOAD`	For backward compatibility with versions of Microsoft SQL Server before 7.0. The database is created with the `dbo use only` database choice on, and the status set to `loading`.
`FOR ATTACH`	Indicates that a database is attached from an existing set of operating system files. You must supply a `<filespec>` entry specifying the first primary file. You must also supply a `<filespec>` for each file with a different path than the path used when the database was first created or last attached.

Now that you have seen the syntax used to create a database, let's use it by actually creating a database. Listing 8.1 is an example of the `CREATE DATABASE` statement.

LISTING 8.1 DDL Used to Create a Car Parts Database

```
USE master
GO
CREATE DATABASE Parts
ON
(NAME = parts_dat,
 FILENAME = 'c:\SQL_Data\partsdat.mdf',
 SIZE = 70MB,
 MAXSIZE = 500MB,
 FILEGROWTH = 10MB )
LOG ON
(NAME = parts_log,
 FILENAME = 'c:\SQL_Data\partslog.log',
 SIZE = 25MB,
 MAXSIZE = 150MB,
 FILEGROWTH = 5MB )
GO
```

The directory path used in Listing 8.1 refers to the directory `SQL DATA` on the C drive. You must create this directory on your computer for the SQL procedure to execute properly.

This example will create a database named Parts using the file c:\SQL_Data\partsdat.mdf with an initial file size of 70MB. It can grow as large as 500MB by 10MB at a time. The log file for this database is stored in c:\SQL_Data\partsdat.log, is 25MB in size, has a maximum size of 150MB, and its growth size is set to 5MB. When you execute this statement in Query Analyzer, you should get the following output:

```
The CREATE DATABASE process is allocating 70.00 MB on disk 'parts_dat'.
The CREATE DATABASE process is allocating 25.00 MB on disk 'parts_log'.
```

To check the information for any of the databases in SQL Server, you can run the system stored procedure SP_HELPDB. In Query Analyzer, type in the command and execute it. The following type of results for the databases that are on your server:

```
name       db_size      owner    dbid   created     status
-------- ------------- -------- ------ ----------- -------------------
master       10.94 MB sa        1      Nov 13 1998 trunc. log on chkpt.
model         1.50 MB sa        3      Sep  3 1999 no options set
msdb         16.25 MB sa        4      Sep  3 1999 trunc. log on chkpt.
Northwind     3.94 MB sa        6      Sep  3 1999 select into/bulkcopy
                                                      , trunc. log on chkpt.
Parts        95.00 MB sa        9      Aug  7 2000 no options set
pubs          1.74 MB sa        5      Sep  3 1999 trunc. log on chkpt.
tempdb       11.44 MB sa        2      Aug  2 2000 select into/bulkcopy
                                                      , trunc. log on chkpt.
```

You should know that the db_size column shows the size of each database by combining the size of the data and log files. Also, notice that the new database you created, Parts, has no options set in the status column. These options are not set during the creation process, but can be set by using this stored procedure:

```
Sp_dboption
```

In addition, because the Model database is used as the template when you create a new database, if you want an option to be used by default, you should set it in the Model database.

Altering a Database

In any design, you can never anticipate everything that might be needed in a database. Fortunately, there is a way to change, or *alter*, the database after it has been created. The command ALTER DATABASE can be used to add files and filegroups and to change the name or size of existent database files. It can also be used to remove files and filegroups from the database. The ALTER DATABASE syntax is

```
ALTER DATABASE database_name
{    ADD FILE <filespec> [,...n] [TO FILEGROUP filegroup_name]
    | ADD LOG FILE <filespec> [,...n]
```

```
    | REMOVE FILE logical_file_name
    | ADD FILEGROUP filegroup_name
    | REMOVE FILEGROUP filegroup_name
    | MODIFY FILE <filespec>
    | MODIFY FILEGROUP filegroup_name filegroup_property}

<filespec> ::=
(NAME = logical_file_name
  [, FILENAME = 'os_file_name' ]
  [, SIZE = size]
  [, MAXSIZE =  ( max_size | UNLIMITED ) ]
  [, FILEGROWTH = growth_increment] )
```

The arguments for this command are described in Table 8.2.

TABLE 8.2 Definition of ALTER DATABASE Command Arguments

Argument	*Explanation*
database_name	Name of the database you are altering.
ADD FILE	Specifies that you want to add a file.
logical_file_name	The logical name used for the file. It must be unique in the database.
os_file_name	The actual path and filename of the database.
size	With ADD FILE, size is the initial size for the file.
max_size	The maximum size to which the new file can grow.
growth_increment	Specifies the growth increment of the defined file.
filegroup_name	Name of the existing filegroup to add the specified file.
ADD LOG FILE	Add a log file to this database with the <filespec> info given.
REMOVE FILE	Removes the file information from the database system tables and deletes the physical file. The file must be empty first.
filegroup_name	With ADD FILEGROUP and REMOVE FILEGROUP, the name of the filegroup to add or remove.
MODIFY FILE	Modifies the given file settings for FILENAME, SIZE, FILEGROWTH, and MAXSIZE. Only one of these properties can be changed at a time.
MODIFY FILEGROUP filegroup_name filegroup_property	Sets the given filegroup name with the given filegroup property. Settings for filegroup_property are READONLY, READWRITE, and DEFAULT.

Let's look at a couple of different ALTER DATABASE examples. Listings 8.2 and 8.3 will show you how this command can be used. Using the new Parts database from the previous CREATE DATABASE command, you can increase the data file size from 70MB to 100MB.

LISTING 8.2 Increasing the Size of a File in an Existing Database

```
Use Master
GO
ALTER DATABASE Parts
MODIFY FILE
 (NAME = 'parts_dat',
 SIZE = 100MB)
GO
```

When you execute this command, SQL Server will display the following output:

```
The command completed successfully.
```

You can use the `sp_helpdb` command to verify that the database size has been changed. Listing 8.3 shows how you can add a secondary file to the existing filegroup in the Parts database.

LISTING 8.3 Adding a File to an Existing Database

```
Use Master
GO
ALTER DATABASE Parts
ADD FILE
 (NAME = 'parts2_dat',
 FILENAME = 'c:\SQL_DATA\parts2dat.ndf',
 SIZE = 50MB,
 MAXSIZE = 100MB,
 FILEGROWTH = 5MB )
GO
```

SQL Server will display the following message after executing the preceding command.

```
Extending database by 50.00 MB on disk 'parts2_dat'.
```

The stored procedure `sp_renamedb` can be used to change the name of the database.

Dropping or Deleting a Database

Deleting or dropping a database is almost too easy. Before you start dropping databases, you should make sure that you have a backup of all your databases, including the master and model. SQL Server will not prompt you with the ever popular `Are you sure you want to do this?` message to stop you from making a potentially huge error. You would use the following syntax for the `DROP DATABASE` command:

```
DROP DATABASE database_name[,    n]
```

To drop the `Parts` database, you would use the following example:

```
DROP DATABASE Parts
```

The result of dropping the database you created in the previous sections would look like this:

```
Deleting database file 'c:\SQL_data\partsdat.mdf'.
Deleting database file 'c:\ SQL_data \partslog.log'.
Deleting database file 'c:\ SQL_data \parts2dat.ndf'.
```

If you need to delete more than one database, you can just type the database names separated by commas as shown:

```
DROP DATABASE Parts, Orders, Customers
```

DDL Versus the Enterprise Manager

You're probably thinking, "Why should I bother using the actual statements when I can just use the Enterprise Manager and do it graphically?" (see Figure 8.1). As a rule, you should use the Enterprise Manager whenever you can. However, from a development standpoint, you'll be glad that you know how to use the DDL statements.

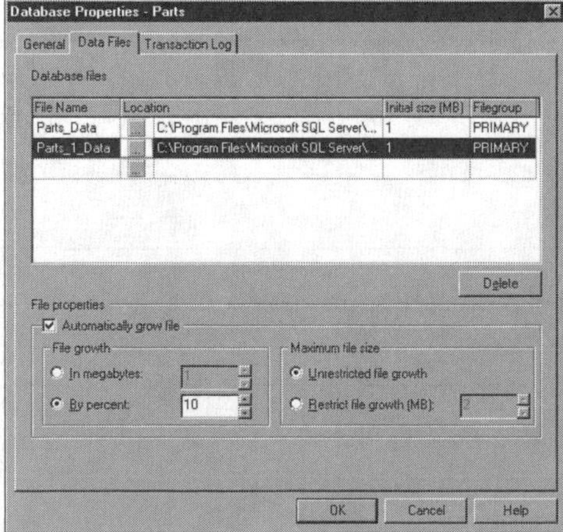

FIGURE 8.1

Using the SQL Server Enterprise Manager.

Suppose that you have to set up two databases. Each database has 150 tables, and each table has several columns. That would be a lot of clicking in Enterprise Manager. If you're a developer, think about all the users of your software having to set up these objects. Having the code to generate objects on the SQL Server can save a lot of time and headaches for you and for your users. You can write programs that automatically build the entire database for new users. You can use code with loops that go through the same generic subroutines for adding certain objects. Then you just change the variables each time the loop is passed.

Knowing the Enterprise Manager is great. It's quick and it's easy. But knowing the code to create and alter the objects can save you a lot of redundant clicking and can get you out of some messy situations.

Working with Tables

A database is nothing but an empty file that will contain the tables our programs will actually use to store data. The data will be stored in the tables as columns and rows that you have been using up to this point in our queries. To put the information in the database, you need objects such as tables and columns to house the data. Table 8.3 lists the information that would be needed for a pet store database.

TABLE 8.3 Sample Table of Pet Store Data in Columns and Rows

Pet Name	*Tags*	*Animal*	*Breed*	*Favorite Food*
Calvin	1325	Dog	Dalmatian	Eats Anything
Sarah	9526	Dog		Steak
Spike	A256	Cat	Fussy	Tuna
Rex	1	Dinosaur	T-Rex	Triceratops (tastes like chicken)

Just as you have to create our databases, you have to create your tables within that database. After a table is created, you will have to consider data similar to the `Pets` table. All columns aren't created equal. Using the sample data in Table 8.3, some questions that must be asked about the properties of the table and columns. For example, how do you name your table and columns? What data type will each column use—for example, which columns are text and which are numeric? Which should, or can't be, integers? How many characters will be allowed in a text column? Should you allow NULLs or blanks? If you don't allow NULLs in a column, should there be a default entry for that column? There are many more questions that need to be addressed in addition to these. As the database developer, you must answer each of these questions in order to create optimal tables. Setting table and column properties is essential for having a well-tuned database that meets the users needs for a long time.

Let's create a simple database and table using the data in Table 8.3 as our rules, and answer some of those questions along the way. Later, we'll go into some of the more detailed ways of creating tables. First, Listing 8.4 takes a quick look at the DDL used to create the database our table will go in.

LISTING 8.4 Creating the Pet Store Sample Database

```
USE master
GO
CREATE DATABASE Pets
ON
(NAME = pets_dat,
 FILENAME = 'c:\sql_data\petsdat.mdf',
 SIZE = 30MB,
 MAXSIZE = 50MB,
 FILEGROWTH = 5MB )
LOG ON
(NAME = pets_log,
 FILENAME = 'c:\sql_data\petslog.log',
 SIZE = 10MB,
 MAXSIZE = 20MB,
 FILEGROWTH = 5MB )
GO
```

After the database is created, make sure that you are working in the new database before creating any other objects that you want in it. In Query Analyzer, the drop-down box next to DB: is used to choose the current database. But to be safe, tell QA the exact database you want to work with by using this command:

```
Use Pets
```

Now, building the table a line at a time, you start with the obvious:

```
CREATE TABLE pets_table
```

The `pet_name` column follows the creation of the table. You can make some educated guesses from the sample data about what this column's requirements need to be. You know the names will be text. Some might be as long as 15 characters. Let's start with the varying characters data type, or `varchar`. Also, you want to make sure that you have a name for each pet and that this field is not left blank, so insert a `NOT NULL` command to ensure that users leave something here. The following section of code sets these properties:

```
(pet_name varchar(15) NOT NULL,
```

The same questions exist for the `tags` column. Try a five-character maximum length and allow NULLs. It is tempting to use the integer data type here because of all the numbers. But notice that Spike's tag is alphanumeric. Setting this field to `integer` would cause invalid data type errors when an alphanumeric tag was entered. So, for this one, stick to `varchar`:

```
tags varchar(5) NULL,
```

You want to make sure that the users have something for the type of animal it is and that the entry could be 10 characters long. (Anyone owning a Siberian tiger will just have to shorten it to Tiger.)

```
animal varchar(10) NOT NULL,
```

You might not know the breed or its favorite food, so let both allow NULLs and be `varchar` types:

```
breed varchar(10) NULL,
```

```
fav_meal varchar(40) NULL )
```

Other data types and choices will be discussed later today. Let's put all these command segments together as shown in Listing 8.5. Execute this statement in Query Analyzer and then look at the table you have just created.

LISTING 8.5 Adding the `pets_table` and Columns to the `Pets` Database

```
Use pets
GO
CREATE TABLE pets_table
 (pet_name varchar(15) NOT NULL,
 tags varchar(5) NULL,
 animal varchar(10) NOT NULL,
 breed varchar(10) NULL,
 fav_meal varchar(40) NULL )
GO
```

You can double-check all the details of the new table by using the `sp_help` stored procedure and passing the table name as a parameter as shown:

```
Sp_help pets_table
```

But if you simply want to see the new table and its columns, you could use the following SQL statement:

```
SELECT * FROM pets_table
```

Don't expect to see any data yet, but at least you can see that you have successfully created the table.

The `CREATE TABLE` command has many more arguments than what you have just used. What follows is the complete syntax of the `CREATE TABLE` command:

```
CREATE TABLE
[
    database_name.[owner].
    | owner.
] table_name
(
    {    <column_definition>
        | column_name AS computed_column_expression
        | <table_constraint>
    } [,...n]
)
[ON {filegroup | DEFAULT} ]
[TEXTIMAGE_ON {filegroup | DEFAULT} ]

<column_definition> ::= { column_name data_type }
[ [ DEFAULT constant_expression ]
| [ IDENTITY [(seed, increment ) [NOT FOR REPLICATION] ] ]
]
[ ROWGUIDCOL ]
[ <column_constraint>] [ ...n]

<column_constraint> ::= [CONSTRAINT constraint_name]
{
    [ NULL | NOT NULL ]
    | [    { PRIMARY KEY | UNIQUE }
        [CLUSTERED | NONCLUSTERED]
        [WITH FILLFACTOR = fillfactor]
        [ON {filegroup | DEFAULT} ]]
     ]
    | [    [FOREIGN KEY]
        REFERENCES ref_table [(ref_column) ]
        [NOT FOR REPLICATION]
     ]
    | CHECK [NOT FOR REPLICATION]
        (logical_expression)
}

<table_constraint> ::= [CONSTRAINT constraint_name]
{
    [ { PRIMARY KEY | UNIQUE }
        [ CLUSTERED | NONCLUSTERED]
        { ( column[,...n] ) }
        [ WITH FILLFACTOR = fillfactor]
        [ON {filegroup | DEFAULT} ]
```

```
]
| FOREIGN KEY
        [(column[,...n])]
        REFERENCES ref_table [(ref_column[,...n])]
        [NOT FOR REPLICATION]
| CHECK [NOT FOR REPLICATION]
    (search_conditions)}
```

Tip

Using SELECT INTO to Create a Table

You might have situations in which you want to build a table and the data already exists in other tables. A SELECT statement can be used to extract the exact data you need from those tables. By using the INTO parameter, another table can be built from the returned data as shown here:

```
SELECT breed FROM pets_table
INTO dogbreed_table
WHERE animal = 'dog'
```

This would create dogbreed_table with a breed column for every record with animal listed as 'dog'.

The SELECT INTO statement is covered in more detail on Day 10, "Views and Temporary Tables."

Caution

The SELECT INTO option must be turned on for the database in use. You can set it in the GUI or just run the stored procedure as in this example:

```
Sp_dboption 'pets', 'select into', true
```

Rules About Table and Column Names

Table and column names fall under the rules of identifiers in SQL. Identifiers, or names, are used to define database objects. They can contain up to 128 characters. (An exception to this is a local temporary table. It can only contain up to 116 characters.) The first character of tables and columns must be a letter, an underscore, the @ symbol, or the # sign. Characters after the first character can be all those, plus a number or the $ sign. If a table name begins with a single # sign, it is defined as a local temporary table. If it starts with ## (two # signs), it is defined as a global temporary table. The combination of *owner.table* must be unique within the database in which the table exists. Each column name must be unique within its table. Several examples of valid table and column names are

- @Table1
- Table$1

- `#Column1`
- `Table_1_#1`

Understanding Column Data Types

During the `CREATE TABLE` discussion earlier today, you used just a few of the data types that are available in SQL Server. To see all the technical details on data types, run the following SQL statement, which lists all the data types stored in the system table systypes:

```
SELECT * from systypes
```

Or, you can use the following statement to list just the data type names in order:

```
SELECT Name from systypes ORDER BY Name
```

Table 8.4 shows you a list of the data types and their details.

TABLE 8.4 SQL Data Types

SQL Data Type Usage	*Type of Data*	*Number of Bytes*
`binary[(n)]`	Binary	0–8000
`bit`	Stores a single 0 or 1	1
`char[(n)]`	Character	0–8000
`datetime`	Date and time	8
`decimal[(p[,s])]`	Exact numeric	2–17
`float[(n)]`	Approximation of entered value due to binary representation	4,8 (depending on precision)
`image`	Binary	0–2GB (>8000 bytes recommended)
`int`	Integer	4
`money`	Currency	8
`nchar[(n)]`	Unicode	8000 (4000 characters)
`ntext`	Unicode	0–2GB
`numeric[(p[,s])]`	Exact numeric	2–17
`nvarchar[(n)]`	Unicode	8000 (4000 characters)
`real`	Approximation of entered value due to binary representation	4

TABLE 8.4 continued

SQL Data Type Usage	*Type of Data*	*Number of Bytes*
`smalldatetime`	Date and time	4
`smallint`	Integer	2
`smallmoney`	Currency	4
`sysname`	Special	256
`text`	Character	0–2GB (>8000 bytes recommended)
`timestamp`	Counter Unique to DB	8
`tinyint`	Integer	1
`uniqueidentifier`	Globally Unique ID Number (GUID)	16
`varbinary[(n)]`	Varying-length binary	0–8000
`varchar[(n)]`	Varying-length character	0–8000

User-Defined Data Types

User-defined data types are created using system data types. They enable you to set data type, length, and nullability for your own data type. User-defined data types are database specific. The system command `sp_addtype` is used to create a user-defined data type. The syntax for this command is

```
sp_addtype [@typename = ] typename,
           [@phystype = ] system_data_type
           [, [@nulltype = ] 'null type']
           [, [@owner = ] 'owner_name']]
```

You could create a user-defined data type called `zipcode` by using the `sp_addtype` command as shown:

```
Sp_addtype zipcode, 'char(10)', 'NOT NULL'
```

You can then use that new data type for all ZIP Code fields in your database:

```
Zip zipcode,
```

Then, for every table that has a ZIP Code entry, you could use the user defined data type instead of setting up those parameters every time.

Choosing Nullability

In prior years, there was no easy way in SQL Server to show a column in a row that was simply not entered. There were, however, some very creative ways to do it. For instance, using a specific number of 9s (99999) for a value or a series of Xs (XXXXX), and hoping that no one ever used that particular combination for anything. A popular way of entering an unknown date field was using 01/01/1900 in the field. Of course, if the four-digit year is turned into a two-digit year, well, you know where this is going…Y2K! Throw all these data elements into many different applications that were written by different programmers using different rules, and it becomes more than a bit confusing. A standard had to be created to handle these situations more effectively.

Nullability determines whether a column can accept a NULL value as data in the column. NULL means no entry was made to the column, or the entry was specifically set to NULL. When a field is left NULL in a column, it usually means the value was not known for that column. NULL is not zero. NULL does not mean blank spaces.

Back when we made our Pets table (refer to Table 8.1), we decided to make the `pet_name` column `NOT NULL` because we didn't want to allow blanks in that column. We wanted to make sure that we had an actual pet name to which to link back all the other information. But we knew some pets might not have an easily identifiable breed, so we allowed NULLs in the `Breed` column.

To determine whether a column should be allowed to be NULL, ask yourself, "Can this field be left with no entry?"

Default Columns

Now think about this: What if the user does not have the information to fill in the data for a column, but you don't want to leave the field as NULL? A default value can be specified and used when this occurs.

You can use `DEFAULT` to specify a value when no value is entered during an `INSERT` or `UPDATE`. A column can have only one `DEFAULT` definition.

What follows are a few examples of different ways of using the default values.

Setting the Field If Left Blank

You work for a small company whose customers are all in your state. The state field for their addresses should default to your state of Texas (TX).

```
state char(2) NOT NULL DEFAULT 'TX',
```

The company's employee information program has a field for entering a secondary email address. Not everyone has email at home, so this field might sometimes be left blank. Because reports on employee information are always wanted, but you don't want this field to just show up blank if it hasn't been entered, you would set up a `DEFAULT` for it:

```
secondary_email varchar(40) NOT NULL DEFAULT 'No secondary email given.',
```

8

Using Server Information as the Default

An `Entered By` column in the table keeps track of who enters each row. This info is obtained from SQL Server by using the system command `SYSTEM_USER` to get the user who was logged in to the SQL Server:

```
user_entered varchar(40) NOT NULL SYSTEM_USER,
```

Remember not to use quotes or parentheses around the system command `SYSTEM_USER`.

Using the `GETDATE()` Function to Default the Current Date

Our company has a database of invoices. When a new invoice is entered, we want to fill the Creation Date column using the current date:

```
create_date datetime NOT NULL DEFAULT (getdate()),
```

Computed Columns

A computed column is not really a column that is stored in the table. It is a computation usually based on other columns in the same table. A computed column can be derived from other columns, a constant, a variable, a function, or a combination of any or all of these. Computed columns can't be used for `PRIMARY KEY`, `UNIQUE`, `FOREIGN KEY`, and `DEFAULT` constraints. You cannot `INSERT` or `UPDATE` a computed column. The computation takes place whenever a `SELECT` statement references that computed column.

Using an Expression in a Computed Column

You have a table that contains retail prices and sale prices. You also have a computed column that figures the difference between the two prices:

```
CREATE TABLE prices
 (retail money,
 sale money,
 cost_diff AS (retail - sale))
```

Using a Function in a Computed Column

You can use the `GETDATE()` function to fill a date column:

```
CREATE TABLE invoice_due_table
 (invoice_num int NOT NULL,
 date_due datetime NOT NULL,
 currentdate AS GETDATE())
```

Altering Tables

As your application development progresses, you might realize that you should have used a different length or data type. Or maybe you shouldn't have allowed NULL in a particular column. The ALTER TABLE command can be used to make these changes. In previous versions of SQL Server, you had to drop most objects and re-create them to make any changes. As I have already said, "Things change!" It's time to figure out how to modify and add new objects or settings to a table, and how to change what is already there. The ALTER TABLE command is used to perform this work. The syntax of the command is

```
ALTER TABLE table
{    [ [ALTER COLUMN column_name
        {    new_data_type [ (precision[, scale] ) ]
                       [ NULL | NOT NULL ]
            | {ADD | DROP} ROWGUIDCOL
        }
    ]
    | ADD
        {    [ <column_definition> ]
            |  column_name AS computed_column_expression
        }[,...n]
    | [WITH CHECK | WITH NOCHECK] ADD
        { <table_constraint> }[,...n]
    | DROP
        {    [CONSTRAINT] constraint_name
            | COLUMN column
        }[,...n]
    | {CHECK | NOCHECK} CONSTRAINT
        {ALL | constraint_name[,...n]}
    | {ENABLE | DISABLE} TRIGGER
        {ALL | trigger_name[,...n]}
}
<column_definition> ::= { column_name data_type }
[ [ DEFAULT constant_expression ]
| [ IDENTITY [(seed, increment ) [NOT FOR REPLICATION] ] ]
]
[ ROWGUIDCOL ]
[ <column_constraint>] [ ...n]
<column_constraint> ::= [CONSTRAINT constraint_name]
{[ NULL | NOT NULL ]
    | [    { PRIMARY KEY | UNIQUE }
        [CLUSTERED | NONCLUSTERED]
        [WITH FILLFACTOR = fillfactor]
        [ON {filegroup | DEFAULT} ]]
     ]
    | [    [FOREIGN KEY]
        REFERENCES ref_table [(ref_column) ]
        [NOT FOR REPLICATION]
```

8

```
    ]
   | CHECK [NOT FOR REPLICATION]
      (logical_expression)
}
<table_constraint> ::= [CONSTRAINT constraint_name]
{    [    { PRIMARY KEY | UNIQUE }
        [ CLUSTERED | NONCLUSTERED]
        { ( column[,...n] ) }
        [ WITH FILLFACTOR = fillfactor]
        [ON {filegroup | DEFAULT} ]
]
   |    FOREIGN KEY
           [(column[,...n])]
           REFERENCES ref_table [(ref_column[,...n])]
           [NOT FOR REPLICATION]
   |    DEFAULT constant_expression
           [FOR column]
   |    CHECK [NOT FOR REPLICATION]
        (logical_expression)}
```

The arguments for ALTER TABLE are almost identical to those of CREATE TABLE. Everything that is created in CREATE TABLE can be added, changed, or removed in ALTER TABLE. Let's look at some examples of using the ALTER TABLE command to work with columns in a table.

Adding and Dropping Columns

The table already has a column for phone numbers, but a column for tracking cell phone numbers is also needed. To add this new column, use the following statement:

```
ALTER TABLE customers
 ADD cell_phone char(10) NOT NULL DEFAULT 'None' WITH VALUES
```

This statement will add an additional column called cell_phone to the existing table. This column will be a 10-character field that does not allow nulls. In addition, because it is being added to an existing table, the value 'None' is used in the column for all the existing rows in the table.

Note

When you add a column to a table that already has data in it, you must allow NULLs or specify a default. This allows existing data rows to have a NULL in the new column or to be filled in with the default value. Using WITH VALUES sets each existing value to the default. Without WITH VALUES, you have to allow NULLs.

Removing Columns

You have a music store that tracks album sales by CD, tape, record, and mini-disk. You realize that the record stock is probably not too sellable, so you need to remove the column. To remove the records column from the `record_sales` table, you would use the following statement:

```
ALTER TABLE record_sales
 DROP COLUMN records
```

Adding a Column Constraint `WITH NOCHECK`

Constraints can be used to keep certain values from being added into a database. Let's say that a fruit company is no longer selling apples. The company doesn't want any more entries for apples, but wants to continue tracking the orders that have already been placed. You can use the `WITH NOCHECK` parameter to keep the constraint from affecting rows that already have apples in them. Without `WITH NOCHECK`, the constraint cannot be added if `apples` already exists in the `fruit_choice` column:

```
ALTER TABLE fruit_sales WITH NOCHECK
 ADD CONSTRAINT no_apples CHECK (fruit_choice <> 'apples')
```

Adding Multiple Columns

Just as when building columns with `CREATE TABLE`, you can use a comma-delimited list to add multiple columns. What if you have an older database of people? You need fields for new technologies:

```
ALTER TABLE people_info
 (cell_phone char(10) NOT NULL DEFAULT 'No Cell' WITH VALUES,
 beeper_phone char(10) NOT NULL DEFAULT 'No Beep' WITH VALUES,
 secondary_email varchar(40) NULL,
 web_page varchar(40) NULL)
```

Renaming Tables and Columns

Renaming tables and columns is easy with the system stored procedure called `sp_rename`. Before you rename a table, you should execute the `sp_depends` command on the table to see any views, stored procedures, or triggers that might be using this table or column:

```
sp_depends old_table_name
```

They should all be adjusted automatically with the new table or column name. To rename a table, use the following syntax:

```
sp_rename 'old_table_name', 'new_table_name'
```

You get the following output after executing the command:

```
Caution:  Changing any part of an object name
could break scripts and stored procedures.
The object was renamed to 'new_table_name'.
```

Rerun sp_depends on the new table name to make sure that all the objects referencing the table are now using the new name:

```
sp_depends new_table_name
```

Using the sp_rename command, you can also change the name of a column as shown in the following command. This example renames the old column to new:

```
sp_rename 'my_table.old', 'new', 'COLUMN'
```

Changing Data Types and Nullability

When your tables and columns are already created, you might simply need to change the data type or nullability.

Any data already in a column that is being changed must be able to be converted to the new data type. You would use the same format for changing the columns as you did for adding them, with the exception of the ALTER COLUMN command:

```
ALTER TABLE my_table
 ALTER COLUMN column1 varchar(20) NOT NULL
```

This sets column1 to a 20-character field that does not allow NULLs.

Defining Constraints

Constraints are defined during the CREATE TABLE or ALTER TABLE command. They are used to enforce data integrity and ensure that valid data is entered into the columns. Constraints can also ensure that integrity is maintained between tables. A column-level constraint applies to a single column, whereas a table-level constraint applies to multiple columns, even if it does not apply to every column. PRIMARY KEY, UNIQUE, FOREIGN KEY, DEFAULT, and CHECK are all examples of constraints. Both PRIMARY KEY and UNIQUE constraints are used to enforce uniqueness on columns. However, a UNIQUE constraint can allow NULLs.

If you need to know the constraints already on a table, you can use the stored procedure

```
sp_helpconstraint table_name
```

to list all the constraint types, names, and columns for the table you specify.

CHECK Constraints

CHECK constraints can be used to restrict data depending on a "pass or fail" test of its requirements. It's similar to using a WHERE condition with the SELECT statement. The following are examples of the CHECK constraint.

Checking for a Phone Number Format

This example can be used to check a phone number to make sure that it fits the standard format of (xxx)xxx-xxxx:

```
ALTER TABLE customer_info
 ADD CONSTRAINT ck_phone CHECK (cell_phone LIKE
 '([0-9][0-9][0-9])[0-9][0-9][0-9]-[0-9][0-9][0-9][0-9]')
```

CHECK Constraint Using an Expression

In this example, assume that you have a job code (56) that is no longer being used and you don't want it added to the database. You could just put a CHECK constraint on the column:

```
ALTER TABLE employee
 ADD CONSTRAINT ck_job_code CHECK (job_code <> '56')
```

Defining Table Relationships

In a relational database, relationships enable you to prevent redundant data from being entered. For example, when you are designing a database that tracks information about books, you might have a table named TITLES that stores information about each book, such as the book's title, date of publication, and author. You might want to store information about the author, such as the author's phone number, address, and ZIP Code. If you were to store all this information in the TITLES table, the author's phone number could be duplicated for every title that the author has written. Instead of duplicating data in a table, you could store the author information once in a separate table, AUTHOR. You could then use a key in the TITLES table that references or points to an entry in the AUTHOR table.

To ensure that your data is not out of sync, you can enforce something called *referential integrity* between the TITLES and AUTHOR tables. Referential integrity relationships help to ensure that information in one table matches information in another. For example, each title in the TITLES table must be associated with a specific author in the AUTHOR table. A title cannot be added to the database for an author who does not yet exist in the database. If this is the case, your application can have the user add the new author before adding the new book.

Referential integrity uses the combination of the FOREIGN KEY and PRIMARY KEY, or the UNIQUE constraint, to ensure that every dependent row in a table is correctly linked to a primary key row in another table. A table of customer numbers and orders doesn't do any good if it doesn't properly link back to another table with corresponding customer numbers and customer information. A foreign key should always hold a value equal to the value of its primary key in another table (or be NULL). Without that connection, the link is broken. If a foreign key refers to a row, the primary key for that row cannot change and the row holding the primary key cannot be deleted. Also, a foreign key cannot be added unless it has an existing primary key. In some situations, you might have an optional foreign key. In that case, the foreign key must be set to NULL.

Primary and Foreign Keys

A table usually has a column or combination of columns whose values uniquely identify each row in the table. This column (or combination) is called the *primary key* of the table and enforces the integrity of the table. You can create a primary key by defining a PRIMARY KEY constraint when you create or alter a table.

A table can have only one PRIMARY KEY constraint, and a column that participates in the PRIMARY KEY constraint cannot accept NULLs. Because PRIMARY KEY constraints require unique data, they are often defined as an identity column. When you specify a PRIMARY KEY constraint for a table, data uniqueness is enforced by creating a unique index for the primary key columns. This index also permits faster access to data when the primary key is used in queries. If a PRIMARY KEY constraint is defined on more than one column, values may be duplicated within one column, but each combination of values from all the columns in the PRIMARY KEY constraint definition must be unique.

A *foreign key* is a column or combination of columns used to establish and enforce a link between the data in two tables. A link is created between two tables when a column or combination of columns that hold one table's primary key values is added to the other table. This column becomes a foreign key in the second table. You can create a foreign key by defining a FOREIGN KEY constraint when you create or alter a table.

The table that holds the primary key is referred to as the *parent* table. The table holding the foreign key is known as the *child* table. The connection these two keep is what gives the database referential integrity.

Primary Keys

You can only have one PRIMARY KEY constraint per table. Any column listed in the PRIMARY KEY constraint must, and will, be set to NOT NULL.

The syntax for a PRIMARY KEY constraint with ALTER TABLE:

```
ALTER TABLE table_name
 ADD [CONSTRAINT constraint_name]
  PRIMARY KEY [CLUSTERED|NONCLUSTERED]
   {(column_name[,...n])}
```

Here is how to add a PRIMARY KEY constraint to an existing table. You will add my_PK_column and make it the constraint in my_table. PK_my_PK_column is the name of the constraint. We will not use [CLUSTERED|NONCLUSTERED] for now because it will be discussed in detail on Day 9, "Indexes and Performance." The default value is CLUSTERED:

```
ALTER TABLE my_table
 ADD my_PK_column INT IDENTITY
 CONSTRAINT PK_my_PK_column PRIMARY KEY (my_PK_column)
```

constraint_name can be left blank and a system-generated name will be assigned. Any error within a constraint will list the constraint_name as a reference.

Foreign Keys

A table can have up to 253 FOREIGN KEY constraints, and can reference up to 253 other tables in the FOREIGN KEY constraint. Foreign keys can be linked only to columns that are primary keys or UNIQUE constraints.

The syntax for the FOREIGN KEY constraint with ALTER TABLE is

```
ALTER TABLE table_name
 ADD [CONSTRAINT constraint_name]
   FOREIGN KEY {(column_name[,...n])}
     REFERENCES ref_table [(ref_column_name[,...n])]
```

You can have multicolumn constraints. Each column listed for the child table (foreign key) must have a corresponding column in the parent table (primary key). In the following example, the PRIMARY KEY constraint is built by combining company_ID and customer_ID. This is referenced in the FOREIGN KEY constraint as well. Listing 8.6 creates a database, a couple of tables with columns, and then sets their constraints so that you can get the "big picture."

LISTING 8.6 Creating a Database, Tables, Columns, and Associated Constraints

```
/* Create the database and log */
USE master
GO
CREATE DATABASE Main
ON
(NAME = main_dat,
```

LISTING 8.6 continued

```
 FILENAME = 'c:\mssql\data\maindat.mdf',
 SIZE = 50MB,
 MAXSIZE = 200MB,
 FILEGROWTH = 10MB )
LOG ON
(NAME = main_log,
 FILENAME = 'c:\mssql\data\mainlog.log',
 SIZE = 15MB,
 MAXSIZE = 75MB,
 FILEGROWTH = 5MB )
GO
/* Create the 'customers' and 'orders' tables */
Use main
GO
CREATE TABLE customers
 (company_ID int NOT NULL,
 customer_ID int NOT NULL,
 customer_name varchar(30) NOT NULL)
GO
CREATE TABLE orders
 (comp_ID int NOT NULL,
 cust_ID int NOT NULL,
 order_item int NOT NULL,
 order_descrip varchar(30) NULL,
 item_amount int NOT NULL DEFAULT 1)
GO
/* Set primary key */
Use main
GO
ALTER TABLE customers
 ADD CONSTRAINT PK_comp_cust_ID
 PRIMARY KEY (company_ID, customer_ID)
GO
/* Set foreign key and relationship to primary key */
Use main
GO
ALTER TABLE orders
ADD CONSTRAINT FK_comp_cust_ID
 FOREIGN KEY (comp_ID, cust_ID)
 REFERENCES customers (company_ID, customer_ID)
GO
```

You should notice in this example that the columns in the parent table and the child table have to be related, but the column names do not have to be the same in each table. The only output you will receive is

```
The CREATE DATABASE process is allocating 50.00 MB on disk 'main_dat'.
The CREATE DATABASE process is allocating 15.00 MB on disk 'main_log'.
```

Constraint names follow the same rules for identifiers that databases, tables, columns, and other database objects do. The special rule for constraints is that they cannot start with a # sign.

A table cannot be dropped if it still has a constraint attached. Use `ALTER TABLE DROP CONSTRAINT` in this format:

```
ALTER TABLE table_name
  DROP CONSTRAINT constraint_name
```

Using Declarative Referential Integrity (DRI)

We have talked about the parent and child tables and their links with primary keys and foreign keys. This is referred to as *declarative referential integrity* (DRI).

SQL Server builds a clustered index for the primary key when the primary key constraint is added. Again, we'll get more into indexes on Day 9. A table can reference itself with a DRI constraint. There might be a need to have a foreign key link to a primary key with the same table. The declarative referential integrity on SQL Server allows optional or required foreign key specifications.

Summary

Today you learned about the Data Definition Language (DDL) that is included in every relational database system now available. Using DDL, you can create, alter, and drop databases and tables. When creating or altering these tables, you can add or remove columns or change any of their properties.

You also learned about the importance of setting data types and column constraints to help ensure database integrity. Columns can be set up with specific data types to force the type of data that can be inserted into a column. You can set columns to allow or not allow NULL values. You also saw how primary and foreign keys can be used together to maintain data integrity between tables.

Q&A

Q How will I know what tables, columns, and properties to have for my database?

A Draw a picture of your database to help you see the relationships in the data. Know as much as you can about what you need to accomplish with the database before you even start adding the database and tables. Sample data can often give you ideas about the tables you will need and the constraints on the columns, but in the real world, these aren't set in stone. That's when the `ALTER DATABASE` and `ALTER TABLE` commands come in handy.

Q What's the difference between a primary key and a foreign key?

A The primary key is referenced by a foreign key. The primary key can not be a NULL value. A foreign key can be NULL or it can be linked to the primary key. A table can have multiple foreign keys but only one primary key. By itself, the primary key can maintain data integrity within a table. A foreign key can be linked to a primary key to provide data integrity between tables.

Q What is a unique constraint?

A The unique constraint is exactly like the primary key with a couple of differences. First, you can have multiple unique columns per table. Second, unique columns will allow a NULL value in one row per unique column.

Workshop

The Workshop provides quiz questions to help you solidify your understanding of the material covered and exercises to provide you with experience in using what you've learned. Try to answer the quiz and exercise questions before checking the answers in Appendix A, "Answers to Quizzes and Exercises," and make sure you understand the answers before continuing to the next lesson.

Quiz

1. In the following code, what will the database size be increased to the first time it runs out of allocated space?

```
CREATE DATABASE Customer
  ON
  (NAME = cust_dat,
  FILENAME = 'c:\SQL_Data\custdat.mdf',
  SIZE = 100MB,
  MAXSIZE = 500MB,
  FILEGROWTH = 20MB)
```

2. What would happen if you tried to insert the value `123abc` into a column defined with a data type of `integer`?
3. How many primary keys can you have per table?

Exercises

1. Write the code to create a table with the following columns and specifications:

   Call the new table "`employees2`," and add columns for peoples' names as `first`, `middle`, and `last`; allow NULLS for the middle name only.
2. Now write the code to add a four-digit, numbers-only column called `emp_number` to the table in exercise 1.

WEEK 2

DAY 9

Indexes and Performance

So far, you have learned how to use T-SQL to access and manipulate data in your SQL Server database. In Day 8, "Defining Data," you were introduced to the Data Definition Language, or DDL, which is used for creating and modifying the definitions and structures of the tables used in a database. What we haven't looked at yet, is how to make your database perform better. There are many database programmers who have spent years working with SQL without any real understanding of how the SQL Server works or what decisions it makes for them.

However, in these days of ever growing databases, you are required to write faster, more efficient application systems. To do this, you need to know more about how the server processes queries. Today, we are going to develop an understanding of the different types of indexes available to you in SQL Server, and then see how the server uses them to optimize query performance. Some of the topics that are going to be covered are

- Index types
- Creating indexes
- Taking a brief look at optimization
- Using performance tools

How SQL Server Uses Indexes

Indexes are used to provide fast access to data. An index in a database is much like an index in a book. When you are looking for a specific topic in a book, you would use the index to find the page or pages where the topic is located. In a database, when you are looking for a specific row of data in a table, SQL Server uses an index to find where that row is physically located. There are two main differences between a book index and one that exists in SQL Server. First, with a book, you decide whether or not to use the book index. This option does not exist in SQL Server. The database system itself decides whether to use an existing index or not. Second, a book index is edited together with the book and does not change after the book has been printed. This means that each topic is exactly where the index says it is on the page. In contrast, a SQL Server index changes every time the data referenced in the index is modified.

There is one other method for accessing data in a database table, which is called sequential access. *Sequential access* means that each row of data is retrieved and examined in sequence and returned in the result set if the condition in the `WHERE` clause is true. All the rows in the table are read according to their physical position in the table. (Sequential access is sometimes called a *table scan.*)

Using an index to access the data is the preferred method for accessing tables with many rows. By using an index, SQL Server will usually take only a few I/O operations to find any row within a table, in a very short time. Sequential access, on the other hand, requires much more time to find a row in the table.

Why Use Indexes?

If you haven't already figured it out, indexes speed up the processing of your SQL query. There are really three main reasons for SQL Server to make use of an index. These are

- Organizing data
- Improving performance of all data retrieval and data modification queries
- Enforcing uniqueness of data

To see this, we are going to look at the different types of indexes that SQL Server uses, how the data is organized within them, and how the server uses them to improve performance. When you create a table, SQL Server will create it without adding any indexes to the table. The reason for this omission is that unless you specify a primary key or unique constraint (these will be discussed later in this lesson), the table is created with no indexes. Every time a query references this table, the server has no choice but to examine every row to find the required data using tables scan.

As an example, if you were to submit the following query to an orders table with no indexes, the server would perform a table scan to determine which rows meet the criteria:

```
Select Count(*)
From [Order Detail]
Where Quantity > 50 and
      ProductID = 41
```

As the server reads each page of data into memory and retrieves a row, it inspects the values for `quantity` and `productID`, to determine which rows should be included in the final result set.

It doesn't matter if 10 rows or 1 million rows are returned. Without an index, the server must inspect every row in the table to build the result set.

This increased performance does come with a cost. Tables that have indexes require more storage space in the database. In addition, any commands that insert, update, or delete data can take longer and require more processing to maintain the indexes. When designing and creating an index, you should make sure that the performance benefits you get outweigh the extra cost.

Understanding Optimization

Optimization is the process of selecting the best access path for resolving a SQL query. To understand what this means, let's look at what the server does when it processes a SQL query. When you execute a query, SQL Server performs the following four-step process:

1. Parse—SQL Server verifies the syntax of the SQL query and all the objects referenced in it.
2. Optimize—SQL Server chooses how to execute the query.
3. Compile—An executable module or plan is created.
4. Execute—The compiled module or plan is executed by SQL Server.

In step 2 of this process, the server will make several decisions regarding how the query should be processed and which if any indexes will be used to enable the query to run more efficiently. Now that you have seen the different types of indexes and how SQL Server actually uses them when executing a query, we will take a look at how the process of optimization really works.

Understanding that SQL Server decides when and where to use indexes to optimize the execution of a query will be the hardest thing for you to do. As we look at the decision process, you will see how it is affected by the data you are accessing. You will see that the server is far more flexible and efficient over time than you could be when writing the actual SQL code.

Remember, that the server is seldom wrong about which path is the most efficient when retrieving data, but this increase in efficiency brings with it a loss of control to the programmer.

To decide how to optimize a query, SQL Server uses a method called *cost-based optimization*. This means that the server will focus on the cost (in terms of the physical resources needed—disk and memory reads) of performing a query using a certain plan. The optimization process itself consists of the following four steps:

1. Find the current Search ARGuments (SARGs).
2. Match the SARGs to one or more indexes.
3. Estimate the work required by the server to resolve the query using each of the identified indexes (as well as without using an index).
4. Choose the most effective way to resolve the query from the list of indexes or table search found by the server as described in the previous 3 steps.

The following example demonstrates how the optimization process works:

```
Use northwind
select count(*) as 'Count',
       sum(Quantity) as 'Total Sold'
From [Order Details]
Where orderid between 10250 and 10700
      and ProductID like '6%'
```

Finding the SARGs

SQL Server will first try to find the elements of a query that will allow the server to use an index. These are the search arguments, or SARGs.

A *SARG* is the portion of a `WHERE` clause that contains the actual condition in the form of

```
<column name> <operator> <constant | expression>
```

An example of this is

```
orderid between 10250 and 10700
```

Only SARGs can take advantage of indexes.

Whenever possible, you should use constants instead of expressions or variables in the `WHERE` clause to increase the use of indexes.

Also, try not to use functions with columns in a `WHERE` clause. Of course, there will be many times when you must use functions and expressions. SQL Server will do its best to optimize the query.

Getting back to our original example, there are two SARGs that the server will use to locate an index. These are the `BETWEEN` and `LIKE` keywords that were discussed on Day 2, "Filtering and Sorting Data."

Matching the SARGs to Available Indexes

The next step is for the server to look for any indexes that might be useful for the query. Each column that is referenced by a SARG might have one or more relevant indexes. For our example, the server finds two candidate indexes, one for each SARG.

An index is used only if one of the search arguments is the `First` column in the index. Most programmers expect that an index will be effective for a query because a column is included in an index. This, of course, is not true unless that column is the `First` column.

Estimating the Work Using Each Index

In order for the server to estimate the work needed to perform a query, it checks several of the statistics about the table and the indexes. First, it determines how many pages and rows are in the table. Second, it looks in a *distribution page* for each index to determine about how many rows will fit the condition for each SARG.

NEW TERM An index has a *distribution page* that enables the server to estimate the selectivity of a `WHERE` clause. These pages allow the server to quickly scan the values contained in the index and determine exactly how many rows might match the condition.

The distribution page statistics are set up one time, when the index is created. There is no automatic method to get SQL Server to rebuild the information on the distribution page. On a periodic basic, someone (probably the database administrator) should execute the following statement for every table in the database.

```
Update Statistics <table name>
```

When executing this command, the process might take a while to complete when run on larger tables. You should plan to do this work after hours, when the tables are not being used.

Using the distribution page, the server would determine that about 9% of the table's rows matched the `WHERE` clause conditions. A table itself might contain more than 500,000 rows on 9,572 pages. If a clustered index on the `OrderID` is used, on the same percentage, it might find about 10,567 rows on approximately 425 pages. Finally, if a nonclustered index on the ProductID is used, the server might find 975 rows on about 1000 pages.

The numbers used in this example are completely fictional and do not represent actual values in the `Northwind` database.

Choosing the Optimal Way to Resolve the Query

The server will use the statistics calculated in the previous step to decide on the most efficient approach. In addition to the index methods, the cost of performing the query with a table scan is also considered. Based on this information, the server does a comparison of estimated cost, as shown in Table 9.1.

TABLE 9.1 Comparing the Estimated Costs for Each Method

Execution Method	*Estimated Cost*
Table scan	9,572 pages
Clustered index on OrderID	425 pages
Nonclustered index on ProductID	1,000 pages

Although the nonclustered index approach is less costly than a table scan, the clustered index scan is the fastest method to use for this query.

Of course, this is a very simple overview of how the server determines the best way to execute a query, and which index or indexes to use. In the remaining sections of this lesson, we will be learning about the different indexes available, how to create them, and how to use the tools provided in SQL Server 2000 to enhance their performance.

Understanding Clustered and Nonclustered Indexes

There are two main types of indexes used by the server to organize data: clustered and nonclustered. A *clustered index* sorts the actual rows of data by the index key specified, whereas a *nonclustered index* creates a separate, sorted list of keys that contains pointer to the actual rows in the table.

Clustered Indexes

A clustered index actually determines the physical order of the data in a table. Only a single clustered index is allowed per table in SQL Server because the rows of data in the table cannot be physically ordered more than one way. If you define a primary key for a table when you create it, a clustered index is automatically created for that table.

The first thing that the server does when you create a clustered index is to sort the existing rows in the order specified in the clustered index. If you created an index for last name on a telephone directory, the server would automatically re-sort all the rows in the directory by the values in the last name column. If you then dropped that index, and created a new clustered index based on the telephone number, the server would again re-sort the table. Although the system or database administrator controls most index maintenance, everyone who might perform maintenance on an index should be aware of some of the maintenance issues associated with indexes. Some of these questions are

- How often should the indexes be rebuilt to remove fragmentation?
- How long does it take to re-sort the data on a large table?
- Can presorting the data before loading it speed up the creation of the index?

The clustered index on OrderID forces SQL Server to sort the table by OrderID and to maintain that sort throughout any other operations that might be performed on that table. Figure 9.1 shows the first level of the clustered index on Order Details. After sorting the rows by the index key (`orderID`), the server will build the index by recording the first value of orderID on each data page, along with a pointer to that page. In the figure, the orderID value on the first page in the table (page 7420) is 17. The first value on the first page of the clustered index is also 17. The row in the index includes a pointer value to the page number in the table.

Note

> In SQL Server 2000, a page is defined as an 8kb area of storage that is used both on disk and in memory to contain rows of data in a SQL table and index.
>
> Depending on the size of a row of data, many rows can fit into one page of storage. As an example, if your data row is 200 bytes, then you would be able to fit 40 rows on one page.

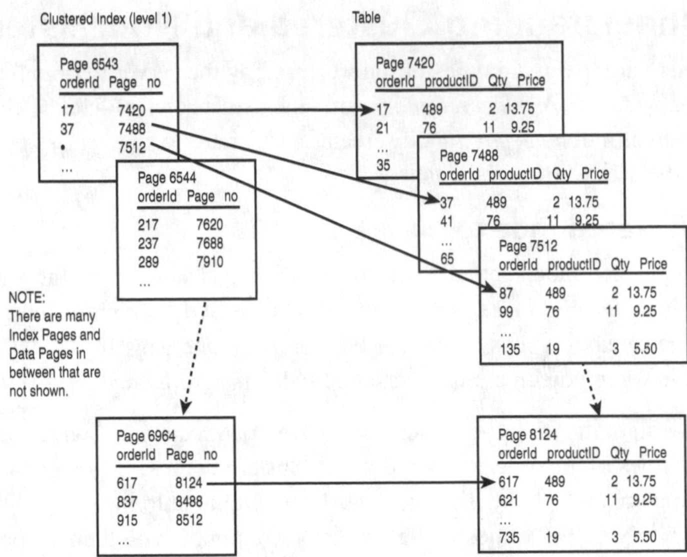

FIGURE 9.1
An Order Detail table and its Level 1 clustered index.

Because the data in the table is already sorted by orderID, the server does not need to store a pointer to each row to know what values are on each page. Because of this, the number of rows in the first level of a clustered index is dramatically lower than the number of rows in a table.

Clustered indexes use several levels to reduce the amount of searching the server must perform to find a particular set of data. Figure 9.2 displays the rest of the structure for the clustered index. Level 1 includes one row per page which is faster to search than the actual data pages. The server continues to generate additional index levels until it is able to store pointers to all the pages at the next index level on a single page, which is called the root page.

The *root page* is the index page where all the rows in a single index level are stored. Almost all index-based searches will start at the root page.

To understand how a clustered index really works, let's consider how the server actually uses the index to resolve the following query.

```
Select ProductID
From [Order Details]
Where OrderId = 10260
```

Using the index shown in Figure 9.2, the server looks at the root page to see where the value 41 falls. You can see that it is between the first entry and the second entry on the page. The server uses the page pointer 6543 to find the right page at the next level of the index, Again, it decides the 41 would fall between the second and the third entries on that page, so it follows the chain for 41 to page 7488, which is the table itself.

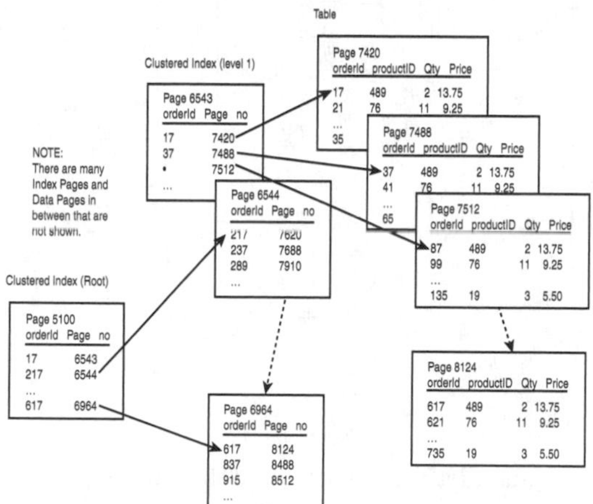

FIGURE 9.2

A Level 3 clustered index structure.

After the server has found the correct page, it will scan each row on the page. As soon as a row is retrieved that has a value that does not match 41, the server will stop the search immediately. As you can see in the previous example shown in Figure 9.2, the server scanned two index pages and one table page to retrieve the data.

> **Note**
>
> To give you an idea of how this all saves time for the server, a clustered index on a 1 billion-row table that has a 4-byte key will only have six levels in the index.

Nonclustered Indexes

A nonclustered index is a bit different from the clustered index. Remember that you can only have one clustered index on a table because of this restriction; a nonclustered index will build a separate table of key values. When you create a nonclustered index, the server always starts by building a sorted list of the values in the specified index column, with page and row pointers to each value. Figure 9.3 displays a completed nonclustered index.

You can see that the diagram looks almost the same as a clustered index. The only real difference is that the leaf or final level of the nonclustered index contains one row for each row in the table.

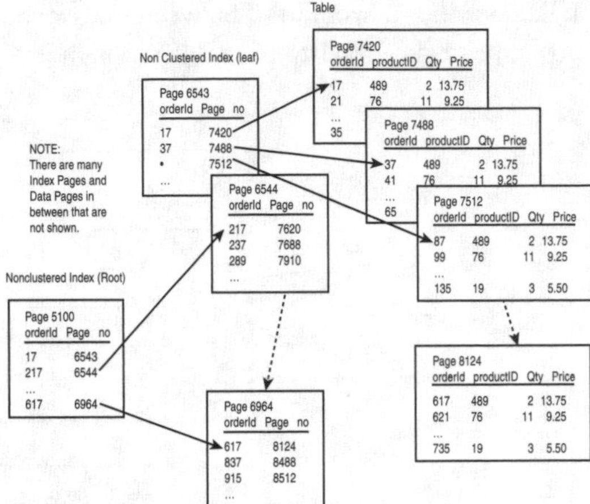

FIGURE 9.3
Data and index levels of a nonclustered index.

Using the following query, let's take a quick look at the search process using the nonclustered index.

```
Select count(*)
From [Order Details]
Where productID = 21
```

The server starts at the root page of the index, and then follows the chain to pages 6543 and 7420. Page 7420 displays the values for the productID value, 21.

Here is where the real difference between a clustered and nonclustered index becomes clear. Instead of going to a single page in the table and doing a table scan for occurrences of productID 21, the server scans the index leaf page, reading one data page per row on the index leaf page.

You are probably asking yourself, "How do I know which type of index to use?" The following list can help you to answer that question.

- Clustered indexes are best at range searches, mostly for larger quantities of data.
- Clustered indexes are most likely to help with a query requesting sorted data.
- Nonclustered indexes are almost as fast as clustered indexes at finding a single row of data.
- Nonclustered indexes enable the server to use an index containing all the columns required to resolve the query without accessing the table itself. This can run substantially faster than a query accessing a table, even with a clustered index.

Understanding Unique Indexes

A unique index ensures that the indexed column contains no duplicate values. In the case of multicolumn unique indexes, the index ensures that each combination of values in the indexed column is unique. For example, if a unique index *fullname* is created on a combination of *lname*, and *fname* columns, no two people could have the same full name in the table.

Both clustered and nonclustered indexes can be unique. Therefore, provided that the data in the column is unique, you can create both a unique clustered index and nonclustered indexes on the same table. Specifying a unique index makes sense only when uniqueness is a characteristic of the data itself. If uniqueness must be enforced to ensure data integrity, create a `UNIQUE` or `PRIMARY KEY` constraint on the column, rather than a unique index.

Creating a `PRIMARY KEY` or `UNIQUE` constraint will automatically create a unique index on the specified columns in the table.

Indexing Computed Columns

A computed column is nothing more than a column in a table that is used to store the result of a computation of a table's data. The following example shows the creation of a table with computed columns:

```
Create Table OrderDemo (
    Orderid Int Not Null,
    Price Money Not Null,
    Qty Int Not Null,
    SaleTotal AS Price * qty,
    OrderDate DateTime Not Null,
    ShippedDate AS Dateadd(DAY,7,OrderDate))
```

You can see that this table contains two computed columns; `SaleTotal` and `ShippedDate`. They are both computed using other columns in the table.

New to SQL Server 2000, you can now define indexes on a computed column if the following conditions are true:

- The computed column must always return the same result for a given set of inputs.
- The result value of the computed column cannot evaluate to a text or image data type.

Forcing Index Selection

One of the last topics I want to discuss is how to tell the server which index to use. Take a look at the following example:

```
Use pubs
Select count(*) as 'Count',
       sum(qty) as 'Total Sold'
```

```
From Sales
Where Stor_id between 6000 and 7000
and   Title_id like 'PS2%'
```

Normally, SQL Server chooses to use the clustered index that is defined for the `Sales` table. If you wanted to override that choice, you would specify an optimizer hint by using the following syntax in the `FROM` clause:

```
From Sales (index = <index name>)
```

This will tell the server the actual index you want to use instead of what was selected.

Defining and Managing Indexes

Now that you have seen what indexes are and what they can do for the performance of your SQL queries, you will learn how to create and maintain any indexes on your database. Before you start creating indexes, you need to consider where you need indexes and on which columns. In addition, you also must decide whether to use clustered or nonclustered indexes. When considering whether to create an index on a column, you should consider whether and how an indexed column is going to be used in a query. What follows are some suggestions in deciding if indexes are useful in a query:

- Searches for rows that match a specific search key value (an exact match query). An exact match comparison is one in which the query uses the `WHERE` statement to specify a column entry with a given value.
- Searches for rows with search key values in a range of values (a range query). A range query is one in which the query specifies any entry whose value is between two values.
- Searches for rows in a table that, based on a join predicate, match a row in another table.
- Queries that produce sorted query output without an explicit sort operation.
- Queries that scan rows in a sorted order to permit an order-based operation, such as a merge join.
- Queries that scan all rows in a table with better performance than a table scan because of the reduced column set and overall data volume to be scanned.
- Searches for duplicates of new search key values in insert and update operations, to enforce `PRIMARY KEY` and `UNIQUE` constraints.
- Searches for matching rows between two tables, for which a `FOREIGN KEY` constraint is defined.

In the following sections, you will learn how to create an index and then how to set up automatic maintenance of an index.

Creating an Index

After you have determined what indexes you want, they can be created on the tables in a database. As you have probably figured out by now, this can be done is several different ways. The first way is to use the DDL SQL code to create a SQL script that will define an index on a table. The `CREATE INDEX` statement is used to create an index. The following is the syntax for this statement:

```
CREATE [UNIQUE] [CLUSTERED | NONCLUSTERED] INDEX <index name>
    ON [table name | view name]
       (column name [ASC | DESC] [,..n])
[WITH
    [PAD_INDEX | FILLFACTOR = fillfactor]
    [[,] IGNORE_DUP_KEY]
    [[,] DROP_EXISTING]
    [[,] STATISTICS_NORECOMPUTE]
    [[,] SORT_IN_TEMPDB]]
[ON filegroup]
```

Table 9.2 lists each argument and its description.

TABLE 9.2 Defining the `CREATE INDEX` Statement

Argument	*Description*
`UNIQUE`	Specifies that no duplicates are allowed for this index. The default is nonunique, and duplicate index entries are allowed.
`CLUSTERED`	Specifies that the data itself will be physically sorted. Clustered index values must be unique.
`NONCLUSTERED`	Specifies that an index will be created as a completely separate object. This is the default type of index.
Index name	Specifies the unique name for an index.
Table name	Specifies the name of the table that contains the columns you want to index.
View name	Specifies the name of the view that contains the columns you want to index.
Column name	Specifies the name of the column or columns to be indexed. An index can be created with up to 16 columns.
ASC|DESC	Indicates whether the column is to be sorted in ascending or descending order. Ascending is the default.
Filegroup	Specifies the name of the filegroup on which the index should be created. If it is not specified, the index is created on the default filegroup.

To create an index on the `Employees` table in the Northwind database, you could use the following SQL statement:

Don't try to actually execute this statement on the database. The `Employees` table already has a clustered index defined to it. You will receive an error from the server telling you that the index already exists.

```
CREATE UNIQUE CLUSTERED
  INDEX [PK_Employees] ON [dbo].[Employees] ([EmployeeID])
WITH
    DROP_EXISTING
ON [PRIMARY]
```

As you will see, the `CREATE INDEX` statement is a little more difficult to work with than the next two methods you will look at.

Creating an Index Using the Index Wizard

The Index Wizard in the Enterprise Manager will walk you through the process of creating an index on an existing table. To access the wizard, start the Enterprise Manager, and then either select Tools, Wizards from the menu, or click the Run a Wizard button. (Both are shown in Figure 9.4.)

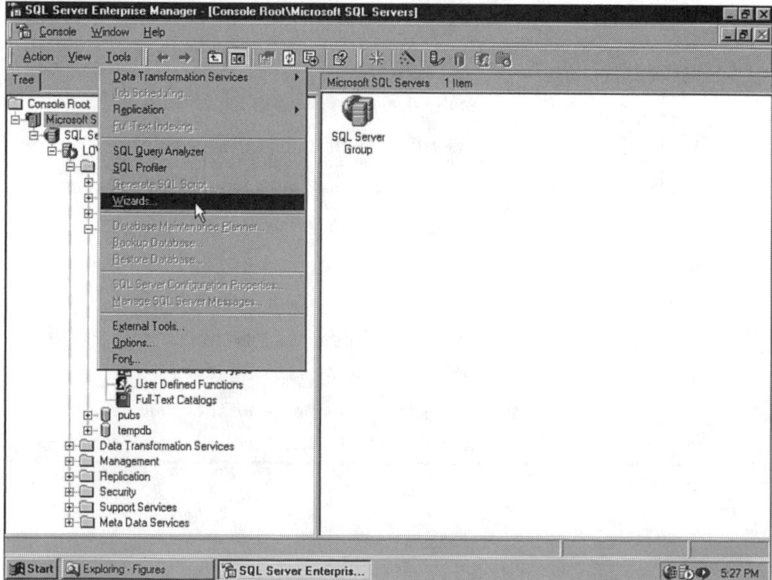

FIGURE 9.4
Starting the Index Wizard.

Next, open the Database folder and click the Create Index Wizard. This will display the Welcome to the Create Index dialog form. Click the Next button to continue to the Select Database and Table dialog as shown in Figure 9.5.

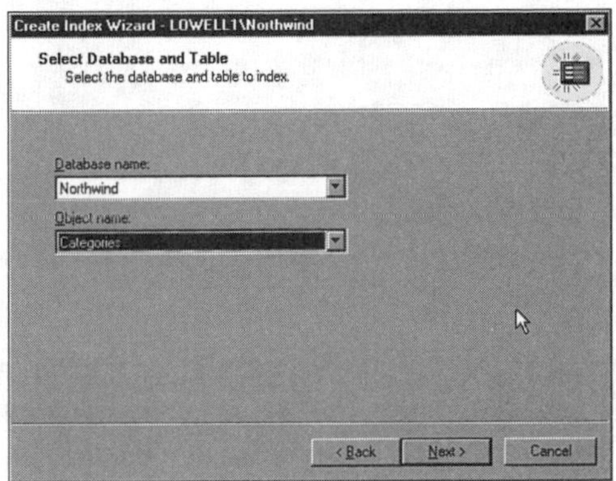

FIGURE 9.5

Selecting the database and table to create an index on.

For this example, select the `Northwind` database and the `Employees` table, and then click Next to continue. The next dialog (see Figure 9.6) will display the current indexes on the selected table. This enables you to check whether the index you are creating already exists for this table.

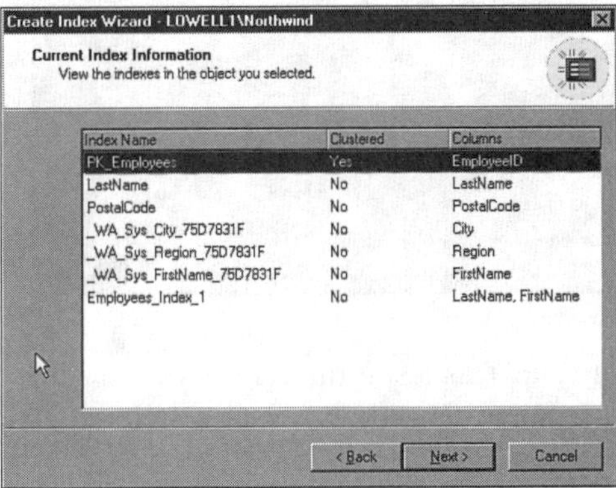

FIGURE 9.6

Verifying the existing table indexes.

If you do not see an existing index that satisfies your requirements, click Next to continue on to the creation process. Figure 9.7 enables you to select the columns you want in the index. In addition, you can specify the sort order for each column.

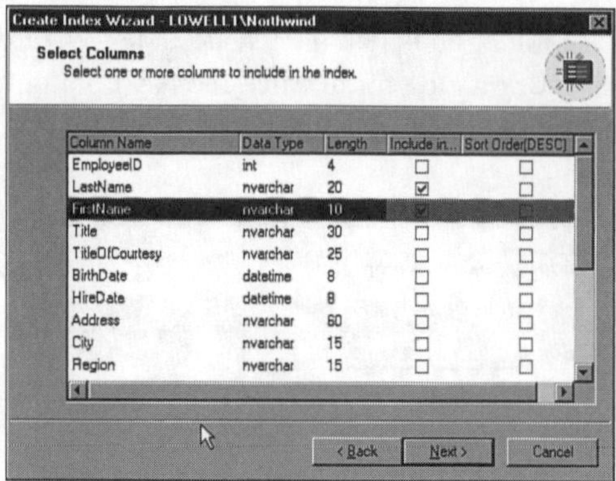

FIGURE 9.7
Selecting the columns for an index.

For our sample index, select the `FirstName` and `LastName` columns as shown. Then click Next to continue. The next dialog (see Figure 9.8) enables you to specify the options you want for the index. Because there is already a clustered index, you can click Next to bypass this form.

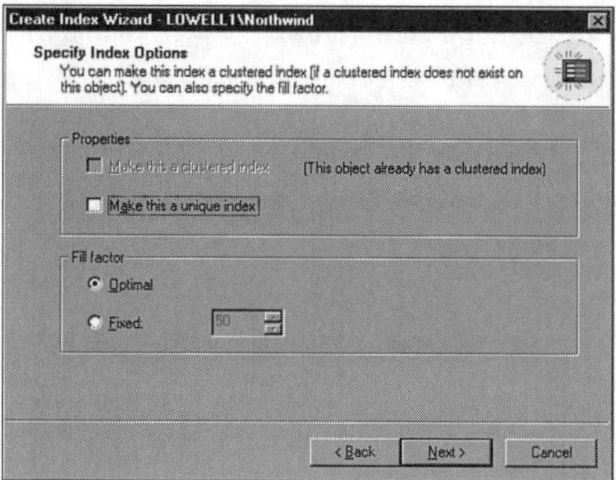

FIGURE 9.8
Specifying the options for an index.

You are in the home stretch. This last form enables you to name the index and specify the order in which the columns you selected will be indexed, as shown in Figure 9.9.

Click the Finish button to complete the process and add the index to the table in the database. To view the indexes for the table, open the Query Analyzer, the Northwind database folder, the Employees folder, and, finally, the indexes folder. You will see the new index that was just created (see Figure 9.10).

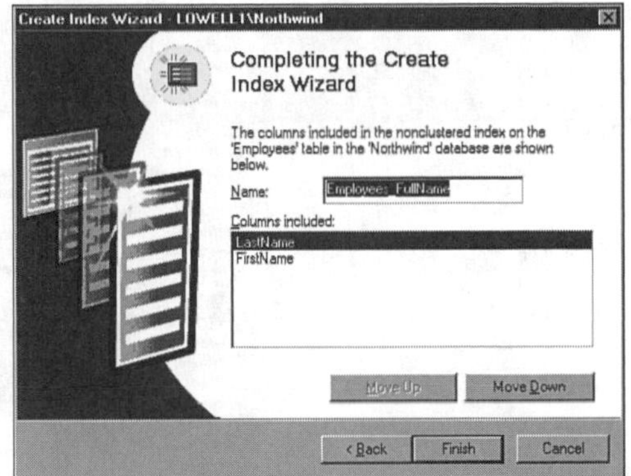

FIGURE 9.9

Naming and ordering the index.

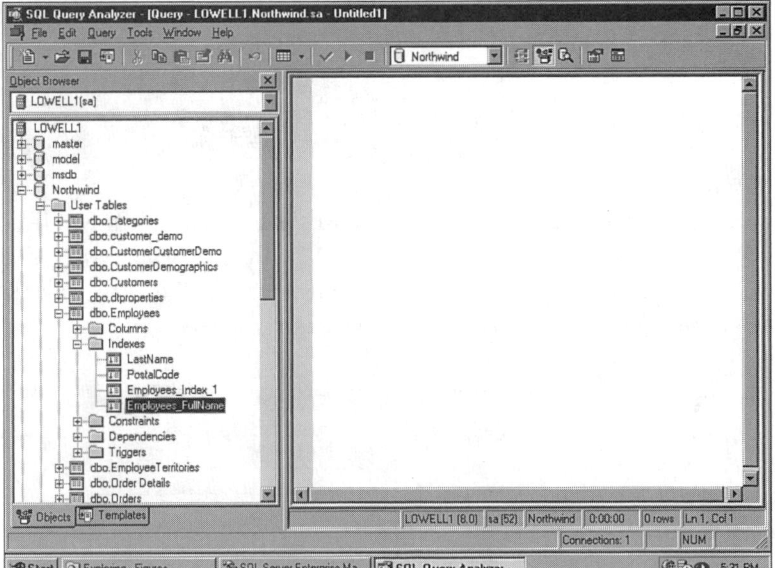

FIGURE 9.10

Displaying indexes in Query Analyzer.

Creating an Index in Enterprise Manager

Besides creating an index using the Index Wizard or the `CREATE INDEX` statement, you have a third way of performing this task. From Enterprise Manager, you can right-click the table that you want to add the index to and select All Tasks, Manage Indexes from the pop-up menu as shown in Figure 9.11.

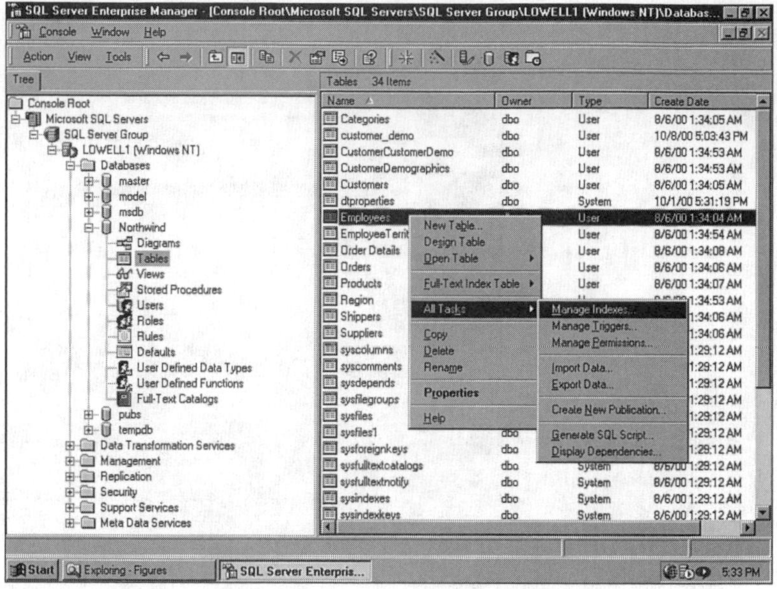

FIGURE 9.11

Select Manage Indexes in Enterprise Manager to either modify an existing index or create a new one.

This will display the Manage Indexes dialog. This form will list all the current indexes for the selected table (see Figure 9.12). To modify an existing index, select the desired index and click the Edit button at the bottom of the form. To create a new index, simply click the New button to start the creation process.

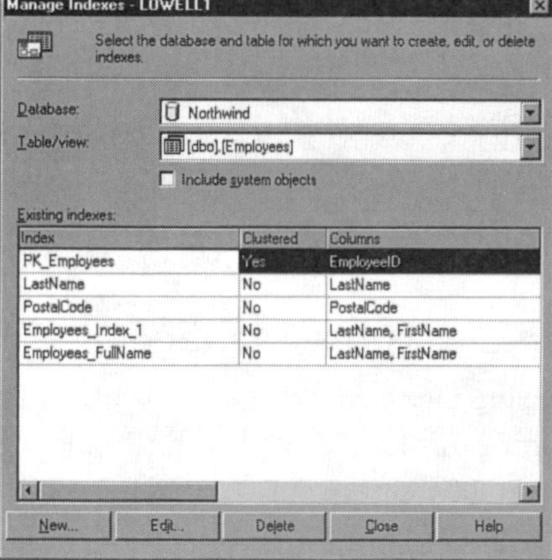

FIGURE 9.12

Existing Indexes list is displayed by the Manage Indexes dialog.

You can see that when you have this form open, you can change either the database you are working in, or the table you want to add an index to, using the two drop-down selection boxes at the top of the form. Let us create another new index for the `Employees` table. To start, click the New button to display the Create New Index dialog as shown in Figure 9.13.

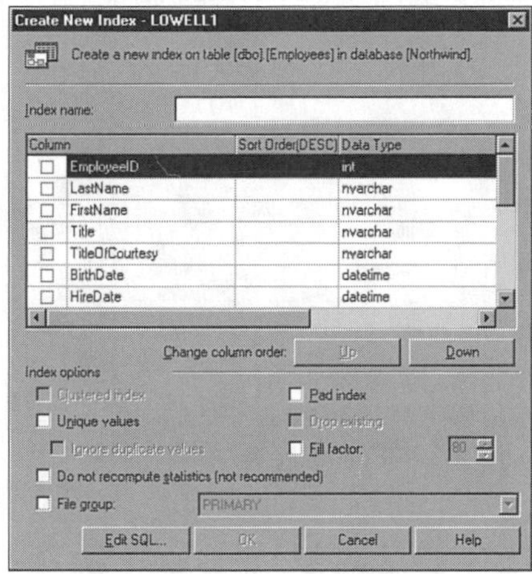

FIGURE 9.13

Creating a new index is as simple as filling in the blanks.

To create the index, enter the name of the index and then select the columns you want to include in the index as shown in Figure 9.14. On this same form, you can also change the order in which the columns are indexed using the Up and Down buttons.

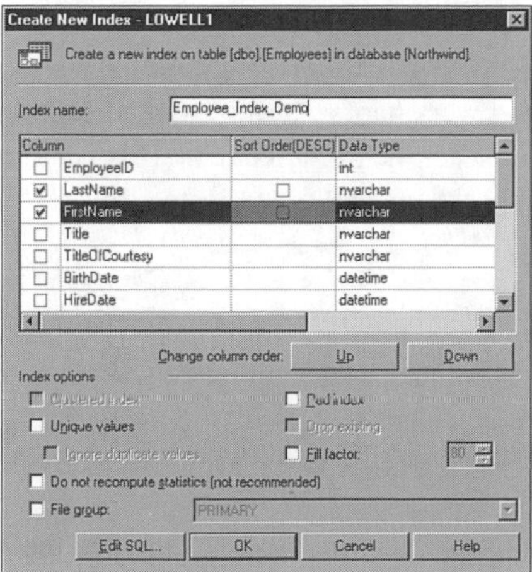

FIGURE 9.14

Defining the new index.

You should notice the Edit SQL button at the bottom of this form. This enables you to view and/or modify the actual SQL that will be used to create the index. Figure 9.15 shows the Edit SQL dialog. You can execute the `CREATE INDEX` statement right here, or close this form and click OK to have SQL Server do it for you automatically.

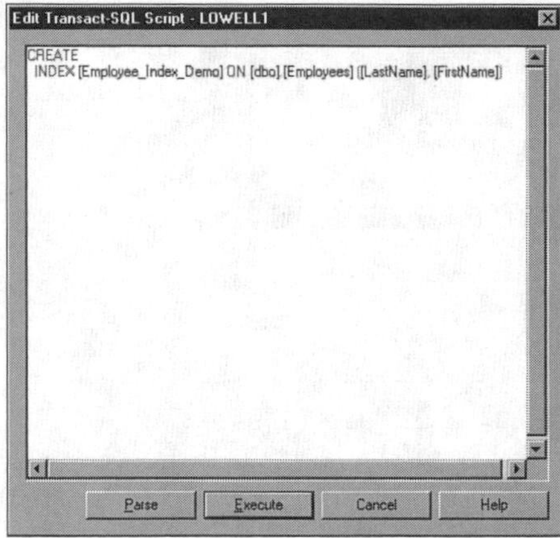

FIGURE 9.15

Working with the generated SQL for the `CREATE INDEX` *definition you have just created.*

After the Create New Index form is closed, you will see the new index appear in the Existing Index list.

Using Full-Text Indexing

As you have already seen in the previous lessons in this book, the `WHERE` clause enables you to reduce the amount of data returned from your database. By defining conditions in the `WHERE` clause, the server will then select the required rows of data from the database. However, when you use the `CONTAIN` keyword to look for a selection of text in a larger text column, the server must work harder. It must look at each value in the specified text column and then scan the text for the specified text. This is a time-consuming task. In SQL Server 2000, you now have the ability to create a full-text index on any text column in a table.

This feature is installed by default unless you are running SQL Server on Windows 9x.

This feature is only possible because Microsoft has merged the Microsoft Index Server technology into SQL Server 2000. In addition, it also requires that the Microsoft Search service is running. (This is also installed and started as the default if you installed full-text indexing.) Finally, it requires a unique index be created on each table you want to use full-text indexing with.

> **Caution**
>
> Only the owner of the table can create a full-text index on it.

There can be only one full-text index on a table, and the index itself is stored outside of SQL Server (in `\mssql\FTData`). Unlike normal indexes, a full-text index does not update itself. After you create the index, it remains static unless you schedule a job to update it. (You will see how to do this in the next section.)

Creating a full-text index is a little different from creating a normal index. First, there is no DDL statement that you can use to create the index. However, there is a wizard available in the Enterprise Manager to take you through the process (of course!).

To start the wizard, in the Enterprise Manager, select the table for which you want to create the full-text index. You then have three ways of starting the actual wizard:

1. Right-click the table and select Full-Text Index Table, Define Full-Text Indexing on a Table from the pop-up menus.
2. Select Full-Text Indexing from the Tools menu.
3. Click the Wizard button on the Toolbar, open the Database folder, and click Full-Text Index Wizard.

For this example, I will be using the PUBS database table, `Pub_Info`. (This table contains a book title as a text data type column.) Although you can create indexes on columns with a data type of `varchar`, you cannot create one on a `text` data type. After you have started the wizard, click Next to bypass the intro form. The form shown in Figure 9.16 enables you to select the unique index to associate with this full-text index.

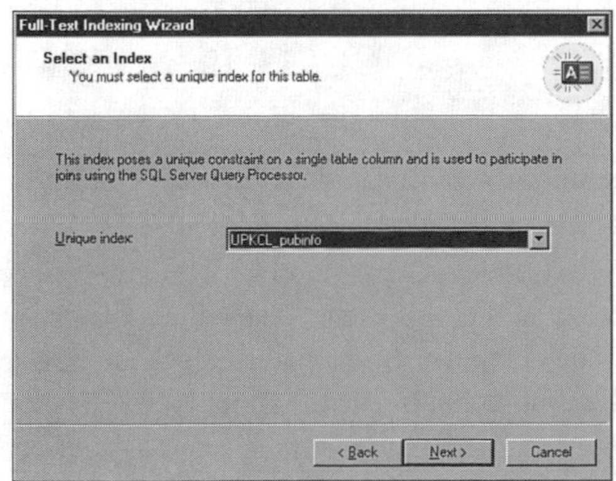

FIGURE 9.16

Specifying the unique index to be associated with the full-text index for the table.

Select the unique index you want to use from the drop-down list. (There should be only one in the `Pubs_info` table.) Click Next to select the columns to index as shown in Figure 9.17.

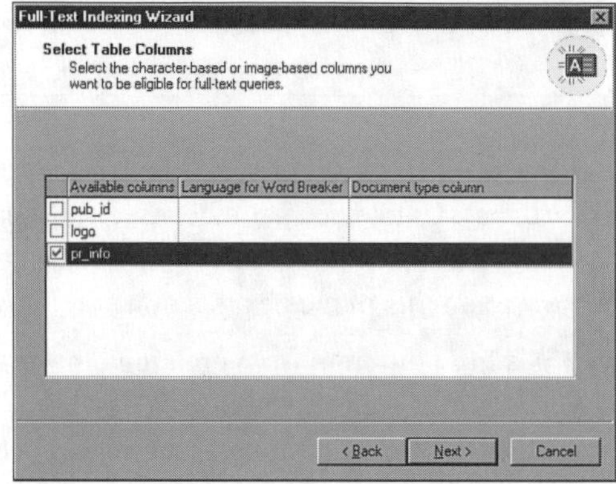

FIGURE 9.17
Selecting the table columns you want to index.

Select the `pr_info` column (this is the only text data type in the table) by clicking the box in front of the column name. The other options on the form are new features of SQL Server 2000. They enable you to index documents that have document filters available. An example would be a Microsoft Word document. You can even specify the language of the document. Click Next to select a catalog for the index as shown in Figure 9.18.

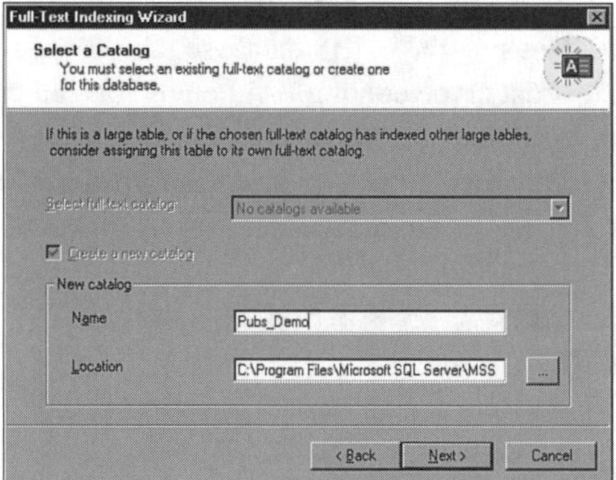

FIGURE 9.18
Selecting a catalog to store the index in.

If this is your first full-text index, then you probably do not have a catalog defined. Enter a name for a new catalog and, if you want, change the location of where you want to physically place it on the computer. If you had catalogs already created, you could have selected them from the drop-down list on the form. Now, click Next to display the

optional schedules dialog. We are going to cover scheduling these tasks in the next section, so for now, just click Next to bypass this form. Click Finish to enable the wizard to perform the process of creating the full-text index. Figure 9.19 will be displayed when this process is completed. However, it also reports that your full-text index has yet to be populated.

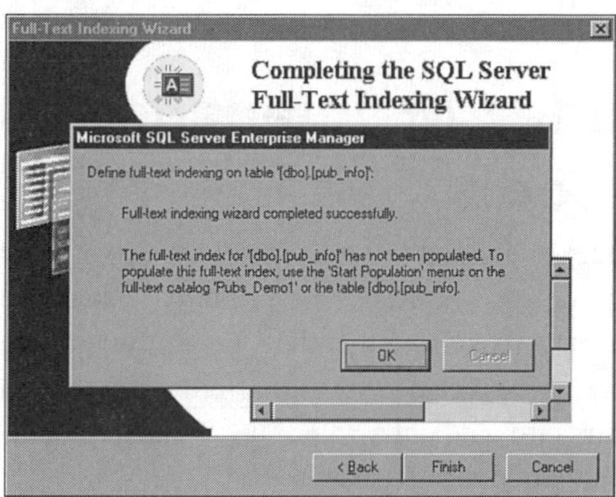

FIGURE 9.19
The completion dialog from the wizard.

To populate the index manually, open the Pubs database, if it is not open, and then select Full-Text Catalogs. Now, right-click the catalog you just created (it should be displayed in the right pane), and select Start Full Population from the pop-up menu as shown in Figure 9.20.

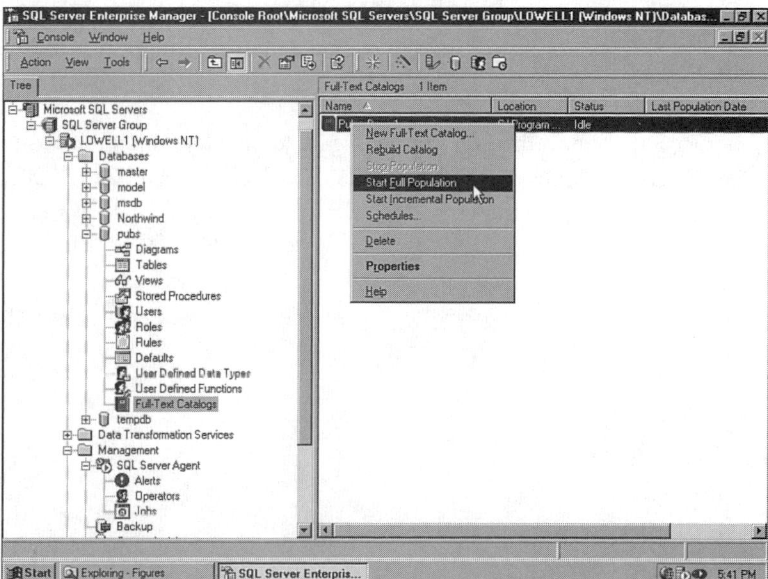

FIGURE 9.20
Starting the population process for your new full-text index.

Congratulations! You have just created and populated the index and can now query against it. The following example shows a simple query using the full-text index:

```
use pubs
Select pub_id,
       substring(pr_info,1,50) as pr_info_50
From Pub_info
Where Contains (pr_info, 'sample')
```

Performing Index Maintenance and Using Performance Tools

Now that you have indexes defined for the tables in your database, the next step is to see how to maintain them. Because indexes are constantly changing, their structure must be inspected every so often to make sure that they are still working efficiently. In addition, you have also learned how to create two very different types of indexes. The first type includes the indexes that are contained within the SQL Server, and the second includes the full-text indexes that are outside of the server.

In this section, you will learn how to use several of the tools available in SQL Server 2000 to investigate how the indexes are performing. In addition, you will see how to set up automatic, scheduled maintenance for both of these index types.

Full-Text Indexing Scheduling

To maintain a full-text index, two separate tasks must be performed. These are

- Populating the catalog where the index is stored
- Populating the index that is defined on the table

To add a job to the SQL Server Agent to populate the index, right-click the table in Enterprise Manager, display the table properties form, and then click the Schedules tab to display the form shown in Figure 9.21. If there are any tasks already scheduled, they will be listed here.

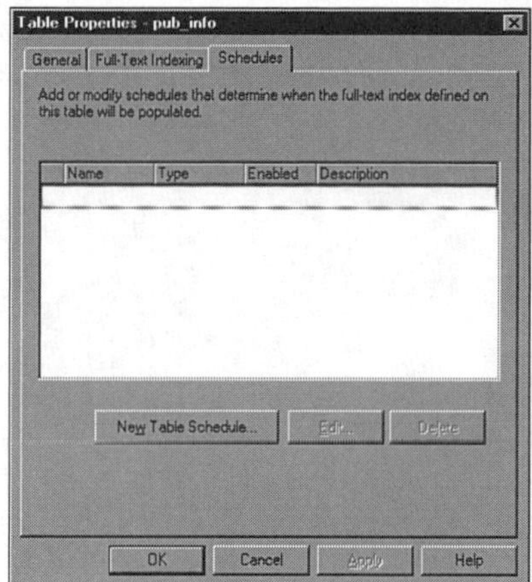

FIGURE 9.21

Defining a scheduled task for a table's full-text index.

Click the New Table Schedule button to display the form shown in Figure 9.22. On this form, enter a name for this job and then specify the update you want performed. Finally, enter the frequency of when you want to run this job.

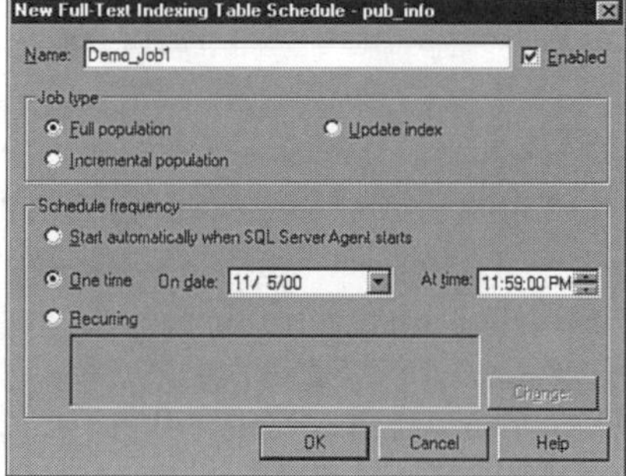

FIGURE 9.22

Defining a new job to SQL Server Agent.

When you are satisfied with your entries, click OK to finish the definition. Now that you have added a job for the table, you also want to add one for the catalog. Highlight the Full-Text Catalogs for the Pubs database, and then right-click the catalog and select schedules from the pop-up menu. This will display the form shown in Figure 9.23. As you can see, it is the same form displayed when you started to add a schedule for the table. In fact, you should see the job you previously added in this list.

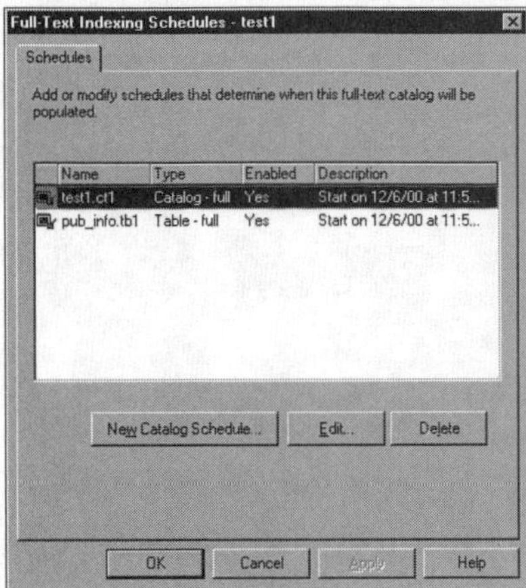

FIGURE 9.23
Displaying the jobs defined for the full-text index on the `pub_info` *table.*

When you click the New Catalog Schedule button, you will see the same definition form that was used for the table. Complete this form the same way and click the OK button.

Now, the SQL Server Agent will run these jobs at the times you have specified. This will keep your full-text index current with the information in the table, taking into account any updates, deletes, or inserts that might have been performed.

Using Server Statistics

SQL Server can record statistical information about your data and store this information in a special object in the database. This object, which I will call a *statistics object*, contains information about how the data is distributed throughout each table and also calculates the average number of duplicates for the indexed columns. When you create an index, if any data exists in the table, a statistics blob will be created and populated with information about the columns that you are indexing. If you create an index on a table and then add the data, and did not turn off the recording of the statistics, a statistics blob will be created for you. If you have turned off the recording of the statistics about an index, this statistics blob won't be created. SQL Server used this information to determine the proper index to use for any given query. The more current the statistics, the better job SQL Server will do selecting the proper index.

To turn these automatic statistics off or on, you would use the following system stored procedure:

```
Sp_Autostats <table name>, 'Off' | 'On'
```

If you want to know the last time that the statistics were recorded, you can use the function STATS_DATE() as shown in the following example:

```
use pubs
declare @tabid int
declare @indid int
select @tabid = object_id('titles')
select @indid = 2  /* non clustered index */
Select Stats_date(@tabid,@indid)
```

When you execute this script, you should see the following:

```
------------------------------------------------------
2000-08-06 01:34:00.123

(1 row(s) affected)
```

Using the Query Analyzer Tools

When executing a query in the Query Analyzer, you have the ability not only to work with T-SQL, but also to view the result sets interactively. You can also analyze the query plan, and receive assistance to improve the performance of the query. The Execution Plan options will graphically display the data retrieval methods chosen by the server. This enables you to examine the plan being used and to make changes to the query itself or possibly to the indexes of the query, if the performance of the query is inefficient. The server investigates all the different plans that are available to execute the query.

When you run the query, you can display the execution plan for the query by selecting Show Execution Plan from the Query menu in Query Analyzer. Then, when you run the query, an additional tab will be available. To see how this works, start the Query Analyzer and execute the following SQL statement after turning on the Execution Plan option:

```
Select *
from [order details]
Where Quantity > 20
```

After execution, click the Execution Plan tab to see how the query was executed as shown in Figure 9.24.

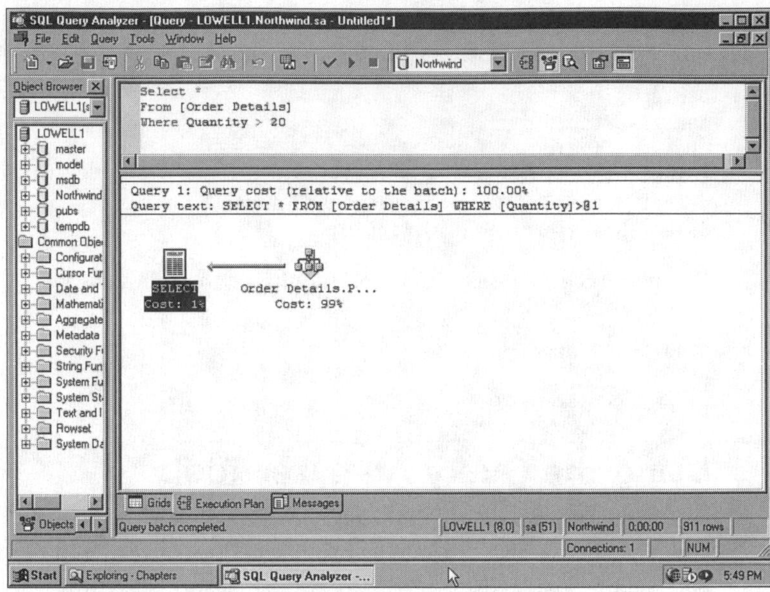

FIGURE 9.24

Accessing the execution plan for a query in the Query Analyzer.

While you are displaying the Execution Plan, you can display detailed information about any of the objects displayed by simply placing and holding the mouse over the object. Figure 9.25 shows the information about the clustered index used for the query.

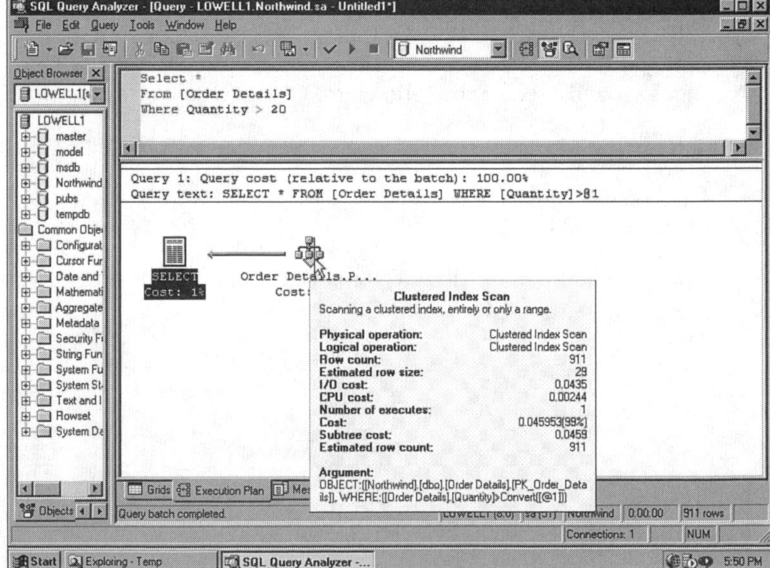

FIGURE 9.25

Displaying the execution statistics for the current query.

Another feature of the Query Analyzer is being able to capture statistics about the query, such as the number of rows affected. You can turn on this option in the same way as the Execution Plan, from the Query menu. Figure 9.26 shows the statistics for the query we have been working with.

FIGURE 9.26

Displaying the client statistics for the current query.

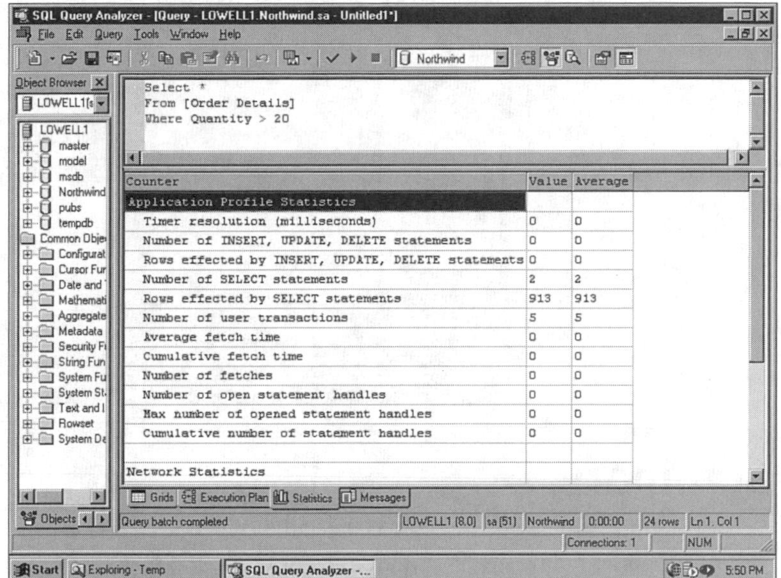

The information displayed in these forms will help you decide whether you need another index or maybe need to modify an existing one. The following SQL statement accesses the `Invoices` view in the `Northwind` database. Figure 9.27 shows the execution plan after executing the view.

```
Select * from Invoices
```

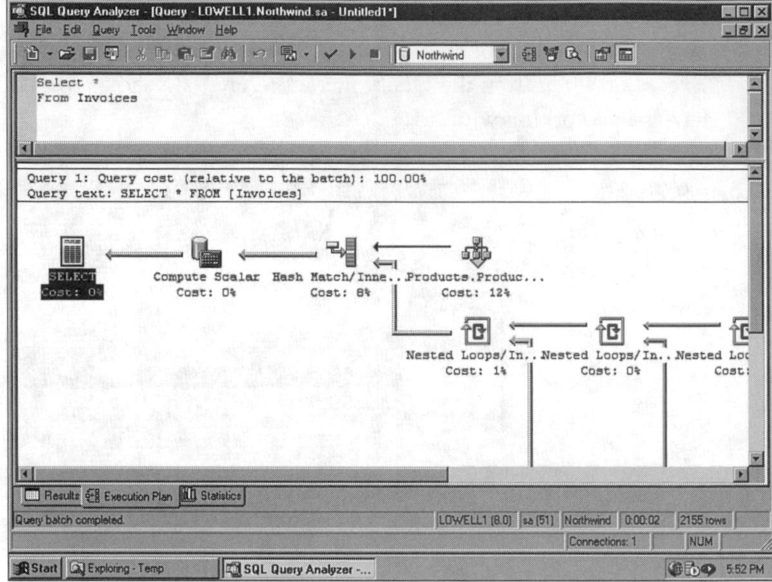

FIGURE 9.27

Displaying the execution plan for a view.

Summary

Congratulations, you made it to the end of the day. In this lesson, you have learned quite a bit about indexes, what different types exist, and how to create them. In addition, you also took a quick look at some of the tools available to you to see how the server executes a query and what statistics are generated when the query is run. Finally, you saw how the Execution Plan option in the Query Analyzer displays graphically how the server actually executes a query.

Q&A

Q What are some of the differences between clustered and nonclustered indexes?

A The number of indexes available (1 for clustered, 249 for nonclustered) and the contents of the leaf level of the index (data for the clustered index, rows pointing to the data for the nonclustered index).

Q Does SQL Server give you a warning if the index being created is not useful?

A No. The only warning you might get is when your queries take forever.

Q How do you override SQL Server's choice of indexes?

A With optimizer hints such as `SELECT ... FROM <table> (index = 1)`.

Q How do you enable the Execution Plan display in the Query Analyzer?

A Select Show Execution Plan from the Query menu.

Workshop

The Workshop provides quiz questions to help you solidify your understanding of the material covered and exercises to provide you with experience in using what you've learned. Try to answer the quiz and exercise questions before checking the answers in Appendix A, "Answers to Quizzes and Exercises," and make sure that you understand the answers before continuing to the next lesson.

Quiz

1. Which is larger, a nonclustered or clustered index?
2. How do you force a table scan in SQL Server?

Exercises

1. Write a query to output the contents of the Employees table in the Northwind database. Display the Execution Plan for this query.
2. Add a `WHERE` clause to the query based on the `LastName` column and see whether the execution plan has changed.
3. Force the use of the nonclustered index on the PostalCode. Check the execution plan to see what the effect is.

WEEK 2

DAY 10

Views and Temporary Tables

Up to this point in your reading, you have learned quite a lot about the SELECT statement and how you can use it to retrieve and manipulate data from a database. You have also learned how to use the INSERT, UPDATE, and DELETE statements to further manipulate the data in the database. In fact, you used a SELECT statement to retrieve data from one table and insert it into another table. Along the way, you also learned about joins, indexes, and the functions that you can use in a SQL query. In today's lesson, you will learn about two unique and very different features of SQL that you can use: temporary tables and views.

Temporary tables are very much like regular tables, except that you create them as needed and they are cleanly deleted at the end of the process. A *view* is just what its name implies: a way of looking at or viewing columns from one or more tables as a single entity.

The topics that we will cover today include

- What is a view?
- Working with views

- Using the SQL UNION keyword
- What is a temporary table?
- Creating a temporary table
- Real versus temporary tables
- Local and global temporary tables

Using Views to Access Data

A view is nothing more than a virtual table whose columns are defined by using a SELECT statement. As with a real table, a view consists of a set of named columns and rows of data. However, a view does not actually exist as a physical table in the database. The rows and columns of data come from the tables referenced in the SELECT statement that defines the view, and are produced dynamically whenever the view is referenced.

Views enable you to look at data in the database without duplicating that data. A view provides you with a method to filter the data referenced in the SELECT statement used to define the view. This SELECT statement can reference one or more tables or other views in the current database or other databases.

Just about now, you might be wondering, "What can I really use views for?" The answer is, "Everything." Views can be used to limit the data that can be accessed by an application's process or as a way of simplifying access to the data.

Because a view is defined in the database, a user or application program can access a view as if it were a regular table. So, views are used to restrict the data, or index the data, or even filter the data with a WHERE clause.

The types of views that you can create range from the very simple to the very complex. In the next several sections, you will see how to create and work with both types of views. Along the way, you will also see how to create and modify views by using both the Query Analyzer and the Enterprise Manager, which actually has two different ways of creating a view.

Creating a Basic View

A basic view is nothing more than a simple SELECT statement that retrieves data from a single table. When creating a view, you use a specific syntax, which is shown here:

```
Create View [<database name>.] [<owner>.] view_name
[(Column [ ,...n])]
```

```
[With <view_attribute> [ ,...n]]
As
Select_statement
```

Each of the arguments in this syntax is listed in Table 10.1 along with a brief explanation.

TABLE 10.1 The Arguments for Creating a View

Argument	*Description*
`View_name`	The name of the view you are creating. You can optionally specify the owner and database names as well (for example, `Northwind.dbo.newView`).
`Column`	One or more columns that will be included in the view when executed.
`Select_statement`	The `SELECT` statement that actually defines the view.

10

To understand views, we will start with a standard `SELECT` statement as shown:

```
use northwind
SELECT * FROM Employees
```

Results:

```
EmployeeID  LastName    FirstName  Region    (...)      Extension ReportsTo
----------- ----------- ---------- ---------(...)----- --------- ----------
1           Davolio     Nancy      WA        (...)      5467      2
2           Fuller      Andrew     WA        (...)      3457      NULL
3           Leverling   Janet      WA        (...)      3355      2
4           Peacock     Margaret   WA        (...)      5176      2
5           Buchanan    Steven     NULL      (...)      3453      2
6           Suyama      Michael    NULL      (...)      428       5
7           King        Robert     NULL      (...)      465       5
8           Callahan    Laura      WA        (...)      2344      2
9           Dodsworth   Anne       NULL      (...)      452       5

(9 row(s) affected)
```

> **Note:** Although I selected all the columns from the `Employees` table in this example, I displayed only a few columns to keep the output readable and so that it would fit on one page.

As you can see, the `SELECT` statement returns all the columns requested in the `Employees` table. Now, let's trim this down a little. Suppose that the process you are working on needs only the name of the employee and his region. The new SELECT statement would look like this:

```
use northwind
SELECT EmployeeID, LastName, FirstName,
       Region
FROM Employees
```

Results:

```
EmployeeID  LastName             FirstName  Region
----------- -------------------- ---------- --------
1           Davolio              Nancy      WA
2           Fuller               Andrew     WA
3           Leverling            Janet      WA
4           Peacock              Margaret   WA
5           Buchanan             Steven     NULL
6           Suyama               Michael    NULL
7           King                 Robert     NULL
8           Callahan             Laura      WA
9           Dodsworth            Anne       NULL

(9 row(s) affected)
```

Okay, so far so good. But, what if you know that your application will need this selection of data over and over again? Well, one way to resolve this is to keep rewriting this SELECT statement whenever you need it. Or you can create a view that will return only this data. The following will create such a view when you execute this code in Query Analyzer.

```
USE Northwind
Go
CREATE VIEW Employees_VIEW
AS SELECT EmployeeID as Emp_ID, LastName as Lname,
          FirstName as Fname, Region as State
FROM Employees
```

The preceding CREATE statement consists of the CREATE VIEW command and the associated SELECT statement. You might notice that a new statement is included in this code. The GO statement tells the server to execute all the commands that precede it before continuing. This is required because a CREATE VIEW statement must be the first statement in a batch.

The preceding SELECT statement also provides alias names for the columns. When you use this view, you can reference those alias names as though they were the actual column names or use the star (*) notation to select all the columns in the view.

```
Use Northwind
Select * from Employees_View
```

Results:

```
Emp_ID      Lname                  Fname      State
----------- ---------------------- ---------- ---------------
1           Davolio                Nancy      WA
2           Fuller                 Andrew     WA
3           Leverling              Janet      WA
4           Peacock                Margaret   WA
5           Buchanan               Steven     NULL
6           Suyama                 Michael    NULL
7           King                   Robert     NULL
8           Callahan               Laura      WA
9           Dodsworth              Anne       NULL

(9 row(s) affected)
```

As you can see, the star (*) notation returns only the columns that were referenced in the creation of the view, not all the columns in the table.

After you create a view, it will continue to exist in the database until you explicitly delete it.

To see what views exist in the database, you can use the Object Browser in the Query Analyzer. When you start Query Analyzer, click on the database you are working with to expand its objects. Then, click on the folder named `Views` to see all the views in the database (see Figure 10.1).

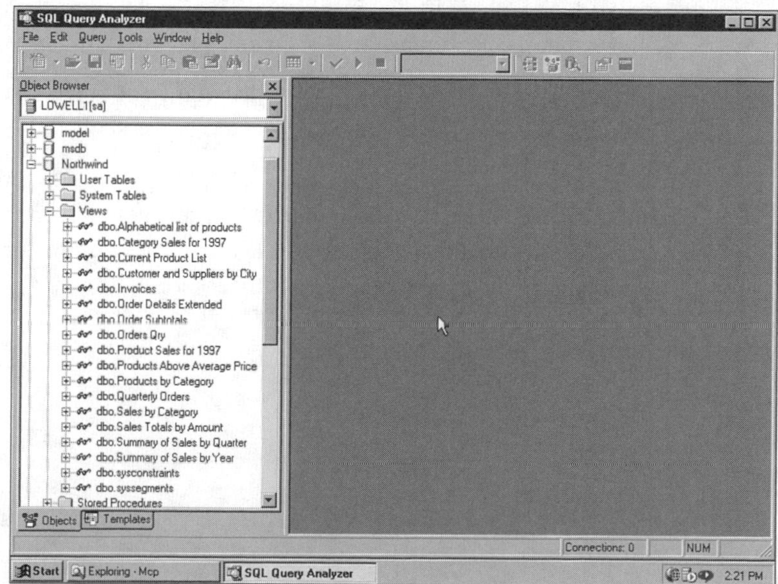

FIGURE 10.1

Listing all views contained in a database.

Any syntax that you can use for accessing a table with a SELECT statement can be used to access a view.

When you create a view, you can create it with many of the options that are available in a normal SELECT statement. However, you should know about a few restrictions, which are

- You may not use an ORDER BY or a COMPUTE clause when creating a view, but you can use one of them when accessing a view.
- If you create aliases for the column names in a view, the aliases must be valid column names according to the naming rules.

As you can probably figure out, if you want to prevent a SQL query from accessing some of the columns in the database, you simply create a view that doesn't reference those columns.

Now that you have seen how to create a basic view using the CREATE VIEW statement, let's take a look at how the Enterprise Manager makes it easier to perform these actions.

Using Enterprise Manager Query Builder to Create Views

The Enterprise Manager actually has two different ways to create a view. The first method uses a SQL Query Builder, which provides you with a visual method of creating a view. To access this tool, start the Enterprise Manager and double-click on the database you are working with to display its objects. Then, right-click the Views node, and choose New View from the pop-up menu as shown in Figure 10.2.

The next step is to add the table or tables that you want to include in the view. To do this, you click the Add Tables button on the toolbar as shown in Figure 10.3, which will display the Add Table dialog.

To build the same view as we did before, either double-click on the Employees table name or select the Employees table name and click the Add button. This will add a list of all the columns in the table to the SQL Builder (see Figure 10.4).

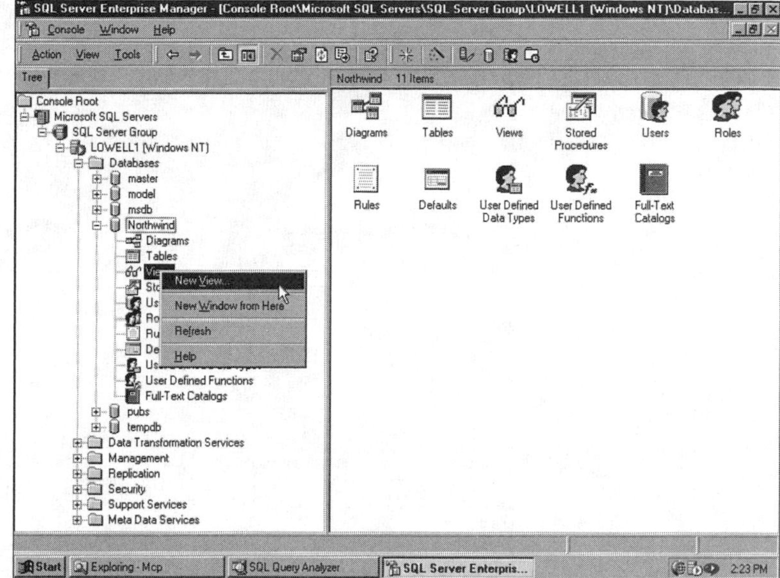

FIGURE 10.2

Starting the `CREATE VIEW` *process.*

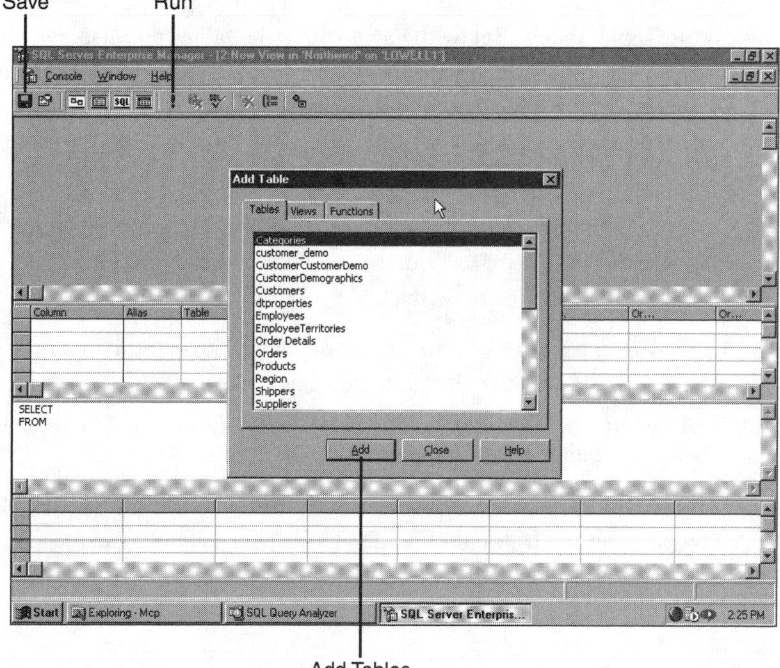

FIGURE 10.3

Displaying the Add Table dialog.

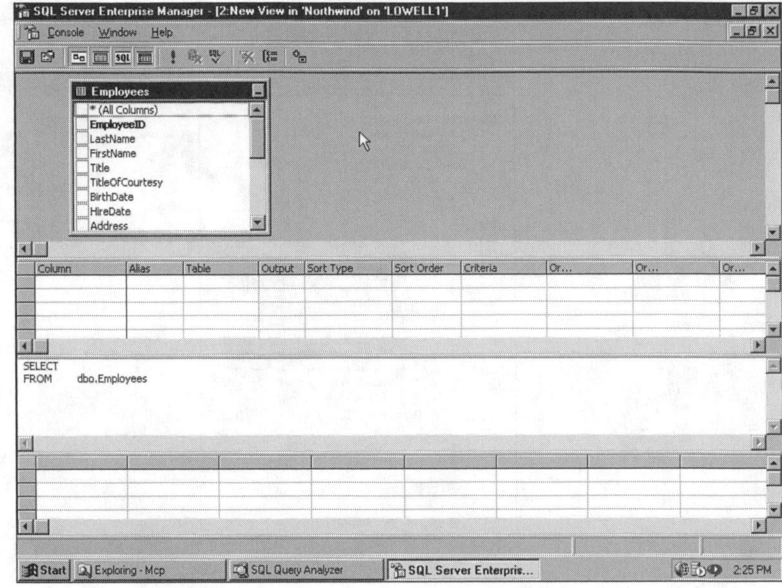

FIGURE 10.4

Tables added to the SQL Builder are displayed at the top of the screen and list all the available columns in the table.

After you have selected all the tables that you need, click the Close button to close the Add Table dialog. Below the area where the tables are displayed are three distinct sections. The first section will display the columns selected for the view, and the second section will display the actual SQL code for the `SELECT` statement used in the view. The third and final section will display the data from the `SELECT` statement if you choose to run the `SELECT` statement to test the results (always a good idea!).

To select the four required columns, click the empty box next to the column names as shown in Figure 10.5. As you select these columns, you will see them displayed in the column list section below the tables.

Of course, we also want to change the names. To do this, you would simply type in the new names for each column in the Alias column of the Column List section as shown in Figure 10.6. Again, as you type in the aliases, you will see the `SELECT` statement code below it change to reflect your modifications.

When you are satisfied with your selection, you should run the query to test it. Do this by clicking the Run button on the toolbar. You should see results similar to what is displayed in Figure 10.7.

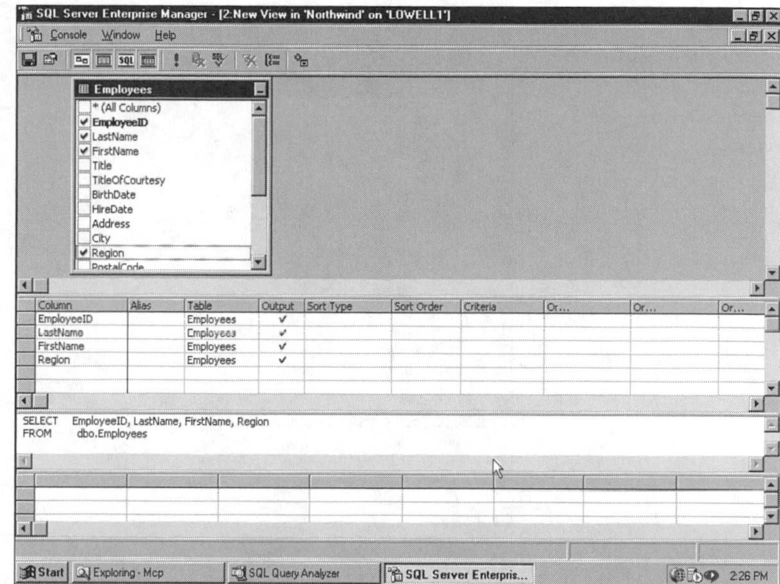

FIGURE 10.5

Selecting the columns for the view.

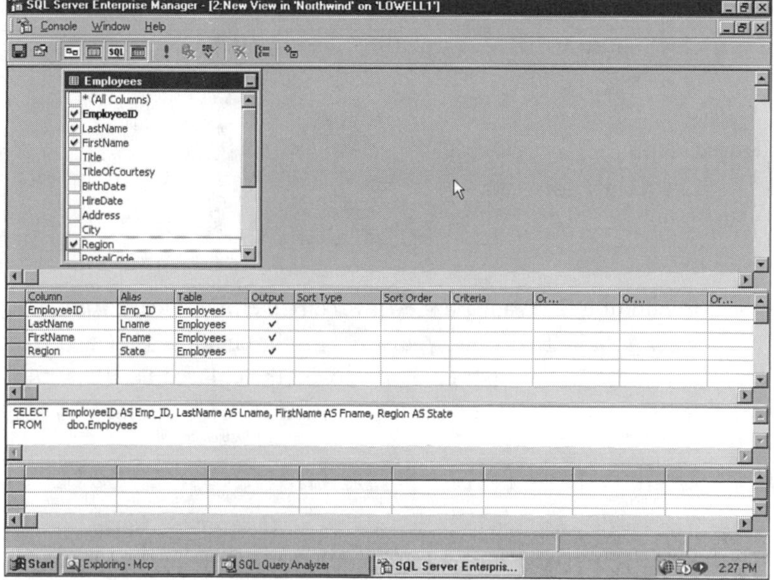

FIGURE 10.6

Adding aliases to a view.

10

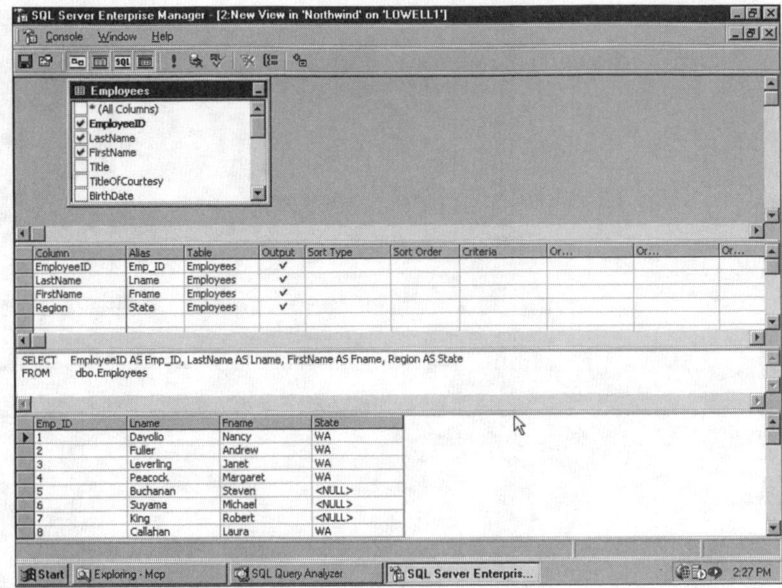

FIGURE 10.7
Testing the final `SELECT` *statement before creating the view.*

If you are ready, click the Save button, and you will be prompted for a name for the view (see Figure 10.8). After entering a name, click OK to save the view and complete the process.

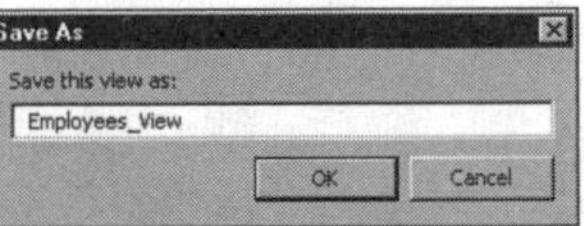

FIGURE 10.8
Specifying a name for a new view.

In addition to creating a view by using the SQL Query Builder, you can also modify a view with it. To do this, you simply right-click the view and select the Design View option from the pop-up menu. You are then placed back into the SQL Query Builder with the view displayed in the `SELECT` statement area as shown in Figure 10.9.

Using the Enterprise Manager Create View Wizard

The second method to create a view in Enterprise Manager is by using the Create View Wizard. To access this wizard, click the wizard button (which has a wand displayed on the button), which will display the Select Wizard dialog as shown in Figure 10.10.

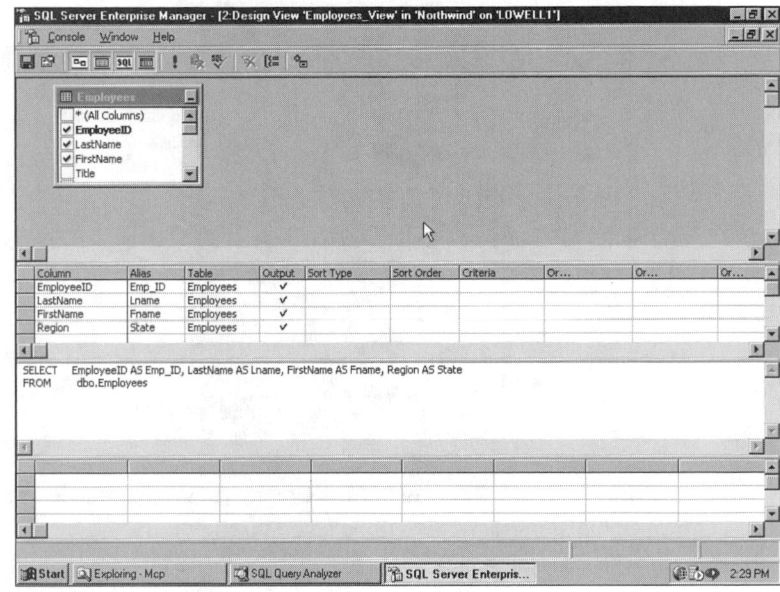

FIGURE 10.9

Editing a view by using the SQL Query Builder.

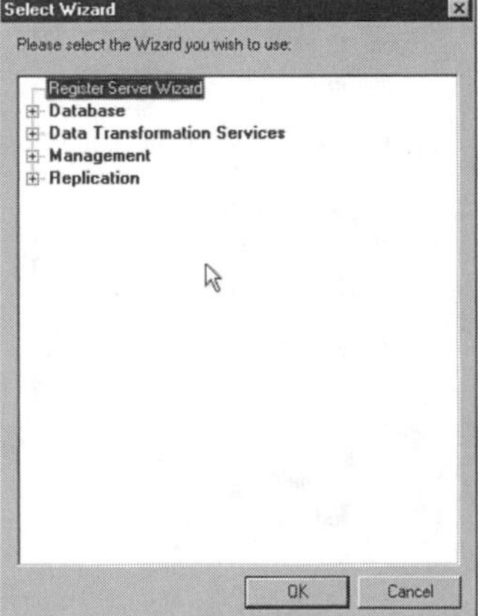

FIGURE 10.10

Accessing the Create View Wizard tools.

Expand the Database object and select the Create View Wizard option as shown in Figure 10.11.

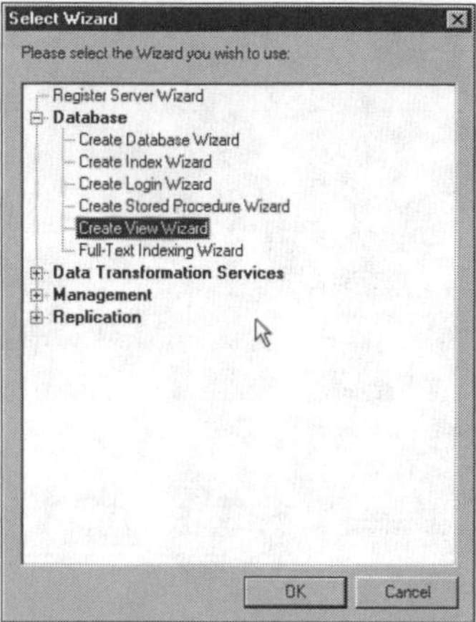

FIGURE 10.11
Selecting the Create View Wizard.

This will display the first page of the Create View Wizard (see Figure 10.12). This page describes the steps that you will be taken through to create the new view. Click Next to continue to the next page.

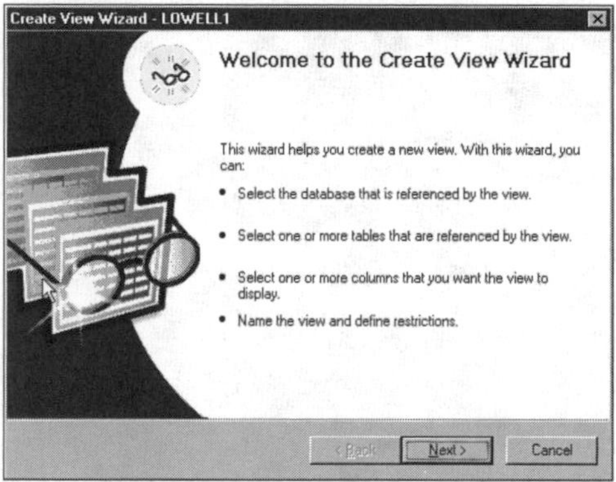

FIGURE 10.12
The first page of the Create View Wizard.

This page (see Figure 10.13) displays a drop-down list box that lists the available databases on the server to which you are connected. Select the database to which you want to add the view, and click Next to continue.

This page displays the available user tables in the selected database, as shown in Figure 10.14. To select the `Employees` table, simply click in the box next to the name. After you have selected all the tables you need, click Next to continue.

FIGURE 10.13

Selecting the database in which to create the view.

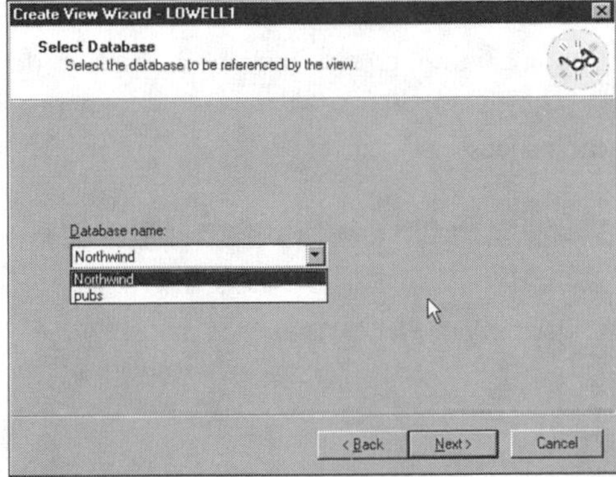

FIGURE 10.14

Selecting the tables required for the view.

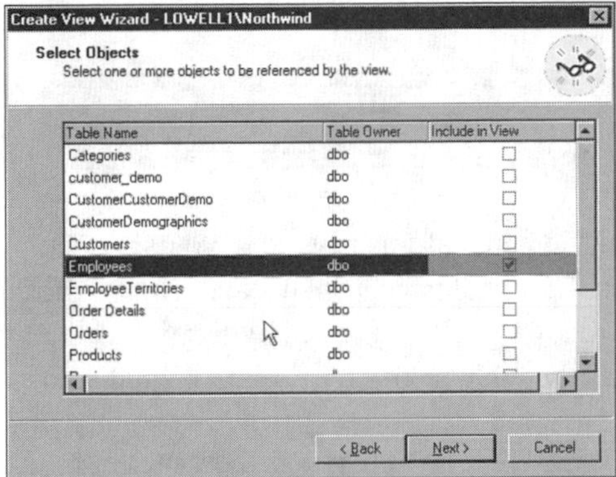

The next page is very similar to the preceding page; it displays all the available columns in the table or tables you have selected. Figure 10.15 shows this list and the columns that were selected for this view. After you have selected these columns, click Next to continue.

FIGURE 10.15

Selecting the columns to include in the view.

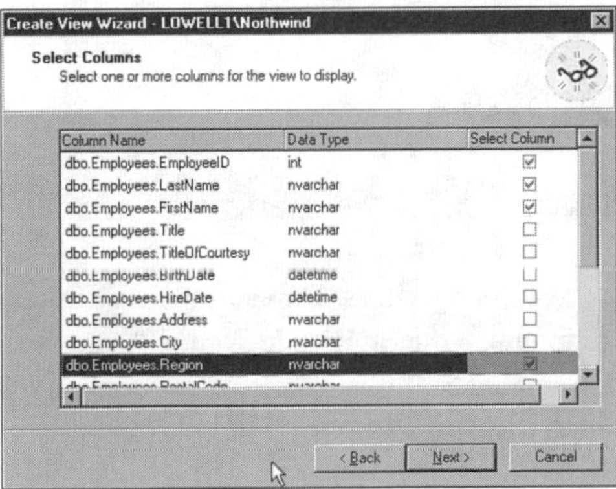

Next, you have the option of adding restrictions to the view by adding a `WHERE` clause to the `SELECT` statement you are building (see Figure 10.16). You do not need this option yet, but you will learn about the `WHERE` clause in a view later in this lesson. Click Next to go to the next step in the process.

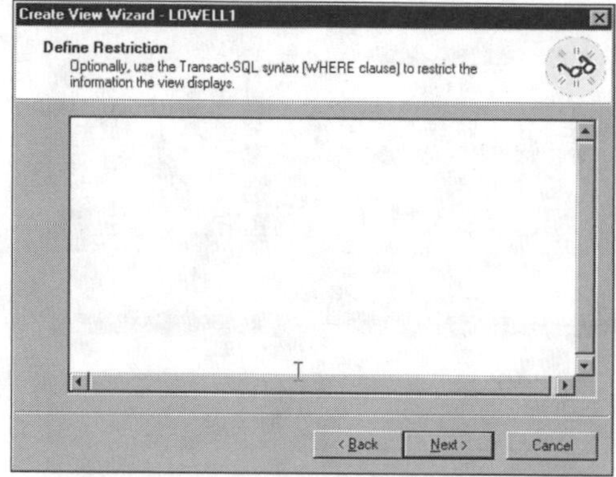

FIGURE 10.16
Adding a `WHERE` *clause to the* `SELECT` *statement.*

You are now asked for the name of this new view you are creating. Enter a name and click Next to continue. This final page displays the actual SQL code that will create the view. As Figure 10.17 shows, the syntax used by the wizard includes the database name, owner name, as well as the table names for each table and column in the view.

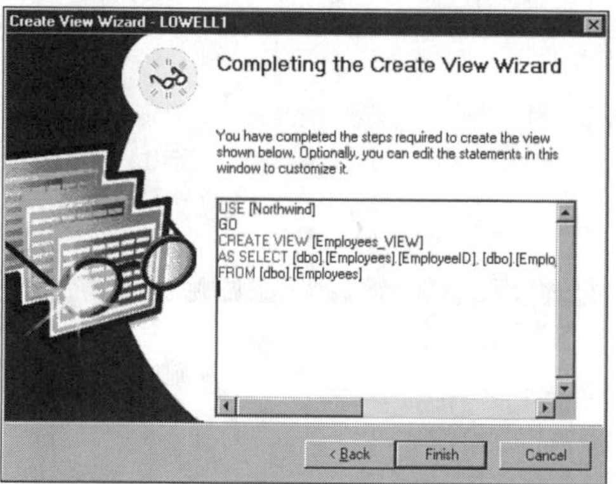

FIGURE 10.17
The final SQL code to create a new view.

You now have a choice in creating views. Depending on your level of knowledge and time, you could choose to create the SQL code yourself, use the SQL Query Builder, or use the wizard. For the remainder of this discussion on views, I will use the Query Analyzer and SQL code for the examples.

Editing Views in Query Analyzer

Although you cannot create a view in the Query Analyzer, you can edit one. To edit a view, right-click on the view name in the Object Browser and select Edit from the pop-up menu as shown in Figure 10.18.

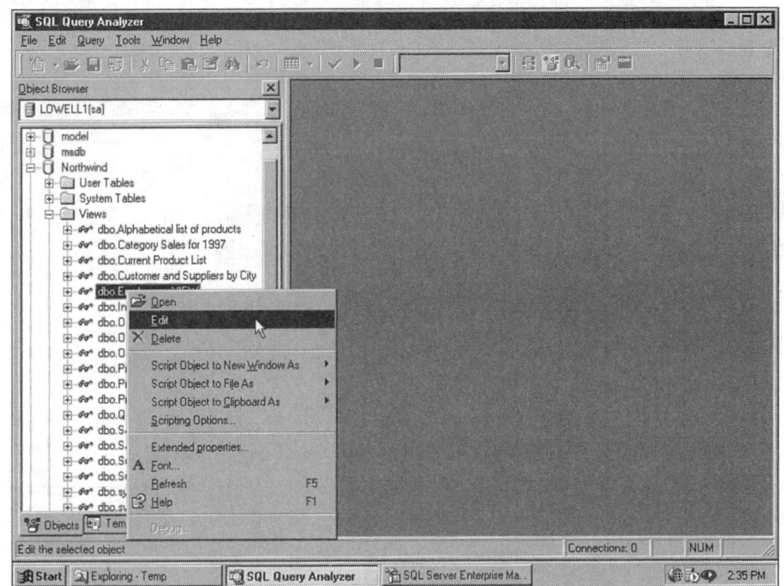

FIGURE 10.18
Editing a view in Query Analyzer.

What will be displayed is the SQL code for the view, but instead of the `CREATE VIEW` statement, the code has been modified to an `ALTER VIEW` statement, as shown in Figure 10.19. The Query Analyzer assumes that when you selected the Edit option on the pop-up menu, you wanted to alter the view. In addition, a few other statements were added that assist in the alteration process.

Using Views for Security

You have just learned how to create a basic view that limits the number of columns that can be accessed in a SQL query. Now, you will see how to further limit access by using the `WHERE` clause in the `SELECT` statement you used to create the view. To see how this works, assume that you want to retrieve only employees who are from the state of Washington. You would add a `WHERE` clause as follows:

```
USE Northwind
Go
CREATE VIEW Employees_WA
AS SELECT EmployeeID as Emp_ID, LastName as Lname,
```

```
            FirstName as Fname, Region as State
FROM Employees
WHERE Region = 'WA'
```

In the `WHERE` clause, you must still use the original names of the columns. When you execute this statement, you will receive no result set, only a message telling you that the command was processed. The `Employees_WA` view can now be used in lieu of the `Employees` table.

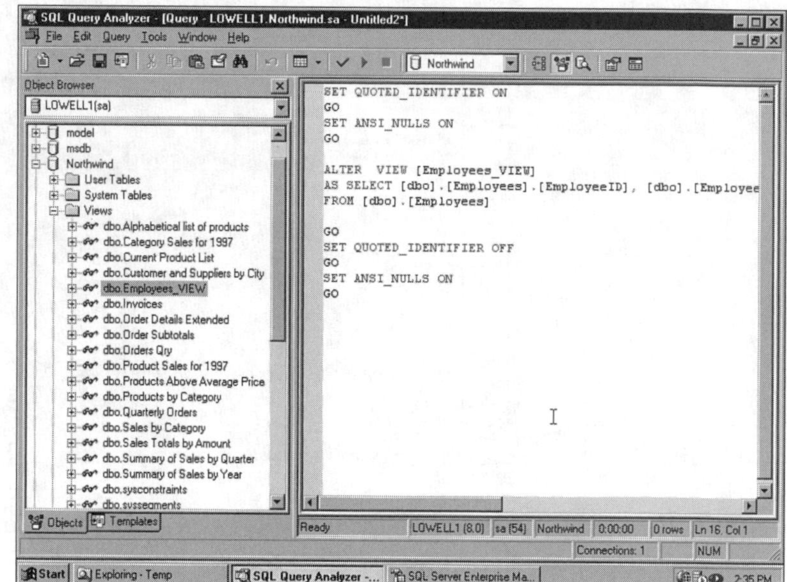

FIGURE 10.19
Working with the view's SQL code in the Query Analyzer.

When you are altering a view using the Create View statement, you might get an error message as shown:

```
Server: Msg 2714, Level 16, State 5, Procedure Employees_VIEW1,
Line 3
There is already an object named 'Employees_VIEW1' in the database.
```

To prevent this, you should add the following code before the `CREATE VIEW` statement:

```
If exists (Select Table_Name from Information_Schema.Views
      Where Table_Name = 'Employees_VIEW1')
      Drop View Employees_VIEW1
```

This code will check whether the view name exists in the system table where view information is stored. If the view exists, it will be deleted. (The `DROP` statement will be discussed later today.)

Of course, this is true only if you are trying to create a new view and you did not realize that a view with that name already exists. If you are trying to modify an existing view, remember to use the `ALTER VIEW` statement instead. Using the `ALTER VIEW` statement will not produce this error message.

Note

A user could have permission to access only the view you have created, but not the original tables on the database. This enables the view to restrict access to specific columns or specific rows in the table.

Creating Views with Multiple Tables

You know how to create a basic view by using a single table, so now let's see how you can create more complex views using the `JOIN` syntax of a `UNION` statement. You have seen how to use these clauses on Day 5, "Joining Tables." Using them to create views enables you to create very specific access to the data.

Views and Joins

You can specify a `SELECT` statement in the view creation that joins tables together. Although this provides no real performance benefit when the view is executed, it does make your SQL code simpler to read and write. The following example shows how to bring together two or more tables but select only a few columns from each table:

```
SELECT LastName as Lname, FirstName as Fname, substring(Region,1,5) as State,
       substring(TerritoryDescription,1,15) as Terr_Desc,
       substring(RegionDescription,1,15) as Region_Desc
FROM Employees as E
     INNER JOIN
        EmployeeTerritories as ET
        ON E.EmployeeID = ET.EmployeeID
     INNER JOIN
        Territories as T
        ON ET.TerritoryID = T.TerritoryID
     INNER JOIN
        Region as R
        ON T.RegionID = R.RegionID
where (E.Region = 'WA')
```

In addition to the standard coding for the `SELECT` statement, I also added the `SUBSTRING` function to the three long strings to reduce the amount of blanks I am displaying. When this view is executed, the following output is returned:

```
Lname                Fname      State Terr_Desc       Region_Desc
-------------------- ---------- ----- --------------- ---------------
Davolio              Nancy      WA    Wilton          Eastern
Davolio              Nancy      WA    Neward          Eastern
Fuller               Andrew     WA    Westboro        Eastern
Fuller               Andrew     WA    Bedford         Eastern
Fuller               Andrew     WA    Georgetow       Eastern
Fuller               Andrew     WA    Boston          Eastern
Fuller               Andrew     WA    Cambridge       Eastern
Fuller               Andrew     WA    Braintree       Eastern
Fuller               Andrew     WA    Louisville      Eastern
Leverling            Janet      WA    Atlanta         Southern
Leverling            Janet      WA    Savannah        Southern
Leverling            Janet      WA    Orlando         Southern
Leverling            Janet      WA    Tampa           Southern
Peacock              Margaret   WA    Rockville       Eastern
Peacock              Margaret   WA    Greensboro      Eastern
Peacock              Margaret   WA    Cary            Eastern
Callahan             Laura      WA    Philadelphia    Northern
Callahan             Laura      WA    Beachwood       Northern
Callahan             Laura      WA    Findlay         Northern
Callahan             Laura      WA    Racine          Northern

(20 row(s) affected)
```

Refreshing this view would create a result set that contains only those columns specified, without requiring you to code the join in your SQL query.

Views and a UNION

Using a `UNION` when creating a view enables you to combine the results from multiple `SELECT` statements in a single result set. The following example shows how to combine the `Employees` table and the `Suppliers` table:

```
Create  VIEW vw_Name
AS
SELECT LastName + ' ' + FirstName as Fullname, city
FROM Employees
UNION
SELECT ContactName as Fullname, City
FROM Suppliers
```

Results:

```
Fullname                        city
------------------------------- ---------------
Anne Heikkonen                  Lappeenranta
Antonio del Valle Saavedra      Oviedo
Beate Vileid                    Sandvika
Buchanan Steven                 London
Callahan Laura                  Seattle
Carlos Diaz                     Sao Paulo
```

```
...
Regina Murphy                    Ann Arbor
Robb Merchant                    Boston
Shelley Burke                    New Orleans
Suyama Michael                   London
Sven Petersen                    Cuxhaven
Wendy Mackenzie                  Sydney
Yoshi Nagase                     Tokyo

(38 row(s) affected)
```

Note

If you have any questions about using Unions, review the section on views in Day 5.

All the employee and supplier contact names are listed together. You can also combine multiple result sets with several UNIONs. The result sets that each SELECT statement returns must contain the same number of columns, and those columns must contain compatible data types.

A view that contains a UNION opens up some powerful opportunities. It is very useful in data warehousing operations. As an example, the following describes a real-life requirement. You have four databases, one for each region in the country where your company operates. These databases are named East, West, South, and Central. Each database contains identical table structures except that the data is relevant only to each region.

You need to produce reports on sales for October. Operating on just the base tables in each database would require you to run the following SELECT statement four times, one for each of the separate databases:

```
Select sum(Sales_amt) as Sales_Total
From Order_Detail
Where Order_Date >= '10/01/2000'
      And Order_Date < '11/01/2000'
```

You would then have to enter the data into another tool, such as Excel, and calculate the final total yourself. Instead of doing all that work, you could create a view similar to the following. This view uses a UNION to combine the four SELECT statements.

```
Create View vw_All_Sales as
     Select * from East.Order_Detail
     Union
     Select * from West.Order_Detail
     Union
     Select * from South.Order_Detail
     Union
     Select * from Central.Order_Detail
```

You now have a view that combines the data from all four regions, and you can use it to return the final sales total. The following shows the final result of this example:

```
Select sum(Sales_amt) as Sales_Total
From vw_All_Sales
Where Order_Date >= '10/01/2000'
      And Order_Date < '11/01/2000'
```

Modifying Data in a View

You are allowed to insert rows into a view. This actually adds rows into the table that the view references. Using the view `Employees_WA` from earlier, the following will insert a row into the `Employees` table:

```
INSERT vw_Employees_WA(Lname, Fname, State)
VALUES('Mauer', 'Lowell', 'WA')
```

To insert rows into a view, keep the following restrictions in mind:

- If all the columns in the table are not listed by the view referencing it, you cannot insert data into those columns, and they must accept NULLs or have a default value defined.
- If the view is performing a join, make sure that you are inserting into only one table at a time.

Updating a View

You may update data in tables by referencing the view, but restrictions apply here as well. You may not update columns in two tables at once. However, with `UPDATE` you can always run multiple updates on the same row.

The view cannot group or aggregate the data. Calculated results do not physically exist in a table. To update data in a view that joins tables together, you must execute an `UPDATE` statement for each table in the view independently of the others.

Most times, it is much easier to update the base tables themselves than to figure out all the restrictions on updating a view.

Deleting from a View

To delete data by using a view, the view must not perform any joins. If it did, you would be trying to delete rows from two tables at the same time, which is not possible at this time. In addition, the view cannot perform any groupings, aggregates, or unions.

Using INSTEAD OF Triggers and Views

The only way to update and delete rows from a view without worrying about restrictions is by using a feature called a *trigger*. A trigger enables you to intercept an action—an INSERT, UPDATE, or DELETE—and perform a process on the tables being accessed. You will learn all about triggers on Day 18, "Writing and Testing Triggers." This section is just to let you know that there is another way of modifying data in a view.

INSTEAD OF triggers can be created on a view to make that view updateable. These triggers are executed instead of the data modification statement that was originally executed. That means if you execute an INSERT statement on a view that uses a join, the trigger will be executed instead of the standard INSERT procedure. This enables you to write your own procedure for that join—executing multiple INSERT statements on each of the tables referenced in the join.

Modifying and Renaming Views

You have already seen how to modify a view by using both the SQL Query Builder in the Enterprise Manager, as well as by using the ALTER VIEW statement. To rename a view, you can use the Enterprise Manager, renaming the view just as you would a filename in Windows Explorer, or you can re-create the view with the new name. The easiest way is to use the Enterprise Manager, but I will show you how to re-create the view by using the Query Analyzer.

In the Query Analyzer, locate the view that you want to rename in the Object Browser and right-click on that view. Then select Script Object to New Window As from the pop-up menu, and select Create from the next pop-up menu, as shown in Figure 10.20.

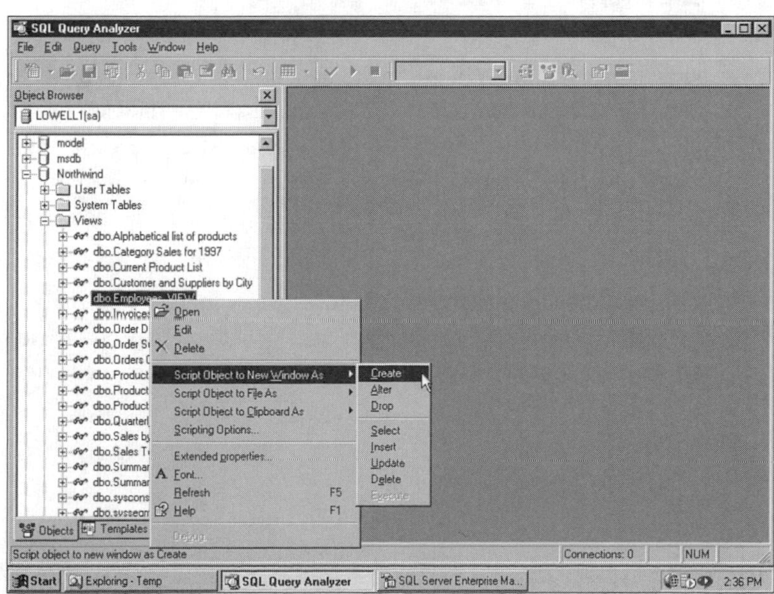

FIGURE 10.20

Displaying a view's code for creation.

This will display the SQL editor with the view definition, as shown in Figure 10.21. Change the name of the view in the code and execute it to create the new view.

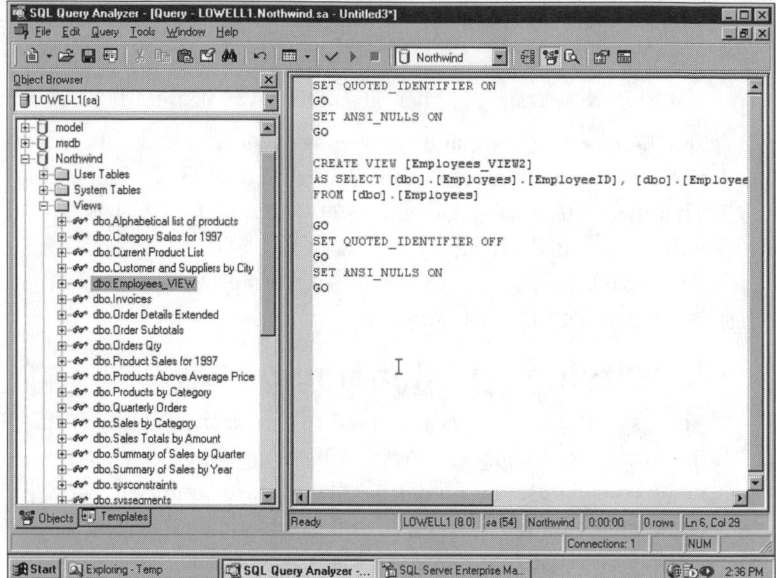

FIGURE 10.21
Modifying the view's SQL code.

The next step is to drop the old view. To see how this is done, continue to the next section.

Deleting a View

After you have created a view, you should delete it if it is no longer needed. When a view is deleted, the tables and the data are not affected. Any queries that use objects that depend on the deleted view will fail the next time they are executed. Before deleting a view, it is a good idea to look at the dependencies the view might have. To do this, you would use the Enterprise Manager. Find the view you want to delete and right-click on it. Select the All Tasks option from the pop-up menu and then select the Display Dependencies option, as shown in Figure 10.22.

This will display a dialog (see Figure 10.23) that contains two unique lists. The list on the left side of the dialog displays all objects that depend on the selected view. The list on the right side displays all the objects on which the select view depends.

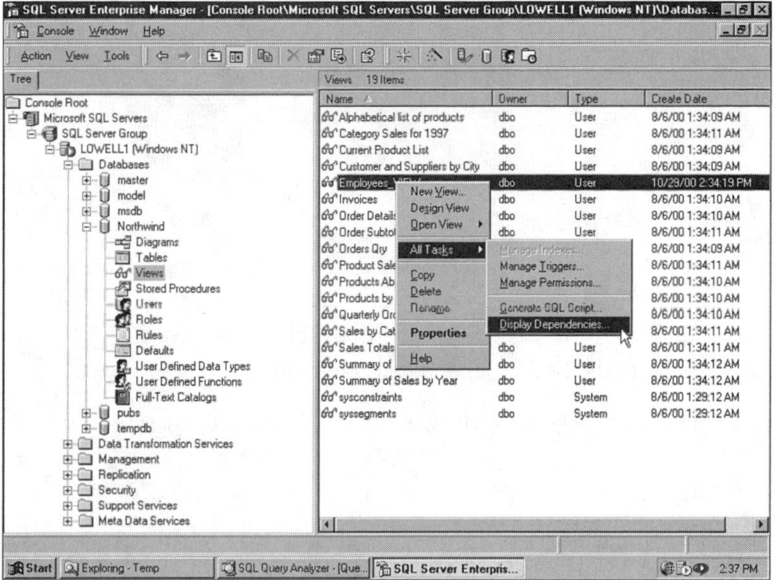

FIGURE 10.22

Selecting the Display Dependencies option.

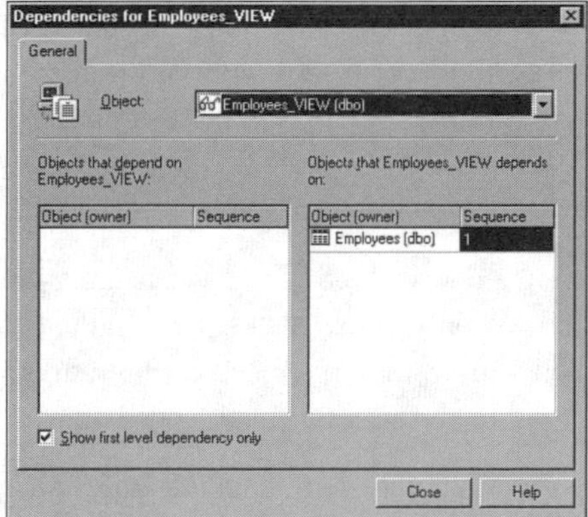

FIGURE 10.23

Displaying the dependencies of a view.

After you know whether you can really delete a view, close the Dependencies dialog and perform the actual deletion. You can, of course, select the view in the Enterprise Manager and press the Delete key. This will display the Drop Objects dialog as shown in Figure 10.24. If you agree with what is displayed, you can click the Drop All button to complete the process.

> **Note**
>
> You must be careful when choosing to click the Drop All button. After you delete or Drop a view, it is gone forever.

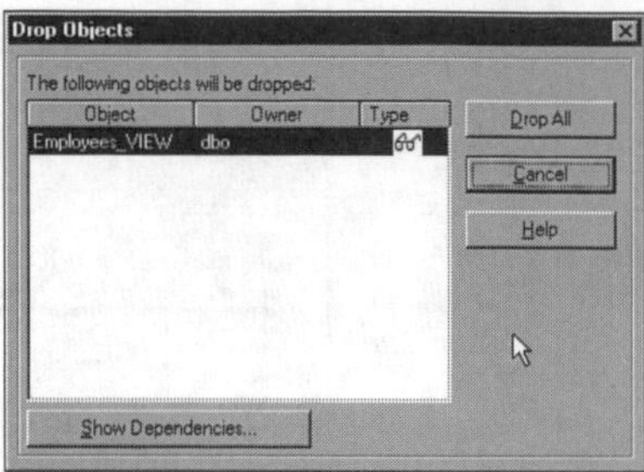

FIGURE 10.24
Deleting a view from the database.

You can display the view's dependencies from this dialog by selecting a view and then clicking the Show Dependencies button.

The other way of deleting a view is by using the `DROP` statement as shown here:

```
Drop View vw_Employees_WA
```

Using Temporary Tables for Storing Data

As you use T-SQL to perform more complex processing, you will sometimes need to temporarily save data that you have selected so that you can work with and possibly modify it. This is done using temporary tables. Temporary tables exist, as their name implies, for a limited amount of time. Temporary tables come in three variations: local, global, and permanent. All temporary tables are created in the `TEMPDB` database, no matter which database you are using when you create it.

Whenever you are processing a query, the SQL Server usually creates temporary tables behind the scenes as needed. When you use `ORDER BY` and the data you are sorting does not have an index associated with it, the server will use a temporary table to perform the sorting.

In this section, you will learn how to create temporary tables and how to use them. Of the three types of temporary tables, you probably will work most often with local temporary tables. Each type is listed in Table 10.2 along with a short explanation.

TABLE 10.2 Temporary Table Types

Type	*Description*
Local	These tables last only as long as your connection to the server. Other users on the server cannot access these tables. They are created with a # sign as the first character of the name as shown here: `Create table #temp1(KeyCode int Null)`

TABLE 10.2 continued

Type	*Description*
Global	Similar to local temporary tables, except that they allow all users on the system to access them. They are created with two # signs at the beginning of the name: `Create table ##temp1(KeyCode int Null)` A global temporary table exists until the connection that created it is closed.
Permanent	These tables last until the server is shut down and restarted. These are real tables, created using the same syntax you learned on Day 8, "Defining Data." The difference is that permanent temporary tables are created in `TEMPDB`. `TEMPDB` is cleared out automatically every time the server restarts.

Table 10.3 outlines the differences between temporary tables and standard tables.

TABLE 10.3 Differences Between Temporary and Standard Tables

Local Temp Table	*Global Temp Table*	*Permanent Table*	*Standard Table*
Created in `TEMPDB`	Created in `TEMPDB`	Created in `TEMPDB`	Created in any database
Uses # to create	Uses ## to create	Created like a standard table but in `TEMPDB`	Created in any database
Reference using #	Reference using ##	Reference using `TEMPDB` `..tablename`	Reference using table name
Exists until connection that created it is closed	Exists until connection that created it is closed or until all connections have stopped accessing it	Exists until the server is restarted	Exists until explicitly deleted
Accessible only from the connection that created it	Accessible from any connection	Accessible from any connection	Accessible from any connection

Creating a Temporary Table

There are two ways to create a temporary table. The first way is to use a `CREATE TABLE` statement as shown here:

```
Create Table #TP_Demo1 (Fname varchar(10), Lname varchar(20))
```

The other method of creating a temporary table is by using the `SELECT ... INTO` statement.

Using the `CREATE TABLE`

When using the `CREATE TABLE` syntax to create a temporary table, you must define each column that you want to add to the table by using the rules that you learned on Day 8 when creating standard tables.

A temporary table created this way is empty, waiting for further SQL statements to insert data into it. An example of creating a temporary table using the `CREATE TABLE` is shown here:

```
Create Table #Tp_Jobs (
    Job_id smallint Identity(1,1) primary key clustered
    Job_desc varchar(50) not null default 'New position'
)
```

Using the `SELECT ... INTO` Statement

Temporary tables are very useful for holding a subset of data from a standard table. The easiest way to copy that data from a standard table into a temporary table is by using the `SELECT ... INTO` statement. The following example makes a copy of the entire `Employees` table:

```
select *
into #tpEmployees
from Employees
```

Results:

```
(10 row(s) affected)
```

The output from executing this SQL statement is a single line displaying the number of rows that were affected. After this statement is executed, there will be two identical tables. The `Employees` table itself, which is unaffected by this action, and the new local temporary table, `#tpEmployees`, in `TEMPDB`. To see the new table, you can display it in Query Analyzer by expanding the `tempdb` database folder and the `User Tables` subfolder as shown in Figure 10.25.

FIGURE 10.25

Displaying the temporary tables in Query Analyzer.

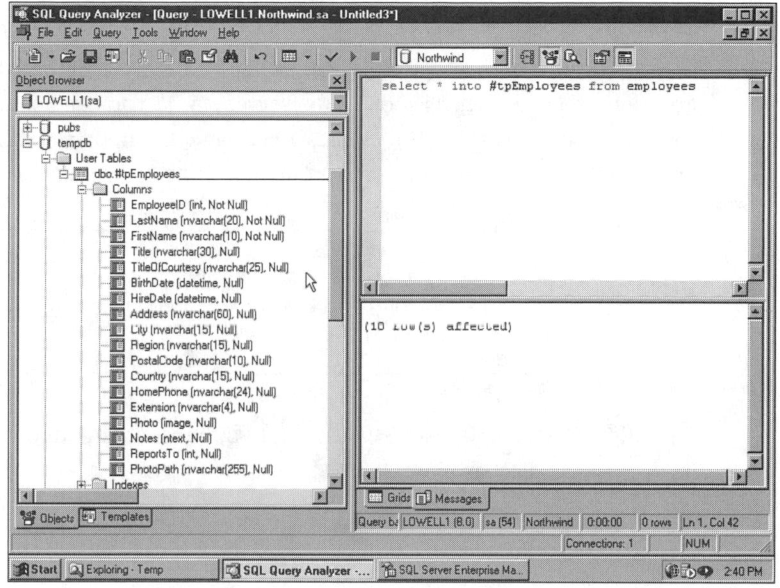

In addition to creating exact copies of tables, the `SELECT ... INTO` statement can also create tables that contain a few rows, or just a few columns, from the original table. This is done by specifying the columns you want from the original table and, if needed, a `WHERE` clause to limit the amount of data being returned, as shown in the following example:

```
Use Northwind
drop table #tpemployees
select firstname as fname,
       lastname as lname,
       region as state
into #tpEmployees
from Employees
```

Note

Remember to drop the temporary table before you try to re-create it.

This statement creates a new, local temporary table, called `#tpEmployees`, in the `TEMPDB` database. However, this time, the temporary table will only contain three columns: `fname`, `lname`, and `state`. You should know that when you alias a column name in the `SELECT ... INTO` statement, this new name is used in the temporary table.

Creating a Temporary Table on System Startup

The stored procedure sp_procoption enables the system administrator to create a stored procedure that executes as soon as the server starts. You can use this function to create a stored procedure that, in turn, creates a permanent temporary table. The permanent temporary table could be used to support queries in heavy volume, multiuser environments.

Don't worry about what stored procedures are; you will learn about them in Days 15, "Writing and Executing Stored Procedures," and 16, "Optimizing Stored Procedures."

The following example lists the steps that you must take to duplicate the Orders table in the Northwind database into TEMPDB:

Step 1—Create a stored procedure in the master database. The following is an example of this procedure:

```
Create Procedure sp_Startup_Orders_Table as
Select *
Into tempdb..orders
From Northwind..orders
```

Step 2—You must notify the server that you want this procedure executed when the server starts. You do this by executing the sp_procoption procedure as shown here:

```
Exec sp_procoption sp_Startup_Orders_Table
```

Now, the next time the server restarts, a copy of the Orders table will be created automatically. It is important to remember that each time the server is restarted, this table will be re-created with the most current data from the original table.

Determining When to Use a Temporary Table

Temporary tables are used to reduce the amount of processing the server must perform when working with large amounts of data. Suppose that you have some work to do related to the Customers and Orders tables. But today, you are only responsible for the orders that are from the United States. You also know that you will be working with this information all day long. Instead of asking the server to sort through all the customer data, you can make the process faster and easier by making a copy of only the customers from the United States.

The following example creates a local temporary table that will contain only a few columns from the Customers and Orders tables:

```
Drop Table #mycustomers
select     CompanyName,
    Phone,
    RequiredDate
into #myCustomers
From Customers inner join
    orders on
    customers.customerid = orders.customerid
Where customers.country = 'USA'
```

Results:

```
(122 row(s) affected)
```

Remember to use `DROP TABLE` when you first work with a temporary table. This enables you to change the temporary table quickly, without worrying about duplicate object names.

Now, if you selected everything from this new table, it would display the following:

```
Select * from #myCustomers
```

Results:

```
CompanyName                    Phone                    RequiredDate
------------------------------ ------------------------ -----------------------
Rattlesnake Canyon Grocery     (505) 555-5939           1996-08-19 00:00:00.000
White Clover Markets           (206) 555-4112           1996-08-14 00:00:00.000
Split Rail Beer & Ale          (307) 555-4680           1996-08-29 00:00:00.000
Rattlesnake Canyon Grocery     (505) 555-5939           1996-08-30 00:00:00.000
Rattlesnake Canyon Grocery     (505) 555-5939           1996-09-27 00:00:00.000
Old World Delicatessen         (907) 555-7584           1996-10-11 00:00:00.000
Lonesome Pine Restaurant       (503) 555-9573           1996-10-15 00:00:00.000
The Big Cheese                 (503) 555-3612           1996-10-18 00:00:00.000
...
Save-a-lot Markets             (208) 555-8097           1998-05-15 00:00:00.000
White Clover Markets           (206) 555-4112           1998-05-15 00:00:00.000
Old World Delicatessen         (907) 555-7584           1998-06-01 00:00:00.000
Great Lakes Food Market        (503) 555-7555           1998-05-20 00:00:00.000
Great Lakes Food Market        (503) 555-7555           1998-06-11 00:00:00.000
Save-a-lot Markets             (208) 555-8097           1998-05-29 00:00:00.000
White Clover Markets           (206) 555-4112           1998-05-29 00:00:00.000
Rattlesnake Canyon Grocery     (505) 555-5939           1998-06-03 00:00:00.000

(122 row(s) affected)
```

Using `SELECT ... INTO`, I created a new table with columns and data from `Customers` and `Orders`. You can use any legal `SELECT` statement with the `INTO` clause, so summary tables can be created by performing aggregates and `GROUP BY`. In the preceding example, the new table used the column names from the original table because I did not specify any alias names for the columns.

After the temporary table is created and populated, you can use it later in the process. Most of the time, temporary tables will be used in both stored procedures and triggers. (Both are covered later in this book.)

Temporary Tables Versus Views

Now that you have learned what temporary tables and views are and how to create them, it is up to you to decide which is better to use and when. Remember that a view does not actually store any more or duplicate data in the database. However, whenever a view is accessed, the `SELECT` statement contained in the view is executed and the current data is returned.

In contrast, when a temporary table is created, it contains a duplicate of the data you are working with. If the underlying tables are changed, the data in the temporary table will not reflect these changes unless you drop and re-create it.

Summary

Today you learned what views are and how to use them. Views are one of the most useful features that you will use in programming T-SQL applications. They enable you to control everything from the number of columns to the amount of data returned to the user.

In addition to working with views, you also learned how to work with temporary tables. In fact, you could use any one of three types of temporary table, depending on the type of work you want to use it for. You also learned how to create temporary tables by using the `SELECT ... INTO` statement, which creates copies of the existing tables.

Finally, you were briefly exposed to stored procedures in order to create a permanent temporary table when the server starts. Tomorrow you will take the first steps in learning the basic programming aspects of T-SQL. Those steps include how to use variables and how to deal with errors.

Q&A

Q When I tried to use `SELECT ... INTO` to create a table in a database at work, I got a permissions error. Why?

A To execute a `SELECT ... INTO` statement, the database requires certain options to be set. In addition, you must have permission to read the source table and to create a table in the destination database.

Q If I modify a row using a view, does that change the data in the table on which the view is defined?

A Yes. A view is simply a way of looking at the original tables. The actual data you see when accessing a view still resides in the standard tables.

Q Why should I use a temporary table instead of the original table?

A There are several reasons, but the real reason is performance. If you use a table for reference while many others are updating it, you would work much faster if you created a temporary table that no one else is using.

Workshop

The Workshop provides quiz questions to help you solidify your understanding of the material covered and exercises to provide you with experience in using what you've learned. Try to answer the quiz and exercise questions before checking the answers in Appendix A, "Answers to Quizzes and Exercises," and make sure that you understand the answers before continuing to the next lesson.

Quiz

1. What are the three different types of temporary tables and how do you create them?
2. If I need to append 10 tables together, how can I do it?
3. Who can access a global temporary table? A permanent temporary table?
4. How can I make changes to a view?

Exercises

1. Using the `Pubs` database, create a global temporary table that includes the author names along with the revenue they have generated.
2. Create a view that shows sales information for the United States only. This should include the company name, order date, product name, and the total sales for each.

WEEK 2

DAY 11

T-SQL Programming Fundamentals

In the previous 10 lessons, you have learned how the basics of T-SQL work when accessing and modifying data in a relational database. You have seen how to create the actual database and how to create and use views and temporary tables. With this knowledge and a tool such as the Query Analyzer, you can write simple, SQL queries. By simple, I mean with little or no logic built into them.

In today's discussion, you will learn about the different programming structures that T-SQL provides to handle the expected tasks of conditional execution and program looping. In addition, you will learn how to define and use variables. If you are familiar with any of the object-oriented programming languages, such as Visual Basic, Delphi, or PowerBuilder, you will probably find today's discussion fairly easy to follow. However, if you do not have a programming background, take the time to review the exercises at the end of this lesson.

You will also see how errors are handled by T-SQL and what you need to create error-handling routines. Finally, we will look at some of the options you can set to control how your SQL queries are handled. Some of the topics we will cover are

- Defining and using variables
- Batch processing

- `BEGIN...END` blocks
- Looping statements
- Conditional statements
- Using comments
- Displaying error messages
- Error handling

Handling Variables

Before we can discuss how to handle variables, we first need to define what a variable is. A *variable* is an area of memory that you use to store information during the execution of a SQL script. This information could be data that you recently retrieved from the database or a value that you entered, to be used by the SQL script, such as the `WHERE` clause. Using variables in your SQL scripts will make it easier to maintain this code later. There are two basic types of variables: local and global, both of which are described in the following sections.

Declaring and Setting Local Variables

Local variables are needed to do any serious work within a stored procedure or trigger. As the SQL you write becomes more complex, you will need variables to keep specific values for later processing. Local variables are also used as counters in loop processing as you will see later today. They are also used to hold the values of a global variable for use in a specific process. Finally, they can be used to hold column values from tables for testing. Some of the more common uses for local variables are

- Counter in `WHILE` loops.
- Holding return values from a stored procedure. When a stored procedure returns a value to indicate the success or failure, the local variable must be used to hold this value to test it.
- Holding a value from a table for use later in the batch or procedure.
- Passing parameters to and from a stored procedure.

A local variable is defined by using a `DECLARE` statement as shown:

```
Declare @cntr int
```

The `DECLARE` statement specifies the name of the variable (which consists of an @ sign and the variable name). The second parameter specifies the data type of the variable. In the preceding example, we declare a variable called `@cntr`, which is an integer. You can use any data type to declare a variable, except a user-defined data type. When a variable is declared, its value is null until used.

> If you are using more than one local variable, you should declare all the variables in one DECLARE statement, separated by commas, as shown:
>
> `Declare @cntr int, @sales-total money, @full_name varchar(50)`
>
> While declaring the variables this way does not provide you anymore functionality, it does reduce the amount of work the server needs to perform.

The most used method for assigning a value to a variable is by using a SELECT statement. The following example shows how a variable is defined, initialized, and then displayed:

```
declare @cntr int --Define counter variable @cntr
Select @cntr = 1 --Assign @cntr to the value of 1
Select @cntr --Access the value in @cntr and display it
```

Results:

```
-----------
1

(1 row(s) affected)
```


The DECLARE statement creates the local variable which is then assigned the value of 1 in the first SELECT statement. The second SELECT statement displays the value of @cntr.

Note

> In the preceding example, you should also see that I used comments to describe the function of each statement.

Caution

> Because the value of a variable is null when it is created, you must initialize it to a starting value before using it. For example, if you had the following statement in the SQL script without initializing the @cntr variable first, you would encounter a problem later in your code:
>
> `Select @cntr = @cntr + 1`
>
> You might assume that the first time this statement is executed, the value in @cntr would be 1. You would be wrong, null + 1 is still null. If you were testing the value of @cntr, the test would always fail since the value would always be null. However, you would not know this because no error message would be returned.

In the previous example, you saw how the SELECT statement is used in two different ways. You cannot combine SELECT statements so that you are setting a variable at the same time as you retrieve data from a table. The following example shows what would happen if you tried this:

```
declare @cntr int --Define counter variable @cntr
Select @cntr = 1, au_lname
from authors
```

Results:

```
Server: Msg 141, Level 15, State 1, Line 2
A SELECT statement that assigns a value to a variable
must not be combined with data-retrieval operations.
```

This error is slightly incorrect because you can assign table values to a variable. This error is really saying: "A SELECT statement that assigns a value to a variable can not also return data to the client." The following example shows how to assign a variable with the value from a table column:

```
use northwind
declare @sales_total money
Select @sales_total = sum(unitprice) * sum(quantity)
from [order details]
where productid = 54
Select @sales_total as 'Sales Total'
```

Results:

```
Sales Total
---------------------
184937.2500

(1 row(s) affected)
```

Because the SELECT statement is assigning a value to @sales_total, it does not return data, other than what is assigned to the variable. You can also see that I have used aggregates in the first SELECT statement and a column alias in the second SELECT statement. If the query that is assigning a variable returns more than one row of data from the table, the value for the last row is placed in the variable. If the query returns no rows, the variable's value is unchanged.

A local variable will last for the duration of a batch process. A batch is a set of commands that are sent to the server, and executed together. The GO statement can be used to separate batches when you are using the Query Analyzer to execute the SQL scripts as shown in the following example.

```
Use northwind
Declare @msg varchar(25)
```

```
Select @msg = 'This is a Demo'
Select @msg as Comment
Go
Select @msg
Go
```

Results:

```
Comment
-------------------------
This is a Demo

(1 row(s) affected)

Server: Msg 137, Level 15, State 2, Line 1
Must declare the variable '@msg'.
```

You can see that the declaration of `@msg` lasts only until the first `GO` statement is encountered. After that batch is completed, the variable is destroyed and its memory is released.

> **Tip:** When returning messages from procedures, you should use the `PRINT` statement instead of the `SELECT` statement. A `SELECT` statement will create a separate result set for each message.

Using Global Variables

Global variables are used by SQL Server to communicate information to the client. Global variables are read-only and are set automatically by the server. A global variable can be identified by the double `@@` signs before their names. The following example uses the `@@Version` variable to retrieve the current version of the SQL Server you are working with:

```
Select @@version
```

Results:

```
----------------------------------------------------
Microsoft SQL Server  2000 - 8.00.194 (Intel X86)
       Aug  6 2000 00:57:48
       Copyright (c) 1988-2000 Microsoft Corporation
       Enterprise Edition on Windows NT 4.0
       (Build 1381: Service Pack 5)


(1 row(s) affected)
```

Global variables are used to retrieve important information when inside a stored procedure or trigger. The most important of these variables is the @@ERROR variable as discussed later today. There are two types of global variables: connection-specific and server-specific variables. Tables 11.1 and 11.2 list some of the more useful global variables that you could use.

Table 11.1 Connection-Specific Global Variables

Variable Name	*Description*
@@ERROR	Indicates the type of error that occurred. If the value is not zero, an error has occurred.
@@CURSOR_ROWS	Returns the number of rows in the last opened cursor. This is discussed on Day 14, "Using Cursors."
@@FETCH_STATUS	Returns the status of the last fetch operation against a cursor. This is discussed on Day 14.
@@IDENTITY	Returns the last value automatically inserted by the server. This is discussed on Day 7, "Adding, Changing, and Deleting Rows."
@@NESTLEVEL	Returns the nesting level of a stored procedure or trigger. Every time a new procedure is called from within another procedure, the nest level is increased by one.
@@ROWCOUNT	Returns the number of rows that were affected by the last statement executed.

Most of the server-specific variables are used to track statistics for the SQL Server since the last time the server was started.

Table 11.2 Server-Specific Global Variables

Variable Name	*Description*
@@CONNECTIONS	Number of logins
@@CPU_BUSY	Number of ticks spent doing work. 300 ticks to a second
@@IDLE	Ticks spent not doing work
@@SERVERNAME	The name of the server to which you are currently connected
@@VERSION	The current version of the server to which you are connected

Reviewing Programming Structures

Every programming language, including T-SQL, has a set way of performing multiple actions, checking whether an action is needed, or performing the same action multiple times. Because a computer processes commands linearly—that is, in a straight line—and program code or SQL script must be presented in a structured format, you will find the different topics in this section very useful. What you will learn in this section are the basic building blocks for this structured style of programming in T-SQL.

Understanding Batches

A *batch* is a collection of one or more SQL statements that are sent to the server as one group by a client application, such as Query Analyzer. Each batch is then compiled or translated into a single executable unit and plan. If the batch contains multiple SQL statements, all the optimized steps needed to perform the statements are built in the single plan. The ways to specify a batch process are

- All the statements in a stored procedure or trigger comprise a single batch.
- The string executed by an `EXECUTE` statement.
- All SQL statements send as a single execution unit.

11

NEW TERM A *batch* is one or more SQL statements that are sent to the server to be compiled and executed.

When using batches, there are a few rules you must know. They are

- The `CREATE` statement must begin the batch. All other statements that follow in that batch will be interpreted as part of the definition of the first `CREATE` statement.
- A table cannot be altered and then have the new columns referenced in the same batch.
- If an `EXECUTE` statement is the first statement in a batch, the `EXECUTE` keyword is not required.

In the Query Analyzer, a batch is sent by one of the following methods:

- Selecting Query, Execute from the menu
- Clicking the green run arrow button
- Pressing Ctrl+E

If you include the word `GO` anywhere in the executed text, this will indicate that the client program should send all the SQL statements that precede the `GO` command, wait for a result, and then continue with the commands that follow it.

Execution Order

Whenever a batch of commands is sent to the server, the SQL code that is sent is processed in order according to the following five steps:

1. Parse:Syntax—The SQL statements are checked to ensure that they are syntactically correct.
2. Parse:Object References—If the statements are syntactically correct, the referenced objects are checked to see if they exist and that the user has the permission to access them.
3. Optimize—The server decides what plan to use for the best performance.
4. Compile—The query plan (SQL statements) is compiled.
5. Execute—The compiled plan is executed by the server.

Multiple SQL Statements in a Single Batch

When the server accepts a batch of T-SQL commands, those commands are then put through the process outlined earlier. If any errors are found at any step, with any command in that batch, the process is terminated and an error is returned.

You can place multiple commands in a single batch, which can be compiled and executed as a single group. By taking a look at the following commands, you will be able to get a better idea of how batches work.

```
use pubs
Select title
From titles
Where title like '%cooking%'
select au_id, au_lname
From authors
Where au_lname = 'Green'
```

Results:

```
title
--------------------------------------------------------------------------------
Cooking with Computers: Surreptitious Balance Sheets
Onions, Leeks, and Garlic: Cooking Secrets of the Mediterranean
The Psychology of Computer Cooking

(3 row(s) affected)

au_id       au_lname
----------- ----------------------------------------
213-46-8915 Green

(1 row(s) affected)
```

The two SELECT statements in the example were parsed, compiled, and executed as a group. Each of the SELECT statements returns a result set. However, the server returns the results as a single result set as shown.

To execute these SELECT statements separately, you need to add only a single statement to the script. By adding the word GO to the script, you are instructing the Query Analyzer to process this script as two distinct batches.

```
use pubs
Select title
From titles
Where title like '%cooking%'
GO
select au_id, au_lname
From authors
Where au_lname = 'Green'
```

I am not showing you the output for this example because it is identical to the previous output. The difference is how the statements are sent to and processed by the server. The Query Analyzer sent the first SELECT statement to the server and then waited for the results to be returned. When the results were completely retrieved, the second command was sent to the server for execution.

> Batching commands will improve performance on the server because the server will have less work to do. If you compile and execute one set of ten INSERT statements, it will be faster than compiling and executing ten separate INSERT statements.

Controlling Program Flow

When working in a procedure that contains more than one SQL statement, such as a stored procedure, you need to be able to group multiple SQL statements together according to function. By controlling the flow of execution, you can choose which statements to execute and which ones to skip over, even when to exit a procedure. Table 11.3 lists the T-SQL keywords you can use to control the flow of your SQL scripts.

TABLE 11.3 Flow of Execution Keywords

Keyword	*Description*
BEGIN...END	Defines a program block
BREAK	Exits the innermost WHILE loop
CONTINUE	Restarts a WHILE loop

TABLE 11.3 continued

Keyword	*Description*
`GOTO label`	Continues processing at the statement following the `label`
`IF...ELSE`	Defines conditional and, optionally, alternative execution when a condition is `FALSE`
`RETURN`	Exits unconditionally
`WAITFOR`	Sets a delay for statement execution
`WHILE`	Repeats a group of statements while a specific condition is `TRUE`

By combining one or more of these keywords, you can create very complex SQL programs that will perform the required processing for a database.

Using the `IF...ELSE`

The `IF` statement enables you to choose to execute one or more statements if a specified condition is `TRUE`. Additionally, if that same condition is `FALSE`, you can execute a different set of SQL statements. The syntax of the `IF` statement is

```
IF Boolean_expression
    {sql_statement | statement_block}
[ELSE
    {sql_statement | statement_block}]
```

This statement can be used to test a variety of conditions within a stored procedure or trigger. The following is a simple example that will test the value of a local variable and then print a different message depending on the value of that variable:

```
Use northwind
Declare @price money
Select Unitprice
From products
Where productid = 44
Select @price = unitprice
From products
Where productid = 44
If @price < $10
    Print 'Under $10'
Else
   Print 'Equal to or Over $10'
```

Results:

```
Unitprice
---------------------
19.4500

(1 row(s) affected)

Equal to or Over $10
```

The IF test is composed of three basic sections. Immediately after the IF keyword is the Boolean expression that will be tested. If the expression is TRUE, the statement following the test is executed. If the expression is FALSE, the statement following the ELSE is executed. The ELSE clause is optional; if it is not specified and the expression is FALSE, processing will continue by skipping the statement after the IF keyword.

The Boolean expression can consist of one or more expressions that are combined by using the AND and OR keywords. The following IF statement tests two unique expressions and will only execute the following statement if both conditions are TRUE:

```
If ((@price > $25) and (@type = 'business'))
```

Using the BEGIN...END

In the syntax of the IF statement, you might have noticed that you can execute one or more statements after the condition is tested. To execute more than one statement in an IF statement, you must group the SQL statements together. This is done by using the BEGIN and END keywords to block a section of code for use with the IF statement or the WHILE loop. Using the BEGIN and END keywords is actually quite simple. To block a group of statements together, simply precede the code with a BEGIN statement and follow it with an END statement. The following example shows an IF statement that executes multiple statements after the test:

11

```
USE pubs

IF (SELECT AVG(price) FROM titles WHERE type = 'mod_cook') < $15
BEGIN
   PRINT 'The following titles are excellent mod_cook books:'
   PRINT ' '
   SELECT SUBSTRING(title, 1, 35) AS Title
   FROM titles
   WHERE type = 'mod_cook'
END
ELSE
   IF (SELECT AVG(price) FROM titles WHERE type = 'mod_cook') > $15
BEGIN
   PRINT 'The following titles are expensive mod_cook books:'
   PRINT ' '
   SELECT SUBSTRING(title, 1, 35) AS Title
   FROM titles
   WHERE type = 'mod_cook'
END
```

If the average price of the select book type is less than $15, one message is printed, whereas another message is printed if the price is greater than $15.

I want to stop here for a moment and mention programming style. In the previous example of the BEGIN and END keywords, I indented the SQL statements that were contained within the BEGIN block. There are many ways to format the SQL code as you type it in. The method I use comes from my background as a mainframe programmer. I indent the SQL within the BEGIN block because doing so makes it easier for me to identify what statements are in the BEGIN block and which aren't. When you learn about the WHILE loop, you will see how this indenting of statements increases the readability of your SQL scripts.

Never use a BEGIN...END statement to group a single SQL statement. It is unnecessary and increases the amount of work the server must perform.

Using the WHILE Statement

Using the WHILE command enables you to repeat a series of SQL statements as long as the condition specified by the WHILE command is TRUE. When you are processing many rows of data, but need to look at the data one row at a time and perform the same actions on each row, the WHILE command provides you with the method for doing so. The following example shows how the WHILE statement works:

```
Use Northwind
Declare @cntr int
Select @cntr = 1
While @cntr < 6
Begin
       Select Productid, Productname From products Where productid = @cntr
       Select @cntr = @cntr + 1
End
```

Results:

```
Productid  Productname
---------- ----------------------------------------
1          Chai

(1 row(s) affected)

Productid  Productname
---------- ----------------------------------------
2          Chang

(1 row(s) affected)
```

```
Productid   Productname
----------- ----------------------------------------
3           Aniseed Syrup

(1 row(s) affected)

Productid   Productname
----------- ----------------------------------------
4           Chef Anton's Cajun Seasoning

(1 row(s) affected)

Productid   Productname
----------- ----------------------------------------
5           Chef Anton's Gumbo Mix

(1 row(s) affected)
```

In this example, I first declared the variable `@cntr`, which is used to hold the value that is used to select the `ProductID` in the `WHERE` clause. The `WHILE` command specifies to continue while the `@cntr` variable is less than `6`. A `BEGIN...END` block of SQL is then started where a `SELECT` statement retrieves the single row of data from the `Products` table. Finally, the `@cntr` variable is incremented by `1`. When the `END` statement is executed, the process goes back to the `WHILE` statement, the condition is tested, and if it is still `TRUE`, the program block is executed again.

11

Caution

It is very easy to accidentally create an infinite `WHILE` condition. If this happens, the code will execute until you close the connection to the server, or cancel the query.

Two extra keywords can be executed within a `WHILE` loop. If you tried to use them outside of a `WHILE` loop, an error would occur. These keywords are

`CONTINUE`	Immediately jumps to the top of the `WHILE` loop and re-tests the condition
`BREAK`	Immediately exits the `WHILE` loop regardless of the condition

Using the `PRINT` Statement

The `PRINT` statement can be used to display any type of message to the user. The `PRINT` statement returns a single line of output instead of a result set as the `SELECT` statement returns. To show you the difference, the following example will display the same message; first by using the SELECT statement, and then with the PRINT statement:

```
select 'The following titles are expensive mod_cook books:'
print 'The following titles are expensive mod_cook books:'
```

Results:

```
--------------------------------------------------
The following titles are expensive mod_cook books:

(1 row(s) affected)

The following titles are expensive mod_cook books:
```

You can see that the SELECT statement displays a column title and the row count message, whereas the PRINT statement will display only the requested message. To use the PRINT statement, you would simply pass a string to it. In fact, using many of the available functions, you can create very sophisticated messages with the PRINT statement. The following is an example of this:

```
print 'The last error number to occur was ' +
       convert(varchar(5), @@error)
```

Results:

```
The last error number to occur was 0
```

Using Comments

Comments are nonexecutable text strings that you place in the program code (they are also called *remarks*). Comments are used to document the functionality of the SQL code or to temporarily disable sections of T-SQL statements and batches that you are testing. Using comments to document SQL code makes any future changes easier. You can use comments to add the following information to a SQL script:

- SQL program name
- Author name
- Date of code changes
- Describe complicated calculations
- Explanation of programming method

SQL Server 2000 supports two different types of commenting syntax:

- -- (double hyphens)—These comment characters can be used on the same line as the code to be executed or by themselves. All text entered after the double hyphen to the end of the current line is part of the comment. If you want multiple-line comments using double hyphens, they must appear at the beginning of each line.

```
Select * from Products --This is a comment
```

- `/* */` (forward slash-asterisk pairs)—These characters can be used anywhere in a SQL script. Everything enclosed between the starting and ending pairs is considered a comment. Using this method of creating comments enables you to have a comment that spans multiple lines.

```
/* this is also a comment
on different lines */
```

Caution

> The only restriction that you should be aware of is that the multiple-line `/*...*/` comments cannot span a batch. The complete comment must be contained within a single batch.

> Comments are the best way to document what a SQL script does, or what certain variables are used for by a stored procedure. I highly recommended that you use comments at all times.

Trapping Errors and Implementing Error Handling

When working with T-SQL batch processing, errors will occur. You can either learn to handle them or let them handle you. That means when writing your T-SQL scripts, you need to ask yourself, "What should the SQL code do if something goes wrong?" If your batch is a multi-step process and something goes wrong in the middle, should the batch reverse the previous statements, just end, or continue as if nothing happened? Learning how to detect, display, and respond to errors that might occur is very important to the programming process. In this section, you will learn how to use the available global variables that return error information in your SQL scripts.

Communicating Error Messages

When an error occurs during the execution of T-SQL code, the server will determine what error has occurred, assign the appropriate number, and then display the message describing that error. An error number uniquely identifies each error message that the server knows about. Each of these descriptions is kept in the sysmessages table. The following SQL statement will display all the known error messages in the sysmessages table:

```
use master
select * from sysmessages
```

Results:

```
error       severity dlevel Description
----------- -------- ------ ------------------------------
1           10       0      Version date of last upgrade:
21          10       0      Warning: Fatal error %d occurr
102         15       0      Incorrect syntax near '%.*ls'.
103         15       0      The %S_MSG that starts with '%
104         15       0      ORDER BY items must appear in
105         15       0      Unclosed quotation mark before
106         16       0      Too many table names in the qu
...
21510       10       0      Data changes are not allowed w
21511       10       0      Neither MSmerge_contents nor M

(3782 row(s) affected)
```

When an error does occur, it is associated with the appropriate error number, and then the server reads the sysmessages table to retrieve the correct text description of that error to display. This process is called *raising an error*. When an error is raised, the server provides several attributes to assist in determining where and why an error has occurred. These attributes are

- Error Number—A unique number that identifies the error.
- Message String—A text string that provides diagnostic information about the cause of the error.
- Severity—Specifies the severity of the error. Low severity errors are usually informational, whereas high severity errors indicate problems that should be addressed immediately.
- State Code—Some errors can be raised at multiple locations in the source code for SQL Sever. Each location where an error code is raised assigns a unique state code. This state code can be used by a Microsoft support engineer to find the location in the source code where that error code is being raised.
- Procedure Name—The name of the stored procedure in which the error occurred, if available.
- Line Number—The line number in the stored procedure where the error occurred.

To determine the current error, you would use the @@ERROR variable or system function. This variable returns a zero if the last T-SQL statement executed successfully. If the last statement generated an error, @@ERROR returns the error number. The value contained in @@ERROR changes at the completion of each T-SQL statement. The @@ERROR variable can be displayed by using either the SELECT statement or the PRINT statement as shown in the following example:

```
print 'Error #: ' + str(@@error)
select @@ERROR
```

Results:

```
Error #:          0

-----------
0

(1 row(s) affected)
```

Or, you can use @@ERROR to identify that an error occurred and take action depending on the error. The following example shows how to use the IF...ELSE statement to check for a specific error:

```
If @@error = 547
   Print 'A check constraint violation has occurred'
```


Raising an Error Message

In addition to using the error messages that are included with SQL Server, you can use your own error messages when writing T-SQL code in stored procedures and triggers. You can raise an error by using the RAISERROR statement. This statement enables you to return a user-defined error message and set the system flag to record that an error has occurred. Using RAISERROR, you can either retrieve an entry from the sysmessages table or build a message yourself. After the message is defined, it is sent back to the client as a server error message. The syntax for the RAISERROR is as follows and Table 11.4 lists each of the arguments and their descriptions.

```
Raiserror ( {msg_id | msg_str}{,severity, state}
    [,argument[,…n]])
    [With option [,…n]]
```

Table 11.4 RAISERROR Arguments and Descriptions

Argument Name	*Description*
Msg_id	A user-defined error message that was stored in the sysmessages table.
Msg_str	An error message of up to 400 characters.

TABLE 11.4 continued

Argument Name	Description
`Severity`	User-defined severity level associated with this error. There are two sets of severity levels. Levels 0 through 18 can be used by any user. Levels 19 through 25 are used only by a system administrator defined user.

> Severity levels `20–25` are considered fatal and will terminate the client connection if they are encountered.

Argument Name	Description
`State`	An arbitrary number from 1 through 127 that represents the state of the error.
`Argument`	A parameter value used to substitute for variables that are defined in the `Msg_str` or the message identified by the `Msg_id` number.
`Option`	A custom option for the error. This option can be `Log`, `Nowait`, or `Seterror`.

Any error message can contain placeholders that will be replaced with values in the `RAISERROR` argument list. A placeholder is specified by a percent sign (`%`) followed by one of the following:

- `d`—Placeholder for a number
- `ls` or `*ls`—Placeholder for a string

The following example shows how to use the `RAISERROR` statement to display a custom error message:

```
Declare @dbid int, @dbname nvarchar(128)
Set @dbid = db_id()
Set @dbname = db_name()
Raiserror ('The current database ID is: %d, the database name is: %ls.',
          16,1,@dbid, @dbname)
```

Results:

```
Server: Msg 50000, Level 16, State 1, Line 4
The current database ID is: 6, the database name is: Northwind.
```

The `RAISERROR` statement is very useful when detecting errors in your SQL logic or in the data. Neither one of these conditions will trigger an error from the server. In the next section, you will see how to create code that will detect these types of errors as well as system-generated errors.

Creating an Error Message

In addition to using the error messages that are defined in SQL Server, or creating a custom error message displayed with the `RAISERROR` for a single event, you can create custom error messages and store them in the `sysmessages` table to be used by any SQL program that will execute on the server. This also enables you to define custom error messages once and use them in multiple locations in your SQL programs. As always, there are two ways that you can define a new error message. You can use the Enterprise Manager, or use the `sp_addmessage` system stored procedure to add messages to the `sysmessages` table.

Using Enterprise Manager to Create an Error Message

To define a new error message using the Enterprise Manager, expand the SQL Server Group folder to display the database servers. Then right-click on the database server you want to create the new error message. To display the Manage SQL Server Messages dialog box, select All Tasks, Manage SQL Server Messages from the pop-up menu, as shown in Figure 11.1.

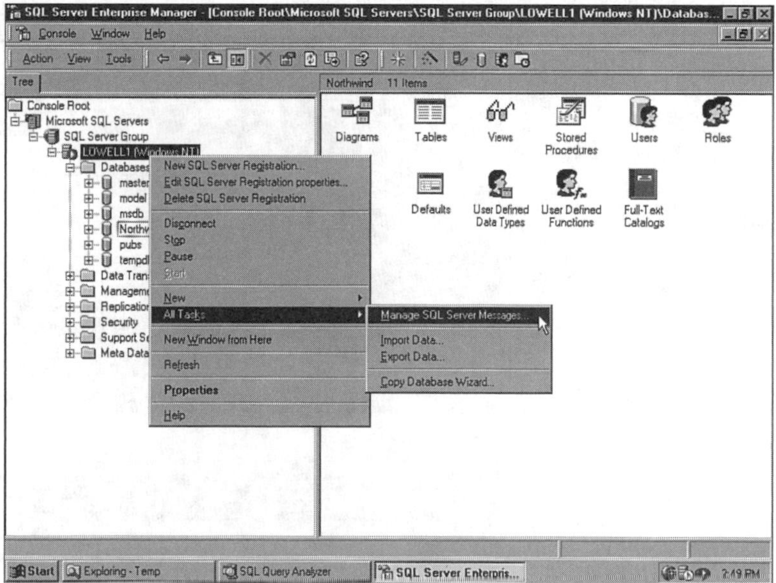

FIGURE 11.1

Selecting the Manage SQL Server Messages option.

In the Manage SQL Server Messages dialog, click on the Messages tab to display any customer error messages already defined, as shown in Figure 11.2.

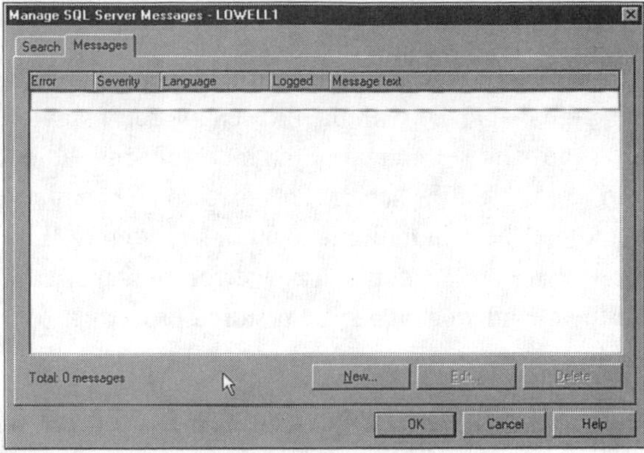

FIGURE 11.2
Displaying any custom error messages.

Now, to define a new error message, click the New button to display the New SQL Server Message dialog box as shown in Figure 11.3.

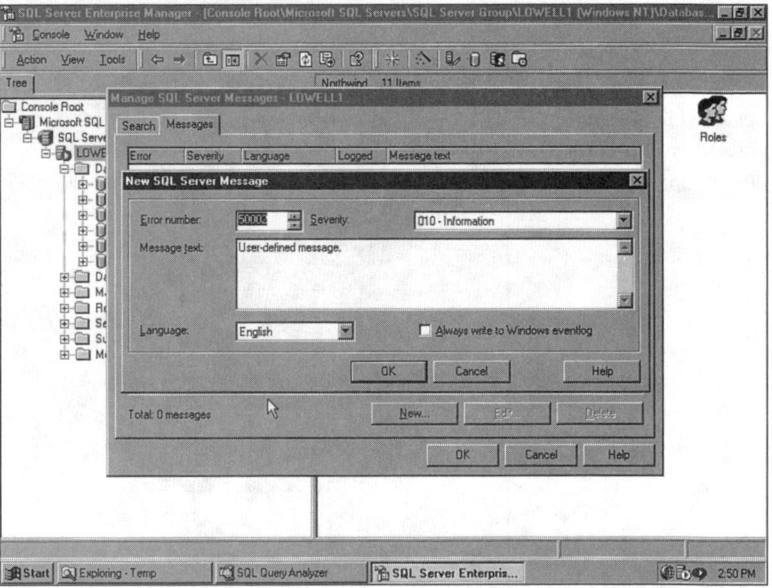

FIGURE 11.3
Defining a new server error message.

In this dialog, you can specify the error number (which must be greater than `50000`), the severity level, the language, and the actual message. Change the message text from `'User-defined message'` to `'This is a demo of Defining an Error Message'`. Now, click OK to save this new message and you will see it displayed in the Manage SQL Server Messages dialog (see Figure 11.4).

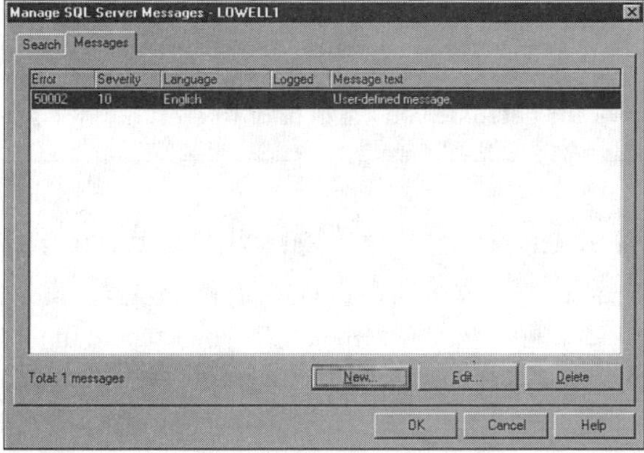

FIGURE 11.4
The new error message displayed in the Messages list.

You can now use your newly defined error in the `RAISERROR` statement as shown:

```
Raiserror (50002,0,1)
```

Results:

```
This is a demo of Defining an Error Message
```


Finally, you can also define a new error message using the stored procedure `sp_addmessage`. The syntax for this procedure is

```
Sp_addmessage [ @msgnum = ] msg_id,
    [@severity = ] severity,
    [@msgtext = ] 'msg'
    [,[@lang = ] 'language']
    [,[@with_log = ] 'with_log']
    [,[@replace = 'replace']
```

The following example shows the previous error message being defined using this stored procedure:

```
Use Master
Sp_addmessage 50002,
    10,
    'This is a demo of Defining an Error Message2',
    @replace='REPLACE'
```

Finally, if you want to delete an error message that you have previously defined, you would use the `sp_dropmessage` stored procedure as shown in the following example:

```
Use Master
Sp_dropmessage 50002
```

It is important to make sure that you are using the `master` database when adding or dropping a message. The `USE MASTER` statement should be used to set the database you are in prior to executing the stored procedure.

Coding Standard Error Handling Methods

Standard error handling is done using many of the programming techniques you have learned earlier today. For every statement that you execute in a SQL script, you must check the `@@ERROR` variable to see whether an error has occurred. By using the `@@ERROR` variable, you can

- Detect specific errors
- Conditionally exit a stored procedure or trigger
- Determine whether to commit or rollback a transaction
- Use local variables to check several statements at once

Depending on the type of processing the stored procedure or trigger is performing, you could check for and handle errors differently. If a procedure is not updating any tables, you could check for errors after each statement and store the value of any errors found to return to the calling routine. This will work only if you do not need to reverse any of the commands that were processed. The following is an example of this type of stored procedure:

```
Use Northiwnd
CREATE PROCEDURE SampleProcedure @EmployeeIDParm INT,
            @MaxQuantity INT OUTPUT
AS
DECLARE @ErrorSave INT
SET @ErrorSave = 0

SELECT FirstName, LastName, Title
FROM Employees
WHERE EmployeeID = @EmployeeIDParm

IF (@@ERROR <> 0)
    SET @ErrorSave = @@ERROR

SELECT @MaxQuantity = MAX(Quantity)
FROM [Order Details]

IF (@@ERROR <> 0)
    SET @ErrorSave = @@ERROR

RETURN @ErrorSave
```

The entire procedure will be executed whether or not an error occurs. This is okay as long as no data is invalid because of the error. This stored procedure could be modified to exit and return the error value anytime a non-zero error is detected by making use of the `BEGIN...END` statement logic. The following example shows those changes:

```
Use Northiwnd
CREATE PROCEDURE SampleProcedure @EmployeeIDParm INT,
            @MaxQuantity INT OUTPUT
AS

SELECT FirstName, LastName, Title
FROM Employees
WHERE EmployeeID = @EmployeeIDParm

IF (@@ERROR <> 0)
BEGIN
    RETURN (@@ERROR)
END

SELECT @MaxQuantity = MAX(Quantity)
FROM [Order Details]

IF (@@ERROR <> 0)
BEGIN
    RETURN (@@ERROR)
END
```


Finally, if you have a SQL statement that modifies data, such as an UPDATE statement, and you are using transaction processing, you might want to `ROLLBACK` or `COMMIT` the transaction depending on the value of the `@@ERROR` variable. The following is an example of this type of error processing:

```
Use northwind
Begin Transaction
Update Products
Set UnitsInStock = UnitsInStock - 1
Where ProductID = 1
If @@Error <> 0
Begin
    Rollback Transaction
    Return (@@ERROR)
End
Insert [order details](orderid, productid, unitprice, quantity, discount)
       Values(1002,1,3.50,1,.25)
If @@Error <> 0
Begin
    Rollback Transaction
    Return (@@Error)
End
Commit Transaction
Return (0)
```

This routine updates the Products table to decrease the quantity of a product. If this update generates an error, you do not want to insert a new order row. If an error is encountered anywhere in the routine, a ROLLBACK TRANSACTION statement is executed and the error number is returned to the calling routine. If there was no error, a COMMIT TRANSACTION is executed and a 0 is returned.

This is only the tip of the iceberg when it comes to error processing. However, you can see that you need to check for errors after every SQL statement that you execute.

Summary

Many topics covered in today's lesson. The first topic we discussed today was how to define and use variables in your SQL programs to store data for later use. You also learned many of the fundamental concepts of using T-SQL as a programming language. This includes controlling the flow of your program code as it is executed by using the IF and WHILE statements to test conditions. In addition, you learned how to group statements together in blocks using the BEGIN...END statements.

In the second half of the day, you learned about error processing and the variables and features that SQL Server provides you with to identify errors and even add your own features to the system. Finally, by combining many of today's concepts, you saw how to test for an error and then execute a grouping of SQL code if an error did occur.

Q&A

Q Does SQL Server allow me to create an array of variables?

A No, arrays are not supported by SQL Server.

Q I have used Visual Basic. Aren't there more program flow statements that I could use, such as CASE and FOR-NEXT?

A No. The IF and WHILE statements will provide you with as much control as you would need. The CASE statement is not used for controlling the flow of execution in T-SQL. It is most often used for conditional execution inside a SELECT or UPDATE statement.

Workshop

The Workshop provides quiz questions to help you solidify your understanding of the material covered and exercises to provide you with experience in using what you've learned. Try to answer the quiz and exercise questions before checking the answers in

Appendix A, "Answers to Quizzes and Exercises," and make sure that you understand the answers before continuing to the next lesson.

Quiz

1. Name the five steps that the server must perform when a batch of SQL statements is sent for execution.
2. What are two of the major flow of control statements that you can use?
3. What value does the variable `@@ERROR` contain?

Exercise

1. Write a SQL statement that displays the current version of SQL Server.

DAY 12

Understanding Database Locking

In yesterday's lesson, you learned how to write more complex programs and handle variables. Today, you will learn how SQL Server locks data to isolate work in your applications. The most fundamental job of a relational database is to maintain data integrity, especially when many users are working in and around the same data. Databases use locks to make certain that the work you do is always complete and consistent.

By the end of this lesson, you will

- Understand how SQL Server uses locks
- Be able to use different transaction isolation levels to manage lock persistence
- Know how to read locking output to find blocking locks
- Be able to control lock types through query hints
- Understand and be able to avoid deadlocks

Lock Fundamentals

So far, we've concentrated on the internal consistency maintained by a transaction. We've seen how the automatic begin, commit, and rollback transaction mechanisms make certain that entire transactions are completed or no work is done at all.

It's also important that a transaction be *isolated* from other activity. A transaction uses locks to prevent others from changing relevant data while the transaction is active.

In this section, you will learn about many characteristics of locks. Let's define some terms before we get started:

- *Lock mode* defines how a lock interacts with other processes and locks. We'll look closely at shared, exclusive, update, shared intent, and exclusive intent locks.
- *Lock scope* refers to how much data is locked. Locks can be acquired at the database, table, extent, page, and row levels.
- *Lock persistence* describes how long a lock lasts.

Let's consider an example: My wife and I both carry ATM cards that access the same account. What if each of us makes a $50 withdrawal at the same time, but we have only $75 in the bank? If there were no locking to isolate each transaction, each of us could make a withdrawal at the same time and together we would overdraw the account. You can see in Figure 12.1 that the second withdrawal proceeded because the first withdrawal did not block its access to the account.

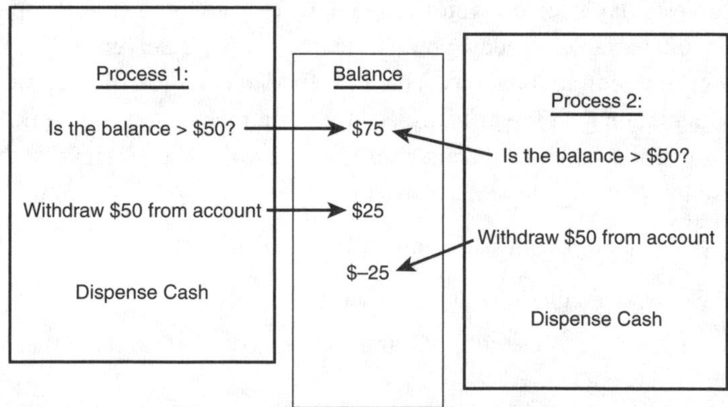

FIGURE 12.1

Without transaction isolation, the account is overdrawn.

The first transaction needs to lock the account to prevent further access. Only when the process is complete should another transaction be permitted to proceed. Figure 12.2 shows how transaction isolation prevents the overdraft problem discussed earlier.

FIGURE 12.2

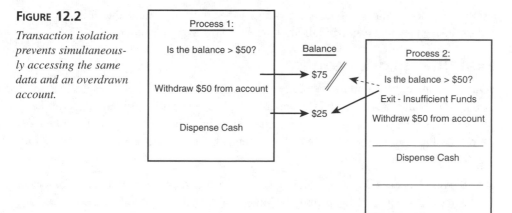

Transaction isolation prevents simultaneously accessing the same data and an overdrawn account.

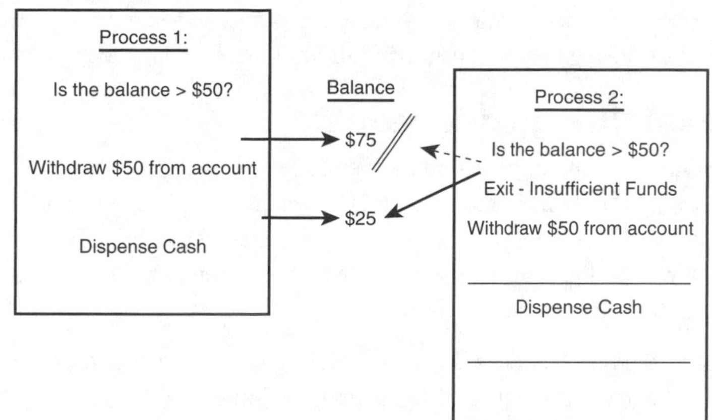

Just as with transactions, locks are automatically managed by SQL Server. The server decides when to lock data, how much to lock, and the type of lock to use. The server also determines when to release a lock. We will look at each of these aspects of locking to understand how your programs will interact with locks, and how you can influence how the server manages them.

Even though you don't actually create or drop locks in SQL Server, understanding how they work will help you avoid mistakes and understand better what's going on under the covers.

Understanding Lock Modes

There are two broad categories of locks: shared locks (also called *read locks*) and exclusive locks (also called *write locks*). Shared locks are obtained whenever a process reads data. Select statements obtain read locks, but so do update, delete, and insert statements when they use information in one table to update another.

Exclusive locks are obtained whenever a process modifies data. Typically, exclusive locks are assigned during insert, update, and delete processes. Select statements get exclusive locks on temporary worktables. Create, alter, and drop statements also get exclusive locks.

Shared and exclusive locks behave the way their names imply. Another user can read (select) through another user's shared lock. Both users will hold shared locks at that point. You cannot write through another user's shared lock because you would need an exclusive lock; you usually wait until the shared lock frees up, and then acquire the exclusive lock.

Exclusive locks permit only one user at a time to see a unit of data. Other users' shared and exclusive lock requests will fail until the exclusive lock is released.

Examining Lock Scope

SQL Server records and manages locks at many levels. Database locks are obtained to record activity and prevent certain maintenance operations until all users are out of the database. Table-level locks are used to manage large operations. A very common type of table-level lock is the *extent lock*, which prevents other table-level operations from occurring until the extent lock is released.

SQL Server also locks data at the eight-page level and at the row level. Page-level locks can be very efficient. Usually, page-level locks don't interfere with other users, especially where there is a large amount of data and a fairly small number of users updating the data. Where you have a unique index or primary key defined for a table, SQL Server can use row-level locks to manage multi-user concurrency one row at a time. This is the smallest lock that the server will obtain on a table.

During table creation and the allocation of space, SQL Server will also lock eight-page (64KB) *extents*. When tables or indexes require more space, SQL Server provides it one extent at a time (rather than one page at a time). During the allocation, other processes cannot access that space.

Note

> Remember that an extent is made up of eight pages of storage.

SQL Server makes a decision during query optimization about the locking level that makes sense for each query. The server looks at the likely hit percentage (rows found per rows scanned) for the row retrieval method planned, and decides what level of locking would balance performance and concurrency. Some locking strategies minimize resource usage (table locks are cheap; row locks are expensive). Other strategies maximize concurrency (table locks block all users; row locks block almost nobody). In the section "Using Hints to Control Lock Types," you will learn to use table-level hints to suggest locking levels to SQL Server.

Examining Locks

Let's experiment with locks a little bit. To do that, we need to make the locks stay around long enough for us to see them. Ordinarily, and particularly on small tables such as those in the `Northwind` database, processes run so quickly that you can't see their locks.

This experiment will help you understand lock *persistence*, or how long locks stick around. Under different circumstances, different kinds of locks last for more or less time. We'll actually take advantage of that to inspect locks.

Later in the lesson, you will learn to use `BEGIN TRANSACTION` and `COMMIT TRANSACTION` to group sets of statements together into a single transaction. You will also learn to use `ROLLBACK TRANSACTION` to reverse the work in a pending transaction. We'll use those statements now to hold open a transaction so that we can query the locks created by various operations. We'll also see how locks affect other processes.

We'll start by deleting rows from the `Order Details` and `Orders` tables. The delete operation requires an exclusive lock to guarantee the consistency of its own operations. Open a window in the Query Analyzer and execute this query:

```
begin transaction
delete [Order Details]
where OrderID = 10258
delete Orders
where OrderID = 10258
```

The first line starts a transaction, but the transaction is not completed. That would require a `COMMIT TRANSACTION` statement at the end. Until you commit the transaction, SQL Server holds any locks obtained during the deletion. After you execute this query, you can examine the locks it created.

Examining Locks with the Enterprise Manager

You can examine locks in SQL Enterprise Manager or using `sp_lock` in the Query Analyzer. We'll start with SQL-EM, and then look at `sp_lock` output. Both return the same information.

12

To observe lock information in SQL-EM, use the tree control to open the current server. Under Management, Current Activity, you will find two locking options. You can observe locks by process ID or by object. Let's look at locks by object first.

Figure 12.3 shows the lock information for the `Orders` table after the delete has occurred. By default, the list is sorted on the `ProcessID` column. By clicking twice at the top of the `Lock Type` column, I've resorted the list of locks in descending order by lock type. This will help you more easily understand the list.

Note

> Most of the time, when you look for locks on the server, you won't find many. That's because locks are maintained only as long as the transaction takes. Most simple transactions take hundredths of a second, so your chances of finding locks aren't too good. We found these locks because we executed a transaction and did not commit our work. Don't do this in real life.

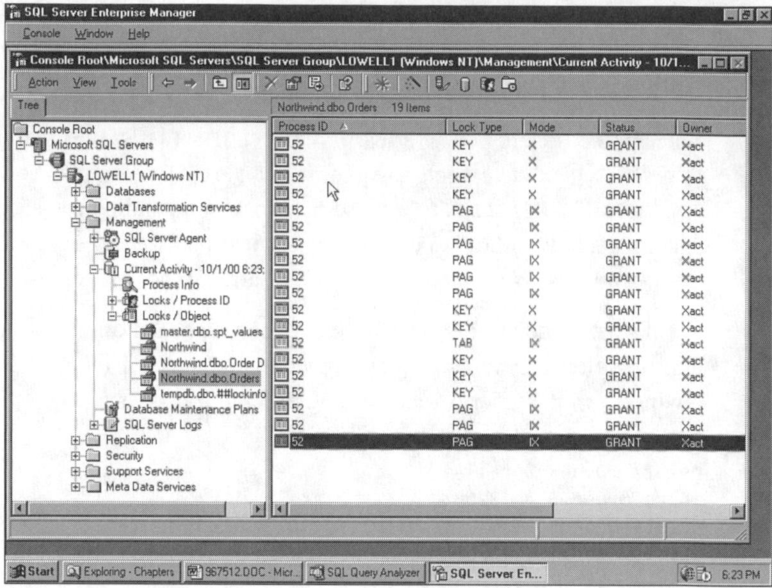

FIGURE 12.3
Enterprise Manager enables you to look at locks by process ID or object. This list of locks on the `Orders` *table was obtained during a delete statement.*

The first lock in the list—after the list is sorted in reverse order by lock type—is a table lock (lock type `TAB`) on the `Orders` table. Don't worry! SQL Server won't lock an entire table to delete one row unless there are no indexes on the table, or if you delete all the rows. This lock is an intent lock, which you can determine because of the mode, `IX`. An intent lock tells other processes that this process intends to do work somewhere in this table. The mode `IX` means that the process intends to do exclusive work (`I` for *intent*, `X` for *eXclusive*); that is, the process intends to update one or many rows in the table.

Intent locks block other processes from getting table-level locks that would conflict with the work being done somewhere inside the table. Many processes can all hold a mix of exclusive and shared intent locks for a single table. (Shared intent locks are identified with the mode `IS`.) The intent locks only indicate that many processes are working in the table, but nobody else can obtain an exclusive table-level lock until the intent locks are cleared.

SQL Server can also obtain an intent lock on a page. These locks warn other processes that work is going on within the page. The nine page locks in the list (lock type `PAG`) are all intent locks. Why nine locks? There is one page lock for each index on the `Orders` table. Each index is stored in a separate allocation structure and requires a lock on the page where the entry for `OrderID 10258` is stored, and will be deleted. The actual page number is displayed in the `Resource` column.

Exploring Page Headers

Why are all the page entries marked with the index value `PK_Orders`? Each page entry should have the name of a different index.

It might be a bug or a deficiency in the table in the `master` database that stores locking information, `syslockinfo`. I wondered about it, so I asked the server to display the header for each page. In the page header, you can find the object ID and index number.

This is a little technical, but there's an undocumented command to display page headers. To display the header from the fifth item in the list, page 1:252, I ran this query:

```
dbcc traceon (3604)
dbcc page ('Northwind', 1, 252, 0)
dbcc traceoff (3604)
```

The dbcc, or Database Console Commands, enable you to check the physical and logical consistency of a database. Many DBCC statements can even fix detected problems.

Here is the page header displayed by the `dbcc page` command:

```
1: Page @0x1B9B0000
2: ----------------
3: m_pageId = (1:252)       m_headerVersion = 1  m_type = 2
4: m_typeFlagBits = 0x0     m_level = 0          m_flagBits = 0x0
5: m_objId = 1781581385     m_indexId = 5        m_prevPage = (0:0)
6: m_nextPage = (1:206)     pminlen = 9          m_slotCnt = 290
7: m_freeCnt = 4036         m_freeData = 7092    m_reservedCnt = 0
8: m_lsn = (106:396:31)     m_xactReserved = 0   m_xdesId = (0:59945)
9: m_ghostRecCnt = 1        m_tornBits = 2
```

Line 5 includes both the object ID and the index ID. As you saw back on Day 3, "Working with Columns," metadata functions can convert these numeric IDs into meaningful names. This query converts the object ID to an object name:

```
select
        object_name(1781581385) 'Object Name'
```

As you would expect, this query returns the name `Orders`. The easiest way to get the index name for index `5` is to query the `sysindexes` system table:

```
select
        indid, name
from
        sysindexes
where
        id = 1781581385
```

Results:

```
indid  name
------ ----------------------------------------
     1 PK_Orders
     2 CustomerID
     3 CustomersOrders
     4 EmployeeID
```

```
5 EmployeesOrders
6 OrderDate
7 ShippedDate
8 ShippersOrders
9 ShipPostalCode
```

I've displayed the complete list of indexes. There are nine real indexes, which corresponds to the number of page locks in the lock display. Index 5 is Employee Orders.

Caution

You must be a system administrator to use `dbcc page`. If you have a local instance of the server on your machine, you can try it there.

This command is mostly used by Microsoft's technical people to diagnose problems and find bugs.

The next nine rows are key locks. *Key locks* are locks on individual rows in the database. The mode of the key locks is `X`, which means that they are (finally) real locks, not intent locks. These exclusive locks block other readers and writers attempting to access these individual rows in the database.

Each of the nine key locks points to the deleted row in one of the nine indexes. Notice that the indexes are properly named in this case. The key resource identifiers are hexadecimal identifiers, used internally by the server.

Examining Locks with `sp_lock`

You can also use the stored procedure `sp_lock` to get locking information. You can execute the stored procedure on its own, or you can pass one or two server process IDs (spids) to limit the results to display locks for only specific processes.

Server process IDs are assigned when you log in to the server. They are managed in the system table `sysprocesses` in the `master` database.

To get your current server process ID, use

```
select @@spid
------
    57
```

You can get a list of current users from the Current Activity, Process Info tab in SQL-EM. To get a list of current users and their process IDs from a stored procedure, use `sp_who`. Figure 12.4 displays the output from `sp_who` for my test server. When many sessions are logged in for a single user name, it can be difficult to tell processes apart.

> One important note about `sp_who`: Whenever you look at the list of processes, there will always be at least one runnable process; that is, a process currently executing. That runnable process is the `sp_who` query itself. I have seen people spend hours trying to eliminate the running process, only to have it reappear every time they run the query again.

FIGURE 12.4

The stored procedure `sp_who` *reports a list of current users and their process identifiers. The only runnable process is the* `sp_who` *query itself (process* `52`*).*

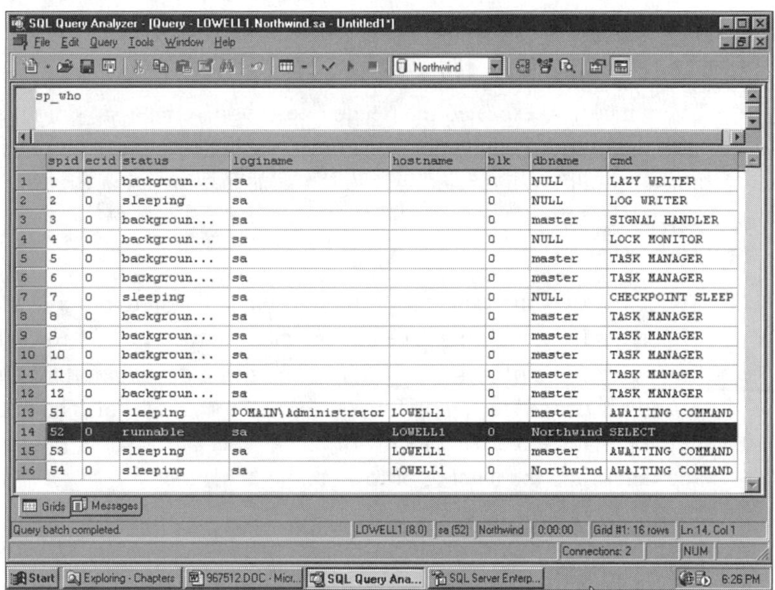

	spid	ecid	status	loginame	hostname	blk	dbname	cmd
1	1	0	backgroun...	sa		0	NULL	LAZY WRITER
2	2	0	sleeping	sa		0	NULL	LOG WRITER
3	3	0	backgroun...	sa		0	master	SIGNAL HANDLER
4	4	0	backgroun...	sa		0	NULL	LOCK MONITOR
5	5	0	backgroun...	sa		0	master	TASK MANAGER
6	6	0	backgroun...	sa		0	master	TASK MANAGER
7	7	0	sleeping	sa		0	NULL	CHECKPOINT SLEEP
8	8	0	backgroun...	sa		0	master	TASK MANAGER
9	9	0	backgroun...	sa		0	master	TASK MANAGER
10	10	0	backgroun...	sa		0	master	TASK MANAGER
11	11	0	backgroun...	sa		0	master	TASK MANAGER
12	12	0	backgroun...	sa		0	master	TASK MANAGER
13	51	0	sleeping	DOMAIN\Administrator	LOWELL1	0	master	AWAITING COMMAND
14	52	0	runnable	sa	LOWELL1	0	Northwind	SELECT
15	53	0	sleeping	sa	LOWELL1	0	master	AWAITING COMMAND
16	54	0	sleeping	sa	LOWELL1	0	Northwind	AWAITING COMMAND

This is a partial result set from `sp_lock` command:

```
sp_lock 53
```

Results:

```
spid dbid ObjId      IndId Type Resource   Mode  Status
---- ---- ---------- ----- ---- ---------- ----- ------
  53    6          0     0 DB              S     GRANT
  53    6  325576198     1 PAG  1:148      IX    GRANT
  53    6  325576198     1 PAG  1:183      IX    GRANT
  53    6  325576198     1 PAG  1:189      IX    GRANT
  53    6  325576198     1 PAG  1:187      IX    GRANT
  53    6  325576198     3 PAG  1:185      IX    GRANT
  53    6  325576198     1 PAG  1:199      IX    GRANT
  53    6  325576198     1 PAG  1:198      IX    GRANT
  53    6 1781581385     1 PAG  1:207      IX    GRANT
  53    6 1781581385     1 KEY  (1200...   X     GRANT
...
```

```
53    6    325576198         3 KEY   (1700…    X        GRANT
53    6    325576198         1 KEY   (1700…    X        GRANT
53    6    325576198         4 KEY   (1700…    X        GRANT
53    6    325576198         5 KEY   (1700…    X        GRANT
```

This is the same information you saw in SQL-EM. Table names and index names are displayed as object and index IDs, and database names are listed as numbers. The data is not as carefully sorted as in SQL-EM, but the information about each lock is the same.

Testing Lock Interaction

Ever since you executed the delete query, you've been holding the locks open. The session that performed the delete can read through the locks it created. Try running this query from the same window where the delete operation occurred:

```
select count(*)
from Orders
```

You should get the value `830`, but don't panic if you don't; a row might have been added or deleted from the table. The `Orders` table starts with 831 rows, but the current transaction deletes one of those rows. This demonstrates an important point about transactions: *A process is not blocked by its own locks.* Process `53` holds an exclusive lock on a page in the `Orders` table. That lock will block other readers, but process `53` can read the page and determine the number of rows in the `Orders` table.

Try opening a new window and running the same query. Even though you log in with the same username and are accessing the server from the same workstation and application, SQL Server isolates each process. The query window appears to hang, waiting for a response from the server. Figure 12.5 shows the Query Analyzer waiting for results after the query is executed from a second window.

How long will this lock hang around? And how long will the query run until it fails? The lock will last until the transaction is committed or rolled back. If the server goes down, the user exits the session or the server or administrator kills the session, the transaction will roll back and the changes will be reversed.

Setting the Lock Timeout

How long will the query wait for a lock to be released? That depends on the application. Every session can define a *lock timeout*, which is the amount of time that the session should wait for a response before declaring a failure and returning a timeout error. Common timeouts for data entry applications run from 10,000 milliseconds to a minute or two. The default value is `-1`, which means that the application should wait indefinitely. A value of `0` means that the application will never wait for a lock, and the server should return an error immediately if it encounters a blocking lock.

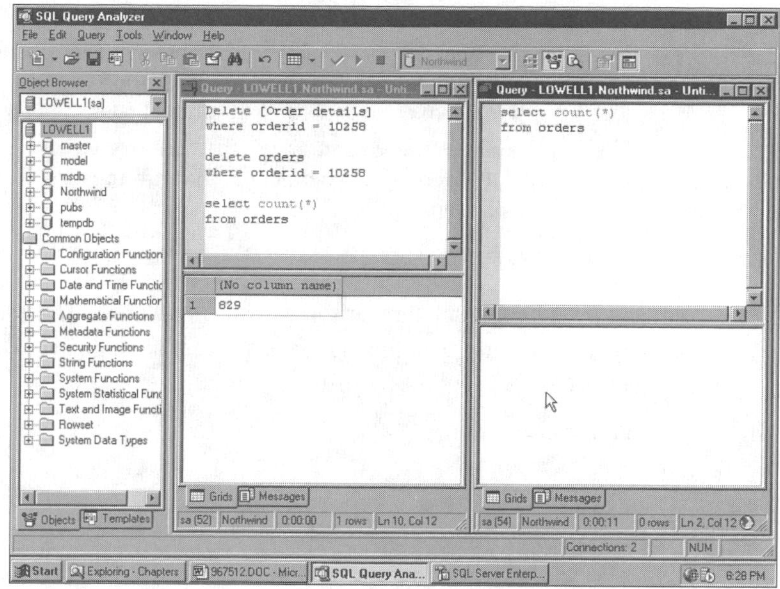

FIGURE 12.5

The window on the left can select from the `Orders` *table, but the window on the right cannot. The spinning globe icon in the lower-right corner of the window on the right tells you that the process is still executing.*

You can set the lock timeout for the Query Analyzer in the Connections tab of the Options dialog, which is displayed by selecting Tools, Options in the Query Analyzer (see Figure 12.6). A value of `-1` means that the query should wait indefinitely when it encounters a lock.

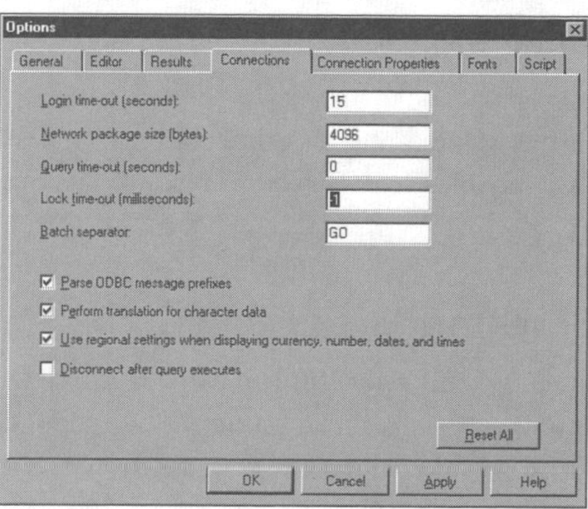

FIGURE 12.6

Set the lock timeout in this dialog. Notice that the query is still running in the background (the globe is still turning).

In the same Options dialog are two other timeout parameters. The *login timeout* determines how long an application should look for a server before returning an error. Sometimes a value of `60` is useful on large networks.

The *query timeout* determines the time to wait for a slow query. This is a useful governor to avoid queries that run too long without meeting a locking problem.

You can also manage lock timeouts in a T-SQL statement. The `lock_timeout` setting enables you to define a lock timeout for a session, an application, or a specific query. This query sets the lock timeout to 10 seconds:

```
set lock_timeout 10000
```

The timeout is specified in milliseconds, so `10000` represents only 10 seconds.

When you run the `SELECT COUNT(*)` query in a new window with the lock timeout setting, you will get this response after 10 seconds:

```
Server: Msg 1222, Level 16, State 49, Line 2
Lock request time out period exceeded.
```

If you plan to monitor timeouts in your application, you will need to trap error 1222 and deal with it. You might decide to warn the user or to wait a certain amount of time before re-executing.

You can access the current value of the lock timeout on your session with the `@@lock_timeout` global variable. To report the value, use this query:

```
select @@lock_timeout
```

Monitoring Blocking Locks

If you are working along with me, you still have that blocking lock hanging around your system. My blocked process has now been waiting for 28 minutes. Let's look at some resources available for seeing blocking locks and blocked processes.

The Process Info list under Current Activity in SQL Enterprise Manager enables you to unravel complex locking chains. Figure 12.17 shows the Process Info list while the select process waits for the transaction to complete.

> **Note** When you look at the following figures, the process numbers might be different on your computer and SQL Server database.

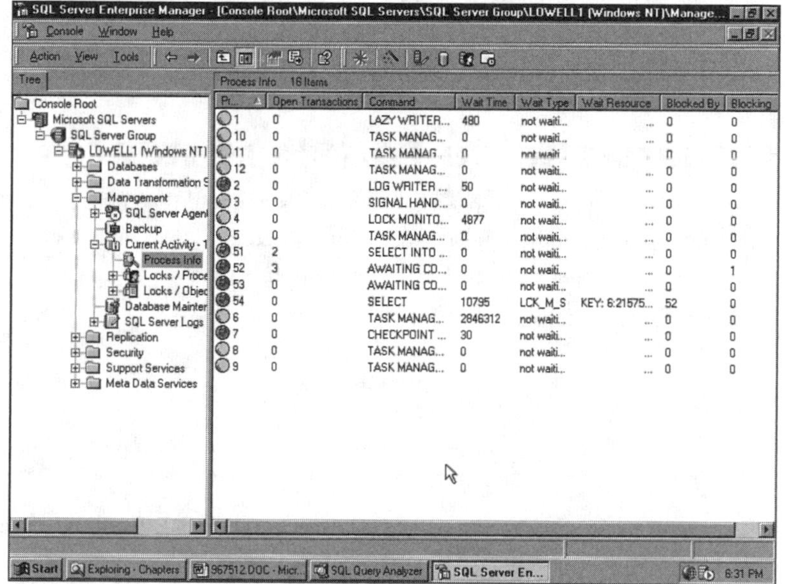

FIGURE 12.7

The Process Info list has a number of useful data elements about each process. A number of columns were hidden to display the lock-related information. Notice how the highlighted process, number `51`*, is blocked by process* `53`*.*

The only running processes are `51` and `54` (the rest of the user processes are `AWAITING COMMAND`). Our process is `51`, which is blocked by process `53` (see the Blocked By column). It has been waiting for 1.7 million milliseconds or almost 30 minutes. Process `53` is idle (`AWAITING COMMAND`), and is blocking one process. It has an open transaction pending (see the Open Transactions column).

12

If I were assigned to troubleshoot in this situation, I would look for the blocked process (non-zero in the Blocked By column), and use that process ID to determine whether the blocking process is running or idle. If the process is idle, someone made a mistake (idle processes should generally not hold locks). I would notify that person by phone or ask an administrator to kill the process.

> **Note** For this to work properly, do not delete the BEGIN TRANSACTION query before running the Select Count query. For the ROLLBACK TRANSACTION to work, it has to be executed in the same connection or window as the BEGIN TRANSACTION.

Go ahead and release the select statement by rolling back the transaction in the first window. To do that, execute this statement:

```
Rollback Transaction
```

Almost instantly, the select query should return a result. (How many rows did it find?) If you check with sp_lock or in the SQL-EM, all the locks held by that process should be gone.

Understanding Lock Persistence

You've already seen that exclusive locks are held throughout a transaction and are released when the transaction is committed or rolled back. Let's try a similar experiment with a select statement. We'll start with this query:

```
begin transaction
select CustomerID
  from Orders
 where OrderID = 10258

CustomerID
----------
ERNSH
```

The first line of the query creates a transaction. The select statement acquires a shared lock on the row in the Orders table. Intent locks are acquired. Let's look at the locks held by this process:

```
spid   dbid   ObjId      IndId  Type Resource Mode     Status
------ ------ ---------- ------ ---- -------- -------- ------
    57      6          0      0 DB            S        GRANT
```

Even though the process acquired locks during the select process, the locks are gone. In its default mode, SQL Server releases shared locks after they are used, regardless of whether a transaction is running (the *transaction state*). This helps improve concurrency when many users are working.

This characteristic of locks is called persistence. *Persistence* is the length of time a lock is held. Locks can be held throughout the transaction, released after they are used, or never acquired. You will manipulate lock persistence with transaction isolation levels (which are covered later in the next section) and with table hints.

Working with Transaction Isolation Levels

The default transaction isolation level in SQL Server is called *read committed.* In that mode, exclusive locks persist throughout the transaction, but shared locks are released as soon as the page is no longer needed. If the process needs to refer to a page a second time, it acquires the select lock again. This is also known as isolation level 1.

The transaction isolation level determines lock persistence. The ANSI standard calls for databases to support four transaction isolation levels. We'll take a minute to review the four levels, and then experiment with them so that you understand how transaction isolation level might affect your applications.

The four transaction isolation levels refer to the way that shared locks are acquired and held. (Data modifications always obtain exclusive locks and the exclusive locks are always held throughout the transaction.) The isolation levels are listed here in order from least restrictive to most restrictive.

- Read uncommitted—(Level 0) Read operations do not obtain locks. You can read through any lock (even an exclusive lock), known as a *dirty read*. Processes can modify data while it is being read. A dirty read is one that contains uncommitted data.
- Read committed—(Level 1) Read operations obtain locks, but they release them immediately after the page is read. Exclusive locks are respected. If a page is read a second time, a new lock is obtained, but the data might have changed in the meantime. This is the SQL Server default.
- Repeatable read—(Level 2) Read operations obtain locks and the locks are held through the transaction. This prevents other transactions from modifying values, in case they need to be read again (repeatable) or modified by the process later in the transaction.
- Serializable—(Level 3) Read operations obtain locks and the locks are held through the transaction, making the read repeatable. Phantom inserts and updates are blocked using a range lock on the data set. This is the most restrictive level, and is most likely to create a blocking lock.

All the examples you have seen so far have demonstrated the default behavior of the server: using the read uncommitted isolation level. To change the isolation level, use one of these commands:

```
set transaction isolation level read uncommitted

set transaction isolation level read committed

set transaction isolation level repeatable read

set transaction isolation level serializable
```

Let's look at how the other isolation levels work.

Experimenting with Dirty Reads

The read uncommitted isolation level, also called isolation level 0, implements dirty reads. Dirty reads allow select statements to read through a data set without creating or respecting locks. The reads are called "dirty" because the pages being read might be in the midst of being modified by a transaction.

We'll create another pending transaction and change the supplier, `Escargot Nouveaux`, to `Joe's Rib Joint`. Execute this script in your current window:

```
begin transaction
update Suppliers
       /* two '' to store one in the string */
   set CompanyName = 'Joe''s Rib Joint'
 where SupplierID = 27
```

This process obtains exclusive locks in the table and indexes on the `Suppliers` table. As you've already seen, another process coming to look at supplier 27 will be blocked by the exclusive lock.

If you select the modified row without first changing the transaction isolation level, the update will block your select. This is the same situation we created earlier after a delete. Before you execute the select, set the transaction isolation level for dirty reads. Here's the command:

```
set transaction isolation level read uncommitted
```

Now execute a test query in the same session:

```
select CompanyName
  from Suppliers
 where SupplierID = 27
```

Results:

```
CompanyName
----------------------------------------
Joe's Rib Joint
```

Despite the exclusive lock, your process reads the modified data before the transaction is committed.

When should you use isolation level 0? Dirty reads are useful when you need to perform large queries on a table that is heavily updated. Any time you can accept an answer that's "close enough," you can use dirty reads.

If you need absolute precision, as with bank balances or inventory control, dirty reads will return data in a partial or inconsistent state. Avoid level 0 in those circumstances.

The transaction isolation level settings are specific to a connection. They characterize the way that a session (a window in Query Analyzer) will obtain and keep locks. The easiest way to reset the transaction isolation level when you are working in Query Analyzer is to close the window and reconnect to the server. I suggest that you close any open transactions by exiting all your open connections before continuing.

Understanding More Restrictive Isolation Levels

The isolation levels that support repeatable reads and serialized work are also known as levels 2 and 3. These higher isolation levels obtain and keep shared locks throughout a transaction.

In a new window, execute this query:

```
set transaction isolation level repeatable read
begin transaction
select CompanyName
  from Suppliers
 where SupplierID = 27
```

Here are the locks that `sp_lock` reported for this process:

```
dbid   ObjId       IndId  Type Resource        Mode  Status
------ ----------- ------ ---- --------------- ----- ------
     6           0      0 DB                   S     GRANT
     6  2137058649      1 PAG  1:292           IS    GRANT
     6  2137058649      1 KEY  (1b007df0a359)  S     GRANT
     6  2137058649      0 TAB                  IS    GRANT
```

There are four locks.

- The database lock indicates that a user is working in this database. It is a shared lock.
- The table-level shared intent lock (mode `IS`) reports that a user holds a shared lock somewhere in this table. This lock prevents another user from obtaining a table-level exclusive lock until it is released. Another process could obtain a table-level exclusive intent lock (mode `IX`), indicating that the process is updating something in the table.
- A shared key lock (mode `S`) indicates a real lock on this row. Other users may read the row, but no one may modify it until the transaction completes.
- The page-level shared intent lock (mode `IS`) reports that a user holds a shared lock on a key within the page. This prevents other users from obtaining an exclusive page-level lock until this transaction completes.

12

Because the transaction is running at this transaction isolation level, shared locks are held instead of being released immediately. We can now see three shared locks on the table, page, and key.

What is the value of holding shared locks? If a process needs to reread or modify information about a row later in the transaction, the repeatable read setting guarantees that the data will not change. Without this setting, another user could modify the data or even delete the row.

Listing 12.1 deletes an order and all of its associated order detail rows if the total value of the order is less than $2000.

LISTING 12.1 Deleting Rows for Order Less Than $2000

```
 1: declare @OrderID int
 2: select @OrderID = 10258
 3: begin transaction
 4: if  (
 5:         select sum(Quantity * UnitPrice * (1 - Discount))
 6:           from [Order Details]
 7:          where OrderID = @OrderID
 8:     ) < $2000
 9:
10: begin
11:         delete [Order Details]
12:          where OrderID = @OrderID
13:
14:         delete Orders
15:          where OrderID = @OrderID
16: end
17:
18: commit transaction
```

In this query, lines 5 through 7 read from the `Order Details` table. Based on this result, the process either quits or deletes the rows from `Orders` and `Order Details`. The sequence *read-validate-write* is specifically what transaction isolation levels are meant to handle.

Listing 12.2 is a query that another user is trying to run at the same time. We'll look closely at the interaction between these operations to understand transaction isolation better.

LISTING 12.2 Updating the Value of a Row in the `Order Details` Table

```
begin transaction
update [Order Details]
   set Quantity = 100
 where OrderID = 10258
   and ProductID = 2
commit transaction
```

Using the default isolation level, read committed, can cause significant consistency problems in this situation. What happens if the first user gets the total dollar value of the order, but before he has a chance to delete the rows, a second user increases the total value of the order? In Figure 12.8, Step 1_ is the external user performing a data modification. Without a persistent shared lock, other users can change data conditions while you are working, making a later update invalid.

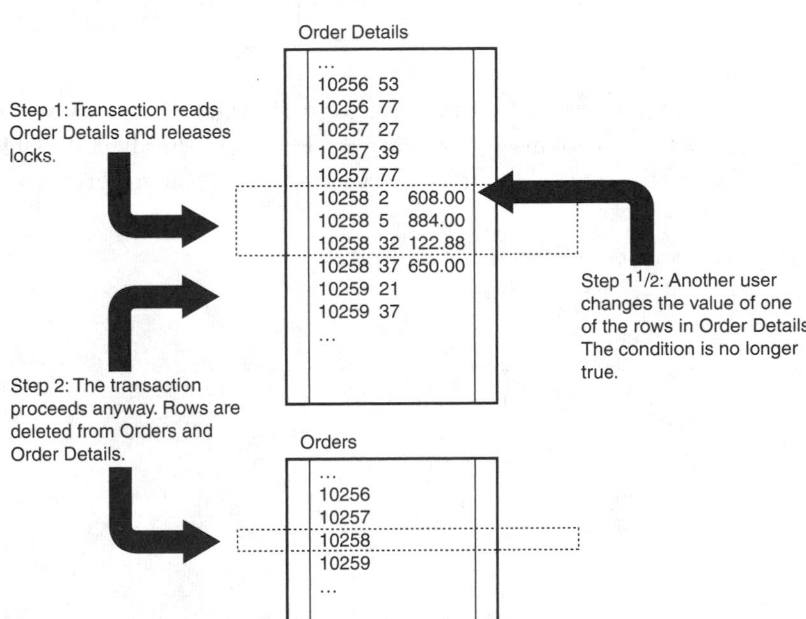

FIGURE 12.8
Using the read committed isolation level, the first query releases the shared lock on the `Order Details` *table before the transaction is complete.*

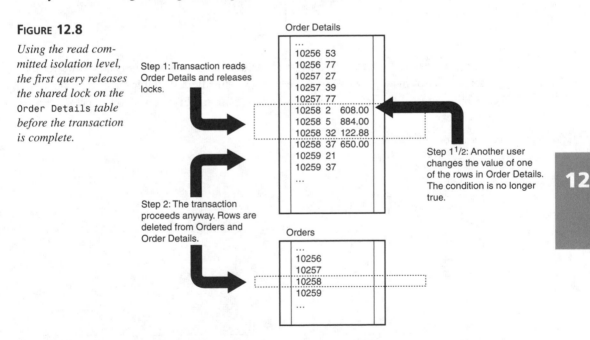

If the transaction isolation level is raised to repeatable read, shared locks are held throughout the transaction. In Figure 12.9, you can see how the shared locks block the other user, preventing him from obtaining an exclusive lock. In this case, the data is safe from modification after it has been read.

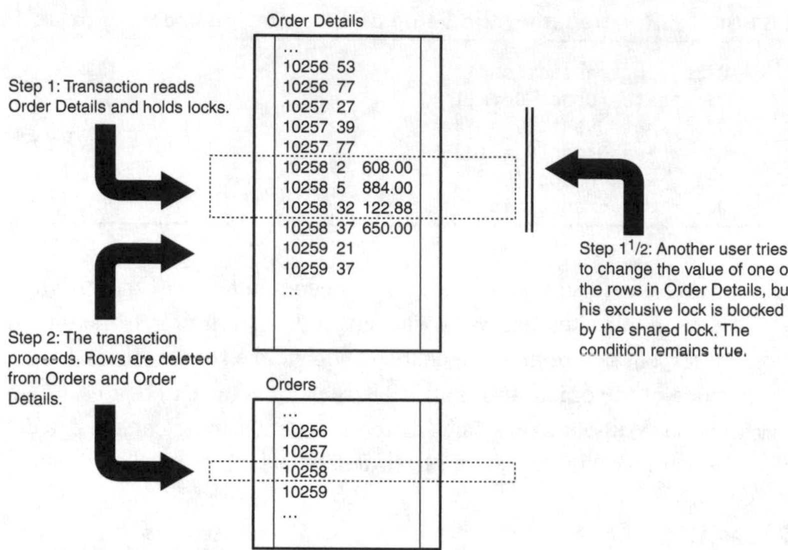

FIGURE 12.9
Using the repeatable read isolation level, the first query holds the shared lock on the `Order Details` *table throughout the transaction.*

There is a weakness in the repeatable read method. What if a user adds new rows for the order instead of modifying `Order Details` rows already in the table? This query could cause the value of the order to exceed $2000 without modifying any rows that are currently locked:

```
insert [order details] (
       orderid,
       productid,
       unitprice,
       quantity,
       discount
) values (
       10258,
       7,
       25,
       10,
       .2
)
```

> **Note** The `orderid` that is used in this example must exist in the `Orders` table. If it does not exist in the `Orders` table, you will receive an error.

The insert would need an exclusive intent lock on the table and a page, and a key lock on the new row. After it is in the table, further operations with this order will include the new order detail row. Figure 12.10 illustrates the addition of a new row, known as a phantom because it appears mysteriously in the midst of a transaction.

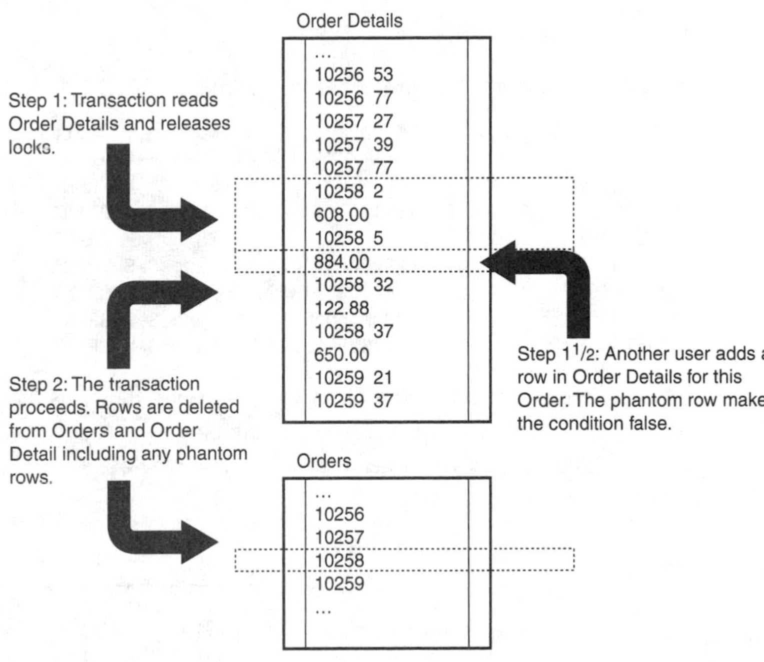

FIGURE 12.10

Using the repeatable read transaction isolation level, the first query holds the shared lock on specific rows in the `Order Details` *table throughout the transaction.*

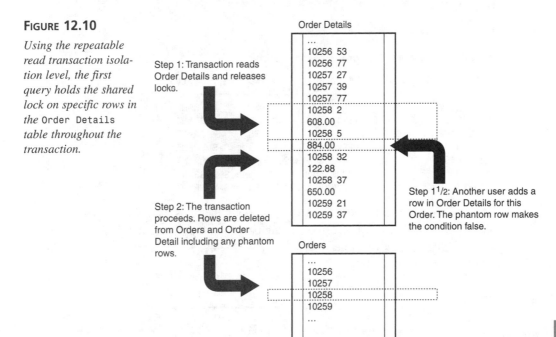

The highest level of transaction isolation, serializable, blocks phantom rows by locking not only individual rows but also the range of rows represented by a query. The select query that obtains the shared locks uses this condition:

```
where OrderID = @OrderID
```

With serializable transactions, the server guarantees that the query will return the same result set if it is run again later in the transaction. Figure 12.11 illustrates the blocking of phantom rows.

You can see the range locks created by serializable transactions. Execute this query from a new session, and then look at the locks on the `Order Details` table.

```
set transaction isolation level serializable
declare @OrderID int
select @OrderID = 10258
begin transaction
```

12

```
if  (
        select sum(Quantity * UnitPrice * (1 - Discount))
          from [Order Details]
         where OrderID = @OrderID
    ) < $2000
print 'lower'
else
print 'higher'
```

Here are the locks for this process from `sp_lock`:

```
ObjId       IndId  Type Resource         Mode     Status
----------- ------ ---- ---------------- -------- ------
          0      0 DB                    S        GRANT
  325576198      1 PAG  1:148            IS       GRANT
  325576198      0 TAB                   IS       GRANT
  325576198      1 KEY  (280008c67cf3)   RangeS-S GRANT
  325576198      1 KEY  (1400b0a918f2)   RangeS-S GRANT
  325576198      1 KEY  (320005ce23f8)   RangeS-S GRANT
  325576198      1 KEY  (17000991cf6f)   RangeS-S GRANT
```

The range locks prevent other users from modifying the rows matching the search condition, but they also prevent users from adding new rows that would match the condition. If you try to insert a new order detail row for `OrderID 10258`, the insert will wait for this transaction to complete.

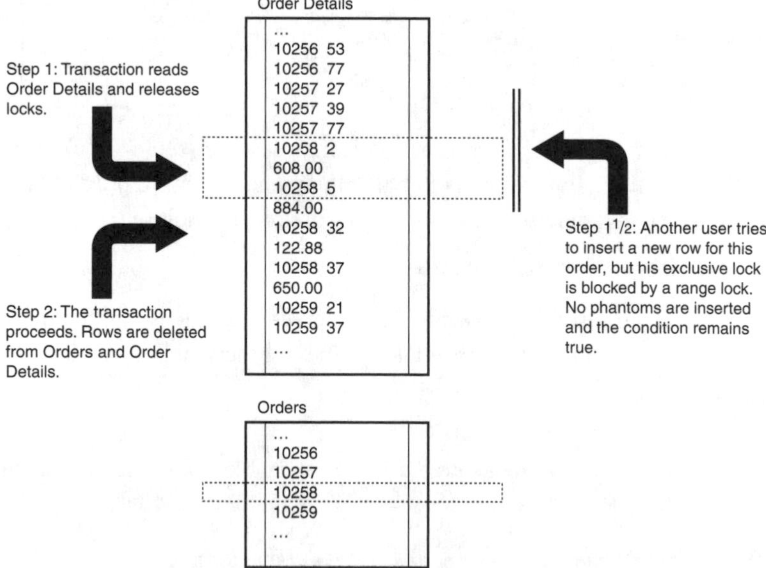

FIGURE 12.11

Using the serializable transaction isolation level, the first query holds the shared lock on specific rows in the `Order Details` *table and holds a range lock throughout the transaction.*

Caution Don't forget to rollback this transaction when you are finished.

Using Higher Transaction Isolation Levels

The default isolation level works well and is very efficient in most circumstances. You will seldom write applications that need repeatable reads or protection against phantoms. Level 2 is used infrequently because the phantom problem is hard to manage. If you need repeatable reads, you probably need serializable reads as well.

You need to recognize the situations when higher transaction isolation levels are required and consider ways to code around them. For example, a read-reread or read-validate-write sequence creates the need for higher isolation levels. Instead, use a locking hint (see the section "Using Hints to Control Lock Types") to obtain exclusive locks instead of shared locks in a query.

You'll see in the section "Deadlocks" that higher isolation levels frequently lead to deadlocks. First, you need to learn about using table hints to control lock types.

Using Hints to Control Lock Types

You saw on Day 9, "Indexes and Performance," how to use table hints to specify an index or table scan for a table in a query. Locking hints provide the programmer with the flexibility to manage the locking behavior for individual tables in a query.

For example, in this query, the `Orders` table is read without locks (dirty reads), but the `Order Details` table uses read committed (the default isolation level):

```
select o.OrderID, o.CustomerID, od.ProductID
  from Orders o with (readuncommitted)
    inner join
       [Order Details] od with (readcommitted)
          on o.OrderID = od.OrderID
 where o.OrderID = 10258
   and od.OrderID = 10258
```

Here is a list of locking hints regarding isolation level and the behavior they specify:

- `readuncommitted` (or `nolock`)—This implements dirty reads for a table (isolation level 0). Locks on this table held by other processes are ignored. This process places no locks on the table.
- `readcommitted`—The default transaction isolation level (isolation level 1). Exclusive locks will be held throughout a transaction, and shared locks will be released. Use this hint only when you are set to a different isolation level and require default behavior for this table.

- `repeatableread`—Exclusive and shared locks are held throughout a transaction, but phantoms can still appear (isolation level 2).
- `serializable` (or `holdlock`)—Exclusive and shared locks are held throughout a transaction, and phantoms are prevented (isolation level 3).
- `readpast`—This hint tells the query to skip locked rows (isolation level 4). In this query, the server requests all orders between `10256` and `10260`, but if any specific rows are locked, return only the available rows:

  ```
  select OrderID, CustomerID
    from Orders with (readpast)
   where OrderID between 10256 and 10260.
  ```

  If another process were holding a lock on `OrderID` `10258`, the server would return `10256`, `10257`, `10259`, and `10260`.

You can also request specific locking levels by using hints:

- `rowlock`—If the process would normally obtain shared page- or table-level locks, you can request shared row locks instead.
- `paglock`—If the process would normally obtain a shared table-level lock, you can request page locks.
- `tablock`—This requests a shared table-level lock to be held throughout a transaction. This hint enables you to get a snapshot in time of a table, but the table lock will slow down other users.

Finally, you can request locking modes by using hints. You can escalate locks only with hints. (Shared locks can be promoted to exclusive locks, but not vice versa.)

- `updlock`—This hint causes a query to obtain update locks instead of shared locks. Update locks are locks indicating an intent to modify data. They are used to prevent deadlocks. (For more on update locks, see the next section, "Deadlocks.")
- `xlock`—This hint requests exclusive locks instead of shared locks. Using the `xlock` hint will help you avoid deadlocks and should be considered as an alternative to higher isolation levels.
- `tablockx`—This hint tells the server to acquire an exclusive lock on the table. It is the equivalent of combining the `tablock` and `xlock` hints.

Deadlocks

What is a deadlock? A *deadlock* occurs when two or more users are stuck waiting for resources held by each other. None of the processes can proceed until a lock is released. Let's look at an example. In earlier database systems, deadlocks were a serious problem that required administrative intervention to resolve. SQL Server detects deadlocks before they occur and automatically resolves them. You need to understand deadlocks for two reasons:

- First, deadlocks generate error states that you need to understand and respond to. This is a programming problem. Normally, when you get a deadlock error (server error 1205), your application should just go ahead and retry the query.
- Second, deadlocks have a definite performance impact. The more deadlocks your application encounters, the slower work will proceed. (One client years ago was dealing with a 95% deadlock rate. 95% of all attempted updates were failing on deadlocks!) Deadlock avoidance is a separate programming challenge. That's what we'll focus on here.

Examining Deadlocks

Most of the time, you can create a deadlock by imagining two users, each running the same program. The program needs to use the read-validate-write sequence you saw earlier, with repeatable read or serializable isolation level.

Listing 12.3 is a copy of Listing 12.1 with the serializable locking hint added to the query. In addition, the `OrderID` is hard-coded in each statement.

LISTING 12.3 Code for Testing Deadlocks

```
declare @TotalDollars money
begin transaction
    select @TotalDollars = sum(Quantity * UnitPrice * (1 - Discount))
      from [Order Details] with (serializable)
     where OrderID = 10258

    if  @TotalDollars < $2000
    begin
            delete [Order Details]
             where OrderID = 10258
            delete Orders
             where OrderID = 10258
    end
commit transaction
```

To perform the test, you will need to simulate concurrent execution. I do that by executing a small part of the query at a time from each of two windows. Figure 12.12 shows how my Query Analyzer looks as I prepare to execute this test. To do deadlock testing, I single-step each query to keep the queries synchronized.

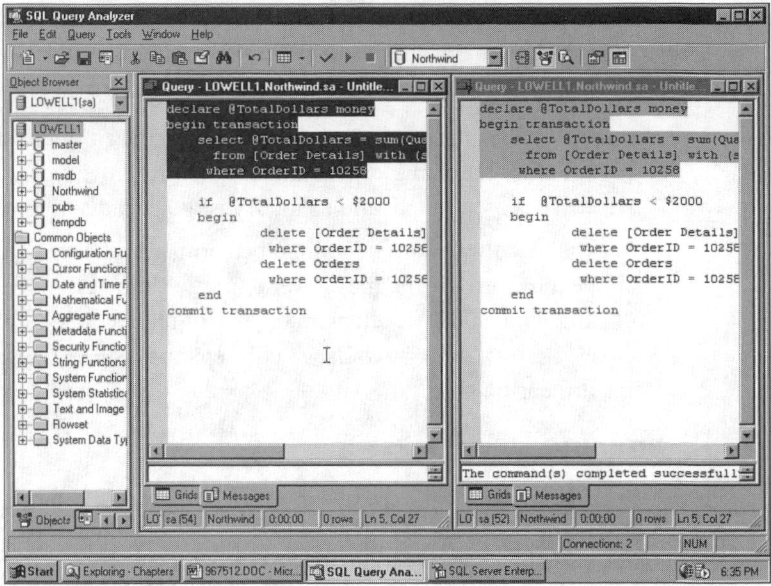

FIGURE 12.12

In the Query Analyzer, the same query is run from two separate windows.

To single-step the query, highlight the portion you want to run, and then execute. In the figure, I've highlighted the `BEGIN TRANSACTION` statement and the select query. Execute the select statement from both sessions, and then check the locks on the `Order Details` table. You should find persistent shared intent locks on the table and page, and shared range locks on individual keys. If the locks don't appear in the list, you might have forgotten to execute the `BEGIN TRANSACTION` statement as well.

Now, skip the `if` condition and just highlight the delete statement on `Order Details` (lines 9 and 10 in the Query Analyzer). When you execute the delete in one of the windows, that window will go into a lock sleep state, waiting for the lock on the `Order Details` table to release. Figure 12.13 shows the locking sequence on the `Order Details` table.

Before we go ahead, you should look at the list of locks for the table. Here is the output from `sp_lock` for these two sessions:

```
spid   ObjId       IndId  Type Resource    Mode     Status
------ ----------- ------ ---- ----------- -------- ------
    51   325576198      0 TAB              IS       GRANT
    55   325576198      0 TAB              IX       GRANT
    51   325576198      1 PAG  1:148       IS       GRANT
    55   325576198      1 PAG  1:148       IU       GRANT
    55   325576198      3 PAG  1:185       IU       GRANT
    51   325576198      1 KEY  (280008c6   RangeS-S GRANT
    55   325576198      1 KEY  (280008c6   RangeS-S GRANT
    51   325576198      1 KEY  (1400b0a9   RangeS-S GRANT
```

```
55    325576198        1 KEY  (1400b0a9   RangeS-U GRANT
55    325576198        1 KEY  (1400b0a9   X        CNVT
55    325576198        3 KEY  (1400b0a9   U        GRANT
51    325576198        1 KEY  (320005ce   RangeS-S GRANT
55    325576198        1 KEY  (320005ce   RangeS-S GRANT
51    325576198        1 KEY  (17000991   RangeS-S GRANT
55    325576198        1 KEY  (17000991   RangeS-S GRANT
```

I've manually sorted the output to make it easier to read. Each process holds an intent lock on the table, although the first process (spid 55) has escalated the lock to an exclusive intent lock. It plans to modify data in the table.

FIGURE 12.13

Almost ready for the deadlock. Each user holds a shared lock on the `Order Details` *rows, and both users need exclusive access to delete the rows. When the second user executes a delete statement, the deadlock will be detected.*

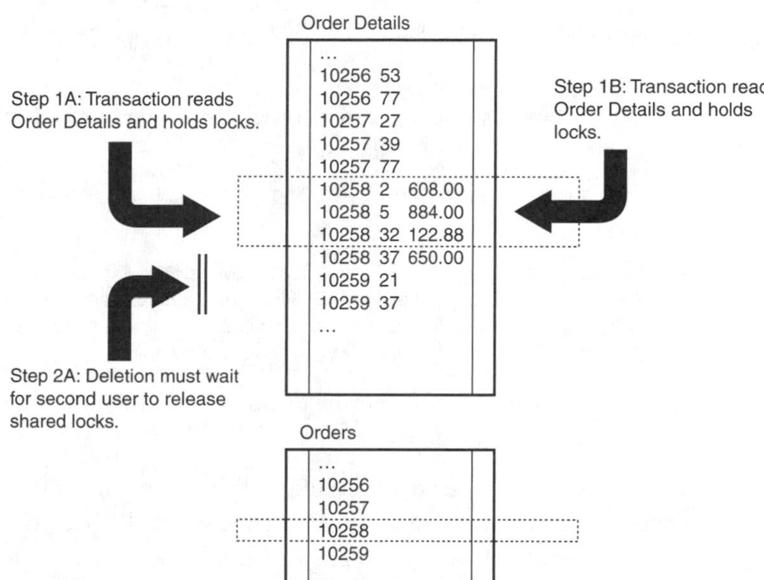

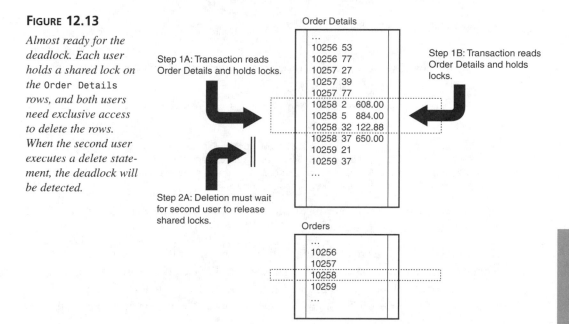

The page locks are also modified. Process 55 holds two page locks, one for the clustered primary key index and one for a second, nonclustered index. These are update intent locks. *Update intent locks* are held when the server plans to perform exclusive work but needs to wait for another lock to clear. These update locks are specifically used to prevent deadlocks. (Update locks are special shared locks: Other users can read through an update lock.)

At the key level, we can also see update locks on one key, resource number `1400b0a9`…. The original shared range lock has been converted to an update range lock (`RangeS-U`), an update lock has been added for this row, and an exclusive lock is waiting to be acquired. Note the status of the exclusive lock (`CNVT`). The server is waiting for the shared locks from process 51 to clear so that it can convert a prior shared lock to an exclusive lock.

Normally all this work takes place in the blink of an eye. We've slowed it down to see the details. Now let's push this forward one last step.

To complete the deadlock chain, highlight and execute the delete statement in the second window. The second process (process `51`) will try to obtain an update lock on the same row, but that lock will be blocked by process `55`. The server sees the blocking chain (`55` blocks `51`, `51` blocks `55`) and detects a deadlock before it occurs.

Two things happen immediately:

- First, one of the processes will report success (`3 rows deleted`). (The transaction will still be alive, so you can roll back the deleted rows if you don't want to make changes to the sample database.)
- Second, the other process will report error 1205, a deadlock. Here's the actual error message:

```
Server: Msg 1205, Level 13, State 50, Line 1
Your transaction (Process ID 51) was deadlocked on {lock}
resources with another process and has been chosen as the
deadlock victim. Rerun your transaction.
```

Which process will succeed and which will fail? The choice of a deadlock victim is essentially chosen at random.

What happens when you are the deadlock victim? The server terminates your current command, rolls back any current work, and releases all locks. If you are running a multi-statement batch or a stored procedure, deadlock detection will abort your work immediately. The process will not go on to the next step. The logical next step for the application is simply to try again.

Avoiding Deadlocks

To avoid deadlocks, try to obtain exclusive locks in the first step of a batch. For instance, modify the data before you read it. Here is a typical programming problem that can be easily solved with a simple change in the code.

In Listing 12.4, the user checks the balance in the account before deducting $50.

LISTING 12.4 An Example of Incorrect Transaction Usage

```
begin transaction
if (
        select Balance
          from Checking with (serializable)
         where AccountNum = 12345
    ) >= $50
    begin
        update Checking
           set Balance = Balance - $50
         where AccountNum = 12345
        print 'Withdrawal approved'
    end
else
    begin
        print 'Account balance insufficient'
    end
commit transaction
```

The query validates the balance first, and then updates the checking account. Because this follows the read-validate-write sequence, you need to use the `serializable` hint to prevent data consistency problems.

Listing 12.5 shows an alternative approach, where the update is performed, and then the resulting balance is checked. Notice that the balance must be greater than $0 *after* the withdrawal occurs.

LISTING 12.5 Updating the Account and then Validating the Modification

```
begin transaction
        update Checking
           set Balance = Balance - $50
         where AccountNum = 12345
if (
        select Balance
          from Checking with (serializable)
         where AccountNum = 12345
    ) >= $0
    begin
        print 'Withdrawal approved'
        commit transaction
    end
else
    begin
        print 'Account balance insufficient'
        rollback transaction
    end
```

If the withdrawal was successful, the transaction is committed. If the withdrawal failed, the transaction is rolled back. This "shoot first, ask questions later" approach acquires an exclusive lock in the first step. Other users wait for the entire transaction to complete. There is no danger of deadlock.

This approach is supported in an alternative form of the update statement, which returns the modified value of a column to a variable. Here is the same example, this time using the `@Balance` variable to store the contents of the modified `Balance` column.

```
declare @Balance money
begin transaction
        update Checking
            set @Balance = Balance = Balance - $50
         where AccountNum = 12345
if @Balance >= $0
    begin
        print 'Withdrawal approved'
        commit transaction
    end
else
    begin
        print 'Account balance insufficient'
        rollback transaction
    end
```

Whenever possible, use this approach to avoid locking problems and improve performance. Here is an example of a query that retrieves the next value in a sequential counter:

```
declare @NextKey int
update CounterTable
   set @NextKey = NextKey = NextKey + 1
 where TableName = 'Ledger'
```

Normally, getting the next key requires a read and a write. By writing both the read and the write at once, the query can be performed in a single step with no transactional coding at all and no danger of deadlock.

Summary

SQL Server balances concurrency, performance, and lock overhead in the way that it defines locks. You can manipulate locks with locking hints to influence the kinds of locks your process obtains. In tomorrow's lesson, you will learn to use transactions to group statements and improve error handling. Once again, here are a few Do's and Don'ts for you to use:

Do	Don't
DO	**DON'T**
Use dirty reads to get quick, approximate results.	Overuse lock hints.
Use lock hints and isolation levels to improve performance.	Use serializable and repeatable read too often—they lead to deadlocks.
Write data first, and then read it, to avoid deadlocks.	
Test for deadlocks in your programs.	

Q&A

Q Can I lock tables and rows myself?

A No. Locking is automatic. You can execute statements that obtain locks, and you can use locking hints to change locking modes and levels, but you cannot explicitly lock tables or rows.

Q When does it make sense to use dirty reads? It sounds like that will just create problems.

A Dirty reads (isolation level read uncommitted) help you perform large-scale selects against a database without running into locks or creating locks of your own. I use them to monitor performance on a production system, with the idea that I don't want to slow people down while I look around. If you need absolutely correct answers, you should avoid read uncommitted, but dirty reads are a lifesaver for quick, large selects.

12

Q In the locking hints, you list both `nolock` and `read uncommitted`, as well as `holdlock` and `serializable`. Why are there multiple terms for the same hints?

A The terms `nolock` and `holdlock` are left over from earlier versions of SQL Server. In those earlier versions, there was no formal set of transaction isolation levels. You had only a few keywords to manipulate locks in special situations. They appear in this version of SQL Server to maintain compatibility with legacy programs. Avoid the older terms in favor of the ANSI standard ones.

Q Why not always set transaction isolation as high as possible? Won't that improve data integrity?

A There's no question that the higher the transaction isolation level, the greater the guarantee of data integrity. The problem is that higher isolation levels cause performance and concurrency problems. The more resources you lock and the more restrictive those locks, the more likely another user will need to wait for a lock to clear. It's a balancing act.

Q Can I always avoid deadlocks?

A Not really. Most heavily used systems will have some level of deadlocking. Some deadlocks occur within a single table when two processes need to perform maintenance on a single index page. (This is more common when many users are actively modifying a small table.)

Q Can I choose which process becomes the deadlock victim when a deadlock occurs?

A No. The server selects a victim on the basis of accumulated CPU time.

Workshop

The Workshop provides quiz questions to help you solidify your understanding of the material covered and exercises to provide you with experience in using what you've learned. Try to answer the quiz and exercise questions before checking the answers in Appendix A, "Answers to Quizzes and Exercises," and make sure that you understand the answers before continuing to the next lesson.

Quiz

1. What is the difference between a shared and an exclusive lock?
2. What statements (select, insert, update, delete) will acquire a shared lock?
3. What is an intent lock, and what exactly gets locked?
4. Does an exclusive intent lock block other users from reading or writing?

Exercises

1. Write a query to retrieve a list of the five worst-selling products. You'll want to update the `products` table when your query is complete, so get and retain exclusive locks on the low-selling products. (You will need to examine the locks in the next exercise.)

```
ProductID   ProductName                  Total Dollars
----------- ---------------------------- ------------------
         48 Chocolade                      1368.7125244140625
         33 Geitost                                  1648.125
         15 Genen Shouyu                   1784.8249969482422
         67 Laughing Lumberjack Lager      2396.8000183105469
         74 Longlife Tofu                              2432.5
```

2. Find out the spid of your process.
3. In a new session, get a list of products in category 1.
4. Find a blocking and a blocked session. Clear the locks from the blocking session.

```
spid status     loginame    blk dbname    cmd
---- ---------- ----------- --- --------- ---------------
   1 background sa          0   NULL      LAZY WRITER
   2 sleeping   sa          0   NULL      LOG WRITER
   3 background sa          0   master    SIGNAL HANDLER
   4 background sa          0   NULL      LOCK MONITOR
   5 background sa          0   master    TASK MANAGER
   6 sleeping   sa          0   NULL      CHECKPOINT SLEEP
   7 background sa          0   master    TASK MANAGER
   8 background sa          0   master    TASK MANAGER
   9 background sa          0   master    TASK MANAGER
  10 background sa          0   master    TASK MANAGER
  51 sleeping   northwind_d 0   Northwind WAITING COMMAND
  52 sleeping   northwind_d 0   Northwind WAITING COMMAND
  53 sleeping   northwind_d 51  Northwind SELECT
  54 runnable   northwind_d 0   Northwind SELECT
```

WEEK 2

DAY 13

Programming with Transactions

In the last lesson, you learned all about locking. You saw the different kinds of locks the server uses to maintain transaction isolation and how the automatic transaction mechanisms work. Today, you will see how to manage transactions and locks in your own programs.

After completing this lesson, you will be able to

- Understand automatic transaction management mechanisms
- Manage transactions in your applications
- Write effective error-handling routines
- Use alternative locking approaches with optimistic locking and application resource locking
- Understand and work around long-running transactions

Understanding Transaction Basics

The definition of a transaction is "a logical unit of work." In real terms, a transaction is one or more statements that are executed together as a group. SQL Server guarantees that a transaction will succeed or fail completely. You will never get a partial transaction.

When you go to an ATM to make a $50 withdrawal, that act is treated as a transaction. The transaction consists of two parts:

- The debit of $50 from your bank account
- The delivery of $50 cash into your hand

It's clear that both parts of the transaction should be completed, or neither should occur. If you get $50 but your account is not debited, the bank is unhappy. If your account is debited, but no money comes out of the machine, you are not happy. In the design of the ATM system, it was critical to implement transaction control.

Transactions: An ACID Test

Transactions need to pass an "ACID" test. ACID is an acronym standing for the four critical qualities of transactions: atomicity, consistency, isolation, and durability.

Transactions are *atomic* because they cannot be split. They either succeed or fail as one.

Transactions enforce *consistency* because they restore a consistent state at the end of a data modification. For example, a double-entry accounting system needs to make multiple entries to complete each complete transaction. The ledger remains consistent because the transaction ensures consistency before and after the transaction. Notice that there is no guarantee of consistency within a transaction.

Transactions use locks to *isolate* work. Programmers can be confident that modified data will not be affected in the middle of a transaction. Other programmers should never be able to retrieve in-process data. Isolation helps enforce consistency.

Transactions use a transaction log to ensure *durability*. This makes certain that each completed data modification is written to a secure location.

Understanding Automatic Transactions and the Transaction Log

SQL Server automatically uses transaction management to ensure the completeness and consistency of all work performed on the server. Every SQL Server statement is a transaction.

This is a key point. You cannot step outside of the transaction management system. Even a simple `insert` statement or a `select` statement will be governed by transactions.

Consider this statement, that raises the unit price for all products by 10%:

```
update Products
set UnitPrice = UnitPrice * 1.1
```

There is no `where` clause in the statement, so all rows in the table are affected. SQL Server guarantees that all rows in the Products table will be modified, or, if that fails, no changes will be written.

How does the server guarantee this? Through the use of a write-ahead transaction log and automatic commit and rollback mechanisms. Let's see how that works.

Understanding the Write-Ahead Log

SQL Server uses a *write-ahead log* to manage database consistency during transactions. It's a write-ahead log because the log entries are written first, before changes are made to the tables and indexes.

To understand this better, let's step through the process of changing a set of rows in the Products table. In Figure 13.1, I've set up four areas. On the left are disk areas for the transaction log and for permanent data storage. On the right are similar areas within the data cache. SQL Server performs work in cache first to improve performance. It is only when the work is complete, or when the work is too large to fit entirely into memory, that the server will write changes to disk.

FIGURE 13.1

Data modifications are made in RAM first, and then saved to disk.

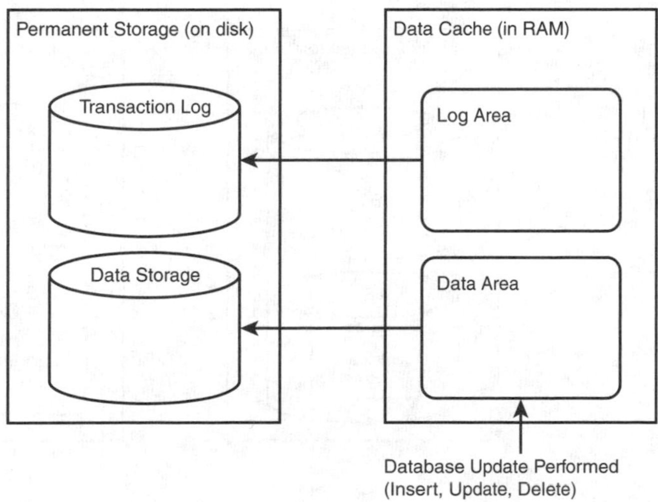

When the server performs work on data, the first step is to retrieve that data into the cache. Data sets are retrieved gradually, as required. Figure 13.2 shows the data all in cache, where all modifications occur.

FIGURE 13.2

When rows are to be modified, the first step is to retrieve the data from disk into cache.

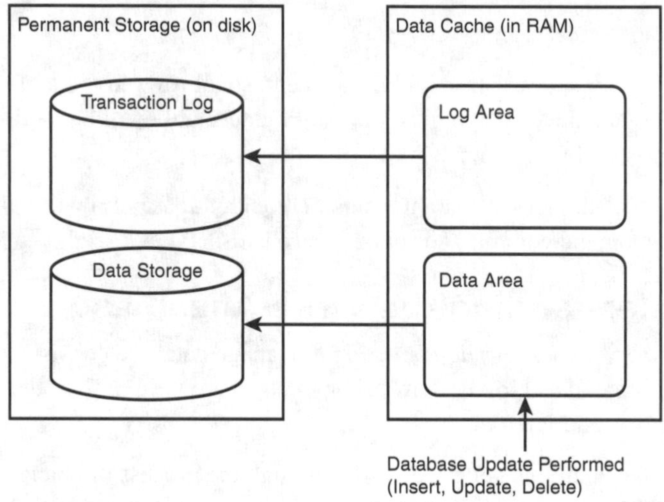

The first part of a transaction occurs when the server writes a Begin Transaction marker in the transaction log (see Figure 13.3). A time stamp identifies transaction markers. Time stamps don't include a time component. They are sequential hexadecimal keys for rows in the transaction log.

FIGURE 13.3

Before changing data, the server makes a transaction in the log. All subsequent changes will be associated with this transaction marker.

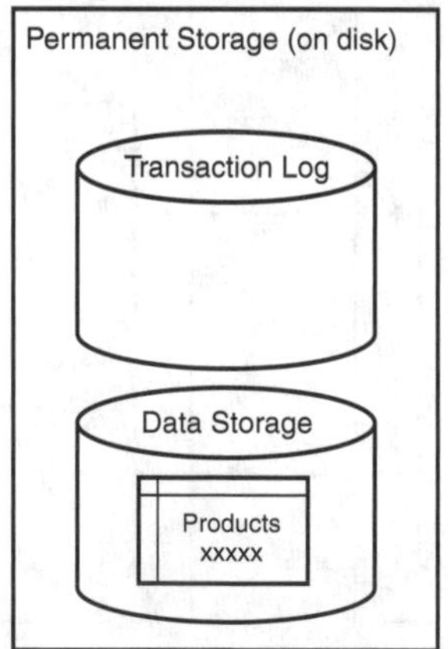

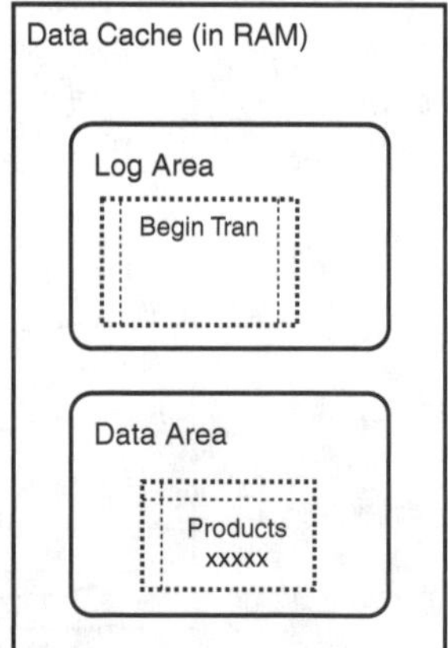

The transaction marker log record does include date and time information, which the server can use to do "as-of" database restores. For instance, you could restore the database to its state on Thursday at 4 p.m. That would restore all transactions completed by that time.

Some updates can occur in place, when only the modified part of a row is replaced. Most updates occur in two steps—a delete followed by an insert. The server decides the method based on what is changing about the row. We'll look closely now at how the server performs the delete/insert sequence of an update statement.

Don't get confused. The server deletes, and then reinserts the row, but it's not a regular `DELETE` or `INSERT` statement. For instance, you don't need the `DELETE` or `INSERT` permission on a table to perform an update.

When the server deletes the old version of the row, it first writes that version to the transaction log (see Figure 13.4). The old version of the row is a useful resource. If the update fails for any reason, the row in the transaction log can be reinserted to the table.

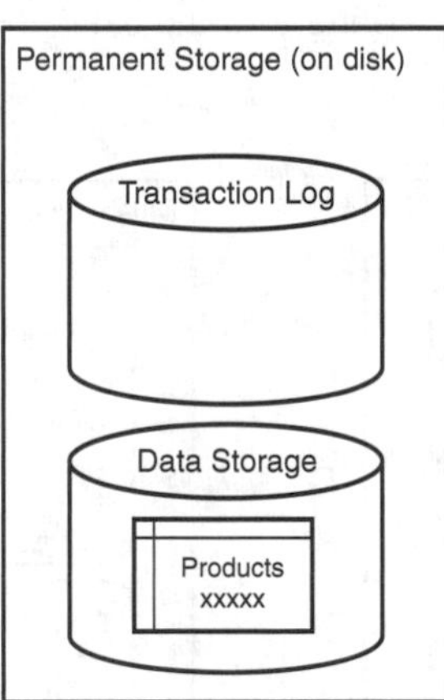

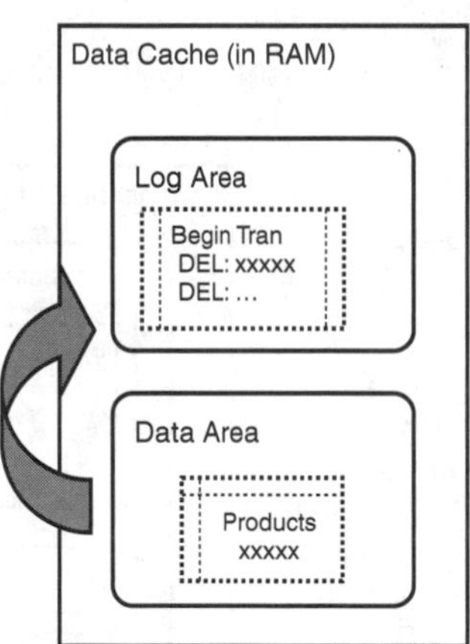

FIGURE 13.4

The next step is to save the original data values prior to modification. If something goes wrong, the server can restore those values.

13

As part of the deletion, the server also deletes all index entries that point to the row. The index deletions themselves are also logged.

When the deletions are complete, the server then inserts the modified values. The inserts are logged first, and then written to the table in cache (see Figure 13.5). Any index changes are written at this point.

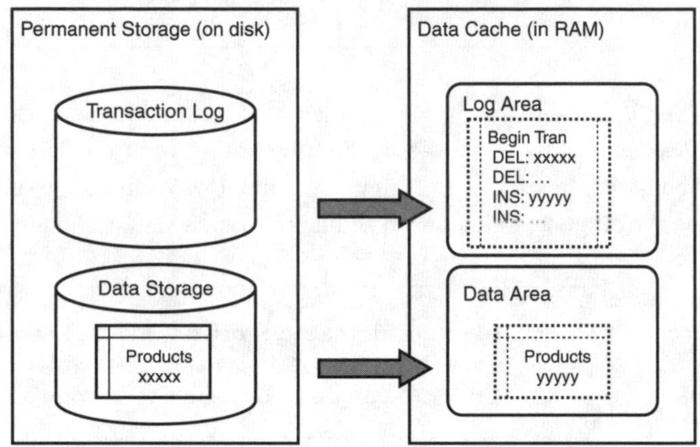

FIGURE 13.5
Now the server records changes to the log and makes the changes to the data in cache.

The rows have been updated, and it's time to write the work to disk. The server writes a *commit marker* to the log in cache, and then flushes the changes to the log out of cache to the disk (see Figure 13.6).

NEW TERM When you *commit* data, you are writing it to the database permanently, without any opportunity to back out.

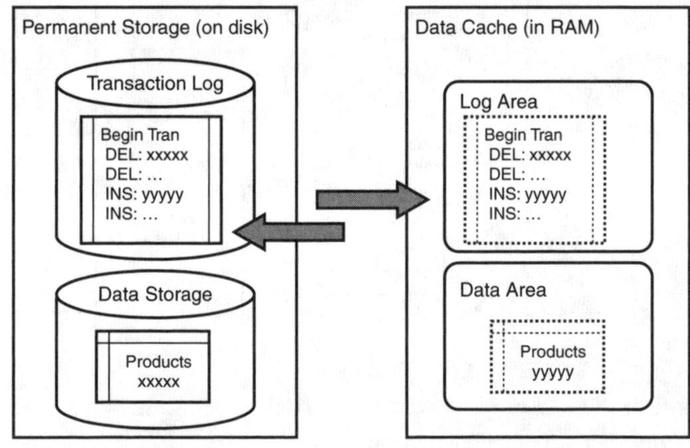

FIGURE 13.6
The server writes a commit marker to the log in cache, and then flushes the changed log pages to disk. Notice that the data area on disk still contains the original data.

That's all. The changes have been made, and the new values in the table are ready for use.

Rolling Back Changes

If something goes wrong when a transaction is partially completed, the server automatically rolls back the transaction. What might go wrong? You could have a constraint limiting the `UnitPrice` column to $150, and the update might attempt to set a `UnitPrice` higher than that value. You might violate a unique index, or insert an invalid foreign key.

When the server rolls back work, it re-creates the state of the data before the transaction started. If an update or delete was underway, any deleted rows are restored to the table. If an insert was underway, rows added to the table are removed. Indexes are restored. When all the changes are completely removed, a `ROLLBACK TRANSACTION` marker is written to the log to indicate that the work was backed out.

An automatic rollback is usually fast, unless the transaction was enormous. That's because almost all of the work associated with a rollback takes place in cache.

Controlling Transactions in Your Programs

You used `BEGIN TRANSACTION`, `COMMIT TRANSACTION`, and `ROLLBACK TRANSACTION` in batches throughout yesterday's lesson on locking. You should have a pretty good idea what they do at this point. This section will present the transaction control statements more formally, and then we'll look at transaction nesting and transaction modes.

Transaction Control Statements

SQL Server supports four transaction control statements. (You can use the words `TRANSACTION` and `TRAN` interchangeably.)

- `BEGIN TRANSACTION`—Starts a transaction block. Locks are held from this point forward. Optionally, name the transaction, like this:

  ```
  begin transaction my_tran
  ```

- `COMMIT TRANSACTION`—Ends a transaction block. Work is completed and written to permanent storage. Locks are released. Also written as `COMMIT WORK`.
- `ROLLBACK TRANSACTION`—Ends a transaction block. Work is rolled back, and a log record is written to permanent storage. Locks are released. Also written as `ROLLBACK WORK`.
- `SAVE TRANSACTION`—Marks a transaction savepoint. Only valid while a transaction is active. `SAVE TRAN` requires a savepoint name, as in this example:

  ```
  save transaction my_savepoint
  ```

Rolling back a tran to a named savepoint does not release locks or end a transaction block:

```
rollback transaction my_savepoint
```

It returns the data state to its condition prior to the `SAVE TRANSACTION` statement. Locks are not released.

Most database programming layers provide corresponding database connection methods to manage transactions. In Active Data Objects (part of ODBC), the ADO Connection object supports `BeginTrans`, `CommitTrans`, and `RollbackTrans` methods. There is no ADO version of the `SAVE TRANSACTION` statement in T-SQL.

You've seen plenty of examples using `BEGIN`, `COMMIT`, and `ROLLBACK TRANSACTION`. Let's look at a couple of examples with `SAVE TRANSACTION` to see how that works.

In Listing 13.1, I've modified the checking account tasks we were discussing earlier. In addition to approving or rejecting the withdrawal, we will also record the request to an `AuditTrail`, whether it is approved or not.

LISTING 13.1 Processing Checking Account Transactions

```
declare @Balance money
begin transaction
save transaction BeforeUpdate
        update Checking
           set @Balance = Balance = Balance - $50
         where AccountNum = 12345
if @Balance >= $0
    begin
        print 'Withdrawal approved'
        insert AuditTrail (AccountNum, Amount, Approved)
         values (12345, $50, "Yes")
        commit transaction
    end
else
    begin
        print 'Account balance insufficient'
        rollback transaction BeforeUpdate
        insert AuditTrail (AccountNum, Amount, Approved)
         values (12345, $50, "No")
        commit transaction
    end
```

Line 2 starts a transaction, and line 3 writes a marker in the log named `BeforeUpdate`. Later we will be able to roll back to the data state at that marker.

The next step is to update the account and retrieve the new balance (lines 4 through 6). In line 7, the batch makes certain that the balance is still above water. If it is, it prints a message (line 9), inserts an audit trail record (lines 10 and 11) and completes the work.

If the balance is negative, the batch reports an error (line 16). In line 17, the work since the savepoint is backed out, but the transaction and locks remain active. The $50 withdrawal that was debited from the account is restored. The batch records the failed withdrawal in the audit trail as part of the transaction (lines 18 and 19), and then commits the work. In this case, the commit only applies to the `AuditTrail` entry.

By using the `SAVE TRANSACTION`/`ROLLBACK TRANSACTION` pair, the application kept the transaction alive while still backing out unwanted changes. Then the audit trail record could be part of the original transaction, maintaining data integrity.

In Day 16, "Optimizing Stored Procedures," you will learn how to use `SAVE TRANSACTION` and `ROLLBACK TRANSACTION` to maintain transactional integrity in stored procedures.

Nesting Transactions

SQL Server supports *syntactic nesting* of transactions. Each session can have only one live transaction. Within that transaction, a session can `BEGIN TRANSACTION` and then `COMMIT TRANSACTION` repeatedly. As long as each `BEGIN TRANSACTION` is matched with a `COMMIT TRANSACTION`, the last matched `COMMIT TRANSACTION` will commit all the work.

Here is a simple example. A transaction starts and executes an update. A second transaction starts (actually, another level within the same transaction), and then does another update, as follows:

```
 1: begin transaction
 2: update Orders
 3:    set OrderDate = getdate()
 4:  where OrderID = 10258
 5:     begin transaction
 6:        update [Order Details]
 7:           set Quantity = Quantity * 2
 8:         where OrderID = 10258
 9:     commit transaction
10: commit transaction
```

When the first `COMMIT TRANSACTION` statement is executed (line 9), no actual work is completed. Only after the second `COMMIT TRANSACTION` is executed—balancing the outermost `BEGIN TRANSACTION`—is the work written and locks released.

SQL Server manages transaction nesting using a global transaction control variable, `@@trancount`. `@@trancount` begins each session with a value of 0. When `@@trancount` is incremented by a `BEGIN TRANSACTION` statement, work is committed only when `@@trancount` returns to 0. If you log out or your connection is lost before `@@trancount` returns to 0, your work is rolled back, and locks are released.

Table 13.1 displays the effects of transaction control statements on `@@trancount`. Each time you execute a `BEGIN TRANSACTION` statement, the `@@trancount` for your session is incremented. Each `COMMIT TRANSACTION` statement decrements `@@trancount`. Notice that `ROLLBACK TRANSACTION` ignores all nesting layers and sets `@@trancount` back to 0. No matter how deeply nested your transaction, a single `rollback` statement immediately ends the transaction.

TABLE 13.1 Effects of Transaction Control Statements on `@@trancount`

Statement	*Effect on* `@@trancount`
`begin transaction`	+1
`commit transaction`	–1
`rollback transaction`	=0
`save transaction <savepoint>`	+0
`rollback transaction <savepoint>`	+0

We'll talk more about transactions and nesting in Day 16, when we look at the problems stemming from incorrect transaction handling in procedures.

Implicit, Explicit, and Autocommit Transactions

We've spent today discussing *explicit* transactions, that is, transactions that you declare with `BEGIN TRANSACTION`. We've also looked at *autocommit* transactions, or the automatic transactions that manage data consistency when a single statement executes outside of a transaction. SQL Server optionally supports *implicit* transactions, or transactions that start whenever you execute a SQL statement (sometimes called *chained mode*).

Statements that implicitly start a transaction fall into these categories:

- Data modification language (DML): SELECT, INSERT, UPDATE, DELETE
- Data definition language (DDL): CREATE, ALTER, DROP
- Data control language (DCL): GRANT, REVOKE

Statements that do not start transactions include

- Control of flow: WHILE, IF, BEGIN, END, BREAK, CONTINUE, RETURN
- Error and message: RAISERROR, PRINT
- Variable declaration and assignment: DECLARE, SET

You can turn on the session option, `IMPLICIT TRANSACTIONS`, to change the way SQL Server defines a transaction. The syntax is similar to the other set options you have seen so far:

```
set implicit_transactions <on | off>
```

When you turn on implicit transactions, every statement issued when `@@trancount` is 0 automatically begins a transaction. In order to commit any work, you need to include an explicit `COMMIT TRANSACTION` statement. By default, implicit transactions are turned off.

Implicit Transactions and Transaction Nesting

For the most part, implicit transactions do not change the way you will write transaction programs with nested transactions. Let's look closely at `@@trancount` to understand what implicit transactions do to transaction handling and transaction nesting. Listing 13.2 demonstrates the effect of implicit transactions on `@@trancount` without nesting.

LISTING 13.2 Implicit Transactions Change Transaction Behavior, Requiring `commit` After Any DML Statement

```
 1: set nocount on
 2: set implicit_transactions on
 3: declare @msg varchar(25)
 4: declare @silentselect int
 5: set @msg = 'Starting value: '
 6:         + convert(varchar(2), @@trancount)
 7: print @msg
 8: select @silentselect = count(*)
 9:   from Products
10: set @msg = 'After select statement: '
11:         + convert(varchar(2), @@trancount)
12: print @msg
13: commit transaction
14: set @msg = 'After commit: '
15:         + convert(varchar(2), @@trancount)
16: print @msg
```


Results:

```
Starting value: 0
After select statement: 1
After commit: 0
```

I've used `PRINT` statements to display the value of `@@trancount` at each stage. The first `PRINT` statement, in line 7, displays the value of `@@trancount` before the `SELECT` statement is executed. The second `PRINT` (line 12) returns the transaction nesting level after the SELECT. Because IMPLICIT TRANSACTIONS is turned on, the transaction is still open. The final PRINT statement (line 16) returns the value after the transaction is committed.

Listing 13.3 tries a similar test, but first starts an explicit transaction with BEGIN TRANSACTION.

LISTING 13.3 Testing a Transaction Process

```
1: set nocount on
2: set implicit_transactions on
3: declare @msg varchar(25)
4: declare @silentselect int
5: set @msg = 'Starting value: '
6:          + convert(varchar(2), @@trancount)
7: begin tran
8: print @msg
9: set @msg = 'After begin tran: '
10:         + convert(varchar(2), @@trancount)
11:print @msg
12:select @silentselect = count(*)
13:  from Products
14:set @msg = 'After select statement: '
15:         + convert(varchar(2), @@trancount)
16:print @msg
17:commit tran
18:set @msg = 'After commit: '
19:         + convert(varchar(2), @@trancount)
20:print @msg
```

Results:

```
Starting value: 0
After begin tran: 2
After select statement: 2
After commit: 1
```

In this case, the BEGIN TRANSACTION statement increments the transaction counter to 1. The SELECT statement detects the open transactions, so it doesn't need to open a new transaction. The net effect of running a select statement on @@trancount is 0.

The bottom line is this: Setting implicit transactions will affect the behavior of the server whenever you are running SQL statements outside of any transaction context. Within a transaction context, implicit transactions have no effect.

Transaction Error Handling

It's up to you to handle errors that arise during transaction programming. When a statement in your batch fails, raising an error, it is up to you to detect that error and recover.

In many situations, that means you will need to roll back work and close out the transaction.

In Listing 13.4, an error in any statement in the batch will not cause the batch to fail.

LISTING 13.4 Transaction Process Without Error Handling

```
 1: begin transaction
 2: insert [Order Details]
 3:       (OrderID, ProductID, UnitPrice, Quantity, Discount)
 4:    values
 5:        (10258, 3, $22, 10, .02)
 6: insert [Order Details]
 7:       (OrderID, ProductID, UnitPrice, Quantity, Discount)
 8:    values
 9:        (10258, 3, $15, 25, .02)
10: insert [Order Details]
11:       (OrderID, ProductID, UnitPrice, Quantity, Discount)
12:    values
13:        (10258, 17, $15, 30, .02)
14: commit transaction
```

The second `INSERT` statement (lines 6 through 9) duplicates the primary key combination (Order ID `10258`, ProductID `3`) in the first `INSERT` (lines 2 through 5). Even though the second `INSERT` fails, the batch will continue. The third `INSERT` (lines 10 through 13) will work, and the transaction (line 14) will commit.

This is a transactional nightmare. The whole purpose of using transactions is to commit all three statements or none at all. Without proper error checking, you will frequently end up with partial transactions.

We need to add error handling to this batch. To do that, check for an error after each statement. If an error is encountered, we need to roll back the transaction and report an error to the user. Listing 13.5 shows the revised batch with the error handlers included.

LISTING 13.5 Processing Errors in a Transaction

```
begin transaction
insert [Order Details]
      (OrderID, ProductID, UnitPrice, Quantity, Discount)
   values
       (10258, 3, $22, 10, .02)
   if @@error <> 0 goto err_handler
```

LISTING 13.5 continued

```
 7: insert [Order Details]
 8:       (OrderID, ProductID, UnitPrice, Quantity, Discount)
 9:    values
10:        (10258, 3, $15, 25, .02)
11:    if @@error <> 0 goto err_handler
12: insert [Order Details]
13:       (OrderID, ProductID, UnitPrice, Quantity, Discount)
14:    values
15:        (10258, 17, $15, 30, .02)
16:    if @@error <> 0 goto err_handler
17: commit transaction
18: return
19: err_handler:
20:    rollback transaction
21:    raiserror ('Failed to insert. Transaction aborted.', 16, 1)
22:    return
```

The `@@error` global variable reports the success or failure of the previous statement. A zero value means the statement succeeded. Any non-zero value means the statement failed. In this example, the second `INSERT` (lines 7 through 10) fails. The `if @@error` test sends program control to the error handler (lines 19 through 22). In the error handler, the transaction is rolled back, and the batch raises an error to alert the user.

The important thing to remember is that most errors do not abort a batch. For example, DRI constraint violations and unique index violations will not cause a batch to fail. The individual statement will fail, but subsequent statements will be executed.

Listing 13.6 shows the checking account example again. This time, there is more complete error handling.

LISTING 13.6 Adding Error Processing to the Checking Process

```
declare @Balance money
declare @errornum int, @errormsg nvarchar(100)
begin transaction
save transaction BeforeUpdate
        update Checking
           set @Balance = Balance = Balance - $50
         where AccountNum = 12345
         select @errornum = @@error
         if @errornum <> 0
              goto Err_CheckingUpdate
if @Balance >= $0
   begin
```

LISTING 13.6 continued

```
13:           print 'Withdrawal approved'
14:           insert AuditTrail (AccountNum, Amount, Approved)
15:            values (12345, $50, 'Yes')
16:           select @errornum = @@error
17:           if @errornum <> 0
18:                goto Err_CheckingUpdate
19:           commit transaction
20:     end
21: else
22:     begin
23:          print 'Account balance insufficient'
24:          rollback transaction BeforeUpdate
25:          insert AuditTrail (AccountNum, Amount, Approved)
26:           values (12345, $50, 'No')
27:           select @errornum = @@error
28:           if @errornum <> 0
29:                goto Err_CheckingUpdate
30:          commit transaction
31:     end
32: return
33: Err_CheckingUpdate:
34:     select @errormsg = 'Non-standard error detected: ' + str(@errornum)
35:     print @errormsg
36:     rollback transaction
37:     return
```

This example is looking more and more like a real program. It has complete error checking and an error handler. Let's review the changes:

- In the declaration area, we need variables to preserve the value of the error number and to build an error message to pass to the user in a `PRINT` statement.
- After each data modification statement, we check the value of `@@error`. In order to retain the value and report it to the user, we need to store the value in a variable (line 16) before testing it.
- We use the `GOTO` statement to direct processing into the error handler (lines 10, 18, and 29). There is no formal error handler, and no subroutines. Everyone frowns on `GOTO`, but it is the best approach here.
- The `RETURN` statement in line 32 prevents successful executions from also executing the error handler.
- In the error handler section (lines 33 to 37), you use `ROLLBACK TRAN` to make certain that all work is rolled back.

Using xact_abort to Avoid Transaction Errors

We've seen how to use an @@error test to check for errors and manually abort a batch. SQL Server also offers a setting to automatically abort a batch and roll back when any runtime error occurs in a transaction.

The xact_abort setting terminates the current batch and rolls back work if a T-SQL statement raises a runtime error. This setting is off by default. Here is the syntax:

```
set xact_abort < on | off >
```

When you use xact_abort, you can avoid the need for complex error checking. Here is the earlier example shown in Listing 13.5 rewritten using xact_abort. Remember that you will receive an error as shown:

```
Server: Msg 2627, Level 14, State 1, Line 1
Violation of PRIMARY KEY constraint 'PK_Order_Details'.
Cannot insert duplicate key in object 'Order Details'.
```

```
set xact_abort on
begin transaction
insert [Order Details]
      (OrderID, ProductID, UnitPrice, Quantity, Discount)
   values
       (10258, 3, $22, 10, .02)
insert [Order Details]
      (OrderID, ProductID, UnitPrice, Quantity, Discount)
   values
       (10258, 3, $15, 25, .02)
insert [Order Details]
      (OrderID, ProductID, UnitPrice, Quantity, Discount)
   values
       (10258, 17, $15, 30, .02)
commit transaction
```

When the error occurs in the second insert statement, the transaction is rolled back, and the batch is aborted. This simplifies programming enormously, but applications are responsible for reporting batch failure and transaction rollback to the user.

Your own T-SQL error handlers will not fire after an error when you use xact_abort.

Managing Concurrency

SQL Server provides two additional methods for handling multiuser programming situations:

- Optimistic locking, using time stamp tokens
- Application resource locking

Optimistic Locking

So far we have discussed active locks that block other users. Optimistic locks aren't really locks at all. Instead, when a user reads a row from a table, he also reads a `rowversion` column. The `rowversion` is a version stamp: It uniquely identifies a version of the row. Every time a row is updated, the server applies a new `rowversion` value to the column. If a user tries to update the row after the `rowversion` changes, the server will refuse the update.

Here is a simple example. The first query creates, populates, and retrieves the rows from a new `RVTest` table, a table containing a unique key and a `rowversion` column:

```
 1: create table RVTest (
 2:         id int identity primary key,
 3:         col2 int not null,
 4:         rv rowversion not null
 5: )
 6: go
 7: insert RVTest (col2) values (19)
 8: insert RVTest (col2) values (-10)
 9: insert RVTest (col2) values (7)
10: go
11: select * from RVTest
12: go
```

Results:

```
id          col2        rv
----------- ----------- ------------------
          1          19 0x000000000000012E
          2         -10 0x000000000000012F
          3           7 0x0000000000000130
```

The create statement includes a definition of a `rowversion` column, `rv` (line 4). `rowversion` is a system datatype based on the `binary(8)` datatype. When you define a column with the `rowversion` datatype, it has special properties:

- You cannot insert the column directly or refer to it in the set clause of an `UPDATE` statement.

- Every time the row is modified, the `rowversion` is automatically updated with the unique transaction log row identifier.

The `INSERT` statements (lines 7 through 9) only include a value for the `col2` column. The other columns are automatically maintained by the server. In the output, you can see the values applied by the `rowversion` datatype.

Optimistic locking was useful before SQL Server implemented row-level locking. It was a method for managing concurrency at the row level instead of the page-level or higher. Nowadays, it is still a useful method of managing multiuser concurrency without leaving locks open while waiting for a user to complete work.

The obvious drawback to optimistic locking is that users will be livid if several hours' work is discarded on a `rowversion` problem. Using optimistic locking requires you to work hard to avoid simply discarding work after a `rowversion` has changed, and that often isn't worth the effort.

For more on optimistic locking, see the next chapter, Day 14, "Using Cursors."

Application Resource Locking

Application resource locking is new to SQL Server. The server will enable you to define your own resources and will manage the locks on the resources within its existing lock management subsystem.

This is a useful approach for handling process-level locks. For example, accounting systems frequently need to lock out certain functions while posting or other maintenance operations are running.

For example, in an accounting system, posting the general journal to the general ledger should prevent other processes from interfering. You might want to get an exclusive lock on the general journal and an exclusive intent lock on the general ledger (preventing others from locking out the whole ledger).

Getting Application Locks with `sp_getapplock`

You use the `sp_getapplock` stored procedure to lock your own application resources. Here is a batch to acquire the two locks:

```
exec @ret = sp_getapplock
        'General Ledger',
        'IntentExclusive',
        'Session',
        0
exec @ret = sp_getapplock
```

```
            'General Journal',
            'Exclusive',
            'Session',
            0
```

`sp_getapplock` takes four parameters:

- Resource name—You choose an alphanumeric value (`nvarchar`(255)). You will use this name to release the lock later.
- Lock mode—Your choices are `Shared`, `Update`, `Exclusive`, `IntentExclusive`, and `IntentShared`. These lock modes interact the same way that standard system locks interact. Shared locks block exclusive locks, exclusive blocks lock all other locks, and so on.
- Lock owner—This isn't a name. It describes whether the lock will be held by the current `Transaction` or by the `Session`. If the lock is held by a transaction, then committing or rolling back the transaction will release the lock. If it's owned by the session, you will need to release the lock manually with `sp_releaseapplock`. The lock will be released when you log out. The default value is `Transaction`.
- Lock timeout—The default value is the value of `@@lock_timeout` (as discussed previously). If the lock timeout is set to 0, the procedure will fail immediately. This is probably your best choice when working with application resource locks.

Releasing Application Locks with sp_releaseapplock

To release an application lock, use the stored procedure, `sp_releaseapplock`. To release the two locks obtained with `sp_getapplock`, you would run these two statements:

```
exec sp_releaseapplock "General Journal", "Session"
exec sp_releaseapplock "General Ledger", "Session"
```

If you run `sp_getapplock` multiple times for the same named resource, you will have to run `sp_releaseapplock` the same number of times to release the lock.

Examining Application Locks

You can use `sp_lock` to get information about application locks, too. Here is the output from `sp_lock` after I obtained the General Ledger lock shown previously:

```
spid   dbid   ObjId       IndId  Type Resource         Mode     Status
------ ------ ----------- ------ ---- ---------------- -------- ------
    53      6           0      0 DB                    S        GRANT
```

```
55      6          0       0 DB                         S        GRANT
55      1   85575343       0 TAB                        IS       GRANT
55      6          0       0 APP  Gene3786c2e5          IX       GRANT
```

The last lock in the list is an application lock. Notice that the server hashed my resource name into a unique identifier.

Handling Long-Running Transactions

Long-running transactions are transactions that create and hold locks for a long time. They include large-scale updates, deletes, and massive inserts. Monthly maintenance programs that move data into an archive directory are a typical example. For instance, Listing 13.7 would move the `Orders` and `Order Details` for a month from active to (make-believe) archive tables.

LISTING 13.7 An Example of a Long-Running Transaction

```
set xact_abort on
begin transaction
declare @OrderList table (OrderID int)
insert @OrderList (OrderID)
select OrderID
  from Orders with (readpast)
 where OrderDate >= '8/1/2000' and
       OrderDate < '9/1/2000'
insert into Orders_Archive (
       OrderID, CustomerID, EmployeeID, OrderDate,
       RequiredDate, ShippedDate, ShipVia, Freight,
       ShipName, ShipAddress, ShipCity, ShipRegion,
       ShipPostalCode, ShipCountry, OrderClosed
)
select
       OrderID, CustomerID, EmployeeID, OrderDate,
       RequiredDate, ShippedDate, ShipVia, Freight,
       ShipName, ShipAddress, ShipCity, ShipRegion,
       ShipPostalCode, ShipCountry, OrderClosed
  from Orders
 where OrderID in (select OrderID from @OrderList)
insert [Order Details_Archive]
      (OrderID, ProductID, UnitPrice, Quantity, Discount)
select OrderID, ProductID, UnitPrice, Quantity, Discount
  from [Order Details]
 where OrderID in (select OrderID from @OrderList)
delete [Order Details]
 where OrderID in (select OrderID from @OrderList)
delete Orders
 where OrderID in (select OrderID from @OrderList)
commit transaction
```

Line 3 declares a table variable. Lines 4 through 8 write a list of `OrderIDs` to the table variable. We'll use that list of IDs as a reference in the rest of the batch. Notice the use of the `readpast` hint. If an `OrderID` is locked, the query will ignore the lock and continue to find orders. You might also want to use the `xlock` table hint to acquire persistent, exclusive locks.

The `INSERT` statement in lines 9 through 21 moves the Orders rows to the `Orders_Archive`. Lines 22 through 26 moves Order details to the `Order Details_Archive`. Lines 27 through 30 deletes the rows, first from `Order Details`, then from `Orders` (to preserve DRI). The batch is written as a transaction to avoid performing partial work.

Long-running transactions are a significant performance concern for system designers and application programmers. Here's why:

- These processes typically modify a large percentage of the data in a table. When that happens, the server often promotes row and page locks to a table lock to minimize lock maintenance overhead. Live, exclusive table locks on active tables force all other processes to wait.
- When you update a large amount of data, you also write a significant number of entries to the transaction log. A large active log takes up more space. The log segment will expand until the transaction is complete, or the disk is full.

Note

> When you create a database, you decide whether to restrict the growth of the log file(s). If you choose unrestricted file growth, the log file(s) can grow until the logical volume is full. At that point, you get a log-full error message and possibly an out of disk space error as well.

- If you are running on a single-CPU system, long-running transactions tend to monopolize the processor.

To avoid long-running transactions, break up work into smaller chunks. For instance, when you perform a monthly archive, write the work one day at a time in a loop. Commit the transactions after each day's work, and consider adding a statement to truncate the log in the loop. Listing 13.8 contains the skeleton of a revised statement, with the inserts and deletes omitted.

LISTING 13.8 Example of Breaking Up a Long-Running Transaction

```
 1: set xact_abort on
 2: declare @StartDate datetime
 3: declare @OrderList table (OrderID int)
 4: set @StartDate = '8/1/2000'
 5: while @StartDate < '9/1/2000'
 6: begin
 7:     insert @OrderList (OrderID)
 8:     select OrderID
 9:       from Orders with (readpast)
10:      where OrderDate >= @StartDate and
11:            OrderDate < dateadd(dd, 1, @StartDate)
12:     begin transaction
13: /*
14:    inserts and deletes performed here for one day
15:  */
16:     commit transaction
17:     backup transaction Northwind with truncate_only
18:     set @StartDate = dateadd(dd, 1, @StartDate)
19: end
20: backup database Northwind [ ... ]
```

The `while` loop breaks down each of the large queries into a smaller set of queries. The `BACKUP TRANSACTION` statement (line 17) truncates the transaction log without performing a backup. This will keep the size of the log under control by freeing up log space between transactions. The `BACKUP DATABASE` command (line 20) would perform a full backup when the process is complete. Truncating the transaction log disables transactional disaster recovery from that point forward, so you will need to make a new database backup as soon as the process is complete.

Whenever possible, perform long-running and large-scale work when other users are not working. Your processes will run more smoothly because your table locks won't be blocked by other users. They will be more cheerful because they won't need access to data while you have it locked.

Summary

In this lesson, you learned how to execute statements within a transaction. Transactions are groups of statements that either succeed or fail as a single group. You saw why the database server needs locking and how it affects the performance of the server. The server automatically uses transaction control to manage the integrity of single SQL statements.

Q&A

Q Can I turn off transaction management for a while?

A No.

Q Is there real stuff I can look at to help me understand transactions? Can I read log records? Can I see a `BEGIN TRAN` or `COMMIT TRAN` marker?

A There are methods of dumping pages from the log to examine them, but I won't go into them here. These are advanced methods, and they can cause some disruption or corruption of your database. When you need to know that stuff, Microsoft tech support can walk you through it.

Q You said that every SQL statement is a transaction itself. Does the server use a different mechanism for those transactions from the way that my explicit transactions are performed?

A No. Every statement, whether within an explicit transaction or not, includes an implied `BEGIN TRANSACTIONS` and `COMMIT TRANACTIONS`. On Day 17, "Debugging Stored Procedures," when we look at triggers, we will examine the value of `@@trancount` while we are running the trigger. You'll see that `@@trancount` is automatically incremented at the start of every SQL statement (by the implied `BEGIN TRANSACTIONS`) and decremented at the end (by the implied `COMMIT TRANSACTIONS`).

Q When should I use implicit transactions?

A Implicit transactions are particularly useful when you are porting SQL code from another database environment when the default is to use implicit transactions. Instead of rewriting every single query to remove extra `COMMIT` statements, you simply set the `IMPLICIT TRANSACTIONS` option in each session and run it.

Workshop

13

The Workshop provides quiz questions to help you solidify your understanding of the material covered and exercises to provide you with experience in using what you've learned. Try to answer the quiz and exercise questions before checking the answers in Appendix A, "Answers to Quizzes and Exercises," and make sure that you understand the answers before continuing to the next lesson.

Quiz

1. What is the difference between `ROLLBACK TRANSACTIONS` and `ROLLBACK TRANSACTIONS <savepoint>`?

2. How do the following settings affect your programming?

   ```
   set implicit_transactions on
   ```

   ```
   set xact_abort on
   ```

   ```
   set lock_timeout 0
   ```

Exercise

In the following exercise, correct this batch to avoid a common transaction programming problem. Describe the problem and then suggest a solution.

```
begin transaction
if (
    select avg(UnitPrice)
    from Products
    where Category = 1
) > 15
update Products
   set UnitPrice = UnitPrice * .90
 where CategoryID = 1
/* implement 30-day price protection */
update [Order Details]
   set UnitPrice = UnitPrice * .90
 where ProductID in (
       select ProductID
       from Products
       where CategoryID = 1
       )
   and OrderID in (
       select OrderID
       from Orders
       where datediff(dd, OrderDate, getdate()) <= 30
       )
commit transaction
```

WEEK 2

DAY 14

Using Cursors

In the last few days you have learned about the different topics that help you in working with the data in your database. All the operations that you perform on the data in the database are performed on a complete set of rows. The set of rows, or *result set*, that is returned by a `SELECT` statement includes all the rows that satisfy the `WHERE` clause of the statement. Most applications cannot always work effectively with the entire result set as a unit. You need a way to work with one row or a small set of rows at one time.

Cursors give you the ability to request a result set, using a `SELECT` statement, and then to deal with the data on a row-by-row basis. Today, you will learn what cursors are and how to use them, including the following topics:

- What is a cursor?
- Creating a cursor.
- Using cursors in SQL scripts.
- Using cursor variables.
- Enhancing performance with cursors.

Defining Cursors

If you have been using a computer for any length of time, you might be familiar with the term *cursor*. When a cursor is mentioned in relation to a computer, it generally means the blinking line that tells you were the next character will appear when you type. A cursor in terms of database access is a completely different concept. A *database cursor* is a programming feature that allows each row in a table to be processed separately from the rest of the rows in the result set. Another way to look at cursors is that they are the closest things you can get to an array when using T-SQL programming. This can be very useful when the rows in the table cannot be manipulated easily with the standard set of SQL commands.

The standard SQL commands (`INSERT`, `UPDATE`, and `DELETE`) all operate on an entire result set at once. To see this, take a look at the following example:

```
Use Northwind
Update employees
Set city = 'New York'
```

The set on which this query operates is the whole table. The server has received instructions that say: "For every row in the table, change the value in the city column to `'New York'` no matter what was there before."

A cursor will accept commands for processing each row independently, rather than processing the whole result set. For each row in the `Employees` table, for instance, a set of operations can be carried out based on the values in the row. In addition, different operations can be performed on the same row, at the same time. One benefit to using a cursor is that you could perform many operations on a single row of data before moving on to the next row.

> If you are a programmer and you understand array processing, you can see that cursors allow you to use the power of the server and its usually larger memory capacity to process each row, instead of your program reading in the entire result set into an array and then processing it.

Creating a Cursor

Cursors work in multiple statement SQL scripts where the cursor provides a row of data to the remaining statements in the script. Because of this, the best places to use cursor processing are in SQL scripts, stored procedures, and triggers. The latter two will be discussed later in this book.

In order to use cursors—meaning to create, use, and destroy cursors—you must perform a series of commands in a particular order. These commands are

1. Define T-SQL variables to contain the data returned by the cursor.
2. Define the cursor by associating it with a `SELECT` statement.
3. Open the cursor.
4. Use the `FETCH INTO` statement to retrieve individual rows of data.
5. Close the cursor.
6. Deallocate the cursor.

If you take a close look at these steps, you can see the basic structure of most computer programs. That is, define memory, connect to the data, request data, close the connection, and release memory.

Cursor Types

There are two ways that you can define and use cursors in a client/server environment. A client/server environment describes the types of cursors: client-side and server-side cursors. *Server-side* cursors are defined, opened, and scrolled by submitting a SQL program to SQL Server, where that program is compiled and executed. Output of the program is returned to the client.

Client-side cursors are cursors that request normal SQL results from the server but then buffer those results on the client machine, where they can be stepped through on a row-by-row basis. Choosing which type of cursor to use depends on how you will be processing the data in your application.

Using a cursor is less efficient that using a default result set. In a default result set, the only packet sent from the client to the server is the packet containing the statement for the server to execute. When using a server cursor, each `FETCH` statement you associate must be sent from the client to the server, where it must be translated by the server and compiled before being executed.

If a T-SQL statement will return a relatively small result set that can be stored in the memory available on the client computer, and you need to retrieve the entire result set, you should use a default result set. You should use server cursors only when cursor operations are required to support the functionality of the application, or when only part of the result set is likely to be retrieved.

A potential drawback of using server-side cursors is that they do not support all T-SQL statements. Because server-side cursors do not support any statements that generate multiple result sets, they cannot be used when the application executes a stored procedure or a batch that contains more than one `SELECT` statement. In addition, they do not support T-SQL statements containing the keywords `COMPUTE`, `COMPUTE BY`, `FOR BROWSE`, or `INTO`.

Table 14.1 lists the advantages of using a server cursor instead of a client cursor.

TABLE 14.1 Advantages of Server Cursors

Advantage	*Explanation*
Performance	If you plan on accessing only a fraction of the data in the cursor (typical for browsing applications), using server-side cursors provides optimal performance because only fetched data is sent over the network. Client-side cursors cache the entire result set on the client.
Additional cursor types	If the SQL Server ODBC driver used only client-side cursors, it could support only forward-only and static cursors. By using API server-side cursors, the driver can also support keyset-driven and dynamic cursors, which are defined in Table 14.2.
More accurate updates	Server-side cursors directly support positioned operations, such as the `UPDATE` and `DELETE` statements.
Memory usage	When using server-side cursors, the client does not need to cache large amounts of data or maintain information about the cursor position.
Multiple active statements	When using server-side cursors, no results are left outstanding on the connection between cursor operations.

Cursor Scope

A cursor exists throughout the life of a connection. A cursor declared early during a connection's existence is available until either the connection is closed or the cursor is destroyed. Unless you destroy or deallocate a cursor, it not only remains available for use, but it can even be left open with data being fetched from it as needed while the connection is maintained. For example, you can declare a cursor in one batch, open it in another, and then fetch data from it in a third batch. The cursor remains open until you close it and remains available until the cursor is destroyed.

Working with Cursors

In order to understand how to use a cursor, we will build a T-SQL script that uses a cursor, one step at a time, explaining the process as we go. The example will read rows from the `Products` table. If the product is from Germany, it will add 25% to the unit cost of the product. It will also produce a report of all unit costs and any changes that were made.

> The final code for this example can be found at the end of this section and on the CD-ROM.

Declaring the Cursor

The first step you must perform is to declare or create the cursor, associating it with a `SELECT` statement. The syntax of the `DECLARE` statement used to create a cursor is

```
Declare <cursor name> [insensitive] [scroll] cursor
For <select statement>
[for <read only | update [of <column list>]>]
```

This syntax is the ANSI-92 standard for declaring a cursor. Microsoft SQL Server 2000 provides a T-SQL extended syntax for the `declare cursor` statement, which is shown in the following code. Table 14.2 lists each of the different keywords and their descriptions.

```
Declare <cursor_name> cursor
[ local | global ]
[ forward only | scroll ]
[ static | keyset | dynamic | fast_forward ]
[ read_only | scroll_locks | optimistic ]
[ type_warning ]
For <select_statement>
[ for update [ of <column list>] ]
```

TABLE 14.2 Cursor Declaration Keywords

Syntax Type	*Keyword*	*Description*
SQL-92	`INSENSITIVE`	Defines a cursor that makes a temporary copy of the data to be used by the cursor. All requests to the cursor are answered from this temporary table, therefore, any changes made to the base tables are not reflected in the data returned by fetches made to this cursor. This cursor does not allow modifications.

TABLE 14.2 continued

Syntax Type	Keyword	Description
	SCROLL	Specifies that all fetch options (FIRST, LAST, PRIOR, NEXT, RELATIVE, ABSOLUTE) are available. If SCROLL is not specified, NEXT is the only fetch option supported. SCROLL cannot be specified if FAST_FORWARD is also specified.
	READ_ONLY	Prevents updates made through this cursor
	UPDATE	Defines updateable columns within the cursor. If OF *column_name* [,...*n*] is specified, only the columns listed allow modifications. If UPDATE is specified without a column list, all columns can be updated.
T-SQL Extensions	LOCAL	Specifies that the scope of the cursor is local to the batch, stored procedure, or trigger in which the cursor was created. The cursor name is only valid within this scope. The cursor is implicitly deallocated when the batch, stored procedure, or trigger terminates.
	GLOBAL	Specifies that the scope of the cursor is global to the connection. The cursor name can be referenced in any stored procedure or batch executed by the connection. The cursor is only implicitly deallocated at disconnect. If neither the GLOBAL nor the LOCAL argument is specified, the default is controlled by the setting of the default to the local cursor database option. This option defaults to FALSE.
	FORWARD_ONLY	Specifies that the cursor can be scrolled only from the first to the last row. FETCH NEXT is the only supported fetch option. If FORWARD_ONLY is specified without the STATIC, KEYSET, or DYNAMIC keywords, the cursor operates as a DYNAMIC cursor. When neither FORWARD_ONLY nor SCROLL is specified, FORWARD_ONLY is the default, unless the keyword STATIC, KEYSET, or DYNAMIC is specified. STATIC, KEYSET, and DYNAMIC cursors default to SCROLL.
	STATIC	Defines a cursor that makes a temporary copy of the data to be used by the cursor. All requests to the cursor are answered from this temporary table, therefore, any changes made to the base tables are not reflected in the data returned by fetches made to this cursor. This cursor does not allow modifications. (This is the same as the ANSI-92 keyword INSENSITIVE.)

TABLE 14.2 continued

Syntax Type	Keyword	Description
	KEYSET	Specifies that the membership and order of rows in the cursor are fixed when the cursor is opened. The set of keys that uniquely identify the rows is built in to a table in tempdb, known as the keyset. Changes to nonkey values in the base tables, either made by the cursor owner or committed by other users, are visible as the owner scrolls around the cursor. Inserts made by other users are not visible.
	DYNAMIC	Defines a cursor that reflects all data changes made to the rows in its result set as you scroll around the cursor. The data values, order, and membership of the rows can change on each fetch. The ABSOLUTE fetch option is not supported with dynamic cursors.
	FAST_FORWARD	Specifies a FORWARD_ONLY, READ_ONLY cursor with performance optimizations enabled. FAST_FORWARD cannot be specified if SCROLL or FOR_UPDATE is also specified. FAST_FORWARD and FORWARD_ONLY are mutually exclusive; if one is specified the other cannot be specified.
	READ_ONLY	Prevents updates made through this cursor.
	SCROLL_LOCKS	Specifies that positioned updates or deletes made through the cursor are guaranteed to succeed. SCROLL_LOCKS cannot be specified if FAST_FORWARD is also specified.
	OPTIMISTIC	Specifies that positioned updates or deletes made through the cursor do not succeed if the row has been updated since it was read into the cursor. SQL Server does not lock rows as they are read into the cursor. OPTIMISTIC cannot be specified if FAST_FORWARD is also specified.
	TYPE_WARNING	Specifies that a warning message is sent to the client if the cursor is implicitly converted from the requested type to another.

You cannot mix the two forms of the DECLARE CURSOR statement. If you specify the SCROLL or INSENSITIVE keywords before the CURSOR keyword, you cannot use any keywords between the CURSOR and the FOR *<select_statement>* keywords. If you specify any keywords between the CURSOR and the FOR *<select_statement>* keywords, you cannot specify SCROLL or INSENSITIVE before the CURSOR keyword.

If you use T-SQL syntax when declaring a cursor and do not specify READ_ONLY, OPTIMISTIC, or SCROLL_LOCKS, the default actions are as follows:

- If the SELECT statement does not support updates (insufficient permissions, accessing remote tables that do not support updates, and so on), the cursor is READ_ONLY.
- STATIC and FAST_FORWARD cursors default to READ_ONLY.
- DYNAMIC and KEYSET cursors default to OPTIMISTIC.

You can select all the columns or specify some of the columns for the cursor, but allow updates to only some of those columns by providing an update column list, as shown in line 3 of the following syntax.

```
Declare <cursor name> [insensitive] [scroll] cursor
For <select statement>
[for <read only | update [of <column list>]>]
```

To declare the cursor for our example, the following SQL code is used:

```
use northwind
declare crs_products cursor
for
select p.productid, p.productname, p.unitprice,
       s.country, s.supplierid, s.companyname
from products as p inner join
     suppliers as s on
     p.supplierid = s.supplierid
where s.country = 'Germany'
order by s.companyname, p.productname
for update
```

This example is the same DECLARE keyword that you used on Day 11, "T-SQL Programming Fundamentals," to declare local variables. You can declare variables or declare a cursor with a single DECLARE statement, but you cannot do both. To declare both variables and cursors, you must use two DECLARE statements, as you will see in this example.

You must provide a name for the cursor in the DECLARE statement. After you have named the cursor, you would next specify the set of rows you want the cursor to have access to. This is defined as a regular SELECT statement, whether you intend to use the cursor to modify the rows or not. This cursor is defined as an UPDATE cursor because we intend to update the rows we are working with. If you wanted to just read the rows using the cursor, you would declare the cursor for read only instead of for update.

When naming a cursor, use a convention that you are comfortable with. Remember, I like to use crs_ as a prefix to the cursor name. I would use the name of the table in which most of the processing is being done. In the example, the cursor name is crs_products.

If you do not specify a cursor type, either by design or by accident, it will default to READ_ONLY.

Opening the Cursor

After declaring the cursor, be sure that the statement is executed before the Open statement. When this has been done, you are ready to open the cursor. This is a very simple step, requiring a single line of code as shown:

```
Open Cursor crs_products
```

Declaring the Variables

In order for the cursor process to work properly, you must declare one variable for each column that is returned by the SELECT statement. The following shows the DECLARE statement for our example.

```
Declare @product_ID int, @product_name varchar(40),
        @product_Price money, @product_country varchar(15),
        @Supplier_ID int, @Supplier varchar(40),
        @old_product_price Money, @tempstr varchar(60)
```

Besides declaring a unique variable for each of the columns being selected, we have also declared a second unit price variable to contain the old unit price. Finally, a temporary string variable is declared for use when printing the results.

Fetching the Rows

Now that you have set up the elements for using the cursor, you need to actually instruct the server to fetch a row of data for you. This is where the fun begins. The FETCH statement is the key to using cursors. The following shows the syntax for the FETCH state ment:

```
Fetch
[[Next | Prior | First | Last |
  Absolute {n | @n} |
  Relative {n | @n}]
```

```
from]
[Global] <cursor name> | <@cursor variable name>
[Into @variable1, @variable2, ...]
```

The only required elements are the actual word `FETCH` and the name of the cursor that you are using. The different keywords are described in Table 14.3.

TABLE 14.3 Fetch Keywords

Keyword	*Description*
`NEXT`	Returns the result row immediately following the current row, and increments the current row to the row returned. If `FETCH NEXT` is the first fetch against a cursor, it returns the first row in the result set. `NEXT` is the default cursor fetch option.
`PRIOR`	Returns the result row immediately preceding the current row, and decrements the current row to the row returned. If `FETCH PRIOR` is the first fetch against a cursor, no row is returned and the cursor is left positioned before the first row.
`FIRST`	Returns the first row in the cursor and makes it the current row.
`LAST`	Returns the last row in the cursor and makes it the current row.
`ABSOLUTE {`*`n`*` | `*`@n`*`}`	If *n* or *@nvar* is positive, returns the row *n* rows from the front of the cursor and makes the returned row the new current row. If *n* or *@nvar* is negative, returns the row *n* rows before the end of the cursor and makes the returned row the new current row. If *n* or *@nvar* is 0, no rows are returned. *n* must be an integer constant, and *@nvar* must be smallint, tinyint, or int.
`RELATIVE {`*`n`*` | `*`@n`*`}`	If *n* or *@nvar* is positive, returns the row *n* rows beyond the current row and makes the returned row the new current row. If *n* or *@nvar* is negative, returns the row *n* rows prior to the current row and makes the returned row the new current row. If *n* or *@nvar* is 0, returns the current row.
`GLOBAL`	Specifies that *cursor_name* refers to a global cursor.

If you use any of the `FETCH` keywords, you must also use the `FROM` clause. The last line of the syntax specifies where to store the data from the row being fetched. The number of variables must match the number of columns, and each variable must match in size and data type of the corresponding column from the selected column list.

The following code will fetch a row into the local variables that you have previously defined. You can also fetch the columns directly, which will print them to the screen just as a standard `SELECT` statement would. In this example, we will use the `PRINT` statement to send the results to the screen. Because the `PRINT` statement doesn't add column headers automatically, we will need to add them ourselves. Many cursor programs are used strictly for server-side processing and do not return rows the way this example does. As you can see, it is a lot less convenient than a simple `SELECT` statement.

Note

Although I should be printing everything that I selected, I am printing only the product name, the old unit price, and the new, updated unit price.

Caution

The following example will not execute by itself; several statements must be added, as you will see later in this section.

```
print 'Product Name                          Old Unit Price New Unit Price'
print '------------------------------------- -------------- --------------'
fetch next from crs_products into @product_ID, @product_name,
        @product_Price, @product_Country, @Supplier_ID,
        @Supplier
while @@fetch_status = 0 begin
set @old_product_price = @product_price
if @product_price > 40
        set @product_price = @product_Price * 1.25
if @product_price is null
        set @tempstr = convert(char(40), @product_name) +
        convert(char(7),@old_product_price,1) + '--no pricing--'
else
      set @tempstr = convert(char(40), @product_name) +
      convert(char(7),@old_product_price,1) + convert(char(7),@product_price,1)
print @tempstr
fetch next from crs_products into @product_ID, @product_name,
        @product_Price, @product_Country, @Supplier_ID,
        @Supplier
end
```

After the headings are printed, you would execute the initial `FETCH` statement to retrieve the first row from the cursor keyset.

NEW TERM A *cursor keyset* refers to the set of rows that are accessed by the open cursor specified by the `SELECT` statement attached to the cursor.

You might have noticed a strange-looking variable that you did not declare. The `@@FETCH_STATUS` variable is really a function that reports on the status of the last `FETCH` statement. This status information should be used to determine the validity of the data

14

returned by a `FETCH` statement prior to attempting any operation against that data. The `@@FETCH_STATUS` variable will always have one of three values as shown in Table 14.4.

TABLE 14.4 Fetch Status Codes

Value	*Description*
0	The most recent fetch statement succeeded.
-1	The most recent fetch failed because there were no more rows to get.
-2	The row requested no longer exists.

The loop that was set up using the `WHILE` statement will continue to fetch rows until a `-1` or `-2` is returned by the `@@FETCH_STATUS` variable. Inside the loop, the original price of the product is saved in the variable `@old_product_price` before any action is taken. Then, the value of `@product_price` is tested. If the current row's price is greater than $40, it is increased by 25%. Next, the `@product_price` is tested, and, if the price is null, it will print a custom message rather than null values. Finally, the messages are all gathered together in a temporary string and printed to the screen. The next row is fetched, and the loop begins from the top.

Closing the Cursor

After all the rows have been processed, the `WHILE` loop will end, and you can now close the cursor that was being used. It is very simple to close a cursor as the following statement shows:

```
close crs_products
```

Closing the cursor will destroy the cursor keyset, meaning that it will wipe out the result set that the cursor was using. The cursor declaration will still be active, however, and can be reopened with a new `OPEN` statement after it has been closed. If you are using an insensitive or static cursor, you could close and then reopen the cursor in order to refresh the result set.

Destroying the Cursor

Finally, if the process is complete, you should destroy or deallocate the cursor. This is done using the following syntax:

```
deallocate crs_products
```

If you do not deallocate the cursor, memory will remain in use until your connection is closed. If you have declared a cursor, you cannot declare another with the same name until you have deallocated the original one. Listing 14.1 illustrates declaring, using, closing, and destroying a cursor.

LISTING 14.1 Using Cursors in T-SQL Scripts

```
use northwind
declare crs_products cursor
for
select p.productid, p.productname, p.unitprice,
       s.country, s.supplierid, s.companyname
from products as p inner join
     suppliers as s on
     p.supplierid = s.supplierid
where s.country = 'Germany'
order by s.companyname, p.productname
for update
open crs_products
Declare @product_ID int, @product_name varchar(40),
        @product_Price money, @product_country varchar(15),
        @Supplier_ID int, @Supplier varchar(40),
        @old_product_price Money, @tempstr varchar(60)
print 'Product Name                              Old Unit Price New Unit Price'
print '------------------------------ -------------- --------------'
fetch next from crs_products into @product_ID, @product_name,
    @product_Price, @product_Country, @Supplier_ID,
    @Supplier
while @@fetch_status = 0 begin
set @old_product_price = @product_price
if @product_price > 40
    set @product_price = @product_Price * 1.25
if @product_price is null
    set @tempstr = convert(char(40), @product_name) +
        convert(char(7),@old_product_price,1) + '--no pricing--'
else
    set @tempstr = convert(char(40), @product_name) +
   convert(char(7),@old_product_price,1) + convert(char(7),@product_price,1)
print @tempstr
fetch next from crs_products into @product_ID, @product_name,
    @product_Price, @product_Country, @Supplier_ID,
    @Supplier
end
close crs_products
deallocate crs_products
```

Results:

```
Product Name                       Old Unit Price New Unit Price
---------------------------------- -------------- --------------
Gumbär Gummibärchen                         31.23  31.23
NuNuCa Nuß-Nougat-Creme                     14.00  14.00
Schoggi Schokolade                          43.90  54.88
Nord-Ost Matjeshering                       25.89  25.89
Original Frankfurter grüne Soße             13.00  13.00
Rhönbräu Klosterbier                         7.75   7.75
```

LISTING 14.1 continued

```
Rössle Sauerkraut                              45.60  57.00
Thüringer Rostbratwurst                       123.79 154.74
Wimmers gute Semmelknödel                      33.25  33.25
```

Other Cursor Functions

There are three main variables that are associated directly with the use of cursors:

`@@FETCH_STATUS`	Returns the status of the last cursor `FETCH` statement issued against any cursor currently opened by the connection.
`@@CURSOR_ROWS`	Returns the number of rows currently in the last cursor opened on the connection.
`CURSOR_STATUS`	Returns to the caller of a stored procedure whether or not that procedure has returned a cursor with a result set for a given parameter.

You have already seen how to use the first cursor variable in the previous examples.

Using the @@CURSOR_ROWS Function

The `@@CURSOR_ROWS` function allows you to determine the number of rows that a cursor has retrieved at the time the function was called. This number can change because SQL Server can populate a large keyset and static cursors asynchronously to improve performance. To see how this really works, try executing the following code in Listing 14.2 to see the output that is generated.

LISTING 14.2 Working with the `@@Cursor Rows` Function

```
use northwind
select @@cursor_rows as 'Cursor Row Cnt'
declare crs_employees cursor
for
select firstname
from employees
open crs_employees
Fetch next from crs_employees
select @@cursor_rows as 'Cursor Row Cnt'
close crs_employees
deallocate crs_employees
```

Results:

LISTING 14.2 continued

```
Cursor Row Cnt
--------------
0

(1 row(s) affected)

firstname
----------
Nancy

(1 row(s) affected)

Cursor Row Cnt
--------------
-1

(1 row(s) affected)
```

Listing 14.2 declares a cursor and uses the `SELECT` statement to display the value of the `@@CURSOR_ROWS` function. The value of the function is `0` before the cursor is opened, and a value of `-1` indicates that the cursor keyset is populated asynchronously. Table 14.5 lists the different return values of the function and the description of each.

TABLE 14.5 `@@CURSOR_ROWS` Return Values

Value	*Description*
`-n`	The cursor is populated asynchronously. The value returned (`-n`) is the number of rows currently in the keyset.
`-1`	The cursor is dynamic.
`0`	No cursors have been opened, no rows have been qualified for the last-opened cursor, or the last-opened cursor is closed or deallocated.
`n`	The cursor is fully populated. The value returned (`n`) is the total number of rows in the cursor.

Using the `CURSOR_STATUS` Function

The `CURSOR_STATUS` function is used in conjunction with a stored procedure. It allows you to check whether a cursor that was declared and opened in a stored procedure actually returned data in its keyset. You will see how to create and use stored procedures in the next few lessons. However, you will take a quick look at how this function works so that you will be able to use it in the future.

The syntax for the use of this function is

```
Cursor_Status
({'local', '<cursor name>'}
|{'global', '<cursor name>'}
|{'variable', '<cursor variable>'})
```

The arguments of this function are listed in Table 14.6 along with their descriptions.

TABLE 14.6 `Cursor_Status` Arguments

Argument	*Description*
Cursor name	The name of the declared cursor
Cursor variable	The name of the declared cursor variable
Local	Indicates that the cursor name is a local cursor
Global	Indicates that the cursor name is a global cursor
Variable	Indicates that the source of the cursor is a local variable

When this function is used, it returns a single value indicating the status of the cursor. Depending on whether the function is referencing a cursor or cursor variable, the values can have slightly different meanings. These values and their meanings are listed in Table 14.7.

TABLE 14.7 `Cursor_Status` Return Values

Value	*Cursor Use*	*Cursor Variable Use*
`1`	For insensitive and keyset cursors, the result set has at least one row.	For insensitive and keyset cursors, the result set has at least one row.
	For dynamic cursors, the result set can have zero, one, or more rows.	For dynamic cursors, the result set can have zero, one, or more rows.
`0`	The result set is empty (except for dynamic cursors).	The cursor allocated to this variable is open, but the result set is empty (except for dynamic cursors).
`-1`	The cursor is closed.	The cursor allocated to this variable is closed.
`-2`	N/A	No cursor was assigned to this output variable, or a cursor was assigned but was closed upon completion of the procedure.
`-3`	The cursor does not exist.	The cursor variable does not exist, or there is no cursor allocated to it yet.

Listing 14.3 shows how this function can be used. The first section of code creates a stored procedure (remember that you will learn how to do this tomorrow). Then, you will see how the actual code will make use of this stored procedure and the `Cursor Status` function.

Listing 14.3 Using the Cursor Status Function

```
 1:USE pubs
 2:IF EXISTS (SELECT name FROM sysobjects
 3:      WHERE name = 'lake_list' AND type = 'P')
 4:   DROP PROCEDURE lake_list
 5:GO
 6:CREATE PROCEDURE lake_list
 7:   ( @region varchar(30),
 8:     @size integer,
 9:     @lake_list_cursor CURSOR VARYING OUTPUT )
10:AS
11:BEGIN
12:   DECLARE @ok SMALLINT
13:   EXECUTE check_authority @region, username, @ok OUTPUT
14:   IF @ok = 1
15:      BEGIN
16:      SET @lake_list_cursor =CURSOR LOCAL SCROLL FOR
17:         SELECT name, lat, long, size, boat_launch, cost
18:         FROM lake_inventory
19:         WHERE locale = @region AND area >= @size
20:         ORDER BY name
21:      OPEN @lake_list_cursor
22:      END
23:END
24:DECLARE @my_lakes_cursor CURSOR
25:DECLARE @my_region char(30)
26:SET @my_region = 'Northern Ontario'
27:EXECUTE lake_list @my_region, 500, @my_lakes_cursor OUTPUT
28:IF Cursor_Status('variable', '@my_lakes_cursor') <= 0
29:   BEGIN
30:   /* Some code to tell the user that there is no list of
31:   lakes for him/her */
32:   END
33:ELSE
34:   BEGIN
35:      FETCH @my_lakes_cursor INTO -- Destination here
36:      -- Continue with other code here.
37:END
```


Looking at Listing 14.3, you can see that the stored procedure is called in line 27. Then, when execution is returned, the following `IF` statement uses the `Cursor_Status` function to check whether the cursor variable `'@my_lakes_cursor'` has returned any data. Depending on the value in the `Cursor Status` function, your SQL code can perform the required actions.

Cursor Locking

On Day 12, "Understanding Database Locking," you learned all about how SQL Server uses locks to prevent accidental changes to the database. When you use cursors, the `SELECT` statement in the cursor `DECLARE` is subject to the same transaction-locking rules that you have seen applied to other `SELECT` statements in Day 12. In cursors, however, you can acquire an additional set of scroll locks based on the cursor concurrency level.

As a review, the transaction locks that are used by any `SELECT` statement, including those in a cursor definition, are controlled by

- The transaction isolation level setting for the connection
- Any locking hints specified in the `FROM` clause

These locks are maintained until the end of the current transaction for both standard `SELECT` statements and for cursors. Although cursors must obey the same set of rules that standard `SELECT` statements do, regarding the type of transaction locks being used, the locks themselves are acquired at different times. Although a lock is generated when a row is retrieved, for a standard `SELECT` statement, all the rows are retrieved when the statement is executed. In contrast, a cursor retrieves rows at different times depending on the type of cursor. Table 14.8 lists the different types of cursors and when they acquire a transaction lock.

TABLE 14.8 Acquiring Locks with Cursors

Cursor Type	*Lock Description*
Static	Retrieves the entire result set at the time the cursor is opened. This locks each row of the result set at open time.
Keyset-driven	Retrieves the keys of each row of the result set at the time the cursor is opened. This locks each row of the result set at open time.
Dynamic	Does not retrieve any rows until they are explicitly fetched. Locks are not acquired on the rows until they have been fetched.

Summary

What you have learned in today's lesson is how cursors make your job as a SQL programmer easier. You have also gotten an understanding that using cursors requires you to do a bit more design and analysis of what actions you want to perform on the data before creating the SQL code. Remember that, although you might think that cursors are the best way of doing things, they require a great deal more effort, and, more importantly, they often provide you with poorer performance when executing the SQL scripts.

At this point, you have probably figured out that cursors allow you to use SQL statements just like a regular programming language. In addition, you saw that there are several things to watch out for when using cursors. Cursors can be created as read-only or for update. However, to update or delete the current row in a cursor keyset, you must use the `WHERE CURRENT OF` *<cursor name>* clause. Cursors have slightly different rules for locking and performance than do normal SQL statements.

In Day 15, "Writing and Executing Stored Procedures," you will be taking your first look at stored procedures and triggers, which as you have seen is where you could use cursors to perform complex processing.

Q&A

Q Can I have more than one cursor active in a SQL script at a time? Using the same tables?

A There is no limitation on the number of cursors that you can have active and open in a SQL script. In addition, you can access the same table or tables from the different cursors.

Q Can cursors fetch more than one row at a time?

A The answer is a little more complicated than a yes or no. If you are using server-side cursors, then no, you can only fetch one row at a time. However, if you are using client-side cursors, you could fetch multiple rows at a single time. This is because of the way client-side cursors retrieve the data from the database.

Q Can I use cursors inside triggers or stored procedures?

A Although you can use cursors inside both triggers and stored procedures, it is strongly discouraged in regards to triggers. By definition, cursors create overhead when used. Triggers run every time an `INSERT`, `UPDATE`, or `DELETE` is executed on a table. If a trigger had to create, run, and destroy a cursor for each of these operations, it would take longer than most users would want to wait.

Workshop

The Workshop provides quiz questions to help you solidify your understanding of the material covered and exercises to provide you with experience in using what you've learned. Try to answer the quiz and exercise questions before checking the answers in Appendix A, "Answers to Quizzes and Exercises," and make sure that you understand the answers before continuing to the next lesson.

Quiz

1. Name the six navigation operations that are possible with cursors.
2. Can a cursor select data from joined tables?
3. Name the six steps required to use a cursor.

Exercise

Create a cursor on the `Employees` table in the Northwind database. Read in each employee's last name, birth date, and hire date. If an employee is more than 40 years old, then print his last name, and hire date.

```
Employee Name         Birth Date  Age  Hire Date
--------------------  ----------  ---  ---------
Buchanan              03/04/1955   45  10/17/1993
Callahan              01/09/1958   42  03/05/1994
Davolio               12/08/1948   52  05/01/1992
Davolio               12/08/1948   52  05/01/1992
Fuller                02/19/1952   48  08/14/1992
Fuller                02/19/1952   48  08/14/1992
Fuller                02/19/1952   48  08/14/1992
Peacock               09/19/1937   63  05/03/1993
Peacock               09/19/1937   63  05/03/1993
```

WEEK 2

In Review

You've reached the end of the second week. To review what you have learned, let's quickly recap each day. If you see something you don't remember, go back to the day in question and review the topic.

Day 8, "Defining Data": You found that a database is a logical container for many related objects. You learned how to create new databases on SQL Server using Data Definition Language or DDL. In SQL Server, the `master` database contains data about the server itself, such as the names of all the databases on the server. You also found that the `model` database is used as a template when you create new databases.

Day 9, "Indexes and Performance": This was a discussion of how indexes are used by SQL Server. You learned how the server uses indexes to optimize the manipulation of data in a database. You also saw how clustered and nonclustered indexes are used to enforce uniqueness and to help the server find data quickly. In addition, you learned how to create and manage indexes for a table in a database. Finally, you worked with some of the performance tools that are available in SQL Server 2000.

Day 10, "Views and Temporary Tables": In Day 10, you learned how to create and work with views and temporary tables. Views provide you with a way to restrict access to the columns in a table. Finally, temporary tables enable you to store data temporarily as needed, including creating reference tables when the server is started.

Day 11, "T-SQL Programming Fundamentals": On this day, you learned how to batch your SQL statements together for better performance. Also, you worked with the different SQL commands that enable you to create complex SQL code using `BEGIN-END` blocks, `IF` statements, and `WHILE` loops. Finally, you learned how to detect errors in a SQL script and how to display them to the user.

Day 12, "Understanding Database Locking": To prevent more than one user from updating a given row of data, you learned today that SQL Server locks rows and tables to ensure the proper updating of data.

Day 13, "Programming with Transactions": Transactions make sure that a group of statements you have sent to the server either succeeds or fails as a group. You learned that a transaction is started with the `BEGIN TRANSACTION` statement and ended with the `COMMIT TRANSACTION` statement, unless there is a problem, in which case you would use the `ROLLBACK TRANSACTION` statement to undo the actions taken.

Day 14, "Using Cursors": The last day of the week covered the use of cursors. Cursors require lots of SQL programming. They often result in longer query execution because of the high CPU usage they require. To use a cursor, you use the following statements in order: `DECLARE`, `OPEN`, `FETCH`, `CLOSE`, `DEALLOCATE`.

WEEK 3

Procedures and Triggers

Congratulations on finishing your second week! The third and final week will teach you how to write stored procedures and triggers. It also goes beyond syntax to prepare you for the real world of T-SQL programming. On Days 15 through 17, you will focus on stored procedures, which are T-SQL batches stored on the server that you can execute by name. On Days 18 and 19, you will learn how to write and test triggers.

On Day 15, "Writing and Executing Stored Procedures," you will learn the basic concepts of how to write and execute a simple stored procedure.

Then, on Day 16, "Optimizing Stored Procedures," you will see how to optimize a stored procedure so that they will run more efficiently.

On Day 17, "Debugging Stored Procedures," you will learn how to test and debug a stored procedure that you are creating.

On Day 18, "Writing and Testing Triggers," and Day 19, "Solving Special Trigger Problems," you will learn how to write and test triggers. These are special stored procedures that are fired automatically by the server whenever you make a change to a row in a table by using one of the following commands: `INSERT`, `UPDATE`, or `DELETE`.

On Day 20, "User-Defined Functions in SQL," you will learn about a new feature available in SQL Server 2000 that will enable you to define your own functions that can be used in SQL.

Day 21, "Handling BLOBs in T-SQL," deals with a special data type called BLOBs. These are large binary objects that are stored in a column of a table. You will learn how to work with and modify BLOBs using SQL scripts.

WEEK 3

DAY 15

Writing and Executing Stored Procedures

Today, you are going to learn how to write and manage stored procedures and how the server uses them. Stored procedures are nothing more than T-SQL statements that have been saved within the database and can be executed by referencing the name with which it was saved. To see this, some of the topics that are covered in today's lesson are

- Understanding stored procedures
- Writing your first stored procedure
- Working with parameters
- Returning procedure status

After learning the basics of stored procedures in this lesson, you will then learn some of the more advanced issues of stored procedures in tomorrow's lesson.

Stored procedures are batches of T-SQL statements that SQL Server stores in the database and then executes by name. They provide a number of benefits, including enhanced control of data, straightforward access to complex data operations, and improved performance. In some applications, a database administrator (or DBA) might decide that procedures should be the only interface to the data.

A stored procedure should contain a logical set of commands that are executed more than once for that database. They enable the SQL programmer to simply call the stored procedure as a function instead of repeatedly executing the same statements inside a SQL script. However, stored procedures have additional advantages.

Benefits of Stored Procedures

As you've worked through this book, you've learned to use a number of stored procedures to get information about system objects or about the status of SQL Server. Some of those stored procedures include

- `sp_help`
- `sp_helptext`
- `sp_helpdb`
- `sp_helprotect`
- `sp_helpuser`

These procedures are used for reporting and provide several benefits. First, they enable us to extract useful information from the server even though we don't really understand the structure of the tables themselves. Look at `sp_help`. It draws information from `sysobjects`, `syscolumns`, `systypes`, `sysindexes`, and `master..spt_values`.

Second, procedures reduce your workload by reducing the amount of typing and maintenance you must perform. The `sp_help` procedure contains about 350 lines of SQL code, and it calls three other procedures (`sp_helpconstraint` [600 lines], `sp_helpindex` [350 lines], and `sp_objectsegment` [30 lines]). So, if you wanted to write the code by hand to duplicate the functionality of `sp_help`, you would need to compose about 1300 lines of SQL. The annoyance of finding and managing that much SQL code in your client program would drive you crazy; writing similar amounts of code specific to your application would cost a fortune in programming time.

Third, procedures help network performance. The network impact of sending 1300 lines of SQL every time you want a simple query result would be devastating. Many stored procedures are run constantly, all day long, by dozens or hundreds of users.

The last benefit comes in security and data integrity. In addition to the system procedures that select data, there are several system-stored procedures used by administrators to manage users (`sp_adduser`, `sp_dropuser`), logins (`sp_addlogin`, `sp_droplogin`), databases (sp_changedbowner, sp_dboption), and tables (sp_bindrule, sp_rename). These stored procedures provide a simple and carefully managed point of entry to sensitive tables, such as the system tables that maintain all the information about the objects we use.

Let's consider the example shown here. You can't directly execute this statement that would change the name of a column:

```
update syscolumns
set name = 'PhoneNumber'
where  id = object_id('Customers')
and    name = 'Phone'
```

Instead, the only way to rename a column through SQL is to use the sp_rename stored procedure as shown here:

```
sp_rename 'Customers.Phone', 'Telephone'
```

The code we just wrote to do the update seems pretty simple. Even though the sp_rename procedure is more than 1200 lines of SQL, its UPDATE statement looks pretty much the same as ours:

```
UPDATE
             syscolumns
      set
             name        = @newname
      where
             id          = @Tab_id
      and    name        = @UnqualOldName
```

So what do the other 1193 lines in the procedure do? They check to make certain that every aspect of the update is correct. Does the old column exist? Is the new name a valid name for a column? Is the new name unique in the table? Is this user permitted to change it? Every possible error gets a unique error message.

By carefully controlling the modifications to the system tables, SQL Server avoids data corruption that might cause the system to fail and data to be lost. The data managed by your application is equally important and probably merits the same level of care.

The rest of this lesson shows you how to write stored procedures so that you can introduce the same kind of data security and integrity into your database environment.

Writing Your First Stored Procedure

This week, we'll look at various approaches to handling orders and the related order details records in the Northwind database. We'll use the Shopping Cart analogy used by most commerce Web sites, in which you can freely add and remove items from your "cart" (that is, your order) until you close the order. We will require five procedures:

- Add an item to the cart
- Remove an item from the cart
- Display the contents of the cart
- Cancel the order
- Close the order

First, we'll write the first two procedures, and then you will write the next two as part of the exercises at the end of this lesson. We'll write the final procedure in Day 16, "Optimizing Stored Procedures."

In order to use the shopping cart method, we'll need to know when an order is closed. If the customer has an open order, we'll assume that the order is in his cart. Let's add a new column, `OrderClosed`, to the `Orders` table using the following code:

```
alter table Orders
add OrderClosed nchar(1) default 'Y' not null
```

By defaulting the value to `'Y'`, we'll declare all the existing orders closed and make sure that anyone using this table in a non-shopping-cart way won't leave open orders lying around by mistake.

The `INSERT` Statement

Let's start with the procedure that adds an item to the cart. The procedure will need to check to see whether the current customer has an open order. If an order is found, use that orderID. If not, create a new order. For now, let's keep it simple. We'll add a new open order for the customer, `QuickStop` (CustomerID `'QUICK'`) and use the open orderID in the Order Details `insert` procedure. Listing 15.1 shows the `INSERT` statement to add the new order.

LISTING 15.1 Opening a New Order

```
INSERT INTO [Northwind].[dbo].[Orders] (
    [CustomerID],
    [EmployeeID],
    [OrderClosed]
) VALUES(
    'QUICK',
    2,
    'N'
)
```

Listing 15.1 adds a row to the `Orders` table for the customer `'Quick'` and employee #2. The `'N'` is the `OrderClosed` field; it tells us that this is an open order.

We'll allow the details of the order (dates, shipping method, addresses) to be null until we close the order.

`OrderID` is an identity column, so when the order is added we can get the new order number by using the `@@identity` global variable. This variable contains the value of the most recently added row number using the following syntax:

```
Select @@identity
```

This query returned the value 11078 for the order in the new order row, so I'll use that as we continue by adding a detail row. Your value could be different if you have been entering data into the `Orders` table.

The `insert` Procedure

At the core of the procedure is a simple `INSERT` statement:

```
INSERT INTO [Northwind].[dbo].[Order Details] (
    [OrderID],
    [ProductID],
    [UnitPrice],
    [Quantity],
    [Discount]
) VALUES (
    11078,
    3,
    10.00,
    6,
    0
)
```

If you execute the statement by itself (not as a procedure), you'll add a row to the `Order Details` table.

Let's write the `insert` statement as a procedure using the `CREATE PROCEDURE` statement. Procedures are objects, so the procedure will require a name. The name must be unique among all objects in the database (so that a procedure can't have the same name as a table or view that it accesses).

Tip

> You need to develop useful naming standards for procedures and then stick with them. Here are some suggestions for standards from the dozens I've come across over the years.

Have a procedure identifier at the start of the name, as in the following examples:

- `pInsertOrderDetails`
- `pr_AddOrderDetails`
- `prAddCartItem`

Use lowercase and uppercase characters in a consistent way. If a new word should start with an uppercase letter, do so everywhere. If you want to add a procedure identifier at the start of the name (`p`, `pr_`, `pr`), that might help you quickly distinguish procedures, views, tables, and so forth. Don't use `sp_`! That means "system procedure" (not "stored procedure") and has special powers.

If you plan to use a verb in the procedure name (`get`, `add`), use that verb in the same way every time. Don't start with get one time, then use `return`, `select`, or `find` in a similar situation.

We'll use `prAddItemToCart` for the name of the procedure. Listing 15.2 provides the statements that create the new procedure.

LISTING 15.2 A Simple Stored Procedure

```
create proc prAddItemToCart
as
INSERT INTO [Northwind].[dbo].[Order Details] (
    [OrderID],
    [ProductID],
    [UnitPrice],
    [Quantity],
    [Discount]
) VALUES (
    11078,
    3,
    10.00,
    6,
    0
)
return
```

When you successfully create a procedure, it does not insert or return data, and it does not return any messages. It does create a new object in your database.

First, let's look at the procedure itself.

Lines 1 and 2 declare the type and name of the object. You can use the words `proc` and `procedure` interchangeably. After the name, you indicate that the actual batch of statements follows with the keyword `AS`.

Lines 3 through 15 are the query itself.

Line 16 contains a `RETURN` statement. `RETURN` statements are optional at the end of procedures, but they are recommended. In the section titled "Returning Procedure Status" later in this lesson, you will see how you can use the `RETURN` statement to let a calling program know whether the procedure worked properly.

The syntax for the `CREATE PROCEDURE` statement is

```
create proc[edure] <procedure-name>
as
<SQL statements>
return
```

What about the output? SQL Server responds in the same way to all `CREATE` statements: total silence. No "procedure created" or "attaboys" here. In SQL Server, no news is good news.

Getting Information About Procedures

You might want to check to make sure that your procedure was really created. Figure 15.1 shows how you can use the Object Browser in SQL Query Analyzer to see whether the new procedure appears in a list of procedures in the database.

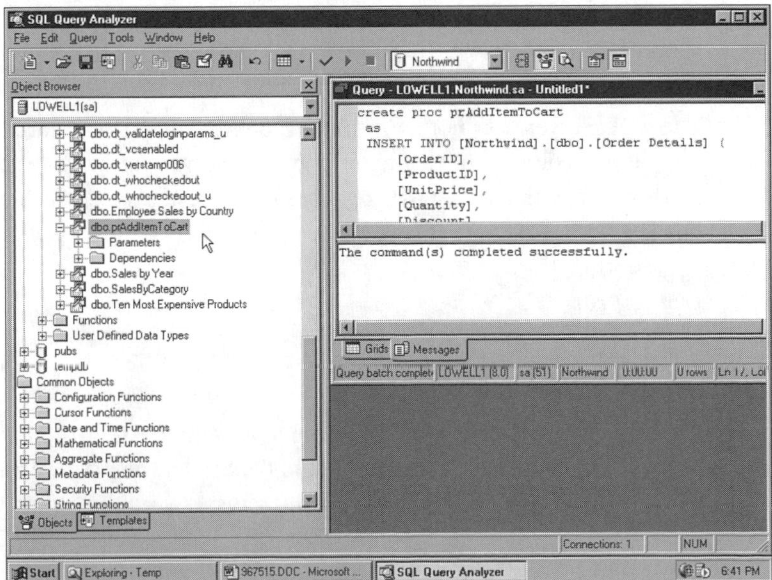

FIGURE 15.1

The name of your new procedure will appear in the Object Browser after you refresh the list.

SQL Server stores the text of your procedure in a system table, and you can easily retrieve the text with the object browser or the stored procedure `sp_helptext`. Nevertheless, to save yourself a lot of grief, save the script of stored procedures, triggers, views, table creations, and just about every other thing you do in separate script files on a file system that you back up regularly. You can also use SourceSafe or a similar code repository to manage stored procedures. This will avoid your trying to reconstruct (or worse, remember!) a vital stored procedure.

Executing Procedures

Now that the procedure has been created, the next step is to run it. You've already run several stored procedures, including `sp_help`. To run a procedure, simply type its name:

```
prAddItemToCart
```

The procedure reports that one line was affected.

Problems with Procedure Execution

If you try to run a procedure in a batch after another statement, you can run into problems.

```
select OrderID
from   Orders
where  CustomerID = 'QUICK'
  and  OrderClosed = 'N'
prAddItemToCart
```

```
Server: Msg 170, Level 15, State 1, Line 5
Line 5: Incorrect syntax near 'prAddItemToCart'.
```

The SQL Server does not know that `prAddItemtoCart` is a stored procedure. In order to run the procedure, you need to tell the SQL Server parser that it is a stored procedure by preceding it with the `EXECUTE` keyword (you could also use the abbreviated version of this keyword, `EXEC`). That tells the server that what follows is a procedure name.

```
select OrderID
from   Orders
where  CustomerID = 'QUICK'
  and  OrderClosed = 'N'
execute prAddItemToCart
```

It's never wrong to use `execute` to run a procedure. `EXECUTE` is only optional when the procedure name is the first statement in the batch. The parser expects that the first word in every batch will be a SQL keyword (that is, a word that it knows, like `SELECT`, `DELETE`,

EXECUTE, CREATE, or SET). If it does not recognize the first word, it assumes that that word is a stored procedure name.

As we step through the development of procedures, the syntax for procedure creation and execution will become increasingly complex.

Remember: EXECUTE is required only if the procedure is not the first statement in the batch. However, I recommend that you always use it for consistency and better readability.

Working with Parameters

Let's get back to our procedure—there's a serious problem. It works great if we have only one customer who buys only one item, but what if that customer wants to buy something else? What if we have another customer? Should we write a separate procedure to handle each customer? Each product? Of course not. Instead we'll change the procedure to enable you to pass the customer ID, the order ID, and the product ID as parameters.

A *parameter* is a mechanism enabling a calling program to pass a value to a procedure so that the procedure can operate in response to that value.

An example of a parameter can be seen in the stored procedure sp_help that you have used in previous lessons. The table name in the statement shown here is a parameter that is passed to the stored procedure.

```
Execute sp_help Orders
```

Here is the syntax for creating or altering procedures that accept parameters:

```
create | alter proc[edure] <procedure-name>
[ ( @parameter-name datatype [, ...] ) ]
as
<SQL statements>
return
```

To use a parameter in a stored procedure, it needs to be declared in the CREATE PROC statement or added later using the ALTER PROCEDURE statement. You can then use the parameter in the same way as you would use any value or variable in the procedure.

Listing 15.3 shows you how to modify the procedure to access parameters for each of the insert values. Notice that you use ALTER PROC to change an existing procedure.

Listing 15.3 Using Parameters to Pass Item Information to the Stored Procedures

```
 1: alter proc prAddItemToCart (
 2:     @OrderID int,
 3:     @ProductID int,
 4:     @UnitPrice money,
 5:     @Quantity smallint,
 6:     @Discount real
 7: ) as
 8: INSERT INTO [Northwind].[dbo].[Order Details] (
 9:     [OrderID],
10:     [ProductID],
11:     [UnitPrice],
12:     [Quantity],
13:     [Discount]
14: ) VALUES (
15:     @OrderID,
16:     @ProductID,
17:     @UnitPrice,
18:     @Quantity,
19:     @Discount
20: )
21: return
```

In Listing 15.3, you can see that lines 2 through 6 define the list of parameters used in the stored procedure. The declaration of a parameter requires a system or user-defined data type. The data type should match the column data type if it will be used in a `WHERE` clause or in a `VALUES` list, as in lines 15 through 19 in the example.

Query performance is considerably better if the data type of the parameter is an exact match for the column data type. You should take the time to look up the data type in the Query Analyzer when you are writing a stored procedure.

Execution Using a Parameter

How do you pass a parameter to a procedure? (You have already been doing it with the system procedures.) Parameters are passed in the same statement after the parameter name. In the following statement, all the values that follow the stored procedure name are treated as parameters.

```
Execute prAddItemToCart
    11078,
    4,
    10.00,
    6,
    0
```

The procedure now enables the user to add any item to any cart based on his parameters.

To find out the parameters of a stored procedure, run `sp_help` against the procedure. You can also use the Object Browser to get information about a procedure's parameters, including their data types (see Figure 15.2).

FIGURE 15.2

The Object Browser displays the names and data types of procedure parameters.

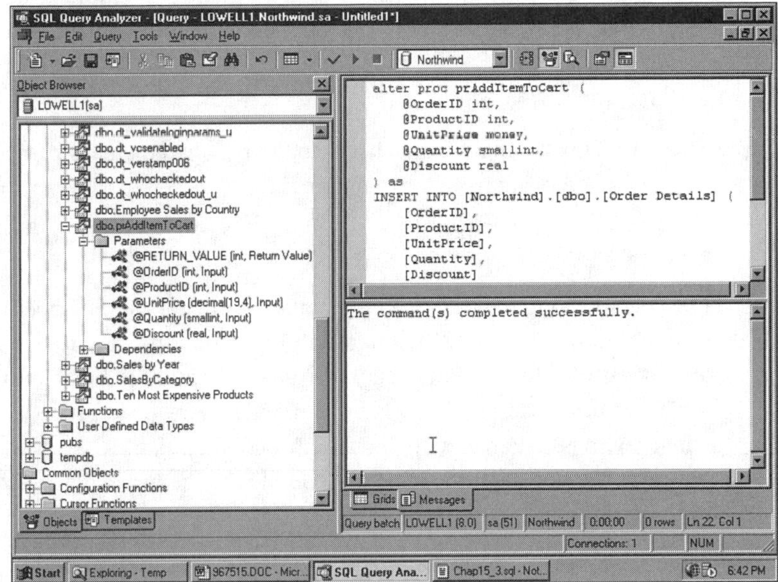

There's a bit more you need to know about passing parameters. Let's consider the following procedure that uses three parameters:

```
create proc sample
(@a int, @b int, @c int)
as
select c1, c2, c3
from   t1
where  a = @a
and    b = @b
and    c = @c
return
```

To execute this procedure, you can pass the parameters by position, as we've been doing, or you can pass the parameters by name. To pass by position, just provide values for each parameter, in order:

```
execute sample 1, 2, 3
```

To pass values by name, you provide the parameter names defined in the procedure header:

```
execute sample @b = 2, @a = 1, @c = 3
```

You can mix both styles, but when you start passing by name, you must pass all of the remaining parameters in the list by name. The next example is wrong because it passes by position a parameter that is later in the list than the one passed by name:

```
/* This won't work */
execute sample @b = 2, 1, 3
```

The following example works because the first parameter is passed by position, and only later parameters are passed by name:

```
/* This will work */
execute sample 1, @c = 3, @b = 2
```

For years I thought that passing by name was better than by position, and, from a coding standpoint, it is better. It's not unusual for a stored procedure to have 20 or 30 parameters. It's useful for someone reading your application to be able to tell immediately which values correspond to which parameters. However, procedure execution is faster when you pass parameters by position rather than name. If you want to get the best of both worlds, consider documenting complex procedure calls with the parameter name, as in this example:

```
execute sample
    1,          -- @a
    2,          -- @b
    3           -- @c
```

Although there are two different ways to pass parameters, you should pass them by position when you can because of its increased performance over the by name method. This is especially true with long, complicated stored procedures using many parameters.

Parameters and Quoted Values

When you pass a char (`nchar`) or varchar (`nvarchar`) parameter to a procedure, quotes aren't required unless one of these three conditions is true:

- The parameter value contains any punctuation, special character, or a space (`'.'`, `','`, `'-'`).
- The parameter value is a reserved word (`'default'`, `'null'`).
- The parameter value is a string consisting entirely of numbers (`'1234'`).

Notice that dates need to be passed as quoted strings because date strings require a slash, dash, or space.

Default Parameters

What happens if you try to execute the procedure without passing any parameter values? Then the parameter execution will fail. The following code shows an example of this scenario:

```
Execute prAddItemToCart
```

```
Server: Msg 201, Level 16, State 3, Procedure prAddItemToCart, Line 0
Procedure 'prAddItemToCart' expects parameter '@OrderID', which was
not supplied.
```

A parameter is required, so the execution fails.

But let's think about system procedures, such as `sp_help`. They operate in multiple modes, always working whether you pass a parameter or not. What is the difference? The key is that in the system procedures, the parameters are defined with default values, making those parameters *optional*.

To make a parameter optional, assign it a default value in the parameter declaration, like this:

```
(@parameter-name datatype = default-value)
```

How does that apply to our procedure? Unit price, quantity, and discount all have reasonable default values. Quantity defaults to 1, discount defaults to 0, and unit price can default to the unit price in the `Products` table.

Listing 15.4 shows the revised `prAddItemToCart` procedure with defaults for quantity, unit price, and discount. (We will continue to require values for `OrderID` and `ProductID`.)

LISTING 15.4 Default Parameters Provide Additional Flexibility

```
alter proc prAddItemToCart (
    @OrderID int,
    @ProductID int,
    @UnitPrice money = null,
    @Quantity smallint = 1,
    @Discount real = 0.0
) as

/* get the unit price from the products table
   only if unit price is null (default value) */
if @UnitPrice is null begin
    select @UnitPrice = UnitPrice
    from Products
    where ProductID = @ProductID
```

LISTING 15.4 continued

```
15:
16: /* exit the procedure if price is not found   */
17:     if @UnitPrice is null or @@error != 0 or @@rowcount = 0 begin
18:         raiserror ('Product %d not found or no price available',
19:              16, 1, @ProductID)
20:         return 99      /* non-zero return means error */
21:     end
22: end
23:
24: /* insert the row */
25: INSERT INTO [Northwind].[dbo].[Order Details] (
26:     [OrderID],
27:     [ProductID],
28:     [UnitPrice],
29:     [Quantity],
30:     [Discount]
31: ) VALUES (
32:     @OrderID,
33:     @ProductID,
34:     @UnitPrice,
35:     @Quantity,
36:     @Discount
37: )
38:
39: if @@error != 0
40:     return 99
41: else
42: return 0
```

In the preceding code, not only are we adding to the declaration statements, we are also adding code to get the unit price from the `Products` table, if a value was not passed to the procedure. The declarations now include the assignment of three default values for the parameters. These values are only assigned to the parameters when no value is provided in the execution string.

In lines 11 through 14, the procedure gets a default value for the unit price if none was provided. (We don't really want to insert a product with no price.) Notice that the default value for the unit price parameter, and the value we test for when we run the procedure, is a null value. This is a common default value.

Lines 17 through 21 perform a necessary error check. Was there a default unit price for that product? Did the `SELECT` query work? Remember to check for errors between steps in a procedure. If you don't check, the procedure will continue to process after errors as if everything was fine. (I've also added an error check at the end of the procedure to make certain that the INSERT step worked. We'll learn how to retrieve those return values in the next section.)

Executing Procedures with Default Values

To use a default value, omit the parameter from the parameter list. The following example shows how you can add an item to the cart by just providing the OrderID and ProductID.

```
prAddItemToCart 11078, 5
```

Let's check the Order Details table to see what's in the cart by executing the SELECT statement shown:

```
select * from [Order Details] where orderID = 11078
```

Results:

```
OrderID     ProductID   UnitPrice             Quantity Discount
----------- ----------- --------------------- -------- ------------------------
11078       3           10.0000               6        0.0
11078       4           10.0000               6        0.0
11078       5           21.3500               1        0.0
```

The first two rows (products 3 and 4) were added by our earlier efforts. The last row (product 5) has the correct default values for Quantity (1) and Discount (0). You'll have to find the Unit Price for product 5 in the Products table to check the default unit price.

You can also use the keyword default to insert a default value. Here are a few of the possible parameter combinations for executing a procedure with default parameters:

```
prAddItemToCart 11078, 5
prAddItemToCart 11078, 5, @Quantity = 5
prAddItemToCart 11078, 5, default, 5, default
prAddItemToCart 11078, 5, 15, default, .05
prAddItemToCart 11078, 5, @discount = .05
```

Returning Procedure Status

So far we have been writing very optimistic code: only a little error checking and very few validations. Unfortunately, there's plenty that could go wrong here.

Let's look closely at the prAddItemToCart procedure we just finished writing. If something goes wrong, we shouldn't insert an order, and the user or her application should be warned. What if we couldn't access the default unit price because of database problems, network problems, and so forth? You can't insert an order without a price. All these circumstances are handled with the procedure return status.

The *procedure return status* describes the state of the procedure when it ended. It tells the calling program why the procedure stopped executing.

Under normal circumstances, a procedure ends its execution because it reaches the end of the procedure, or the procedure executes a `RETURN` statement. This normal end of a procedure has a return status of `0` by default. Almost all SQL Server application developers agree to use the value of `0` to mean that the procedure executed successfully.

To retrieve the return status from a procedure, declare a variable and use it in the `EXECUTE` statement. Then report the value of the return status in the next step. For example, if I try to enter another item to this order for `ProductID 5` using `prAddItemToCart`, the insert will fail. (There's a primary key constraint on `OrderID` and `ProductID`.) This can be seen in the Listing 15.5.

LISTING 15.5 Retrieving a Return Status

```
declare @retstatus int
exec @retstatus = prAddItemToCart 11078, 5
print 'Return status is ' + cast(@retstatus as nchar(10))
```

Results:

```
Server: Msg 2627, Level 14, State 1,
Procedure prAddItemToCart, Line 25
Violation of PRIMARY KEY constraint 'PK_Order_Details'.
Cannot insert duplicate key in object 'Order Details'.
The statement has been terminated.
Return status is 99
```

The server returned an error alerting me to the primary key violation. The `INSERT` statement failed, and the return status is `99`. What if we had not inserted an error check (lines 39 through 40 in Listing 15.4, `if @@error != 0` …) after the insert statement? The error would have been raised, but the program calling the procedure might not have been aware that the procedure call had failed.

How did I choose the value `99`? `99` is my standard "something went wrong" return value. In your own application environment, you will need to define standard return values and agree on what they mean.

By now, you probably realized that writing stored procedures is real programming. Up to this point, it wasn't all that bad, but now we have real error checking, and the code is getting longer.

The fact is, a stored procedure is seldom longer than two or three pages, and almost never longer than ten. If you find yourself writing a ten-page procedure, you probably made a mistake in the design that needs to be corrected. SQL is such a compact language that there is seldom need to write a whole lot of it, even with solid error checking and plenty of commentary.

Using Output Parameters

So far, you have used parameters to send data to the procedure. Now you will learn to return data from the procedure using an output parameter. We'll write a procedure, `prGetCustomerCart`, to return the Order ID for a shopping cart if one exists, or create a shopping cart if one doesn't exist. Then we'll call the `prGetCustomerCart` from inside the `prAddItemToCart` procedure and use an output parameter to pass the value back to the calling procedure.

Let's be clear on the logic for `prGetCustomerCart`. You pass it as a Customer ID and it returns an Order ID. To find the Order ID, it finds an open order for the customer (if one exists), or it creates a new open order. Listing 15.6 shows the completed `prGetCustomerCart` procedure.

LISTING 15.6 Default Parameters Provide Additional Flexibility

```
create proc prGetCustomerCart (
    @CustomerID nchar(5),
    @OrderID int output
) as

/* find an open order if one exists */
select @OrderID = OrderID
from   Orders
where  CustomerID = @CustomerID

if @@error != 0 begin
    raiserror ('Error finding an open order', 16, 1)
    return 99     /* non-zero return means error */
end

if @OrderID is null begin
    /* row not found so add a new open order */
    INSERT INTO [Orders] (
        [CustomerID],
        [EmployeeID],
        [OrderClosed]
    ) VALUES(
        'QUICK',
```

LISTING 15.6 continued

```
24:         2,
25:         'N'
26:     )
27:
28:     /* check for error in the insert */
29:     if @@error != 0 begin
30:         raiserror ('Error inserting a new order', 16, 1)
31:         return 99     /* non-zero return means error */
32:     end
33:
34:     /* Otherwise set OrderID = last identity value */
35:     set @OrderID = @@identity
36: end
37:
38: return
```

There are a couple of key points in the `CREATE` syntax. First, the parameter declaration in line 3 includes the keyword `OUTPUT`. In order to get a variable value to return to the user, you need to declare it with `OUTPUT`. (Note that if you declare a parameter for `OUTPUT`, it can still be used to accept values.)

Second, to actually output the variable, you don't need to do anything special. Just assign it a value as in line 35 and the value is passed back to the calling program.

Putting Output Parameters to Work

You can test the procedure directly from a SQL batch. You need to provide a local variable as a parameter in order to provide a container for returning the OrderID. The following code shows you how to use the stored procedure that was created and how to check the `@ret` value to see if the stored procedure worked.

```
declare @ret int
declare @MyCustomerID nchar(5)
declare @MyOrderID int
select @MyCustomerID = 'QUICK'
exec @ret = prGetCustomerCart @MyCustomerID, @MyOrderID output
if @ret = 0
    print 'The cart for ' + @MyCustomerID + ' is: '
        + cast(@MyOrderID as nchar(5))
else
    print 'Error'
```

```
The cart for QUICK is: 11078
```

When SQL Server executes the procedure, it retrieves the OrderID for CustomerID `'QUICK'` and puts it into the `@OrderID` parameter. When the procedure returns, the value is assigned to the variable `@MyOrderID` by position.

Notice that the keyword, `OUTPUT`, is also included in the execution string. Both the procedure programmer and the user need to include `OUTPUT` in order for the value to be returned.

Communicating Between Stored Procedures

When we say that stored procedures communicate with each other, we really mean that stored procedures pass parameter values back and forth to each other. Now we can create the `prAddItemToCustomerCart` procedure. Instead of taking an OrderID for a parameter, the procedure accepts a CustomerID. Then it uses the `prGetCustomerCart` procedure to retrieve the active OrderID for the order detail insert. Listing 15.7 shows how this is done.

LISTING 15.7 Modular Systems Often Call Procedures Within Other Stored Procedures

```
create proc prAddItemToCustomerCart (
    @CustomerID nchar(5),
    @ProductID int,
    @UnitPrice money,
    @Quantity smallint,
    @Discount real,
/* OrderID is optional parameter;
        can output OrderID if necessary */
    @OrderID int = null output
) as

declare @ret int
exec @ret = prGetCustomerCart
    @CustomerID,
    @OrderID output

if @ret != 0 begin
/* error getting an OrderID - quit now */
    return @ret
end

INSERT INTO [Northwind].[dbo].[Order Details] (
    [OrderID],
    [ProductID],
    [UnitPrice],
    [Quantity],
    [Discount]
) VALUES (
```

LISTING 15.7 continued

```
29:     @OrderID,
30:     @ProductID,
31:     @UnitPrice,
32:     @Quantity,
33:     @Discount
34: )
35:
36: /* check for error in insert */
37: if @@error != 0
38:     return 99
39: else
40:     return
```

There is not a lot of new material here. Perhaps the most important point is how important it is to check the return status of the inner procedure (`prGetCustomerCart`) lines 13 through 21, before going ahead with the insert. If you don't check the value, you could end up trying to insert a null or incorrect value for OrderID in Order Details.

Using Output Parameters with Remote Procedure Calls

Output parameters enable two-way communication between a stored procedure on one server (a *local* server) and a procedure on another server (a *remote* server).

For example, what if the Order Details table was stored on a local server, but the Orders table was on a remote server? In that case, the user or application would execute the `prAddItemToCustomerCart` procedure locally. When the procedure ran, it would call the `prGetCustomerCart proc` remotely, passing in a CustomerID and retrieving an OrderID. The OrderID would be returned as an output parameter.

Here's the crucial point: The results of a `SELECT` statement in a remote procedure are returned directly to the calling program (that is, the client application). The output parameter is the only method of returning a value to the calling procedure or batch; that value could be put to use immediately.

To invoke a remote procedure, fully qualify the procedure name when it is called. In this case, the name includes the server name as well as database, owner, and object name. In Listing 15.7, we invoked the `prGetCustomerCart` procedure locally. To invoke the `prGetCustomerCart` procedure on another server, you would replace the `execute` statement in line 13 (leaving the parameters in lines 14 and 15) with the following statement:

```
execute @ret = OrderServer.Northwind.Northwind_DBO.prGetCustomerCart
```

There are a couple of setup and security issues to be resolved to implement remote procedures, but when they are implemented, the Remote Procedure Call (or RPC) mechanism provides a fast and reliable cross-server communications method.

Five Ways to Communicate Between Stored Procedures and Client Programs

You can return information from a procedure to a calling program, a client application, or a user in any of five ways. It's important to understand what those return methods are for, and how they are different:

- `SELECT` is for data. Try to use it only to return data to the client application that's intended for processing, printing, or displaying onscreen.
- `PRINT` is for messages. Use it when you want to send a noncritical message to the user (not the programmer) about status, progress, or success.
- `RAISERROR` is for errors. Use it when you want to send a critical message to the user about a failed process or invalid choice. Notice that this statement changes the value of `@@error`. If the server has already raised an error, you might choose not to.
- Output parameters return a value to a program (not a user). They are not shipped immediately to the client program; instead, they are returned to the program that called a stored procedure.
- Return status tells the programmer whether a procedure worked or failed. Return status is only available to the program or procedure that calls a stored procedure. By convention, any non-zero return status means that a procedure failed.

Summary

Today you've learned how to write and execute stored procedures. Here is a quick summary of the full `CREATE PROCEDURE` syntax:

```
create proc[edure] <procedure-name>
[ ( @parameter-name datatype [= default-value] [output] [, ...] ) ]
as
<SQL statements>
return [return-status]
[exec[ute]] [return-status = ] procedure-name
    [@parameter-name =] parameter-value [output] [, ...]
```

In Day 16, you are going to look at some detailed programming and optimization issues associated with stored procedures. Until then, here is some general advice about writing stored procedures.

Do	**Don't**
Test procedures rigorously.	Use return status to return real data values (use output parameters instead).
Check parameters before using them.	
Permit optional parameters where possible.	
Return a meaningful status code.	
Check return codes after every procedure execution.	
Check `@@error` after every data modification statement.	
Comment your code.	
Maintain scripts to create your procedures offline.	

Q&A

Q Where are stored procedures stored?

A A stored procedure is a database object, so it is stored in the database in which it is created. There are references to a stored procedure in several system tables, including `sysobjects` (one line per procedure), `syscolumns` (one line per parameter), `sysdepends` (one line per referenced table, view, or procedure), and `syscomments` (one line per block of 255 characters of source SQL).

Q Is a stored procedure faster than a batch?

A Tomorrow, we'll look more closely at procedure performance issues. For now, I'll say, "Yes, most of the time."

Q How do I get a list of all stored procedures in the system?

A On a database-by-database basis, you can execute this statement to retrieve a list of stored procedures:

```
select name
from sysobjects
where type = "P"
```

You can also use the object browser in the Query Analyzer.

Q Can I write a system-stored procedure?

A Yes. You will learn how tomorrow.

Q What does "group number" refer to?

A If you try to create a procedure whose name already exists, you get this error message:

```
Msg 2729, Level 16, State 1
Object 'oops' group number 1 already exists in the database.
Choose another procedure name
```

Group numbering enables you to create sets of procedures with the same name, but different sequence numbers. For instance, to add a procedure oops to group 2, I would execute

```
create proc oops;2
as
...
```

This creates a maintenance nightmare because (1) you can't run any stored procedures against the procedure, and (2) you have to drop all the procedures belonging to a group at once.

Workshop

The Workshop provides quiz questions to help you solidify your understanding of the material covered and exercises to provide you with experience in using what you've learned. Try to answer the quiz and exercise questions before checking the answers in Appendix A, "Answers to Quizzes and Exercises," and make sure you understand the answers before continuing to the next lesson.

Quiz

1. What is the correct method to return a data value to a calling program?
2. I have the following procedure and batch, but when I run the batch, the value of `@out_x` is always null. What's wrong?

```
create procedure p1 (@x int output)
as
select @x = 1
return

declare @out_x int
execute p1 @out_x
select @out_x
```

3. In this procedure and batch, my return status is always null. Why?

```
create procedure p2
as
declare @x int
select @x = 1
if @x = 1
   return 1
else
   return 0

declare @retstat int
execute p2
select @retstat "return"
```

4. How do I get a list of parameters for a procedure?

Exercises

1. Write a stored procedure to display the contents of the shopping cart for a customer. Call the `prGetCustomerCart` procedure in your procedure.
2. Write a stored procedure to delete the current shopping cart for a customer. Delete both the order details and the order itself.

WEEK 3

DAY 16

Optimizing Stored Procedures

In yesterday's lesson, you learned the basics of creating stored procedures. As always, a little knowledge can be very dangerous. Unless you understand the effect that a stored procedure can have on the performance of the SQL Server, you might create very poorly optimized SQL scripts. Today, you will learn the following topics as they relate to stored procedures:

- Optimizing stored procedures
- Using temporary tables
- Controlling compilation
- Transaction processing

Understanding Stored Procedure Optimization

When working with any computer program, the way it performs is very important. This is even more important when you start working with database procedures that can be executed many times by many users at one time. In this section, we will look at how to make procedures run better, faster, and more efficiently. Along the way, we will see what makes a good stored procedure and what makes a bad one. Learning how to design and code a stored procedure that performs well will allow your application to execute that much faster.

Because many different users execute stored procedures many times a day, the performance of the stored procedures is very important. It is easy to see that if a stored procedure is written poorly and slows the processing of the server, by multiplying the effect over a long period of time, your users might become very frustrated waiting for an answer from the server. That is why learning how to optimize their performance is so critical. In this section, we will look at some methods of understanding and optimizing procedure performance.

Using Good Procedure Performance Practices

To understand how to write a good stored procedure, we must first understand how a procedure is processed and executed by the server. In the lesson on Day 9, "Indexes and Performance," you were introduced to performance and some of the tools available to you to see what is happening when a query is executed. Stored procedures are also subject to the same steps that were described on Day 9, but they don't occur all at the same time. Knowing when each of these steps is performed will help you in understanding how to make the stored procedure better. To review these steps, here is a summary of what they are.

- Parse—Verify the syntax and check for valid object names.
- Optimize—Decide on the most efficient execution path.
- Compile—Create the executable SQL code.
- Execute—Execute the SQL script or batch.

These steps are taken whenever a batch, script, trigger, stored procedure, or single SQL statement is executed. Now, let's review these steps and change the definition to reflect when they are performed.

- Parse—The stored procedure's syntax and object names are checked at creation time.
- Optimize—Whenever a new procedure plan is needed by the server, the procedure is optimized using the current parameters.
- Compile—Immediately after the stored procedure is optimized, the server will compile it, but only when a new plan is required.
- Execute—Every time a procedure is executed.

When is a stored procedure actually optimized by the server? When you execute a procedure, the server generates an optimization plan for the SQL script (batch) that is calling the stored procedure, but not for the *procedure* itself. Optimization of the procedure is not done until the procedure itself is executed. To help demonstrate where a stored procedure is actually optimized, we will build a small SQL script (batch) that includes two distinct steps. In the example in Listing 16.1, you will see that the first step is to create the stored procedure and the second step consists of two code blocks.

LISTING 16.1 Test SQL Script to Work with Stored Procedure

```
use Northwind
Drop procedure demo_performance
go
create procedure Demo_Performance (@ordID int)
as
select count(*) as sp_order_count
from orders
where orderid = @ordID
return 0
go
--This will not be executed
if 1 = 2
begin
print 'executing the procedure'
print ''
exec demo_performance 10260
print ''
select count(*) as Order_count_1 from orders
end
--This will be executed
if 1 = 1
begin
print 'executing without the procedure'
print ''
select count(*) as Order_count_2 from orders
end
go
```

The DROP PROCEDURE statement is in this SQL batch to enable me to re-execute the entire batch, including the CREATE PROCEDURE statement, without receiving any error messages about the procedure already being defined.

Before executing this SQL batch, turn on the Show Execution Plan option in Query Analyzer. After you have done this, execute the script. The output you receive will include the actual output as shown and an execution plan as shown in Figure 16.1.

```
executing without the procedure
```

Results:

```
Order_count
-----------
830

(1 row(s) affected)
```

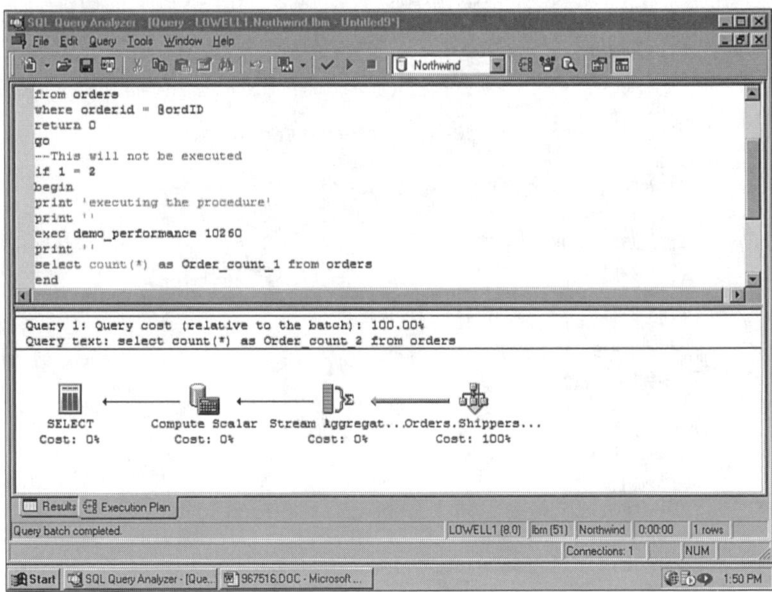

FIGURE 16.1
The execution plan created by SQL Server for the SQL batch.

From this example, you can see that the creation of the stored procedure does not generate an execution plan. Only when the procedure is actually executed is a plan generated for it. In addition, you can see that the server did not optimize the procedure when it optimized the batch in which it was executed. The `CREATE PROCEDURE` statement is not optimized as a part of an execution batch.

Notice that the optimizer did generate an execution plan for the `SELECT` statement in the first `BEGIN` block. Only the `SELECT` statement in the `BEGIN` block that was actually executed generated an execution plan.

Now, change the `IF 1=2` statement to `IF 1=1` to allow the first `BEGIN` block to be executed. After executing the batch, the output displayed is


```
executing the procedure
```

Results:

```
sp_order_count
--------------
1

(1 row(s) affected)


Order_count_1
-------------
830

(1 row(s) affected)

executing without the procedure

Order_count_2
-------------
830

(1 row(s) affected)
```

When you look at the execution plan that was generated as shown in Figure 16.2, you will see that three separate execution plans are generated by the server: one for each `SELECT` statement in the `BEGIN` blocks and one for the `SELECT` statement in the stored procedure.

The most important point to this example is that the stored procedure is not optimized until it is actually executed inside of a batch.

Every time a stored procedure is executed, the server looks first in the procedure cache to see whether there is already a compiled plan for the procedure. A plan would already exist in the procedure cache if the stored procedure had been executed at least once while SQL Server has been running. If that plan still exists, the server uses it and entirely skips the optimization step for the procedure.

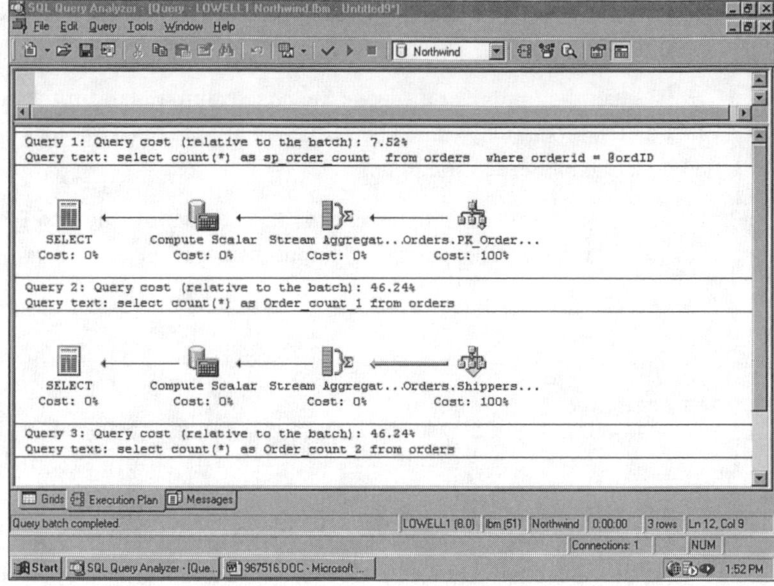

FIGURE 16.2

Execution plans generated for the stored procedure and the other SELECT *statements in the batch.*

Figure 16.3 shows the basic logic used by SQL Server for determining how a stored procedure will be processed. First, the server will check the procedure cache for an available plan. If one is found, the server will pass the parameter values to the procedure and then execute it. If a plan is not found, the server will substitute the parameter values into each statement in the procedure and will generate a plan, compile that plan, pass the parameters, and finally execute the procedure.

Understanding the Compilation Process

Because the process of optimizing a stored procedure takes time and work on the server, it is a good thing that stored procedures can reuse the optimization plans that are already in the procedure cache. If the optimization plan for a procedure never changes, it is wasteful to recompile that procedure every time it is executed. However, there are stored procedures that need to be reoptimized each time that they are executed. Look at the following example of a stored procedure:

```
select sum(unitprice * quantity)
from [order details]
where orderid = @ordID
```

Depending on the value of `@ordID`, this SQL query could find all the rows in the table (`*`) or very few (`orderid = 10260`). When the server generates a plan for this query, it might select a table scan or one of the available indexes for use. After the plan is selected, it will remain in cache until either the server is shut down, or the server needs the space the plan takes up for another procedure being executed.

FIGURE 16.3

Stored procedures are optimized only when a new plan is needed.

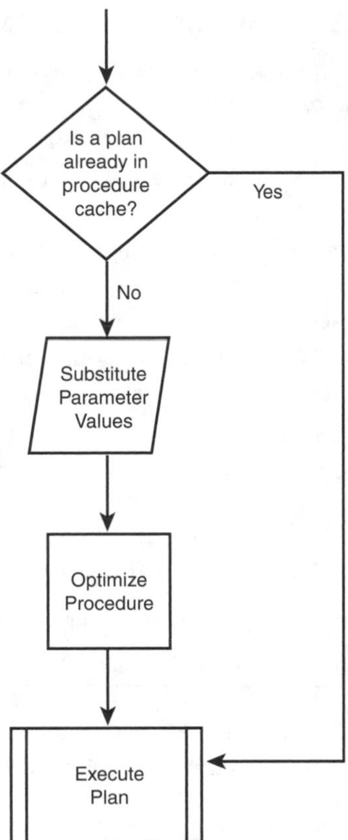

The problem is this: The first time you execute a procedure with a query containing a `WHERE` clause that returns a variable number of rows depending on the value passed, the value is substituted into the `SELECT` statement and it is then optimized for that parameter. If you execute the procedure at a later time and the optimization plan is still in the procedure cache, you will get the previous optimization plan, even if it is not correct for the new value being passed.

Using the RECOMPILE Option in Stored Procedures

One way to avoid the problem described in the previous section is use the `WITH RECOMPILE` option with the stored procedure. By specifying this option, you can have the server generate a new optimization plan before the procedure is executed.

You can add this option in either the `CREATE PROCEDURE` statement or in the `EXEC PROCEDURE` statement. Where you place this option affects how the stored procedure is processed and executed.

Using the WITH RECOMPILE in the CREATE PROCEDURE Statement

When you use the WITH RECOMPILE option in the CREATE PROCEDURE statement, the execution plan will not be saved in the procedure cache. This option will instruct the server to recompile the stored procedure every time it is executed. This is very similar to the way that a standard query is processed, and it can be useful if parameters being passed to the stored procedures make the default execution plan run poorly. By recompiling every time, the procedure can be optimized for the new parameters. Of course, if the procedure is recompiled every time it is executed, there will be many plans in memory, which fills up the procedure cache and could actually impact performance. The following example shows a stored procedure with the WITH RECOMPILE option. Notice that it is placed between the parameter list and the AS keyword.

```
CREATE PROCEDURE sp_demo_proc (@ordID int)
WITH RECOMPILE
AS SELECT * FROM Orders
Where OrderId = @ordID
```

Using the WITH RECOMPILE in the EXEC PROCEDURE Statement

Instead of specifying the WITH RECOMPILE option in the CREATE PROCEDURE statement, you can use it in the EXEC PROCEDURE statement. Using it in the EXEC PROCEDURE statement causes the stored procedure to be recompiled in that single execution, and the new plan is stored in the procedure cache for later EXEC PROCEDURE commands. Here is an example of using the WITH RECOMPILE option in an EXEC PROCEDURE statement:

```
Exec sp_demo_proc 10260
With Recompile
```

The downside of this option is that it does not solve the original problem. Any plans generated by using the WITH RECOMPILE are left in the procedure cache to be used by other users, again causing possibly unanticipated results.

Forcing All Stored Procedures to Be Recompiled

You can tell the server to recompile all stored procedures and triggers associated with a particular table the next time they are executed. You do this by executing the system-stored procedure SP_RECOMPILE as shown:

```
EXEC sp_recompile Orders
```

This command is also used to optimize existing plans when new indexes are added to a table.

Run the `sp_recompile` procedure on a table after creating indexes or you won't see the effect of the new indexes on the stored procedures until you restart the server.

Automatically Running Your Stored Procedures at SQL Startup

You can have stored procedures automatically executed when SQL Server is started. You can execute as many stored procedures as you want, but each individual stored procedure executed will use up a user connection.

If you do not have many user connections available, you can have one stored procedure call other stored procedures and thus use only one user connection to the server.

The execution of these stored procedures will begin after the last database has been recovered at startup.

To tell the server which stored procedures to execute at startup, you use the system stored procedure `SP_PROCOPTION`. The syntax of this procedure is

```
Exec sp_procoption [@ProcName = ] <procedure name>
    ,[@OptionName = ] <option>
    ,[@OptionValue = ] <value>
```

Using this stored procedure is actually quite easy. `'Startup'` is the default option (it is the only one) and the `value` parameter can be either `'on'` or `'off'`, with `'on'` being the default. So, if I needed the `SP_PROCOPTION` procedure to execute at startup, I would execute the following statement:

```
Exec sp_procoption sp_demo_proc
```

Using Table Variables and Temporary Tables with Procedures

You have seen how to use both table variables and temporary tables earlier in this book on Day 10, "Views and Temporary Tables." When you begin using them in stored procedures, you need to understand how they affect the performance of the stored procedure when executed. Temporary tables provide you with the ability to store data from a table in a temporary area to allow access to the data during the stored procedure. Then, when the procedure is finished, the table variable or temporary table is deleted.

In the next few sections, you will see how each of these features is used in a stored procedure and what to watch for in optimization and performance.

Using Table Variables in a Stored Procedure

A *table variable* is a special data type that can be used to store a result set for later processing. It can be used in the same fashion as a temporary table. The real power of a table variable is that it can be used like an ordinary table, or like a local variable in any stored procedure, function, trigger, or batch. Whenever possible, a table variable should be used instead of using a temporary table. The benefits of using a table variable are

- A table variable is used like a local variable. The scope of the variable remains in the function, stored procedure, trigger, or batch in which it was declared. Within its scope, the table variable can be used like a regular table. It can be referenced in `SELECT`, `INSERT`, `UPDATE`, and `DELETE` statements. However, you cannot use it in an `INSERT INTO` or `SELECT...INTO` statement.
- Table variables are automatically deleted at the end of the stored procedure, trigger, function, or batch.
- Fewer recompiles are needed when a table variable is used in a stored procedure than when a temporary table is used.
- Transactions involving table variables last only for the duration of an update on the table variable. This means that using a table variable requires less locking and logging resources.

You declare a table variable like any other local variable, as shown in the following example. Then, you use the `INSERT` statement to load data into this variable. Finally, you can use the table variable later in the stored procedure, even joining it to other tables to provide the final result needed.

```
Declare @table_Var Table (
            OrderId Int Not Null,
            ProductID Int Not Null,
            CustomerID Int Not Null)
    Insert @table_var
      Select ord.orderid, od.productid, ord.customerid
      From Orders as ord inner join
           [order details] as OD on
            ord.orderid = od.orderid
```

This SQL code enables you to create a table of information that you can use later, as shown in the following example:

```
Select ProductID
from @table_var
Where CustomerId Like 'H%'
```

Understanding the Scope of a Temporary Table

A *temporary table* is a physical table that is created in the TEMP database area and then deleted when the transaction process is completed. There are two types of temporary tables: local and global. The scope of a local temporary table is the same as a table variable. While the stored procedure, trigger, function, or batch is being executed, the temporary table is available within that process. After the process is completed or the connection is dropped, the temporary table is deleted. However, global temporary tables are available to all users until the connection is dropped.

There is one problem with using a local temporary table in a stored procedure. Remember from earlier in this lesson that the stored procedure is not optimized until it is executed. But what if a procedure creates a temporary table? SQL Server does not know the size or distribution of the data in the temporary table at optimization time. Because the table is not yet created, the server must estimate the information.

Note

> The server will estimate the size of a temporary table at 100 rows on 10 data pages. Of course, this is usually very wrong.

This entire issue is important only if you plan on using the temporary table in a join later in the procedure. The following example shows a stored procedure that uses a temporary table to provide information to be used in an outer join in the procedure.

```
Create Procedure sp_sales (@City char(15))
As
Select ORD.CustomerId, OD.productId, OD.quantity
Into #tp_products
From [Order Details] as OD inner join
     Customers as CT on
     CT.City = @City
     inner join
     Orders as ORD on
     ORD.OrderID = OD.OrderID
```

```
Select Companyname,
       tpp.CustomerID,
       sum(quantity) as 'QTY'
From Customers as CT Left Outer Join
     #tp_products as tpp on
     tpp.customerid = CT.customerid
Group by Companyname, tpp.customerid
```

Because both SELECT statements are compiled at the same time, the server must estimate the information for the temporary table used in the second SELECT statement.

If this process were being done in a batch, you could simply place a GO statement between the two SELECT statements. For a stored procedure, the process is more complicated than you might think. To understand how to resolve this problem, let's first look at how the server determines the proper execution method for this query.

Because it uses an OUTER JOIN, the outer table must be processed first. The server scans the outer table once. Each time it finds a row that is not excluded by the WHERE clause, it then scans the inner table once. This inner scan uses an index when possible; where an index is not available, it does a table scan. If the server determines that an index could be useful, it will create a temporary one in the TEMPDB. To prevent the server from guessing the size of the temporary table, you use a subprocedure to perform the OUTER JOIN on the temporary table. The subprocedure will be optimized after the temporary table is created, allowing the server to use actual size information.

It is still a little more complex than just using a subprocedure. The inner procedure expects the temporary table to exist already when it is created. However, the outer procedure doesn't expect the temporary table to be created. To have the server optimize both stored procedures properly, you would create the objects in the following order:

1. Drop both procedures.
2. Create the temporary table.
3. Create the inner procedure.
4. Drop the temporary table.
5. Create the outer procedure.

You should save the entire SQL as a single script, which will enable you to create the procedures any time you need to use them. Listing 16.2 is the final SQL script for this example.

LISTING 16.2 Final SQL Script Using Temporary Tables

```
If Exists (Select * From sysobjects where name = 'Sp_sales_inner')
    Drop Procedure sp_sales_inner
Go
If Exists (Select * From sysobjects where name = 'Sp_sales_outer')
    Drop Procedure sp_sales_outer
Go
--  Create the Temporary Table
Select ORD.CustomerId, OD.productId, OD.quantity
Into #tp_products
From [Order Details] as OD inner join
     Customers as CT on
     CT.City = 'New York'
     inner join
     Orders as ORD on
     ORD.OrderID = OD.OrderID
GO
--Create the inner procedure
Create Procedure sp_sales_inner
With Recompile
As
Select Companyname,
       tpp.CustomerID,
       sum(quantity) as 'QTY'
From Customers as CT Left Outer Join
     #tp_products as tpp on
     tpp.customerid = CT.customerid
Group by Companyname, tpp.customerid
If @@Error <> 0
    Return 99
Else
    Return 0
Go
--Drop the Temporary Table
Drop Table #tp_products
Go
--Create the Outer procedure
Create Procedure sp_sales_outer (@City char(15))
As
Declare @Ret_Code Int
Select ORD.CustomerId, OD.productId, OD.quantity
Into #tp_products
From [Order Details] as OD inner join
     Customers as CT on
     CT.City = @City
     inner join
     Orders as ORD on
```

LISTING 16.2 continued

```
47:      ORD.OrderID = OD.OrderID
48:If @@Error <> 0
49:    Return 98
50:Execute @Ret_Code = sp_sales_inner
51:Drop Table #tp_products
52:If @Ret_Code <> 0
53:    Return 99
54:Else
55:    Return 0
56:Go
```

This is the best way to guarantee that you will not experience any problems as the temporary table increases or decreases in size. The important thing to remember when doing this type of process is to place a `GO` command after each unique operation. This allows the server to process each command separately, providing the server with the information it needs to optimize the next step in the process.

> You should notice in the example that the temporary table is dropped at the end of each process (lines 34 and 51). This is done even though the table will be deleted when the connection is closed. However, it is good programming practice to drop the table explicitly. This ensures that it is dropped just in case there is a problem closing the connection.

Indexing Temporary Tables

Temporary tables can be indexed like any other table in the database. However, if you index a temporary table after a stored procedure has been optimized, the index will not be used in the stored procedure. You should remember to create the index on the temporary table before creating the stored procedures that will use it. The index created on the temporary table, as with the table itself, is deleted at then end of the session.

Handling Transactions in Stored Procedures

The way that a transaction is processed in a stored procedure forces you to handle transaction processing differently within the stored procedure. Using a transaction process within a stored procedure is tricky because you will generally be using transactions in the batch that calls the stored procedure. To make sense of this, we will first create a stored procedure and see how the problems could occur. Then, I will make changes to the procedure and look at how this solves the transactional problems. For this section, we will be using the Northwind database tables. However, to save the original data, I will create two new tables using the data from the `Products` table.

```
Create Table Demo_OrderDetails (
    OrderID int Identity ,
    ProductID int NOT NULL ,
    Quantity smallint NOT NULL)
Create Table Demo_Products (
    ProductId int,
    Productname nvarchar(40) NOT NULL ,
    Quantity smallint NOT NULL)
Insert Demo_Products
Select ProductId, productName, UnitsInStock
From Products
GO
```

The preceding code creates two new tables for the order detail and product information. We then use the information in the original `products` table to initialize the `demo_products` table. The stored procedure that we will use for this example is

```
Create procedure Order_Ins (
       @ProdId Int,
       @qty Int)
As
Declare @in_Stock smallInt
Begin Transaction
   Update Demo_products
     Set @in_stock = Quantity = Quantity - @qty
   Where productId = @prodID
   If @in_stock < 0
   Begin
     RollBack Transaction
     Raiserror ('Not enough Stock', 16, 1)
   End
Insert Demo_orderdetails (productID, Quantity)
       Values(@prodID, @qty)
Commit Transaction
```

In this procedure, the `demo_products` table is updated before a new order detail row is inserted into the table. By updating the `demo_products` table first, you set a page lock on that table preventing anyone else from changing that product's information until the procedure is completed and the transaction ends.

The SET statement should appear a little strange to you. In the statement as shown, we are performing two actions at the same time. The statement used is

```
Set @in_stock = Quantity = Quantity - @qty
```

It could also have been written this way:

```
Set Quantity = Quantity - @qty
Set @in_stock = Quantity
```

Either way the result is the same. However, the first one is more elegant.

If the updated stock level is less than zero, the procedure reverses the process performed and raises an error, returning a non-zero return code that signifies a problem in the procedure. Otherwise, a new row is inserted into the `demo_orderdetails` table. It should be noted that this stored procedure lacks some of the code needed for proper error checking and will fail if no rows are found in the `UPDATE` statement.

To perform this process properly, a transaction is needed inside the procedure. Now, let's run the stored procedure several times within a batch transaction to insert some more data as shown.

```
Begin Transaction
   Execute Order_ins 1,2
   Execute Order_ins 1,8
   Execute Order_ins 2,9
Commit Transaction
Select *
From demo_products
Where productid in (1,2)
Select *
From demo_orderdetails
Where productid in (1,2)
```

Results:

```
ProductId   Productname          Quantity
----------- -------------------- --------
1           Chai                       29
2           Chang                       8

(2 row(s) affected)

OrderID     ProductID  Quantity
----------- ---------- --------
2           1          2
3           1          8
4           2          9

(3 row(s) affected)
```

This all works fine as long as nothing fails within the procedure. The following SQL code forces a failure to occur by trying to sell more of product 2 than exists in the inventory.

```
Begin Transaction
   Execute Order_ins 2,9
   Execute Order_ins 1,9
Commit Transaction
Select *
From demo_products
Where productid in (1,2)
Select *
From demo_orderdetails
Where productid in (1,2)
```

Results:

```
Server: Msg 50000, Level 16, State 1, Procedure Order_Ins, Line 13
Not enough Stock

(1 row(s) affected)

Server: Msg 3902, Level 16, State 1, Procedure Order_Ins, Line 17
The COMMIT TRANSACTION request has no corresponding BEGIN TRANSACTION.
Server: Msg 266, Level 16, State 1, Procedure Order_Ins, Line 17
Transaction count after EXECUTE indicates that a COMMIT or
ROLLBACK TRANSACTION statement is missing.
Previous count = 1, current count = 0.

(1 row(s) affected)


(1 row(s) affected)

Server: Msg 3902, Level 16, State 1, Line 4
The COMMIT TRANSACTION request has no corresponding BEGIN TRANSACTION.
ProductId   Productname                              Quantity
----------- ---------------------------------------- --------
1           Chai                                     20
2           Chang                                    8

(2 row(s) affected)

OrderID     ProductID   Quantity
----------- ----------- --------
2           1           2
3           1           8
4           2           9
6           2           9
7           2           9
8           1           9

(6 row(s) affected)
```

You should notice that only half of the order made it to the server. Instead of selling both products, only the first EXECUTE statement completed successfully. To understand how this happened, you need to examine the error messages that were transmitted.

```
Server: Msg 50000, Level 16, State 1, Procedure Order_Ins, Line 13
Not enough Stock
```

This is the error message from the stored procedure. It informs us that a failure has occurred in the procedure using the RAISERROR statement.

```
Server: Msg 3902, Level 16, State 1, Procedure Order_Ins, Line 17
The COMMIT TRANSACTION request has no corresponding BEGIN TRANSACTION.
Server: Msg 266, Level 16, State 1, Procedure Order_Ins, Line 17
Transaction count after EXECUTE indicates that a COMMIT or
ROLLBACK TRANSACTION statement is missing.
Previous count = 1, current count = 0.
```

These messages warn us that the procedure has changed the status of the global variable @@trancount. It also tells us that the transaction control for this batch is not correct. The @@trancount variable is used by the server to keep track of how many BEGIN TRANSACTION statements have been issued by incrementing the variable for each BEGIN TRANSACTION that is executed, and decrementing the variable for each COMMIT or ROLLBACK TRANSACTION that is executed.

When the procedure is called in this example, the @@trancount is already set to 1 because of the BEGIN TRANSACTION in the first line of the batch. When the procedure issues the ROLLBACK TRANSACTION statement because of the failure, it resets the @@trancount variable to 0 before exiting the procedure. This change in the transaction level triggers the message informing you that transaction control is failing. Finally, when the COMMIT TRANSACTION command in the procedure tries to decrement the value in @@trancount, the second error is sent because the @@trancount variable cannot be negative.

Solving the Transactional Problem

There are many different ways of solving this problem. Any solution you come up with should follow the principles listed here:

- A stored procedure must be able to undo all the work it has performed.
- A stored procedure must be able to manage its own transaction work regardless of any transactions being used outside the procedure.
- There must be no net change to the @@trancount variable at the end of a procedure.

The following approach is but one way of solving this problem. In the procedure, I use a transaction savepoint to mark the beginning of the work in the procedure. Then if there is an error, the procedure will rollback to the savepoint and then use the `COMMIT TRANSACTION` statement, returning a non-zero status to warn that there was a failure in the stored procedure. This will not have any effect on the `@@trancount` variable. What follows is the final SQL script for the stored procedure with these changes.

```
Create procedure Order_Ins (
       @ProdId Int,
       @qty Int)
As
Declare @in_Stock smallInt
Begin Transaction
   Save Transaction sp_StartWork
   Update Demo_products
     Set @in_stock = Quantity = Quantity - @qty
   Where productId = @prodID
   If @in_stock < 0
   Begin
     RollBack Transaction sp_StartWork
     Commit Transaction
     Raiserror ('Not enough Stock', 16, 1)
     Return 99
   End
Insert Demo_orderdetails (productID, Quantity)
       Values(@prodID, @qty)
commit Transaction
Return 0
```

Finally, the batch that uses this stored procedure must also be modified to check the return status for a non-zero value and roll back the entire batch if a failure is detected. Doing so prevents a partial order from being processed (see Listing 16.3).

LISTING 16.3 SQL Script That Solves Transactional Problems by Committing or Rolling Back the Transaction at the Appropriate Points

```
Declare @ret_code Int
Begin Transaction
   Execute @ret_code = Order_ins 2,9
   If @ret_code <> 0
   Begin
     Print 'Order Entry has Failed'
     Rollback Transaction
     Return
   End
   Execute @ret_code = Order_ins 1,9
   If @ret_code <> 0
   Begin
     Print 'Order Entry has Failed'
     Rollback Transaction
     Return
```

LISTING 16.3 continued

```
16:   End
17:Print 'Order has been completed'
18:Commit Transaction
19:Select *
20:From demo_products
21:Where productid in (1,2)
22:Select *
23:From demo_orderdetails
24:Where productid in (1,2)
```

Results:

```
(1 row(s) affected)

Server: Msg 50000, Level 16, State 1,
Procedure Order_Ins, Line 15
Not enough Stock
Order Entry has Failed
```

If this process fails, the actual `ROLLBACK TRANSACTION` in lines 7 and 14, will be performed in the batch instead of within the stored procedure.

Summary

In today's lesson, you looked at several different topics that will help the performance of your stored procedures. There were many tips throughout this lesson on how to create better procedures. One of the ways in which you can ensure that the procedure is being processed properly is to determine when to have the server recompile its execution plan. When using temporary tables or table variables, pay close attention to any logic that would cause the server to guess at the statistics that it needs to determine the best execution plan.

Finally, remember to use return codes to make certain that the procedures are ending properly, and pay close attention to error handling within the procedure. Of course, you should also pay attention to error handling anywhere in your SQL script processing. Finally, you should try to test any transactional processing you are using to ensure that you will not accidentally stop the transaction process if a procedure fails.

In tomorrow's lesson, you will learn the different techniques that you can use to test and debug your stored procedures. In fact, some of these techniques can be used on any procedure, such as a trigger or function.

Q&A

Q Why are multiple execution plans kept in memory for a single procedure?

A Each execution of a stored procedure requires its own execution space to store any session information (temporary table names, cursor information, or variable names). This space is also where the procedure actually runs. To allow multiple users to execute the same procedure at the same time, the server needs to load multiple versions of the procedure into memory.

Q There is a lot of work involved in using stored procedures. Do their benefits outweigh the amount of work required?

A Absolutely! Stored procedures provide performance benefits that include less network traffic and the storing of the procedures' optimization for use by many users. Many of the actions taken within the stored procedure, such as error trapping, would be performed by your application if they were not included in a stored procedure.

Q Why is it necessary to use transaction processing in a stored procedure?

A Transaction processing is needed any time you want to ensure that an entire process is completed successfully before committing the actions to the database. When using a stored procedure to perform a complex process, the transaction process should be included within the procedure and the calling SQL script should identify any failures that might have occurred.

Q Using variables in the `WHERE` clause would create a problem during the optimization process. How can using variables be avoided in queries within a stored procedure?

A Whenever there is a variable in the `WHERE` clause, the server guesses which optimization method it should use. Because the server doesn't know the value of the variable at optimization time, it cannot look up its value and determine how the `WHERE` clause will behave. The following example shows how the values of the variables are not known when the procedure is optimized:

```
Declare @start_date datetime,
        @end_date datetime
Select @start_date = '10/24/1996'
Select @end_date = '12/31/1997'
Select *
from [Order Details] as OD inner join
      orders as ORD On
      ORD.orderid = OD.orderid
Where ORD.OrderDate between @start_date and @end_Date
```

If you modify this procedure code so that the server knows the values of the variables before the optimization is performed, the values can be substituted in the query to develop the optimization plan. The following example shows how this is done:

```
    Create Procedure Get_Orders
    (@start_date, @end_date)
As
Select *
from [Order Details] as OD inner join
      orders as ORD On
      ORD.orderid = OD.orderid
Where ORD.OrderDate between @start_date and @end_Date
```

By passing the values of the variables as parameters, the server can now successfully optimize the procedure.

Workshop

The Workshop provides quiz questions to help you solidify your understanding of the material covered and exercises to provide you with experience in using what you've learned. Try to answer the quiz and exercise questions before checking the answers in Appendix A, "Answers to Quizzes and Exercises," and make sure that you understand the answers before continuing to the next lesson.

Quiz

1. When could a stored procedure cause serious performance problems?
2. Can you give a example of the previous answer?

Exercises

1. The following procedure seems to take a long time to process. Can you identify the reason and correct it?

```
        Create Procedure Sales_by_State
  (@start_date datetime, @end_date datetime)
As
Select od.productid, od.quantity, od.unitprice, ord.customerid
  into #tp_Sales
From orders as ORD inner join
     [Order Details] as OD on
     ord.orderid = od.orderid
Where ORD.orderdate between @start_date and @end_date
Select cst.region,
       sum(tp.quantity * tp.unitprice)
From Customers as cst left outer join
```

```
     #tp_sales as tp on
     cst.customerid = tp.customerid
Group by tp.region
```

2. Create a procedure that updates the price of a product, passing the price and its product ID. This update must verify that the product is available (quantity > 0) and the new price is greater than $12.00. If the update fails for any reason, return an error. Make sure to use transaction processing.
3. Extra Credit: Create a system procedure that displays the usernames and login names of everyone using the current database.

WEEK 3

DAY 17

Debugging Stored Procedures

On Day 15, "Writing and Executing Stored Procedures," you learned what stored procedures are, how to create them, and how to execute them. In fact, you saw that stored procedures are the way to package a piece of logic for use by any application that is written to access your database. Then, on Day 16, "Optimizing Stored Procedures," you learned how the optimization process works and what the server does when it validates and then compiles the stored procedure. In the process, you saw how you can use temporary tables and the many programming structures and variables in a stored procedure.

Now that you have written a stored procedure, the last thing you need to know is how to test, locate, and fix any problems that might crop up in a stored procedure. This process is called *debugging* and can be used for triggers, functions, and batches as well as for stored procedures. In this lesson, we will cover the following topics:

- Simple debugging techniques
- Using the print statement

- Tracking elapsed time
- Using temporary tables for debugging
- Error checking a stored procedure
- Using the T-SQL interactive debugger

Debugging Explained

The process of debugging is the least favorite task that a programmer must perform. Debugging means nothing more than finding the problems that are preventing your program code from performing properly and fixing it. To prevent these problems from occurring when the application is executed, you must take the time to test your stored procedures, triggers, functions, and batches. The best way to debug your SQL code is to take the time to plan and design the code before you start writing it. In addition, you should create a list of the conditions that you want to test in the code. As your SQL programs become more complex, you will find that testing will also become more difficult.

It is very important for you to take the time to understand the impact that poor debugging and testing will have on your SQL applications. In this lesson, you will see several different methods of testing and debugging your SQL code. Although most of the techniques and suggestions in this lesson can be used for any of the different SQL scripts you want to debug, I will be using stored procedures to provide the examples. A special tool, called the T-SQL debugger, is provided with the Query Analyzer; the T-SQL debugger can be used with stored procedures.

Finding the Problems

Finding where a problem has occurred in your SQL code isn't as easy as you might think. The SQL Server will stop the execution of your code for many different reasons (as you will see later in this lesson). Even more confusing is that the actual error might have occurred in an entirely different section of code, but manifested itself later. What this means to you is that you have to start at the point of the problem and work backward through the code until you find the real problem. You will find that the testing and debugging process will be easier if you follow the following simple suggestions:

- Include well-designed error-handling routines when possible.
- Keep the procedures, triggers, and functions short and easy to follow.
- Indent all loops and `IF` statement code to make them easier to read.
- Use a naming convention for all procedure names and variables that you create or declare.

These suggestions will help you solve many of the problems that might pop up. In most cases, there are three distinct types of errors that can occur: syntax, compile time, and execution errors.

Syntax errors are found very quickly because the server will provide you with an error message that describes what is wrong with the code, as shown in the following example:

```
select * employees Where city = 'London'
```

```
Server: Msg 170, Level 15, State 1, Line 1
Line 1: Incorrect syntax near 'employees'.
```

Although the server tells you that a syntax problem exists, it is up to you to figure out exactly what is missing.

The next type of error occurs at compile time. These errors are generally caused when you misspell a variable or use the wrong data type. You have probably seen this type of error several times while reading this book.

The final type of error, the execution or logic error, is the hardest to find because your SQL code is syntactically correct. The server has found no compile problems and the procedure executes, but the results are incorrect.

There are no magic tricks to help you find these problems. Time and patience will help you resolve them. Other things that will also help include good testing and debugging skills, and a little bit of luck. The rest of this lesson will show you some good techniques and coding skills that can help you to debug your SQL code.

Creating a Good Work Environment

When creating stored procedures, a good work environment goes a long way in helping to make your job easier when and if you need to debug a stored procedure. One of the first habits you should get into is to use comments in your procedures. T-SQL supports two different types of comments: multi-line and single-line comments. Multi-line comments enable you to comment out sections of code when you want to bypass them during testing. One occasion to use this technique is when you are writing the `CREATE PROCEDURE` code. Commenting out the `CREATE` statement enables you to test the actual procedure code as a batch. The following example shows how this is done:

```
/*
Create Procedure sp_UpdateProduct
   (@prodID int,
    @Qty int,
    @Units int,
    @endQty int Output)
```

```
As
*/
-- This declaration is for testing only
Declare @prodID int, @qty int, @units int, @endqty int)
-- This declaration is required for the procedure
Declare @Priceval money, @ret_code int
...
Return -- 0
```

Remember that a RETURN statement can return only a value from within a procedure. When you are testing your procedure as a batch as shown in the previous example, you need to remember to comment out the value that should be returned.

Single-line comments are used to add or remove any debugging commands you might have included in the procedure such as DECLARE and PRINT statements. Using the previous example, if I were ready to create the procedure, I would remove the comment marks from the CREATE statement and comment out the DECLARE statement that I put in the procedure for testing.

```
Create Procedure sp_UpdateProduct
   (@prodID int,
    @Qty int,
    @Units int,
    @endQty int Output)
As
-- This declaration is for testing only
-- Declare @prodID int, @qty int, @units int, @endqty int)
-- This declaration is required for the procedure
Declare @Priceval money, @ret_code int
...
Return 0
```

You should leave any testing commands in the procedure, but commented out, so that you can use them later if you modify the procedure.

One very important thing to remember is that an error that occurs at the beginning of a procedure could cause more errors later in the process. The later error could occur either at compile time or at execution time. You should always resolve the first error listed in the messages, and then re-execute the procedure to see what happens. The following is an example of a procedure with several errors:

```
Create  Procedure SalesByCategory
    @CategoryName nvarchar(15), @OrdYr nvarchar(4) = '1998'
```

```
as
If @OrdYear != '1996' and @OrdYear != '1997' and @OrdYear != '1998'
Begin
    Select @OrdYear = '1998'
End

Select ProductName,
    TotalPurchase=Round(Sum(Convert(decimal(14,2),
          OD.Quantity * (1-OD.Discount) * OD.UnitPrice)), 0)
From [Order Details] OD, Orders O, Products P, Categories C
Where OD.OrderID = O.OrderID
    and OD.ProductID = P.ProductID
    and P.CategoryID = C.CategoryID
    and C.CategoryName = @CategoryName
    and Substring(Convert(nvarchar(22), O.OrderDate, 111), 1, 4) = @OrdYear
Group By ProductName
Order By ProductName
```

Results:

```
Server: Msg 137, Level 15, State 2, Procedure SalesByCategory, Line 5
Must declare the variable '@OrdYear'.
Server: Msg 137, Level 15, State 1, Procedure SalesByCategory, Line 8
Must declare the variable '@OrdYear'.
Server: Msg 137, Level 15, State 1, Procedure SalesByCategory, Line 17
Must declare the variable '@OrdYear'.
```

This was a working stored procedure in which I made one simple spelling error when typing it in. When the `CREATE` statement executed, the server displayed several error messages about a nonexistent variable. You might look at this for a while, not understanding what the server is trying to tell you. Of course you declared the variable. It will take you a bit to figure out that you misspelled it. You should fix that error and re-execute the `CREATE` statement to see whether there are any more problems.

Tip

When you create stored procedures, you should take time to test each unique component of the procedure, and then finally put the procedure together when all its parts are error free.

The Query Analyzer provides you with a method to execute pieces of a procedure independently of the complete procedure. To do this, simply highlight the section of SQL code that you want to execute and click the Execute button or press the F5 key. This will execute the highlighted section of code. Of course, if the section you highlighted contains a variable, you will get an error message.

Displaying Debugging Messages

One of the most common issues when debugging any software is to know where an error has really occurred. One of the simplest methods of debugging is to use the PRINT statement to report on the progress or to track the performance of the sections of the procedure. However, you need to be aware of a weakness in the use of the PRINT statement. Try executing the following example:

```
Print 'Starting Test Now'
Waitfor delay '00:00:25'
Print 'Ending Test Now'
```

This example will take a while to execute. The output, when it is finally displayed, will look like the following:

```
Starting Test Now
Ending Test Now
```

If you were staring at the monitor, you should have noticed that both messages were displayed at the same time. This is because the server builds data packets of 512 bytes at a time before returning any information for your query. When the packet is full or the query is completed, the packet is sent. This means that debugging message will not help you observe the behavior of the procedure while it is running.

Although you can increase the size of the data packet, you cannot change the way the server processes batched information. Instead, simply by using the GO statement, you can change the way your debugging messages are printed. The following example uses the previous code with only a minor change:

```
Print 'Starting Test Now'
Go
Waitfor delay '00:00:25'
Print 'Ending Test Now'
```

This time, you should see the first message immediately because the first PRINT statement is its own batch. Although this method works when you need to debug a SQL batch, you cannot use it when debugging a stored procedure because the GO statement is not available in a stored procedure.

Using the PRINT Statement

In the previous section, you saw that the PRINT statement could be used to display information about the execution of the procedure. The PRINT statement can also be used to return any string of text to the user, as you have already seen. In addition, you can combine text strings with system functions, such as GETDATE(); system constants, such as

@@ROWCOUNT; and local variables. The following example shows a PRINT statement that combines a local variable, a system constant, and a text string:

```
Declare @pcname varchar(20)
Select @pcname = @@Servername
Print 'The Computer ' +
      Rtrim(@pcname) +
      ' is using ' +
      Rtrim(@@version)
```

Another way you can use the PRINT statement is in conjunction with the IF statement. Using the IF statement, you can have information printed only when certain conditions occur. The following example shows you how to print a message only if the condition is true:

```
If Exists (Select * from Employees Where city = 'London')
   Print 'There are Employees from London'
```


Tracking Time

One of the hardest things to find out is why a procedure takes a long time to execute. The first step is to determine how much time each process in the procedure takes to execute. You could use the RAISERROR statement to display the timing of a batch. The following example shows how to print the starting and ending time:

```
Declare @time varchar(30)
Select @time = convert(varchar(30), getdate(), 109)
Raiserror ('Starting now %s', 0, 1, @time)
Declare @cntr int
Select @cntr = 0
While @cntr < 2000
Begin
   Select @cntr = @cntr + 1
End
Select @time = convert(varchar(30), getdate(), 109)
Raiserror ('Ending Now %s', 0, 1, @time)
```

The WHILE loop in this example is used to slow down the batch enough so that the starting and ending times are different, as shown here:

```
Starting now Nov 18 2000  3:54:06:550PM
Ending Now Nov 18 2000  3:54:06:650PM
```

The RAISERROR statement in this method uses the severity of 0 to suppress the error component. You can use the PRINT statement in the same way, as shown here:

```
Declare @time varchar(30)
Select @time = convert(varchar(30), getdate(), 109)
Print 'Starting now ' + @time
Declare @cntr int
```

```
Select @cntr = 0
While @cntr < 2000
Begin
   Select @cntr = @cntr + 1
End
Select @time = convert(varchar(30), getdate(), 109)
Print 'Ending now ' + @time
```

Remember that the output from these debugging statements will not be displayed until the batch is completed.

Tracking Elapsed Time Using Temporary Tables

One of the ways in which you can track the performance of the server is by creating a procedure that you run many times during the day, and which writes these timing statistics to a table. The following table stores information about server performance:

```
Create Table wk_Time_Perf (
   Module varchar(20) not null,
   Exec_ID int not null,
   Step_ID int not null,
   Start_time datetime,
   End_time datetime,
   Elapsed int)
```

This table can be created as either a permanent worktable in the database, or as a global temporary table at startup time. Either way, it will be used to track the performance of the server. Now that the table is created, we can add rows of information to it by using the `INSERT` statement within a stored procedure shown in Listing 17.1.

LISTING 17.1 Using the `INSERT` Statement

```
Create procedure Get_Perf_Trk
As
--Get Exec ID
Declare @exid int,
        @start_time datetime
Select @exid = isnull(max(exec_id) + 1,1)
From wk_Time_Perf
Where module = 'Demo'
--Get Starting Time
Select @start_time = getdate()
Select count(*) from [order details]
--Insert performance record
Insert wk_Time_Perf (
```

LISTING 17.1 continued

```
        Module, Exec_ID, Step_ID, Start_time, End_time, Elapsed)
Values ('Demo', @exid, 1, @start_time, Getdate(),
         datediff(ms, @start_time, getdate()))
--Get next Start Time
Select @start_time = getdate()
Select count(*) from [order details]
--Insert performance record
Insert wk_Time_Perf (
        Module, Exec_ID, Step_ID, Start_time, End_time, Elapsed)
Values ('Demo', @exid, 2, @start_time, Getdate(),
         datediff(ms, @start_time, getdate()))
```


Now, execute this stored procedure and then display the data in the `wk_time_perf` table.

```
Exec Get_Perf_Trk
select * from wk_time_perf
```

Results:

```
-----------
2155


-----------
2155

Exec_ID  Step_ID  Start_time               End_time                 Elapsed
-------- -------- ------------------------ ------------------------ --------
1        1        2000-11-18 16:39:52.020  2000-11-18 16:39:52.050        30
1        2        2000-11-18 16:39:52.060  2000-11-18 16:39:52.060         0

(4 row(s) affected)
```

The output includes two rows in the `wk_time_perf` table and the time required to perform each step in the procedure. Storing this type of information in a permanent table provides you with a method for identifying any performance problems that might pop up.

Performing Error Checking in a Stored Procedure

Whenever you create a stored procedure that modifies data, you need to check the value of the `@@ERROR` system function in case a trappable error has occurred during execution of the procedure. This is even more important when you are using transactional processing. Unfortunately, there are times when an error immediately ends the stored procedure and returns a negative value to the calling procedure or batch. Other errors end both the procedure in which the error occurred and the procedure or batch that executed it.

The common errors you will encounter when executing stored procedures are listed in Table 17.1.

TABLE 17.1 Common Errors When Executing Stored Procedures

Where Trapped	*Type of Error*	*Error Number*	*Error Trapped (proc)?*	*Return Value*	*Error Trapped (batch)?*
Procedure	Unique index violation	2601	Yes	<user defined>	Yes
	Rule violation	513	Yes	<user defined>	Yes
	Constraint violation	547	Yes	<user defined>	Yes
	Security violation (table)	229	Yes	<user defined>	Yes
Batch	Missing or bad parameter	201	No	-6	Yes
	Table missing	208	No	-6	Yes
Application	Deadlock	1205	No	-3	No
	Data conversion error	8114	No	-6	No
Application error handler	Security violation (proc)	229	No	0	Yes
	Trigger rollback	<user defined>	No	0	No
User trapped	Data overflow	None	No	None	No

The first type of errors (those with "Yes" in the Error Trapped (proc) column) in the table is comprised of those errors that are trappable in the procedure. They are the easiest to trap because the server knows the current context and location of the instruction that caused the error. Simply return a nonzero return code from the procedure to let the batch know that a problem has occurred.

The second type of errors (those with "No" in the Error Trapped (proc) column) causes the procedure to quit, but it returns a nonzero value to the batch. Data errors (error #201) tell you to look at the application code for the cause of the error. Missing tables (error #208) tell you to check the database and any maintenance routines that might have accidentally deleted or renamed a table.

The third type of errors terminates both the procedure and the batch. These must be trapped in the application by checking the return value using the available application functions.

The fourth type of errors terminates the procedure and the batch, but does not return a meaningful value. You must then use either the error or message handlers.

Finally, if there are data overflow errors, the procedure and batch are terminated and a message that there was an overflow is sent. You will not receive any other message.

Basically, you should watch the return status from both the batch and the application in case of any error that has caused a termination of the procedure.

Using the T-SQL Debugger

If none of the previous techniques helps to solve the problems in the procedure, there is one tool you can use that will definitely help. Microsoft SQL Server 2000 provides a debugging tool within the Query Analyzer that will assist you in finding the problems. The T-SQL debugger provides the traditional functionality that most current debugging tools support, such as the following:

- Assigning parameter values
- Single-stepping through the stored procedure
- Observing the changes to the variables during execution
- Setting breakpoints on any statement to stop when executing

The T-SQL debugger will assist you when testing your procedure with valid or invalid data. In addition, if the procedure is returning the wrong result with valid data, it will even help you to figure out why. To start the debugger, you need to do several things:

1. Determine which procedure you want to debug.
2. Create a list of the values you want to use as parameters for testing.
3. Start the debugging session for that procedure.

The first two actions are really the most difficult. However, if you do not have your computer and security environment set up correctly, the debugger will not work.

When reading this section, if you have any difficulties getting the T-SQL debugger to work, go to the Online Books and start the Troubleshooting section for the debugger. This will help you identify the issue that is preventing the debugger from working.

Before attempting to troubleshoot your debugger configuration, you should verify the following:

- Make sure that you have permission to execute the `SP_SDIDEBUG` extended procedure (which can be found in the `MASTER` database).
- Make sure that the SQL Server service is using an account that has Administrator privileges on that computer when it is started.
- Check the Event Viewer's Application and System logs for any error messages.

Starting the Debugger

The first step in starting the debugger is to start the Query Analyzer. After you have started the Query Analyzer, open the folder for the database you are working with. For the remainder of this lesson, we will work with the `Northwind` database and one of the procedures that were created on Day 15. After you have the database open, click on the Store Procedure folder to open the list of available procedures as shown in Figure 17.1.

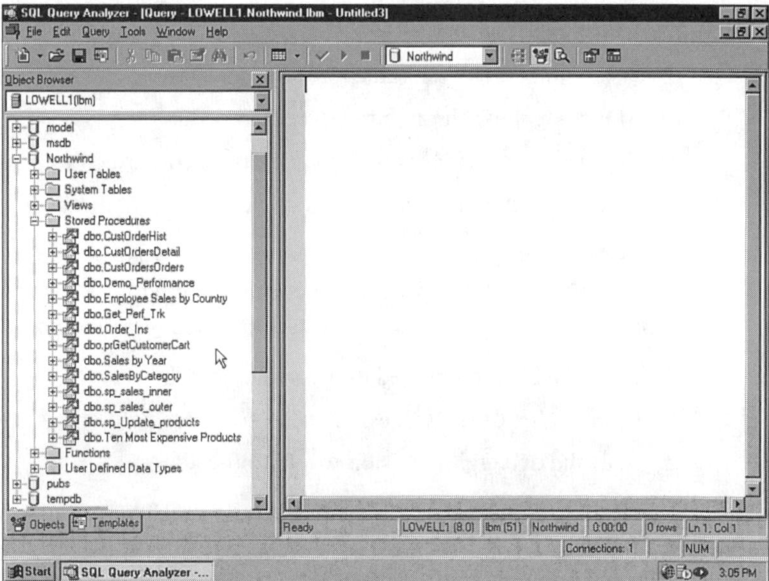

FIGURE 17.1

Listing the stored procedures created in a database.

The stored procedure that I will use to show you how the debugger works was created on Day 15 (refer to Listing 15.6) and is shown in Listing 17.2:

LISTING 17.2 Using the T-SQL Debugger

```
create proc prGetCustomerCart (
    @CustomerID nchar(5),
    @OrderID int output
) as

Declare @ret_Code int
/* find an open order if one exists */
select @OrderID = OrderID
from   Orders
where  CustomerID = @CustomerID

Select @ret_Code = @@error
if @@error != 0 begin
    raiserror ('Error finding an open order', 16, 1)
    return 99     /* nonzero return means error */
end

if @OrderID is null begin
    /* row not found so add a new open order */
    INSERT INTO [Orders] (
        [CustomerID],
        [EmployeeID],
        [OrderClosed]
    ) VALUES(
        'QUICK',
        2,
        'N'
    )

    /* check for error in the insert */
    if @@error != 0 begin
        raiserror ('Error inserting a new order', 16, 1)
        return 99     /* nonzero return means error */
    end

    /* Otherwise set OrderID = last identity value */
    set @OrderID = @@identity
end

return
```


Locate this procedure in the list; if you did not save it or you deleted it, re-create it now. After you have the procedure available in the list, right-click on it and select the Debug option from the pop-up menu as shown in Figure 17.2.

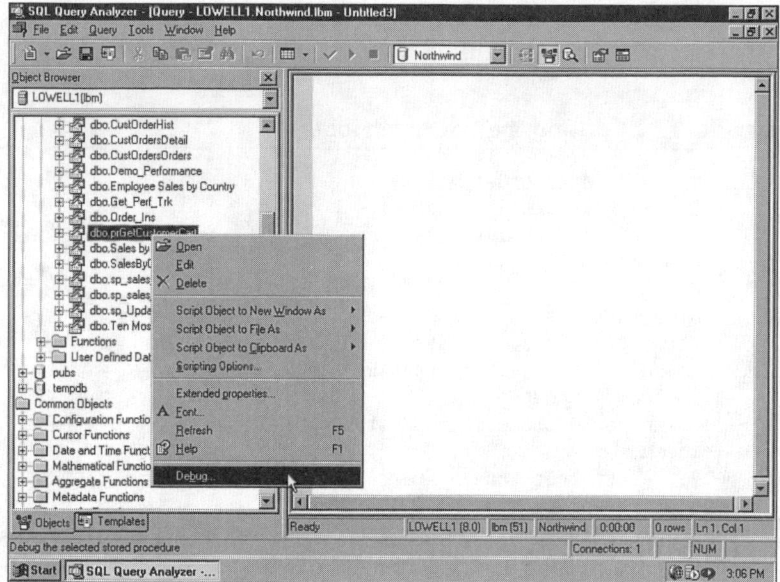

FIGURE 17.2
Starting the debugger for the selected procedure.

This will display the Debug Procedure dialog that enables you to enter starting parameters for the procedure (see Figure 17.3). This dialog enables you to select the stored procedure that you want to test by using the drop-down list at the top of the form. As you select each of the different parameters in the list, the dialog will display the data type of the parameter and whether it is an input or output parameter. The Debug Procedure dialog also enables you to enter a value. If you want the parameter set to NULL, simply click the Set to null check box.

Output parameters should always be set to NULL.

The second drop-down list on the dialog enables you to select the database to work with. However, this drop-down is available only when you are debugging a system stored procedure. The last option you set is the Auto roll back option to roll back all work performed during the execution of the procedure automatically.

For our sample debugging session, enter **`VINET`** as the value for the `@customerid`, select the `@OrderID` parameter, and click the Set to null check box. Now, click the Execute button to continue to the debugging session. What is now displayed is the T-SQL debugging interface.

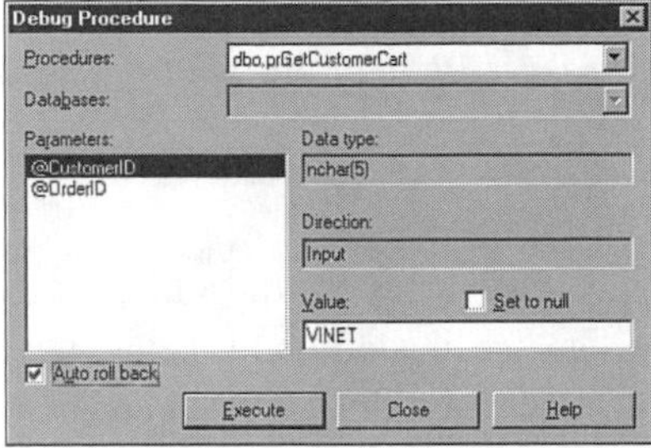

FIGURE 17.3

Setting the parameter values for the procedure.

Using the T-SQL Debugger Interface

The debugger interface (see Figure 17.4) consists of several different sections that are used to display information about the procedure that you are debugging.

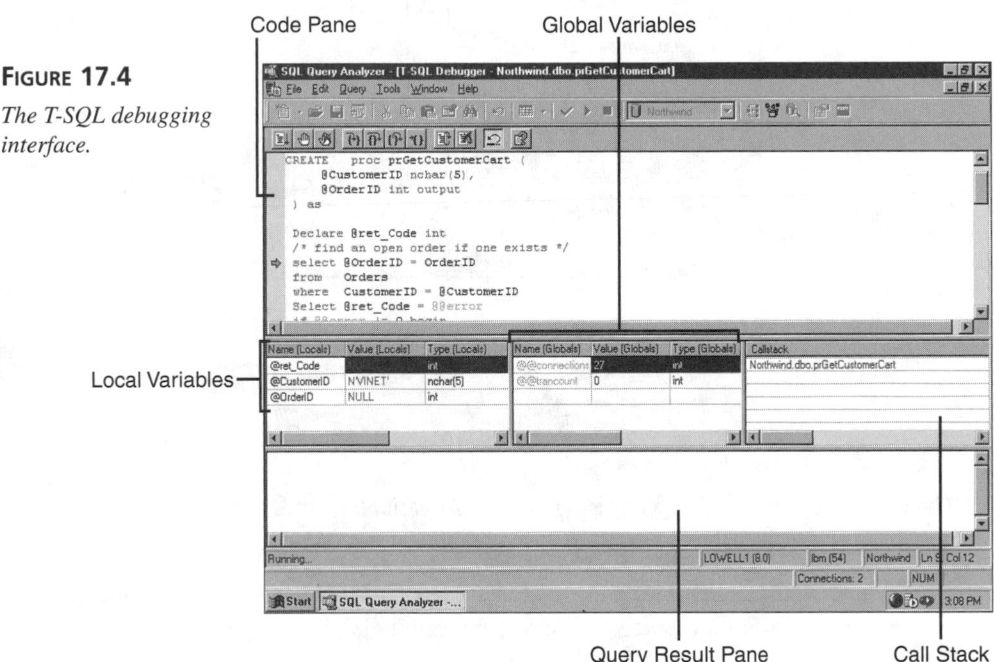

FIGURE 17.4

The T-SQL debugging interface.

The code pane displays the SQL statement that you are debugging. In addition, you should see a yellow arrow, which points to the first executable statement in the procedure. This arrow will always identify the statement that will be executed next. Separate output panes are provided for the local and global variables, the result set of the query, and the call stack.

Global variable is a legacy term for the built-in Transact-SQL functions whose names start with `@@`.

The Local Variables pane displays the values of all parameters that are declared or used in the procedure at any given moment. In addition to seeing what is happening to the values as the procedure executes, you can use this pane to change these values if needed. Simply click on the value you want to modify and change it as shown in Figure 17.5.

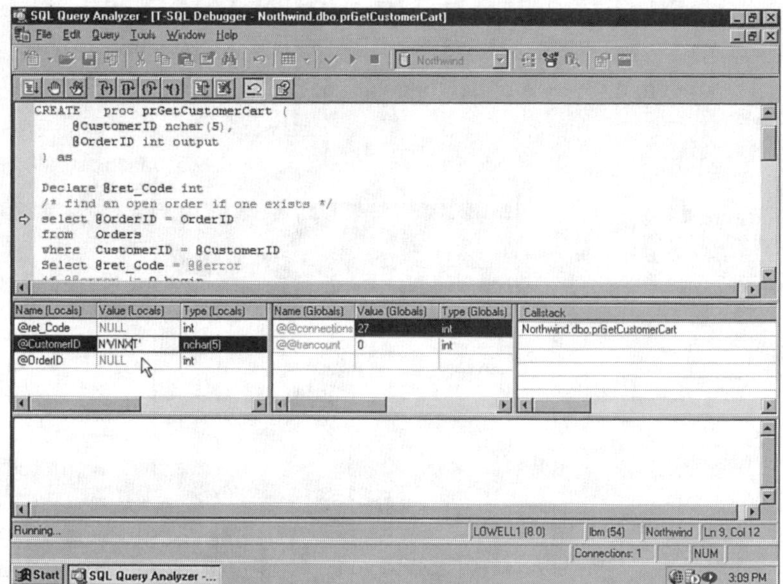

FIGURE 17.5
Displaying and modifying local variables.

The Global Variables pane will display only two variables by default. These are

- `@@connections`—This variable displays the number of connections, or attempted connections, since the server was last started. This value should increase every time you restart the procedure during the debugging session.
- `@@trancount`—This variable displays the number of active transactions for the current connection. This value will help you to find any problems that are caused by incorrect transaction processing.

If you want to track another system variable, such as `@@Error`, you can simply type it into the Global Variables area as shown in Figure 17.6.

FIGURE 17.6

Adding additional global variables to the debugging display.

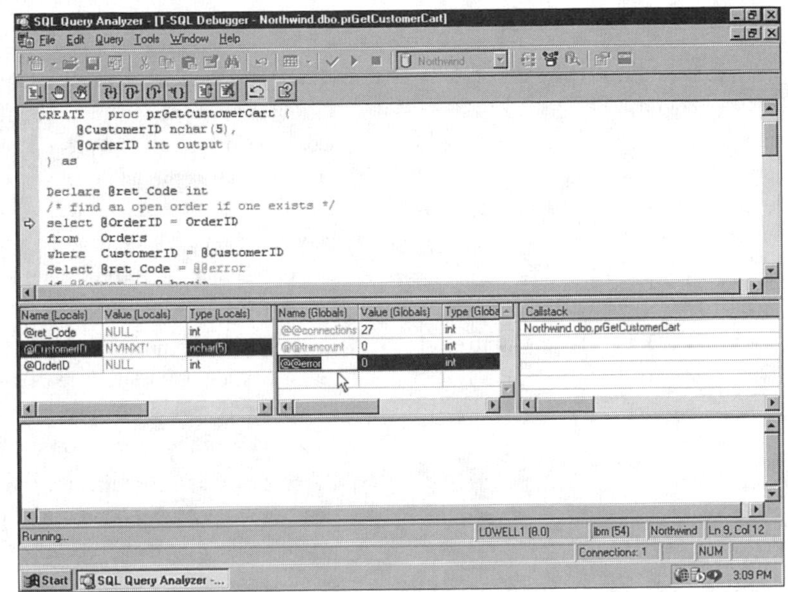

17

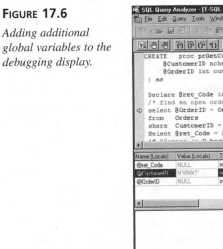

The Call Stack pane will show you the list of all procedures that have been started but have not yet been completed in relation to the procedure you are testing.

The final tools that you will use when debugging your procedure are the different options you have available from the Debugging toolbar. Table 17.2 lists the options that are available from the Debugging toolbar, and the toolbar is shown in Figure 17.7.

TABLE 17.2 T-SQL Debugging Options

Option	*Key*	*Description*
Go	F5	Runs the stored procedure in debugging mode.
Toggle Breakpoint	F9	Sets or removes a breakpoint at the current line. You cannot set a breakpoint on lines containing nonexecutable code such as comments, declaration statements, or blank lines.
Remove All Breakpoints	Ctrl+Shift +F9	Clears all breakpoints in your code.
Step Into	F11	Executes one code statement at a time. If the statement is a call to a procedure, the next statement displayed is the first statement in the procedure.

TABLE 17.2 continued

Option	*Key*	*Description*
Step Over	F10	Executes one code statement at a time. If the current statement contains a call to a procedure, Step Over executes the procedure as a unit, and then steps to the next statement in the current procedure. Therefore, the next statement displayed is the next statement in the current procedure regardless of whether the current statement is a call to another procedure.
Step Out	Shift+F11	Executes the remaining lines of a function in which the current execution point lies. The next statement displayed is the statement following the procedure call. All the code is executed between the current and the final execution points.
Run to Cursor	Ctrl+F10	Specifies a statement further down in your code where you want execution to stop. This option enables you to avoid stepping through large loops.
Restart	Ctrl+Shift +F5	Restarts execution from the beginning of the stored procedure.
Stop Debugging	Shift+F5	Stops the debugging process.
Auto Rollback	n/a	Automatically rolls back all work performed during execution of the procedure.
Help	n/a	Displays the Help topic for the debugger.

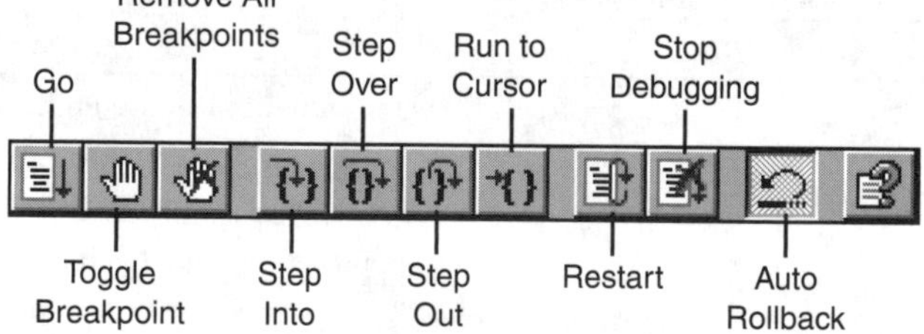

FIGURE 17.7
The T-SQL Debugging toolbar.

In addition to the buttons and keys you can choose from to select any of these options, you can simply right-click in the Code pane to display the pop-up menu shown in Figure 17.8.

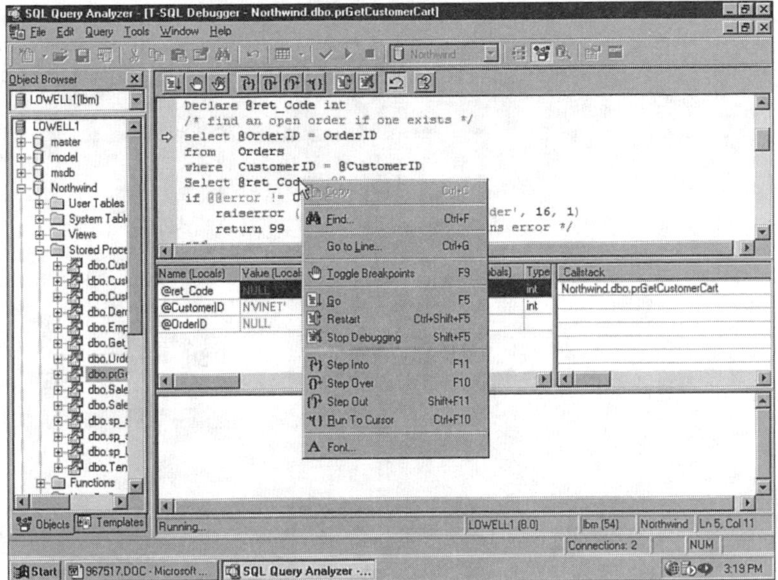

FIGURE 17.8

Using the pop-up menu to select a debugging option.

Setting Breakpoints

Now that you understand what is available to you in the debugging interface, take the next step and learn how to debug the procedure. Although you can execute the procedure simply by pressing F5 or clicking the Run button, doing so will not help you find any problems. What you should do is step through the procedure to see how it executes. One of the strongest tools available to you is the breakpoint. You can instruct the server to stop the execution of the procedure at a specified statement temporarily. This enables you to execute large amounts of SQL without having to step through them and stop where you think the problem is occurring. To set a breakpoint, select a statement in the Code pane and click the Set Breakpoint button or press F9 as shown in Figure 17.9.

A red dot will appear in the left margin, specifying that a breakpoint has been set for this statement. To see how this works, press the F5 key or click the Run button. The procedure will stop at the breakpoint. Processing has stopped at the breakpoint when both the yellow current statement arrow and the breakpoint indicator are on the same statement, as shown in Figure 17.10.

When you are at a breakpoint, you can change the values of any of the local parameters in the procedure to see what effect doing so would have on the execution.

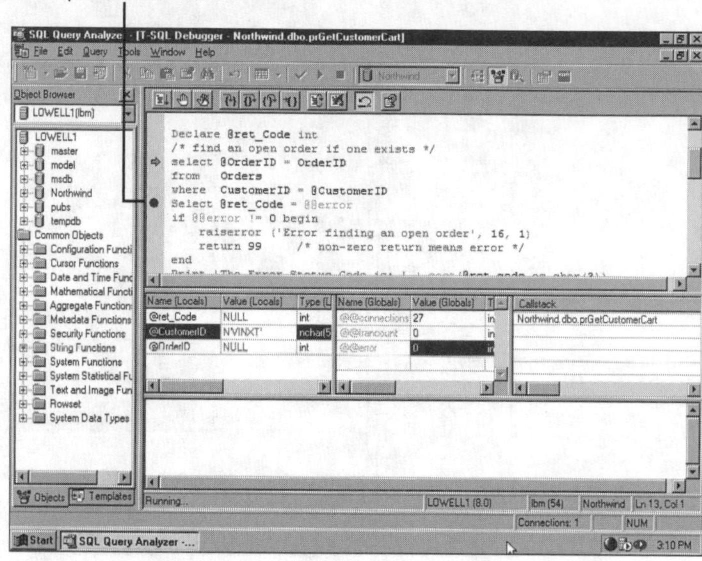
Breakpoint On Indication
SQL Query Analyzer - [T-SQL Debugger - Northwind.dbo.prGetCustomerCart]
Declare @ret_Code int
/* find an open order if one exists */
select @OrderID = OrderID
from Orders
where CustomerID = @CustomerID
Select @ret_Code = @@error
if @@error != 0 begin
raiserror ('Error finding an open order', 16, 1)
return 99 /* non-zero return means error */
end

FIGURE 17.9

Setting a breakpoint in the procedure.

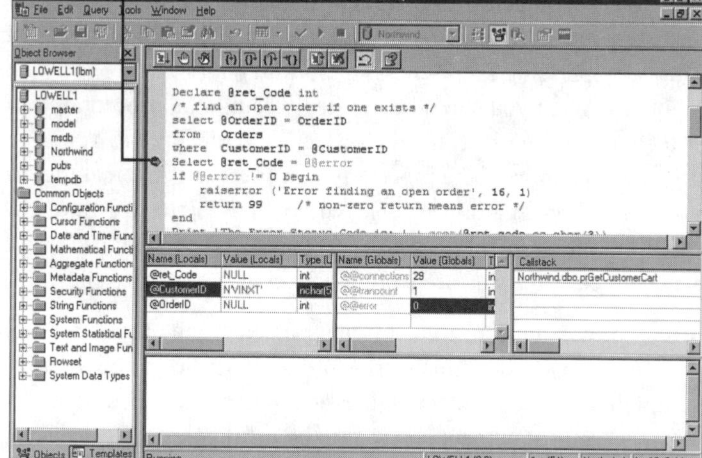
Breakpoint Stop Indication
SQL Query Analyzer - [T-SQL Debugger - Northwind.dbo.prGetCustomerCart]
Declare @ret_Code int
/* find an open order if one exists */
select @OrderID = OrderID
from Orders
where CustomerID = @CustomerID
Select @ret_Code = @@error
if @@error != 0 begin
raiserror ('Error finding an open order', 16, 1)
return 99 /* non-zero return means error */
end

FIGURE 17.10

Stopping at a breakpoint during execution.

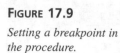

Note When you find a problem and want to fix it, you need to close the debugging session, alter the procedure, and then reopen the T-SQL debugger. You cannot fix the code directly in the debugger window.

Single-Stepping in a Procedure

Wherever you are in the procedure, the different STEP options permit you to execute the procedure slowly to watch how the process proceeds. Restart the procedure you are working with and instead of clicking the Run button or pressing the F5 key, click the Step Into button or press the F11 key. You will see one statement executed and you will then stop at the next statement. You can then check all the parameters, change any if needed, and continue execution. This process of single stepping enables you to check each statement in the procedure as it executes and to verify that the result you expected is correct.

Getting Output

Finally, the Query Result pane at the bottom of the form will display any output from the procedure. This includes any PRINT statements you might have placed in the procedure for testing purposes or for information to the user. Figure 17.11 shows the output of a PRINT statement that I inserted into the procedure as an example.

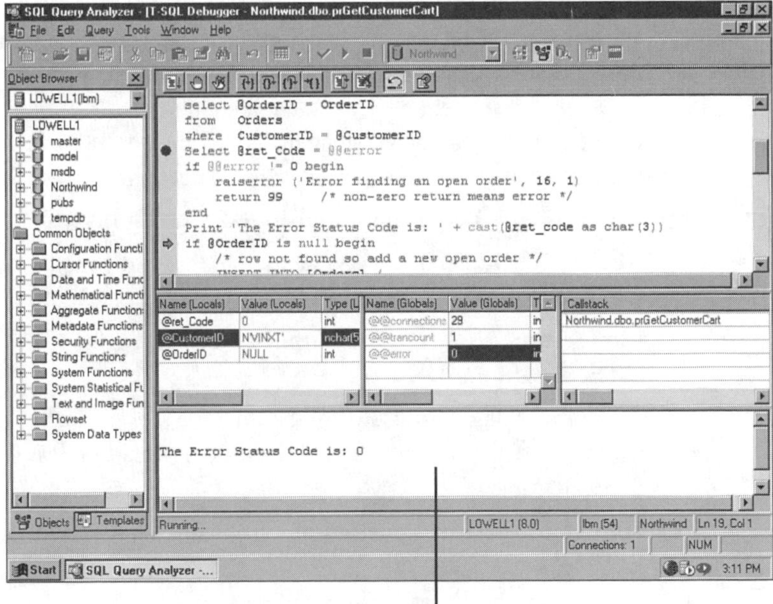

FIGURE 17.11
Displaying information in the Query Result pane.

Summary

Today you have learned several concepts and techniques that should help you to create better more efficient triggers, functions, and stored procedures. You learned that tracking the elapsed time of a procedure will help to determine whether there is a problem in performance. You also saw how to use the `RAISERROR` and `PRINT` statements to display information about the SQL code that you are testing. In addition, you worked with a permanent worktable to store information about the procedure, such as start and end times.

Finally, you learned about the T-SQL debugging tool that is available in the Query Analyzer. The T-SQL debugging tool enables you to work with the stored procedure slowly; one statement at a time, if required. It also enables you to test for conditions (parameter values) that might be very difficult to test for under normal circumstances. This enables you to find many more problems or errors before your users do.

Q&A

Q What is the difference between the `RAISERROR` and `PRINT` statements?

A When using the `RAISERROR` statement, you must use a severity code of 0 if you do not want the procedure to terminate early. When using a severity code of 0, the `RAISERROR` statement behaves much like the `PRINT` statement. But the real difference between these two statements is that the `PRINT` statement enables you to display many of the system variables and functions.

Q Can I use the T-SQL debugger to test a function?

A No. The T-SQL debugger can be used to test and debug only a stored procedure.

Q I have used `PRINT` statements to display information about the procedure that I am testing. However, the output I am looking for takes a long time to print. What is wrong?

A There is nothing wrong. Remember that the server batches output together in packets of 512 bytes. The server will not send a packet until it is full, unless the procedure has completed.

Q How can I execute a portion of a procedure instead of the entire procedure?

A In the Query Analyzer, you can execute a portion of any procedure (function, trigger, or stored procedure) while testing it by selecting the portion you want to execute and then pressing the F5 key or clicking the Run button.

Workshop

The Workshop provides quiz questions to help you solidify your understanding of the material covered and exercises to provide you with experience in using what you've learned. Try to answer the quiz and exercise questions before checking the answers in Appendix A, "Answers to Quizzes and Exercises," and make sure that you understand the answers before continuing to the next lesson.

Quiz

1. What is a breakpoint?
2. What is being displayed in the Local Variables pane?
3. How can comments help in the testing process?

Exercises

Because of the nature of testing and debugging, it is almost impossible to provide exercises for you. I suggest that you work with several of the functions, triggers, and stored procedures to see how the different techniques help. Finally, using the T-SQL debugger, select a stored procedure and test it using the debugger.

WEEK 3

DAY 18

Writing and Testing Triggers

Triggers, a feature of most SQL languages, enable you to attach SQL code to an event such as an `INSERT` request. Triggers enable SQL Server to verify data modifications before they are written and committed to the database. With a trigger, you can check complex data integrity rules, and then perform actions of all kinds on the dependent data. Today, we will cover the following topics:

- What triggers are
- How to create triggers
- How the system executes triggers

In addition to the simple concepts of writing triggers, you will also learn how triggers work. After you have that information, you will learn when triggers are the correct solution to a problem and when they should be avoided.

Understanding Triggers

A trigger is a special class of stored procedure that is defined and designed to execute automatically when an UPDATE, INSERT, or DELETE statement is issued against a table or view in the database. In addition, a trigger can query other tables and can include complex SQL statements. For example, you could control whether to allow an order to be added to the database based on the customer's current account status.

Some of the advantages of using triggers are

- Because triggers are automatic, they are activated immediately after any modification to the table's data, such as a manual entry or an application action.
- They can cascade any changes through related tables in the database.
- They can be used to enforce restrictions that are more complex than can be defined in the table definitions.

Finally, although most T-SQL statements can be used when creating a trigger, the following is a list of statements that cannot be used:

- ALTER DATABASE
- RESTORE LOG
- CREATE DATABASE
- DROP DATABASE
- RECONFIGURE
- RESTORE DATABASE

Writing Your First Trigger

The best way to see how a trigger works is to create one. Let's create a simple trigger for the Employees table on the Northwind database. A CREATE TRIGGER statement looks a lot like the CREATE PROCEDURE statement, with two exceptions:

- A trigger is associated with a table or view, and with one or more actions that will be performed on that table or view.
- A trigger takes no parameters for input or output.

The following is a sample trigger on the Employees table in the Northwind database, which we will use to see how triggers work:

```
Use Northwind
Create Trigger trg_employees
On Employees
For insert, update
```

```
As
Raiserror ('%d rows modified (This is the trigger message)', 0,1,@@rowcount)
```

This trigger will execute whenever you insert or update rows in the `Employees` table. When the trigger executes, it will display the number of rows modified by the statement calling the trigger (`@@rowcount`); that is, when it is called by an `INSERT` or `UPDATE` statement.

To make this trigger known to the database, you need to execute the `CREATE TRIGGER` statement in the Query Analyzer. In addition to executing this statement in the Query Analyzer, you can also create triggers in the Enterprise Manager by right-clicking on the table you want the trigger to be associated with and selecting All Tasks, Manage Triggers from the pop-up menus displayed (see Figure 18.1).

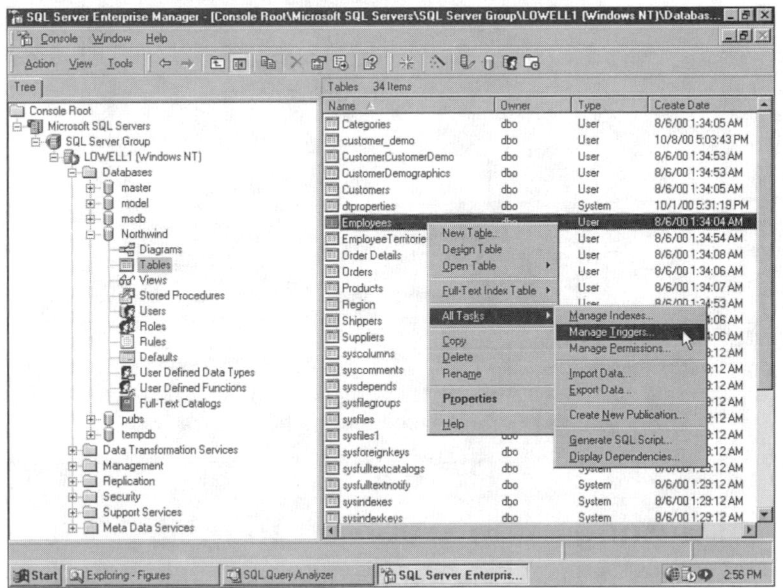

FIGURE 18.1

Displaying the Triggers Properties dialog for a table.

The Trigger Properties dialog displays as shown in Figure 18.2 and allows you either to modify an existing trigger or enter a new trigger for a given table.

After a trigger is created, you can view and modify it in both Enterprise Manager and Query Analyzer. When you want to modify an existing trigger in Enterprise Manager, you would display the Trigger Properties dialog as before, and then select the trigger you want from the drop-down list (see Figure 18.3). This drop-down list also displays icons that specify the actions with which the trigger is used.

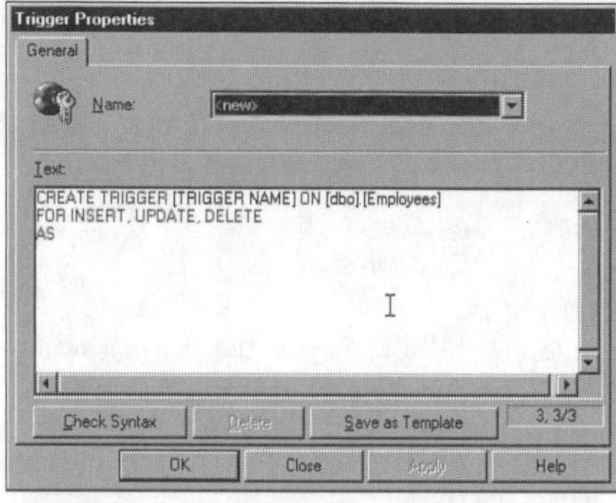

FIGURE 18.2
Creating triggers using the Trigger Properties dialog.

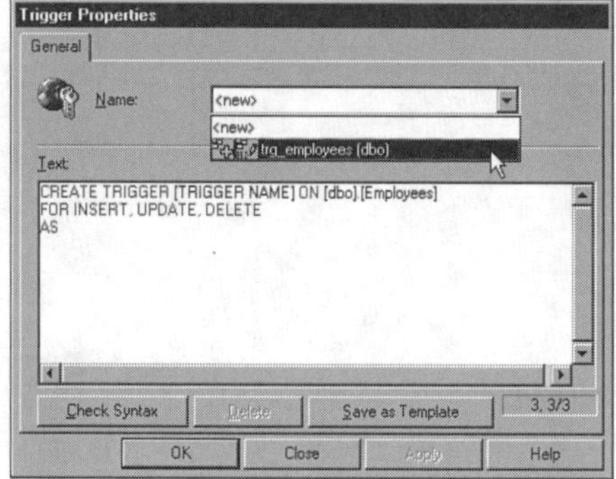

FIGURE 18.3
Selecting a trigger to modify.

> **Note**
>
> It is important to remember that a trigger is not executed directly, but is executed by the server when the `FOR` clause is met.

Getting Information on Triggers

Before we go any further with the discussion of triggers, it is important for you to learn how to see what triggers are associated with which tables, and to look at the code contained in those triggers. You can get this information from the Query Analyzer simply by expanding the database and table you are interested in, and selecting the `Triggers` folder to see what triggers are associated with that table. Figure 18.4 shows this for the `Employees` table and the trigger that we have just created.

FIGURE 18.4

Displaying triggers associated with tables.

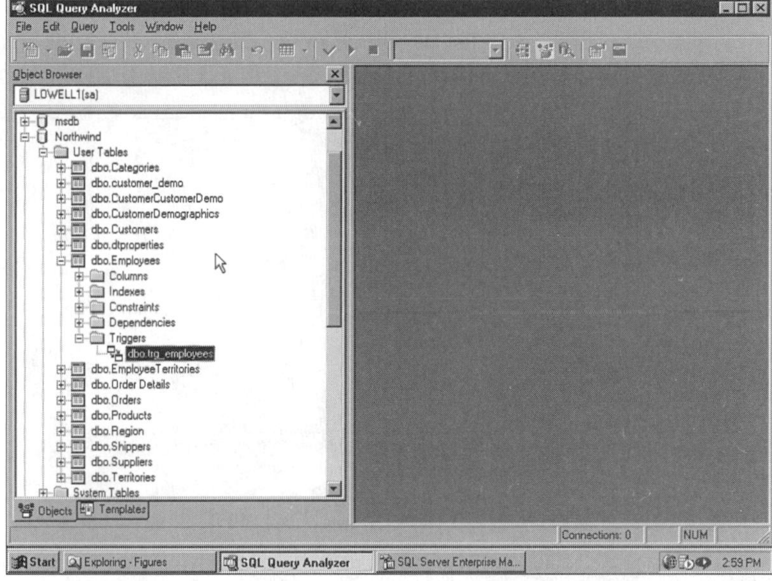

If you right-click on the trigger and select Edit from the pop-up menu, you can modify the SQL code in the trigger as shown in Figure 18.5.

FIGURE 18.5

Editing a trigger in the Query Analyzer.

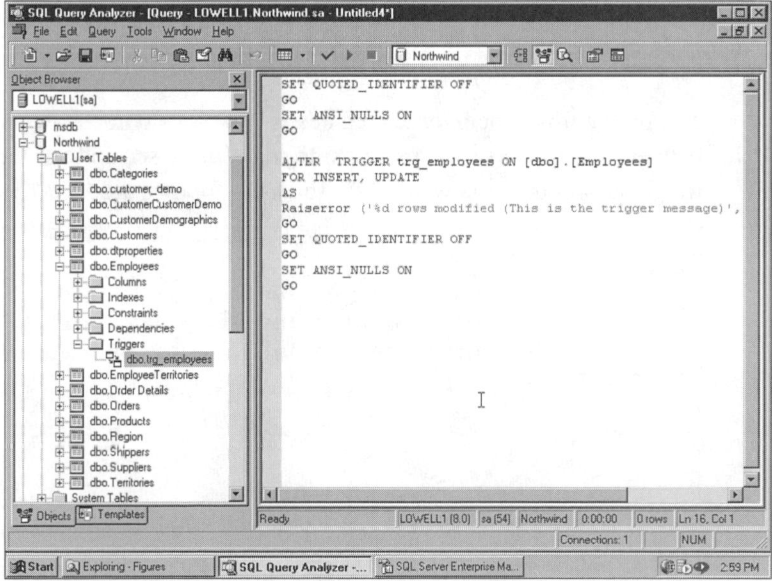

The other way to get information about triggers is to use several of the system stored procedures. To see a list of objects in the database, you would use the `sp_help` procedure. This list will include any triggers defined. The following example shows only the name, owner, and object type. Although there are many more columns and rows, I did not show them for ease of reading.

```
Sp_help
```

Results:

```
Name                                 Owner                      Object_type
------------------------------------ -------------------------- -----------
Alphabetical list of products        dbo                        view
Employees                            dbo                        user table
tr_test1                             dbo                        trigger
```

To see only a list of triggers, try this `SELECT` statement:

```
Select substring(name,1,20) as Name,
       substring(user_name(uid),1,10) as Owner,
       type
From sysobjects
Where type = 'TR'
```

Results:

```
Name                 Owner      type
-------------------- ---------- ----
trg_employees             dbo        TR

(1 row(s) affected)
```

The problem with both these methods is that they do not show you the relationship between the triggers and the tables. If you want to see a list of the table and the related triggers (of course you want to see this), the following `SELECT` statement would show it to you:

```
Select substring(name,1,20) as Name,
       substring(object_name(instrig),1,10) as 'Insert',
       substring(object_name(updtrig),1,10) as 'Update',
       substring(object_name(deltrig),1,10) as 'Delete'
From sysobjects
Where type = 'U'
      and (instrig <> 0 or updtrig <> 0 or deltrig <> 0)
```

Results:

```
Name                 Insert     Update     Delete
-------------------- ---------- ---------- ----------
Employees            trg_employees   trg_employees   trg_employees

(1 row(s) affected)
```

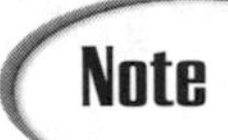

I have been using the SUBSTRING function as discussed on Day 3, "Working with Columns," to reduce the number of blanks that are being displayed by the output.

The system table, SYSOBJECTS, contains a list of all objects, including tables and triggers. The columns INSTRIG, UPDTRIG, and DELTRIG store the object ids of the triggers for each table. If the trigger id is 0, there is no trigger for that action, for that table.

Finally, if you know the name of the trigger (and you should), you can display the text of the trigger by using the sp_helptext procedure as shown here:

```
Sp_helptext trg_employees

Text
---------------------------------------------------------------------------
CREATE TRIGGER trg_employees ON [dbo].[Employees]
FOR INSERT, UPDATE, DELETE
AS
Raiserror ('%d rows modified (This is the trigger message)', 0,1,@@rowcount)
```

The sp_helptext procedure displays the text of the trigger at the time it was created. Remember to save the SQL scripts that you wrote to re-create triggers, procedures, views, and other objects in case of a system failure.

Maintaining Triggers

You have already seen how to actually modify, delete, or rename triggers by using the Query Analyzer or Enterprise Manager. However, there are a couple of things to know about maintaining triggers. In addition to the tools you can use to delete a trigger, you can also use the DROP TRIGGER statement as shown:

```
Drop Trigger trg_employees
```

This statement would remove the trigger from the table. After this statement is executed, there would be no INSERT or UPDATE trigger for the table.

Instead of dropping a trigger, you could replace it with another (differently named) one without first dropping the old trigger. The newly defined trigger would replace the old one, but only for the actions specified in the new trigger. If you created a new trigger as shown, it would replace the update action of the previous trigger.

```
Create Trigger trg_employees
On Employees
For update
As
Raiserror ('%d rows have been updated (This is the trigger message)',
            0,1,@@rowcount)
```

At this point, the new trigger is responsible for handling any updates, but the old one still handles inserts.

Naming Triggers

Although there is no required way to name a trigger, you should create a convention that you understand and stay with it. If you will be using T-SQL at work, you should find out whether your company has any naming standards that you must follow. If your company doesn't have naming standards, let me explain the conventions I use for naming.

For each of the different objects that I work with, I prefix the actual name with an abbreviation that tells me the type of object it is. For example, all my views start with `vw_`, whereas all my stored procedures begin with `sp_`. You can probably figure out how I name my triggers, but I add a little extra for triggers. In addition to a prefix of `tr_`, I add a suffix that consists of one to three letters, telling me what actions this trigger is for. An example of a trigger that works for all three actions is

```
Tr_Employees_IDU
```

This tells me that the trigger works for `INSERT`, `DELETE`, and `UPDATE`.

If you follow this convention or invent your own, the name of the trigger will provide you with a good deal of information and enable you to scan the objects more quickly when you need to find triggers referencing a particular table.

Executing Triggers

Triggers are very much like stored procedures in that you must define them to store them in the database. It is also true that like a stored procedure, triggers are not executed when you create them. However, the difference between stored procedures and triggers comes in when they are executed. You control when a stored procedure is executed, whereas the SQL Server controls when a trigger is executed. To see how this works, we will execute an `UPDATE` statement on the `Employees` table for which we created a trigger in the previous section. The following `UPDATE` statement will make a minor change to the `Employees` table:

```
Update Employees
Set City = 'New york'
Where City = 'Seattle'
```

Results:

```
2 rows modified (This is the trigger message)

(2 row(s) affected)
```

The first line that is displayed in the output is our trigger message; the second is the standard row count information that is displayed by Query Analyzer. If you look at the output, it seems as if the trigger executed before our rows were updated, but that is not true. The Query Analyzer, not the SQL Server, generates the line `(2 rows affected)`, telling how many rows have been modified, inserted, or deleted. The trigger was actually executed after the `UPDATE` statement was processed.

When Do Triggers Fire?

A trigger is executed based on how you have defined that particular trigger. You can specify one of the following options:

`AFTER`	Specifies the action that, when performed, will fire the trigger. The trigger will execute after the action is performed on the database. This is the default option.
`FOR`	Specifies the action that, when performed, will fire the trigger. The trigger will execute after the action is performed on the database. Specifying `FOR` is the same as specifying `AFTER`.
`INSTEAD OF`	Specifies that this trigger should execute instead of the triggering action.

To get a better picture of when the trigger actually fires, let's execute an `UPDATE` statement. However, let's look at the data in the table first.

```
select city, region
from employees
where region = 'WA'
```

Results:

```
city            region
--------------- ---------------
New york        WA
Tacoma          WA
Kirkland        WA
Redmond         WA
New york        WA
NULL            WA

(6 row(s) affected)
```

```
Update Employees
set city = 'Seattle'
Where city = 'New york'
```

Results:

```
2 rows modified (This is the trigger message)
(2 row(s) affected)
```

Two rows met the `WHERE` condition in the `UPDATE` statement. The trigger executes only once, when it reports the number of rows modified.

> The key to remember is that no matter how many rows were modified by the triggering action, the trigger itself executes only one time.

Even if the triggering statement modified no rows, the trigger will still execute. This is important to remember because when you start writing triggers, you will need to take into account all of the following possibilities:

- One row was modified.
- Two or more rows were modified.
- No rows were modified.

You will find that the trigger code you write will be more complex than most of the other code because of these possibilities.

How Does a Trigger Fire?

To write better triggers, let's review what really happens when a trigger is fired. After you have an understanding of the methods that are used to manage and execute a trigger, you will be better able to understand how the system behaves and write better SQL code. Let's take a closer look at an `UPDATE` statement and its related trigger. An update is the most complex action that is performed by the server, and from this process, you can probably guess how inserts and deletes work.

Figure 18.6 shows an action flow diagram that lists the tasks performed while a trigger is being executed. An update actually consists of two separate steps: the deleting of the original rows (tasks 2–5) and the inserting of the updated rows (tasks 6–9). After all nine tasks are completed, but before the transaction has been committed (task 11), the server will execute the trigger (task 10).

Note

> In terms of what actually happens, an `UPDATE` is treated as a `DELETE` followed by an `INSERT`. From a logical point of view, the `DELETE` and `INSERT` are not visible to the user. For instance, the `INSERT` trigger is not fired when an `UPDATE` is performed.

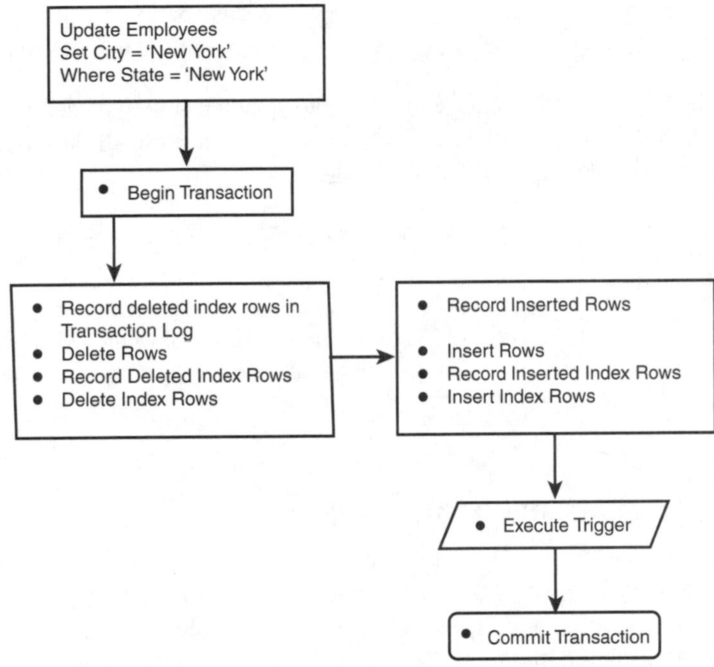
Update Employees
Set City = 'New York'
Where State = 'New York'
• Begin Transaction
• Record deleted index rows in Transaction Log
• Delete Rows
• Record Deleted Index Rows
• Delete Index Rows
• Record Inserted Rows
• Insert Rows
• Record Inserted Index Rows
• Insert Index Rows
• Execute Trigger
• Commit Transaction

FIGURE 18.6
Action flow diagram of how an update is processed.

To see how the resources are used and what is actually happening, let's examine these steps a little closer.

Step 1	Begin Transaction	This step starts a transaction and is used to identify the batch of work that will be performed by this session until either a `COMMIT` or `ROLLBACK TRANSACTION` is executed.
Step 2	Delete Data (Tasks 2–5)	This is the first part of an update. It removes the old version of the rows, along with any index references to those rows. The deleted data is first logged.
Step 3	Insert Data (Tasks 6–9)	SQL Server inserts the now-modified rows into the table, along with any related index values. Before the inserts are done, the inserted rows are logged.
Step 4	Execute Trigger	If there is an `UPDATE` trigger on the table, it is executed now, after the rows are modified, but before the transaction is committed.

Step 5	Commit Transaction	This operation will end the transaction and commit the updates to the database.

If this all seems complex and slow, it actually can be; you are allowed to be concerned. Although it is complex, it is usually very fast because all the work prior to an actual `COMMIT` command takes place in memory.

> From a performance point of view, the most important thing to remember is the locking process. When your trigger is running, there are almost always locks in place. Other users will end up waiting while your trigger executes. This means that trigger processing has to be as quick and small as possible and very efficient.

INSTEAD OF Triggers

`INSTEAD OF` triggers are used to override the standard actions of the triggering statement (`INSERT`, `UPDATE`, or `DELETE`). For example, an `INSTEAD OF` trigger can be defined to perform error or value checking on one or more columns, and then perform any additional actions before inserting the record. For instance, when a new order is being inserted into the `Orders` table, a trigger can first check whether the item being ordered is in stock. If it is, the insert will be performed; if not, an error message can be displayed.

The primary advantage of `INSTEAD OF` triggers is that they give you the ability to update views that would not normally be updateable. A view that contains multiple tables must use an `INSTEAD OF` trigger to support inserts, updates, and deletes that reference data in the tables. Another advantage of `INSTEAD OF` triggers is that they enable you to modify the logic so that you can reject certain rows of data without performing the action, and still allow the other rows to be processed.

An `INSTEAD OF` trigger can take any of the following actions:

- Ignoring parts of a batch
- Not processing a part of a batch and then saving the problem rows in an error table
- Taking a different action if an error occurs

By using the `INSTEAD OF` trigger to code this type of logic, you prevent all applications that access this table from having to duplicate this logic in its code.

The `INSTEAD OF INSERT` trigger is used to replace the standard action of the `INSERT` statement. Usually, the `INSTEAD OF INSERT` trigger is defined on a view to insert data into one or more base tables. Columns referenced in the view can either allow nulls or not. If a column in the view does not allow nulls, the INSERT statement must provide values for the column.

When writing the INSTEAD OF INSERT trigger, you can use the ALLOWSNULL property of the COLUMNPROPERTY function to see whether a view column allows nulls.

As an example, if a view joins two tables together, the INSTEAD OF INSERT trigger would actually perform two separate INSERT statements to perform the requested action.

The INSTEAD OF UPDATE and INSTEAD OF DELETE triggers both work like the INSTEAD OF INSERT trigger, except that you are replacing the UPDATE or DELETE action and not the INSERT action. Both triggers are used on a view to modify or delete data in one or more base tables.

Using Trigger Resources

Triggers have access to resources and information that other T-SQL statements don't. They can roll back transactions, undoing an action. They can look at both the old and new versions of rows that are being modified by a statement. And they can determine which columns were modified. To see how all this works, we will write some simple examples to show how these resources are used.

Accessing the INSERTED and DELETED Tables

In the section where I described the program flow of an UPDATE statement, you saw that all the deletes and inserts are written to a log file. Those logged rows are available to a trigger as the INSERTED and DELETED tables. SQL Server 2000 automatically creates and manages these two tables. You can use the temporary tables to test the effects of certain changes and to set the condition for trigger actions; however, you cannot change the data in the tables directly.

The DELETED table stores copies of the affected rows from the UPDATE and DELETE statements. During the execution of either of these statements, the rows are deleted from the trigger table and written to the DELETED table.

The INSERTED table stores copies of the affected rows from the UPDATE and INSERT statements. During an insert or update transaction, new rows are added simultaneously to both the trigger table and the INSERTED table.

Within the trigger code, you can use a SELECT statement with the INSERTED and DELETED tables just like you can any other table in the database. For example, to get a better idea of what these tables are, you can display their contents when a trigger fires. Create the following trigger on the Customers table:

```
Use Northwind
Go
Create Trigger tr_Table_Demo
On Customers
For Insert, Update
as
Select Customerid, city, country from Inserted
print '****Deleted Table Info****'
Select Customerid, city, country from Deleted
```

> I created the preceding trigger to select only a few of the columns from the INSERTED and DELETED tables to make it easier to display in the book.

Now, execute the following simple update on the Customers table:

```
update customers
set city = 'New York'
Where city = 'Paris'
```

Results:

```
****Inserted Table Info****
Customerid city            country
---------- --------------- ---------------
PARIS      New York        France
SPECD      New York        France

(2 row(s) affected)

****Deleted Table Info****
Customerid city            country
---------- --------------- ---------------
PARIS      Paris           France
SPECD      Paris           France

(2 row(s) affected)
```

The trigger will display the contents of the INSERTED and DELETED tables. If the requested action was an insert, the INSERTED table would have data in it and the DELETED table would be empty. You should also notice that the INSERTED and DELETED tables have the same structure as the table you are working with, right down to the column names.

Using these tables in a trigger, you can validate column values and row consistency and determine whether rows are ready for archiving, maintain an archive, or update derived values, or even create an audit trail of any modifications to a table.

The INSERTED and DELETED tables are only available within the processing scope of a trigger.

Using the UPDATE() Function

The UPDATE() function allows you to check whether a particular column was modified in the triggering INSERT or UPDATE statement. As with the INSERTED and DELETED tables, the UPDATE() function is available only within the scope of a trigger. Listing 18.1 shows an example of a trigger on the Customers table that uses the UPDATE() function to determine whether the City column was updated.

LISTING 18.1 Creating a Trigger on the Customers Table

```
Create Trigger tr_CustTable_Demo
On customers
For Insert, Update
as
If Update(city)
begin
    If (Select Distinct country from Inserted) <> 'USA'
    Begin
         Raiserror('Cannot update International Cities',16,10)
         Rollback Transaction
    end
end
```

To test this new trigger, execute the following SQL statement:

```
update customers
set city = 'New York'
Where city = 'Paris'
```

Results:

```
Validating the City Input
Server: Msg 50000, Level 16, State 10, Procedure tr_Table_Demo, Line 11
Cannot update International Cities
```

You can see that the UPDATE() function is true, so the message stating that the city input was being validated is printed. Because the rows selected do not have 'USA' in the

`Country` column, the update is cancelled using the `ROLLBACK TRANSACTION` statement (you will learn more about that statement in the next section).

Triggers do not sort through the data and inform you which rows failed and which actually worked. They are responsible for managing data integrity and preventing invalid data from entering the system.

Using Rollback in a Trigger

You already know how to use the `ROLLBACK TRANSACTION` statement as well as the `COMMIT TRANSACTION` statement from Day 13, "Programming with Transactions." As you know, when `ROLLBACK TRANSACTION` is executed, the server will reverse all the work performed since the outermost `BEGIN TRANSACTION` statement. If there was no explicit `BEGIN TRANSACTION` statement, `the ROLLBACK TRANSACTION` will reverse all the work since the process was started.

You have already seen how this works in Listing 18.1 where we updated the `Customers` table. But what if you had written a transaction in which you performed three separate updates to the table as shown in the following SQL code?

```
Select City, Country From Customers Where Country = 'USA'
Begin Transaction
    Update Customers Set City = 'New York' Where City = 'Portland'
    Update Customers Set City = 'Albany' Where City = 'Seattle'
    Update Customers Set City = 'New York' Where City = 'Paris'
Commit Transaction
Go
Select City, Country From Customers Where Country = 'USA'
```

When you execute this transaction, you would see the following output:

```
City            Country
--------------- ---------------
Eugene          USA
Elgin           USA
Walla Walla     USA
San Francisco   USA
Portland        USA
Anchorage       USA
Albuquerque     USA
Boise           USA
Lander          USA
Portland        USA
Butte           USA
Kirkland        USA
Seattle         USA
```

```
(13 row(s) affected)

Validating the City Input

(2 row(s) affected)

Validating the City Input

(1 row(s) affected)

Validating the City Input
Server: Msg 50000, Level 16, State 10, Procedure tr_Table_Demo, Line 11
Cannot update International Cities
City            Country
--------------- ---------------
Eugene          USA
Elgin           USA
Walla Walla     USA
San Francisco   USA
Portland        USA
Anchorage       USA
Albuquerque     USA
Boise           USA
Lander          USA
Portland        USA
Butte           USA
Kirkland        USA
Seattle         USA

(13 row(s) affected)
```


If you take a close look, you will notice that none of the updates were actually committed to the table. The reason for this is that the last update was invalid and the trigger executed a `ROLLBACK TRANSACTION` statement. This in effect cancelled all the updates because they were not yet committed. To prevent this from happening, you must be very careful how you code transactions that affect tables with triggers. The following modified SQL code would perform what you expected from the preceding code:

```
Select City, Country From Customers Where Country = 'USA'
Begin Transaction
    Update Customers Set City = 'New York' Where City = 'Portland'
    Commit Transaction
    Update Customers Set City = 'Albany' Where City = 'Seattle'
    Commit Transaction
    Update Customers Set City = 'New York' Where City = 'Paris'
    Commit Transaction
```

```
go
Select City, Country From Customers Where Country = 'USA'
```

This is just one of the possible ways to write transactions with tables that have triggers.

Another way is to change the trigger to commit the update if it is validated correctly, as shown in the following example:

```
Create Trigger tr_CustTable_Demo
On customers
For Insert, Update
as
If Update(city)
begin
    If (Select Distinct country from Inserted) <> 'USA'
    Begin
        Raiserror('Cannot update International Cities',16,10)
        Rollback Transaction
        Return
    end
    Commit Transaction
end
```

Make sure that whatever method you use, you handle any errors that might roll back a transaction without having any 'good' actions cancelled at the same time.

Determining When to Use Triggers

When you are creating a SQL database, you must choose whether you want to write all your table modification scripts using standard SQL, or put many of the modification routines into stored procedures. If you use stored procedures to handle these modifications and you revoke any direct permission to insert, update, and delete rows from the tables, you probably don't need to use triggers. However, if you choose not to use stored procedures, or you cannot use them due to restrictions in the database connection software you are using, triggers are the only way to get things done efficiently.

Triggers become part of the table by attaching themselves to one or more of the standard actions against that table. After you have created a trigger for an action on a table, the trigger will fire every time that action occurs. This doesn't mean that you should use triggers to perform all the validation on the database. There are many other ways to perform many of the data validation tasks. For example, indexes are far quicker to check uniqueness than triggers. What follows is a list of some of the do's and don'ts of using triggers.

Do	Don't
Check `@@rowcount` at the beginning of a trigger and exit the trigger if the value is zero	Make changes to the same table the trigger is on
Check for errors after every statement that modifies data	Return rows of data to the user from a trigger
Raise an error before issuing a rollback	Do anything in a trigger that you can easily do somewhere else
	Avoid triggers because they are difficult

Summary

What you have seen in today's lesson is how to create and use one of the most misunderstood and powerful tools in a SQL database. A trigger enables you to specify a set of SQL statements that you want executed either instead of or after one of the three data modification actions is performed. Remember that a trigger is executed only once per triggering statement, no matter how many rows are being modified by the statement.

The SQL Server will use transactions and locks to ensure that a trigger will run by itself. Your trigger also has access to the `INSERTED` and `DELETED` tables, which give you the information about the data being modified, both before and after the modification.

Finally, because you cannot specify when the trigger should or should not be fired, the code you write for triggers should be optimized for good performance and well tested. This includes a well-planned error handling routine.

Q&A

Q Are there any actions that I cannot do in a trigger?

A There are several things that you cannot do within a trigger. They are

- Creating or dropping objects or databases
- Altering tables or database
- Truncating tables
- Modifying privileges
- Reconfiguring the server
- Loading databases

Q Which is faster, a trigger or a stored procedure?

A Stored procedures and triggers use the same execution methods to run. So, they are actually the same. However, triggers are fired after the data modifications are performed, so if any of the data checks in the trigger fails, the changes must be rolled back. This causes a lot of extra work.

In a stored procedure, you can perform all the checks first, and if everything passes, the data modification can be performed.

Q Can I define a trigger to a system table?

A There are certain system tables on which you can create a trigger, but there is no list that I have found telling me which ones will allow it and work.

Workshop

The Workshop provides quiz questions to help you solidify your understanding of the material covered and exercises to provide you with experience in using what you've learned. Try to answer the quiz and exercise questions before checking the answers in Appendix A, "Answers to Quizzes and Exercises," and make sure that you understand the answers before continuing to the next lesson.

Quiz

1. What is wrong with the following triggers' error handler?

```
If @@Error <> 0
  Raiserror ('Trigger error: Rolling back', 16, 1)
  Rollback Transaction
  Return
```

2. If inserted rows go into the `INSERTED` table and deleted rows go into the `DELETED` table, where do updated rows go?

Exercise

Create a trigger on the `Order Detail` table in the `Northwind` database so that whenever an order is entered, modified, or deleted, `UnitsInStock` is properly updated. However, if an order causes `UnitsInStock` to drop below zero, raise an error and roll back the transaction.

DAY 19

Solving Special Trigger Problems

As you have learned on Day 18, "Writing and Testing Triggers," triggers give you the ability to have SQL code execute automatically whenever an action, `INSERT`, `UPDATE`, or `DELETE` is taken against a table. Now that you know how to create triggers and where you should use them, you will see how they can assist you in solving some special requirements in an application.

When designing and creating a complex application that uses T-SQL to access data in a relational database, there will be times when you will want to ensure that certain business rules are enforced. There will also be a need for a particular update to be made throughout multiple tables. By using triggers, you can accomplish these goals. Some of the topics we will cover in today's lesson are

- Enforcing business rules
- Referential integrity
- Cascading triggers
- Managing summary columns
- Creating an audit trail

Managing Referential Integrity with Triggers

Referential integrity (RI) is used to preserve the defined relationships between tables when rows are inserted or deleted. In SQL Server 2000, referential integrity is based on the relationships between foreign keys and primary keys or between foreign keys and unique keys defined on tables in a database. This process ensures that key values are consistent across all tables in the database. This requires that there are no references to nonexistent values and, if a key value changes, all references to it change consistently throughout the database. When you enforce referential integrity in your database, SQL Server prevents users from

- Adding records to a related table if there is no associated record in the primary table
- Changing values in a primary table that result in orphaned records in a related table
- Deleting records from a primary table if there are matching related records

For example, with the `Customers` and `Orders` tables in the `Northwind` database, referential integrity is based on the relationship between the foreign key (`CustomerID`) in the `Orders` table and the primary key (`CustomerID`) in the `Customers` table. This relationship is shown in Figure 19.1.

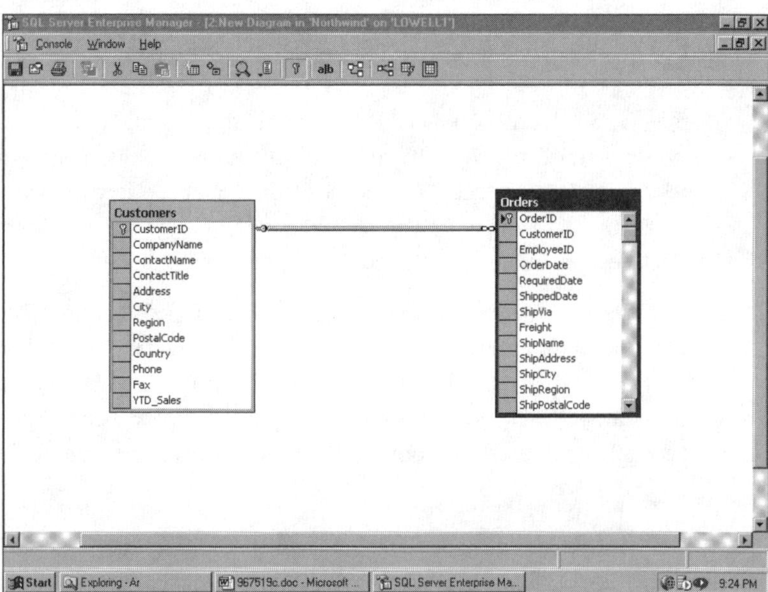

FIGURE 19.1

The Parent Child relationship between the `Orders` *and the* `Customers` *tables over the* `CustomerID` *fields.*

A trigger can be used to maintain referential integrity between two tables in much the same way a foreign key can. Of course, foreign keys are more efficient because they are tested before any data is changed, as opposed to triggers, which are fired after the data changes. The primary benefit of triggers is that they enable you to add complex processing using T-SQL code.

Implementing triggers instead of using foreign keys is vital to the success of cascading delete and update triggers, which will be covered later in this lesson.

Enforcing Referential Integrity with Triggers

In addition to using constraints to define referential integrity within a database, you can also use triggers to perform this task. In fact, the primary function of a trigger is to enforce referential integrity and any business rules that are needed. They are especially useful in cascading updates and deletes, as you will see later in this lesson. Executing triggers and testing their conditions are last in line when any data modifications are made to the database. Constraints, on the other hand, are tested first before the modification is made. If any constraint is violated, the trigger(s) associated with that table would never be executed. Listing 19.1 is an example of a trigger that enforces referential integrity on a database. This trigger will verify that a valid customer number exists in the `Customers` table before an order is added to the `Orders` table.

Listing 19.1 Creating a Trigger on the Orders table

```
Create Trigger tr_Customer_Orders
On Orders
For Insert, Update As
If (
Select Count(*)
From Customers Inner Join
     Inserted on
     Customers.Customerid = inserted.Customerid) = 0
Begin
   Print 'The Customer Number you have entered is invalid!'
   Print ' and does not exist in the Customers table!'
   Print 'The Transaction has been cancelled.'
   Rollback Transaction
   Return
End
```

The trigger in Listing 19.1 will work on any single `UPDATE` or `INSERT` performed on the `Orders` table. It checks whether there is a valid customer number in the `Customers` table.

If you run a `SELECT INTO`, this trigger might not execute properly. When there are multiple rows to be processed, you should check to make sure that the row count of customer numbers that are inserted matches the numbers of orders you are adding. The code to handle multiple rows of data is shown in Listing 19.2, which uses the code in Listing 19.1 as a starting point.

LISTING 19.2 Processing Multiple Rows in a Trigger

```
Create Trigger tr_Customer_Orders
On Orders
For Insert, Update As
If (
Select Count(*)
From Customers Inner Join
     Inserted on
     Customers.Customerid = inserted.Customerid) = 0
Begin
   Print 'The Customer Number you have entered is invalid!'
   Print ' and does not exist in the Customers table!'
   Print 'The Transaction has been cancelled.'
   Rollback Transaction
   Return
End
If (
Select Count(*)
From Customers Inner Join
     Inserted on
     Customers.Customerid = inserted.Customerid) = @@rowcount
Begin
   Print 'There is at least one order referencing an invalid'
   Print ' Customer number!'
   Print 'The Transaction has been cancelled.'
   Rollback Transaction
   Return
End
```

Note

> If you have executed the first `CREATE TRIGGER` in this section, you should remember to `DROP` the trigger before creating the updated version.

As you can see, triggers can be very powerful for testing multiple or complex conditions before allowing a data modification to be applied to the database.

Enforcing Business Rules with Triggers

In addition to testing conditions for referential integrity, such as validating customer numbers as shown in the previous section, triggers also enable you to test and modify any change being made to data in the database. When you need to reference other tables to validate a business rule, you must use a trigger because this type of action is not allowed in a constraint. An example of a business rule is shown in the following T-SQL code:

```
Create Trigger tr_Product_UnitsOnOrder
On Products
For Delete As
If (Select count(*)
    From deleted
    Where Deleted.UnitsOnOrder > 0) > 0
Begin
   Print 'This product has orders against it'
   Print 'That are still waiting for delivery'
   Print 'The delete is cancelled'
   Rollback Transaction
End
```

This trigger will test whether a product being deleted has any orders open against it. If the product has units on order, the delete will not be allowed.

Note

If you try to run a `DELETE` statement against the `Products` table in the `Northwind` database, you will probably get an error message as shown:

```
Server: Msg 547, Level 16, State 1, Line 1
DELETE statement conflicted with COLUMN REFERENCE
constraint 'FK_Order_Details_Products'.
The conflict occurred in database 'Northwind',
 table 'Order Details', column 'ProductID'.
The statement has been terminated.
```

You get an error message because there is a foreign key constraint defined in the `Order Details` table for the `ProductID` in the `Products` table. If you delete this constraint and then test this trigger by executing a delete against the `Products` table, you will get the response you were expecting.

You will see later in this lesson that triggers can also be used to perform calculations with the data and update the same table or other tables with this calculated information.

Cascading Update and Delete Triggers

In many instances, standard referential integrity does not take into account business reasons for performing a particular type of database action. For example, if your database contains large amounts of archived sales data, you might want to allow the deletion of a row in the `Products` table if the product has not been sold for a particular period of time, or if it no longer useful.

The trick to this is that you would have to delete all the related sales data or you would violate the database's referential integrity (`ProductID` in the `Order Details` table that does not have a match in the `Products` table). Triggers are used to solve this problem. A trigger that performs this complicated task is called a *cascading trigger*. The trigger actually cascades the delete from the `Products` table to the `Order Details` table and the `Orders` table.

To see how the different types of cascading triggers work, we will be using the `PUBS` database. However, to bypass any referential integrity that might be defined on the database, we will copy several of the tables without defining any constraints for referential integrity. The following SQL script will make copies of the tables used in the next several examples. We will look at the `Stores` table and its relationships with the `Discounts` and `Sales` tables in the `PUBS` database.

```
Use Pubs
Select * Into ex_stores From stores
Select * Into ex_discounts From discounts
Select * Into ex_sales From sales
```

If you look at these tables in the Query Analyzer, you will see that there are no constraints, dependencies, or triggers defined. This allows us to see how cascading triggers work without any referential integrity rules in place.

Cascading Delete Triggers

A *cascading delete trigger* is a delete that moves down a chain of dependent tables, from a primary key to a set of foreign keys. For this discussion, we will see how a delete trigger on the `Stores` table will cause a corresponding deletion of matching rows in the `ex_Discounts` and `ex_Sales` tables. The trigger will use the `Stor_id` column in the `ex_Stores` table as a unique key to locate and delete all matching rows in the other two tables. The example in Listing 19.3 shows a fairly simple delete trigger.

LISTING 19.3 Deleting Rows in a Trigger

```
Create Trigger tr_Stores_Del
On ex_Stores
For Delete As
```

LISTING 19.3 continued

```
If @@rowcount = 0 Return
Delete ex_Sales
Where ex_Sales.Stor_id in
      (Select del1.stor_id from deleted as del1)
Delete ex_Discounts
Where ex_Discounts.Stor_id in
      (Select del2.stor_id from deleted as del2)
```

This trigger will delete all sales and discounts information for the stores that were deleted. You can test whether this trigger works by using the SQL script in Listing 19.4. The script uses a transaction process to roll back the delete so that the rows of data are not really deleted.

LISTING 19.4 SQL Script to Test a Trigger

```
Use Pubs
Set Nocount on
Begin Transaction

Delete ex_Stores where stor_id = '8042'

Select count(*) as StoresAfterDel from ex_stores where stor_id = '8042'
Select count(*) as SalesAfterDel from ex_sales where stor_id = '8042'
Select count(*) as DiscAfterDel from ex_discounts where stor_id = '8042'

Rollback Transaction

Select count(*) as StoresBeforeDel from ex_stores where stor_id = '8042'
Select count(*) as SalesBeforeDel from ex_sales where stor_id = '8042'
Select count(*) as DiscBeforeDel from ex_discounts where stor_id = '8042'
```


The output of this script is

```
StoresAfterDel
--------------
0

SalesAfterDel
-------------
0

DiscAfterDel
------------
0
```

```
StoresBeforeDel
---------------
1

SalesBeforeDel
--------------
4

DiscBeforeDel
-------------
1
```

You can see that the rows for store number 8042 were all deleted from each table, and after the transaction was rolled back, the rows were replaced.

Listing 19.5 is an example of a cascading delete trigger, we will take the previous example and have it test for a date range before allowing the deletion to occur. Using the same store number, 8042, I first listed all the rows in the `Sales` table as shown:

stor_id	ord_num	ord_date	qty	payterms	title_id
8042	423LL922	1994-09-14 00:00:00.000	15	ON invoice	MC3021
8042	423LL930	1994-09-14 00:00:00.000	10	ON invoice	BU1032
8042	P723	1993-03-11 00:00:00.000	25	Net 30	BU1111
8042	QA879.1	1993-05-22 00:00:00.000	30	Net 30	PC1035

For this example, we will allow the deletion only if there are no orders from the year 1993.

LISTING 19.5 A Cascading Delete Trigger

```
Create Trigger tr_Stores_Del
On ex_Stores
For Delete As
If @@rowcount = 0 Return
If Exists(
    Select * From Deleted as del inner join
                  ex_sales as Sa on
                  del.stor_id = Sa.stor_id
             Where Year(Sa.ord_date) = 1993)
Begin
   Print 'Sales Exists for the year 1993.'
   Print 'The transaction has been cancelled!'
   Rollback Transaction
   Return
End
Delete ex_Sales
Where ex_Sales.Stor_id in
      (Select del1.stor_id from deleted as del1)
```

LISTING 19.5 continued

```
19:Delete ex_Discounts
20:Where ex_Discounts.Stor_id in
21:      (Select del2.stor_id from deleted as del2)
```

As always, the `IF` statement that checks the system variable `@@rowcount` is there and quickly exits the trigger if no rows were affected by the `DELETE` statement. To see how this will change the process, try changing the year in the `WHERE` clause (line 9) to a different year to see how the condition works. The final piece to this trigger is to check for any errors before exiting the trigger. If an error occurred, there is a strong possibility that all of the required deletes might not have happened. The following should be added to the end of the trigger:

```
If @@error <> 0
Begin
 Raiserror ('Store Delete Trigger has Failed, Transaction Rolled back!', 16, 1)
 Rollback Transaction
 Return
End
```

There is a disadvantage in the method shown in Listing 19.5. The server is forced to access the deleted table three times: once to test the condition (line 6), and twice to perform the deletions on the related tables (lines 16 and 19). There is an alternative to this method. You could have the trigger on the `Sales` table check the order dates. This process is called a nested trigger and is described in the section "Using Nested Triggers."

Cascading Update Triggers

Cascading updates throughout related tables provide you even more flexibility than cascading deletes do. In this section, we will take a quick look at one type of cascading update. Later, in the section "Managing Derived Columns," you will see how cascading updates are used to maintain derived data in your database. In the next example, you will see how to update the value of the `stor_id` column in the `Stores` table and then have all its related table references modified to reflect those changes. As in the previous, we will use the copies of the `Stores`, `Sales`, and `Discounts` tables. The trigger shown in Listing 19.6 will update the `ex_Sales` and `ex_Discounts` tables after the unique key (`stor_id`) in the `ex_Stores` table has been updated.

LISTING 19.6 A Cascading Update Trigger

```
Drop Trigger tr_stores_upd
go
Create Trigger tr_Stores_upd
On ex_Stores
For Update As
Declare @row_cnt int
Select @row_cnt = @@rowcount
If @row_cnt > 1
Begin
   If Update(stor_id)
   Begin
      Print 'There is more than one Store being updated!'
      Print 'This transaction has been cancelled!'
      Rollback Transaction
      Return
   End
End
Else
If @row_cnt = 1
Begin
   If Update(stor_id)
   Begin
      Update ex_Sales
         Set ex_Sales.stor_id =
             (Select stor_id From inserted)
         From ex_Sales Inner Join
              deleted on
              ex_sales.stor_id = deleted.stor_id
      Update ex_Discounts
         Set ex_Discounts.stor_id =
             (Select stor_id From inserted)
         From ex_Discounts Inner Join
              deleted on
              ex_Discounts.stor_id = deleted.stor_id
   End
End
```

You can test this trigger by executing the script in Listing 19.7, which is the same type of SQL script you used in Listing 19.4:

LISTING 19.7 Testing a Trigger Using a SQL Script

```
Use Pubs
Set nocount on
Begin Transaction

update ex_Stores set stor_id = '8043' where stor_id = '8042'

```

LISTING 19.7 continued

```
Select stor_id as StoresAfterUpd from ex_stores where stor_id = '8043'
Select stor_id as SalesAfterUpd from ex_sales where stor_id = '8043'
Select stor_id as DiscAfterUpd from ex_discounts where stor_id = '8043'
Rollback Transaction
Select stor_id as StoresBeforeUpd from ex_stores where stor_id = '8043'
Select stor_id as SalesBeforeUpd from ex_sales where stor_id = '8043'
Select stor_id as DiscBeforeUpd from ex_discounts where stor_id = '8043'
Select stor_id as StoresBeforeUpd from ex_stores where stor_id = '8042'
Select stor_id as SalesBeforeUpd from ex_sales where stor_id = '8042'
Select stor_id as DiscBeforeUpd from ex_discounts where stor_id = '8042'
```

Using Nested Triggers

Earlier today, you learned how to create a cascading delete trigger that actually deletes rows from several tables. Now, you will see how to use nested triggers to perform the same task. A *nested trigger* is where the server executes a statement from a trigger (such as a delete), which fires a subsequent trigger. Trigger nesting is limited to 32 levels, which is more than you should ever need. The example in Listing 19.8 shows two triggers, one for the `ex_Stores` table and one for the `ex_Sales` table. This trigger will fire when you issue a delete against the `ex_Stores` table.

LISTING 19.8 Creating the First Nested Trigger

```
Create Trigger tr_Stores_Del
On ex_Stores
For Delete As
If @@rowcount = 0 Return
Delete ex_Sales
Where ex_Sales.Stor_id in
      (Select del1.stor_id from deleted as del1)
If @@error <> 0
Begin
 Raiserror ('Store Delete Trigger has Failed, Transaction Rolled back!', 16, 1)
 Rollback Transaction
 Return
End
```


Note Before testing the trigger in Listing 19.8, you must create the trigger in Listing 19.9.

When the `ex_Stores` delete trigger is fired, it will execute a `DELETE` statement against the `ex_Sales` table, which will fire the following trigger:

LISTING 19.9 Creating the Second Nested Trigger

```
Create Trigger tr_Sales_Del
On ex_Sales
For Delete As
If @@rowcount = 0 Return
If Exists(
    Select * From Deleted as del
             Where Year(del.ord_date) = 1993)
Begin
   Raiserror ('Sales Exists for the year 1993. Transaction Cancelled!', 16, 1)
   Rollback Transaction
   Return
End
```

If either of these triggers fails, either because of a server error or because the condition is false, the entire transaction will be rolled back.

Because triggers are executed within a transaction, a failure at any level of a set of nested triggers will cancel the entire transaction, and all data changes will be rolled back.

You should include `PRINT` statements in your triggers to identify where the failure has occurred. This is especially useful when you are testing the triggers.

The ability to nest triggers is controlled by the server option `'Nested Triggers'` for the database server. You can set this option to true using the following system stored procedure:

```
exec sp_configure 'nested triggers', 1
```

Another way to turn on this option is by using the Enterprise Manager. Right-click the server on which you want to enable the option and select Properties from the pop-up menu. Then click on the Server Settings tab as shown in Figure 19.2. To set the option on, select the Allow triggers to be fired which fire other triggers (nested Triggers) check box.

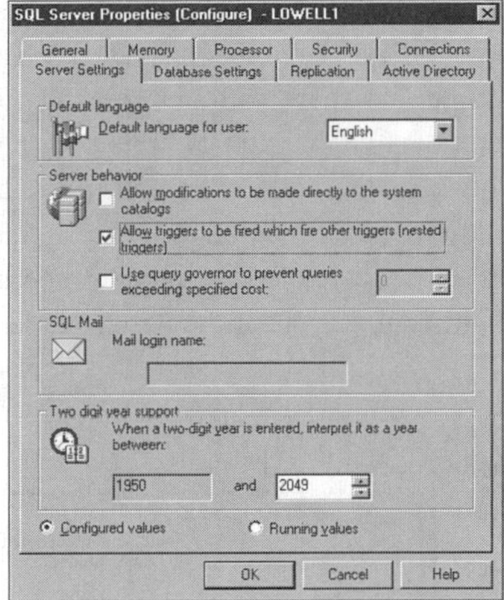

FIGURE 19.2
Setting the nested triggers option on for the server.

Managing Special Database Actions with Triggers

In addition to using triggers to help you enforce the business rules within your database, you can also use them to perform tasks that would be too complicated without them. In this next section, you will learn about three different tasks that you might need to use in any application you create. The first two are important if you will be tracking any type of summary or derived values within the database itself. The second task is more of an administrative task, but creating an audit trail is important if you need to know where, when, and maybe who performed each action against the database. Some of the database actions will use the ability to cascade or nest one or more triggers. This enables you to provide complex capabilities with the database without creating complex application code to support these actions.

Managing Derived Columns

A *derived column* is nothing more than a column that is calculated based on information in other columns from the database. When designing an application and its respective database, you will find that many types of summary information must be stored and displayed. Some application designers will actually create separate tables that store nothing but summary information, whereas others will include the summary information within the data row that it relates to in the original database table. Triggers enable you to update this summary information automatically without having to create unique application code to perform the task. By writing a trigger that calculates the summary data and then performs any action required, you can ensure that the summary information is kept up-to-date.

To make this a more real-life example, we will add a summary column to both the Customers and Products tables. For the customers, it makes sense to store the total amount of money that the customer has spent with our company. From the products side of the business, we want to track the total amount of units that have been sold. To do this without any triggers would require you to place extra code in your application to update these columns every time you made a modification to a row in the tables. Another approach would be to schedule a SQL batch to execute and read both tables updating the summary columns as it went. The SQL script for the Products table is shown in Listing 19.10:

LISTING 19.10 Creating a Derived Column in a Table

```
Select productID,
        sum(quantity) as totqty
Into #tp_Temp
From [order Details] as OD Inner Join
      Orders as ORD On
      OD.OrderID = ORD.OrderID
Where ORD.Orderdate Between '1/1/98' and '12/31/98'
Group by ProductId
Update Products
Set YTD_Qty = totqty
From #tp_temp as TP
Where Products.productid = TP.ProductID
Drop Table #tp_Temp
```

The problem with this approach is that the summary column will be updated only when this SQL script is executed. If you forget to execute the script, the information in the column is incorrect. Another issue you need to think about is that as the tables become larger (your company is growing), the time it takes to perform a complete table update as shown in Listing 19.10 will increase. The most reliable way to keep the information current is to use a trigger.

To see how this would work, we will do the following:

- Add a summary column to the Customers and Products tables in the Northwind database
- Initialize the summary columns
- Create a trigger that will maintain the derived column for any new action taken on the database

Adding the Summary Columns

The first step in working with summary columns is to add them to the tables. The following SQL code will add a summary column to the `Products` and `Customers` tables. The following example shows how to add these columns to the tables:

```
Alter Table products
Add YTD_Qty int NULL

Alter Table Customers
Add YTD_Sales money null
```

After this SQL script is executed, the summary columns will be available to use.

Initializing the Summary Columns

If you add these columns after the application has been in use, you must initialize the columns before the trigger process will be useful. This is done by using a SQL script very much like the one shown in Listing 19.10. The `Products` table would be updated as described. The `Customers` table would be updated much the same way, as shown in listing 19.11:

LISTING 19.11 Working with Summary Columns

```
Select ORD.CustomerID,
       sum(OD.quantity * OD.unitprice) as totsales
Into #tp_Temp
From [order Details] as OD Inner Join
     Orders as ORD On
     OD.OrderID = ORD.OrderID
Where ORD.Orderdate Between '1/1/98' and '12/31/98'
Group by ORD.customerID
Update Customers
Set YTD_Sales = totsales
From #tp_temp as TP
Where Customers.CustomerID = TP.CustomerID
Drop Table #tp_Temp
```

Remember that you are using the actual tables in the database to see how summary columns work. You should drop the summary columns from the tables at the end of this exercise.

Creating the Trigger

Now that you have the summary columns created and initialized, the last remaining step is to create the trigger that will keep these columns updated. The key to this process is remembering that both summary columns need to be updated whenever a change is made to the `Order Details` table. This trigger should be on the `[Order Details]` for `Insert`, `Update`, and `Delete`. There are three steps to this process, which are

1. Create a temporary table from the inserted and deleted tables
2. Create a temporary table for the customers and products updates
3. Apply any updates to the `Customers` and `Products` tables

Listing 19.12 shows the completed trigger, which will perform the updates to the summary columns in both tables whenever the `Order Details` table is modified.

LISTING 19.12 A Completed Trigger

```
Create Trigger tr_Order_Details_YTD
on [Order Details]
For Insert, Update, Delete
As
If @@rowcount = 0 Return
/***********************
PHASE 1
Create a single temporary table
that contains all of the
inserts and deletes
performed on the
Order Detail table,
***********************/
Select ORD.CustomerID,
       ProductID,
       isnull(sum(Quantity),0) as TotQty,
       isnull(sum(Unitprice * Quantity),0) as TotSales
Into #tp_OrdDetails
From Inserted as INS inner join
     Orders as ORD on
     ORD.orderID = INS.orderID
Where ORD.orderdate between '1/1/98' and '12/31/98'
Group By ORD.CustomerID, ProductId
Union
Select ORD.CustomerID,
       ProductID,
       -isnull(sum(Quantity),0) as TotQty,
       -isnull(sum(Unitprice * Quantity),0) as TotSales
From Deleted as DEL inner join
     Orders as ORD on
```

LISTING 19.12 continued

```
     ORD.orderID = DEL.orderID
Where ORD.orderdate between '1/1/98' and '12/31/98'
Group By ORD.CustomerID, ProductId
If @@Error <> 0
Begin
  Raiserror
 ('Error in YTD Trigger Phase 1: All Changes Rolled Back', 16,1)
  Rollback Transaction
  Return
End
***********************
PHASE 2
Create a temporary table
for the customers table
and one for the products
table that contains a
single list of net changes
performed
*********************/
--STEP 1: Create the Products summary table
Select productID,
       Sum(TotQty) as TQ
Into #tp_ProdTQ
From #tp_OrdDetails
Group By productid
If @@Error <> 0
Begin
   Raiserror
  ('Error in YTD Trigger Phase 2: Step 1: All Changes Rolled Back', 16,1)
   Rollback Transaction
   Return
End
--STEP 2: Create the Customers summary table
Select customerID,
       Sum(TotSales) as TS
Into #tp_CustTS
From #tp_OrdDetails
Group By customerID
If @@Error <> 0
Begin
   Raiserror
  ('Error in YTD Trigger Phase 2: Step 2: All Changes Rolled Back', 16,1)
   Rollback Transaction
   Return
End
/**********************
PHASE 3
Apply updates to the
Customers and Products
```

LISTING 19.12 continued

```
77  Tables
78***********************/
79  --Step 1: Apply updates to Customers
80  Update Customers
81  Set YTD_Sales = isnull(ytd_sales,0) + TS
82  From #tp_custTS as CustTs
83  Where customers.customerID = CustTs.CustomerID
84  If @@Error <> 0
85  Begin
86     Raiserror
      ('Error in YTD Trigger Phase 3: Step 1: All Changes Rolled Back', 16,1)
87     Rollback Transaction
88     Return
89  End
90  --Step 2: Apply updates to Products
91  Update Products
92  Set YTD_Qty = isnull(ytd_Qty,0) + TQ
93  From #tp_ProdTQ as ProdTq
94  Where Products.productID = ProdTq.productID
95  If @@Error <> 0
96  Begin
97     Raiserror
      ('Error in YTD Trigger Phase 3: Step 1: All Changes Rolled Back', 16,1)
98     Rollback Transaction
99     Return
100 End
```

Looking at this trigger, you can see that it is a little more complex than you have previously seen. The reason for this is that it must be able to handle `INSERT`, `UPDATE`, and `DELETE` processing. You must take into account several issues concerning null values. Remember that a null plus anything is still null. In addition, the inserted and deleted tables will only both be populated after an `UPDATE`. Finally, a single operation may affect many rows in the `Order Details` table, so the code must handle the case of multiple affected rows in all tables, `Order Details`, `Customers`, and `Products`.

Line 5 tests the system variable `@@rowcount` to check the number of rows affected by the last statement executed. If no rows were affected, there is no reason to continue in this trigger. The next step (lines 14 through 39) builds the list of net changes to each product that is recorded in the inserted and deleted tables.

The result set of the `SELECT` statement in lines 14–39 is a single four-column temporary table, with one or more rows per product and customer. As you should be aware, there can be many rows for each customer depending on how many products that customer has bought. Of course, there can be many rows of the same product, one for each customer who bought it. Finally, there is a row for each addition (from inserted) and one with total subtractions (from deleted).

Even though you can decrease the size of this trigger by using subqueries, I recommend that you do not use a subquery in this instance because you are updating to separate tables in PHASE 2 and you would need to run the subquery twice. This would actually reduce the performance instead of enhancing it.

In addition, this trigger will only act upon the current year's year-to-date summary. Any changes to prior years will not affect the summary columns. The second phase (lines 41 through 73) creates two new temporary tables, one for `Products` and one for `Customers`. Each provides one row for each product or customer and the summary value for that respective table. The final phase (lines 74 through 100) updates each of the tables with the appropriate values using the key value to match the rows.

Again, you should remember that this is not the only approach you can use to perform this task. You might want to consider using a cursor inside the trigger to remove the need for temporary tables, looking closely at the performance issues of cursors within a trigger.

Synchronizing Real-Time Updates Between Databases

There will be times when you need data copied from one table to another within a single database or from one database to another. To understand why this would be done, assume that your company has a database that tracks the inventory for your European sales and another database that tracks the inventory for your U.S. sales. The European sales database is located in London, England, and the U.S. database is located in New York. Both these databases contain information for the entire company. The problem is that both must be updated whenever a sale is made, otherwise the inventory information would not be correct. This task could be done in your application code, but it would be simpler to have the server perform this task using triggers.

Placing a trigger on the `Inventory` table of both databases that performs an update on the other database would provide you with the result you need. For both databases, when an action is taken in the `Inventory` table, the corresponding `Update`, `Insert`, or `Delete` trigger would fire and send the identical change to the other database. This way, you can ensure that the databases are kept in sync with each other.

Caution

Be careful not to use recursive triggers. A recursive trigger would cause the same database change to be sent between the databases multiple times.

When sending updates from one database to another, you must make sure that the update performed by the trigger does not in itself cause the trigger in the target database to be executed, thus sending an update back to the source database. This causes a loop to occur, which could result in a severe error that would cause SQL Server to stop executing, or at the very least, incorrect data to be added to the database.

Another issue to be careful of is how many times this trigger process might be performed. Remember that any action sent from one database to another will require the information to be sent on the network. You should carefully design and analyze any real-time update that you want to implement to reduce the network traffic to a minimum.

Maintaining an Audit Trail

Another task that you can use triggers to perform is creating an audit trail by writing audit transaction information to a table. For example, in designing your application, you do not want the users to delete any information actually. Instead, you would prefer to move the deleted information into an archive table. Another type of audit transaction is to keep a running record of changes made to a table.

Archiving Table Deletions

When archiving table deletions, the first step is to create a table with the same structure as the table you want to archive. For this discussion, we will archive the `Sales` table in the `PUBS` database. The following shows the SQL script that will create the archive table for `Sales`:

```
CREATE TABLE [Archive_Sales] (
    [stor_id] [char] (4) NOT NULL ,
    [ord_num] [varchar] (20) NOT NULL ,
    [ord_date] [datetime] NOT NULL ,
    [qty] [smallint] NOT NULL ,
    [payterms] [varchar] (12) NOT NULL ,
    [title_id] [tid] NOT NULL)
```

Transferring the deleted rows to this archive table enables you to query this data in the future, and even to restore it into the `Sales` table if needed. The final step is to create the `Delete` trigger to transfer the deleted sales information to the sales archive table as shown in Listing 19.13.

LISTING 19.13 Archiving Data

```
Create Trigger tr_Sales_Archive_Delete
on Sales
For Delete
As
Insert Archive_Sales
   Select stor_id,
          ord_num,
          ord_date,
          qty,
          payterms,
          title_id
   From Deleted
```

This trigger is both very simple and very powerful. After this trigger is in place, every sale that is deleted from the `Sales` table is subsequently transferred to the `Archive_Sales` table. It doesn't matter how the data might be deleted from the `Sales` table, it will always be archived to the `Archive_Sales` table.

Logging Table Changes

Besides the archiving type functionality that you have just seen, you can also use triggers to log activity on a table. To see how this works, we will add an update trigger to the `Products` table in the `Northwind` database to record any changes to the `UnitPrice` column. As with the example in Listing 19.13, the first step you need to take is to create the table that will contain the log information. The following is one example of the information that could be captured in the log table:


```
Create Table Log_Products
    (ProdID      Int                                 Not Null,
     Spid           Int                                 Not Null,
     Change_Date    DateTime  Default Getdate()  Not Null,
     Logged_user    Varchar(30) Default User     Not Null,
     Old_UnitPrice Money                           Null,
     New_UnitPrice Money                           Null)
```

As you can see, we use default values in two columns. The defaults are for the user who is performing the action, and the date and time that the change was made. In addition, the `spid` column will contain the server process ID or the task number for the change being made.

The trigger that you need to create is much less complicated than the archiving trigger. First, using the `UPDATE()` function, you should check whether the `UnitPrice` was updated. If it was, the trigger should write the update to the audit table, `Log_Products`. Listing 19.14 shows how this is done:

LISTING 19.14 Logging Data in a Trigger

```
Create Trigger tr_Product_UnitPrice_Log
On Products
For Update
As
If @@Rowcount = 0 Return
If Update(UnitPrice)
Begin
   Insert Log_Products (ProdId, spid, Old_UnitPrice, New_UnitPrice)
   Select ins.productId,
          @@spid,
          del.Unitprice,
          ins.Unitprice
   From Inserted as ins inner join
        Deleted as del on
        ins.productId = del.productId
/***The following condition filters out any extra data***/
     And ins.Unitprice != del.Unitprice
   If @@Error <> 0
   Begin
      Raiserror ('Audit Insert Failure: Rolling Back Changes', 16, 1)
      Rollback Transaction
      Return
   End
End
```

The `UPDATE()` function checks only whether the column was referenced, not whether the column was actually modified by the query. That is why the `UnitPrice` column is tested to see if what was inserted was different from the value that was deleted.

Summary

What you learned in today's lesson are some of the unique tasks that you can perform using triggers. Triggers enable you to create complex business rules for your database without having to code them into your application program. You saw how cascading triggers and nested triggers provide slightly different abilities to your application. In addition, you saw how to use triggers to maintain derived information within the database tables, and how to keep multiple copies of that database updated. Finally, you learned how to use triggers to create an audit log for any modifications in the database.

Q&A

Q I am trying to create a group of nested triggers, but they aren't working. What's wrong?

A If you have coded your triggers properly and they still do not work, check whether the database option for allowing nested triggers is enabled. You can enable it with the following statement:

```
Exec sp_configure 'nested triggers', 1
```

Q What is the difference between a nested trigger and a recursive trigger?

A A trigger is nested when it performs an action that would fire another trigger, which in turn would fire another trigger, and so on. A recursive trigger occurs when a trigger fires and performs an action that causes the same trigger to fire again.

Q Why should derived columns be maintained within a trigger?

A Most derived columns are calculations that require more information than is available in the column. You will probably want to get information from other tables, or update a calculated column in a second table when the first one is modified.

Workshop

The Workshop provides quiz questions to help you solidify your understanding of the material covered and exercises to provide you with experience in using what you've learned. Try to answer the quiz and exercise questions before checking the answers in Appendix A, "Answers to Quizzes and Exercises," and make sure that you understand the answers before continuing to the next lesson.

Quiz

1. What can triggers be used to enforce?
2. How many levels of nested triggers are allowed?
3. What happens when a statement in a trigger fails?

Exercise

Using the `Northwind` database, create a trigger that prevents you from adding a new product without having a valid supplier.

DAY 20

User-Defined Functions in SQL

In every programming language, there is a group of prewritten routines that can be used by anyone using the language. These routines are called *built-in functions*. During most of this book, you have used or have seen many of the functions available to you when coding T-SQL scripts. However, there probably will be many times when these functions do not supply the functionality you need.

When you start writing complex T-SQL applications, you will find that many of the actions and calculations that you perform are repetitive. Of course, you could decide to use stored procedures to perform some of these tasks, but you might also want to consider creating your own functions so that you can then use them elsewhere in the application.

Microsoft SQL Server 2000 provides a powerful new feature that enables you to define your own reusable functions, which are called user-defined functions or UDFs. In today's lesson, I will cover the following topics:

- Creating a user-defined function
- Using a UDF in views and queries

- Returning a table data type
- Handling errors
- Performance and the UDF

Understanding User-Defined Functions

When you start creating complex T-SQL programs or use T-SQL in another programming language such as Visual Basic, you will probably use the same calculations over and over again. Most languages give you the ability to define your own subroutines or functions to be reused in multiple places in your application. T-SQL is no different when it comes to defining your own functions. These user-defined functions provide you with the ability to create any type of function you might need. SQL Server 2000 supports three types of UDFs:

- Scalar functions
- Inline single table value functions
- Multi-statement table value functions

User-defined functions can be created to return either a scalar (single value) or a table (either single or multiple tables). In a UDF, the `RETURNS` clause determines whether the function is a scalar or a table function. When deciding what actions your functions will take, you should be aware of the SQL statements that you can use in a function. These include

- `DECLARE` statements (for defining data variables and cursors local to the function).
- Cursor operations that reference local cursors.
- `FETCH` statements that return data to the client are not allowed, only `FETCH` statements that assign values to a local variable can be used.
- Flow of control statements, such as `BEGIN...END`.
- Assignments of values to local objects.
- `SELECT` statements that contain select lists with expressions that assign values to local variables.
- `UPDATE`, `INSERT`, and `DELETE` statements that modify `TABLE` variables local to the function.
- `EXECUTE` statements that call an extended stored procedure.

The number of times that a function is actually executed in a query will vary between execution plans. An example of this is a function that is invoked by a subquery in a `WHERE` clause. The number of times the subquery and its function are executed can vary with different access paths chosen by the server.

When returning a single value, your function is considered a scalar function. If the UDF returns a table from a single `SELECT` statement, it is referred to as an inline table value function. If you create a table using this type of function, all the column names and data types are determined by the columns returned by the `SELECT` statement. If you specify new column names and different data types in your function, you are creating a multi-statement table value function.

Creating a Function

User-defined functions are created using the `CREATE FUNCTION` statement. Of course, there is no way for me to tell you what to create in a UDF. That is because a UDF is created to perform a unique function in an application. In the following sections, you will learn how to create all three of the different UDFs. In each, I will use a simple functional requirement as an example to show you how it is done.

You can create UDFs in the Query Analyzer by writing the `CREATE FUNCTION` code as described in the following sections. Or, you can choose to create UDFs in the Enterprise Manager by opening the database you are working with and then right-clicking on the User Defined Functions icon, which will display any UDFs already defined to the database. From the pop-up menu, select New User-Defined Function to display the User-defined Functions Properties dialog as shown in Figure 20.1.

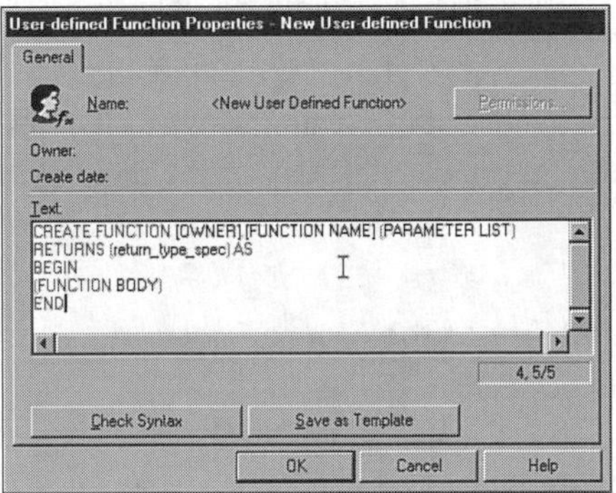

FIGURE 20.1
Creating a new user-defined function in the Enterprise Manager.

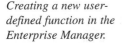

This dialog form enables you to enter the code for the function, and then to verify the code by clicking the Check Syntax button. When you are satisfied with the function, click OK to create it.

Creating a Scalar Function

Creating a function might seem a bit confusing, so to start with, let's create a basic function that will return a single value. The scalar function is the easiest function to create and work with. The syntax to create a scalar function is shown along with Table 20.1 which lists the arguments and their descriptions.

```
CREATE FUNCTION [owner name.] function_name
([{@parameter_name [AS] scalar_parameter_data_type [ = default]} [,...n]])
RETURNS scalar_return_data_type
[WITH ENCRYPTION | SCHEMABINDING]
[AS]
BEGIN
   <function body>
RETURN scalar_expression
```

TABLE 20.1 Arguments of a Scalar Function Definition

Argument	*Description*
Owner name	The object owner.
Function_name	The name of the UDF.
Parameter_name	The name for any parameters that you might need passed to the function. The maximum number of parameters is 1,024.
Scalar_parameter_data_type	The data type of the return value of this function. Nonscalar data types are not supported. This includes TABLES, CURSORS, ROWVERSION, or TIMESTAMP.
Scalar expression	SQL code that performs an action either by calculating or selecting data and returning a single value.

Now that you have seen the syntax, let's create a simple UDF. Listing 20.1 shows you how to create a function that returns the last day of the month when you pass a date to the function.

LISTING 20.1 Creating the Last Day of the Month Function

```
Use Northwind
Go
Create Function fnLastDayMonth (@inDate datetime)
Returns datetime
As
Begin
  Declare @mm int
  Declare @dd int
  Declare @yy int
  Declare @tempdate datetime
  Declare @tempstr varchar(10)

  Set @mm = Datepart(mm, @inDate)
```

LISTING 20.1 continued

```
Set @dd = Datepart(dd, @inDate)
Set @yy = Datepart(yy, @inDate)

If @mm = 12
   Begin
     Set @mm = 1
     Set @yy = @yy + 1
   End
Else
   Begin
     Set @mm = @mm + 1
   End

Select @tempstr = Convert(varchar(2), @mm) +
        '/01/' + Convert(varchar(4), @yy)
Set @tempdate = Convert(datetime, @tempstr)
Set @tempdate = Dateadd(dd, -1, @tempdate)

Return @tempdate
End
```

After you have entered the `CREATE FUNCTION` code and executed it, the function is available in the database as shown in Figure 20.2.

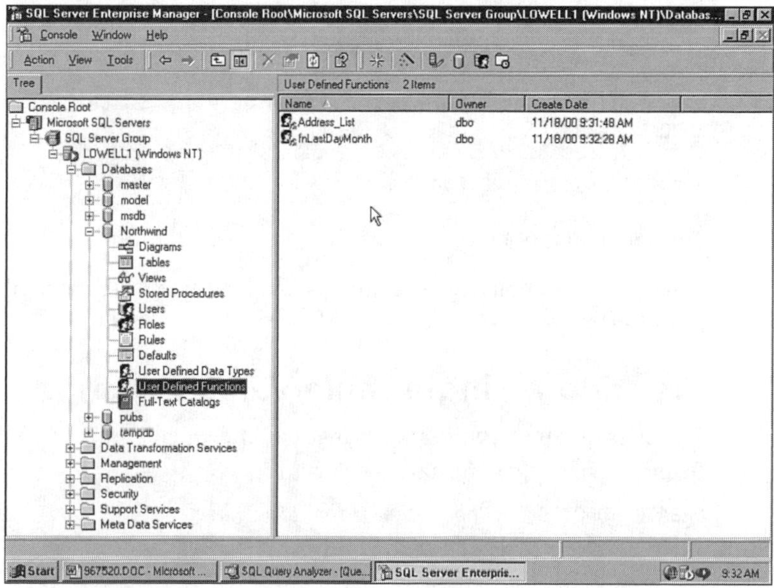

FIGURE 20.2
Listing the user-defined functions defined to a database.

To execute the function, you simply reference it in a `SELECT` statement as shown.

When executing any user-defined function, you must specify the owner name as shown here:

```
Dbo.function_name()
```

Otherwise, you will get the following error message:

```
Server: Msg 195, Level 15, State 10, Line 1
'fnlastdaymonth' is not a recognized function name.
```

```
Use Northwind
Select dbo.fnLastDayMonth('3/21/00') as 'EndOfMonth1'
Select dbo.fnLastDayMonth('2/31/00') as 'EndOfMonth2'
Select dbo.fnLastDayMonth('2/4/00') as 'EndOfMonth3'
```

The results you get from the preceding statements will probably surprise you. The first and third statements will execute correctly, but the second statement will cause an error. Here is the output:

```
EndOfMonth1
------------------------------------------------------
2000-03-31 00:00:00.000

(1 row(s) affected)

Server: Msg 242, Level 16, State 3, Line 2
The conversion of a char data type to a datetime
data type resulted in an out-of-range datetime value.
EndOfMonth3
------------------------------------------------------
2000-02-29 00:00:00.000

(1 row(s) affected)
```

Later in this section, I will briefly discuss how errors are handled in a User-Defined Function.

Creating a Single Table Value Function

The `CREATE FUNCTION` syntax changes a little when you are defining an inline table value function. The syntax for this statement is

```
CREATE FUNCTION [owner_name.] function_name
([{@parameter_name scalar_parameter_data_type [ = default]} [...,n]])
RETURNS TABLE
```

```
[WITH ENCRYPTION | SCHEMABINDING]
[AS]
RETURN [(] select_statement [)]
```

The big difference in the syntax is that the `RETURNS` clause specifies `TABLE`. This tells the server that instead of returning a single value, a table will be returned that is populated with the data returned from the specified `SELECT` statement. Of the two table functions you will look at in the next sections, the inline table value function is the easier of the two. It uses the same parameters as the scalar function with one exception: The *`select_statement`* is used instead of the *`scalar_expression`*. This is a single standard `SELECT` statement. Keep in mind that all columns in the `SELECT` statement must be named, including your computed columns.

In the following example, you will create a function that will return the total sales to date for a provided `ProductID`.

```
Use Northwind
Go
Create Function fnTotalSalesProduct (@inPrd int)
Returns Table As
Return (select productId,
        sum((quantity * unitprice) -
            ((quantity * unitprice) * discount)) as TotSales
        From [Order Details]
        Where ProductId = @inPrd
        group by productid)
```

When executing this UDF, you can reference it by itself or join with other tables using standard join syntax. The following two examples show you both of these options.

```
Select * from dbo.fnTotalSalesProduct(22)
Select fn.productid, productname, totsales
from dbo.fnTotalSalesProduct(21) as fn
     inner join products
     on products.productid = fn.productid
```

The output would look like this:

```
productId   TotSales
----------- ------------------
22          7122.3600082397461

(1 row(s) affected)

productid   productname            totsales
----------- ---------------------- -----------
21          Sir Rodney's Scones    9104.0

(1 row(s) affected)
```

One last thing about an inline table value function. If you know that you will need data from two or more tables that you can join together, you could create the UDF with this join defined as shown in the modified sample function that follows. What you did here was move the join to the `Products` table to get the product name in the UDF, instead of doing the join later in the `SELECT` statement.

```
Use Northwind
Go
Create Function fnTotalSalesProduct (@inPrd int)
Returns Table As
Return (select od.productId,
        prd.productname,
        sum((od.quantity * od.unitprice) -
            ((od.quantity * od.unitprice) * od.discount)) as TotSales
        From [Order Details] as od inner join products as prd
        on prd.productid = od.productid
        Where od.ProductId = @inPrd
        group by od.productid, prd.productname)
```

The execution of this UDF would look like:

```
Select * from dbo.fnTotalSalesProduct(22)
```

With the output:

```
productId   productname           TotSales
----------- --------------------- -----------------
22          Gustaf's Knäckebröd   7122.3600082397461

(1 row(s) affected)
```

Creating a Multi-Table Function

A multi-table function differs from a scalar function in that you reference more than one table within the function itself. Creating a multi-table function is basically the same as creating a scalar function. Once again, the `CREATE FUNCTION` syntax changes slightly. The syntax shown here now requires you to define the structure of the table being returned.

```
CREATE FUNCTION [owner_name.] function_name
([{@parameter_name scalar_parameter_data_type [ = default]} [...,n]])
RETURNS @return_variable TABLE <table_type_definition>
[WITH ENCRYPTION | SCHEMABINDING]
[AS]
BEGIN
    function_body
    RETURN [(] select_statement [)]
END
```

In this type of UDF, the change to the syntax is a combination of both the scalar and inline table value functions. You create a SQL script that inserts data into a variable defined as a table data type. You use the multi-statement table value functions to return a table. However, the table that is returned does not need to be created by a single SELECT statement. For example, you might want to do some processing on data and create a temporary table. Then you can do some additional processing based on that temporary table and return a new table with your results.

To see how the multi-statement function works, you will create a function in the PUBS database that returns the royalties to date based on books sold. However, this is not as simple as it sounds. The problem is that a book might have more than one author. If a book has multiple authors who split their royalties, incorrect results would be returned if you simply calculated the royalty by row of data and returned it associated with each author.

To fix this problem, you should figure out the royalties by title, divide those royalties by the number of authors on each title, and return a table with the author's name, the title, and the newly modified royalties. You are assuming that the royalties are divided evenly among multiple authors.

To execute this UDF, you would use the following syntax:

```
SELECT * FROM dbo.fnRoyaltySplitByAuthor()
```

Caution

Even if the function does not require any parameters, you must include the opening and closing parentheses. Otherwise, you will receive the following error message:

```
Server: Msg 208, Level 16, State 3, Line 1
Invalid object name 'dbo.fnRoyaltySplitByAuthor'.
```

The output of this SELECT statement is

```
au_fname         au_lname      title                     RoyToDate
---------------- ------------- ------------------------- ----------
Cheryl           Carson        But Is It User Friendly?  32240.16
...
Michael          O'Leary       Sushi, Anyone?            2046.135
Burt             Gringlesby    Sushi, Anyone?            2046.135
Akiko            Yokomoto      Sushi, Anyone?            2046.135

(25 row(s) affected)
```

Reviewing Advanced UDF Topics

Although creating a user-defined function is a fairly simple process, using them is a bit more interesting. Of course, to repeat myself, when you decide to create a UDF for your database, you need to do some analysis on what you really want the function to do and what type of information the function will return when it is executed. In addition, when you create user-defined functions, the performance of the function is very important because it will be used by many programs to access information from the database.

Finally, you saw earlier in this lesson that errors must be accounted for in a UDF just as in triggers and stored procedures. However, the server responds to errors in a UDF in a slightly different way. In this section, you will look at some performance recommendations, what you need to know when accessing a UDF from a view, and error checking.

Rewriting Stored Procedures as Functions

On Days 15, "Writing and Executing Stored Procedures," and 16, "Optimizing Stored Procedures," you learned what stored procedures are, how to create them, and how to use them in your SQL programming. However, one of the places you cannot use a stored procedure is from within a query. If you want to invoke a stored procedure directly from a query, you should to repackage the code in the stored procedure as a user-defined function. In general, if the stored procedure returns a single result set, you can define a table-valued function; if it returns a single value, you can define a scalar function.

To see whether a stored procedure can be converted to a user-defined function, compare it to the following criteria. If the stored procedure meets all the following requirements, it is a good candidate to be converted.

- A single `SELECT` statement is used in a stored procedure, rather than a view, because it requires parameters, so a scalar function can be used.
- The stored procedure does not perform any update operations.
- Dynamic `EXECUTE` statements are not needed.
- Only one result set is returned.
- The primary purpose is to build a temporary result set that is loaded into a temporary table, which is then used in a `SELECT` statement.

UDF Performance and Recommendations

To help you produce good quality user-defined functions, this section provides some recommendations and tips for working with them.

Using Scalar Functions

Scalar functions are useful for situations in which you need to do the same math calculations in more than one place in the SQL code. For example, if calculating interest based on percent rate, principal, and years is done throughout your application, it can be coded as a user-defined function, as shown in the following example:

```
Create function calcInt (@prin int,
                         @rate numeric(10,5),
                         @yrs int)
Returns int
As
Begin
     Declare @interest int
     Set @interest = @prin * @rate * @yrs / 100
     Return @interest
End
```

Using System Functions in UDFs

System functions can be used as building blocks for a user-defined function. For example, if you need to calculate the quadrupled value of a number, use the `SQUARE` system function to arrive at the value instead of writing the entire function from scratch.

Nesting Functions to Simplify a Complex Function

If you are trying to create a very complex function, you can break down the complexity of the process into several smaller functions that can then be used together in a larger function. The advantage of breaking complex functions into smaller functions is that this code can be reused in more places in the application.

For example, suppose that you need to calculate the area of a plot of land and the input can be in either meters or feet, but the area must always be displayed in square feet. Instead of writing one function that does all the work, you can break up the task into two functions:

- `cvt_meters_feet()` does the conversion from meters to feet.
- `calc_area_feet()` calculates the area in feet.

This way, you can use the `cvt_meters_feet()` function at other places in the code.

```
Create Function cvt_meters_feet (@inVal numeric(10,3))
Returns numeric(10,3)
As
Begin
    Declare @ret_feet numeric(10,3)
    Set @ret_feet = @inVal * 3.281
    Return(@ret_feet)
End
```

In the second function, `calc_area_feet()`, you can use the `cvt_meters_feet()` function as shown here:

```
Create Function calc_area_feet (@inLength numeric(10,3),
                               @inWidth numeric(10,3),
                               @inUnit char(1))
Returns numeric(10,3)
As
Begin
    Declare @area numeric(10,3)
    If @inUnit = 'm'
    Begin
        Set @inLength = dbo.cvt_meters_feet(@inLength)
        Set @inWidth = dbo.cvt_meters_feet(@inWidth)
    End
    Set @area = @inLength * @inWidth
    Return @area
End
```

Now, you can use the final function to calculate either meters or feet. The following shows how to execute this function for both types of measurements:

```
Select dbo.calc_area_feet (95,45.5, 'M') As 'Area in Meters'
Select dbo.calc_area_feet (95,45.5, 'F') As 'Area in Feet'
```

The output from these statements would look like this:

```
Area in Meters
--------------
46531.700

(1 row(s) affected)

Area in Feet
------------
4322.500

(1 row(s) affected)
```

Considering the Effects of Changes to the Schema

If `SELECT * FROM` <*table*> is used in a function, effects of changes to the structure of the database after the creation of the function should be taken into account. If the function is not created with the `SCHEMA_BINDING` option, changes to the structure are not reflected in the result.

For example, if a new column is added to the table after the function was created and the function is not `SCHEMA` bound, the new column will not show up in the result set. If a column is removed after creation of the function and the function is *not* `SCHEMA` bound, a NULL value will show up in the result set for the deleted column.

Using Functions Instead of Views

Any user-defined function that returns a table can be a very powerful replacement to a view. Views are limited to a single SELECT statement. However, a user-defined function can contain any number of statements that enable you to create much more powerful logic than is possible in a view. If your SQL application requires a complex set of data, you used to be required to create two or more views that you would then join together to get the appropriate data. Using user-defined functions, you could build a temporary table in the function code that can include many tables and, more importantly, complex calculations and data manipulation all rolled up together.

As an example of how using a UDF instead of a view can provide you with extended capabilities, let's take a look at the following view:

```
Create View vw_CustomerOrdersSAVEA As
select *
from orders
inner join [order details]
on orders.orderid = [order details].orderid
Where Orders.customerID = 'SAVEA'
```

By using a user-defined function, you can create a more general version of this view by replacing `WHERE orders.customerId = 'SAVEA'` with `WHERE orders.customerId = @custId` and letting the user supply the customer if he wants to do so. Views, on the other hand, do not support parameters in the WHERE condition. The following is the same query rewritten as a user-defined function:

```
Create Function fn_CustomerOrders (@CustId varchar(10))
Returns Table
As
Return (
        Select *
        From orders
        Inner join [order details]
        On orders.orderid = [order details].orderid
        Where Orders.customerID = @CustId
       )
```

20

Error Trapping and Functions

Any T-SQL statements that would cause a statement to be cancelled with execution continuing on to the next statement in the script (such as triggers and stored procedures) are treated a little differently when they occur inside a user-defined function. In a UDF, such errors will cause the execution of the function to stop. This will in turn cause the statement that invoked the function to be cancelled.

Summary

In today's lesson, you learned about the new feature in SQL Server 2000 that enables you to create user-defined functions. You have seen how powerful UDFs are in providing expanded capabilities to you and your users. They will take a little practice to get used to, but I predict that user-defined functions will be one of the most often used additions to SQL Server 2000.

If you return a single value from your function, it is called a *scalar function*. If you return a table with a simple `SELECT` statement, your function is known as an *inline table value function*. The `SELECT` statement defines the table being returned. If the table is defined not by the `SELECT` statement, but explicitly in the function itself, it is called a multi-statement table value function.

Q&A

Q I tried to use a `RAISERROR` statement in the UDF to notify me about any errors. Why won't it work?

A The `RAISERROR` and `PRINT` statements are not valid within a UDF. To detect any errors, you must use the `RETURN` statement and check for any errors when the UDF returns to the calling routine.

Q What can I use a user-defined function for?

A A user-defined function can be used to provide a complex calculation to all users of the database. This would prevent requiring everyone to create his own.

Workshop

The Workshop provides quiz questions to help you solidify your understanding of the material covered and exercises to provide you with experience in using what you've learned. Try to answer the quiz and exercise questions before checking the answers in Appendix A, "Answers to Quizzes and Exercises," and make sure that you understand the answers before continuing to the next lesson.

Quiz

1. User-defined functions can return scalar values as well as tables and can be used as part of the `SELECT` statement or in the `FROM` clause of a query. True or False?
2. What are the three different types of user-defined functions?

Exercise

1. Using the `Northwind` database, create a function that accepts a ZIP Code and returns a table of customer names and addresses.

WEEK 3

DAY 21

Handling BLOBs in T-SQL

As you have learned, Microsoft SQL Server 2000 supports many different data types that you can use to store data in the database. Most of these data types should have been familiar to you. Whether or not you have programmed before, integers, decimals, characters, and money are pretty standard types of data that you work with all the time. However, we have not really taken a look at one other group of data types that SQL Server 2000 supports. These are the large object data types or LOBs. In this lesson, we will take a look at the following:

- How BLOBs are stored
- Modifying BLOB data

Understanding Large Data Types

Before we discuss large data types, let's take a brief look at the history of why they are useful. Prior to SQL Server Version 7.0, the largest character, text, or binary field allowable was 255 bytes. Of course, as applications became more sophisticated, this became a restriction. Since Version 7.0, the maximum size of these data types has expanded to 8,000 bytes. This was a large jump, but it is still a bit lacking for some application requirements. Many applications have the need to store more than 8,000 bytes of data. Some of the more common reasons are

- Long comments
- Detailed descriptions
- Resumes
- Digitized photographs or pictures
- Audio
- Video

These are only the most common uses for large data types (greater than 8,000 bytes). If you have a requirement for this type of storage in your database, SQL Server 2000 provides the capability for storing binary large objects (BLOBs) as large as 2 gigabytes per row. This can be done by using one of the following three data types described in Table 21.1.

TABLE 21.1 Large Object Data Types

Data Type	*Description*
`TEXT`	Variable-length (non-Unicode) data that can contain a maximum length of 2,147,483,647 characters
`NTEXT`	A variable-length Unicode field that can contain a maximum length of 1,073,741,823
`IMAGE`	Variable-length binary data field that can contain a maximum length of 2,147,483,647 bytes

Working with BLOBs and using BLOBs are two very different actions. What you will learn in this section is how large objects are stored and how they are indexed inside a database. In the next section, you will learn how to manipulate them within your SQL scripts and how to gather information about them.

How Large Data Is Stored

When storing data in a database table, you usually do not worry about the size of the data. However, individual `TEXT`, `NTEXT`, and `IMAGE` data type columns can be a maximum of 2GB, which is too large to store in a single data row. In SQL Server 2000, smaller values of these data types can be stored directly in the row, but the values that are too large to fit are stored in a separate area than where the data for the other columns in the row are stored.

The 'TEXT IN ROW' option (which is set within a SQL Script) is used to specify how data contained in a TEXT, NTEXT, or IMAGE column is stored in the table. Storing text directly in the row would reduce the work performed by the server whenever this data was accessed. The server administrator uses the system stored procedure sp_Tableoption to turn on or off this option. To turn on this option for the Employees table, you would use the following syntax:

```
Exec sp_Tableoption 'Employees', 'text in row', 'ON'
```

In addition to just turning on this option, you could also specify the maximum amount of data that can be stored in the row, from 24 up to 7,000 bytes as shown:

```
Exec sp_Tableoption 'Orders', 'Text In Row', '1000'
```

If you set this option 'ON' without specifying a limit, the default limit of 256 bytes will be used.

You can turn off this option by using the statement shown here:

```
Exec sp_tableoption 'Employees', 'text in row', 'OFF'
```

Although you will always work with each of these columns as if it were a single string of bytes, the data is not stored in that format. The data will be stored in a collection of 8KB pages, which are organized logically in an index-like structure to provide faster access to the data.

Data Storage Options

Although SQL Server 2000 allows the storage of small- to medium-sized TEXT, NTEXT, and IMAGE values directly in a data row, it is best to use this 'in row' feature where the data is usually read or written in one unit, and most SQL statements that access the table use the data in these large object columns. Unless the 'text in row' option is specified, any data for these three data types will be stored outside the data row. What will be stored in the row is a 16-byte text pointer that points to the root node of internal pointers for the pages that contain the large object data.

Text Not in Row Data

When the 'text in row' option is not set, any large data strings will be stored outside the data row. The server will insert a 16-byte text pointer into the data row that will point to the actual location of the large object. Although you will not see any difference in how you process these strings, the internal structure that SQL Server uses will vary slightly if there is less than 32KB of data or if there is more than 32KB of data. If the data is smaller than 32KB, the 16-byte text pointer in the data row points to a root structure that is 84 bytes long. This structure forms the root node of the tree structure that will be used to point to the different blocks that hold the actual data. The structure shown in Figure 21.1 is how the actual data row points to the root structure, which in turn points to the data blocks.

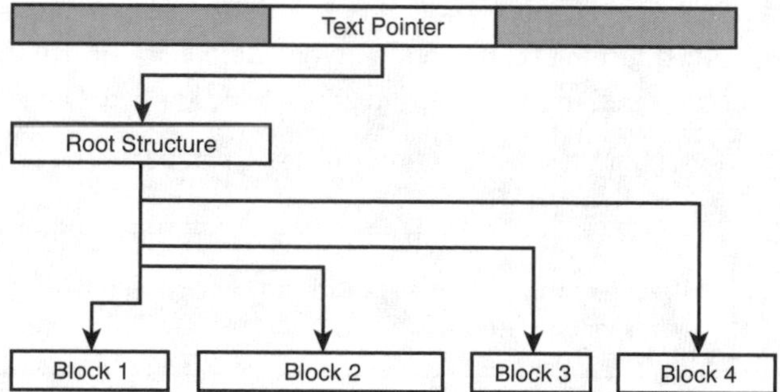

FIGURE 21.1

Storing BLOBs that are less than 32KB in length.

Although the data for a BLOB column is arranged logically, both the root and individual blocks are spread throughout the chain pages for the table. They are placed anywhere space is available. The size of each block is determined by the size of the data written by the application using the BLOB. Smaller blocks of data will be combined to fill a page. If there is less than 64 bytes of data, the entire object is stored in the root structure.

If the amount of data in a BLOB exceeds 32KB, SQL Server will start building intermediate nodes between the data blocks and the root node, as shown in Figure 21.2.

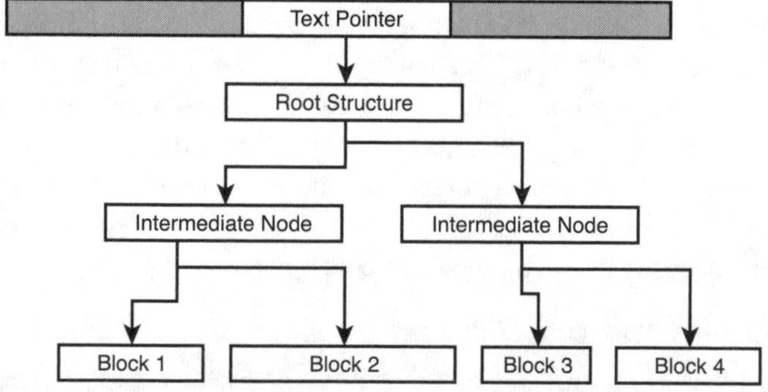

FIGURE 21.2

Storing BLOBs that are greater than 32KB in length.

The root structure and the data blocks are stored throughout the `TEXT`, `NTEXT`, or `IMAGE` pages; however, the intermediate nodes are stored in pages not shared between occurrences of BLOB columns. A page that contains intermediate nodes is not used to store any other types of data.

Text in Row Data

When the `'text in row'` option is set, `TEXT`, `NTEXT`, and `IMAGE` strings are stored directly in the data row if

- The length of the string is shorter than the specified limit or the default of 256 bytes if a length is not specified.
- There is enough space available in the data row to hold the string.

When these strings are stored in the data row, the server does not need to access a separate page or set of pages to read or write the string. This means that the access to the large data columns is about as fast the standard-size character columns. However, if the string is longer than the `'text in row'` option limit or the space available in the row, the pointers to the large object is stored in the row itself. These pointers are stored in the row if

- The amount of space needed to store the pointers is smaller than the `'text in row'` limit.

Note

> The techniques the server uses when pointers are required for large strings that are stored in the row are the same as those when the `'text in row'` option is `OFF`.

You should be aware of the effects that enabling this option will have on your database and performance. The effects of how the option `'text in row'` is set are

- You cannot use `READTEXT`, `UPDATETEXT`, or `WRITETEXT` statements with any `TEXT`, `NTEXT`, or `IMAGE` stored in the table. This requires you to work with the entire string at all times. You will not be able to modify portions of the string.
- If the option is turned on after the table contains data, any existing large object columns will not be converted to in-row strings until they are updated.
- If the option is turned off after the table contains data, the table will be locked and any in-row `TEXT`, `NTEXT`, or `IMAGE` strings will be immediately converted to regular `TEXT`, `NTEXT`, or `IMAGE` strings. The amount of processing required to perform this conversion depends on how many strings must be converted.

Managing BLOB Data

Depending on whether the BLOB data is stored in the data row or outside of the data row, the way you manage it will be different. When BLOB strings are stored in the data row, reading and writing the data strings can be as fast as reading and writing character and binary strings. SQL Server does not have to access separate pages of data to read or write the BLOB string. Unless the `'text in row'` option is specified, BLOB strings are stored outside the data row with only the text pointers to these strings in the data row. These text pointers point to the pages that contain the string fragments that contain the actual BLOB data in multiple pages, as discussed earlier in this lesson.

Using the Large Object System Functions

Whenever you access data stored in any of the large object data types, you will use one of the following system functions. These system functions are used exclusively for the large object data types.

- `TEXTPTR()`—Returns a binary value that represents a pointer to the `TEXT`, `NTEXT`, or `IMAGE` object. The pointer remains valid until the row is deleted.
- `TEXTVALID()`—Checks whether a specified text pointer is valid.

Text pointers are used in the `READTEXT`, `WRITETEXT`, and `UPDATETEXT` statements to reference the BLOB strings that are not stored in the row itself. In addition, you can also use several other functions to access data stored in a BLOB. These are

- `PATHINDEX()`—Returns the starting position of the first occurrence of the specified pattern, or zeros if the pattern is not found. This can be used on all character and text data types including `TEXT` and `NTEXT`.
- `DATALENGTH()`—Returns the number of bytes used to store the data in the BLOB.
- `SUBSTRING()`—Returns part of a character, binary, text, or image expression.

Using the `DATALENGTH()` and `SUBSTRING()` functions is the same with BLOBs as when they are used with smaller text objects. The following example shows you how to use both functions with a BLOB data column:

```
Select pub_id,
       Datalength(pr_info) as 'DataLen',
       Substring(pr_info,30,15) as 'short_pr_Info'
From pub_info
```

The output will display the actual number of bytes in each `pr_info` column and 15 characters from the data for each row.

```
pub_id DataLen     short_pr_Info
------ ----------- ---------------
0736   65071       New Moon Books,
0877   675         Binnet & Hardle
1389   1476        Algodata Infosy
1622   18518       Five Lakes Publ
1756   131         Ramona Publishe
9901   114         GGG&G, publishe
9952   135         Scootney Books,
9999   544         Lucerne Publish

(8 row(s) affected)
```

Using the TEXTPTR() Function

The TEXTPTR() function is used to retrieve the pointer value for a BLOB from the data row in the database table. A valid text pointer can be obtained even if the text value in the column is NULL. If the table is not storing the BLOBs in the data row and the BLOB column has not been initialized, the TEXTPTR() function will return a NULL pointer. To retrieve a text pointer, you must declare a variable to hold the pointer value to be used later in the SQL script. As shown here, the syntax for the TEXTPTR() function is very simple:

```
TEXTPTR (<column name>)
```

The following example shows how to use this function to retrieve the TEXT BLOB 'logo' from the Pubs database:

```
Use pubs
Declare @ptrval varbinary(16)
Select @ptrval = textptr(logo)
From pub_info
Where pub_id = '0736'
```

The only output you would get from this script is the message telling that the command completed successfully. The TEXTPTR() function was used to locate the IMAGE column logo associated with the publishers ID of '0736'. The text pointer is stored in the local variable @ptrval, which can then be used later in the SQL script.

Caution

In SQL Server 2000, if you use an 'in row' text pointer, it must be used inside a transaction. If you try to use it outside a transaction, the following message will be displayed:

```
Server: Msg 7101, Level 16, State 1, Line 2
You cannot use a text pointer for a table
with option 'text in row' set to ON.
```

To display a text pointer, you simply specify the function in the `SELECT` statement as shown:

```
Use pubs
Select textptr(logo) as 'Text Pointer'
From pub_info
Where pub_id = '0736'
```

When you execute this statement, the following output will be displayed:

```
Text Pointer
----------------------------------
0xFFFF6E00000000005C00000001000000

(1 row(s) affected)
```

As you can see, displaying the text pointer is not really useful, but you will see how the text pointer is used to access the BLOB data stored in the table.

Using the `TEXTVALID()` Function

Before you actually use the value stored in the text pointer for a BLOB, you must make sure that it is a valid pointer. Otherwise, any statement in which you use the pointer variable will fail. The `TEXTVALID()` function will check the specified text pointer variable to verify that it is a valid pointer. The syntax of this function is

```
TEXTVALID ('Table.column', text_ptr)
```

The function will return an integer value of `1` if the pointer is valid and a `0` if it is not valid. Using this information, you can set a local variable with the returned value and then use it to conditionally perform one or more SQL statements as shown in the following example:

```
Use pubs
Declare @val int
Declare @ptrval Varbinary(16)
Select @ptrval = Textptr(pr_info) from pub_info
Set @val = Textvalid('pub_info.pr_info', @ptrval)
If @val = 0
    Begin
        Raiserror ('This pointer is invalid', 1, 15)
    End
if @val <> 0
    Begin
        Readtext pub_info.pr_info @ptrval 0 15
    End
```

If the pointer value returned were invalid, this SQL script would display the following output:

```
Msg 50000, Level 1, State 50000
This pointer is invalid
```

Otherwise, the text contained in the column would be displayed as shown here:

```
pr_info
----------------------
This is sample

(1 row(s) affected)
```

Caution

> You cannot use a UPDATETEXT, WRITETEXT, or READTEXT statement without a valid text pointer.

Working with the `PATINDEX()` Function

The `PATINDEX()` function enables you to search a large text string for the first occurrence of a specified pattern. Here is the syntax for this function, along with the description of the two arguments:

```
Patindex ('%pattern%', expression)
```

- *`pattern`* This is a literal string, which can contain wildcard characters. However, if you use the `'%'` character, it must precede and follow the pattern unless searching for the first or last characters.
- *`expression`* This is usually a column that is searched for the specified pattern.

The `PATINDEX()` function can be very useful when used with any text data type. It can be used in a `WHERE` clause as shown in the following example:

```
Use Pubs
Select pub_id,
       title
From titles
Where Patindex('%wonderful%', notes) > 0
```

In this example, only titles with the word `wonderful` will be returned in the result set and displayed as shown.

```
pub_id
------ --------------------------------------------------------------
0877   Onions, Leeks, and Garlic: Cooking Secrets of the Mediterranean

(1 row(s) affected)
```

Using the READTEXT, WRITETEXT, and UPDATETEXT Statements

When working with BLOB data that is stored outside the data row, you must use the SQL statements that are designed specifically for this purpose. These statements provide you with the standard functionality you are familiar with as it relates to reading, writing, and updating the information in the BLOB. Table 21.2 lists each of the three functions and a description of how they are used.

Both the READTEXT and UPDATETEXT statements enable you to work with chunks or blocks of a text column at a time. The WRITETEXT statement does not allow you to work with chunks, only with the entire column. In addition, the WRITETEXT and UPDATETEXT statements will not log the operation by default, although you can specify that you want logging to be active.

TABLE 21.2 Using the Large Data Statements

Statement	*Description*
READTEXT	Used to read values from a TEXT, NTEXT, or IMAGE column, starting from a specified offset and a specified length.
UPDATETEXT	Updates an existing BLOB field. This allows you to change only a portion of a BLOB column in place.
WRITETEXT	Permits interactive updating of an existing BLOB column. This statement completely overwrites any existing data in the column it affects. WRITETEXT cannot be used on any BLOB columns in views.

Using the WRITETEXT Statement

The WRITETEXT statement completely overwrites an existing text or image column by providing the column name, the text pointer for the column of a specific row, and the actual data to be written. The syntax of this statement is

```
WRITETEXT {table.column text_ptr}
          {data}
```

Remember that for the WRITETEXT statement to work properly, the column must already contain a valid text pointer. If the column does not contain a valid text pointer, you must initialize it by using a variation on one of the following:

- Explicitly insert a non-NULL value in the text column when you use an INSERT statement. The WRITETEXT statement will overwrite whatever you put in that column anyway.

- Define a default on the column with a non-NULL value.
- Explicitly update the row after inserting it, and then set the column to NULL.

The following example shows how to use the WRITETEXT statement along with the TEXTPTR() function to ensure that the text pointer is valid:

```
Use Pubs
Declare @ptrval varbinary(16)
Select @ptrval = Textptr(pr_info)
From pub_info
Where pub_id = '999'
If @ptrval Is Not Null
    Writetext pub_info.pr_info @ptrval 'Test Data'
```

You can see that we check for a valid text pointer value by using the 'Is Not Null' condition. If the text pointer were valid, the following statement would overwrite the text data of the row where the pub_ID is 999. Because you can reference only one text pointer at a time, you would normally use cursor processing when working with BLOBs.

Using the READTEXT Statement

The READTEXT statement is very similar to the WRITETEXT statement, except that it enables you to specify a starting position and the length of data to be read. The basic syntax for this statement is

```
Readtext [table_name.column_name
          Text_ptr offset size [Holdlock]
```

With the READTEXT statement, you can work with either the entire contents of the data or with any specified portion of the data. The following example shows how you can retrieve any part of the contents; in fact, you can see how to retrieve the entire contents even if you do not know the length of the data. The DATALENGTH() function provides you with the actual length of the data in the column and you can use it in the READTEXT statement.

```
Use pubs
Declare @ptrval varbinary(16)
Declare @dataLen int
Select @ptrval = TEXTPTR(pr_info),
       @dataLen = datalength(pr_info)
From pub_info
Where pub_id = '9901'

Readtext pub_info.pr_info @ptrval 0 25

Readtext pub_info.pr_info @ptrval 0 @datalen
```

The output displayed by this example is

```
pr_info
----------------------------------
This is sample text data

(1 row(s) affected)

pr_info
------------------------------------------------------------
This is sample text data for GGG&G, publisher 9901 in
 the pubs database. GGG&G is located in München, Germany.

(1 row(s) affected)
```

Using the UPDATETEXT Statement

The UPDATETEXT statement enables you to work with the text in pieces to insert, overwrite, or append data to the BLOB. You can also copy data from another text column and append it or overwrite the column with it. The syntax of this statement is a bit more complex than the other two statements we have looked at. Table 21.3 describes the arguments of the UDPATETEXT statement.

```
UPDATETEXT { table_name.dest_column_name dest_text_ptr }
    { NULL | insert_offset }
    { NULL | delete_length }
    [ inserted_data
        | { table_name.src_column_name src_text_ptr } ]
```

TABLE 21.3 Using the UPDATETEXT Statement

Argument	*Description*
table_name.dest_column_name	The name of the table and BLOB column to be updated.
dest_text_ptr	The text pointer value that points to the BLOB column being updated.
insert_offset	A zero-based starting position for the update. It represents the number of bytes to skip from the start of the existing column before inserting the new data.
delete_length	The length of data to delete from the existing BLOB column.
inserted_data	Data to be inserted into the existing BLOB column.
table_name.src_column_name	The name of the table and BLOB column being used as the source of the inserted data.
src_text_ptr	The text pointer value that points to the BLOB column being used as the source of the inserted data.

The following example shows how to use the UDPATETEXT statement to modify a single character in the pr_info column. In addition, it displays the section of text before and after the update to show the change.

```
Use pubs
Declare @ptrval binary(16)
Select @ptrval = TEXTPTR(pr_info)
From pub_info pr, publishers p
Where p.pub_id = pr.pub_id
      AND p.pub_name = 'New Moon Books'
Readtext pub_info.pr_info @ptrval 80 10
Updatetext pub_info.pr_info @ptrval 88 1 'b'
Readtext pub_info.pr_info @ptrval 80 10
```

Results:

```
pr_info
------------
. New Moon

(1 row(s) affected)

pr_info
------------
. New Mobn

(1 row(s) affected)
```

Summary

What you learned in today's lesson is one of the least used features of SQL Server. BLOB data is seldom used because of the complexity of manipulating it. The only tables I have seen that use BLOB data are employee tables that store a photo or formatted resume. For most application databases, there are usually better, easier, faster, and less complicated ways of storing data. You just have to think about how you are going to be using the data before deciding on how to store it.

Q&A

Q What are Large Data Types really used for?

A A Large Data Type would be used in a database table to store very large pieces of information. The Northwind database uses a Large Data Type to store the pictures of each employee. Other applications use these data types to store an entire document that is associated with a particular row of data, such as a resume with an employee.

21

Q What function can I use to find a particular string within a Large Object Field?

A The `PATINDEX()` function enables you to search a large text string for the first occurrence of a specified pattern.

Q Can I change a portion of a Large Object Field?

A Yes. Using the `UPDATETEXT()` function, you can update a portion of an existing Large Object Field.

Workshop

The Workshop provides quiz questions to help you solidify your understanding of the material covered and exercises to provide you with experience in using what you've learned. Try to answer the quiz and exercise questions before checking the answers in Appendix A, "Answers to Quizzes and Exercises," and make sure that you understand the answers before continuing to the next lesson.

Quiz

1. What is the difference between the data types `TEXT` and `NTEXT`?
2. What amount of data can be stored before it is considered a large object?
3. How do I tell the server to store the text in the row, instead of using separate pages?

Exercises

There are no exercises for this lesson.

WEEK 3

In Review

Congratulations! You have reached the end of Week 3 and you are still standing. The topics that were covered in this last week are usually the stuff most SQL programmers do not want to deal with. If you were able to understand the topics and do some of the exercises, you are ready to get down to business as a SQL Server programmer. For the record, you covered the following topics this week.

Day 15, "Writing and Executing Stored Procedures": In the first section of this lesson, you learned what makes a stored procedure and how to use the tools available to create your own. You also saw how to make the stored procedures more flexible by using local variables to pass parameters into the stored procedure. Finally, you discovered how to pass the status of the stored procedures.

Day 16, "Optimizing Stored Procedures": Today you learned about how stored procedures are compiled for performance. In addition, you saw how to use temporary tables and table variables to assist in making the stored procedure more efficient. Finally, you learned that some stored procedures should really be split up into subprocedures to allow the server to compile the correct execution plan.

Day 17, "Debugging Stored Procedures": Now that you have learned all the different topics relating to stored procedures, the final piece of the puzzle is learning how to debug them. When something doesn't work properly in a stored procedure, you need to know what your options are in figuring out what went wrong. Many of these techniques are useful when debugging triggers and functions as well. The last topic

15
16
17
18
19
20
21

covered today was the T-SQL Debugger, a tool that is available in the Query Analyzer to assist you in debugging your stored procedures.

Day 18, "Writing and Testing Triggers": Triggers are special stored procedures that do not accept any parameters, do not return any status codes, and cannot be executed directly by the user. They are executed by the server only when one of the three actions (`INSERT`, `UPDATE`, `DELETE`) executed against a table is performed. You were shown how triggers are written and what they can do for you in a complex application. You also learned when triggers should be used. Any ordinary functions that can be handled by rules, constraints, or defaults should not be included in trigger processing.

Day 19, "Solving Special Trigger Problems": Today was the second half of the trigger discussion. You learned how to use triggers to assist in enforcing referential integrity or to maintain an audit trail. Finally, you also saw how to use triggers to maintain summary columns in a database table.

Day 20, "User-Defined Functions in SQL": One of the newest features in SQL Server 2000 is the capability to define user-defined functions (UDF). This feature enables you to create standard routines that anyone can access and use in their application SQL scripts.

Day 21, "Handling BLOBs in T-SQL": On the last day of our discussion, you looked at a group of data types that are rarely used in everyday database applications. Binary large object data types, or BLOBs, are used to store very large (>8000 bytes) data in a database table. In particular, you saw how to use SQL to access any piece of this large object to read, write, or update the information. These objects are generally used to store data such as

- Pictures
- Audio
- Video
- Documents (such as resumes)

APPENDIX A

Answers to Quizzes and Exercises

Day 1

Quiz

1. How can I tell whether the words I type into the Query Analyzer editor are keywords?

   Answer: Any words that you enter in the Query Analyzer editor which are keywords will be changed to the color blue. These default colors can be changed in the Options dialog within the Query Analyzer.

2. Identify the column and table names in the following `SELECT` statement:

```
select OrderID,
          CustomerID,
          OrderDate,
          ShipName,
          ShippedDate
From Orders
```

   Answer: The columns in the `SELECT` statement are all listed between the `SELECT` and `FROM` keywords. The table name follows the `FROM` keyword.

3. The following query does not work. Why?

   ```
   Select * Employees
   ```

   Answer: The `SELECT` statement requires the keyword `FROM` before the actual table names.

Exercises

1. Using the `Employees` table from earlier today, write a query to return just the `EmployeeID` and title for each employee.

   Answer:

   ```
   Select EmployeeID,
          Title
   From Employees
   ```

Day 2

Quiz

1. Can you use wildcards with `IN`, as in this example?

   ```
   select ProductName, UnitPrice
   from Products
   where ProductName in ('%tofu%', '%cereal%', '%grain%')
   ```

   Answer: No. The server will treat the wildcards (`%` characters) as literal characters and will try to find products whose name is literally `'%tofu%'` or `'%cereal%'`. To combine multiple wildcard searches, use `OR` to connect `LIKE` clauses:

   ```
   select ProductName, UnitPrice
   from Products
   where ProductName like '%tofu%'
       or ProductName like '%cereal%'
       or ProductName like '%grain%'
   ```

2. When do you need to group conditions using parentheses?

   Answer: Parentheses are required when your `WHERE` clause consists of more than two conditions and there is a combination of `OR` and `AND` conjunctions.

3. In this query, is the sort order on the `EmployeeID` ascending or descending?

   ```
   select EmployeeID, OrderDate, OrderID
   from Orders
   order by EmployeeID, OrderDate desc
   ```

   Answer: The sort order is ascending. The scope of the `ASC` and `DESC` keywords is only over a single column or expression, not over the entire list of columns.

4. In this query and result set featuring `DISTINCT`, why are there multiple rows with the value `'Sales Representative'` in the title column? Isn't `DISTINCT` supposed to eliminate those duplicates?

```
select distinct Title, LastName
from Employees
```

Result:

```
Title                          LastName
------------------------------ --------------------
Inside Sales Coordinator       Callahan
Sales Manager                  Buchanan
Sales Representative           Davolio
Sales Representative           Dodsworth
Sales Representative           King
Sales Representative           Leverling
Sales Representative           Peacock
Sales Representative           Suyama
Vice President, Sales          Fuller
```

Remember that `DISTINCT` removes duplicate rows, not duplicate values. Each combination of title and last name is unique.

Exercises

1. List all customers in Mexico. How many are there?

There are 5 customers.

```
select CustomerID, CompanyName, Country
  from Customers
 where Country = 'Mexico'
```

2. Find Andrew Fuller's home phone number.

His phone number is (206) 555-9482.

```
select FirstName, LastName, HomePhone
  from Employees
 where FirstName = 'Andrew'
   and LastName = 'Fuller'
```

3. What product costs the same as Chang?

(For now, this problem requires two steps. Answer: Inlagd Sill.)

```
select UnitPrice
from Products
where ProductName = 'Chang'
```

(The intermediate result is $19.00.)

```
select ProductName
from Products
where UnitPrice = 19
```

4. Produce a list of different countries shipped to in May of 1998.

```
select distinct ShipCountry
  from orders
 where orderdate >= '5/1/98'
   and orderdate < '5/31/98'
```

Result:

```
ShipCountry
---------------
Austria
Brazil
Denmark
France
Germany
Mexico
Switzerland
USA
Venezuela
```

5. Find the youngest employee. When was he (she) born?

Anne Dodsworth was born in 1966.

```
select LastName, FirstName, BirthDate
  from Employees
 order by BirthDate Desc
```

Day 3

Quiz

1. What function enables you to provide a value for nulls?

   Answer: The function you would use to determine whether a column is NULL and then replace it with a value is the `ISNULL()` function.

2. What is the result of this query?

```
Use Pubs
Select 'My name is ' + au_fname
From authors
Where au_id = '172-32-1176'
```

   Answer: The first name of the author with this `au_id` would be appended to the string, `"My name is "`. The output would be

```
My name is Johnson
```

3. What column name is displayed by this query?

```
Use Pubs
Select au_fname as 'First Name'
From authors
```

Answer: The column name that would be displayed is

```
First Name
```

4. What would be the result of the following query?

```
Use Pubs
Select 'My price is ' + price
From titles
Where title like '%Computer%'
```

Answer: This was really a trick question. The query will produce an error message only because the price column data type is Money and you are asking to concatenate it with a string constant. The error message is

```
Server: Msg 260, Level 16, State 1, Line 2
 Disallowed implicit conversion from data type varchar
 to data type money, table 'pubs.dbo.titles',
 column 'price'. Use the CONVERT function to run this query.
```

Exercises

1. When was the first employee hired by Northwind?

Answer: The first employee who was hired will have the lowest or minimum date in the hiredate column of the employees table:

```
Select min(hiredate)
From Employees
```

Results:

```
------------------------------------------------------
1992-04-01 00:00:00.000

(1 row(s) affected)
```

2. What is today's date and what day of the week is it?

Answer: You would use the GETDATE() function to retrieve today's date. Then, to get the day of the week, you could use either the DATEPART() or DATENAME() functions. The SELECT statement you would use is as follows:

```
Select getdate(), datepart(dw, getdate()), datename(dw, getdate())
```

Results:

```
--------------------------- ----------- ------
2000-10-08 13:11:09.723     1           Sunday

(1 row(s) affected)
```

3. How many hours until New Year's Day?

Answer: The answer to this question is calculated by asking for the DATEDIFF() between now and 1/1/2002. To specify hours in the function by using the hh DATEPART() code:

```
select datediff(hh,getdate(), '1/1/2002')
```

Day 4

Quiz

1. Put the following keywords in order to make a `SELECT` statement work properly:
   - `GROUP BY`
   - `HAVING`
   - `SELECT`
   - `DISTINCT`
   - `WHERE`
   - `FROM`
   - `ORDER BY`
   - `ROLLUP`

   Answer:
   - `SELECT`
   - `DISTINCT`
   - `FROM`
   - `WHERE`
   - `GROUP BY`
   - `ROLLUP`
   - `HAVING`
   - `ORDER BY`
2. What is the difference between `COUNT(*)` and `COUNT(`*`expression`*`)`?

   Answer: `COUNT(`*`expression`*`)` evaluates the expression in each row. Only non-null values are counted. `COUNT(*)` counts every row. It does not examine any columns.
3. Is the following query permitted? If not, how would you correct it?

```
select ProductID, ProductName
  from Products
 where UnitPrice > avg(UnitPrice)
```

   Answer: The query is not permitted. An aggregate function (`AVG`) cannot appear in a `WHERE` clause unless it is part of a subquery. Here is the corrected query:

```
select ProductID, ProductName
  from Products
 where UnitPrice >
      (
      select avg(UnitPrice)
        from Products
      )
```

4. Is the following query permitted? If not, how would you correct it?

```
select Country, Region, Count(*) as 'Customers'
  from Customers
 group by Country
```

Answer: All nonaggregate columns in the query need to be included in the grouping clause. `Region` is included in the select list, but is not listed after `GROUP BY`. Here is the correct query:

```
select Country, Region, Count(*) as 'Customers'
  from Customers
 group by Country, Region
```

5. What is the difference between `HAVING` and `WHERE`?

Answer: A `WHERE` clause is evaluated before the results are grouped. A `HAVING` clause is evaluated after grouping has occurred.

6. What is the difference between `ROLLUP` and `CUBE`?

Answer: `ROLLUP` provides a set of subtotals and totals, traversing the hierarchy of the grouping expressions. `CUBE` provides a complete set of subtotals and totals, representing a complete set of all possible combinations of grouping expressions.

Exercises

1. Who is the oldest employee, and when was he or she born?

```
select LastName, FirstName, BirthDate
  from Employees
 where BirthDate =
       (
       select min(BirthDate)
         from Employees
       )
```

Margaret Peacock, 9/19/1937

2. How many customers are located outside the United States?

```
select count(*) as 'Foreign customers'
  from Customers
 where Country <> 'USA'
```

Result:

```
78
```

3. Prepare a report showing a breakdown of suppliers by country.

```
select Country, count(*) as 'Suppliers'
  from Suppliers
 group by Country with rollup
```

Results:

```
Country         Suppliers
--------------- -----------
Australia                 2
Brazil                    1
Canada                    2
Denmark                   1
Finland                   1
France                    3
Germany                   3
Italy                     2
Japan                     2
Netherlands               1
Norway                    1
Singapore                 1
Spain                     1
Sweden                    2
UK                        2
USA                       4
NULL                     29
```

4. Which countries have more than one supplier? Sort the countries by number of suppliers, from greatest to least.

```
select Country, count(*) as 'Suppliers'
  from Suppliers
 group by Country
having count(*) >= 2
 order by count(*) desc, Country
```

Results:

```
Country         Suppliers
--------------- -----------
USA                       4
France                    3
Germany                   3
Australia                 2
Canada                    2
Italy                     2
Japan                     2
Sweden                    2
UK                        2
```

5. How many different categories of product are there?

```
select count(distinct CategoryID)
  from Products
```

Results:

```
8
```

6. Display the top selling product ID (by dollars sold, including discounts) and the total dollar sales.

```
select top 1
       ProductID,
       sum(Quantity * UnitPrice * (1.0-Discount))
                 as 'Dollar Sales'
  from
       [Order Details]
 group by
       ProductID
 order by
        sum(Quantity * UnitPrice * (1.0-Discount)) desc
```

Results:

```
ProductID   Dollar Sales
----------- ------------------------------
         38 41396.73522949219
```

Day 5

Quiz

1. For each of the following items, identify the database name, owner, table name, and column name (if available). Where the value will default, indicate that.

   a. `CompanyName`
   b. `Customers.CompanyName`
   c. `Northwind.dbo.Products.QuantityPerUnit`
   d. `Northwind..Products.UnitPrice`
   e. `dbo.Suppliers.City`
   f. `Mary.Suppliers.City`
   g. `Suppliers`
   h. `dbo.Suppliers`

   Answer:

   a. `CompanyName`—Column name in a table in query. Unqualified, so cannot determine other information.
   b. `Customers.CompanyName`—Column name in `Customers` table. Current database is assumed. Table is owned by current user or `dbo`.
   c. `Northwind.dbo.Products.QuantityPerUnit`—Fully qualified column name of `QuantityPerUnit` column in `Products` table owned by `dbo` in the `Northwind` database.
   d. `Northwind..Products.UnitPrice`—Same as (c), except that owner is allowed to default. Table owned either by current user or database owner.

e. dbo.Suppliers.City—City column in Suppliers table owned by dbo in current database.

f. Mary.Suppliers.City—City column in Suppliers table owned by Mary in current database.

g. Suppliers—Unqualified table name, owned by current user or dbo in current database.

h. dbo.Suppliers—Suppliers table owned by dbo in current database.

2. How many join conditions are required to perform a three-table join?

   Answer: Two join conditions are required.

3. What is a cross join?

   Answer: A join whose result set includes every combination of rows from the tables.

4. How do you decide whether an outer join should be a right or left outer join?

   Answer: The "side" of the join depends on the syntactic table order. Use a left outer join when you want to include rows from the first table in the list. Use right outer join when you want to include rows from the second table in the list.

5. How many ORDER BY clauses can appear in a query containing the UNION keyword?

   Answer: Only one ORDER BY clause may appear at the end of the query.

Exercises

1. Display the names and hire dates of five sales representatives.

```
select top 5
        e.LastName,
        e.FirstName,
        e.HireDate
from
        Employees e
where
        e.Title = 'Sales Representative'
```

   Results:

```
LastName             FirstName  HireDate
-------------------- ---------- --------------------------
Davolio              Nancy      1992-05-01 00:00:00.000
Leverling            Janet      1992-04-01 00:00:00.000
Peacock              Margaret   1993-05-03 00:00:00.000
Suyama               Michael    1993-10-17 00:00:00.000
King                 Robert     1994-01-02 00:00:00.000
```

2. Modify the query in exercise 1 to include a list of order numbers for each employee. Display the first five rows.

A

```
select top 5
        e.LastName,
        e.FirstName,
        e.HireDate,
        o.OrderID
from
        Employees e
    inner join
        Orders o
            on e.EmployeeID = o.EmployeeID
where
        e.Title = 'Sales Representative'
```

Results:

```
LastName             FirstName  HireDate   OrderID
-------------------- ---------- ---------- -----------
Davolio              Nancy      1992-05-01       10258
Davolio              Nancy      1992-05-01       10270
Davolio              Nancy      1992-05-01       10275
Davolio              Nancy      1992-05-01       10285
Davolio              Nancy      1992-05-01       10292
```

3. Modify the last query to include the product IDs and the total dollar value of each sale item. Display five total rows.

```
select top 5
        e.LastName,
        e.FirstName,
        e.HireDate,
        o.OrderID,
        od.ProductID,
        od.UnitPrice * od.Quantity * (1 - od.Discount) 'Dollars'
from
        Employees e
    inner join
        Orders o
            on e.EmployeeID = o.EmployeeID
    inner join
        [Order Details] od
            on od.OrderID = o.OrderID
where
        e.Title = 'Sales Representative'
```

Results:

```
LastName    FirstName  HireDate   OrderID ProductID Dollars
----------- ---------- ---------- ------- --------- -------
Davolio     Nancy      1992-05-01   10258         2   608.0
Davolio     Nancy      1992-05-01   10258         5   884.0
Davolio     Nancy      1992-05-01   10258        32  122.88
Davolio     Nancy      1992-05-01   10270        36   456.0
Davolio     Nancy      1992-05-01   10270        43   920.0
```

4. Group the last result by employee and show the five employees with the worst sales overall.

```
select top 5
        e.LastName,
        e.FirstName,
        e.HireDate,
        sum(od.UnitPrice * od.Quantity * (1 - od.Discount)) 'Dollars'
from
        Employees e
    inner join
        Orders o
            on e.EmployeeID = o.EmployeeID
    inner join
        [Order Details] od
            on od.OrderID = o.OrderID
where
        e.Title = 'Sales Representative'
group by
        e.LastName,
        e.FirstName,
        e.HireDate
order by
        'Dollars' asc
```

Results:

```
LastName             FirstName  HireDate   Dollars
-------------------- ---------- ---------- ----------------
Suyama               Michael    1993-10-17         73913.12
Dodsworth            Anne       1994-11-15         77308.06
King                 Robert     1994-01-02        124568.23
Davolio              Nancy      1992-05-01        192107.60
Leverling            Janet      1992-04-01        202812.84
```

5. Challenge: Modify the previous query to display five employees with the worst average yearly performance. Hint: Use the employee hire date to determine the number of years the employee has worked for the firm.

```
select top 5
        e.LastName,
        e.FirstName,
        e.HireDate,
        datediff(yy, e.Hiredate, getdate()) 'Years of service',
        sum(od.UnitPrice * od.Quantity * (1 - od.Discount)) 'Dollars',
        sum(od.UnitPrice * od.Quantity * (1 - od.Discount))
                  / datediff(yy, e.Hiredate, getdate())
                  'Average Sales Per Year'
from
        Employees e
    inner join
        Orders o
            on e.EmployeeID = o.EmployeeID
```

A

```
    inner join
        [Order Details] od
            on od.OrderID = o.OrderID
where
        e.Title = 'Sales Representative'
group by
        e.LastName,
        e.FirstName,
        e.HireDate
order by
        'Average Sales Per Year' ascLastName     FirstName  HireDate
Years Average Sales
```

Results:

```
------------ --------- --------- ----- --------------
Suyama       Michael   1993-10-17    7        10559.01
Dodsworth    Anne      1994-11-15    6        12884.67
King         Robert    1994-01-02    6        20761.37
Davolio      Nancy     1992-05-01    8        24013.45
Leverling    Janet     1992-04-01    8        25351.60
```

Day 6

Quiz

1. How many tables can appear in a single query?

   Answer: In previous releases of SQL Server, there was a limit of 16 tables. However, Microsoft has increased this limit to 256, which is probably more than any query you write will ever need.

2. Can a subquery be run as a join or vice versa?

   Answer: Yes, in most cases, a subquery can be implemented as a join or vice versa.

3. In which SQL clauses may a subquery appear?

   Answer: A subquery can be used in any `SELECT`, `WHERE`, and `HAVING` statement or clause.

Exercises

These exercises use the `Pubs` database.

1. List the authors who have at least one book priced above the average price.

   Answer: This one is a bit harder than it looks. To answer it, you must use the `Authors` table to get the author names, the `Sales` table to find the books that have sold, the `Titles` table for the book prices, and the `TitleAuthor` table to relate the authors and titles tables to each other. You would then use the `WHERE` clause to compare the price of a book against the average book price, which you retrieved using a subquery. In addition, the `EXISTS` test was used to eliminate any duplicate rows that the join to the `Sales` table produced.

```
use pubs
select au_lname, au_fname, t.title_id
from authors as a inner join
     titleauthor as ta
     on a.au_id = ta.au_id
     inner join
     titles as t
     on t.title_id = ta.title_id
where exists (
      select * from sales as s inner join
                    titles as t2
                    on t.title_id = s.title_id)
      and t.price > (
          select avg(price) from titles)
```

Results:

```
au_lname                                 au_fname             title_id
---------------------------------------- -------------------- --------
O'Leary                                  Michael              BU1111
MacFeather                               Stearns              BU1111
MacFeather                               Stearns              PS1372
Karsen                                   Livia                PS1372

(4 row(s) affected)
```

2. Using a subquery, list the sales information for all books with the word *Computer* in the title.

   Answer: The subquery will run against the `Titles` table, selecting the `Title_ID` for books that have `Computer` in the title. This information is placed in a list. Then, select everything in the `sales` table where the `Title_ID` matches a `Title_ID` in the `IN` list:

```
use pubs
select *
from sales
where title_id in(
      select title_id
      from titles
      where title like '%Computer%')
```

Day 7

Quiz

1. What is wrong with the following statement?

```
DELETE * FROM customer_demo
```

Answer: This statement should not be using the '*'. In addition, the FROM keyword is optional. The correct syntax of this statement is

```
DELETE FROM customer_demo
```

Or

```
DELETE customer_demo
```

Remember that this would delete all the data in the table.

2. What is wrong with the following statement?

```
UPDATE customer_demo (
    'John', 'smith', 34)
```

Answer: This statement mixes the UPDATE command with the INSERT command. To UPDATE values into the customer_demo table, you use the following syntax for an update:

```
UPDATE customer_demo
SET Fname = 'John',
    Lname = 'smith'
    age = 34
```

And for an insert, the following syntax would be used:

```
INSERT INTO customer_demo
            (Fname, Lname, Age)
       Values('John', 'smith', 34)
```

3. What would happen if you executed the following statement?

```
DELETE * from customer_demo
```

Answer: Nothing would be deleted because this is incorrect syntax. The * is not needed in the DELETE statement.

4. Will the following SQL statement work?

```
INSERT INTO customer_demo
SET VALUES = 758
WHERE ITEM = 'CAR'
```

Answer: No, this statement would not work. The syntax is incorrect. The SET clause is not part of the INSERT statement.

Exercises

1. Create a table called `customers_demo` with the following columns: an identity column called `cust_id`; `fname` and `lname` as required fields; `email`, which is an optional email address; and `cust_new` to specify whether the customer is new. The `cust_new` column should default to `'Y'` to specify that the customer is new to the company.

   The following code will create the table as described:

```
Create table customers_demo(
Cust_id int identity,
Fname varchar(30) not null,
Lnamc varchar(30) not null,
Email varchar(20) null,
Cust_new char(1) not null default 'Y'
)
```

2. Insert the following data into your table:

First Name	*Last Name*	*Email*	*New Customer?*
John	Smith	Jsmith@aol.com	Y
Julie	Pinter		N
Bill	Buckley	BillyB@wb.com	Y
Seven	Nine	Sevenof9@st.com	N

   The following shows how to insert the specified data:

```
Insert customers_demo (fname, lname, email, cust_new)
    Values('John', 'Smith', 'Jsmith@aol.com')
Insert customers_demo (fname, lname, cust_new)
    Values('Julie', 'Pinter', 'N')
Insert customers_demo (fname, lname, email)
    Values('Bill', 'Buckley', 'BillyB@WB.com')
Insert customers_demo (fname, lname, email, cust_new)
    Values('Seven', 'Nine', 'Sevenof9@ST.com', 'N')
```

   For email addresses that were not specified, I left them out, and let the server insert a NULL. When the new customer flag is `'Y'`, I left it out so that the server will insert the default value of `'Y'`.

3. Try inserting values with the incorrect data types into the table. Note the errors and then insert values with correct data types into the table.

Day 8

Quiz

1. In the following code, what will the database size be increased to the first time it runs out of allocated space?

```
CREATE DATABASE Customer
  ON
  (NAME = cust_dat,
  FILENAME = 'c:\SQL_Data\custdat.mdf',
  SIZE = 100MB,
  MAXSIZE = 500MB,
  FILEGROWTH = 20MB)
```

   Answer: The initial size starts at 100MB. When that 100MB is used up, the database will automatically increase 20MB to 120MB.

2. What would happen if you tried to insert the value `123abc` into a column defined with a data type of `INTEGER`?

   Answer: The record would not be inserted. The SQL server would return an invalid data type error.

3. How many primary keys can you have per table?

   Answer: One.

Exercises

1. Write the code to create a table with the following columns and specifications:

   Call the new table "`employees2`," and add columns for peoples' names as `first`, `middle`, and `last`; allow NULLS for the middle name only.

```
CREATE TABLE employees2
  (first varchar(15) NOT NULL,
  middle varchar(15) NULL,
  last varchar(20) NOT NULL)
```

2. Now write the code to add a four-digit, numbers-only column called `emp_number` to the table in exercise 1.

```
ALTER TABLE employees
  ADD emp_number INT
```

Day 9

Quiz

1. Which is larger, a nonclustered or clustered index?

   Answer: A nonclustered index is usually larger than a clustered index on the same key. This is because the leaf level requires one row in the index for each row in the table.

2. How do you force a table scan in SQL Server?

   Answer: By specifying an index number of 0 in the optimizer hint.

Exercises

1. Write a query to output the contents of the `Employees` table in the `Northwind` database. Display the Execution Plan for this query.

   Answer: The following is the SQL statement you can use to display the `Employees` table. Remember to set the option in the Query Analyzer to display the Execution Plan.

   ```
   Select * From Employees
   ```

2. Add a `WHERE` clause to the query based on the `LastName` column and see whether the execution plan has changed.

   Answer: The following is the SQL statement that adds the `WHERE` condition to the previous exercise answer. Remember to set the option in the Query Analyzer to display the Execution Plan.

   ```
   Select *
   From Employees
   Where LastName Like 'M%'
   ```

3. Force the use of the nonclustered index on the `PostalCode`. Check the execution plan to see what the effect is.

   Answer: The following is the SQL statement that adds the hint to force the use of the `PostalCode` index. Remember to set the option in the Query Analyzer to display the Execution Plan.

   ```
   Select *
   From Employees (index = 'PostalCode')
   Where LastName Like 'M%'
   ```

Day 10

Quiz

1. What are the three different types of temporary tables and how do you create them?

   Answer: Local temporary tables are created with a single `#` symbol as the first character in the table name; global temporary tables are created with two `#` symbols; permanent temporary tables are created by creating the table in the `TEMPDB` database.

2. If I need to append 10 tables together, how can I do it?

   Answer: You would create a view with 10 `SELECT` statements that are joined together using a `UNION` clause. This will work only if all the tables have the same number and type of columns.

3. Who can access a global temporary table? A permanent temporary table?

   Answer: Global temporary tables can be accessed by anyone connected to the server. Permanent temporary tables are not accessible until permission to that table is granted. By default, most users get Guest access to `TEMPDB`, so they can access a permanent temporary table.

4. How can I make changes to a view?

   Answer: A view can be modified either by using the tools in the Enterprise Manager or by using the `ALTER VIEW` statement.

Exercises

1. Using the `Pubs` database, create a global temporary table that includes the author names along with the revenue they have generated.

   Answer: By using a mixture of columns and aggregates, you can easily create this temporary table. The SQL code required is as follows:

```
Select a.au_lname, a.au_Fname,
       Sum(t.price * s.qty) as 'Revenue'
Into ##tp_Revenue
From authors as a
    Inner Join Titleauthor as ta
    On a.au_id = ta.au_id
    Inner Join Sales as s
    On ta.title_id = s.title_id
    Inner Join titles as t
    On s.title_id = t.title_id and
       Ta.title_id = t.title_id
Group by au_lname, au_fname
Order by revenue
```

2. Create a view that shows sales information for the United States only. This should include the company name, order date, product name, and the total sales for each.

   Answer: The answer to this exercise is a view that contains four tables joined together:

```
Create view vw_sales as
select     c.CompanyName,
    o.OrderDate,
    p.ProductName,
    sum(od.UnitPrice * od.Quantity) as sales
from customers as c
    inner join orders as o
    on o.customerid = c.customerid
```

```
    inner join [order details] as od
    on o.orderid = od.orderid
    inner join products as p
    on p.productid = od.productid
where c.country = 'USA'
group by c.companyname, o.orderdate, p.productname
```

Day 11

Quiz

1. Name the five steps that the server must perform when a batch of SQL statements is sent for execution.

   Answer: Parse:syntax, Parse:object references, Optimize, Compile, and Execute.

2. What are two of the major flow of control statements that you can use?

   Answer: `IF`, `WHILE`.

3. What value does the variable `@@ERROR` contain?

   Answer: It contains the last error code returned by the server. If no error has occurred, it will contain a zero.

Exercise

1. Write a SQL statement that displays the current version of SQL Server.

   Answer: The `@@Version` system stored procedure is used to display the current version of the SQL Server

```
Select @@Version
```

Day 12

Quiz

1. What is the difference between a shared and an exclusive lock?

   Answer: A shared lock, acquired during a read process, prevents other users from changing data, but permits other processes to read the data. An exclusive lock, acquired during a write process, prevents other users from reading or writing data.

2. What statements (select, insert, update, delete) will acquire a shared lock?

   Answer: All select statements acquire shared locks. Insert, update, and delete statements that rely on other tables will use shared locks to read from those tables in addition to exclusive locks on the affected table.

3. What is an intent lock, and what exactly gets locked?

   Answer: An intent lock is a bookmark that a process uses to tell other processes that it holds real locks within a resource. For example, a shared table-level intent lock means that the process holds page or key locks within the table. Other resources will be able to obtain their own page or key locks within the table, but they will not be able to get an exclusive table-level lock until the intent lock is cleared.

4. Does an exclusive intent lock block other users from reading or writing?

   Answer: No. An exclusive intent lock tells other processes that there is an exclusive lock within the resource. Other processes can read and write within the same resource. An exclusive intent lock will block table-level shared and exclusive locks until the intent lock is cleared.

Exercises

1. Write a query to retrieve a list of five worst-selling products. You'll want to update the `products` table when your query is complete, so get and retain exclusive locks on the low-selling products. (You will need to examine the locks in the next exercise.)

```
begin tran
select top 5
        p.ProductID,
        p.ProductName,
        sum(od.Quantity * od.UnitPrice * (1 - od.Discount))
              as 'Total Dollars'
from
        Products p with (xlock)
    inner join
        [Order Details] od
            on p.ProductID = od.ProductID
group by
        p.ProductID,
        p.ProductName
order by
        'Total Dollars' desc
```

Results:

```
ProductID   ProductName                  Total Dollars
----------- ---------------------------- ------------------
         48 Chocolade                    1368.7125244140625
         33 Geitost                                1648.125
         15 Genen Shouyu                 1784.8249969482422
         67 Laughing Lumberjack Lager    2396.8000183105469
         74 Longlife Tofu                            2432.5
```

2. Find out the `spid` of your process.

```
select @@spid
sp_lock 51
```

This is the `spid` when I ran this exercise on my computer.

```
------
    51
```

Based on that process ID, I get a list of locks for that `spid`.

```
spid dbid ObjId       IndId Type Resource     Mode     Status
---- ---- ----------- ----- ---- ------------ -------- ------
  51    6           0     0 DB                S        GRANT
  51    6   17575457      0 TAB               IX       GRANT
  51    6   17575457      1 KEY  (3b00435f91  X        GRANT
  51    6   17575457      1 KEY  (3e0071af4f  X        GRANT
  51    6   17575457      1 KEY  (260001d0e2  X        GRANT
  51    6   17575457      1 KEY  (1d00a1afc8  X        GRANT
  51    6   17575457      1 PAG  1:276        IX       GRANT
  51    1   85575343      0 TAB               IS       GRANT
  51    6   17575457      1 KEY  (3c00fa6746  X        GRANT
```

3. In a new session, get a list of products in category 1.

```
select
        ProductName
from
        Products
where
        CategoryID = 1
```

Results:

```
There is no response because the Products table is being blocked by a
transaction that has not been committed yet.
```

4. Find a blocking and a blocked session. Clear the locks from the blocking session.

```
sp_who
```

Results:

```
spid status     loginame    blk dbname     cmd
---- ---------- ----------- --- ---------- ----------------
   1 background sa          0   NULL       LAZY WRITER
   2 sleeping   sa          0   NULL       LOG WRITER
   3 background sa          0   master     SIGNAL HANDLER
   4 background sa          0   NULL       LOCK MONITOR
   5 background sa          0   master     TASK MANAGER
   6 sleeping   sa          0   NULL       CHECKPOINT SLEEP
   7 background sa          0   master     TASK MANAGER
   8 background sa          0   master     TASK MANAGER
   9 background sa          0   master     TASK MANAGER
  10 background sa          0   master     TASK MANAGER
  51 sleeping   northwind_d 0   Northwind  WAITING COMMAND
```

```
52 sleeping   northwind_d 0   Northwind  WAITING COMMAND
53 sleeping   northwind_d 51  Northwind  SELECT
54 runnable   northwind_d 0   Northwind  SELECT
```

Session 51 is blocking session 53.

In session 53, type:

```
rollback transaction
```

Day 13

Quiz

1. What is the difference between ROLLBACK TRANSACTIONS and ROLLBACK TRANSACTIONS <savepoint>?

   Answer: When you roll back a transaction to a savepoint, the transaction remains active, and any locks that existed before are still available. Without a savepoint, ROLLBACK TRANSACTIONS reverses all work in the transaction, ends the active transaction, and releases locks.

2. How do the following settings affect your programming:

   ```
   set implicit_transactions on
   ```

   Answer: Implicit transactions omit the automatic COMMIT record that would normally be included with single-statement transactions. Whenever you are executing single-statement transactions, you need to include an explicit COMMIT TRANSACTIONS statement to commit your work. Otherwise, your work will never be permanently saved, and locks will be held until you log out.

   ```
   set xact_abort on
   ```

   Answer: When you use the xact_abort setting, you can omit error-trapping code in your transactions. As long as a transaction is active, the server will abort any batch and roll back all work whenever a runtime error occurs.

   ```
   set lock_timeout 0
   ```

   Answer: The lock_timeout setting should not affect your programs. Setting the lock timeout to 0 tells the query to quit if it is blocked by any locks.

   The lock_timeout setting should not matter because your programs already need to be able to react to a query timeout, when a query runs too long. Behavior when the process fails on a lock timeout error should be the same as the query timeout.

Exercise

In the following exercise, correct this batch to avoid a common transaction programming problem. Describe the problem and then suggest a solution.

```
begin transaction
if (
    select avg(UnitPrice)
    from Products
    where Category = 1
) > 15
update Products
   set UnitPrice = UnitPrice * .90
 where CategoryID = 1
/* implement 30-day price protection */
update [Order Details]
   set UnitPrice = UnitPrice * .90
 where ProductID in (
       select ProductID
       from Products
       where CategoryID = 1
       )
   and OrderID in (
       select OrderID
       from Orders
       where datediff(dd, OrderDate, getdate()) <= 30
       )
commit transaction
```

Problem: There are partial transactions. `Products` is not being updated, but `Order Details` is.

Solution: There is no error trapping in transaction allows updates to continue after error.

Run the batch using the `xact_abort` setting.

```
set xact_abort on     --   <<--
begin transaction
if (
    select avg(UnitPrice)
    from Products with (xlock)
    where Category = 1
) > 15
update Products
   set UnitPrice = UnitPrice * .90
 where CategoryID = 1
/* implement 30-day price protection */
update [Order Details]
   set UnitPrice = UnitPrice * .90
 where ProductID in (
       select ProductID
       from Products
```

```
        where CategoryID = 1
        )
    and OrderID in (
        select OrderID
        from Orders
        where datediff(dd, OrderDate, getdate()) <= 30
        )
commit transaction
```

Day 14

Quiz

1. Name the six navigation operations that are possible with cursors.

   Answer: The six operations are `NEXT`, `PRIOR`, `FIRST`, `LAST`, `ABSOLUTE`, and `RELATIVE`.

2. Can a cursor select data from joined tables?

   Answer: Yes, a cursor can select data from a joined table. In addition, it can be declared for update as well. However, when updating a cursor like this, only the columns in the table listed in the `UPDATE` statements are affected. You can update columns in all the tables, but you must do it in separate `UPDATE` statements.

3. Name the six steps required to use a cursor.

   Answer: The six steps are

   1. Declare cursor variables.
   2. Declare a cursor and associate it with a `SELECT` statement.
   3. Open the cursor.
   4. Fetch a row of data from the cursor keyset, and then loop to process the entire keyset.
   5. Close the cursor.
   6. Deallocate the cursor.

Exercise

Create a cursor on the `Employees` table in the `Northwind` database. Read in each employee's last name, birth date, and hire date. If an employee is more than 40 years old, then print his last name, and hire date.

```
use northwind
declare crs_employees cursor
for
select lastname, birthdate, hiredate
```

```
from employees
order by lastname
open crs_employees
Declare @Emp_Name varchar(20), @Birth_Date datetime,
        @Hire_Date datetime, @tempstr varchar(50),
    @age int
print 'Employee Name         Birth Date  Age  Hire Date'
print '-------------------- ----------  ---  ----------'
fetch next from crs_employees into @Emp_Name, @Birth_Date,
        @Hire_Date
while @@fetch_status = 0 begin
set @age = datediff(yy,@birth_date,getdate())
if @age > 40
    set @tempstr = convert(char(22),@Emp_Name) +
    convert(char(13), @birth_date,101) +
    convert(char(4), @age) +
    convert(char(10), @hire_date,101)
print @tempstr
fetch next from crs_employees into @Emp_Name, @Birth_Date,
        @Hire_Date
end
close crs_employees
deallocate crs_employees
```

Results:

```
Employee Name         Birth Date  Age  Hire Date
--------------------- ----------  ---  ----------
Buchanan              03/04/1955   45  10/17/1993
Callahan              01/09/1958   42  03/05/1994
Davolio               12/08/1948   52  05/01/1992
Davolio               12/08/1948   52  05/01/1992
Fuller                02/19/1952   48  08/14/1992
Fuller                02/19/1952   48  08/14/1992
Fuller                02/19/1952   48  08/14/1992
Peacock               09/19/1937   63  05/03/1993
Peacock               09/19/1937   63  05/03/1993
```

Day 15

Quiz

1. What is the correct method to return a data value to a calling program?

   Answer: You should define a variable as output to return a data value to the calling program. Then you must set the variable to the value you want to pass.

   ```
   create proc p1 (@x int output)
   as
   select @x = 1
   return
   ```

2. I have the following procedure and batch, but when I run the batch, the value of @out_x is always null. What's wrong?

```
create procedure p1 (@x int output)
as
select @x = 1
return

declare @out_x int
execute p1 @out_x
select @out_x
```

Answer: The reason you are getting a null returned is that you must include the output keyword in the Execute statement as well as the procedure.

```
declare @out_x int
execute p1 @out_x output
select @out_x
```

3. In this procedure and batch, my return status is always null. Why?

```
create procedure p2
as
declare @x int
select @x = 1
if @x = 1
   return 1
else
   return 0

declare @retstat int
execute p2
select @retstat "return"
```

Answer: You need to include a reference to `@retstat` in the `EXECUTE` statement as shown:

```
declare @retstat int
execute @retstat = p2
select @retstat "return"
```

4. How do I get a list of parameters for a procedure?

   Answer: Parameters are listed in the object browser. You can also use `sp_help` to see a list of parameters.

Exercises

1. Write a stored procedure to display the contents of the shopping cart for a customer. Call the `prGetCustomerCart` procedure in your procedure.

```
create proc prShowItemsInCustomerCart (
    @CustomerID nchar(5)
) as
```

```
declare @ret int
declare @OrderID int

exec @ret = prGetCustomerCart
    @CustomerID,
    @OrderID output

if @ret != 0 begin
/* error getting an OrderID - quit now */
    return @ret
end

Select
    [OrderID],
    [ProductID],
    [UnitPrice],
    [Quantity],
    [Discount]
From
    [Northwind].[dbo].[Order Details]
Where
    [OrderID] = @OrderID

/* check for error in select */
if @@error != 0
    return 99
else
    return 0
```

2. Write a stored procedure to delete the current shopping cart for a customer. Delete both the order details and the order itself.

```
create proc prDeleteCustomerCart (
    @CustomerID nchar(5)
) as

declare @ret int
declare @OrderID int

exec @ret = prGetCustomerCart
    @CustomerID,
    @OrderID output

if @ret != 0 begin
/* error getting an OrderID - quit now */
    return @ret
end

Delete
    [Northwind].[dbo].[Order Details]
Where
    [OrderID] = @OrderID
```

A

```
/* check for error in select */
if @@error != 0
    return 99
else
    return 0
```

Day 16

Quiz

1. When could a stored procedure cause serious performance problems?

   Answer: Stored procedures can cause problems when a stored optimization plan is unsuitable for the current set of parameters.

2. Can you give an example of the previous answer?

   Answer: Certain parameter sets will call for the use of an index, and others are better suited to a table scan. Use of the wrong optimization plan will cause a significant performance problem. You should use the `RECOMPILE` option. A typical example is a search based on a date range as shown.

```
Create procedure sp_datename (@startdate Datetime, @enddate Datetime)
As
Select *
From tablename
Where date Between @startdate and @enddate
```

Exercises

1. The following procedure seems to take a long time to process. Can you identify the reason and correct it?

```
        Create Procedure Sales_by_State
  (@start_date datetime, @end_date datetime)
As
Select od.productid, od.quantity, od.unitprice, ord.customerid
  into #tp_Sales
From orders as ORD inner join
     [Order Details] as OD on
     ord.orderid = od.orderid
Where ORD.orderdate between @start_date and @end_date
Select cst.region,
       sum(tp.quantity * tp.unitprice)
From Customers as cst left outer join
     #tp_sales as tp on
     cst.customerid = tp.customerid
Group by tp.region
```

Answer: As you have seen in this lesson, the reason this procedure is performing poorly is because the optimization of the procedure must guess at how large the temporary table will be. To fix this procedure, you need to break it up into two steps. First, you create two procedures; the first inner procedure will retrieve data from the temporary table, and the outer procedure will call the inner one to perform the complete process. The following SQL batch is an example of how this can be done:

```
        Select od.productid,
       od.quantity,
       od.unitprice,
       ord.customerid
Into #tp_Sales
From orders as ORD inner join
     [Order Details] as OD on
     ord.orderid = od.orderid
Go
Create Procedure Sub_Sales_by_State
With Recompile
As
Select cst.region,
       sum(tp.quantity * tp.unitprice)
From Customers as cst left outer join
     #tp_sales as tp on
     cst.customerid = tp.customerid
Group by tp.region
Go
Drop Table #tp_sales
Go
Create Procedure SP_Sales_by_State
  (@start_date datetime, @end_date datetime)
As
Select od.productid,
       od.quantity,
       od.unitprice,
       ord.customerid
Into #tp_Sales
From orders as ORD inner join
     [Order Details] as OD on
     ord.orderid = od.orderid
Where ORD.orderdate between @start_date and @end_date
        Execute Sub_Sales_by_State
        Go
```

2. Create a procedure that updates the price of a product, passing the price and its product ID. This update must verify that the product is available (quantity > 0) and the new price is greater than $12.00. If the update fails for any reason, return an error. Make sure to use transaction processing.

Answer: There are many ways to work with transactions within a procedure. Using the methods discussed in this lesson, the following is an example of one way to use transactions:

```
    Create Procedure sp_Update_products
  (@prodID int, @price Money)
As
Declare @err int, @rowcount int
If @price <= $12
Begin
   Raiserror ('Price entered must be greater than $12 dollars', 16,1)
   Return 99
End
Begin Transaction
   Save Transaction sp_update_products
     Update products
       Set unitprice = @price
       Where productid = @prodID
     Select @err = @@error
     Select @rowcount = @@rowcount
     If @err <> 0
     Begin
       Rollback Transaction sp_update_products
       Commit Transaction
       Return 98
     End
     If @rowcount = 0
     Begin
       Print 'Product ID does not exist, exiting procedure'
       Commit Transaction
       Return 97
     End
     If Isnull((Select UnitsInStock
        From Products
        Where productid = @prodID), 0) <= 0
     Begin
       Raiserror ('Product is no longer available', 16, 1)
       Rollback Transaction sp_update_products
       Commit Transaction
       Return 96
     End
Commit Transaction
Return 0
```

To test this procedure, you can use the following batch:

```
    Declare @ret_code int
Execute @ret_code = sp_update_products 146, $15
If @ret_code <> 0
Begin
  Raiserror ('Return Code is %d', 0, 1, @ret_code)
```

```
  Return
End

      Product is no longer available
Return Code is 96
```

3. Extra Credit: Create a system procedure that displays the usernames and login names of everyone using the current database.

   Answer: The usernames are in the system table `Sysusers` and the login names are in the `Master..Sysusers` table. (Hint: to create a system stored procedure, you must log in to the `Master` database as the system administrator SA, using the assigned password.)

```
    Create Procedure sp_Users_New
As
Select users.name, login.name
From sysusers as users Inner Join
     Master..sysusers as login on
     users.uid = login.uid
```

Day 17

Quiz

1. What is a breakpoint?

   Answer: A breakpoint is a method of setting automatic stops within a stored procedure to halt the execution of the procedure at a particular statement in order to debug a problem.

2. What is being displayed in the Local Variables pane?

   Answer: The Local Variables pane displays all the parameters that were passed to the procedure as well as any variables that you declared within the procedure.

3. How can comments help in the testing process?

   Answer: You can use comments to prevent sections of SQL code from being executed when testing the procedure. Comments also enable you to leave testing code, such as `PRINT` statements and parameter assignment statements, in the procedure without concern that they will be executed accidentally.

Exercises

Because of the nature of testing and debugging, it is almost impossible to provide exercises for you. I suggest that you work with several of the functions, triggers, and stored procedures to see how the different techniques help. Finally, using the T-SQL debugger, select a stored procedure and test it using the debugger.

Day 18

Quiz

1. What is wrong with the following triggers' error handler?

```
If @@Error <> 0
  Raiserror ('Trigger error: Rolling back', 16, 1)
  Rollback Transaction
  Return
```

   Answer: The `IF` statement is missing a `BEGIN...END` block. This causes only the `RAISERROR` statement to be executed if the `@@Error` value is not equal to zero. Unfortunately, the `ROLLBACK TRANSACTION` statement will always be executed. This means that the trigger would perform the rollback no matter what the condition of the data is.

2. If inserted rows go into the `INSERTED` table and deleted rows go into the `DELETED` table, where do updated rows go?

   Answer: This is a trick question. An updated row is recorded in both places. The original row is placed in the `DELETED` table and the new version of the row is placed in the `INSERTED` table.

Exercise

1. Create a trigger on the `Order Detail` table in the `Northwind` database so that whenever an order is entered, modified, or deleted, `UnitsInStock` is properly updated. However, if an order causes `UnitsInStock` to drop below zero, raise an error and roll back the transaction.

   Answer: The following is an example of one way to perform this task:

```
Create Trigger tr_OrderDetails_StockIn
On [Order Details]
For Insert, Update, Delete As
If @@Rowcount = 0 Return
Select ProductID,
       sum(TotQty)
Into #temp
From (Select ProductID,
       isnull(sum(quantity), 0 ) as TotQty
      From inserted
      Group By productID
      union
      Select ProductID,
       -isnull(sum(quantity), 0 ) as TotQty
      From deleted
      Group By productID) as prdtable
```

```
If @@Error <> 0
Begin
   Raiserror ('Error in Table creation', 16, 1)
   Rollback Transaction
   Return
End
If exists
   (Select *
    From products as prd Inner Join
         #temp as tp on
         prd.productid = tp.productid and
         prd.UnitsInStock < tp.TotQty)
Begin
   Raiserror ('Not enough units in stock', 16, 1)
   Rollback Transaction
   Return
End
Update Products
Set UnitsInStock = UnitsInStock - TotQty
From #temp as tp
Where products.productId = tp.productid
If @@Error <> 0
Begin
   Raiserror ('Error in Update', 16, 1)
   Rollback Transaction
   Return
End
```

Day 19

Quiz

1. What can triggers be used to enforce?

   Answer: A trigger can be used to enforce the following in a database: data integrity, referential integrity, and business rules. In addition, triggers can be used to maintain derived columns, logs, and audit trails.

2. How many levels of nested triggers are allowed?

   Answer: You can nest triggers up to a maximum of 32.

3. What happens when a statement in a trigger fails?

   Answer: Whenever a statement in a trigger fails, the transaction that caused the trigger to fire will be rolled back.

Exercise

Using the Northwind database, create a trigger that prevents you from adding a new product without having a valid supplier.

```
Create Trigger tr_Prod_Supplier
On Products
For Insert
As
If (Select Count(*)
    From Inserted as Ins Inner Join
         Suppliers as Supp On
         Ins.supplierID = Supp.supplierID) <> 1
Begin
   Raiserror ('The Supplier specified in new product does not Exist', 10,
1)
   Rollback Transaction
   Return
End
```

Day 20

Quiz

1. User-defined functions can return scalar values as well as tables and can be used as part of the SELECT statement or in the FROM clause of a query. True or False?

   Answer: True

2. What are the three different types of user-defined functions?

   Answer: The three types of UDFs are

   - Scalar—Returns a single value
   - Inline single table value—Returns a table of data from a single table
   - Multi-statement table value—Uses joins to return data in a table from multiple tables in the database

3. Can I use a user-defined function instead of a view?

   Answer: Yes! In fact, by using a UDF instead of a view, performance will actually increase because the database does not have to maintain the view.

Exercise

1. Using the Northwind database, create a function that accepts a ZIP Code and returns a table of customer names and addresses.

Answer: This exercise needs only an inline table function as shown here:

```
CREATE FUNCTION Address_List (@zip nvarchar(10))
RETURNS Table AS
Return (Select CompanyName,
       ContactName,
       Address,
       City,
       Region,
       PostalCode,
       Country
From Customers
Where PostalCode = @zip)
```

Day 21

Quiz

1. What is the difference between the data types TEXT and NTEXT?

   Answer: The main difference between these two data types is that the TEXT data type is used to store non-Unicode data up to a length of 2,147,483,647 bytes. The NTEXT data type is used to store Unicode data up to a length of 1,073,741,823 characters.

2. What amount of data can be stored before it is considered a large object?

   Answer: Whenever character or binary data is larger than 8,000 bytes, it should be stored in a large data object.

3. How do I tell the server to store the text in the row, instead of using separate pages?

   Answer: You should use the sp_tableoption stored procedure to turn the 'text in row' option ON or OFF for a specified table as shown:

   ```
   Exec sp_tableoption 'Customers', 'text in row', 'ON'
   ```

Exercise

There are no exercises for this lesson.

INDEX

B

C

D

F

J-K

L

M

N

O

Q

R

S

V

W

X-Y-Z

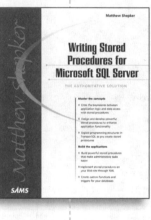

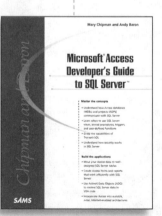